GENTLEMAN RIDER
A *Life of Joyce Cary*

GENTLEMAN RIDER

A Life of Joyce Cary

by
Alan Bishop

MICHAEL JOSEPH LONDON

MICHAEL JOSEPH LTD

Published by the Penguin Group
27 Wrights Lane, London W8 5TZ, England
Viking Penguin Inc., 40 West 23rd Street, New York, New York 10010, USA
Penguin Books Australia Ltd, Ringwood, Victoria, Australia
Penguin Books Canada Ltd, 2801 John Street, Markham, Ontario, Canada L3R 1B4
Penguin Books (NZ) Ltd, 182–190 Wairau Road, Auckland 10, New Zealand

Penguin Books Ltd, Registered Offices: Harmondsworth, Middlesex, England

First published 1988

Typeset in 10½ on 11½pt Linotron Electra by Goodfellow and Egan Ltd, Cambridge

Printed and bound in Great Britain by Richard Clay Ltd, Bungay, Suffolk

A CIP catalogue record for this book is available from the British Library

ISBN 0 7181 2330 1

For Isabel Cary, Winifred Davin, Edith Haggard,
my wife and mother,
and in memory of Anthea Joseph

'Remembered goodness is a benediction'

CONTENTS

LIST OF ILLUSTRATIONS

INTRODUCTION

'as memorable as his work'

It was a noble death. By the end of March 1957 newspapers and popular magazines had carried the story around the world. 'A Great Author Faces up to Death.'[1] 'Undaunted by paralysis, Joyce Cary works to the end.'[2] 'And if death has touched his spirit it has done so magnificently. He is almost unafraid . . . "I look upon life as a gift from God. I did nothing to earn it. Now the time is coming to give it back I have no right to complain."'[3]

On all who knew him well in his later years, or saw him on his deathbed, Cary made an indelible impression. The obituary notice written by one of his closest friends, Lord David Cecil, movingly attests this:

> the man was as memorable as his work. He made a picturesque and exhilarating first impression. His elegant, virile handsomeness, his light athletic movements, his racy, vivid, appreciative talk, and something at once heroic and debonair in his whole personality, suggested a gentleman rider in the race of life, risking his skin for sport rather than for a prize, and looking on every crisis of existence as a hurdle to be surmounted gaily and gallantly, however many bruises and spills might be incurred in the process.[4]

A splendid sketch. However, in talking about Cary twenty-five years later, Cecil himself shaded in its sharp outlines. He spoke of Cary's gentleness, his kindness to children; his even temper, 'sense of fun' and utter lack of malice; his love of tradition and of the appurtenances of 'living well' ('candlesticks on the dinner-table', for instance). Cary was 'a great man with very impressive moral qualities'. But Cecil said also that, despite a delight in eccentricities of human behaviour, he was often very unobservant; that, although a serious writer, he did not seem to take criticism of his writing seriously and 'never reread his old books'; that his literary judgements were surprisingly simple. In fact, Cecil concluded, Cary was 'a simple soul in many ways'.[5]

Enid Starkie, another close friend, also found him 'surprisingly simple'. But she noted strong signs of internal tension, endorsing her mother's amazement that 'the man with the pensive expression, the noble, aristocratic features, and the courteous manner, could possibly have written some of the passages in his books'. Recurrent violence in Cary's novels, Starkie speculated, was the 'romanticism . . . of a man incapable himself of any violence'; for he was a 'gentle, sensitive creature'. Yet – 'There was also in him a strange contrast, a mixture of the conventional in his habits of life, and the unconventional in his climate of thought'.[6]

Other friends suspected an even more complex personality. To Julian Fane, Cary 'gave an impression of completeness through joining in himself many opposite characteristics. He was gay and melancholy, tough and vulnerable, self-sufficient and somehow helpless, robust and refined, obtuse and subtle, sociable and solitary – or so I found him.'[7] And, writing a few years after Cary's death, Pamela Hansford Johnson commented that 'He was, of course, a far odder fish than most people realised – in a sense, than *he* realised . . .'[8]

Cary had many friends in Oxford, especially in the last two decades of his life. Their testimony adds to the sense of an emphatic but elusive personality. Jean Bannister described him as a 'disciplinarian', formal and Edwardian in his behaviour;[9] Peter Ady always felt uneasy in his presence because he gave her so strong an impression of detached observation;[10] Kathleen Stahl referred to his 'simplicity and extroverted habit of thinking, the aristocratic and sometimes tradition-bound side' of his personality;[11] Audrey Beecham remembered him as 'an odd perplexing sort of person' who, when she first met him, was so contained and aloof that she thought him totally lacking in warmth and enthusiasm.[12]

For many friends his characteristic manner was 'gay and gallant',[13] 'a mixture of almost boyish eagerness and reserve'.[14] Interviewers invariably found him ebullient. In 1952 one described him in terms that suggest a vitality almost beyond control:

> . . . Cary is a spry, trim little man, who will plump on his knees beside a chair to point out a passage in a book, crawl on the floor to find a place on a map or, standing near a door, suddenly grab the top in the middle of a conversation . . . Sitting, he squirms, crosses his legs this way and that, and squints his good left eye at his listener as the thoughts skip and jump across a dozen subjects from Africa to Ireland, from yesterday to the 17th Century without transition or pause. He seems so overwhelmed with the teeming ideas and images of his own brain that he has a hard time tumbling them out in a reasonable order . . .[15]

Yet Dan Davin testified that Cary always 'ate and drank sparingly, being a notably temperate man. Nothing in him was out of control. He was a soldier not far from his campaign, austere but without puritanism', impressive 'in his calm and in his good manners'.[16] And Elizabeth Lawrence of Harper found him 'a publisher's dream': 'He was prompt and to the point in the conduct of business, and a respecter of deadlines'; 'always direct, always personal, he was not given to baring his soul, unburdening himself of intimate problems', and his letters were those of 'a busy man in a busy household'.[17]

Several non-Oxford friends who saw him infrequently admired Cary's conversation. Sylvia Lynd thought it 'brilliant'.[18] J. B. Priestley appreciated him as 'a good talker with a quick staccato manner, and utterly without affectation'.[19] Dan Davin, in Oxford, first heard of Cary in 1940 when the Warden of Rhodes House, C. K. Allen, mentioned him, not as a novelist, but as a 'fascinating conversationalist'.[20]

Here again there is quick disagreement. Audrey Beecham and Molly Mahood mentioned his frequent 'absurd generalisations'[21] and 'conversation stoppers'.[22] To W. W. Robson he 'often sounded like a self-educated man: dogmatic, a holder-forth'.[23] And Helen Gardner, who admired Cary deeply for 'his lively, wide-ranging talk, his quick sympathies, his generous response to human idiosyncracy',[24] also sighed that 'he was a compulsive talker, talked at enormous length'.[25] T. S. Matthews, of *Time* magazine, found Cary's conversation 'not very interesting . . . but he was always intently interested; a watcher, a listener, not a talker'.[26]

Dan Davin, who often saw Cary listening patiently to Enid Starkie in full flow, 'one eye screwed up' and smiling his 'merry quizzical fond smile', thought him superlative both as talker and listener: 'though loving to talk himself he was not a greedy talker. He was a skilful listener and gave his companions the feeling that they were talking well . . .'.[27]

Opinions on his success as a lecturer differed similarly. Elizabeth Lawrence remembered how, 'confronted by ideas and an eager audience, his whole being lit up' and he would send his listeners home rejoicing.[28] But both Enid Starkie and Walter Allen thought him, on the whole, a poor lecturer who did not prepare adequately and (Allen) 'talked jerkily and disconnectedly'.[29]

Examples of varied response to Cary's personality and behaviour could be multiplied. Even his appearance and dress were evaluated differently by those who knew him well. His eyes were often called blue (they were brown), and he was usually described as a small man (he was only two inches short of six feet). However, there was general unanimity about his 'bird-like, quizzical expression', his 'slightly arched and very strong' nose, his 'sensitive and well-shaped' mouth, his very firm chin, his lean, compact body. His appearance made W. W. Robson think of a retired colonial sea-captain: 'there was a weather-beaten, hard-bitten air about him . . . He was obviously a gentleman, but there was no suggestion of the aristo-crat . . .'.[30]

Some friends observed that he dressed like a dandy; his son Tristram remembered that when, on a visit to London, a button fell off his coat, he insisted on going into Selfridges to have a new one sewn on immediately (he wrote to thank them afterwards).[31] Helen Gardner pictured him as a 'handsome, exquisitely groomed North Oxford gentleman'.[32] On the other hand, to Robert Lusty of Michael Joseph he never gave 'the impression of being other than mildly careless about his appearance';[33] and an American interviewer noted, with apparent distaste, that Cary's clothes were very 'British': 'baggy, loose-fitting, ancient, permanent tweeds'.[34] Dan Davin to some extent reconciled these divergent observations: Cary's formal dress was precise, self-conscious, he explained, but 'even when dressed in the loose tweeds he preferred . . . he was never without a kind of elegance, an air of unconscious quality'.[35]

Of course the varied comments are partly determined by differences in perspective, relationship, time, situation. And it is also true that Cary was 'very much his own man, gregarious but essentially private, even solitary. Perhaps this accounts for the peculiarly diverse pictures that we get from friends and acquaintances.'[36]

But Cary's personality seems to have puzzled even members of his family. He loved children, and in his later years became 'a kind of godfather' to the Davins' three daughters, welcoming their company, telling them serial stories, attending their birthday parties; Dan Davin would come home to find Cary surrounded by clamour, 'missing nothing of the detail of their minute dramas and enjoying every shift in the kaleidoscope of childish emotions'.[37] Yet he had been a rather severe father to his four sons, particularly the elder two. Tristram, his third son, though temperamentally close to Cary and, during his teens, a frequent companion on long walks, believed that his father had little interest in children until they were old enough to participate in wide-ranging discussion; 'You had to be about sixteen before he accepted you as a human being'.[38] And those who knew him best were divided on the question of whether he was a good husband, some suggesting that he had exploited his wife's hardworking generosity. Cary's four daughters-in-law, although they all respected him deeply, remembered him as often preoccupied and remote in his later years;[39] at family meals he would speak almost exclusively to his sons.[40]

Elizabeth Lawrence felt that Cary eluded definition: 'Such bits and pieces as I and other friends can dredge out of memory will not add up to a definitive portrait of the man or artist. He was too varied. Yet this is as it should be. He was the last person to want any image of him fixed and authenticated for eternity.'[41] About some personal characteristics, however, all who knew Cary were agreed. He was vigorous and courageous, physically and mentally. He was honest. He was generous and considerate. Above all, he was unselfconscious – utterly so, according to Enid Starkie;[42] and Edith Haggard, his American literary agent, who knew him very well in the last few years of his life, said he was 'the most unselfconscious person I ever came across'.[43]

It was perhaps Cary's unselfconsciousness that led some of his best friends to underestimate his abilities and achievement. Enid Starkie's account of his personality, although penetrating and genuinely affectionate, has a damagingly derogatory subtext. This is most obvious when, defending him from charges of self-centredness, she compared him to a child 'entirely engrossed in his newest "craze"'. At other points naïveté was implied – for instance, she suggested that Cary was 'an uncomplicated and unsophisticated person' who 'never analysed himself, nor looked into himself', was 'unaware of the atmosphere around him', 'saw human beings as simple, and set in motion by fairly obvious springs', 'understood symbolism in a very simple, concrete, and unspiritual way'. She even revealed that, when expecting a visit from him, she would 'remove all loose and unsteady objects out of his range, for he was liable, thrusting out his legs or arms suddenly, to sweep them on to the floor'![44]

Like his son Peter, Enid Starkie did not believe Cary capable of true religious feeling, even though several of his novels are explicitly concerned with religious belief. Peter felt that his father lacked a sense of awe and was convinced he had 'pinned down' religion;[45] Starkie stated bluntly 'I would not, myself, have considered that he was gifted religiously' (he told her that he 'considered anxiety on the score of personal spiritual salvation as selfish, and a foolish waste of time').[46] Yet Helen Gardner insisted that his novels were 'designed to express a religious apprehension of human beings as objects of delighted contemplation'.[47]

Starkie was convinced that, for all the comic vitality of his fiction, Cary's was essentially 'a very sad view of life' as 'unjust and finally disappointing'. His 'gusto for life was . . . a kind of whistling in the dark to keep his spirits up, a deliberate attitude of courage . . . .'.[48] Yet Pamela Hansford Johnson thought Cary's responses joyous: he was 'dead certain that all saw as he did, twice as large and nine times as lovely'.[49]

While many readers and critics have found wisdom in his philosophical and analytical thought, Starkie was sceptical. 'Joyce Cary talked a good deal about the philosophy on which his novels were grounded, but, as he expressed it, it did not seem to me profound, and I thought that it boiled down to very little in the end, to something rather obvious.'[50]

Peter Cary felt that his father's analytical thought was too dependent on his reading,[51] and Helen Gardner said, in conversation, that Cary's 'philosophy of life' was a 'mishmash' of ideas taken from other sources.[52] Yet that could be said of the myths created by some of Cary's most respected and ambitious literary contemporaries to express their interpretation of human experience: T. S. Eliot, W. B. Yeats, James Joyce. That Cary's myth has not been recognised and valued is primarily, perhaps, because it was often presented independently of his imaginative writing, and because it is inherently metaphysical rather than mystical or literary. He was strongly influenced, positively or negatively, by many thinkers, including Plato, Kant, Spinoza, Bergson, Blake, Tolstoy, Dostoevsky, Whitehead, MacMurray; but the comprehensive myth he created was ultimately his own.

'a marvellous writer'

Cary never belonged to a self-publicising coterie like the Bloomsbury Group, never became a reviewer, never set out to promote his novels by literary backscratching. Living as a 'gentleman writer'[53] in self-consciously intellectual Oxford, without the cachet of an academic position (Enid Starkie revealingly commented that he had 'no profession'[54]), he constantly exposed himself to the University's sharp (and often malicious) wits – and enjoyed doing so. Always broad in his interests, he also implicitly challenged the academic experts by writing philosophical and political texts in addition to his novels.

In 1975 Helen Gardner recalled that, during his lifetime, Cary 'was on the whole ignored by academic critics, and not taken seriously by the most influential writers on the art of fiction. But he was not, on the other hand, a really popular novelist.'[55] Essentially the same point had been made a quarter-century earlier by Donald Barr, an American critic, when he noticed, with surprise, that Cary's reputation 'did not accumulate, but had to be renewed with every book. Why has this been? Probably because he is too versatile and too enjoyable.'[56]

Other explanations have been proffered. That his writing was 'robustly affirmative' in a period dominated by *Angst* and pessimism. That he was 'old-fashioned' when his most respected contemporaries were experimental, 'modernist'. That his novels lacked shape and rhythm, were packed, picaresque and improvisatory. That their characters were types or caricatures. That his thought and narrative technique were confused and finally obscure – 'You don't know where to have him.'

Each of those statements is questionable. But so is the question they seek to answer. A novelist whose work is still widely read and who has inspired over twenty critical books, numerous articles and many dissertations in the thirty years since his death does not seem in danger of oblivion. It is true that some critical comments have been dismissive; it is also true that (to quote Helen Gardner again) in some 'recent studies of the novel in the twentieth century he is hardly mentioned'.[57] Cary has always been a controversial novelist.

The first full-length study of his novels after Andrew Wright's judiciously admiring introductory survey (1958)[58] was Robert Bloom's stimulating attack *The Indeterminate World* (1962), which accused Cary of avoiding 'moral discrimination' to satisfy a 'captivating but disquieting philosophical and moral largesse'.[59] Among the seven critical books that have appeared so far in the present decade, the two published in 1983 similarly clash. Hazard Adams, in *Joyce Cary's Trilogies*, regretted the influence of Bloom's study; paying close attention to Cary's theoretical and critical statements, he submitted the six novels to rigorous analysis, and found that they have 'the depth of ethical speculation that characterizes a great work'.[60] Dennis Hall, on the other hand, argued in *Joyce Cary: A Reappraisal* that 'there were two Joyce Carys', one a confused thinker, the other an able novelist; so it was necessary to set 'the thinker aside . . . to do the novelist a service'.[61] I have no doubt that, however much in disagreement with Bloom's and Hall's arguments, Cary would have enjoyed them, and would have wished them to be given a hearing equal to Wright's and Adams's. That, after all, is the method of his trilogies. And conflict is a sign of life.

Cary's novelist contemporaries were among the first to recognise his talent, so it is not surprising to find successors praising his work. John Updike: 'a splendid writer'.[62] Doris Lessing: 'This novelist has exemplified the rule that when a writer dies, he or she may suffer a lapse in attention. You say to someone, "Joyce Cary" and they say, "Who?" Amazing! He was a marvellous writer, fresh, funny, popping with life.'[63] And Paul Theroux: 'Whenever I am idle I choose a Cary novel in the way I might seek a friend's company, and it is not long before I am encouraged, inspired to write.'[64]

Two unusual qualities of Cary's work are its independence and diversity. Because he worked in comparative isolation, only occasionally mixing with writers beyond those in his circle, he maintained throughout his career a powerful individuality. So he cannot easily be categorised. Moreover, he strikingly combines the traditional with the experimental. He was influenced by great predecessors (most explicitly Conrad, Hardy, Tolstoy, Dostoevsky), but also by James Joyce. And he himself has influenced prominent novelists like Graham Greene, Chinua Achebe and the New Zealander Maurice Gee.

In fact, Cary has not one but three reputations: he is an Irish writer, by virtue of birth, family and early experience, and two of his novels; he is a Nigerian writer, for he spent a formative part of his life there and wrote several books out of that experience; and he is an English writer, who lived most of his life in Oxford and set all his later novels in England. This has tended to diminish recognition of his achievement by fragmenting critical response.

From Irish literature he has often been excluded – perhaps because, being of Ascendancy stock, he is politically unpalatable. But James Simmons has cogently insisted that *Castle Corner* and *A House of Children* made 'a very significant contribution to Irish (Anglo-Irish?) literature',[65] and it seems likely that literary values will in time prevail.

As a Nigerian writer, Cary has fared better, although after Independence in 1960 there was a tendency to reject him as a colonialist relic – prejudiced or irrelevant. Perhaps the shrillest attack was made by an American Marxist who in 1971 described Cary as a paternalistic neo-colonialist who 'knows very little about the African'.[66] Over a decade earlier, however, the Nigerian Davidson Nicol judged that Cary's 'books on Africa, whether fiction or fact, always had the dominant note of fairness, and a critical observation which was at once affectionate and artistic'.[67] More generally, it has been claimed that 'No [other] British writer . . . has brought into fiction the culture of a developing country so substantially, understandingly and skilfully'.[68] Fine critical books have come from Michael Echeruo and S. H. Kanu.[69] And Chinua Achebe was spurred into writing novels by the 'provocation' of *Mister Johnson*; for, disagreeing with aspects of the novel, Achebe yet acknowledged that 'Cary was good, he was sympathetic, he knew Africa'.[70] Cary, who was similarly inspired by Tolstoy, would have relished the compliment.

Cary has been considered primarily as an English writer – even a *very* English writer, whose great success in the United States surprised his publishers. Yet his range is unusual, for, although he is thought of first as a novelist, beyond the fifteen novels published in his lifetime (and the two published posthumously) are many short stories and essays, two long poems, a memoir, five treatises in politics, history and aesthetics, and a large body of unpublished works (including plays and screenplays, lectures, letters); all of some relevance to the novels, and some of intrinsic value.

There are signs that Cary's reputation is again on the rise as the centenary of his birth arrives; that readers are again recognising Cary's distinctive gifts – his brilliance in narrative and characterisation; his deep but unpretentious exploration (moral, metaphysical, religious, political) of the human condition; his acknowledgment of injustice and suffering as endemic, but his insistence that we can counter them through our natural creativity, our joy in being alive. Cary was ultimately, but not without a very full look at the worst, an optimist.

In that and other qualities, he reminds me, among all the writers he respected, of the one who earliest and (I suspect) most deeply influenced him. Cary was drawn to writers who fulfilled his axiom 'a writer . . . is a man of action'[71] and who had had extensive practical experience of the world, in another profession, before settling into the lonely task of meditating on moral issues and instilling them into literature: Conrad, Hardy, Tolstoy, Dostoevsky. And his 'precious Chaucer'.[72] Who, like Cary, was a successful man of political affairs before he established a literary career; responded intensely to men and women as both individuals and types, and had a notable capacity to empathise with ostensibly unattractive personalities (one might compare Chaucer's Pardoner with Cary's Jim Latter, the Wife of Bath with Sara Monday); was strongly but 'relativistically' moralistic; and, although his genius was essentially comic and optimistic, rendered superbly the tragic pathos of Troilus, Criseyde and Pandarus. Chaucer, too, has confused and stimulated his critics.

'in the creation'

Although Cary is rightly remembered as a writer, he was also, in earlier life (1914–19), a fine colonial administrator in Northern Nigeria. During that period he fought against German forces in the Cameroons, and earlier he had been a Red Cross orderly during conflict between Montenegrins and Turks in the Balkans. His administrative experience had begun with Horace Plunkett's Co-operative Movement in Ireland, and he had spent four years studying Law at Oxford and Art in Edinburgh. During his youth and childhood there had been excursions to Etaples and Paris, and to Inishowen, his Irish home-land.

Through most of his life Cary attempted to be both man of action and writer: indeed, his life falls into two halves, dominated respectively by those two categories. He was intensely aware of duality, both in his own personality and in general human experience; and this, with early deprivation, and awareness of pervasive injustice, led him to interpret life in terms of conflict. But equally he felt deep happiness and security, apprehended unity and coherence, in his earliest years. Duality, in various expressions, is at the heart of his writing; so is unity.

After years of struggle to resolve his apparently contradictory perceptions of human experience – a world intransigently split among conflicting polarities, tragic; a world of ultimate integrity and coherence, comic – he created the myth that dominates his mature thought and writing, and is most strikingly expressed by his two Trilogies. The keystone of that myth is his conception of human beings as free and creative.

Again and again Cary associated creativity with imagery drawn from horses and horse-riding. One of his friends, herself a horsewoman, noted that even his everyday conversation characteristically included 'horse language' (a secretary, for instance, might be described as always 'jigging');[73] and he even advocated horsemanship in children's education, as evoking courage and confidence.[74] So Lord David Cecil's 'gentleman rider' suggested itself as an apposite title for this biography. As I became more aware of Cary's complexity, however, I abandoned the phrase – to reclaim it finally as a label that, although necessarily restrictive, functions significantly, like the titles of his novels, to stress what seems to me to be the essence of the man, his life and his work. For all three are indelibly marked by the duality implied by 'gentleman' and 'rider'; and indelibly marked by the precarious unity, 'gentleman rider', that he struggled throughout his life to achieve or maintain. As 'gentleman' Cary faced injustice; as 'rider' he found fulfilment in creativity; as 'gentleman rider' he held together the two visions of life, the two parts of his being.

In writing this story of Cary's life, I have wanted him, and those whose personalities and lives mingled with his, to speak in their own voices as often as possible. So I have avoided paraphrase in favour of quotation. At times one voice predominates – Cary's own reminiscences during his early years, for instance; at other times, two voices may be counterpointed, several voices become a choir. Cary wrote autobiographical essays late in his life, and avowedly drew on memories and family history for several novels and short stories: I have used these extensively (together with letters, notes, observations, diary entries, interviews, autobiographical statements) as his voice. (In all quotations I have aimed to preserve idiosyncracies as far as possible, but have not retained the very occasional ampersands, or Cary's later-life abbreviation of 'and' to 'd'.)

Ultimately the reader will decide how much credibility to allow each voice speaking in this book. I have implied my confidence by selection, have clearly identified quotations from Cary's autobiographical fiction, and have generally used the present tense to indicate the possible presence of an imaginative element in such passages. But memory is notoriously wayward. Are the reminiscences or fictionalised memories of a man who had a 'fly-paper' memory[75] less trustworthy than a friend's observant insight or a relative's fifty-year-old anecdote? 'We live . . . in the creation . . .'[76]

I have of course been very aware of my own shaping of event into narrative. Facts remain paramount, dictate outlines; but patterns emerge from them, with their own ordering prerogatives; and, at the simplest level, complexity of event may demand separation and concentration to avoid confusion in the telling, and to identify endeavour. I must hope that my formal decisions have not seriously distorted the personality, life and work of a deeply loved and admired human being who was also a great writer.

ACKNOWLEDGEMENTS

The debts I have accumulated while writing this book are many, and the list below seems a grossly inadequate expression of gratitude; but I hope those who have helped me will know how greatly I have appreciated kindness and generosity that, again and again, went far beyond expectation. I am also very grateful to all who have given permission for the publication of quotations. I apologise for any inadvertent omission of acknowledgement.

The Cary Estate: Lucius and John Cary. Joyce Cary's Literary Executrix: Winifred Davin.

The Cary family: Lady Cary (Isabel, widow of Sir Michael Cary); Lady Ogilvie (Mary, widow of Sir Frederick Ogilvie); Shiela Cary; Peter and Elizabeth Cary; Tristram Cary; Dorse Cary; Margaret Robertson; Antonia and Ruari McLean; Agnes Jackson-Clark; Peter Thompson; David Ogilvie; Lucius and Joanna Cary; Chippy (Tristram) and Kirsten Cary; Anthony and Clare Cary; Kate and James Scott; John Cary; Charlotte Cary.

English or American friends and acquaintances of Joyce Cary, and all who gave me personal information about him in interviews or correspondence: Peter Ady; Walter Allen; Jean Bannister; Audrey Beecham; Sir Isaiah Berlin; Christina Bewley; the late Sir Basil Blackwell; Baron Bullock of Leafield; Phyllis Calvert; the late Lord David Cecil; Dan and Winifred Davin; Delia Davin; Cecilia Dick; the late Thorold Dickinson; Elizabeth Fischer; Baron Franks of Headington; the late Dame Helen Gardner; Sarah Fischer Gleason; Graham Greene; Mrs Sewell Haggard; J. R. Harris; the late Dr Richard Hunt; Earle Hyman; John Jordan; the late Hon. Anthea Joseph; Elizabeth Lawrence Kalashnikoff; Lady Keir; Francis King; Dr Henry Kissinger; Peggy Lamert; Irene W. Laune; John Lehmann; Sir Robert Lusty; Lady MacDougall; Michael and Jean Maclagan; M. M. Mahood; T. S. Matthews; Dame Iris Murdoch; Catherine Middleton Murry; Colin Middleton Murry; Dr Gordon Ostlere (Richard Gordon); B. Evan Owen; Lillian S. Pollock; Orville Prescott; Mrs J. B. Priestley (Jacquetta Hawkes); Tom Priestley; Sir Victor Pritchett; the

ACKNOWLEDGEMENTS

late Wendy Campbell Purdie; the late Will Ready, and Bess; Vivian and Anne Ridler; Prof. W. W. Robson; Tania Rose; Norman Rosten; Prof. Walt Rostow; the late Dr Robert Shackleton; Norman Shrapnel; John Simopoulos; Sir Stephen Spender; Ernest and Kathleen Stahl; Mary Stanford Smith; J. I. M. Stewart; Sir Ronald Syme; Dame Janet Vaughan; the late Rex Warner, and Frances; Dame Veronica Wedgwood; the late Gerald Wilde.

Libraries and institutions: Bodleian Library, Oxford (for the James Osborn Collection of Joyce Cary Papers, Enid Starkie Papers, and other material including photographs) – especially D. W. Porter and Colin Harris; Balliol College, Oxford; BBC Archives, London; British Library (Newspaper Library), London; Cambridge University Library; Canada Council (for a Research Fellowship); Clifton College – especially the Librarian, David Reed; Commonwealth Institute Library, London; Commonwealth Office, London; Corpus Christi College, Oxford; English Faculty Library, Oxford; Ibadan University; Ilorin University; National Library of Scotland (for the Dover Wilson Papers); New College, Oxford – especially Dr Penry Williams; National Archives of Nigeria, Ibadan – especially Mr Unuigbe; National Archives of Nigeria, Kaduna – especially Miss Olehi; Plunkett Foundation for Co-operative Studies, Oxford – especially Elise Bayley, Librarian; Queen Elizabeth House Library, Oxford; Radcliffe Science Library, Oxford; Rhodes House, Oxford – especially the Warden, Robin Fletcher, and Ginny; Rhodes House Library, Oxford (Edwardes and Hoskyns-Abrahall Papers, and other material) – especially the Librarian, Alan Bell; Rhodes University, South Africa; St Antony's College, Oxford; Social Sciences and Humanities Research Council of Canada; Society of Authors; Stanley Spencer Gallery, Cookham-on-Thames; Tate Gallery Archive, London – especially Adrian Glew; Trinity College, Oxford – especially the then-President, Lord Quinton, and his Secretary.

In Ireland: Rose Kane, Neil MacGowran, Rev A. E. T. Harper.

In Nigeria: His Highness Alhaji Musa Muhammadu Kigera III, Emir of Borgu; Alhaji Garuba, Secretary of the Emir's Council; Waziri Mohammed Aliyu; Haliru Kiyaru, ex-Emir of Kaiama; Alhaji Suleiman dan Galadima, ex-Treasurer of Kaiama; Serikin Kaiama; Alhaji Zickiri Mohammed, Serikin Agwarra (Borgu); His Highness Alhaji Shaimbu Yakubu, Emir of Yauri; Fr Peter Otillio, O.P.; Inspector Mohammed Jalingo (Yelwa); Jermanus Opara; Chief Moyo Oboderin; Mervyn Taylaur of Price Waterhouse (Lagos); Niyi and Kemi Osundare; John Ohiorheneran; Bisi Aibijuwoh; the Pastoral Institute (Ibadan); Dr Akanji Nasiru and Dupe; Terna Ahua; Paul Tench; Prof. David Cook (Ilorin); Michael and Mary Etherton (Zaria); Stan Lingwood; L. S. Manampery; Debbie and Jack Rumere (Kaduna); and (especially in Kano) CUSO personnel – Bruce and Audrey Caldwell, Tom Carter, Ray Clarke, David and Anne Currie, Louise Jarrett, Sandy Ockenden, Michael and Debbie Smith, Barbara Switocz, Liz Walker.

Writers, critics, academics, literary executors: Peter Abrahams; Julia Birley (information about Margaret Kennedy and her family); Prof. Guy Butler; W. F. Carey (information about the Cary family); Dr Edwin Christian (much valuable help; his *Joyce Cary's Creative Imagination* has just been published);

Dr Mary Clapinson (Enid Starkie Papers); Dr Cornelia Cook (and her *Joyce Cary: Liberal Principles*); Dr Raymond Davis; Katherine Duncan-Jones (literary executor for Helen Gardner); Cyprian Ekwensi; Dr Barbara Fisher (her two books on Joyce Cary, PhD dissertation on Cary's notebooks, and transcription of two notebooks missing from the Cary Papers); Prof. Malcolm Foster (his *Joyce Cary: A Biography*); Prof. Northrop Frye; Maurice Gee; Dr Douglas Killam; Anthony Kirk-Greene (especially his kind help in colonial Nigerian history); Doris Lessing; David Lytton; Dr M. M. Mahood (especially her *Joyce Cary's Africa* and the generous gift of material connected with its composition); Dr Merja Makinen (information relating to *Men of Two Worlds*; Col. Peter Moody (his PhD dissertation and additions to the Cary Papers); Lady Violet Powell (especially *The Constant Novelist*, her biography of Margaret Kennedy); Joanna Richardson (especially her biography *Enid Starkie*); the late Dr W. D. Terry (who introduced me to Joyce Cary's novels); Dr Royston Tester; Paul Theroux; Prof. Andrew Wright (especially his *Joyce Cary: A Preface to his Novels*).

Friends, acquaintances, colleagues: Maurice and Johanna Pope; Hugh Anson-Cartwright; Ron Ayling; Mark and Merrie Baker; Rabbi Bernard Baskin; Paul Berry; Anne and Porl Born; John and Elizabeth Boyle; the late Richard Brooks; Jill Brown; the late Angus Cameron, and Wendy; Dr Moran Campbell; Derek and Margaret Davies; Christine and Robin Davis; Dennis Driscoll; Cathy Garay; John Michael and Margaret Gibbs; Livia Gollancz; Anthony and Helen Kirk-Greene; Kenneth and Deborah Kirkwood; Clare Leighton; Peter Levi; the late Ray Marshall; Nancy Moller; Bridget and John Perry; Jon and Jill Stallworthy; Cornelia Starks; Richard and Zandra Talbert; Valerie and Bill Thomas; George Wallace; Stephen and Yvonne Wall; Gary and Joy Warner; Judy and Nigel Weiss; Bruce and Deborah Whiteman; Madeleine Wood.

Publication: Felicity Bryan, John Lawton (Curtis Brown, London); Andrew Lownie (John Farquharson Ltd, London); Perry Knowlton, Grace Wherry (Curtis Brown, New York); Jennie Davies, Anne Williams, Gillian Bate, and Roland Philipps – to whom this book owes so much (Michael Joseph Ltd).

And my family: Judith, especially for her encouragement and criticism; Ruth, for retyping a chapter purloined by the word-processor; Ann and Matthew.

Alan Bishop, June 1988

PART ONE

Man of Action/Writer

'The growth of every soul is mysterious and full of chances.' *(Art and Reality)*

'They say that tensions make the artist and the writer. That is certainly true of the Anglo-Irish writers, and my childhood should have been full of tensions.' ('Speaking for Myself')

'Courage is the root of happiness.' (C263/N49)

' . . . a writer cannot drift on a stream; he is a man of action.' ('Morality and the Novelist')

' . . . he is possessed by it, carried away like a rider on a wild horse. But also he possesses it. He can't hold it, but he rides it . . .' *(Charley is My Darling)*

CHAPTER ONE

BEGINNINGS

1066–1887

'A man's life begins before he is born'
'Family influence,' Joyce Cary wrote, is 'stronger than any precept or sermon . . .'[1]

For most of his sixty-eight years, he was strongly influenced by family history and tradition. While still a boy, he was the Cary 'expert' on such matters,[2] and his interest in family portraits and family names was surely a source of his early commitment to creating both art and literature. He became an avid reader of memoirs, diaries, letters; and the 'fascinations of History' became a recurrent topic in his mature thought and writing. Even more important: family history and tradition were roots of the duality that dominated his personality. Although fundamentally conservative throughout his life, Cary valued innovation highly. History had uprooted and scattered his family; innovation was essential if a satisfying new life was to be created; but tradition remained a powerful, consoling ally. 'A man's life begins before he is born . . .'[3]

For Cary, in his class and time, choice of profession was not a merely personal decision. His father had adopted a 'new' profession, civil engineering; but that had depended on the approval and support of wealthy relatives. Family example offered a range of other professions, one of which was art. Two of Cary's aunts became painters; he knew them well from his earliest years, and throughout his life felt affection and admiration for them. But the profession was recent, and entirely feminine, in the family.

Literature was better established. In his monograph *The Cary Family of Inishowen* (1963), Lionel Stevenson, Cary's American cousin, argued that one of the family's most striking characteristics in the twentieth century was 'the sudden outcropping of literary activity', with 'all of a hundred volumes' already published.[4] Like Margaret Kennedy (author of *The Constant Nymph* and other novels),[5] Cary contributed substantially to that number. Moreover, Saki – H. H. Munro – was also connected to Cary, through the marriage of his brother Charles Munro (whom Cary knew well) to Muriel Chambers. Saki spent several summers in Inishowen,[6] as did Cary. They may have met; and as a young man Cary would have known about Saki's writing.

One of the most important family literary influences began when he was in his early thirties, and came, not from the Carys, but from his mother's family, the Joyces. Cary said on at least one occasion that he was related to James Joyce, arguably his greatest literary contemporary.[7] Although the connection was probably distant, Cary followed Joyce's career closely. He read and reread A *Portrait of the Artist as a Young Man* in 1919;[8] and the influence of three Joyce works – A *Portrait*, *Ulysses* and *Finnegans Wake* – is discernible in his fiction.

But writing was an exceptional occupation for Cary men. Traditionally they had been soldiers, administrators, merchants, landlords, magistrates, clergymen; and younger sons might seek their fortunes abroad – an adventurous streak was admired.

The oldest traditional Cary profession was the army. It was embellished in Cary's lifetime by a great name: Field-Marshal the Viscount Montgomery of Alamein, whom he resembled in appearance (and high voice). Cary was aware of his relationship to Bernard Montgomery and mentioned, while recalling delinquencies of his youth, that 'some larger boy (I have an idea it was one of the Montgomeries, perhaps the present Commander-in-Chief) warned me to run for it as the police were coming'.[9] Montgomery found fulfilment in the family's military tradition. Cary was strongly influenced by it.

Another prominent relation also became a soldier – and then an intellectual, writer and administrator as well. There are significant parallels of personality and life; and it seems that to some extent Cary modelled himself on Lucius Cary, second Viscount Falkland, who was born in 1610, and like Cary grew up partly in Ireland, where his father, the first Viscount Falkland, was Lord Deputy from 1622 to 1629. Unsatisfied by attempts to establish a military career, he retired to the family property at Great Tew, about twelve miles from Oxford, 'tooke up to be serious, and then grew to be an extraordinary hard student'.[10] Intelligent, tolerant, courageous, gentle, impulsive, a fine conversationalist, he attracted a circle of the leading thinkers and writers of his day, among them the dramatist Ben Jonson, philosopher Thomas Hobbes, poet John Suckling, and theologian William Chillingworth of Trinity College. Their discussions began a 'new era in English theology'.[11] Falkland was also admired as a writer of poems and treatises – and even more for his political wisdom and integrity. A Royalist, he yet supported Parliament and attacked wasteful expenditure. An Anglican, he yet spoke out against Archbishop Laud's tyranny. 'The desire to secure liberty from spiritual tyranny was the ruling principle of his mind';[12] he was 'a lover of truth beset by bigots'.[13]

In 1642, Charles I appointed him Secretary of State. Desperately trying to preserve peace, Falkland negotiated with Parliament on the King's behalf. When the Civil War broke out, he remained a Royalist; but 'his natural cheerfulness and vivacity grew clouded . . .'[14] As the King's position worsened, Falkland returned to his first profession ('he had to fight with the King, with his friends', Cary wrote)[15] and was killed in 1643 at the Battle of Newbury.

Undoubtedly Cary, when still a boy, knew Clarendon's, Aubrey's and J. R. Green's accounts of Falkland, and he was eighteen when Marriott's biography came out. In later years he made an annual pilgrimage to Great Tew, and to the magnificent Tanfield Monument in Burford Church[16] – the tomb of Sir Lawrence Tanfield, Falkland's maternal grandfather, who had been Queen Elizabeth's Treasurer.

'I am the last of the Irish Carys'

The name Cary (which has several variants, Carey being the most common) is of Celtic origin and means, appropriately enough for a writer, 'a pleasant stream'.[17] By settling beside the small River Cary in Somerset, the family's progenitor in England involuntarily secured its name for his descendants. According to one early account, the progenitor was Robert, a Norman of Breton blood, half-brother of William the Conqueror.

A manor of 'Kari' is listed in the Domesday Book, and by the end of the twelfth century there was a 'Castle Karry' (whose ragged ruins still loom over the town Castle Cary, thirty miles south of Bristol), its Lord recorded in 1198 as Sir Adam de Karry. The family grew rapidly in numbers and influence through the Middle Ages, and fourteenth-century documents show that Carys were prominent in Bristol as cloth merchants and administrators. By the fifteenth century, the family had achieved national prominence, and several prosperous and influential Carys were scattered through the West Country.

The main line of descent is through a fifteenth-century Sir Robert Cary of Cockington in Somerset. One descendant, his namesake, inherited Clovelly, in North Devon, in 1540. (This branch of the family is romanticised in Charles Kingsley's Westward Ho!.) And it was George Cary, a grandson of Sir Robert Cary of Clovelly who, at the end of Elizabeth's reign, became the progenitor of the Irish Carys.

The English roots of Cary's family run deep and wide, then, in West Country soil – Somerset and Devon. It was not by chance that, when Cary's father retired, he settled in Wadeford, near Chard; and that Cary and his brother Jack found there, in rural Somerset, a spiritual home in their own later years. Cary's article 'The Meaning of England', written on his deathbed, begins with a yarn about a Somerset man who, finding himself in hospital after an accident, demands in deep distress to be taken home. Assured that the hospital is in his own county, 'He took another look at the fields and settled down peacefully to sleep . . . – in Somerset he felt at home.'[18]

The Irish fields in which George Cary rooted his family were rather less fertile. In 1604, Sir Arthur Chichester, a West Country friend of the family, had been appointed Lord Deputy of Ireland. Taking advantage of the connection, George Cary joined Chichester, and helped him put down Irish resistance.

In 1608, the Irish chieftain Cahir O'Doherty led a futile rebellion against the English Plantation. He was ruler of Inishowen, the most northerly region of Ireland – a large, remote peninsula in County Donegal, between Loughs

Foyle and Swilly. James I granted the whole peninsula to Chichester as a reward, and Chichester in turn divided much of it among his comrades.

In 1613 George Cary was granted five hundred acres around Redcastle, an Irish fortress on the shore of Lough Foyle roughly half-way between Londonderry and the peninsula's easterly point, Inishowen Head. He quickly prospered. His land was bad – rocky, boggy, it rose sharply towards the 'gray mountains of dark Donegal'[19] – but his political connections could hardly have been better and he rose rapidly. By the time of his death in 1642, he had established his family near the pinnacle of the emerging Ascendancy.

When the eldest son, George, inherited Redcastle in 1642, his brother Robert built Whitecastle two miles north along the shore. In the mid eighteenth century both of these fortified buildings were torn down and replaced, without change of name, by Georgian mansions. And a third mansion, Castle Cary, was built by a Redcastle younger son, Edward, on a hill near Whitecastle, with a magnificent view over Lough Foyle. A four-mile stretch of the shoreline was now dominated by the three Big Houses of the Carys. They marked the high point of the family's prestige and prosperity. According to Lionel Stevenson, 'there were at least seven branches of the Cary family flourishing on separate estates in Inishowen and adjacent territory'.[20]

The Cary heads of family in Inishowen were landlords and magistrates, renting land and dispensing English justice. Their relations with the local Irish were warmed by daily contact and personal regard; but remained essentially feudal, with profound cultural, religious and political differences exacerbating the class cleavage.

Moreover, the Carys, largely cut off from the social and political centres of both English and Irish life, were little aware of shifting intellectual opinion and other forces of change. More and more ingrown as cousin married cousin, they exerted their authority with an apparently confident paternalism. Like most of the Ascendancy families they lived 'in the style of the poorer gentleman farmers in England'.[21] They built Church of Ireland churches – like St Finnian's, near Redcastle, where Cary's paternal grandparents are buried – and attended them every Sunday. During the rest of the week, although they would also see to estate affairs and conduct assizes, their main activity was sport – especially hunting and horse-racing.

This way of life gives point to Brendan Behan's gibe that an Anglo-Irishman was 'a Protestant on a horse'.[22] Terence de Vere White, defining the Anglo-Irish, heard, 'over all, the neigh of horses'.[23] A tassle of Irish bitterness can be traced back to the promulgation of laws like the one that prevented a native Irishman owning a horse worth more than £5: if he disobeyed, any member of the Ascendancy could humiliate him by buying his horse from under him for £5. So the horse was absorbed deep into the Ascendancy's psyche, its daily life and conversation, its economy; 'horses everywhere in Ireland earned the homage or disdain that was their master's due'.

For the Anglo-Irishman, right up to Cary's time, a rider was a gentleman, a gentleman was a rider. Bred into him was the knowledge that 'the conduct of horses had for generations been a career',[24] that the qualities of one's horse and one's ability to ride well were symbolic of class as well as personal ability. (Cary once wrote disparagingly of a fellow writer 'he's never learnt to ride . . .')[25]

The Carys' privileged way of life was to survive for over a hundred years beyond the 1750s; but a long decline began early in the nineteenth century, for reasons largely beyond their control. Ireland's economy deteriorated sharply after the Act of Union in 1800; rising prices and taxes hurt even the Ascendancy families, while poverty lashed the Irish. 'The fatal spirit of evictions, emigration, and famine darkened the first half of the nineteenth century, in Inishowen as in the rest of the country.'[26]

The Carys found it hard to adjust: 'my grandfather was the last of a line of spendthrift squires,' Cary wrote in a gloomy moment; 'Not all spendthrift, perhaps, but they wasted enormous estates in those centuries, little by little.'[27]

His great-grandfather, however, had been an exception. The Reverend Anthony Thomas Grayson Cary – 'the only respectable Cary in history', Cary joked[28] – was a younger son of George Cary of Whitecastle. Rector of Glendermott in Donegal, he inherited Castle Cary in the absence of direct male heirs, and combined pastoral duties with his role as a landlord. Unfortunately his strong sense of social responsibility brought misfortune to his family. Most of his children were still under twenty-one when, during the Famine of the late 1840s, he died after catching 'plague fever' from tenants whom he was tending.

Already, a quarter century before Anthony Cary's death, Redcastle had been lost to the Cary family. (With a nice irony, it was bought by a descendant of Cahir O'Doherty, who had been dispossessed in 1608; and not long afterwards Whitecastle also became a Doherty property.) Although Castle Cary would remain in the family's possession for another forty years after Anthony's death, by the 1850s the future of all the remaining Cary property was looking bleak, its capacity to support a large family greatly reduced. Anthony Cary's two daughters emigrated to Australia. The eldest and youngest of his five sons became Anglican priests like their father, one in Canada. Two of the middle sons trained in medicine: Tristram, the second son, and John, who served as surgeon in the American Civil War.

Anthony Cary's fourth son, Arthur Lunell, did not train for a profession. He went to sea, then he and Tristram sought their fortunes gold-digging in Australia. Apparently they had some success, but returned to take over the family land, Tristram at Ballybrack and his younger brother at Castle Cary. By 1859, Arthur Lunell Cary was married to Jane Sproule of Strabane, and trying to make a go of two thousand acres. He built a new Castle Cary – surely an act of defiant optimism. And there his nine children were born between 1861 and 1875.

A man's man who won respect as magistrate, sportsman and local character, Arthur Lunell Cary was immensely hospitable, an extrovert whose vivid personality and declining circumstances are reflected in John Chass Corner, the character who dominates the opening chapters of Joyce Cary's *Castle*

Corner (a novel partly based on Cary family history). 'The people still tell stories of his humour, his dash, his personal beauty, his reckless, brilliant driving,' Cary reported of his grandfather in 1950.[29] He would often challenge fellow magistrates to race him, after petty sessions, from Moville to Castle Cary. Two miles of narrow, hilly road bordered by stone walls made an exhilaratingly dangerous course for tandems, small, light vehicles drawn by two horses.

While still a child, Cary probably grasped the rudiments of the two very different modes of manhood brought to life in yarns about his great-grandfather and his grandfather. Anthony Cary quiet, responsible; Arthur Lunell Cary flinging himself at life.

But, like his father, Arthur Lunell Cary was cut down by disaster. Easy-going landlord that he was, he slipped into financial ruin. The Irish Land Act of 1881 'controlled rents,' wrote Elizabeth Bowen, 'stopped arbitrary evictions and gave the tenant-occupier at least some degree of security.' It also cancelled tenants' arrears of rent, and so 'bore with unforeseen heaviness on landlords, who with estates heavily charged got no remission of these charges to match enforced reduction of rents. Good landlords (of which there had been many) suffered with, and in some cases more than, those who had been the monsters all landlords appeared'.[30]

Cary learned to sympathise with both sides in this conflict, as the eviction scene early in *Castle Corner* illustrates. The rational argument of old Corner, a patriarch who 'had to be obeyed', and the desperate anguish of Con Foy, the young Irishman driven from his home, are rendered with equal force.[31]

Recognition of such irreconcilable opinion while he was still a child fostered Cary's notable capacity to enter and express the personalities of people whose circumstances, feelings, thoughts, differed radically from his own. It also prepared his mind to accept duality. But preceding his sympathy for both sides was sharp awareness of family loss: for the conflict had been partly resolved, less than a decade before his birth, at the cost of his family's deracination. 'I am the last of the Irish Carys,' he wrote.[32]

Arthur Lunell Cary, unable to repay his extensive debts or keep up his mortgage, unable to maintain Castle Cary in adequate repair, was forced to move his family into a rented house, Falmore, about six miles away. There he died two years later, aged fifty-two – 'of a broken heart,' his grandson wrote. Cary's early knowledge of his family's fate ate deep into his psyche. 'Even as a small child . . . I knew something of real tragedy: the tragedy of social conflict in which personal quality counts for nothing; where a man is ruined not because he has done any wrong, but because he represents a class or race.'[33] In that knowledge was the seed of his lifelong concern with the theme of injustice.

'a forthright people, bold and confident'
Joyce Cary was to be a dispossessed Anglo-Irishman, a gentleman rider who would never ride fine horses in Inishowen, who would never own one of the Big Houses of his people. Until middle age, Cary called himself an Irishman.

But he had to accept rejection while still a young man anxious to give the best of himself to his country. He always gratefully celebrated 'the country people' of Inishowen with their 'Irish love of children and old tales'. [34] But his anatomy of the Inishowen Irish is unsentimental: 'They are a tough race, inclined to keep their own council; jealous in love, and fierce in hatred; bringing to everything they do an uncommon energy and tenacity.'[35] And he would surely have recognised a general truth in David Thomson's observation that, however polite and even affectionate the Irish were, they never forgot that the Ascendancy landlords were 'parvenus who had usurped the master's seat'. 'Behaviour and manners of speech were more relaxed between classes than they were in England, but ignorance of each others' ways was absolute. Like Africans under European rule, the Irish people had lived apart for generations.'[36]

In their remote corner of Ireland, the Carys did not suffer the full fury of late-nineteenth-century Irish nationalism. There was no attack on Castle Cary like the fictional near destruction of Castle Corner. Because he was such a popular landlord, Arthur Lunell Cary's tenants surreptitiously helped him during the 1880s: Cary's father 'cld. remember, as a young man, during the time of the rent struggles, the carts of tenants creaking in the dark as they came by night to fill the stockyard at Castle Cary with turf for the winter. These tenants defied the boycott at their own risk out of loyalty and affection to the old man.'[37]

Cary was not immune to moments of resentment in his later years; occasionally he would make hostile comments about Irish nationalism or Roman Catholicism.[38] But in general he managed to hold a sympathetic balance, in his life and in his writing.

To be Anglo-Irish was also to be proudly conscious of an exceptional contribution to English literature. The roll of Anglo-Irish writers includes Swift, Berkeley, Sheridan, Goldsmith, Burke, Wilde, Shaw, Yeats – dramatists, philosophers, poets, novelists.

Similarly, the Cary military tradition was part of a broad Anglo-Irish military tradition. By the late nineteenth century, 'Anglo-Irish generals sometimes seemed to enjoy a monopoly of British command . . . The flow of Irish recruits was almost essential to the survival of the volunteer British Army, and the part played by the Anglo-Irish in the wars of the Empire was out of all proportion to their numbers.' All three members of the military triumvirate then patrolling the British Empire were Anglo-Irish: Kitchener, Roberts, Wolseley.[39]

More generally, to be Anglo-Irish was to belong to a distinctive community, men and women who, however maligned, however isolated, had found in themselves rich resources of creativity, vitality, pride, humour, courage. Elizabeth Bowen insisted that the Anglo-Irish 'saw courage apart from its context, as an end in itself';[40] Cyril Connolly learned that the Anglo-Irish were 'cleverer than the English and fonder of horses . . . poorer no doubt but with a poverty that brought into relief their natural aristocracy'.[41] Victoria

Glendinning saw as distinctive Anglo-Irish qualities 'a natural warmth and gregariousness which leads to a great sense of hospitality and a liking for celebrations of all kinds', a 'gift for friendship', an 'ability to live in the present and make a good time'.[42]

Of English origin, and always looking over their shoulders to England, the Anglo-Irish were also, after nine or ten generations, Irish. But they could be neither fully Irish nor fully English; and loss of power in the late nineteenth century exposed them as a divided people. They had developed an 'instinct either to take on the colour of the ruling class or to rebel'[43] (though some, like Cary, encompassed those extremes). J. C. Beckett argued that 'The most pervasive Anglo-Irish quality is a kind of ambivalence . . . arising from the need to be at once Irish and English, and leading sometimes to detachment, sometimes to a fierce aggressiveness . . .'[44] This was certainly true of Cary, who struggled throughout his life to resolve that tension within his personality.

Characteristically, he stressed the positive qualities of the Anglo-Irish as a 'forthright people, bold and confident' whose 'whole idea of life' was 'founded on protestant education, on individualism, on the conception of struggle, of competition . . .'[45] He also viewed the duality of his own early experience positively: 'My feeling about England is especially deep and conscious because I was born in Ireland to an Anglo-Irish family, long settled there. My earliest memories are of Donegal, its wild hills and the great sea loughs of Foyle and Swilly. I loved the country and the people, spoilers of children. But my heroes were the great men of English history, many of them Anglo-Irishmen like myself . . .'[46]

'most of me is Joyce'

'Two strains met in [my] parents – Dad the sportsman, the practical man – and my dear Mother who had the Joyce dreaminess, and reflectiveness . . . I have always fancied that most of me is Joyce.'[47] One of Cary's relatives came to a similar conclusion while he was a boy: 'I don't think you are like the Carys, but take after your Mother's Father for whom you are called . . .'[48] (Cary certainly resembled the Joyces in some physical features – in his brown eyes, for instance – though his prominent nose came from the Carys.)

In letters to his wife soon after their marriage, he had a lot to say about the Carys, but little about the Joyces. 'I did not know any of the Joyces well,' he admitted. Moreover, they were not Anglo-Irish but 'strange Mountainy men'[49] in origin. There was no detailed family history or tradition: the whole widespread Joyce family claimed descent from a thirteenth-century Welshman of Norman origin, Thomas de Jorse, who had settled in the 'Joyce Country' of Galway.[50] From there, Joyces had spread south and east. Cary's grandfather, James John Joyce, Manager of the Belfast Bank in Londonderry, may have been born in Omagh.[51]

Charlotte Louisa Joyce was the elder of James John Joyce's two daughters. More attractive than her sister Helen (known as Bay in the family), and high spirited, she liked to be called Charlie. Two early holiday diaries show her relishing travel in France and sailing, climbing and walking in Ireland.[52]

She was twenty-two when she met Arthur Pitt Chambers Cary during the summer of 1883, on one of her family's annual holidays in a rented house near Moville. The second son of Arthur Lunell Cary, he was then nineteen – lively, athletic and (with brilliantly blue eyes and aquiline features) extremely handsome. The Cary family were still living in Castle Cary, though they would soon have to move; and the Joyce and Cary girls quickly took to each other, organising parties, dances, games, picnics, painting expeditions.

It would be surprising if Arthur Cary (chaffingly called 'Frère' by his sisters) was not immediately attracted by this pretty, effervescent girl. She showed a charmingly unselfconscious openness about her feelings in the thank-you letters she wrote after the holiday. To Mrs Cary: 'If Frère has survived his descent from the telegraph pole where we left him: I hope he will look us up one of these days . . .' And to Olive, his eldest sister: 'The dance was good fun but of course Frère told you all about it and the young lady to whom he proposed (in his sleep) on the sofa!!'[53]

It took a while for Arthur Cary to open his eyes and do it again, and they weren't married until 1887. Even then Charlotte's father had reservations; but in 1883 Arthur Cary's prospects must have looked bleak indeed. He was not yet established in a profession; his father was in debt, with no chance of recovery; Castle Cary was about to be vacated; the Cary family was breaking up.

By the time Arthur Lunell Cary died, in August 1885, four of his children had already left Ireland. Olive became a governess and lady's companion in London. Two of the four sons emigrated to North America: Tristram joined the American Army and fought in Cuba during the Spanish-American War; George, at only seventeen, chose Canada, wangled himself into the Northwest Mounted Police, helped to put down the Riel Rebellion, and ended up in British Columbia. After their father's death, the youngest son, Leo, and three of his sisters – Agnes, Hessie and Netta – followed Olive to London. Only the youngest, Mab, remained in Inishowen, to look after their mother. She and her husband Harry Stevenson emigrated to North America after Jane Cary died in 1907.

But this final family exodus had only just begun when, in 1884, the twenty-year-old Arthur Pitt Chambers Cary decided to train as a civil engineer, and set off for London. He was 'aided by generous cousins'.[54] (They were probably the family of his recently dead uncle, John Pitt Kennedy, an influential agricultural expert in Ireland and member of the English Institute of Civil Engineers, after whom Arthur Cary named his second son.) He was at the New Bridge Works, Blackfriars, when, in September 1885, Charlotte Joyce wrote to him on the death of his father.

Arthur Cary had been back in Inishowen that summer and romance had steadied into love. 'I can hardly imagine you are over six weeks gone,' she wrote; 'and yet it seems years since we both sat on a "fish box" on Moville Strand, and tried to keep a grin on in case of tears (at least I did).' But she also teased him ferociously. 'My darling Arthur, I am going to be good . . . and write you a nice kind letter. Did I laugh at him? and make fun of his boots? Well I won't never no more.' And immediately she told him about a young man she had just met. 'I quite fell in love with Lewis . . . and had to get all your photos out and look at them to refresh my memory. Oh! I forgot this was to be "a nice letter"'. Even then she can't resist a final dig: 'I think the first time I heard your name mentioned it was "Oh Arthur Cary is an awful flirt, he would flirt with a broom stick if it had a petticoat on".' (In another letter she reported that a local girl called Peggy had burst out 'How did you do it, what way did you coax him, and all the girls crying about him.')

Arthur Cary was certainly attractive to the women in his orbit. Of one, his cousin Dora Stevenson, Charlotte observed tartly that 'she is very like a German, so fat and round, but she looks a good sort'. Of another, her own friend Memie Agar: 'Even if you had fallen in love with her, which I once thought you did, I don't suppose she would have said "Yes". She has no idea of doing on small means, of "making two ends meet" . . . but she is so good and nice I hope she will care for somebody some day.'

Although she missed Arthur deeply, Charlotte was not one to repine. She went to dances, and continued singing in public despite his objections; after one concert reporting with delight that 'the Derry paper says "Miss Joyce excelled herself"'. But she worried about his impulsiveness and love of physical activity, imagining him 'having a turn at the gloves or standing on your head for half an hour because somebody said "Cary couldn't" . . . I am so nervous when I think of all the mad things you do – and all for bravo!'[55] In fact, Arthur Cary was a good amateur boxer 'who might have won championships,' his elder son recalled, 'if my mother had allowed him to risk his fine delicate beak in the ring . . .'[56]

Charlotte's relations with the Cary girls deepened during her family's Inishowen summer holiday in 1886, and of their mother she wrote affectionately 'Such a treat to meet a woman that never says bad of any person and has a kind word to all.'

Charlotte was keen to leave Ireland. Her politics reflected the local Ascendancy's disenchantment as it contemplated the effects of the Land Act and increasing nationalist agitation. 'Ireland is done,' she wrote to Arthur, 'and we may all clear out as soon as we like and give those wretched Home rulers their own way. No good fighting against fate . . .' When in 1886 Arthur suggested that she visit him and Olive in London, Charlotte jumped at the opportunity, and, as always, enjoyed herself immensely – 'we went and ate beef and "stuff"! in Cheapside and knocked about all day ending with the Alhambra where you behaved most awfully and like anything but a "man of excellent address" – but I will draw a veil over the rest of the picture . . .'

She warned him that she was not a 'sweet lovely sort of person at all': ' . . . I believe I could count on my fingers all the people I really love in the world . . . The only thing is that when I do care for any one I don't deal in half measures . . .' Their life together would be hard – 'how we will manage to live double when you are so tight single is the puzzle . . . I am really anxious'; but 'I will try and make ends meet and I'm quite sure we won't be half so bad as people think.' She was anyway 'rather fond of roughing it'.

She had an ally in her mother. Together they laid siege to the Manager of the Belfast Bank, and soon Charlotte could report that she had wrung from him approval of Arthur's profession: 'I think you are quite right to go in for "Railway work" and so does Father; it is hard not making money, but in the end you will get more . . .' She suggested that Arthur should now write to her father and ask for her hand in marriage.[57] Mr James John Joyce faced facts – especially his daughter's determination. In replying to Arthur Cary's letter he announced a handsome settlement. Charlotte would be assured of £100 per year, and would inherit between £2,000 and £3,000, with a share of his property.[58]

A wedding was arranged. It would of course – for Charlotte was the daughter of one of Londonderry's prominent citizens – take place in the Church of Ireland cathedral, Christ Church. The Reverend Joseph Potter, a family friend who had confirmed Charlotte a few years earlier, would officiate.

Even before the day arrived, the sun shone on the couple: 'Yesterday the Mayor of Derry called on Father saying some people had been speaking to him and wishing to give Father an address for his long residence and goodness to the people of Derry, and they thought this a good opportunity and wished to give Father an address and ME! a purse of gold!!'[59] During his address, the Mayor was to rejoice in the alliance of two great local families: the Joyces, successful, newly rich, lords of the future; and the Carys, 'one of the oldest county families in the North of Ireland', lords of the past.[60]

Charlie Joyce knew exactly what sort of wedding she wanted: 'My idea of weddings is Everyone cries! everyone kisses everyone else! everyone looks hatred at the groom for taking away the bride! everyone says "Amen" now and then! and everyone is immensely relieved when it's all over, as I'm sure we shall be . . .'[61] One would like to think that her every wish was fulfilled on 15 August 1887, for eleven years later she was dead, at the age of thirty-seven, leaving behind a still-youthful husband and two small sons.

CHAPTER TWO

LOSS

1888–1899

'I remember my mother and loved her'

Arthur Joyce Lunel Cary, elder son of Arthur Pitt Chambers Cary and Charlotte Louisa Cary, was born in Londonderry on 7 December 1888. Charlotte had returned home to be near her mother and the family doctor for her first confinement. Their second son, John Pitt Cary (always called Jack), was born in London just over three years later, on 28 January 1892.

Cary once remarked that he had been 'rheumaticky as a small boy';[1] he also suffered early from pleurisy and fainting spells. Later, when he could read, it was noticed that he had a weakness in his right eye; and as an adult he was to suffer, sometimes severely, from asthma. But the baby in a series of sketches made by his Aunt Hessie in the summer of 1889 – blissfully sleeping, dreamily gazing at his observer, sitting on the floor surrounded by dolls – looks contented and healthy. In one sketch, Arthur Cary is stretched comfortably on a sofa with pipe and newspaper while his small son, safely ensconced, reaches upward in confident curiosity.[2]

Clearly Cary was cossetted from birth, enveloped in love and approval. He always insisted that 'I was one of those lucky children who had everything to give him happiness'.[3] And his were not only 'the most devoted, the most delightful parents', they were 'endlessly interesting in themselves'.[4] The sudden loss of his mother when he was nine years old can only have been severely traumatic. 'I remember my mother and loved her,' Cary told his wife.[5] But in his published reminiscences he commented on her rarely, and then vaguely or inaccurately (for instance, he always said that his mother died when he was eight; he was nearly ten).

However, one early memory connected with his mother he repeated several times: 'I learnt my prayers . . . kneeling in my mother's lap. The usual child's prayer for God to bless him and his mother in Christ's name, followed by a verse from the hymn "Gentle Jesus, meek and mild".'[6] As the prayers stretched to include the names of all those closest to him – relatives, friends, servants – he 'gabbled them . . . and climbed eagerly into bed to hear my story'.[7] That evening ritual was, he believed, 'the most important event in my life', for it gave him, immutably, 'the idea as well as the sense of love as a permanent and indestructible element in the world'.[8]

But apparently the memory held no clear image of Charlotte Cary; he had, he wrote, only two memories of her. The first is adumbrated enigmatically in one of his notebooks, as an idea for a group of 'Irish sketches': 'The bell wire and my mother on the old pier.'[9] At the age of seven, holidaying in Inishowen with his family, he had got into mischief:

> I had pulled out some bells, a common trick those days among children, and then, worried that the police were after me, had gone into hiding . . . My father and mother had gone to Derry by the morning boat and I felt that no one else could take their place in this crisis.
>
> As the steamer, the *Earl of Dunraven*, came beating down the lough that evening, I slipped from the mountain back into the lanes of the village, so among the boats on the shore, where I kept under cover till the *Earl* was actually tied up and the passengers were away on the shore, to be met by half the population.

And then he rushed to his mother, threw his arms around her, and 'stammered out my tale'. Immediately comfort and security enfolded him, and he would always afterwards remember 'her smile of welcome', her laughing kiss, her reassurances.[10] That there are differences of detail in his two accounts of the incident is characteristic of Cary's reminiscences (he was often cavalier, like any imaginative writer, with ancillary facts); but the core of the incident is constant.[11]

During his various visits to Inishowen and Londonderry in later life, Cary could still gather information about his mother, for she had been 'greatly loved by all who knew her. Fifty years after her death, I have heard old men speak of her charm, her gaiety, her humour. She was not witty like some of my aunts . . . She was too immediate in her response, too quick to feel, she had a soul at once too tender, too modest and too gay. She could laugh at people but she could not despise them; she laughed at them . . . as much out of sympathy as amusement.'[12] He would also learn about his mother from her diaries, and her love letters to his father: all these Arthur Cary gave him – a moving gesture of love and confidence, and, for a future writer, a gift of inestimable value.[13]

The second memory of his mother was very different from the image of protective strength on the old pier at Moville. It must have cut deeply into the nine-year-old boy's mind. Only twice does he seem to have tried to record it, in drafts of an uncompleted essay and poem.

> My mother died when I was eight, but she was always my refuge. My only memories of her are two, one when she was dying and I, who was ill at the same time, was brought in to see her for the last time. I did not know that I should not see her again, but something in the event, no doubt my father's misery, fixed every detail in my memory. I can see her still, vividly, her white face on a low pillow, among the cloud of her hair, still a young woman's hair, while she looked at me and murmured a few words.[14]

Pale as linen, your face turned to me, your dark eyes
Seeking to know how your work might be accomplished
In one word, in one touch bathing my childhood's flesh
In essence of your spirit, in all your love, your wisdom
[You] knew that I could not learn
That you must leave me to whim, to chance, to fate
Be good, you said . . .[15]

Charlotte Cary died on 1 October 1898 in her London home, of pneumonia. Apparently she had gone out in bitter weather, against advice, to interview a prospective maid – an action characteristic of the independent, high-spirited girl Arthur Cary had fallen in love with fifteen years earlier. She had perhaps always been physically weaker than she allowed others, and herself, to acknowledge. A letter to Arthur Cary before their marriage contains a passing remark that, in retrospect, looks ominous: 'you must not begin to imagine that I am delicate, for I never was ill (very bad) in my life . . .'[16]

Apart from the more direct effects of mother loss at an early age – the sharp sense of disruption and insecurity, and the compensating withdrawal into imagination, which have so often resulted in artistic self-expression – Cary's representation of women in his novels was strongly influenced (he tended to define central female characters as maternal, but carelessly or even destructively so); and several of his protagonists (all three in the Second Trilogy) were motherless as children. Virginia Woolf, who lost her mother at the age of thirteen, confronted obsessive memories by fictionalising her in *To the Lighthouse*; Cary's mother became 'one of those invisible presences who . . . play so important a part in every life'.[17]

'an implacable and all-powerful enemy'

Arthur Cary took Charlotte's death hard. Fortunately he had family near by. His uncle Tristram was living in Gunnersbury, a village in process of becoming a suburb of London; and in London itself three of his four sisters, together with his youngest brother, Leo, had set themselves up in an apartment in Alderney Street in Pimlico that they called (mischievously, after a short story by Bret Harte) 'Poker Flat'. Agnes was still a governess; Hessie now studying painting. Netta, having learned the new-fangled art of typewriting, was working as a secretary (a profession just becoming available and attractive to young women). Leo, though 'handicapped by weak eyesight', also worked in an office.[18]

Netta came immediately to her stricken brother. She took over the household and looked after her two small nephews. This was the beginning of a lifetime's affection between Cary and his aunt, 'a real dear'.[19] The portrait of Delia in *A House of Children* is one of his tributes to her witty, forceful, loving personality. (She smoked heavily as a young woman – when ladies did not, at least in public; and as an old woman set her bed on fire with a cigarette!) Netta was the first of Cary's surrogate mothers, and perhaps the most important.

No doubt the two boys also found consolation in each other. Jack was bigger, stronger, more restrained and conventional than his elder brother. The relative who had pronounced Joyce a Joyce averred that Jack was 'so like your dear Grand Father Cary'.[20] As small boys, they 'had regular battles – in spite of our difference in age'.[21] But Cary's very earliest memory related to Jack, and it was a positive, protective one: he was about three 'when my brother, a baby in long clothes, was put into my arms'. He could recall, he said, the very feel of 'the weight of the child and a certain anxiety, probably due to a warning to hold tight'. And he could *see* himself clearly, the baby on his lap – 'and not only myself, but the chair I sat in, even my position in the room, a double room with folding doors. I daresay the occasion was my brother's christening.'[22] This vivid scene, the earliest instance of Cary's 'fly-paper memory',[24] is pervaded by an urgent awareness of responsibility for the wellbeing of a helpless infant.

For Cary, who from an early age 'wanted to go into the Navy, and could not, on account of my eyes',[25] it must have been galling to see his younger brother become a sailor. It must have been galling, too, to endure Jack's sporting prowess, which far outstripped his own. Yet the two boys drew together steadily as they matured, and always liked and respected each other, in spite of their very different personalities. In letters to his wife, Cary often wrote very warmly about Jack, wanting her to appreciate his sterling qualities. 'He's shy, you know, and has no great fund of conversation', but 'a dear boy, unselfish and affectionate'. And again, ' . . . I never knew him make an enemy in his life.'[26]

For both brothers, it was a secure, comforting and beneficent relationship; and one senses the influence of Jack Cary on a character like Bill Wilcher in *To Be a Pilgrim*, noble in his simplicity, his generosity and courage.

Cary can never have needed Jack's support more than after he endured, within four months of his mother's death, a further intense emotional experience.

The Christmas after Charlotte Cary's death was spent in Ireland, where the Joyce and Cary relatives poured out consolation, distraction, love. Back in England at the beginning of 1899, Cary received letters from both grand-mothers. Grandmother Cary told him about 'a concert in the Temperance Hall. The chief attraction was a phonograph, which sang and talked in different voices – which the country people thought just like magic!'[27]

When he received this letter, the ten-year-old Cary was living with an aunt and cousins at their country estate, Tugwood, near Cookham Dean, Berkshire. These wealthy Irish relatives were Kennedys, the widow and children of John Pitt Kennedy (and close connections of the novelist Margaret Kennedy). Cary was sent to them, on his own, for about three months, from the end of January 1899 until Easter, while his father went to Hastings for a holiday and Jack stayed at home in London with Aunt Netta. Whatever the reasons for this arrangement (Cary remembered it as intended to help him recuperate from an illness, probably the influenza from which he had been suffering when his mother died; and it may well have been intended to lighten Netta's burden), he must have been very deeply, if mutely, distressed by a long separation from his immediate family so soon after his mother's death. His grandmothers' long letters suggest that they feared this.

Soon after he arrived at Tugwood – perhaps the following morning, 'a clear, bright morning' – Cary wandered on his own into nearby woods, attracted by the sound of men, horses and hounds gathering for a fox-hunt: 'the hounds were among the trees, the huntsman and whips were [urging] them on to find the fox, and the attendant horsemen were waiting outside, on their restless beautiful mounts, for the halloo. I was gloriously happy in the midst of things.'

> Then there was a cry of 'gone away', the horn tootled, the horsemen jammed down their hats and came galloping along the green rides. I ran after them as fast as I could, but I was blinded by the clods of mud thrown up at me by the hooves, and though, when out of range of the mud shower, I could run open-eyed, following the sound, the shouts, the horn, I was outdistanced in about two minutes. I stopped to listen, and the horn, now very faint, came to me again, but from quite a new direction. Quite possibly it was not the huntsman's call at all, but I made off after it till the noise of a galloping horse, far behind, made me turn back. A red coat dashed between a couple of trees and vanished. I made my way to the place and followed his tracks . . . I had no idea that I was lost until the tracks ended in a pool from which they did not emerge. That horse seemed to have disappeared into the earth, or the sky, like a spirit. I was startled by this mystery, and almost at the same moment, discovered that I was totally lost. I can still remember that first shock of surprise and alarm, the confident feeling that I should soon find my way out . . .

Gradually his confidence evaporated, as he wandered in circles, losing all sense of direction. Then, panic –

> the slow growth of a special kind of terror, a sense of not merely being helpless, lost, but of being played with, deliberately tricked and abused. I was not a very superstitious child, I was used to being alone in what would be called now wild and gloomy places, in Irish hills and bogs. Our Irish servants' tales of ghosts and demons had been laughed out of my imagination by a sporting and sceptical family. But no amount of reasoning can contradict an experience, and my experience in these woods was of an invisible enemy that was determined to keep me lost.

Dusk fell. 'I had run out, in the excitement of seeing the hounds and the hunt, without a coat, and now, as I began to feel the bitter cold, I understood clearly enough as I shivered and stiffened that I might actually die of cold. But still the greatest terror, that I have never forgotten, was the sense of being played with, of being deliberately tricked and tortured by an implacable and all-powerful enemy.' Eventually, terrified, he 'knelt down and prayed that God would shew me the way out of this fearful wood'.

> I then started rushing about again, more and more panic-stricken, till suddenly I saw a green ride, which ended a few yards away, in a gate. The moon was now getting up and I recognised the gate as the one I had first entered. It was within a half-mile of the house where I was staying with my Kennedy cousins. In less than ten minutes, I was sitting in front of the drawing-room fire and eating sweet biscuits from the nursery box. It was long past my bed-time, and I was supposed to be convalescing after an illness, and I was not allowed to be out at all except well wrapped up . . . I

had only just arrived on my visit, and I had been warned not to wander abroad in the woods by myself until I knew my bearings. I felt extremely guilty. My plan was to get warm, eat anything I could lay my hands on, and steal off to bed before I was discovered.

Fortunately a maid caught me on the stairs. Fortunately because there were search parties out in all directions, the county police had been warned, and my hostess, a nervous woman, who had herself spent the whole afternoon driving here and there on the search, was just off to a neighbouring major to organise a mass hunt which might have gone on all night. A groom sent off a carriage horse, stopped this last grand enterprise in the nick – my aunt came home and put me to bed with a pig, that is to say, a hot bottle of stoneware wrapped up in a flannel petticoat. She also ordered me hot supper in bed . . . So far from being reproached I was received like a hero and I certainly gathered the impression that if a small boy wants to make a nuisance of himself, he had better do it on the largest possible scale.[28]

The repercussions of that episode were probably far greater than Cary's narrative initially suggests. A sign of suppression is the absence of reference, in so detailed an account, to the fact that his mother had recently died. One wonders, too, whether he was at this time beginning to suffer from asthma – a psychosomatic disease that could well have begun during that traumatic winter. Unassuaged anger at his mother's loss, terror in its aftermath, may also have inculcated the propensity to violence that was, intermittently, to mark his life and his writing. Cary's psychological health would now be very dependent on his brother, Aunt Netta, the family – and, above all, his father.

CHAPTER THREE

INISHOWEN

1892–1900

'*I lived between two worlds*'
As a small boy Cary became aware that his life was split between two very different environments: for most of the year, London; in summer, and occasionally at other times, Inishowen. Not only was he an Anglo-Irishman, he grew up in both England and Ireland, in two 'worlds so different that they could not be reconciled'.

His London world was centred in 'a small house . . . among miles of streets in which all the people seemed equally drab and anonymous'.[1] In fact, during his childhood, Cary's family lived in two small South London terrace houses, not far from his father's work as a civil engineer in the firm of Rendell, Palmer and Tritton: until he was about eight, 11 Ivydale Road, near Nunhead Cemetery; then 41 Kitto Road, about half a mile away. His memory blurs the two.

From 41 Kitto Road he sent his first public letter, probably written soon after he had seen Queen Victoria from the 'top of a horse bus'[2] – presumably during a procession celebrating her Diamond Jubilee in 1897, when he was eight. It is an emphatically conservative document:

> Your Majesty the Queen,
> I am writing to you because I heard you liked to hear from your subjects. I want you please, to try and stop the man who started the Strand improvement Scheme and let all those queer, and interesting, old buildings and shops and houses stay where they are.
> I remain,
> Your loving subject,
> A. J. L. Cary[3]

Although his London was predominantly drab, one enjoyable occasion was his visit to Ina Sarratt, sister of his Grandmother Joyce and widow of a naval captain who had commanded the Queen's yacht.[4] She was living in a cottage, one of the Pensioners' Houses at Penge, in South East London. There Cary had 'looked through [the captain's] telescope, handled his sword, and learnt with delight that captains wore cocked hats. I had also been attracted by the cottages, because they had a porter at the great gate. It seemed to me that life could offer no greater happiness than glory in that old quadrangle guarded by a porter.'[5] The account balances insecurity and security, adventurous action and protected peace; suggesting that Cary's thought was already dualistic, that he was strongly attracted to opposite modes of living.

Memories of the annual two-month holidays of his childhood are the essence of Cary's radiant semi-autobiographical novel *A House of Children*. A discarded opening rapturously recalls a series of epiphanies composing 'a life so rich with events that in memory it seems to have been all my life': 'My childhood in recollection is full of spray, boats, the little harvest fields of Donegal, white feet seen in green water, and village wars between the mountain and the beach. Above all I can see the faces of children and none of them in repose. Everyone is laughing, shouting, frowning, demanding. Every expression as it springs into the eye of memory, is full of purpose and eagerness . . .'[6]

The very journey from Liverpool to Inishowen was thrilling. Cary vividly recalled sitting on the boat deck of the steamer, between two Cary aunts. They are gossiping and smoking, oblivious to the boy's exhilaration, terror, vertigo, 'the precipice, within six inches of my feet, and the huge valleys of the Atlantic opening below it'. Decades later he could still feel 'that wonder, that pressure, the sense of being wedged between firm thighs,' could 'see the enormous green waves advancing against the iron sheer of the sides' and 'have again the acute and continuous sense of danger . . .'[7]

Arrival off Moville was a further excitement. In a draft for *Castle Corner*, Cary drew on his memories of the steamer's approach, and the transfer of passengers to tenders that would carry them the short distance to the harbour.

> The throb of the screw stopped and the ship rushed smoothly forward by its own weight. An open boat, pointed at each end, of the build known locally as a druntun, whirled up . . . on the bow waves' back . . . The steersman turned up a face like a piece of the sail, bawled 'Hi yar away widder live dar.' . . .
>
> An inner door opened in the steamer's side, far down. A ladder was thrown down. Two passengers for the shore scrambled on board, and two of the rowers held up their arms; a baby was dropped to them; boxes and bags marched in procession along the upraised heads of the crew like fragments of a leaf upon a stream of ants . . .[8]

In a watercolour, Cary shows the druntun, and some of its crew and passengers among them, gazing dreamily downwards into the water, the small boy Evelyn Corner, who is clearly Joyce Cary.[9]

The Inishowen landscape is a brilliant, insistent presence throughout *A House of Children*. 'Wherever we went in Annish we were among the mountains and saw the lough or the ocean; often, from some high place, the whole Annish peninsula, between the two great loughs; and the Atlantic, high up in the sky, seeming like a mountain of water higher than the tallest of land.'[10] Far away, years later, Cary would yearn for that landscape: Lough Foyle 'runs in my blood'.[11] For Cary, as for Felix Corner, the first view of the Inishowen peninsula after a long absence was, 'because he loved it, the most beautiful in the world'.[12]

'that place was like home and I loved it'

Once ashore, Cary would be joyously welcomed into one of the two family households. During those Inishowen holidays, he wrote, he had 'two different beings',[13] depending on whether he was living with his Grandmother Cary or his Grandmother Joyce.

Jane Cary lived in two houses during the last twenty years of her life, Whitecastle and Clare Cottage. She had begun renting Whitecastle within two years of her husband's death in 1885; then, after about a decade, she had moved to the much smaller Clare Cottage less than a mile below Castle Cary.

The Big Houses which dominate the openings of *Castle Corner* and *A House of Children* are both based on Whitecastle. Castle Corner, 'a Georgian house built about 1760 on the site of the original castle and fort of 1615', is so close to the water that, from a boat out on the lough, it 'seemed to stand in the sea', dazzling 'against the dark trees of the little park; a neat white house, with a grey slate roof'.[14] Dunamara is 'an old, long house with a white face and dark, slate roof, set apart from the trees on the steep hill-side'. It has 'no beauty except the fine proportions of door, window, chimney and roof'; and 'almost no garden, for it stood on a narrow shelf between the hill and the lough'. In storms, 'waves broke as far as the doorstep and spray rattled on the roof like shrapnel'.[15]

For a small boy, Whitecastle was unforgettably romantic. Yet if Cary was disappointed when his Grandmother moved to Clare Cottage during the mid 1890s, he soon learned to love the smaller house even more. In memory it became the heart of Inishowen's glory. 'How I loved Clare,' he told his wife, 'the clouds, the wind, the rain even, and the mountains, with the lovely Lough Foyle below.'[16] Set on a low bluff, Clare Cottage faced, across the Lough, 'the hills of County Derry, an unforgettable view'; its garden 'was full of flowers, and on the house stood a flagstaff [up] which, when any member of the family came by steamer, the family flag was hoisted to the salute of guns'.[17]

A further attraction was the 'small upper chamber' that Cary was always given for his bedroom – 'The first room of my own that I can remember'. On one side was the lough; on the other,

> Its round-topped windows looked out on the trees of a short drive and a graveyard beyond. There was one tree close to the windows whose leaves brushed the glass, and on moonlight nights threw its shadows on the white counterpane and the floor. Those shadows, swaying and driving about the room in an Atlantic gale, are so vivid still in my imagination that I could make a film of their motions, the swing of the big branches, suddenly checked in a gust; the wild tearing of the leaves. All the time I could hear,

under the whistling and howling of the wind, the crash of waves and the rattle of the stones on the shore.

And I remember vividly too the sensation of waking among this turmoil with a sense of alarm which was also exhilaration.

Another room in Clare Cottage was also memorable: 'It was a small room on a half-landing and the books were stacked against the walls to the very ceiling. This room was my refuge in misfortune, and also my den . . . no one ever came there . . .' He remembered 'the excitement of those hours when I could be alone with books', lying

among heaped magazines and reading the *Strand*, the *Wide World*, or deep in Ballantine, Henty, Dickens, Lever or Buffons Beasts . . . But it was not stories that absorbed me, at seven or eight. Even in Ballantine or Henty I was more interested in the illustrations . . . And my favourite reading was not books but magazines, especially the *Wide World*. This magazine . . . guaranteed that all its stories were true. [18]

In early notes for of A *House of Children,* Evelyn Corner is 'a voracious reader and wants to know everything. They drive me out – saying I'm ruining my eyes. I enjoy myself out – but with *impatience*. I feel I'm wasting my time.'[19]

This opportunity to become a voracious reader, to develop an interest in the visual and in excitingly 'factual' narrative, was the gift of his Grandmother Cary, who never 'willingly destroyed a book or even a magazine'.[20] She was 'a very clever and well read woman';[21] Aunt Hersey, in A *House of Children*, is clearly a portrait:

She walked upright, even leaning back from the waist, and had a very smooth step. Her features were dignified; she had a firm chin, a small aquiline nose and well-marked, dark eyebrows, and she carried her chin high. Her dignity, however, was never stiff; she had been very well brought up in the old style which was intended to give a girl social charm. No one could be as charming as Aunt Hersey . . .

She was . . . extremely simple in mind and taste. She had no ambition and her idea of a woman was of someone put into the world to look after a man, and a house, and children. She was therefore completely happy in this task, and kept, to old age, a certain irresponsibility.[22]

Jane Cary loved small boys, and Cary was at ease in her company. She had established a family magazine to help keep her now-scattered family in touch with each other, and encouraged her grandsons to contribute to it. 'My writing began very young, at eight or nine, in the family magazine,'[23] which was 'a treasure of stories and pictures,'[24] Cary remembered. Evelyn Corner's first literary sallies, his poems on 'The Ant' and 'The Microbe', are variations of Cary's own.[25]

Holidays in Grandmother Cary's household encouraged, paradoxically, the 'Joyce' side of Cary's personality – his dreaminess, his artistic sensibility. At Clare Cottage he was often 'the only child' in a house 'full of old portraits and old books. I read enormously and dreamed still more.'

Just half a mile away from Clare Cottage, up the hill, was Castle Cary. Arthur Lunell Cary's large white mid-nineteenth-century house was owned by

37

the businessman who had foreclosed the Carys' mortgage a decade earlier. But the boy could 'wander in the old walled garden' and 'have all the romantic feeling appropriate to the Banished Earl of all the story books'.[26] He felt 'at once deprived, depressed and yet immensely happy'.[27]

Happiness came, too, from his relations with his Grandmother's servants, who gave him affection and told him stories. Like Evelyn Corner, he learned to look 'confidently for friendship among the maids and men of any Irish house wherever I happened to be.'[28]

The kitchen of Whitecastle was a particularly delightful haunt. It was 'at the bottom of fourteen stone steps', a big room with 'dim arched windows, high up in the dirty walls'.[29] For the small boy, 'it was a complete change to go under its smoky ceiling hung with clothes-racks and feel the stone floor under one's feet, to see the work going forward.' An early memory was of 'an old fisherman . . . who used to come to grandmother's kitchen . . . and about whose great boots I hovered at four or five, attracted by the sense of strength and courage and desperation.'[30]

Mrs Fee in *A House of Children* is probably a version of his grandmother's cook Mrs Tobin. 'Her talk fascinated us because of her view of the world. She was a hell-fire Protestant' who might talk about 'some poor woman's pain, two days in labour, or some young man's dying, "a year in bed till you could see through his chest, and he that was the only son, a dear lovely boy. He cries for his mammy still when the fear of death comes on him, but she's dead herself this seven weeks." "But he won't go to hell, Mrs Fee?" "Ah, who could say – who knows what God wants?"' Mrs Fee 'loved cleanliness and felt a kind of tender sympathy towards chairs and tables, baths and carpets, as well as people.'

The gardener, Dan Kane, is represented in *A House of Children* by old Roe, 'gardener, coachman, pumpman and sailor to the house'. A 'melancholy stooping old man', shaky and rheumatic, his greatest pleasure was a nightly stroll while smoking a short clay pipe. Roe's nephew, Oweny, is Cary's 'very close friend' the servant Terence; and the two boys would often 'slip away among the trees or up the creek. Our favourite hiding-place was an old mill on Dunamara upper creek.'[31]

Cary would also accompany Terence in his ass cart, on such chores as fetching turf from the bog for the winter. Another journey might take the boys to a remote farm at Tremone Bay, on the northern coast of the peninsula, where the good-natured farmer's wife, Peggy, would welcome them. The greatest attraction of the farm at Tremone for the young Cary was that it

lay in a semicircle round a bay facing the northern Atlantic: the spray from the big combers left salty crystals on the potato flower and coated the oat stalks, perpetually turned by the wind, like hoar frost . . . One could not tell exactly where the farm ended and the shore began. The sand was as yellow as butter even when it was dry . . . [We watched] the rise of the swell out of a perfectly smooth surface, so that one saw each wave grow from a mere green curve, like a fish's back, into a huge rolling mountain, which seemed about to overwhelm, in its stately motion, the whole land . . . at its final foot one saw suddenly that the water, as if by a new mystery, was flowing uphill into the slopes of the great precipice, so that one saw through its agitated streams . . . the flowing brassy sand; its enormous crown began to lean forward . . .[32]

An occasion at Clare Cottage, when Terence reacted cheekily to an order, 'must have alarmed me or I wouldn't remember it . . . I had just been in England and perhaps I had acquired some new ideas about the proper relation between master and servant.' But the adult Carys responded calmly to Terence's 'provocation'; he

then went and mowed the lawn and the family continued breakfast which, with the spring sun on the table-cloth and the cups and spoons and the flowers, seemed to me the most beautiful and happiest ceremony in life . . . I remember especially a china hen which used to sit on a china nest in which eggs were kept warm in a coil of hay.

I remember it especially as a part of this scene when Terence interrupted the sweet intense delight of eating, with a fresh appetite, in the room full of new sunlight and cool sea air. Perhaps in my very childish feeling the gorgeous fragile hen stood for the things, delightful but easily destroyed, endangered by all rebellious movements. This may seem far-fetched but I had been brought up in the very air of revolution. I can't remember what idea I had, if any, about nationalist movements and secret societies and I certainly didn't think of Terry as a possible rebel; but a child . . . takes in a social atmosphere through the pores of his mind without knowing it. [33]

At times during the summer there would be an influx of Carys and Clare Cottage would ring with the vitality of 'a very vivid and fluent generation'. There were games, conversations, walks, horse-rides and picnics. There was swimming, in the creek near Clare Cottage, or off the rocky shore which, itself, constantly invited exploration. One summer Cary used driftwood to build a hut there. And his first diary entry, in a sketch-book, is from 1898, when he was nine: 'Monday, 1 August. Fishing for 3 hrs in morning. 29 codling, 1 glasson, 10 brazers, 4 flukes.'[34]

Holidays in Grandmother Cary's household were in general orderly, restful; 'routine' and 'regularity' prevailed. In his notes for a projected short story, Cary outlined his moods as 'The small boy at Clare': 'The feeling of boredom at Clare – before going – and the feeling of delight on the return – especially with the creeper coming in at the window and the leaves tapping on it.' He found peace, acceptance; but the security bred, after a while, restlessness.

During those holidays Cary seems to have begun to feel a confident selfhood. His notes for that short story focus on the presence of his mother's cousin in the Cary household. The characterisation of Jim Joyce as a volatile bachelor ('silent for long intervals, then talkative') who fails in his literary endeavours because he is losing 'a terrific struggle with the drink', may have been more imaginative than usual (perhaps through an association with the *other* James Joyce). But it is surely significant that 'Uncle J.' brings Joycean sensibilities into the Cary household, and validates there the name by which Cary was known in the family to distinguish him from his father: Joyce, his mother's surname.

To the world at large, Joyce had become feminine as a first name; it exposed Cary throughout his life to occasional teasing, or misunderstanding, and led in middle age to a quirky acquaintanceship with the actress Joyce Carey (he had her to tea and they exchanged Christmas cards). But Uncle J. 'is bitter against girls called Joyce – and says they have no right to the name – there's no blood in them. How many of them have any right to a great name.'[35] In *A House of Children*, Evelyn Corner meditates to the same effect.[36]

For Cary, with his early recognition of the connotations of names, and with the knowledge that his first name was also his mother's surname, validation of the integrity of both names was important. Tension between his Joyce and Cary 'beings' would recur, but Clare Cottage seems to have posited unity, completion. 'My dearest memories are of Ireland, my grandmother at Clare – that place was like home and I loved it.'[37]

'The two glories'

The Joyce household in Inishowen was very different, but almost as important in the boy's development. Cary had not spent much time in his Joyce grandparents' home after his mother's death, and his memories of Londonderry probably derive from the winter of 1898–9, when the Joyce family drew together in grief. James and Helen Joyce lived above the Belfast Bank, just inside the walls of the old city. Cary remembered exploring the nearby docks:

> Derry quays were then busy and very small steamers unloaded there coal, timber, bricks, cattle food and took away cattle, whisky, potatoes, peat. While we stayed at my grandfather's we loved to wander among the squares of timber, the cattle pens, or steal into the vast sheds. The rattle of cranes, the tremendous noise of dray wheels and the enormous hooves of the Clydesdales . . . suddenly changed to a rolling thunder as they passed from the stone quay to the road.

There was also a memory of political violence – men fighting in one of the old city gates, 'a terrific noise of yelling and cursing'.

After Charlotte Cary's death, her parents continued their custom of renting a house near Moville for a family holiday each summer. One of these houses, which Cary recalled vividly, was the imposing, castellated Ravenscliff (the original of Crowcliff in *A House of Children*). On the north edge of Moville, it was approached by a winding drive from the road, but, standing at the edge of the shore, was open to the sea. There Joyce and Jack Cary would be in a group of several children. Helen Beasley, 'a good looking child with long yellow hair down to her waist',[38] eldest of Aunt Bay's six children, was about Cary's age and became his 'first love (aged 10) but she grew up!!'[39] She remembered him telling 'wildly imaginative tales, notably about his namesake King Arthur, who held court, he claimed, above Ravenscliff'.[40]

Their Grandmother, Cary wrote in a semi-autobiographical short story, 'always engaged a governess to give them morning lessons' in 'a little parlour which looked towards the shore not thirty yards away'. Felix Corner, Cary's surrogate in the story, is aged eight; and is drawing 'on the edge of the table with a pin' the sort of picture that fills Cary's early sketch-books, 'a full-rigged ship'. The current governess, Miss Farrell, is so severe that he 'did not dare, for more than five minutes, to put on the dolphin striker, his favourite spar. But when he can bear no longer to see the naked bowsprit, and tries very cautiously to give the one necessary scratch' – Miss Farrell leaps at him. Standing in the corner he looks at the window and 'suddenly he remembers a picture in the *Wide World Magazine* of a burglar hanging by his hands from a window-sill. He was just about to drop forty feet into a shrubbery.' When Miss Farrell is called out of the room, Felix inspires the other children to emulate the burglar. Waiting till last, he is caught – but the governess, one of several worn out by the lively children, breaks into 'loud helpless sobs'.[41]

While staying with their Grandmother, the Joyce cousins were allowed great freedom. 'We went fishing, exploring, stealing rides on other people's horses, sailing on the lough, often for long journeys. We were as free as the mountain slopes, and often in mischief.'[42]

In *A House of Children* the terrifying rapture of sailing in the lough, whether in the old scow kept below Clare Cottage ('a huge clumsy tub, built for the roughest work,' which 'surged and butted through the water, tearing a huge furrow through the green and leaving a wake like a steamer') or in a smaller boat (which 'galloped and leaped over the fields and banks of water like a race-horse'), is magnificently rendered. 'We triumphed in our scow, and every time it smashed through a sea I felt a personal victory.'[43] With such memories, Cary would always love sailing.

The eldest in the family group, he also became 'a gang-leader of criminal youth . . . I was quite as mischievous as other small boys, and perhaps more enterprising than some of my fellows. One whole summer I was leader of the gang that fought other gangs with stones and sods. And our proudest feat was to steal the coastguard's boat in order to make a surprise landing in enemy territory.'

What he most enjoyed, Cary insisted, was 'the breaking of the law' for 'the glory of leadership among a group of other small boys'. And

> I adored Father for his courage and skill as a sportsman, renowned among the people. But I admired him too as a man of quixotic honour. I had the sharpest sense of right and wrong. When, in the excitement of battle, I stole the boat, I knew I was doing wrong; that was the chief of my pleasure. I knew, too, very well, where the wrong must stop, or it would bring me shame instead of glory. Because I loved my father, I dreaded to lose his good opinion.[44]

Arthur Cary was not able to spend more than short periods of the summer in Inishowen, but his flying visits were filled with exuberant physical activity. He would take his sons sailing, climbing, walking, shooting, fishing, swimming. A characteristic exploit was performed on the shore near Carrig Cnoc, the holiday house of their relatives the Chambers:

> there was a great cleft in the rock [promontory] by which the fishermen would make their way to their night lines, laid out in the sea. When the tide

was in, it was necessary to jump across this cleft, from face to face of rock, that is, taking off from footholds in one face and landing on the other. This was a tricky jump and only the younger more daring men preferred it. Others waited for the tide. But I had seen my father jump it. Afterwards, when some fell and [were] hurt or drowned, he had a plank made at the place, which was for a long time called after him. The people, I've been told, accepted and used the bridge only because it came from him who had not been afraid to jump the cleft.[45]

Cary vividly recalled learning to swim under his father's tutelage (as he had learned to pray under his mother's):

On my first sea bathes, when I was seven, my father used to lever me overboard in a bight of rope, and then row slowly forward to keep the boat from dashing against me . . .
   Those deep sea bathes were at first terrifying to me; as a child they always gave me a sense of nervous tension . . . I could not get over the feeling that the depth of the sea was especially dangerous; that there were monsters in it which might seize me by the legs . . .
   Added to this were the fears, based in experience, of being dashed against the boat, and sucked under it when attempting to climb in. I was a light weight and could not pull myself into the boat; which always sucked my legs beneath its hull. So I was usually bruised and scraped in being dragged aboard . . .

His father would sometimes row out into the Atlantic, beyond the mouth of Lough Foyle. These expeditions made Cary 'apprehensive': 'The reason, I think, was not only the feel of the boat, the company of my father, the sense of expanse, both of sky and sea, which I always loved, but the very fact that I had to screw up my courage to jump over the side.' His mingled fear, excitement, and, finally, sense of manly achievement, were almost overwhelmingly exhilarating.

The breathtaking thrill of the cold water was mixed with the sense 'Here I am in the deep ocean'; and as I trod water, I felt the black depth underneath me and triumphed over it. I believe my father, smiling at me from the boat, perfectly understood my feelings . . . it was part of my keen delight in the bathes, which lasted for a long time afterwards, that he thought me brave. Courage, I knew, was for him the first of the virtues, the foundation of all the rest . . .[46]

In letters to his wife, Cary described his father as very kindhearted, charitable and open-minded; usually cheerful and optimistic (a favourite saying, adopted by his son, was 'It's a poor heart that never rejoices'); extremely practical; warm and indulgent towards his sons, although very concerned that they should not fall into the slack, wasteful ways of some of their ancestors (' . . . Dad never opposes Jack or me . . . whatever he thinks . . . [but] he is always afraid of the old Cary extravagance appearing in any of us'[47] – this was to make Cary extremely susceptible to worries about debt in later years).

During his early manhood, Cary would have to struggle to assert his psychological independence from the father he loved and admired so deeply. In one of his earliest attempts to write a novel, the protagonist is a version of himself, and his 'scheme' for it begins 'Fear of merging personality in others especially Father's. Notes Father's tone of voice recurring in his own and same sort of joke.'[48] Cary's wife once commented that 'Dad . . . has a great admiration for your talents' (though he was probably always more at ease with Jack, who had a similar temperament and similar enjoyment of sports like hunting); but she also wrote 'It is extraordinary how different you and your Father are . . . I don't think your tastes could diverge more than they do, and I suppose you must have developed your artistic side from your mother . . .'[49]

In spite of their personal differences, Arthur Cary, during the decade after his wife's death, was able to give his elder son the great gift of emotional security. And, just as his mother had, when she read stories every night, his father fed Cary's imagination. It is this quality of the man – his imaginative sympathy – that is most profoundly celebrated in A *House of Children*, which was begun not long after Arthur Cary's death.

Appearing unexpectedly in the midst of his family like a god, Mr Corner provokes both joy and awe. He teaches Evelyn 'a dozen arts, knotting, net-making, rifle shooting, stalking and, above all, diving'. And it is as a diver, plunging gracefully from one element to another like a dolphin, that Cary fixes his final image. His sons, shivering 'on the rock steps, slippery with sea moss', 'screwing ourselves up for our diving lesson', look up to see Mr Corner's 'compact powerful figure' diving 'twenty or twenty-five feet into the harbour, at such an angle that there was barely a sound, and only one small plop of water, a little spurting mound like that after a big raindrop. It made me cry out with delight. What a triumph, what a combination of skill, courage, neatness and deliberate mastery. It seemed to me that there was no greater deed than to dive like that.'

Although he is weak and bookish, the eight-year-old Evelyn Corner is surrounded by men for whom sport was the 'principal topic . . . and the chief pleasure in life', and his 'great ambition besides going into the navy, [is] to be a sportsman' like his father. Evelyn has been looking forward to going on his first shoot; but in the early morning, as the hunters are about to start, he faints – having forgotten in his excitement to eat during the preceding eighteen hours. Only his father's quick response and imaginative sympathy turn this disaster into a triumph. 'He was thinking out a new poem,' Mr Corner suggests; and one of the hunters just as quickly responds 'Oh yes, that was a great poem of his you showed me about the ant.' And Evelyn's epiphany is Cary's: 'The two glories were open to me: that of a sportsman and that of a poet.' What had seemed opposites could be reconciled.

Looking back at him, Cary connected his father with the values of the era when his family and his people, the Anglo-Irish, were secure. Mr Corner's unshakable good manners epitomise the eighteenth century, 'the great age of polite forms and social ease';[50] and this enables him to move fluently between two worlds, as Cary would aspire to do – the world of action, and the world of art. That the son was able to succeed, Cary clearly believed, was largely because of the father's sensitivity and generosity of spirit.

'the quality of another life'

The summer of 1900, when he was approaching twelve, ended the long idyll of Cary's holidays in Inishowen.

As he looked back on his childhood from middle age, he was strikingly ambiguous. He wrote of having grown up 'among the bitter recollections of a land war which ruined the good resident landlords even more effectively than the absentees';[51] of 'the emotional and bitter political feeling which had surrounded my childhood' and left him with a 'disgust' for such conflict.[52] Yet he also insisted 'If there were tensions I knew nothing of them, and I do not recognise them now. All those deep, richly-felt contrasts and conflicts remained simply an experience, the more vivid for its light and shade. But it is possible also that they gave me, even as a boy, a certain critical feeling (rather than judgement) about the more complacent views of politics and history which were then common form.'[53]

Evelyn Corner muses 'I don't know when my childhood ended or if it is all ended now':[54] Joyce Cary wrote 'for me, both childhood and the things known by the child I was, however clearly seen, have the quality of another life, a previous existence . . .'[55] What the two statements have in common is recognition of the intensity of his childhood memories.

Cary's childhood was a primary source of his literary creativity. The loss of his mother and the healing influence of his father and family, the intense happiness and the sharp social and political tensions of Inishowen, the dualistic vision promoted by his divided English and Irish 'worlds': all these urged him into self-expression, and initiated some of his central themes.

CHAPTER FOUR

SCHOOL

1900–1904

'To be an Englishman'

In September 1900, Arthur Cary sent his two sons to a small but prominent preparatory school called Hurstleigh, at Tunbridge Wells in Kent. Education there would set them firmly on the road to public school and university, or a career in one of the Services.

A few weeks earlier – and two years after Charlotte's death – he had married again; and was on his honeymoon, at Dieppe, when he received a letter from the eleven-year-old Cary, soon to leave his Grandmother Joyce's holiday house in Inishowen for Hurstleigh:

> Dear Dads,
>   I am enjoying myself. Jack has found an elephant's tooth set in gold. Jack can swim but not dive. I have learnt overhand stroke from Bryne [Byrne]. Bryne won a dressing case at Portknish yesterday. Harold Bryne, in Siam, shot a tiger last Monday all by himself and the skin is being cured in London. Did you get my last letter about Navel engineering. Helen's thought me knitting and has thought me to play the piano by notes in stead of ear. A week ago Cecil Bryne and me (I hope they teach grammer at Tunbridge) were walking to Cockhill for yellow daisys when a boy who was standing near a hedge said don't come here ye'l git stunkted its a wopse nes, we laughed. My love to Dora and the Bullivants and a jolly holiday to you all.[1]

Arthur Cary's second wife was his cousin the 'fat and round' Dora Stevenson, of whom Charlotte had once been mildly jealous. (Her brother Harry married Arthur's youngest sister, Mab, a few months later.) Dora was to bear Arthur two children – Anthony, in October 1902, and Shiela, in January 1904 – and to be a kind, but inevitably preoccupied, stepmother to Joyce and Jack.

When they arrived at Hurstleigh School, Cary was nearly twelve, Jack eight. They had strong Irish accents which at first made them figures of fun.[2] No doubt they would have found the transition difficult anyway, from free-and-easy Irish summers to the rigours of English boarding-school life. In addition, Cary – small for his age, with a weak right eye, and debilitated by a series of ailments – was scholastically handicapped by his late entry into the education system.

He did not shine at Hurstleigh. 'My dear old boy,' his father began a hortatory letter in March 1901, 'I got the Half Term Report – the other day from Mr Buston – and I am afraid you are not trying quite so hard as you did at first; as you are keeping rather low in the division . . .'[3]

Mr Buston was the Headmaster and remembered by Jack as a bad-tempered disciplinarian – though exceeded in violent behaviour by one of the masters, who would bash the boys on the head and then knock them down.[4] If Cary suffered from such attentions, they did not improve his performance in the classroom. While Jack won a prize in Division IIA in 1903, Joyce went through his three years at Hurstleigh without winning any scholastic awards at all.

He had little more success at sports, apart from swimming. On Sports Day in 1903, Jack, though still a Junior, was runner-up for the Challenge Cup after victories in the Hundred Yards, High Jump and Throwing the Cricket Ball. Joyce had to be content with winning the lowly Elephant Race. Even in extra-curricular activities he seems to have been overshadowed by his younger brother. In the school's 1902 Christmas concert, Jack was a rumbustious Fluellen in a scene from *Henry V*; Joyce played Tosser in a one-act farce called 'The Area Belle'.[5]

These indignities must have dented Cary's self-confidence. It soon became clear, too, that he would not be able to fulfil the ambition he had confided to his father shortly before starting school. His physical disabilities would rule out acceptance for naval training.

Was Cary unhappy at Hurstleigh? The description in *A House of Children* of Evelyn Corner's prep. school – apparently based on Cary's memories of Hurstleigh – implies no lasting discontent: 'A sense of crowded life, of friendship, of interesting lessons . . . of emerging knowledge – and of course some bullying.'[6] On the other hand, an unpublished novel he wrote in the 1920s, *Tottenham*, is a painful story of a small boy's suffering, and eventual suicide, at a prep. school.[7] Certainly Cary did not speak or write directly about his early school experiences with the bitterness of some of his literary contemporaries, like George Orwell. No doubt he made the best of a difficult situation; and, however galling his brother's achievements, Jack's presence must have helped him, for the two boys seem to have consolidated at this time the warm comradeship which lasted throughout their lives.

Evelyn Corner's prep. school is 'a plain old house, set among gardens, where the masters [gave] their most useful teaching in the cricket field or strolling under the willows with two or three small boys hanging on their arms'. Even classroom teaching at that school is not invariably formal. 'A lecture from a boy's parent, a sailor, about chasing slave dhows in the Gulf, went to the bottom of our feelings like a flash.' The school's ethos 'entered into our very bones . . . an atmosphere much more truly religious than anything I have known since; for it was one of real purpose' – that purpose being to defend, extend and exalt the British Empire. 'To be an Englishman was to be born to a great destiny; as warrior and guardian of freedom and justice and peace.'[8]

As Cary himself observed, 'the early 1900s, when I was at school, was everywhere a time of romantic patriotism'.[9] At Hurstleigh that was accompanied by a 'wave of religion . . . Some missionary came to lecture to us and we all joined a Bible-reading society. We read our portions every day and subscribed to the mission.'[10]

The most memorable single event of Cary's three years at Hurstleigh also had to do with religion. It was the unexpected visit of a 'huge, red-bearded' priest of the Church of Ireland: Canon Potter, who had confirmed, married and buried Charlotte Cary, and whose visit to her two sons may have been connected with their father's recent remarriage. He appeared before Joyce and Jack Cary 'in the lane when we were deep in the feeling of the school'; and spoke to them, in his 'deep voice with its rich accent', about their mother, urging them to remember her in their prayers. Taken aback, they were unable to respond; and Cary, 'a small boy in a cricket shirt', sensed the priest's disappointment. 'His blue eyes look down on me still, and his weather-beaten face, with puzzled inquiry. I daresay he went away supposing that his journey had been a failure. In fact, he had left such a deep mark on my spirit . . . that his voice and look remained there for ever, and with them, the experience of compassionate love, a true intuition of goodness in its own spirit.'[11]

'a household unforgettable to all who knew it'

A few days after his first Hurstleigh term had begun, Cary received a letter addressed from 'Cromwell House' and signed 'D. M. Cary': 'I hope you like your school, and that you and Jack are quite well. Dad and Dora are gone to Lydart but they will be with us when you come back for the Christmas holidays. Barney misses you and Jack, in the mornings, he wishes he had you both here to go out with him and the dogs. Uncle sends his love to you, he had some games of croquet yesterday . . .'[12]

Lydart was the house – on Pepys Road, South East London – in which Arthur and Dora Cary were then living. They would soon move to 70 Dukes Avenue, Chiswick, to be closer to Cromwell House, the home of Tristram and Doll (Dorothy) Cary. For Cromwell House (71 Thorney Hedge Road, Gunnersbury) – a solid, double-fronted Victorian house 'with the usual basement storey, front steps, and high, pillared porch', about eight miles west of central London and close to open country – had become the spiritual home of all the London Carys in their exile from Inishowen.

It was an Irish household, reminiscent of the Big Houses of the Ascendancy. And it was incalculably beneficent for Cary. If nostalgia coloured Cary's picture of Cromwell House, and his mature analysis of human personality coloured his memories of its dominant personalities, the two radiant accounts he published make utterly clear Cary's recognition of its healing, invigorating effect on his personality.

In the background of Cromwell House drifted many figures. His Cary aunts, who, 'scattered about London in various jobs', came to their Aunt Doll 'with all their problems – to be scolded, to be cherished'. The 'numerous Cary male relations, known commonly as "the nephews"', always chaffing and borrowing money. Kate, the cook, 'rarely quite sober after six o'clock and usually roaring by bedtime' (the obvious original of Sukey Egan in *Castle Corner*). The handsome, mysterious Hildebrand Oakes, Aunt Doll's brother, who arrives from time to time for a short stay; though armoured by his French aristocratic ways and his father's Waterloo sword and medal, he is ultimately ineffectual, defeated, 'an exile and a dreamer'.

Tristram Cary, head of this household, and Cary's great-uncle, had trained as a doctor, sought his fortune in Australia with his younger brother Arthur Lunell Cary, met Dorothy Oakes while travelling in France, married her in 1852, settled on inherited family property in Inishowen, lost it through debt, lived briefly as a gentleman-farmer in Kent, and finally settled in Cromwell House, where he tried to maintain the trappings of Ascendancy life while he 'slowly wasted a fortune on horses and cards'. From a surgery in the house, he kept up a small medical practice, and was said by 'the nephews' to treat patients' complaints by alternating red and blue pills bought by the barrelful!

He was 'A magnificent man to see – tall and handsome', with a 'commanding dignity'; immensely generous and hospitable; a lover and connoisseur of dog-racing – and even croquet was to be taken seriously. He seemed to be 'a monument of power and wisdom', 'a master of life'. But long practice in accepting misfortune had bred in him 'a melancholy charm'. 'He did not much notice children; possibly this was his personal reaction to the loss of his own. And he never punished or even reproached us for any mischief.' He was, Cary came to understand, 'essentially a sad man' whose 'sadness came not only from the loss of his property but the realisation that his order had been thrown aside and was about to suffer the slanders of history'.

Also uprooted is Barney Magonegal, Tristram's 'dog man, coachman-groom, and butler – man of all work', whose fate was decided when he lost an eye as a boy in Inishowen, during a Cary shoot, and was given a permanent place in Tristram's service. But Barney is one of the three dominating personalities of Cromwell House. His vigour, his irrepressible optimism, his forceful personality, all blaze against the ashen grandeur of his master. As unimpressive physically as Tristram is impressive, Barney is 'A thin, dark man with very long arms'; he has 'a thin brown face deeply creased, a drooping tobacco-coloured moustache, and a black patch over the right eye'. His clothes are extraordinary: 'a black morning-coat, black trousers, and yellow gaiters over enormous black boots'; on his head 'a small black cap, like those worn by schoolboys'. But he has an innate dignity, is quite indifferent to stares or laughter.

Unlike Tristram, Barney *does* reproach Cary, when the boy is rude to him. 'That's no way for a gentleman to speak to a servant, Master Joyce. I thought you had more respect for your place, and mine, too . . . you demean yourself, sir . . . I say ye demean yourself.' His values are simple, secure and traditional. He has no sense of humour, but he will throw himself with imaginative intensity into the history of the Cary family ('Ah, Master Joyce, that Lucius was the destruction of half what should be coming to you'), or the personalities of Tristram's greyhounds ('He's the shwiftest we ever pupped and turns like a shwallow'), or even the quality of cabbages. He holds the secret of life: a servant of his people's conquerors, living in a strange land, he is so absorbed in creating the moment that there is no time even to consider indulging a sense of injustice (– but once a year, on St Patrick's Day, he drinks himself blind drunk). This illiterate servant offers rough wisdom ('I tell ye, Master Joyce, cleverness is nothing without you have the heart in it') and his conversation is a fountain of lore, moving 'from dogs to horses, religion, fairies, myth, politics, and family history'.

Aunt Doll has a similar simplicity and verve. She too is an exile: the daughter of an English officer and baronet 'who had fought at Waterloo and then settled in France', she 'never lost her French accent or French turn of speech'. A very small plain woman 'with a very long nose, a prominent chin, and pale-grey eyes', she wears her hair 'parted and swept back over the ears in two cone-shaped protruberances, a mid-Victorian style'. She 'always wore a little black apron with twelve pockets in it – three rows of four', and from these pockets would dispense gifts to children. Among her oddities are 'loud bird-like cries' to express admiration for the children's feats; and when, at dinner, her husband attracts her attention by throwing a biscuit towards her along the table, she utters a parakeet-like scream, 'not so much of protest as of ritual, to please the marksman'.

Far from being soured by the loss of the several children she has borne, she never ceases to give her love to other children – 'that special kind of love that delights in children, that can't have too much of them'. She has a 'generosity that is simply not aware of itself, that gives by nature as by a reflex'. Like her husband, she is sad – 'sad for him, for the loss of her children, for us all, who seemed to her deprived by no fault of our own'; but, like Barney, she does not stop to repine. Because she understood that humanity is 'doomed to insecurity, injustice, and the everlasting revolution of politics', 'love was for her the only constant, the only dependable thing'. She 'did me more than kindness,' Cary wrote, 'and gave me more than love.'

Uncle Tristram epitomised the conservative and Barney the creator – like Anthony Cary and Arthur Lunell Cary; Aunt Doll, in her nurturing role, seems to mediate between them. 'It was life itself she understood.'

'Cromwell House, like other Irish households of the time, had a very definite order, even a rather elaborate routine. Meals were punctual. The cake and Madeira always appeared in the morning room at the same hour, eleven. Everyone and everything had an acknowledged time and place. But the whole atmosphere, the whole effect, was quite different from that of an English household.'

Joyce and Jack were allowed to rig up a complicated aerial railway that ran down the main staircase. They could steal into the back parlour to watch a poker game. They could ride their bicycles in the grounds (and even, on one occasion, damage the croquet pitch with impunity!). They could go with Barney into the nearby fields to exercise the greyhounds. No wonder they rushed to Cromwell House every day during their school holidays.

As he looked back at the household not long before his death, trying to locate its importance in his life, Cary concluded that it had been a

> society highly satisfying to everyone's living needs of body and soul – imagination and affection, humour and pride – a household unforgettable to all who knew it. I suspect, though, that its solidarity, so resilient and tough, owed something also to the outside pressures, to the fact that we were all, except the English housemaids, who came and went, in a sense exiles and refugees. We not only gave way more freely to imagination, to dreams . . . but we had richer sources to feed on, of regrets, of memory. Even the children, ourselves, were never without the sense of a special fate, renewed every year when we went back to the countryside where we were native, proscribed, and yet honoured for our name.

Cromwell House not only nurtured the past, it mediated the present, and prepared, especially for the younger members of the dispossessed family, a viable future. To Cary it gave a paradigm of the family, of a social organisation successfully fulfilling individual and communal needs; solace and confidence, enrichment of the imagination. 'We lived more intensely [than English children], and we set a far higher value on what we had of secure happiness. We were more eager in our attachments. We knew, more consciously than other children, what family affection meant, as the one trustworthy thing among so many treacheries.'

'a new Christian chivalry of patriotic service'

After leaving Hurstleigh in 1903, aged fourteen, Cary was sent to Clifton College, near Bristol. There was a family reason for this choice – apart from the ancient Cary connection with Bristol. A relation, Ada Vining, was living in Clifton, near the school. She was a daughter of Cary's great-aunt Ina Sarratt, the old naval widow he remembered visiting as a small boy.

Founded in 1862 by a group of influential Bristol citizens, Clifton College is a cluster of castellated limestone buildings in twelve acres, close to open country. By the turn of the century, with over five hundred boys, it was one of the top twenty public schools, with a high reputation in sport and scholarship. Its first Headmaster, the Revd John Percival (later President of Trinity College, Oxford, and then Bishop of Hereford), was a protégé of Dr Arnold at Rugby, and had enthusiastically translated to Clifton the ideals and practices of 'muscular Christianity'. But with an increased moralistic fervour. Clifton was to be 'a nursery or seed-plot for high-minded men, devoted to the highest service of the country, a new Christian chivalry of patriotic service'.[13] There was a close connection with Oxford and a particularly close connection with Trinity College, as a result of its Percival Presidency.

The critic and novelist Arthur Quiller-Couch, who was a Clifton schoolboy towards the end of the nineteenth century, defined the school's ethos then as 'a cult of Roman stoicism and service suffused with Christianity' which instilled in the boys 'freedom and curiosity of mind tempered by a severe conscience in all matters of service and duty'.[14] Two especially strong traditions began with the establishment, in 1875, of the Cadet Corps and a Mission (in a poor area of Bristol). Thereafter 'Clifton played a major role in manning the Empire':[15] by 1900, it was better represented in the Indian Civil Service than any other public school, while there were already over five hundred Old Cliftonian officers in the British Army (by 1914 there were over a thousand). When Cary was there, Clifton was widely considered 'the most Empire-minded of English public schools';[16] typically its Old Boys were 'in the army or the colonial service, working loyally for little financial return in remote parts of the Empire'.[17]

During the 1904 Clifton Commemoration, which Cary attended in his uniform of 'black coat and Eton collar',[18] a ceremony took place which gives some insight into the school's ethos at that time. On Saturday 24 June, in the presence of the whole school (with the Cadet Corps participating prominently), a War Memorial, in honour of Old Cliftonians who had been killed in the recently ended Anglo-Boer War, was unveiled. It was a bronze statue of St George – 'that great embodiment of patriotism,' the Headmaster, Canon Michael Glazebrook, told the boys; 'a continual reminder that chivalry is one of the first duties of life'.[19]

On the plinth, beneath the feet of the statue, he continued, was 'a noble quatrain from our own poet', Henry Newbolt: 'Clifton, remember these thy sons who fell / Fighting far over sea: / For they in a dark hour remembered well / Their warfare learned of thee.' Famous from the end of the nineteenth century for his patriotic and nautical verse, Newbolt was the best-known Old Cliftonian of Cary's time. Several of his most popular poems forcefully promoted public-school sentiment ('Play up! play up! and play the game!'[20]).

Another Old Cliftonian exemplar was prominent in the speech of the guest of honour, General Lord Methuen, who had fought in the Boer War. Before unveiling the memorial, Methuen referred warmly to a fellow General, Douglas Haig, who had performed 'work worthy of both his country and his old school'; the British Army was proud of him, 'a man who has zeal, ability, and charm of manner'. It was most important, General Methuen concluded, that schoolmasters should inculcate in the youth of England 'those feelings of patriotism which are absolutely necessary to this country', and he urged every boy to join the Cadet Corps.[21]

Newbolt and Haig, who admired each other greatly, were the 'archetypes' of the Clifton spirit in Cary's time; and in them – the man of action 'to whom words did not come easily'[22] and the poet – Cary may have again perceived opposed, but complementary, temperaments and modes of living.

Clifton College was unusual among public schools in several respects. It admitted day boys as well as boarders, and 'at the very beginning . . . was divided into Classical and Modern sides'[23] of roughly equal numbers. Cary was placed in the Third Form of the Modern side, probably because of his comparatively advanced age and his unimpressive record at Hurstleigh. This meant that he left school with small Latin and no Greek. It also meant that 'he was among a crowd of toughs and rather unhappy'.[24] Indeed, to judge from an apparently autobiographical passage in an abortive early novel, 'Darley', Cary was intimidated at first by the roughness of some of his seniors: 'he had been shocked by the language used by the fifth table, big boys chiefly in the army class, who bellowed at breakfast and in the changing room obscenities which fell upon him like blows . . .'[25]

Towards the end of his life, Cary praised two English masters who had encouraged him. He was taught for one term in his second year by 'an enthusiast, a man of the strongest literary prejudice', the Revd A. St John Gray. The Upper Fourth Form 'consisted of lively young boys of fourteen or so, on their way to the fifth, and enormous blockheads of seventeen . . . Grey made some of them enjoy Shakespeare so much that they read the plays for themselves . . . He would sit upon his desk and act them for us.'[26] A school notebook of Cary's shows that he learned to appreciate Chaucer as well as Shakespeare in Gray's classes.[27]

Sydney Irwin, who taught Cary in his final year, was a very different man: 'nervous, suspicious, clever, whimsical, lazy', according to a character-sketch of Cary's.[28] He was 'a precise and careful scholar . . . And he encouraged me to write.' However, he 'tried so far as possible to leave me to express my own ideas in my own way. The result was that I did not learn to use language with precision.'

The contrast Cary drew, late in his life, between the two English teachers, was probably influenced by his habitual recognition of opposed creative and conservative temperaments – and perhaps unfair to Irwin, who is remembered as one of Clifton's finest teachers. Gray, the enthusiast, 'made no secret of his preferences', while Irwin 'sought to hide' his. Irwin's teaching 'was perhaps more valuable than I supposed', but 'Grey gave me something of the profoundest value'.[29]

Cary also enjoyed his Art classes, and remembered Langley, the Art Master, well : 'his little water colours – an intense feeling . . . with his stride, his beautiful voice and eyes, his moustache, his head to one side, his love of beauty and thoroughness.'

More important for Cary's wellbeing at Clifton, especially in his first year, was his Housemaster. Boarders were accommodated in nearby houses owned by the school, each one named for the master who presided over it. Cary was in Tait's House – which, after Mr Tait's retirement at the end of 1904, became Rintoul's House. 'Charlie' Tait made a lasting impression on Cary: 'his goatee, his squeaky up and down voice, his nervousness, his old fashioned manners. His rubbed hands and little jumps. His laugh with his head turned away. His kindness to children, shyness of them. His little lectures given looking out of a window, and sudden jumps afterwards . . . His real authority and inflexibility. Conservative and religious.'[30]

Life in Tait's House seems to have been pleasant enough; but, small and weak, lonely, older than his peers, and in a class of 'toughs' – Cary must often have been unhappy during his first few months at Clifton College.

CHAPTER FIVE

SHOCK & RECOVERY

1904–1906

'you must be brave now'
Near the end of Cary's first year at Clifton, he was told that his stepmother was dead. Dora Cary had died at home, on 8 May (her husband's birthday), of a four-month anaemia and sudden apoplexy – probably complications following the birth of her second child, Shiela, in January. She was only thirty-five.

Cary wrote to his father immediately after receiving the news and then, without telling anyone, set out for Gunnersbury. It seems that he never got there, but was stopped at Paddington Station and sent back to Clifton. His father wrote:

> My dear old boy,
>   I am sure you are bitterly sorry but you must not make me a greater burden than I already have.
> Your letter was another blow to me for you know old boy there are times in this life when we must not give way no matter how we feel so my dear old boy you must be brave now and do your very best for my sake and the sake of dear Dora – We are going to take her to Rusthall Church tomorrow her Mother and Father are there –
> Goodbye for the present I know you will try to be brave for my sake. Work and play with all your might.
>   Ever your affectionate father
>   Arthur Cary[1]

Dora was Cary's stepmother for less than five years. During most of that time he was away at boarding school and she was preoccupied with husband, household and small son. Cary's grief and confusion in the aftermath of her death probably had less to do with her personality than with the renewal of the trauma suffered over five years earlier in the loss of his mother. His very early conviction of pervasive insecurity and injustice, enforced by family history and Charlotte's death, was endorsed; and when he was feeling desperately vulnerable. His father's letter, mixing reprimand and exhortation with affection, must have helped him in facing the crisis; but at the cost of forcing him to suppress his pain. He learned stoicism, and in later life found it hard to speak about his deepest feelings.

At Clifton he was treated sympathetically, his illegal absence quietly passed over. Arthur Cary's letter was followed by one from 'Charlie' Tait, now retired and living in Edinburgh: 'I have just heard of the terrible blow that has fallen upon you. When such griefs come no words can bring consolation . . . May God support and comfort you and your father and all of you!'[2]

Three letters from his father in June imply Cary's rapid outward recovery. 'I think it is very good to have been placed fifth in the middle fourth so soon,' his father now wrote; 'I hope old boy the weather is better and that you are having ripping good cricket'; 'You will lick Jack and me all to pieces if we have any swimming at Kingsgate – that is if you keep on practising . . . I hope your drawing of Hercules will be a great success.'

Arthur Cary was planning a six-week holiday at Kingsgate (near Margate), with its 'sandy beach where you and Jack could bathe'.[3] But meanwhile, before the end of his first year at Clifton, Cary had assuaged his hurt through the vigorous effort his father had prescribed. As *The Cliftonian* for July 1904 records, his drawing of Hercules had indeed, and appropriately enough, been a great success: it won the Silver Star of the Royal Drawing Society – Cary's first public award.[4] 'Work and play with all your might' was a dictum he applied, especially in crises, throughout his life.

Jack's life was also changing. Less than a month after Dora Cary's death, he was interviewed at the Admiralty and accepted for training at Britannia Royal Naval College, Dartmouth. Cary had longed for a naval career; but 'It was my brother who became the sailor . . . his first appearance, at twelve, in blue and gold, made him my hero'.[5]

'a savage once in France'

When the summer holidays came, Cary did not, after all, go to Kingsgate but to France, where his Aunt Winnie Chambers was living. If this was a reward for his herculean efforts at Clifton, it also gave him an unforgettably exhilarating holiday. In a letter to his wife fifteen years later, Cary told her how he had been

> a savage once in France, on a lonely beach near Paris-Plage. I used to go off with a book, and a dog, and spend all day in and out of the sea, and never dry myself. I was brown all over like an Indian. But once I was carried away and nearly drowned. What a hunt there would have been, for not a soul knew where I was, and no one passed that way once in a fortnight. Besides I always hid my clothes – not only because they reminded me very unpleasantly of civilization – but in case anyone should come when I was far off in the water or racing a mile away over the dunes with the dog.

He always liked and admired his Aunt Winnie. (She was in fact a cousin, 'sister of Sir Newman Chambers, whose grandmother was a Cary'.) 'She is one of the pluckiest women I know, and with a very small income of her own, has run her own shew all her life. She has rather a sudden temper, but also [a] very affectionate loyal heart . . .'[6] An enthusiastic painter, she lived for several years in the artists' colony at Etaples – where she took lessons from a Spanish-born Impressionist painter, Edouard-Leon Garrido – before giving up art to run a little shop in London.

For a fifteen-year-old boy flushed with his first artistic success, life at Etaples must have been intoxicating: 'between bathing at Paris Plage or hunting with the beagles through the woods above Le Touquet . . . I amused myself with sketching. I amused myself above all with the artists and their talk.'[7]

The aesthetic ethos of the time was itself stimulating. A quarter-century after the high flood of French Impressionism, its ripples were turbulent. The new school of 'romantic' realism had triumphed, but only after a long and bitter conflict with the 'classical' realism of the Academy and the older generation of painters and critics. In 1904, Impressionism glittered still with the glamour of revolution, and artists continued to debate its dismissal of monolithic immobility for sinuous movement, and line for the vibrant play of light and colour.

Cary was a quick and total convert: 'I thought that Impressionism was the only great and true art.'[8] Impressionism was glamorous and exuberant, with implicit human values of 'independence, individualism and sincerity'.[9] The Impressionists themselves seemed to epitomise the Romantic concept of the artist as lonely genius battling repressive orthodoxy – which became Cary's paradigm. His Impressionist allegiance also led him to believe that authentic aesthetic creation implied fierce innovation, pitting the artist against those who feared and resented change. Conflict between creators and conservatives was inevitable.

Cary, at fifteen, probably did not perceive the ramifications of his conversion to Impressionism; or see a parallel between the aesthetic conflict in France and the political conflict in Ireland that had ruined his family. But his intense response to both conflicts, with a later recognition of their fundamental similarity, would influence his thought and writing profoundly. It would be significant, too, that in the political conflict he had been committed by family tradition and early experience to the conservative side, while in the aesthetic conflict youthful enthusiasm bound him to the cause of creativity.

By the end of 1904, Cary had decided that he wanted to become an artist. When some of his watercolours were admired by a painter, 'I thought, this is a damn good show'.[10] His independence was increased when, on his sixteenth birthday that December, he came into a small annual income inherited from the Joyce family. The following summer he went back to France, and again stayed with his Aunt Winnie at Etaples.

One incident of that second summer holiday in Normandy became a landmark in his life; and, more than fifty years later, he described it several times, in considerable (if variable) detail. He went to 'fetch a basket of eggs' from an artist near by, a man of over sixty and 'a well-known painter in England' whose paintings had been 'hung, year after year, in the Academy'.

> He painted chiefly girls in gardens. I had gone to the farmhouse where he lived with his ragged family and an exhausted wife, and I had found him standing among the hollyhocks beside an easel on which he had placed his

latest picture, in a new gilt frame. It had just been returned to him after rejection by the Academy. He had now been rejected four or five years in succession – he could not sell his pictures any longer and was in deepest poverty. Apparently he had brought out this picture to compare his painted flowers with the real ones . . .

The man begged Cary to examine the picture, 'a girl on a swing surrounded by garden flowers', and

to agree with him about the excellence of the painting. He pointed out some of the best touches and said, 'But they don't want good work at the Academy, or anywhere else. They don't care for beauty any more. They hate it. They only want this new rubbish. The world has gone mad – it despises beauty and only wants ugliness.' And then he began to cry. I'd never seen a man of that age in tears, and I was greatly upset. I murmured some words of consolation . . . and escaped as soon as I could.

Of course, I did not even comprehend the full despair of this unhappy man. I was all for the Impressionists . . . and I believed that there was no other really valid art. As I came away, I thought, 'Poor old man, but why did he ever become a painter? He could never have done anything worth-while – his pictures are ridiculous in their high finish, mere photographic illustrations . . .'

And Cary went on, in this account, to argue that the 'tragedy', which he could not understand at the time, 'of a man . . . not only ruined financially, but whose whole life and skill had lost meaning', was representative. It 'is taking place all the time, in all the arts'.[11]

'a good pattern as far as it goes'

In September 1904 Cary had begun his second year at Clifton College; and accommodated himself fully to its ethos.

He joined the Cadet Corps, reaching the rank of Sergeant. His enjoyment of the Corps' military activities is expressed in a letter he wrote his father on 11 March 1906: 'Yesterday I had my first Field Day . . . We carried a haversack and bayonet on our left, a rolled cape behind, a waterbottle on our right and a pouch with 55 cartridges (blank) in it . . . I was on picket duty under Sergeant Ogilvie in our House . . . [We] had to defend about 7 miles of country with 200 men and they had about 800.'[12]

The 'Sergeant Ogilvie' of that account, eldest child of a Scottish father and German mother, had a background as unorthodox as Cary's. 'I spent my childhood in Chile,' he wrote. 'I learned to ride as soon as I could walk. I spoke Spanish as freely as English, and rode along the trails with dark-skinned peasants who lived in a world of fantasy and folklore . . .'[13] Not surprisingly, Heneage Ogilvie was something of an athlete, coming second in Clifton's annual ten-mile cross-country race, the Long Penpole. He was a few months older than Cary, and a form above, on the Classical side; but he was a boarder in Tait's House, and the two boys became close, lifelong friends.

And Cary made other friends, clearly taking most pleasure in the company of boys who had serious scholarly interests. But he also became generally popular in Tait's House when it was discovered how well he could entertain the dormitory, after lights-out, with suspenseful serial stories.

Although he was still small for his age, and handicapped by his various physical disabilities, Cary threw himself into sport. Inishowen summers had made him a good swimmer; now he used this skill competitively and for regular exercise. Boxing was a new sport for him, however; one in which he could emulate his father. He hated it, 'but one was rather expected to do it . . . the great thing was to have lots of blood, and I was a good bleeder'.[14] Much of the bleeding was from his nose, which he broke – an injury that caused problems later. He once told a close friend that his was a 'ruined Roman' nose – 'it never recovered from a kick at football and a boxing match on the *same* day'![15] For he even made a successful showing at one of the two big school sports, rugby. His friends encouraged and helped him by simulating games in their dormitory, and Cary was picked for his House XV. Like Evelyn Corner, he 'lived for a couple of winters in the atmosphere of Sparta before Thermopylae; except that we fought our desperate battles every week. We felt like a band of heroes, and so we were regarded'.

His lasting admiration for the 'leaders' of the House XV is attested by Evelyn Corner's glowing portraits. There is 'the elder N., afterwards killed on the Somme, with his pale face and broken boxer's nose, a lively humorous courage like that of a terrier, boundless good humour, and an intelligence both sharp and quick'. There is N.'s younger brother, 'killed at Ypres,' who combined 'a fanatical grim courage' with 'a pondering mind' and 'a dreamy love of poetry'. These are probably the Cleghorn brothers, who played with Cary on the Tait House XV. And there is 'Max, with a glass eye of which he told no one, and in which he played, risking a blow that would have driven it into his brain'; a boy with 'the charm of reckless sincerity, a moral courage which had, when he was a fag, stood up to the heaviest pressure, a mind effervescent with wit and imagination; feelings as quick as a flash, and a tongue which answered your thought before you had put it into speech'.

These three boys had 'true greatness': they 'used to romp in the changing-room like small children', but they also had 'those fundamental values which are the elements of all greatness: courage, independence of will, devotion to a cause larger than one's own; a contempt of mean ambition'.[16] Their fundamental values were also those of his father, family and people; which is surely one reason for Cary's lifelong admiration of public-school education. Public schools, he told his wife, 'certainly do tend to turn out boys to a pattern, but it is a good pattern as far as it goes . . .'[17]

Ironically, Confirmation as an Anglican, during his second year at Clifton, did not strengthen Cary's intuition of 'fundamental values' in religion, but injured it. Already the 'naïve faith' of his childhood had been jolted in Clifton classrooms: 'I found geology incompatible with Genesis, and I was aware that "science" did not accept miracles.' These doubts became virulent when his new Housemaster, Mr Rintoul, who was also his Science Master, began to prepare Cary for Confirmation. 'I was fifteen, and at that age one begins to have judgment and to reason about causes . . . Above all, I was used to be given explanations . . .' But Rintoul's preparation 'was simply a set of dogmatic statements': 'difficult and strange ideas', like the Trinity and the Resurrection, were presented 'without any explanation at all. I did not even get an argument for the existence of God'.

So, although the Confirmation service itself 'had a strong emotional effect' on Cary, soon afterwards 'my faith began to wither like a plant whose root has been cut', and a year later 'I had no belief at all in any doctrine of the Church'.[18]

Meanwhile, Cary's achievements in the classroom had steadily improved. He was able to report to his father on 11 March 1906 'I was 3 in my form last week, which is two or three places up'.[19] And the discovery that he could write as fluently as he could tell stories in the dormitory impressed both his masters and his friends. Some of his essays won prizes.

Cary also had success with poetry during his last two years at school. *The Cliftonian* published two of his efforts, a sonnet 'To My Pen' (1905), and an untitled blank-verse poem (1906). The first, though little more than a schoolboy exercise, has an appropriate theme for a future writer's first appearance in print – but its sentiment is hesitant and negative despite hints of intended humour ('To what base uses has this pen been put . . . What inspirations / Have defiled thy nib . . . my dull memory is failing me, / And I am lost in tangles of translation.').[20]

The second poem shows an advance in assurance as well as technical control. It mingles Miltonic and Keatsian imitation with adolescent sensuality in a vision of ideal happiness. Against a romantic background, 'A lawn, and in the midst a silken pool', appears 'the lissom, sweet-breathed English Eve'. She lingers there, 'ruminating on the darkling woods', until she hears 'a little sigh'. Then,

> Rising all womanly to know the cause,
> She moves slow-seeing round the bank, and last
> Haps on a man behind a plumed bush,
> Strong Adam, and looks conscious down, and then
> Is sudden meshed in love's new made net,
> Her brown eyes glistening dark between the lash
> New-lowered and her soft and curved cheek;
> And so she lightly touched his clear cut brow,
> And he did ope his smiling eyes and look,
> Rose swift and clipt her soft snow-breast to his,
> And lingering prest his warm, red lips against
> Her soft, flushed cheek, and all their eyes were wet;
> And so he took her by the hand – they passed,
> Two children in the garden of sweet peace.[21]

Cary's schooldays, begun in the shadow of his mother's death, then profoundly shaken by the death of his stepmother, ended in sunshine. By his own efforts, he had overcome confusion and despair, had achieved self-respect and friendship, success and happiness. Influenced by his father and family tradition, by the Clifton ethos and his unexpected triumphs in sport, he would seek fulfilment as a man of action. But he had found his greatest consolation and confidence, after Dora Cary's death, in the arts of painting, story-telling and writing.

CHAPTER SIX

ARTIST
1906–1909

'an impressionist world'

In the summer of 1906 Arthur Cary remarried for a second time. 'From what your Father tells me – you approve of what we are going to do?' Cary's stepmother-to-be wrote on 12 June. 'It has been an immense help amidst opposition from my own family that *you* will welcome me into your home-circle.' The wedding would take place in January 1907 – 'and I look forward to being a real pal – and friend of yours, dear'.[1]

Arthur Cary had known Memie (Mary) Agar since before his first marriage in 1887. Charlotte had, indeed, suspected him of falling in love with her. Whatever the Agar family's objections to the marriage, the Cary relations were pleased. 'I think your father has done very wisely in securing a nice kind Mother to look after you, as well as himself, for I am sure he never thinks of himself,' one of them told Cary.[2] But Arthur Cary's third marriage was far less successful than its predecessors, and ended in separation.

He now moved from Chiswick to 42 Grosvenor Road, Gunnersbury, even closer to Cromwell House. Memie, as she had promised, tried to keep good relations with her eldest stepson, writing him long affectionate letters. But there was less sympathy for Tony and Shiela, who in 1907 were four and two years old respectively, and they were largely brought up by a warm-hearted resident nurse and governess, whom Cary liked and admired, Miss Wakeham.

In both Arthur's and Memie's letters to Cary, there were hints of marital strain: 'Your Dad is out late to-night its 9 o'clock. evidently finishing to-day at billiards';[3] 'Memie still away . . . I fancy [she] is absorbing all the gossip of the district'.[4] For Joyce and Jack Cary, now away from home most of the year, the state of their father's household was not of great concern. But Cary seems to have found little pleasure in his returns to 42 Grosvenor Road – and to a Gunnersbury rapidly being suburbanised. There was 'nowhere to walk but in *dead* streets. When I remember my times at Gunnersbury, I turn quite chill.' ' . . . my loneliest dreariest most friendless times were spent there, in spite of Dad. But Dad of course was always away, and I had no friends about the place, no men I knew, and Jack was always at sea – no amusements but reading and writing by myself for myself . . .'[5] Moreover, the death of his Great-Uncle Tristram towards the end of 1907 spelled the end of Cromwell House as he had known and loved it.

Earlier that year, his Grandmother Cary had also died and, in the summer of 1908, Arthur Cary and his two eldest children spent a few weeks with Netta Lawrence, sister of Winnie Chambers – their last family holiday in Inishowen. Cary's childhood experiences in Ireland, his boyhood experiences at Cromwell House, were now memories cut off from his daily life – joyous memories, enriched by nostalgia.

From the summer of 1906, Cary set out to fulfil his decision of two years before to become an artist. He was seventeen, and could support himself modestly on his inherited annual income. So his father, 'having always indulged me, allowed me to leave school very young'.[6]

He went to Winnie Chambers at Etaples. Again he enjoyed the beach and the woods, the company of artists; but he also filled a sketch-book with lively, careful studies. Several of them, pencil drawings of natural scenes, show Impressionist influence – clouds, a haystack, trees, a bridge over a stream. There are also exercises in copying; a striking pencil sketch of two boxers in action; a page of grotesque faces. This sketch-book is a record of talented experimentation; and, especially in depicting people, reveals a persistent attraction towards both realism and distortion, seriousness and humour.[7]

At Etaples Cary had become friendly with a Scottish painter, Charles Mackie, an Associate of the Royal Scottish Academy and ex-Chairman of the Society of Scottish Artists. Mackie gave Cary encouragement and advice. Probably they went on painting expeditions together. A few months after Cary had left Etaples, Mackie wrote 'I go cycling all round the country, set down thinking I have an inspiration and then find it was only an intense desire to produce has made me batter myself into a spurious enthusiasm and off I go with a spoilt canvas.' This letter raises the possibility that Mackie was the artist (disguised in the accounts) whose emotional outburst had so moved Cary one or two summers earlier – and who was the original of Gulley Jimson's father.

> I saw a pig standing in a sapphire blue pond in bright sunshine today. That did warm me up a bit but it was simply a divine harmony, had the pig only been a nymph what a picture might have resulted. I have my eye on a perfect idyllic shepherd just now. He has an incipient beard – unrazored – and the blue eye caught from the little patches between grey clouds. I am refraining from running up to Paris lest I should get some new impetus. I think an artist should beware of getting motive power from anywhere but within himself.[8]

Cary's first visit to Paris may have been in Mackie's company. He spent 'several months' there in the second half of 1906; 'I went to galleries and painted on the quays.'[9] He also became familiar with the Bohemian life of the Left Bank, its cafés and restaurants, its poets, painters, prostitutes.

This was the *belle époque* of 1870–1914. 'One of the remarkable things

61

about life in Paris at this time,' recalled a contemporary of Cary's, 'was not only the brightness and variety of the street scene but the gaiety of the people. The painters sang grand opera as they painted houses. The servants sang.' It was 'the age of feathers and fans, of frou-frou, of accordion-pleated taffeta petticoats, of heavy perfumes'. ' . . . I was always aware of art. I knew artists and watched them. Art and beauty in all its forms became an integral part of my existence . . .'[10]

It was probably in a Paris gallery that Cary encountered his 'first Matisse'. The Fauves had caused a furore the previous year with their violent, arbitrary colours, flat patterns and emphatic distortions. Shocked by the Matisse painting, Cary

> burst out laughing, and then grew annoyed by such cheek. For as a convinced impressionist I had created for myself the world as contemplated for painting in the form of an impressionist world . . . I was extremely attached to it. It was my world, the world I had made for myself, and even as a boy I could feel that Matisse was an enemy to this valuable impression of mine. He was attacking it. Many years passed before I could enjoy Matisse as well as Monet . . .[11]

This was an important moment in Cary's intellectual development. It forced recognition that the categories of aesthetic creativity and conservatism are not permanently distinct. Already he, an Impressionist, was conservative in the face of the next wave of aesthetic creativity. Changes of fashion threatened all aesthetic achievement. The two great conflicts, political and aesthetic, that shaped Cary's life and thought, are also patterns shifting through space and time.

Cary enjoyed himself in Paris, but if he was to become a successful professional artist he needed instruction and supervision. Mackie, whose home and studio were in Edinburgh, suggested that Cary study there.

'that famous old School in Edinburgh'

In January 1907, Cary enrolled as a student at the Board of Manufacturers School of Art – which was about to become the Edinburgh College of Art (Cary was there when its foundation stone was laid by the Prince of Wales in July 1907).

Thirty-five years later, he wrote that he was greatly looking forward to visiting Edinburgh again – 'even tho I can no longer sit on the steps of the Mound, in a dirty painter's blouse, and contemplate the passers, from that Bohemian world which seemed to me then so much better furnished for entertainment, than the Heavenly Mansions'.[12] He was always proud that he had been a student at 'that famous old School in Edinburgh'.[13]

Soon after arriving, he wrote to assure his father that he was comfortably settled. ' . . . judging by your timetable,' his father replied, 'you have enough to occupy you and that – in itself – is a very good thing – and then you are beginning to know some nice people . . .'[14]

One of the nice people was his landlady, Mary Yule, of whom he made some drawings and, much later, a detailed character sketch: 'Miss Y. pale with white hair, short sighted eyes, red face, dreamy, meddler, plays the cello but always strings breaking. takes lodgers but house run by maids and very untidy. Devoted to boys. tells stories. is very religious. her tiny fat hands, not very clean , and her terrors. Her sudden jumps. Quite helpless in hands of beggars or any appeal.'[15] Miss Yule was certainly devoted to Cary, as she told his wife a decade later: 'I came into contact with your husband when he was 17 and he remained beside me for three years . . . meeting Joyce, and being privileged to watch the development and revelation of his character made me wish I had been a mother . . .'[16]

He had two comfortable rooms, as bedroom and studio, in Miss Yule's house, 16 St Bernard's Crescent – less than a mile north of the centre of Edinburgh, in a 'new' suburb. She watched over his wellbeing, tending him during his rather frequent bouts of illness (Edinburgh damp was not good for his ailments). 'Miss Yule,' he reported after recovering from a cold, 'painted me so thoroughly with Iodine that I was nearly burnt alive.'

The household was lively and varied, at one point including among Cary's fellow boarders 'a tea planter from Assam, and a Hungarian person, a young quick blackhaired girl of about twenty, the Harlowes and MacGlashan'.[17] The latter, a young man of about Cary's age, became a friend and the subject of some drawings. But Cary's 'great pal' in Edinburgh was Arch Sturrock, who invited him home to Broughty Ferry, and took him trout fishing. In 1909, after Cary had left Edinburgh, Sturrock emigrated to Edmonton, Alberta, where he had been offered a job in a bank; and the friendship ended. 'Joyce, my lad,' Sturrock wrote, 'you are the only independent fellow I know . . .'[18]

Most of Cary's fellow students at the art school were 'older men, who had nothing to depend on but their profession'; and the teaching was academic. Cary remembered that, during one class '– and I may say here that I drew in pencil with somewhat bold strokes and rather a rugged manner somewhat in the Dürer style – the professor gazed on my work for some time and said to me at last "Mr Cary, we know from the scriptures that all flesh is grass but we are not told that it grew on rocks."'[19] He claimed that

> the man who taught me most about drawing in the art school was the one with strong prejudices. He liked only one kind of drawing, the classical . . .
>
> I don't think this man had much enthusiasm for drawing. But he had a set of principles and he was perfectly sure they were right. He taught me exactly what I needed to know about drawing, the fundamental rules, the logic, the syntax.[20]

Yet Cary's enthusiasm for art, his confidence in himself as an artist, waned quickly in Edinburgh:

> soon I grew tired of drawing and painting. I had always been a great reader and also I was very fond of company. I loved to talk with friends, to pay visits, to go to parties. I was quite happy in what must have seemed like great idleness, and a total lack of ambition. Between going from one friend to another, between parties, dances, visits, and reading, there was very little time for the hard work of studying anatomy.[21]

63

Edinburgh's aesthetic ethos was dominated by the Celtic revivalism of the Scottish renaissance, a movement similar to, and influenced by, the Irish renaissance of the same period. Cary's involvement in it seems to have been superficial and ornamental (he adopted a Celtic monogram as his artist's signature, for instance). A fundamental lack of sympathy with the movement's political tenets (partly because he was a stranger, partly because his response to the parallel Irish Celtic revival was ambiguous) may have promoted his sense 'of an ignorance which rose up about me, on all sides . . . I seemed to be walking into a blind gulley, with no opening in front. I felt its shadow upon all my work . . . though I still delighted to draw and paint, I had always the sense of one lost'.[22]

By October 1907, Cary was becoming despondent about both his art and his ability to manage in Edinburgh on his inherited income. 'Blacklock wants me to commence painting, and that is dearer than drawing,' he told his father. 'I was a little doubtful – I did not think I was drawing well enough.'[23]

What Cary later judged to have been the most significant experience of his years in Edinburgh was only indirectly connected with the art school. It was an 'odd encounter' with Marc-André Raffalovich and Father John Gray, both of whom had been associated with Oscar Wilde, Aubrey Beardsley and the *fin-de-siècle* 'decadence' of the *Yellow Book*.

Of Raffalovich, the son of very rich Jewish-Russian emigrés in Paris, it was said that he was so ugly that his mother could not endure his presence. At the age of eighteen, he had settled in London as a writer and, entertaining lavishly, became a friend of Oscar Wilde; but they quarrelled, apparently over John Gray, a handsome and charming young poet widely rumoured to be the original of Wilde's Dorian Gray. Raffalovich had become a friend and patron of Beardsley in 1895 (soon after the latter's illustrations in the first *Yellow Book* made him notorious). A Catholic convert, he was responsible for Beardsley's conversion shortly before his death in 1895, and then for Gray's conversion and eventual ordination in 1901.

When Gray was sent to Edinburgh, to be curate of St Patrick's Church, Raffalovich followed, bought a house, and financed the building of a new church, St Peter's, in Torphichen Road. When Cary saw this church in 1907, it was newly completed, an imposing building in warm-coloured stone imitating 'a small primitive church in Rome'. It does not seem that Cary was invited to Raffalovich's house, then 'the rendezvous for almost every person of distinction in art and letters in Edinburgh, whether residents or visitors to the city'; he would surely have mentioned its exotic '*fin de siècle* atmosphere'.[24] Cary wrote only of being invited to see the church; and 'I looked upon the whole affair, the church and their attitude, as a kind of aesthetic amusement – which, with them, was perhaps true'.

That derogatory final comment implies disapproval of the views, and perhaps behaviour, of the two men; and disapproval – since he would certainly have known about their connection with it – of the aestheticism of Wilde and Beardsley. But 'I suspect that it was here at the Art School and in this odd encounter with Raffalovich and his friend that I began to uncover a train of thinking and experience which became afterwards important to me. For it was almost entirely through the aesthetic experience that I came to a true faith, that is, a faith which I believe so entirely that nothing has shaken it, or could shake it.'[25]

Verse

By Cary's nineteenth birthday at the end of 1908, he was beginning to face the fact that his heart was no longer in training to be an artist. The eminent James Paterson (like Mackie an Associate of the Royal Scottish Academy), had praised one of Cary's portraits;[26] and some of the drawings in his sketch-books are impressive, both in quality and variety – fine portraits and still lifes jostle with copying exercises and lively caricatures.

'I imagine now that I was bored with art,' he wrote forty years later, 'because I was more interested in people and ideas, but I daresay another strong motive was the . . . restlessness of a boy uprooted from the long romantic tradition of a family domain.'[27] On another occasion, he said simply that he had 'got sick of drawing. I couldn't express myself.'[28]

Before the end of his first year in Edinburgh he was devoting more and more of his time to expressing himself in words. He tried combining words and art, composing a fairy-tale and then illustrating it. This work has not survived; but his drawings for another such project, a play called 'The Tree Folk', have satirical bite.[29] From early in 1907 he was also writing lyrics. A letter to his father in June 1907 included 'a little Elizabethan song' which begins

> Other maid has better song
> But none a better lover
> And e'en this ballad's but half wrong
> Should half my love discover
> So hey nonny, nonny.[30]

James Joyce's *Chamber Music*, a cycle of similarly 'Elizabethan' love lyrics, had been published the previous month, and the sickly taste was widespread. As Cary later pointed out, 'In Edinburgh, I was moving in a peculiar atmosphere of sentimentalism, a kind of hangover of the greenery-yallery period, or even earlier, late Rossetti.'[31]

Cary gathered several of his lyrics to compose a small volume, which was privately printed by an Edinburgh stationer, Robert Grant. *Verse*, by Arthur Cary, appeared late in 1908; it was dedicated 'To Arthur Cary my father'.

In later years, Cary was embarrassed by *Verse*, even as a tyro publication. In 1927, he asked his cousin Lionel Stevenson, who had just published a volume of poetry, 'did you ever see a book of verse I wrote at eighteen. If so, I hope you burnt it. It was worse even than the notorious first work of Shelley's . . . In Shelley's work one sees at least energy, in mine there is nothing but bad metre. My fault was in having nothing to say . . .'[32] And towards the end of his life, he could not be persuaded by Andrew Wright even to glance at the poems – 'real trash,' he insisted, 'really very bad for a boy of my age'.[33]

It is hard to contradict Cary's verdict. Wright has commented that 'The poems are at best conventional';[34] and indeed most are archaic exercises lacking personal conviction. With one exception: a 'Sonnet' which seems to reflect, with dark intensity and in Blakean terms, Cary's own dilemma of the time. The first quatrain runs:

> He built his house with squarely hewed stones
> Upon a shaggy-headed cliff, set high
> That every roof and tower did cut the sky
> Enduringly in old Chaos' bones.

On that exposed height, the protagonist 'meditated old temptations' until 'Earth's blood ran slow / And slower in its walls, and it was cold'.

> But he was strong and said, 'This house doth grow
> Into a prison;' and he took nor gold
> Nor craven jewel, but straitly forth did go
> In's tattered coat, as he had come of old.

Cary could not go 'straitly forth' from Edinburgh, from a School of Art become his prison. But the display of 'old temptations' in his volume of poems seems to have been part of a strategy. To publish Verse patronymically, and to dedicate it to his father, was tantamount to a plea for understanding and support.

Earlier in 1908, he had corresponded with a Clifton friend, Douglas Glenister, and at the end of October he told his father 'The Clifton people want to see me again before everyone I know has left. It is rather a journey but I think I ought to go . . .' He also mentioned receiving a 'charming letter of criticism from S. T. Irwin at Clifton – he is a delightful old scholar'.[35]

In fact, Cary had sent a copy of Verse to his old English master, obviously hoping for useful appreciation. Irwin's response had combined honest criticism with encouragement: 'I see there is plenty of cleverness . . . All the same I think you need to *mature* . . . I always thought that you had any amount of *unused* power, and you would be very unwise to be *afraid of your ambitions*. Still I don't think these verses are quite "good enough" for an ambitious person . . . you are worthy (and they themselves are evidence of it) and capable of much higher work.'[36]

During his visit to Clifton, Cary must have come close to making up his mind to abandon art school for university. His friend Tommy Higham would have told Cary he was going up to Trinity College, Oxford, in 1909, as a Classics Scholar – Trinity, the college to which Cary's family was connected through Falkland. Heneage Ogilvie was already in his second year at Oxford, reading Medicine at New College. Cary was now twenty; time was short if he hoped to change course.

In Gunnersbury over Christmas, he broached the topic cautiously; but his father seems to have urged him to reconsider. Back in Edinburgh at the beginning of January 1909, he tried unenthusiastically to pick up his art studies. 'There was rime on the ground this morning and Edinburgh looked uninviting enough – I wished I was at home . . .'

After an inconclusive exchange of letters with his father, he wrote again, agitatedly, towards the end of February:

> I am very sorry that I have made you anxious about me. Truly I realise the importance of this choice – and that is my only excuse for delay.
> I meant in my last letter to tell you I leant towards the Varsity, and indeed, I have been expecting your advice on that project. So many people – of critical knowledge and some literary standing – advise me to write, since I find I spend most of my time thinking about that kind of work, whatever is going on, and since I seem to labour at it without tiring – as I have done these weeks – I am encouraged to try for it. Will you tell me what you think?[37]

Arthur Cary replied sympathetically 'You did not make me anxious – more than I am always anxious that you should have a happy life – if you are now really sure of yourself there is nothing more to be said . . . I shall do my very best to help you . . .' But, he went on, 'all literary work is suffering . . . from over production in the moderate grades and only the very best – and the very worst – seem to find a market of any kind . . . Of course – dear old boy I hope your stuff will be the very best . . .'[38]

Cary followed his father's advice that he make immediate enquiries, and soon wrote to say 'I ought to enter my name at once, as I shall have a first examination to pass in April or May. I think I might manage it with a big effort . . . and if I fail, I do not know when I will be able to get there . . . I shall read, if I go, for Honours in English Literature . . . Should I write to a Correspondence College about tuition?'

It was decided that he should remain in Edinburgh, where his old Housemaster, 'Charlie' Tait, would help him while he had lessons at a 'crammer'. Soon Cary was able to respond positively to a (probably admonitory) letter from his father:

> You know I am proud of the family name too; and I know how you have succeeded in pulling it undamaged out of the fire, practically alone and unhelped . . .
> My Mathematics are practically safe now . . . Latin Prose is getting very much better (and ought to improve my English style later) and History goes on evenly. Greek of course is the doubtful subject, but if I do well in English, so Blakiston the President says, Trinity will excuse a failure in Greek.

He went home for a short holiday over Easter 1909, then returned to Edinburgh for 'the last effort' before his examinations. 'I am afraid, Dad, I am an expensive son,' he wrote, 'but one month more will end the Edinburgh adventure altogether and I will settle down.'[39] Promise or prediction, the final clause of that sentence – although he did succeed in satisfying his examiners – was premature.

Back in Gunnersbury for the summer after sitting his exam, Cary made a callow attempt to set himself up as a professional writer. In a letter to Jack (now a midshipman on the battleship *London*), he bragged that

I have got a secretary now, my boy, to run my shew. So that I can be as secret as I like. She is a Miss Foot (about 55, and not handsome, so don't grin) and lives in a flat in Hammersmith. I have a private name too – I am Thomas Joyce, only don't tell a living soul, you are the only person, except Miss Foot that knows it. I am going to write under it and play any fool's games I like under it, and have Cary for the drawing-room.

I shall advertise it too. 'Read the Counter-Jumper's Magazine. So-and-So by Thomas Joyce' in all the Railway Stations. [40]

Miss Foot typed at least one short story for him. 'Thus Crime is Punished' by Thomas Joyce appeared in a popular magazine, the *Idler*, in May 1910. A neatly ironic parable, it has a brigand and a policeman destroying an innocent shepherd. The charismatic brigand, who inspires the policeman into a partnership of profitable evil, is the apparent prototype of the many such rogues among Cary's characters; his relationship with the policeman foreshadows that of Mister Johnson and Rudbeck; and the main theme is injustice. The story also indicates Cary's lifelong attraction towards simple didactic forms: in art the cartoon, in literature the parable.

By the end of summer, Cary's career as a writer of fiction was, however, shakily, launched. And his choice of pseudonym – Thomas Joyce, legendary ancestor of his mother's family – is perhaps significant. Beyond its expression of family piety, it suggests, in replacing the patronymic Arthur Cary, an awareness of duality within his personality.

CHAPTER SEVEN

OXFORD

1909–1910

'I gave up my whole time to pleasure'
The Admissions Book of Trinity College, Oxford, records, in Cary's strong, neat handwriting, that he was 'admitted Commoner Oct. 8th 1909'. He was then almost twenty-one – a good two years older than most of his peers.

In Edwardian Oxford the University 'consisted largely of public-school men':[1] three thousand undergraduates dispersed among some twenty-five colleges. Although four women's colleges had been founded recently, undergraduate life was essentially masculine; women disturbed its tenor during the annual summer rituals of Eights Week and Commemoration, and occasional chaperoned dances and 'at homes' during term.

Most undergraduates tended to remain closely attached to groups of school friends. This was especially so at Trinity College, 'the proud possessor of a certain element of Muscular Christianity' (according to a comment of the time) since it 'contains a large number of undergraduates from the best public schools'.[2]

College life was unashamedly patrician. Relations were affable but cool and hierarchical (even among acquaintances). Scouts (college servants) respectfully tended the young men – served breakfast in rooms (and hot baths, as illustrated in a cartoon of Cary's), cleaned clothes and shoes, offered discreetly avuncular advice. The afternoon was for sport, the evening for social activities; education centred on the tutorial, its one-to-one relationship rooted in the medieval monastic houses which inaugurated the University.

Trinity College, founded by Sir Thomas Pope in 1555, had originated three centuries earlier in such a house. The eminent churchman and writer John Henry Newman was an undergraduate there in the early nineteenth century. His opinion of the College was not unstintingly favourable. Of his fellow undergraduates he complained 'I really think, if any qualifications were necessary for Trinity College, I should say there was only one, Drink, drink, drink.'[3]

Cary's early impressions, about a century later, are the basis of a passage intended for the novel *Castle Corner*:

> In *Punch* and their fathers' stories Oxford was all sprees, practical jokes, drunks, smokes and riots; it proved to [be] a quiet little country town peppered with twenty colleges as different from each other as the different houses of a public school, in which intercourse was highly formal. You were called upon. You returned calls. You were asked to breakfasts more grave and formal than any family meal at the vicarage. The noisy men who shouted in the quadrangle at night were possibly bloods whom it would be an honour to know; or possibly nonentities whom acquaintances would damn. Society was much more complex than at school; and much more critical than in the world. The school hierarchy of games was of small account here . . .
>
> Money, rank, snobbery of a hundred kinds here began to operate, because they had importance. To know a millionaire or a lord was of no advantage at school. At Oxford it might make a career . . .[4]

The two extremes of undergraduate behaviour were represented by bloods (who centred their lives on sport and physical activity, drinking and rampaging) and aesthetes (who dressed flamboyantly and flaunted their sensitive creativity). Aesthetes were often attacked by bloods; but not at Trinity – 'As a College we prided ourselves on tolerating eccentrics'.[5]

Cary did not ally himself openly with either aesthetes or bloods. Characteristically, he sympathised with both extremes and found his own middle road. His artistic aspirations and training, his experiences in France and Edinburgh, made him value the aesthetes' cause. He affected some dandyism in his clothes – and bought a monocle to wear in his weak right eye. In drafts for 'Tod', a projected semi-autobiographical novel of the 1930s, Cary's protagonist seems to be an exaggerated and partial version of his undergraduate self. At St Jude's College, where 'eccentrics were safe', Tod is 'irresponsible and volatile', 'with his erratic wild spirits, his moods of depression, his detachment from any rational system of morality or expedience'. 'His gestures, his dramatic stories, his brag' and his 'dandyish' clothes ('a bright green suit with enormous checks, and purple shirt, and dark crimson tie . . .') all define a 'flamboyant' personality. For Tod 'the world was dramatic'. He is 'not only capable of breaking windows but making epigrams'; he is 'the aesthetic type'.[6]

But the influence of his family and his schooling ensured that Cary would also continue to value sport and physical exercise. 'I rowed for my first two terms and would have rowed in the summer races if I had not been so bad a stroke that I pulled my arms to pieces and wrecked a crew.'[7] (It was the 'short pulls' of his Inishowen rowing, 'digging at the water in jerks with a navy stroke', that 'ruined my career as an oarsman', he claimed.[8])

Cary's rowing career at Oxford was not as disastrous as his reminiscences suggest: in November 1909, he stroked a College four which 'beat a heavier boat by a length and half' before losing the final race;[9] and in 1910 he rowed for Trinity's second eight in Torpids (a series of bumping races held every spring). After he gave up rowing in the spring of 1910, 'I took my exercise in riding or driving about the country, or cross-country runs or walks, punting on the river or long bicycle journeys to the Downs'.[10]

Although he had told his father that he wanted to read English Literature, Cary first followed 'a suggestion from my family that I should study history', then decided to read Jurisprudence. 'For it did not seem important to me what I studied so long as I was at Oxford, and exposed to its influence, its friendships'.[11]

He did not work enthusiastically for his weekly tutorials and, even before the end of his first term, was finding his law studies heavy going ('Not hard but long, and tedious').[12] The College authorities and his tutor, J. L. Brierly (Fellow of All Souls and later Professor of International Law at Oxford), treated him 'with the greatest indulgence' and 'I gave my whole time to pleasure'.[13]

'friendship and tradition'

When he came up, Cary had two friends at Oxford, the Old Cliftonians Heneage Ogilvie (reading Medicine and now in his final year of Oxford residence at New College) and Tommy Higham (a Classical Scholar at Trinity). Cary saw both of them frequently, but was also soon friendly with a group of fellow Freshers at Trinity, most of them, like him, non-English and older than the majority.

Three were South Africans: Lennox Broster and Gerhardus Maritz, Rhodes Scholars (later eminent as a London surgeon and the Judge-President of the South African Supreme Court); and Percy Horsfall, 'a brilliant scholar who took a double first' in Greats and became 'an international financier'.[14]

Duncan MacGregor, an Exhibitioner who had studied at Edinburgh University, was also reading for Greats. He became a lifelong friend of Cary's, and is fictionalised as MacOrr in 'Tod': 'a wiry long-chinned little Scotsman, pale-eyed, short legged, with fine kinky hair', who when drunk became 'reckless, affectionate, generous . . . His sharpness of tongue and his shrewdness did not leave him; but behind them there was an unmistakable sympathy'.[15] Years later, Cary wrote 'I am very fond of Duncan . . . He has a charming character, and the more one knows him, the more one likes him.'[16]

And there was Ewan Gawne 'with his pale face, cock nose, loud laugh, sensible advice and immense power of work'. And Lennox Napier: 'tall, stooping, smiling, slightly nasal speech, bursts of laughter, not really clever but reputation, sensible, suddenly violent on occasion . . . Always popular, perhaps because of unfailing good humour.'[17]

For Count Albrecht Bernstorff, a German Rhodes Scholar at Trinity for the 1909–10 academic year, the future held tragedy. After the First World War he became Counsellor of the German Embassy in London, but was recalled in 1933 to Berlin owing to his open hostility towards Hitler and the Nazis. He left the Diplomatic Service in 1937, and 'was one of the very few Germans who had the moral courage openly to protest against the Jewish persecutions; he even for some days gave asylum to a Jewish family whom he hid in his flat . . .'[18] Later he was imprisoned and tortured, released for brief periods from 1943, re-arrested after the July 1944 attempt to assassinate Hitler, charged with involvement in the conspiracy, and, in the last days of the war, hanged.

During Cary's first year at Trinity, Bernstorff was a close friend. In a short manual of advice for German Rhodes Scholars which he wrote in 1912, he commented that 'The young Englishman is far more an individualist than the young German', for he 'is allowed to think what he likes. That is a frame of mind which we should seek to imitate if we are to preserve all the things which Germany has acquired in the last decades.'[19]

None of Bernstorff's friends at Trinity better epitomised those values than Cary, who 'conceived society in terms of friendship and common interests; I liked to be with friends and spent a great deal of time every day in talk which was purely friendly and often trivial; but which seemed to me important as well as pleasant because it was between friends . . . Everything conspired to make me suppose that at Oxford I would learn, by friendship and tradition, a wisdom and insight peculiar to it.'[20]

A turning-point in Cary's intellectual development came about as an ironic effect of friendship and tradition. 'I used to visit the home of a College fellow and tutor in philosophy, a man of great charm, goodness and distinction. I loved to play with his children and tell them stories, and to feel the atmosphere of home.'[21] The Fellow and Tutor in Philosophy was H. A. Prichard, later Professor of Philosophy at Oxford (remembered by Maurice Bowra for his 'rough, shabby clothes' and 'passionate commitment to his subject'[22], and reputed to be 'the most rigorous and minute thinker to be found in Oxford'[23]). He lived at 43 Broad Street, close to the College, and offered Cary hospitality as a fellow Old Cliftonian.

> But one day pointing at a reproduction of a Rossetti, he asked me if I liked it. I made some polite comment, but the truth was that at that time I despised Rossetti and his school. I was drawn to Constable, Turner, the French Impressionists, and I had even seen, at Paris, Matisse and Van Gogh, who puzzled me but excited my curiosity. The tutor asked me why I didn't care for his Rossetti and then examined me in the Socratic manner on the meaning of my words. What did I mean by good art, bad art . . . .[24]
> ' . . . It's a thing you recognise – you know it at once.'
> 'But other people know differently about the same picture?'
> 'Oh yes, oh certainly.'
> 'Then how can you be so sure? How do you know?'
> And so on, until I was completely confused and much humiliated. But I was also indignant. Because I had already noticed Prichard's pictures. And seeing nothing but sepia reproductions of popular sentimental works I thought to myself, 'But what does *he* know about *art*?'
> I was too polite to say, 'But after all, I've studied art – and you know nothing about it. So what is the good of all this nonsense?' I was too polite but I was very much aggrieved.

Cary's annoyance and humiliation deepened when his friends, instead of rallying to him, were amused. 'I discerned . . . that, like Prichard, they looked upon me as an innocent, whose ideas were as naïve as his reactions.'

He continued to believe that he had been right – 'that the quality of a picture was something known directly. Prichard hadn't shaken me there.' But he had no means of countering Prichard's traditional Socratic demonstration of a logical deficiency in his position. And this rankled.

In time he would break the intellectual impasse, partly by applying the implications of his 'odd encounter' with Raffalovich and Father Gray in Edinburgh. 'But I would not have reached this point if Prichard had not made me feel, so deeply, the problem of knowledge. He taught me once and for all that there were realms of aesthetic experience beyond the reach of verbal logic.'[25]

'a great place for clubs'

Christopher Hollis has commented that, in contrast to their successors of the 1920s, Oxford undergraduates before the First World War 'spent a quite inordinate amount of time . . . in debating clubs and in pseudo-intellectual societies for reading one another papers'.[26] Cary was no exception. 'Oxford is a great place for clubs,' he wrote later.

> Many are literary clubs, either general in purpose or with some special object of study – Modern Poetry, for instance, or even the works of a single poet. They elect a complete staff of officers, buy a minute book, and may last a single term or fifty years . . . They meet every week on some evening in term, one member reads a paper . . . and then there is a discussion. Once a year the more famous and old established societies, such as the Gryphon of Trinity or the Florio of Magdalen, give a dinner to some guest chosen for his distinction in the club's special subject. These dinners are invariably excellent and conducted with traditional ceremony.[27]

When in 1952 Cary was guest of honour at a dinner given by the Addison Society of Queen's College, he commented ' . . . I probably learnt more when I was up from Clubs like the Addison than anywhere else; although I did not do very much work anywhere else, I did work both at preparing papers for the several Clubs that I belonged to and for discussion on the papers.'[28]

He was a founding member of Trinity's Elizabethan Club. And among his papers is the notice of a Gryphon Club meeting held on Sunday 5 February 1911 at 8 pm. 'Rooms: Mr Cary's / Business: Mr Cary will read a paper on "Impressionism of Painting".'[29] (That year the Club's members also heard a brilliant paper on 'Studies in the Literature of Sherlock Holmes'[30] by the young Ronald Knox, recently elected a Fellow of Trinity, and later Cary's friend.)

Other clubs were inter-collegiate. The Milton Club, named for John Milton, had been established in 1888, and it seems that Cary was its Secretary for a period. Its founders had been 'interested in Free Church principles', but from the first any undergraduate could be proposed as member so long as the membership did not exceed thirty. The Club's Object was 'the discussion of history, philosophy, social, religious, and other subjects of common interest'.[31]

A fellow member, John Middleton Murry, though some months younger than Cary, had been a Classical Scholar at Brasenose College since 1908. Born in London to a poor, lower-middle-class family (Irish in origin on his father's side), he had early shown intellectual brilliance and was 'fished up by charitable scholarships, which . . . were the first of their kind'.[32]

Through the Milton Club, Murry met 'a group of exceptionally able undergraduates, mostly from Trinity, including Joyce Cary, E. H. W. Meyerstein, Arnold Toynbee, Thomas Higham, Duncan MacGregor, F. R. Barry and Philip Mitchell'.[33] He found them 'vastly stimulating': 'They were a little older than the average undergraduate . . . Something had intervened for them between the public school and the university which made a difference. They were neither overgrown sixth-form boys, like me, nor pass-men up for a good time. There was nothing precious about them, yet their intellectual interests were varied and independent; and they judged for themselves.'[34]

A character in Cary's notes for 'Tod' – Daly, 'a clever youth' who 'had come up on a scholarship' – is clearly based on his memories of Murry as an undergraduate: 'Daly was a good looking boy with brown hair and blue eyes and a marvellously fresh complexion. He appeared four or five years younger than his age' and was notable for 'sudden absurd movements, and loud unexpected bursts of laughter. He appeared always to be wondering what effect his conduct was having upon other people . . . It was his nature to be a social parasite.' A brilliant talker, he is 'always full of odd and curious information . . . He could talk to you about esoteric Buddha, yogis, pearl-fishing, radiology, astronomy, Schopenhauer or psychical research; but always for effect.'[35]

Like others after him, Cary was dazzled, puzzled, fascinated. By late 1910, in the first term of Cary's second year at Oxford, they were becoming close friends. Murry had recently discovered the philosophy of Henri Bergson, and longed to hear the great man lecturing; he had also met a French novelist who urged him to spend some time in Paris, 'the metropolis of criticism', and offered to arrange accommodation for him there during the coming Christmas vacation. Cary 'heartily approved my going to Paris, and said he would join me there'.[36]

CHAPTER EIGHT

BOHEMIAN

1910–1911

'Everyone is poor, all have enough'
Cary had recently spent some weeks in Paris, during January and Easter
1910, on the first occasion living in a pension on the Boulevard du
Montparnasse. (He kept the bill, addressed to 'Monsieur Carré', the French
transcription of his surname which, translated into English, gave him
Corner as his fictional variant of Cary.[1]) Now he and Murry had adjoining
rooms in a little hotel overlooking the Luxembourg Gardens, on the rue
Gay-Lussac.

When Cary arrived in Paris on 27 December 1910, he immediately
plunged into Latin Quarter life. He admired the generosity of the artists'
fraternity. Hardly any of them had enough money 'to pay for next week's
dinners', but 'The sort of general sharing that goes on, whether there is need or
not, provides everyone with something . . . Everyone is poor, all have
enough, no one seems to sell anything and no one is ever so poor that he can't
afford a bottle of wine . . .' 'Talk and friendship, after all, are more necessary
than three meals a day.'

He lived a self-consciously Bohemian life. A typical day:

Waked at eleven and pulled my curtains. A sunny morning, cold. Wrote
the end of last night's sonnet and got up to wash. Still only half-past
eleven, so went to bed again until ten minutes to twelve. Went and
waked M. [Murry] and dressed. Out to [the Café] Biard, two doughnuts
and a café crème. Then up to Montparnasse. Chestnuts from the man at
the corner of the Boulevard Montparnasse and rue de Rennes who gives
you nearly a third more for two sous than the man in the Boule Miche,
but his nuts are smaller. So back at two, buying two small cherry tarts at
three sous on the way; and after an energetic argument on commercial
art, to work at three. B. [Café Biard] again at five. Two madeleines and a
café crème; work till seven. Shaved, and so to Bobardet's for dinner . . .
So to d'Harcourt with three more cigars. Had table opposite side door,
met the two Armenians. Great English lessons, both now adepts at the
worser slang and crying various phrases at everyone the whole night. Girl

in pink to me. She is much the prettiest there. Marvellous throat, and pale rosy cheeks, with no paint.

Soon after his arrival, Cary was invited to a meal:

Today I had a note from Miss Dot Banks saying come to supper at 8 . . . I arrived rather late, and found the rest already there, a tall, dark, clean-shaven fellow with a low skull, and a fair bearded man . . . They were sitting over empty soup plates (Miss B. was grilling a steak) round a little island of lamp-light in the middle of the huge bare old hall, that Miss B. paints and eats and receives and sleeps and does everything in.

Dot Banks, whom Cary had first met in Etaples, was Scottish, 'a large and beautiful woman with a heavy, pale face reminiscent of the photograph of Oscar Wilde'; 'strange and brilliant', she oscillated between mordant wit and tearful hysteria. Her guest, the Scot with the low skull, was the painter John Duncan Fergusson. Cary introduced Dot Banks to Murry, who had already come across Fergusson in a café; and the two Scottish painters became important to both young men, Dot Banks providing food and friendship, Fergusson – the 'philosopher-painter', Murry called him[2] – influencing them both very strongly, if diversely.

Fergusson was a self-taught painter who had been a disciple of both Beardsley and the Impressionists before discovering the Post-Impressionists; and he shared Dot Banks's enthusiasm for the work of a young Spaniard recently arrived in Paris, Pablo Picasso. A lively, generous man in his mid-thirties, who dressed with tasteful flamboyance (Cary noted a red jersey and earrings) but was well-organised and hard-working, Fergusson was also a fluent talker with strong opinions and wide general knowledge. Cary followed his advice that artists should use 'a very soft pencil' to make 'quick rough sketches of anything around you; never correct a sketch, just make another . . .'[3] The sketches Cary made on this holiday – including portraits of Murry and Dot Banks, and several self-portraits – are all in soft pencil, and similar in style to Fergusson's sketches of the same period.

Fergusson's most important influence on Cary came from his aesthetic philosophy. At the time, Cary – perhaps because he was still smarting from Prichard's attack, perhaps because he could not sympathise with Post-Impressionism – seems to have been reluctant to respect Fergusson's opinions; commenting that, 'like most professional artists,' Fergusson 'treats philosophy rather as a game, with ideas [as] counters, and pretty patterns always possible'. But the central tenets of Fergusson's aesthetic must have impressed him even in 1911, for they can be discerned in Cary's mature thought and writing – and especially in *The Horse's Mouth*.

Murry recognised in Fergusson one of those for whom 'Art was their religion . . . in the service of which poverty was to be expected and endured'. Although he did not like Fergusson's recent paintings, and 'a good deal of his philosophizing struck me as rather naïve', he admired the painter's 'singular completeness', self-control, and dedication. And recalled Fergusson's conviction that to be an artist 'was not primarily to paint pictures or to write books: it was to have the courage of one's being and one's faculties in the face of the world'. Anyone in any job could be an artist.[4]

In his own book published in 1943, *Modern Scottish Painting*, Fergusson insisted that the artist's task is to express 'a human impression or feeling about people or things', and that Philosophy – which he defined as an attempt to 'get wise' and justify 'one's own "honest to God" feelings' – is therefore an extremely important discipline for him. Fergusson utterly rejected 'absolutism' in both artistic creation and response. We must judge a work of art 'by our feelings' – 'Art is what you feel it is, *for you*.' And his own standard was simple: 'A really good work of art always makes me laugh . . .'[5]

Fergusson's aesthetic seems to have influenced Cary deeply – more deeply than he recognised; not only in its dominant ideas, but also as an artist's brave attempt to resolve, for himself, and without any professional philosophical training, the crucial issues of his vocation.

'much the nicest woman in the d'Harcourt'

By the time Cary arrived in Paris, Murry (who had been there about four weeks – without attending any lectures by Bergson) had been mildly entangled with two *cocottes*. According to his own account, Murry was at the time very shy despite his volubility; intellectually advanced but emotionally retarded; radically insecure. Not surprisingly, when a young and attractive *cocotte* called Marguerite (Murry's version of her name was Marguéritte) showed sexual interest in him, Murry was quickly 'enveloped in her tenderness'.[6] In Cary's opinion, Marguerite was 'much the nicest woman in the d'Harcourt' – 'Tall, not very pretty, but well-shaped, with a clear voice, and sensible, good-natured eyes and mouth . . .'

Cary's diary entry for 30 December 1910 begins with a scene in the Café d'Harcourt:

> She was all in black, very pale. She looked round a moment before she saw me, then she came at once, and shook hands. I ordered coffee. She has a face very broad at the eyes and pointed at the chin. Her mouth was a little drawn, her eyes heavy.
> 'I am very unhappy,' she told me. She was playing with a match on the table. I took her hand between mine, I asked her what was the matter.
> 'I am in love with your friend,' she said and then, after a little, 'Of course I am very fond of you too, but I love your friend.'
> 'You had much better love me instead.'
> 'Ah! no, I can't do that,' she smiled rather faintly at this.
> 'Don't you find me good-looking enough?'
> 'But that isn't the same at all. Oh please don't make fun of me.'
> 'I'm not making fun of you.'
> 'I shall kill him.'

Marguerite was unpredictable. Murry, feeling out of his depth, was trying to avoid her. Cary was caught in the middle.

> M.'s nerves are all to bits and we passed a wretched time. Marguerite has always said she would put a knife in him if he left her, and I believe she

would. Not that I think this worried M. so much as thinking he had lost her. He went round with flowers, and came back to say she was powdered up to her eyes, and said merely au revoir . . . Refused to let me talk to him, and went off to his room. He did this really, it seems, to get me away, if there was to be a knifing.

Cary was increasingly attracted to Marguerite himself. He talked to her one night at the Café d'Harcourt about 'the chances of coming out at Easter and setting up a little *ménage à trois*. She was interested at once . . . And we discussed rents, and déjeuners and soups and cheap dishes for a long time.' The night before the two young men left Paris to return to Oxford, Cary

Dreamt Marg. came in to see me in bed, so actually, that I thought she had. Went in to M.'s room at 1.30 and she was asleep in his arms, dressed in her clothes outside the coverlet. She woke up and glanced at me. Said something about her not coming to see me, and she said, no, she hadn't but she had only been to bed seven hours in three days. Last night she only went home after Montmartre to doze for a time and then came straight to us. Lay down with them but got very restless. Went and washed and came back. Marg. made me lie in the inside corner next the wall, beyond M. where I sang one or two songs and dozed a little.

Cary's brief but intense experience of a triangular sexual relationship, and his proposed *ménage à trois* with Marguerite and Murry, may have originated a recurrent pattern in his fictional writing – above all, in the two trilogies.

Murry believed that his life was changed. 'What had happened to me in Paris was that I had become quite unfitted to continue at Oxford. I was plunged into a tumult of emotions and ideas which incapacitated me wholly for any serious work of the kind expected of me.'[7] Cary would also find it difficult to readjust to the staider rhythms of Oxford, and to the need to work hard for his degree in Jurisprudence.

'I never saw him do a scrap of work'

During the rest of 1911, Cary and Murry remained on friendly terms. They even shared rooms for several months: Cary had been living at 16 Turl Street; after the summer vacation, he moved in with Murry at 55 Holywell Street. But their relationship was becoming tenuous.

Murry returned to Oxford obsessed not only with Marguerite but also with a project to found a new, avant-garde journal of the arts. He and Michael Sadler (later Sadleir) were to found a literary magazine called *Rhythm*. The word 'rhythm' had recurred in Murry's conversations with Fergusson, and he was now convinced 'that rhythm was the distinctive element in all the arts, and that the real purpose of "this modern movement" – a phrase frequent on F—'s lips – was to reassert the pre-eminence of rhythm'.[8] The time was ripe for an achievement that would lead to Murry's becoming within a decade, by the age of thirty, 'a key figure – perhaps the leading figure – of the post-war literary generation' in England.[9] Modernism was the future – not only in Paris, with the ferment of the Fauves and the Russian Ballet, but in ponderous London, where the first Post-Impressionist Exhibition opened while Murry was away, in that year when, Virginia Woolf pronounced famously, 'human nature changed'.[10] *Rhythm* appeared while 'Pound and Eliot were virtually unknown, James Joyce had published no fiction, D. H. Lawrence had not written *Sons and Lovers*, nor Virginia Woolf her first novel . . .' So Murry 'was present at, indeed assisted in, the birth of English Modernism'.[11]

Why was Cary left out of all this? (Although he helped to finance *Rhythm*, only one piece by him – a short review, in the fourth number – was published.[12]) No doubt his openly expressed criticism of the Post-Impressionists and Fauves was partly responsible. But it seems possible that professional rivalry, and increasing personal antipathy, were other reasons. When Murry returned to Paris for the Easter vacation, his companion was not Cary but Michael Sadler.

Marguerite now came second to *Rhythm*. She had abandoned the Café d'Harcourt, found a job as a typist, and was living respectably with her married sister. Years later, Murry wrote guiltily in his journal 'If I had had any money, even the chance of the tiniest job in Paris – or indeed in England – if, like Joyce Cary, I had had £300 a year of my own – or even a *quarter* of that – I should have married Marguérite.'[13] His final break with her did not come until the summer; after that, 'I never wrote to her again; nor did I read the letters she wrote to me.'[14] But meanwhile, he had to beg money from friends to get back to England. Cary received a postcard at the beginning of April: 'Joyce: for God's sake send me £2 or 3. The very fiends of Hell have dogged me since I've been here . . . And now at the Lilas last night I lost every damned penny in my purse, by leaving it on the table . . .'[15] Cary obliged.

One last service, a curious one, Cary seems to have performed for his friend. Returning to Oxford in the autumn, after ditching Marguéritte, Murry decided that 'the right and proper way to break the spell of Marguéritte was to go to bed with another woman . . . So I hinted to my friend, who had seen something of the beginning of my affair with Marguéritte, that I was prepared for an "adventure". He kindly undertook the arrangements.' They cycled to a brothel 'somewhere in the countryside' near Oxford. 'My friend, who knew one of the girls, was cheerful and casual when we entered: I straightway fell into an abysm of depression; from which I never recovered . . . It was a sordid, miserable business . . .'[16]

The first issue of *Rhythm* came out in June 1911, and by the end of the summer, Murry was a minor celebrity in the English literary world. In December he was introduced to Katherine Mansfield, who had sent him her short story 'The Woman at the Store'. Cary, who according to Murry, 'was a little scornful of what was printed in *Rhythm*, admitted I had made a discovery';[17] but when Cary met Katherine Mansfield herself a few months later, 'He had not liked her, he had found her hard, selfish, and a little sordid'.[18] Those sentiments may be close to Cary's private opinion of Murry himself by the beginning of 1912.

And while Murry was busy promoting a career that would soon bring him into contact with D. H. Lawrence, and Lady Ottoline Morrell's Garsington circle, Cary was unsettled and depressed. He had been doing little work for his looming Jurisprudence examinations, and must have known he faced an academic disaster. Should he leave Oxford now (as Murry was talking of doing), and try to establish himself as a writer? When he put this question to his father at the end of November, the response was swift: ' . . . I am quite sure if you do leave you will regret it very much in after years – of course if you have not any aptitude for Law – or so little that you could only pass with a struggle you could not go on with it – but – none the less a mans Varsity Degree is an asset very much worth making even a sacrifice to obtain . . . .'.[19]

Cary decided to soldier on, but spent much of his time writing poetry and fiction. Murry, now often away from Oxford and taken up with frenetic editorial activity, remembered Cary covering 'the sitting-room floor with foolscap sheets of Caroline lyrics – about eight lines to the page; which was extravagant of paper but gave him a necessary feeling of elbow-room. For the same reason, I suppose, he did most of his writing on the floor, with an exceptionally blunt quill pen'.[20] Otherwise, Murry insisted, 'I never saw him do a scrap of work'; and he remembered Cary as frequently drunk – though 'he was the chap who would see you home'.[21]

Murry left Oxford in March 1912, and was soon living with Katherine Mansfield in London. He returned to take Schools, but after that Cary saw little of him. A note for a possible story suggests his private opinion, then or later, of what had happened to his erstwhile friend: 'Murry captured by the artists . . . goes to the dogs.'[22]

Probably in early 1912, Cary started to write 'a book about the life I had seen in Paris';[23] but never completed it. Less than five years later he found himself reading a review of Murry's first novel, *Still Life*. It was of course based on the author's 1910–11 experiences in Paris, and particularly on his affair with Marguerite. Cary wrote with mingled irritation and envy: 'I see that fellow Middleton Murry I lived with at Oxford has written a novel, very well received in *The Times*. He was a scamp that fellow. The novel sounds just the sort of thing I would have expected from him – confused sex relations, neurotic love-affairs – and a great anxiety for originality at all costs.'[24]

When he read *Still Life*, Cary was surely both annoyed and saddened. In representing his affair with Marguerite, Murry was both self-lacerating and self-indulgent. Dot Banks makes an unprepossessing appearance as Miss Etheridge ('as she slowly walked her heavy body swung round from side to side'). The protagonist, Maurice Temple, notes that 'in the next room lived a man who was a great friend of mine then, called Stephen French. He liked Madeleine. I'm not sure even that he did not love her more than I did – I wonder . . . Anyhow, Madeleine didn't like him. I never quite understood why, but I think it was because she thought he made jokes at us together.' There is even an insinuation that Stephen French spies on Temple: 'his door was always open a little way'.[25]

Cary was to return the brickbat in his characterisation of Nosy Barbon, naïf hanger-on of Gulley Jimson in *The Horse's Mouth*. One of his notes about Nosy Barbon reads: '? M. M. Serious, grave, quiet, long-nosed, looking wise, and suddenly producing nonsense.'[26]

But the effects of the relationship went much deeper. Their association in Oxford, and particularly in Paris, bound Cary and Murry in a mutual influence more important than either seemed willing to admit. A hint of this is a passage in *Still Life* describing Maurice Temple's guilty search for Madeleine, years after their affair. His first step is to locate the married sister. When she answers the door and asks who he is, Temple, 'glib with sudden inspiration', answers 'My name is Monsieur French'. 'Vous-êtes Anglais, peut-être?' she continues. 'He told an unexpected lie, smiling. "Non. Je suis Irlandais," he said. "C'est autre chose."'[27]

CHAPTER NINE

THE OGILVIES

1911–1912

'a pretty strict sort of household'

During his final year at Oxford, Cary again spent much of his time with friends made at Clifton and Trinity.

Heneage Ogilvie, his closest friend, had left Oxford over a year earlier, and was now at Guy's Hospital, London, completing his Bachelor of Medicine and studying surgery. Cary kept in touch with him, especially during the university vacations, and gradually got to know the Ogilvie family.

Since 1908, the Ogilvies had been living in a large house, The Glade, at Harrow Weald, on the north-west outskirts of London. Heneage's father, William Maxwell Ogilvie, a Scotsman from a poor family (seven of his nine siblings died of consumption), had trained as an engineer, like Cary's father, then worked for several years in Bristol. In 1882, he had accepted his brother-in-law's invitation to join the firm of Balfour, Lyon and Company in Valparaiso, Chile; there, four years later, he married a German woman, Mary Anna Wolff, and they had five children, two boys and three girls. He returned to England in 1902 to take over his firm's London agency and, after four years in Bristol, decided to move closer to London. The Glade was built to his and his wife's specifications, with a large landscaped garden and tennis court.[1] Since the Ogilvies were not only rich but very hospitable, Cary, as Heneage's friend, became a frequent visitor.

One of Heneage's sisters, Elsie, though more than a year younger than Cary, was his contemporary at Oxford. He met her, through Heneage, during his first year, and in his second she invited him to a Somerville College 'At Home'. Frederick, their brother (who was four years younger than Cary and had been his junior at Clifton College), was also at Oxford, a Classical Scholar at Balliol College from 1911. With Duncan MacGregor, Cary would often visit his rooms, to 'rifle his cupboard' for Ogilvie comestibles.[2]

Mrs Ogilvie was generous and warm-hearted; but also rigid, a disciplinarian. Her husband had been 'brought up in a very strict way as regards Sunday observance. On Saturday night all our toys and play books were put away. We were taken twice to Church and we spent the rest of the day reading Sunday books, having a home Sunday School, and singing hymns.'[3] Mrs Ogilvie, brought up a Calvinist, was even more firmly committed to Protestant piety. The family, its six servants, and any guests, gathered for a prayer service every morning; Church attendance and a prayer service at home were the rule on Sunday; and there was a remorseless emphasis on high morals, self-control, hard work, respectability. It was 'a pretty strict sort of household,' Cary commented later.[4] His response was ambivalent: attracted by the household's orderliness, and its preservation of values and traditions, he was also irked by its repressive narrow-mindedness.

The Ogilvies responded to him with a similar ambivalence. Although they liked him, they regarded him with suspicion. As Heneage put it years later, 'we thought he was rather harum-scarum'.[5] However much he might strive to accommodate his behaviour to the Ogilvie ethos, Cary's ebullience was not always repressible; he was seen to be emotional, unpredictable; he was Irish, he was known to have trained as an artist, and now he wanted to be a writer; he had lived in Paris – and perhaps hints were dropped about colourful Bohemian exploits.

Still, he was at Oxford. He was also Heneage's closest friend – though this may have brought additional censure if his example was blamed for Heneage's increasingly rebellious conduct. While Freddy, her youngest, satisfied Mrs Ogilvie's ideal of respectable restraint, Heneage, her eldest, was independent and outspoken (he argued vociferously, for instance, against public schools).[6]

Heneage and Cary were alike in temperament. With his 'brilliant brains', Heneage was also 'passionate – capable of strong love and deep feeling'. Freddy was 'cooler and more cautious than Heneage, and less adventurous' – he 'works too much by the head, whereas he had much better trust his heart'. Yet Cary felt that he and Freddy were alike in that both of them 'hate to make our feelings public' – though Freddy 'carries it to extremes'. Cary feared that Freddy's uneasy combination of restraint and impressionability could make him 'the most melancholy of human wrecks . . . the religious fanatic'.[7]

The Ogilvie brothers may have exemplified for Cary, again, the pattern of contradictory creative and conservative temperaments (even their youngest sister thought them 'as different as they can be'[8]). He was always more at ease with the outgoing Heneage; but he formed a secure friendship with Freddy Ogilvie before leaving Oxford, and a few years later spoke of them as being, together with Duncan MacGregor, 'my only friends'.[9]

The strict Ogilvie ethos was generally successful in shaping the two sons for public school and university, and for notably successful careers, but its effect on the three daughters was variable. The eldest, Florence (always called Flo by the family), was two years younger than Heneage, and, according to a rather harsh character sketch by Cary, 'intelligent . . . but deficient [in] sympathy.'[10] (He was perhaps remembering that, after he had danced with her at the New College Commemoration Ball in 1911, she complained to her parents that he had been drunk![11]) In 1913, Flo married Malcolm Venables, an Anglican priest.[12]

He liked and admired Elsie, who was a year younger than Flo; but he found her academic seriousness daunting, and twitted her for her feminist ideals. When in 1917 she married a Scottish doctor, George Carlisle, whom she had met while nursing as a VAD in France, Cary was delighted to hear that she had requested changes in the wedding service: 'Did she really refuse to say obey? Dear Elsie, I shall pull her leg if she did.'[13]

'the most affectionate loving heart in the world'

The third daughter was Gertrude (whom the family called Gertie), a year younger than Elsie and two years older than Freddy. She remembered her early years as very constrained – 'Three innocent or ignorant girls sitting round Mama listening to the words of wisdom which fall from her lips . . . Life then was just a round of lessons, games and walks – and when lessons were done with – the round of house duties – tennis parties and dances where everyone was very polite to each other . . . It is funny to think how absolutely sheltered I was . . .' As a girl, her reading was strictly censored: 'I remember Father finding me reading V*anity Fair* when I was about 13, and saying I had no business to read it . . . With Elsie things have always been different. She has been considered the emancipated member of the family, is clever, and has met numerous people of every sort . . .'

Lively and sensitive, but constantly overshadowed by her two elder sisters, Gertie Ogilvie grew up shy and recalcitrant. At fifteen she was sent to a girls' private boarding school (St Felix, Southwold), under Elsie's wing. ' . . . I wouldn't have missed those years at school for anything,' she wrote later. She enjoyed playing hockey, and 'used to win prizes for running';[14] but she fell far short of Elsie's academic prowess.

A letter from her mother preceded her to St Felix. 'It was *very* hard parting from you, darling, doubly so because there had been a little cloud. I know how sorry you were, and how hard it is for you to speak as you feel when you are sorry. But I *do* trust and believe in you dear Gertie and I know you *will* try to be a good girl in every way.' And when Gertie was about to return home for Christmas, she was urged to 'make a solemn promise in your prayer to God that by His help you will be really good and sweet and loving *all* the holidays . . . take courage and try with all your heart not to have a single regret or self-reproach when the holidays are over.'[15]

Gertie's lack of self-confidence became permanent. Throughout her life, she would 'get such ghastly fits of shyness I can't open my mouth', would think herself 'rather a dunce' and the perennial 'bad girl of the family', and would be chronically uncertain about the validity of her opinions. Underlying the shyness, and insecurity, however, were a down-to-earth sensibility and impetuous independence that led to frequent 'explosions' of temper and 'massamoras' (rows).

Her closest relationship through childhood and adolescence was with her younger brother Freddy. 'When I was about 12,' she recalled later, 'it was my ambition to go out as a missionary to China – Freddie and me to go together!'[16] Throughout their lives, they remained emotionally close to each other.

It was as Heneage's friend that Cary met Gertie Ogilvie towards the end of 1910. He had been romantically interested in several girls – especially Gwen and Magdalen Quilter (daughters of the artist and writer Harry Quilter), whom he had met through Heneage. Magdalen had written to him while he was in Paris, and for some years afterwards they corresponded regularly. But the relationship remained indeterminate. (A few years later she was to marry Heneage, after he had been rejected by her sister.)

Cary paid little attention to Gertie Ogilvie when introduced to her in Heneage's rooms. But *she* remembered the occasion well: 'you sat next Mrs McNulty and discussed music . . . I was terrified of all young mons in those days – in fact I think that time at Oxford was more or less my introduction to them – and I don't expect I had a word with you – I should have been too terrified to open my mouth first!'[17]

Later encounters with Cary – like a dance at the Stanmore Institute in July 1911 – did little to moderate her alarm in his presence. But clearly he was becoming interested in her. He was attracted by her warm contralto voice, both when she spoke and when she sang. Like Freddy, Gertie was very musical, and they often entertained family and visitors together, Freddy (who was an excellent pianist) accompanying his sister as she sang or played the cello. Cary responded to such occasions with the deepest pleasure. 'I don't know what sort of voice yours is,' he once wrote, 'but I know it goes right into the inside of me . . .'

By now Gertie Ogilvie may have been connected in Cary's emotions with his mother; her singing and warm voice, even her nervousness of him, could have strengthened the association. A half-teasing description written for her some years later indicates his conscious reasons for pursuing her: she had

> grey eyes, a round chin, a most charming mouth, a fascinating nose, two little marks on her front teeth that you can see when she laughs, an honest way of looking at you (no wonder, for she is the most candid of girls) and a pretty voice and figure. She can sing so that you are stirred right out of yourself, and play [the cello and piano] – and her thoughts on everyday matters are not at all commonplace. Then she can cook and sew – is understanding, unselfish and has the most affectionate loving heart in the world . . .[18]

In the summer of 1912, Gertie Ogilvie visited Oxford twice, for the 'two chief festivals of the Oxford year, Eights Week and Commemoration'.[19] She remembered Cary arriving in Freddy's rooms for lunch, 'looking bored to tears with everything – and we went to the Ashmolean [Museum], and dragged you round it much against your will . . . Afterwards we sat in Balliol Gardens, and you told me all about the novel you had been asked to write and told me not to tell anyone'.[20] Probably he was depressed about the Jurisprudence examinations he had recently written. But discussing the proposed novel (presumably the one based on his Parisian experiences) was a sign of confidence in her.

A few weeks later, he had recovered his energy and optimism for Commemoration, whose 'glory is the College Balls' that 'take place always within the walls of a College, either in the Hall or, if the Hall is not big enough, in a marquee set up expressly in the gardens'. Each ball lasts through the night and ends 'at seven or thereabouts, when a photograph is taken of the whole assembly. Some colleges provide breakfast. At ten on the same morning members of the party may be seen already in punts on one of the rivers, dozing in the sun under the trees or floating down the current with an occasional stroke of the paddle.'[21]

But Commemoration 1912 was a disappointment for Cary. At the Trinity College Ball, Gertie was reluctant to dance with him (and afterwards complained to her mother that he had held her too tight!).[22] She was also 'fed up' with him because 'you squashed me flat about women and literature' in conversation between dances; 'you tried to speak so scornfully of women, their intellect in particular, and you were prepared to pour ridicule on the fact of my not having heard of "The City of Dreadful Night" . . .'[23]

He had arranged to take her punting that afternoon, her last. But when he got to their meeting place – no Gertie. 'I couldn't find you and when I did you would not speak to me'. She had brought a friend with her, and while the two girls conversed, the humiliated Cary was left to feel like 'a wooden automaton wound up to punt, and otherwise to be ignored . . .' Disaster after disaster. That night, after she had left Oxford, Cary was so upset that he broke down and 'cried in Freddy's arms'. But he also 'stole' from Freddy's rooms (on that occasion or earlier) a photograph of her.[24]

'My ideas were still in a complete muddle'

Cary must have left Oxford with very fixed feelings. He had enjoyed himself making friends, attending club meetings, dancing, partying; but he had not worked hard at Jurisprudence. Nor had he made much progress in his avowed aim to become a writer, though his desultory reading, and his daily conversations with friends, were to be fundamentally important to his ultimate literary achievement.

'At Oxford, though I did not take philosophy as a subject,' he commented, 'I read much for my own amusement and heard a great deal about it'; for his friends 'were most of them philosophers'. But he had 'conceived the feeling that I should not care for [philosophy]. I was turned back towards reflection on art, poetry and friendship.' This, he thought, was because 'I encountered each new philosopher, in the mouths of my friends, undergraduates, as a set of ideas, a system, and never a character. Plato was the Forms and the *Republic*, which I detested as a state which had no freedom and despised artists; Kant was a theory of knowledge, and a copybook maxim about duty . . .' But he remembered being impressed by Bentham's utilitarianism because he had had to study it systematically for a Law paper.[25]

When he left Oxford, 'Scraps from the philosophers, from Bergson and Kant, from my reading, from arguments with my friends, fragments of aesthetic and ethical speculation, my practical training in art, and my discovery that it had opened to me a special kind of knowledge, were embedded in different parts of my memory without any connection. My ideas were still in a complete muddle.' It would be many years before Cary was satisfied that he had created order and coherence to replace that muddle; but without the 'scraps from the philosophers' that had lodged in his mind during his three years at Oxford, the process could not have been so richly creative.

Two philosophical influences encountered at Oxford were to be important. Cary's references to Bergson in later life were mainly pejorative; but this is probably because he was introduced to that philosopher's thought by Murry, who 'was then a Bergsonian'.[26] 'Bergson, who was all the rage then, seemed to me void. He gave me no feeling, no picture; but only vivid metaphors, which, when you sought to grasp them, flowed away . . .'[27] In an interview towards the end of his life, Cary insisted that he was 'no life-force man' – the Life Force was 'rubbish, an abstraction, an idea without character'.[28] Yet the fierceness of his protestations suggests that his thinking was influenced more than he wished to recognise by Bergson.

The other major influence was acknowledged fully and often. At the end of his life, for instance, when illness prevented his attending a Blake Society dinner as guest of honour, Cary wrote to express his admiration for William Blake's poetry and thought. 'I still possess the two volumes of the Ellis edition which I used at College, heavily annotated. He is for me the only philosopher, the only great poet, who had a real understanding of the nature of the world as seen by an artist . . .'[29] Elsewhere, in comparing Blake with the philosophers he had encountered at Oxford, he claimed that 'Blake, whom I read and studied at the time, had more effect on my idea of the world, for he introduced me into a highly complex universe where what is called the material is entirely dissolved into imaginative construction and states of feeling, where matter, mind and emotion, become simply different aspects of one reality'.[30]

'Songs all day'

In July 1912, Cary learned that he had barely scraped through his final examinations. 'CLASS 4 WORDS FAIL US' ran the jocular telegram he received from three friends still in Oxford.[31] Although he must have expected low marks for his Jurisprudence papers, it is doubtful that he found any humour in the result. A Fourth Class B.A. is the lowest possible, a derisory pass notable only because it is comparatively rare.

By the time he heard the news, Cary had moved to London to establish himself as a professional writer. He was renting rooms in raffish Store Street, just off Tottenham Court Road, a few paces from the British Museum and Soho; an appropriate address for an aspiring young writer – especially one still attracted by the Bohemian life he had lived in Paris, and anxious to write about it.

In Heneage's rooms at Guy's Hospital Cary encountered Gertie Ogilvie and her mother. He and Gertie had last seen each other at The Glade, again disastrously, just before he moved to Store Street. She had criticised him for depositing pipe ash on the mantelpiece; suddenly he called her 'a beast, I was fearfully enraged, or I daresay I wouldn't have used such language . . . I think you wondered at my sudden explosion . . . And perhaps suspected a reason for it even then.'

Apparently not. She had glared at him as they sat opposite each other at lunch. And Cary might well have despaired about their relationship if he had not received unexpected support. Mrs Ogilvie was unsympathetic ('I was her bête noire'), and he had an 'awful scene' with her – she accused him of hurting Gertie, and when he blurted out his love merely said 'she had no idea it was as bad as that'.[32] On his way out he encountered Gertie: 'You looked perfectly awful when you came down the stairs after saying good-bye to Mother,' she wrote later; ' . . . I suddenly wished I could have made you happy instead of sad – and I do remember I boldly took your arm as you were going to the door and said "Cheer up Joyce"!'[33] Mr Ogilvie was Cary's 'only friend then. The only one who advised me to hope. He took me out specifically to do it . . .'[34]

Now, in Heneage's rooms, Gertie and Cary were stiff with each other. Unknown to him, it was her twenty-first birthday 'and I was very sad because there hadn't been a single letter for me in the morning'.[35] When she enquired about his activities in London, he told her he was busy with a novel based on his experiences in Paris (presumably the one he had told her about in Oxford). Scornfully she wondered why he didn't try to write a play instead, 'to make some money'.[36]

Cary was, in fact, short of cash, since his annuity had been depleted by loans to friends like Murry and by the rather lavish expenditures of his final year at University. One Oxford friend who visited him at Store Street was moved to expostulate that he was now 'living like a pauper in squalor'.[37] A sporadic daily record that Cary kept during July and August indicates his concern to keep track of finances, and gives a rough sketch of his gregarious Store Street life.

On Saturday 13 July he spent £3.7.0d; 'Smoked and read all day.' He spent £4.6.5d on Monday 15 July; 'Two hrs. work in evening.' The following Monday, after 'week-end at Guy's' with Heneage, he spent £34.0.9d – £19.3.0d of that on a chair (which, judging by the price, was an antique – Cary had a lifelong love of antique furniture). The next day he 'Worked all morning and afternoon,' and in the evening his Oxford friend Napier took him 'to dinner at Rendezvous and then the Empire' (the latter a well-known music-hall of the day).

On Thursday 1 August he had 'Tea and dinner at Guy's', and the next day 'Lunch with Barrow at Comedy. Dinner with Forbes at Rendezvous . . .' And the final entry, for Saturday 3 August: 'M. to tea . . . Songs all day.' Murry, now living with Katherine Mansfield, was hectically busy with his literary career; Cary, scribbling his 'songs', must have felt depressingly unaccomplished.[38] He was independent, he was writing, he was enjoying himself making new and meeting old friends, he was surrounded by the bustle of London life. But one suspects there was an edge of boredom and worry to Cary's days and nights in Store Street.

The fiction Cary wrote there survives only in what may be a fragment of his 'novel about Paris', and in a short story.[39] Both are first-person narratives in a style of heartfelt cynicism (later popularised by Hemingway).

The fragment begins 'she was a good girl, Philippe, as girls go, though of course rather stupid and greedy, as all these girls are.' Although Philippe devotedly nurses the narrator through a serious illness, he quickly tires of her: 'After all, my girl had always been Maria, that Russian, you know, who is Queen of the Chope d'or, in the Boulevard Raspail. All admit that she is one of the finest girls on the left bank. And she always did what I told her.'

The short story is entitled 'The Pantry Door'. Its climactic act of violence, recounted with jarring swiftness, simplicity and matter-of-factness, foreshadows a characteristic of Cary's mature fiction.

The plot is straightforward. A *cocotte* is visited unexpectedly by the lover who narrates the story. A muffled sneeze from behind the pantry door convinces him immediately that she has been entertaining a rival. 'I stayed an hour . . . I saw everything in relation to the pantry door. I complimented her – she seemed to laugh to the pantry door. I played for her – she sang at the pantry door. I asked her how long she would be true – and she said "for ever" to the pantry door. She delighted me with her spirit.'

But, as one recognises with a shudder at the story's climax, he has already made the decision that Jim Latter would make, in the last novel Cary completed, *Not Honour More*:

> She sat with her back to me – 'to be between me and the door' I said to myself. I took a Spanish-knife from the window-sill, and ran it into her back beside the shoulder-blade. Her stays hardly resisted. She did not make a sound. I took care that no blood fell on me, but I wiped the knife on the sleeve of Monot's coat, before I hid it under the fender. 'It will be a clue' I thought.
>
> 'Good-bye, Elise,' I said aloud, so as to be heard in the pantry, 'A demain,' and kissed her . . .
>
> I walked out rather noisily and waited in the lobby a moment – I heard the pantry door open and Monot's cautious whisper. Then I went quietly down the stairs.

A little shocker, a conventional magazine story, largely derivative? But 'The Pantry Door' is nevertheless notable for its convincing expression of a deranged, obsessive mind, its confident handling of first-person narrative, and its effective creation of suspense.

However, Cary was not ready to settle into the lonely labour of serious professional writing. He was restless, and frustrated by his unrewarded love for Gertie Ogilvie. He craved action, excitement.

CHAPTER TEN

MONTENEGRO

1912–1913

'I wanted the experience of war'
Cary later referred to his participation in the First Balkan War, of 1912–13, as 'a holiday', and enjoyed reminiscing about it. But it was a very dangerous holiday which turned his life in a new direction, away from writing as a full-time occupation.

Heneage Ogilvie had heard from an American doctor about the war of liberation that had just broken out in Montenegro; that the Montenegrin army was ill equipped and without medical supplies; that there was but one doctor in the whole country. Cary was just as fired as Heneage by the romantic plight of the Montenegrins, just as anxious to experience war before it disappeared for ever; and, unlike Heneage, unhampered by responsibilities. Their exalted mood was that of the millions of young men who, two years later, would fling themselves into the trenches of the Western Front.

Cary left so precipitately in October 1912 that his father, notified by telegram, could only send to Montenegro a letter of mingled anxiety and pride, advice and affection: 'I am very glad you have a kit of sorts old boy – but what you describe will not stand very long if you have to rough it . . . I do hope old boy that you will take care of yourself as far as keeping dry and feeding well is concerned – for of course if you are assisting at the front, to look after wounded men, you cannot help running risks. All send love and luck to you.'[1]

Cary's intention was to join the Montenegrin Red Cross, since he believed that there was little chance of the British Red Cross (stationed in Antivari) getting to the front line. But, after four days of polite brush-offs in Cettinje, the Montenegrin capital, he travelled to Antivari in the company of a Lieutenant Popovic, a retired Serbian officer who assured Cary that he would be allowed to join the Montenegrin Army as Popovic's orderly.

In Antivari, Cary's war began with a bang. He and Popovic, waiting for their papers and uniforms to be issued, 'decided to fill in time by exploring the old Venetian fortress of Antivari. What we did not know was that part of the building had been modernised for use as a shell-filling casemate. As we were admiring the old towers which stand everywhere on the edge of the cliff, this casemate blew up'.[2] Cary and Popovic were thrown down the slope on which they had been sitting, while 'the shadow of a column of smoke a hundred, two hundred feet high, slid down the grass'.[3] Cary had been stunned by the blast; as huge stones began to rain down, Popovic dragged him to the shelter of a wall.

When they stumbled down towards the gate, both were arrested and held on suspicion of being the saboteurs. Soon a British Red Cross unit appeared, to help treat the wounded, and Cary was able to explain his and his friend's presence. 'This unit, fully equipped for front line service, had just arrived to serve with the Montenegrin Army. It included Captain Martin-Leake, V.C. Leake on entering the guard-house asked if anyone knew the way to the fortress, and I presented myself.'[4] 'Burning munitions were exploding all the time and there were many wounded.' As Cary led the way to the fortress, he noticed 'something like a piece of withered branch with the bark on'; and, when he picked it up, he 'saw that it was a man's arm, the fingers blown away from the palm . . . I handed it over to our guide, who put it in his belt.'[5]

Excited by his first experience of the horrors of war, voluble, hungry, Cary was given a lift down to the centre of Antivari in the carriage of three journalists. One of them wrote an article about the explosion featuring Cary as a 'clean-shaven, curly-headed young man' whose life was guided by 'the Irish love of adventure'.[6] Cary's family was impressed. Aunt Netta, now married and living in Castledawson, wrote excitedly: 'Did you know there was a long column about you in the *Daily Express*, telling all about the Explosion, and headed 'The Man who was Blown Up' . . . You are having dreadfully exciting times but you sound in the best of spirits . . .'[7] Great-aunt Doll was worried: 'I was terribly cut up at your going off to the seat of war the way you did . . . Thank God he has taken so much care of you already . . . I hear you have had a Red Cross uniform given to you and that you might after a time get a salary.'[8]

Cary had in fact been offered a job as a Red Cross orderly, and by the beginning of November was on his way to Rjeka in a field party led by Martin-Leake. There he found the newly arrived Heneage Ogilvie in charge of the hospital, and was put to work dressing wounds. But, burning with impatience to get to the battlefront, he found his duties dull, and was 'glad to be out of [Rjeka] when at last I fell ill, and was sent back to Antivari' – from where any expedition to the front would start.

At last, early in December, he was sent to Zogaj, 'a straggling Albanian village'[9] on the southern shore of Lake Scutari just below the high Tarabos Ridge. 'The Montenegrin Army had by now advanced on both shores of the Lake . . . and were besieging the town [Scutari], once the capital of Albania. Heavy fighting had taken place, especially on the Tarabos range, which was still covered with the dead.'[10]

Scutari and its defending fortress on nearby Tarabos were the last Turkish strongholds in Montenegro. An armistice had been declared by the Montenegrin Army; but both sides were disregarding it in heavy bombardments.

At Zogaj, Cary was cook's mate and house orderly, and quickly became known to his colleagues as 'Cookee'. His duties were to help prepare meals in the hospital kitchen, 'a dark windowless chamber' in what had been a Turkish mosque; and to supervise the cleaning of his colleagues' laundry and living quarters.[11] The hospital was busy, with about fifty in-patients arriving for treatment every day; but otherwise Zogaj was comparatively quiet because 'more or less under cover' from gunfire, and some distance from the fighting.[12] From the mosque, 'at the very shore of that lovely water,' Cary was able to enjoy the view over Lake Scutari. 'I can remember many a dawn when I looked out of a lattice window upon waters as magical in the morning sky as Keats' faery seas.'[13]

But he was there to see warfare; so he was delighted when, after about ten days, he was dispatched to another village, Vilgar, on the southern slope of the Tarabos Ridge. At Vilgar, Cary was cook's mate for a newly arrived Red Cross party under Martin-Leake, again using the local mosque as hospital.

Already Cary had come to admire very greatly the 'gentle and simple' Montenegrins, whom he found invariably kind and polite, their soldiers impressive for courage, independence, endurance; and he meditated on the reasons for the Montenegrins' ability to find happiness in so hard a life. All military equipment had to be hauled by hand up three thousand feet of the Tarabos Ridge; yet there was always a soldier ready to carry a sack of stores to a fort on the other side and to 'return to his own camp by the same route within the morning'.[14] Cary's sympathies were being deepened and broadened by what he saw around him in this remote, rugged land which so often reminded him of Inishowen (even Cettinje had looked 'like a small Irish town').[15]

The fighting was now dying down as wintry weather enforced the armistice. Now there were hours of relaxation during the day, hours Cary 'spent merely sitting on a stone in the sun, too lazy to look for the burst of shells even when they were fired, and that was only at long intervals'. The daily routine of cooking and housekeeping tired his muscles but sharpened his appreciation of simple social pleasures: 'Down again to race with the dark, and the night wind – tea and toast by a roaring fire with bare feet warming on the ashes, and coat and breech unbuttoned – then Williams [the cook] and I to make a pudding and the rest to doze till dinner, a meal with nothing before it, but the delights of pipe and bed.'[16]

Among the lively brush sketches that Cary made while in Montenegro is one that renders superbly just such a night. On one side of a huge fire sits Martin-Leake, in profile, smartly military as he leans forward intently. Opposite him is the other member of the group who made a lasting impression on Cary – Todd, smoking a cigarette, 'his beard in the air and his cap on his nose', meditative. And between them, with his back to us, silhouetted against the blaze, smoking his pipe, Cookee. Their contentment is palpable.[17]

Early in the New Year, they received notice of recall. Before leaving for England, Cary visited Antivari, where Heneage Ogilvie joined him. With several companions, they rowed about ten miles along Lake Scutari in a dinghy. The journey took them nine hours; night fell, and they nearly lost their way amongst a multitude of small islands. Cary never forgot that vast shining dangerous expanse lying against 'an endless chain of jagged mountains'.[18] Some years later, in one of his frequent, vivid dreams, he 'enjoyed a long flight over the lake of Scutari, recognising it perfectly well'.[19]

Before the end of January 1913, the two young men were back in England. The Ogilvie family met them at Victoria Station, where they all had dinner. Gertie later mused 'Do you know the first time I really guessed you cared for me, was at that dinner at Victoria when you and Heneage had arrived back from Montenegro.'[20]

Cary went back to 10 Store Street. He was as unsettled as ever. He went to parties and sought out his friends. One visit was abortive and humiliating. Middleton Murry and Katherine Mansfield were living at 57 Chancery Lane; when Cary called on them, he was 'told they were not at home, though the house above was loud with the noise of a literary party'.[21]

Then, less than a month after his return, Cary received a note from Martin-Leake: 'Am coming to town tomorrow to see you. Please be in during the morning. The Red X want us to return to Montenegro – can you?'[22] He could.

'a magnificent fight'

In January 1913, it had looked as if the First Balkan War was almost over. Scutari was under siege, and from February 'attacked from all sides'. But it had since become clear that, until the Turks were dislodged from their fortress on Tarabos, above Scutari, they would continue to defend the town and so retain a foothold.

Cary returned to Montenegro at the end of February. 'I was now on the strength, with a whole uniform and a kit – no longer to be the tramp, ragamuffin, and outcast of the force.' They were stationed this time at the village of Bobote, east of Vilgar along the southern flank of Tarabos Ridge. Life was calm at first, as is indicated by Cary's humorous summary of his daily duties:

6.30. Get into shirt and breeches and make fire. Roll up sack.
6.40. Go for water – and tell the crowd outside to hold their whist and stop poking their bayonets through the wicker work – the big doctor [Martin-Leake] is asleep.
7. Put on the jug, and smoke a pipe.
7.30. A cup of tea for each man. 'Thank you Cookee,' from Cap [Martin-Leake]. A snore from Lauder [the dresser].
8. Ready with pan and bread for breakfast. Lift Lauder two or three inches by the hair, and wait till he opens his mouth wide enough to say, 'All right, Cookee, go to hell!' . . .
8.5 or 10 or 15. Breakfast.
8.30. Drag Lauder from his bed, and make the bed as far as possible uninhabitable.
9.30. Smoke.
10. Make the stew and put it on.

11.   Sprinkle the floor, sweep, and wash up. In sweeping it is only necessary to rub the dust gently to and fro with a besom, and it will fall through the cracks into the stable. Overhaul the stock of provisions and find out what is wanted. If beans, or rice, or bacon fat, send off one of the guards to find a mule and fetch them. If he does not return in two or three days, send another man.

And so through the rest of the day – including '2.30. Put on boots and puttees, fill a haversack, and march'.

This idyll did not last. With spring, the war resumed and early in April Cary at last saw what he had longed to see – 'a pitched battle'. From Crapaj, a village at the foot of Tarabos, 'only three hundred yards from the Turks and right under their rifles', the Montenegrin Army attacked the Turks' fortress, which was defended by 'German trench work and wire entanglements as tried out in that war by the Turks'. During the preliminary five-hour bombardment, Cary and his companions found 'comfortable places, with plenty of cover and an excellent outlook over the positions . . . We saw one man go up bodily in the dust of a melinite shell, spread-eagled.'[23] 'We were near enough to see the heads of the Turkish sharpshooters through Capt. Leake's glasses as they sniped at us . . . the interpreter was hit in the cap, and the rest sprinkled with splinters of rock.'[24]

Now the attack began, at 2:15 on a Monday afternoon:

A line of men appeared suddenly on the sky line from the far side of the ridge, silhouetted, and ran stumbling towards the wire.

These were the bomb-throwers. There were forty of them, all old men and special volunteers. They offered themselves because as they said it would not matter if they got killed. Several of them were wearing the long white frock, blue breeches and white stockings of civil dress, and their coats blew out ludicrously behind them as they hurried their rheumatic old legs over the stones.

The bombs were tubes about eight feet long, meant to be pushed under the wire and fired by a fuse . . .

It must be understood that the Turks were firing point blank at them from fifty yards . . .

About half these men were killed outright, all but two or three were hit . . .

After this attempt to wreck the barbed-wire defences, the Cettinski infantry battalion were to advance, 'in regular parade order', their first objective a Turkish redoubt. The redoubt was taken, at 2:30. But the attack then failed bloodily under the Turks' maxim-guns. The battalion's commander 'was shot through the skull, and for ten minutes or so his battalion was in confusion. They rushed blindly up the trenches from the redoubt and were caught. The Turks had maxims facing straight down these trenches and shot them down in dozens.'[25]

Soon the wounded were stumbling back to the farm building near Crapaj – only seven hundred yards from the Turkish fortress – in which the Red Cross hospital had been established. 'At one time we had over four hundred casualties in the building, and the wounded were lying on the dead for want of space and mattresses. We could not evacuate even the light wounded because the Turkish howitzers as well as some nests of sharp-shooters commanded all the roads.'[26] 'The wounded lay or stood in a close crowd about and we did not stop from washing, painting, bandaging at all. Outside the maxims never ceased, one took up the refrain from another, there was the report of big guns every minute, and now and then the crash of shrapnel like a thunder clap over the roof, but inside the house was as quiet as a church.'[27] Only when night came could they begin to evacuate the wounded, and return to Bobote.

A few days later, when the post was brought in, Cary received 'a large round parcel'. Inside was a cake; and with it a note from Gertie Ogilvie, who, with her sister, Elsie, had baked it for him a month before. The note he carried with him everywhere he went in Montenegro. The cake 'was burnt here and there, but that was a guarantee of human kneading and baking'; and he and his companions savoured its magnificence: 'it had a fine tawny flesh, firm and just damp enough to keep the bites distinct, while the currants and raisins were very evenly distributed at intervals of a centimetre, no desert places, no unfairly rich pockets to cause jealousy'.[28]

Within weeks, the Turks capitulated; and Cary was with the Montenegrin Army when Tarabos fortress changed hands. 'One Turkish officer was crying. He bent down and kissed the gun, and each of his soldiers followed him in turn.' On their way down to Scutari, the Red Cross unit was met by General Martinovec, who 'made us a little complimentary speech . . . We assured him that we had enjoyed the war very much, congratulated him on the fall of the town, and there was general hand-shaking . . .'[29] (Later Cary received 'a little gold medal from the Montenegrin Government which I prize very much'.[30])

Memoir of the Bobotes

Self-confidence and exhilaration mark Cary's account of his experiences in Montenegro, *Memoir of the Bobotes*, published posthumously but written during the first few weeks after his return to England. His father's admiration must have been particularly delightful; following the trust and approval of other men he respected, like Martin-Leake and Todd, it recognised the main implication of the exploit – that Cary was now 'blooded', had proven himself a successful man of action.

By the end of June, Cary was at Trinity College, Oxford, 'living on the same staircase [as during his first year as an undergraduate] with an old friend, and reading, and writing and playing tennis very happily'.[31] There he may have completed the *Memoir*. The Preface he added to it seems to have been written in the last quarter of 1913 (he had then recently seen Ballinasloe, an Irish town mentioned in passing); it indicates that he intended to try to publish the memoir as a book – though there is no evidence that he actually submitted it to a publisher.

As in Paris with Middleton Murry a year earlier, Cary had kept a diary as well as making a series of sketches during his seven months in Montenegro. These were the basis of his 60,000-word record. As Walter Allen pointed out in his Foreword to the *Memoir*, it does not give a detailed explanation of the background and events of the First Balkan War: Cary's focus was a young man's individual experience and observation of warfare in a foreign country, and in 1913 he could expect the general facts of the War to be widely known.[32]

Memoir of the Bobotes is of historical interest as (to quote Walter Allen) 'an intensely pre-1914 document': 'There is, on the one hand, no repudiation of war, no sense of intolerable personal outrage, or, on the other, any passionate identification with a political cause that must defend itself however horrible war may be.'[33] But there is also no glorification of warfare, no evasion of its horrors and boredom; and in this respect *Memoir* differs strikingly from many military records of its time. It is pervaded, Allen stated, by 'Cary's remarkable objectivity'.[33]

That 'objectivity', already evident in his Paris diary and 'The Pantry Door', was to remain fundamental and definitive in Cary's writing. In *Memoir* it may shock the reader by seeming to abrogate pity: 'The Turks came out . . . and bayoneted the wounded. Some of them were tangled in the wire, and hung there helpless until they were shot to pieces, or spitted.' This apparent heartlessness is heightened by frequent aphorisms: 'The sniper waits for the failure of the imagination and shoots you because you have forgotten that you must believe in him.'

And there is humour, some of it self-consciously literary, as in this description of the Red Cross unit exercising:

> Furious marching and counter-marching all over the mountains, rocks, canyons, cliffs of the known world, hands in pockets, hands swinging, hands climbing, hands clasped behind, hands waggling from thumbs stuck into braces – with meditations, contemplations, reflections, compositions, songs, speeches, whistling, duologues, in which the other parts were severally taken up by Gregor, Panurge, Heneage, Doctor Pangloss, Mr Micawber, Brierly, Lauder, Pope Pius, Mord Emly, the Nigger of the Narcissus, Harry Richmond, Epistemon, The Knight of the Burning Pestle and the Nuremberg Man.

That playful paragraph, with its helter-skelter of lists and its bow to Rabelais, could almost come from Sterne's *Tristram Shandy* – or Joyce's *Ulysses*. Indeed, devices later popularised in Modernist writing are common in Cary's *Memoir*. The very first sentence seems to subvert its own status: 'On Friday morning, therefore, October 25th, 1912, I took carriage from Cettinje . . .' And the deliberately anti-climactic conclusion humorously queries its reader's response: 'The Austrians did not come, as you know, and there is nothing more to write . . . If this proves a disappointing book it must be because there is too much eating, and too little incident in it – too much like life, which is perhaps disappointing for the same reason.'[35]

Walter Allen praised 'the terseness of the prose, the concentration of description in the fewest possible words'.[36] But it is also true that Cary's narrative is marked by deliberate discordances and unfulfilled expectations that indicate the presence of irony. The representation of Cary himself, one notices, deflates him at the merest hint of heroic conduct. For example, on the night after the Antivari explosion, he sets fire to his quilt with a cigarette: 'I found that by stamping not only did I not put it out, but singed my feet. I was forced at last to drag it into the corridor and pour a couple of buckets of water over it, of course disclosing my trouble to all the world, a world that laughed unsympathetically and offered very ribald and useless advice. That was a fine end for the adventurer in his carriage of the morning.' Here the final sentence makes a simple irony explicit. But frequently a more complex irony is implicit – 'You object again that this history is all of meals, of stew and eggs. Anyone will tell you that a war is not made up of fighting, but just exactly of stew, and if you are lucky, eggs.'[37]

Memoir of the Bobotes, Cary's first completed substantial work, was a fine achievement, giving notice of his creative ability. It united his talents as writer and pictorial artist; and his aspiration to be both man of action and creator. Derived from direct experience, it is lively, persuasive reportage – as well as a modernist narrative of imaginative force.

CHAPTER ELEVEN

REJECTIONS

1913

'something useful and practical for the Irish peasantry'

Cary's decision to abandon Store Street was also a decision to abandon his commitment to the life of a professional writer; and he sometimes regretted it in later years. 'I am the man who took the wrong turning like the lady at the Lyceum – I should have gone back to Store Street after the Balkans, and worked as I meant to work. I might have succeeded, I very likely would have failed, but that is what I should have done if I had had the courage.'[1]

He still wanted to be a *writer* – the effort given to composing *Memoir of the Bobotes* is evidence of this. But now he set out to combine writing with another career. After seven exciting months abroad, his Store Street life probably seemed intolerably stale and unprofitable. And then, at nearly twenty-five, he was without a settled occupation, and could not hope to support a wife satisfactorily on his annuity. Certainly not if that wife was to be Gertie Ogilvie – who had so recently revived his hopes by making and sending him 'the famous Montenegran cake'.[2] He must prove to her parents that he was sufficiently steady and respectable; and the complimentary recommendation he had received from Captain Martin-Leake would greatly strengthen his application for any post involving practical service.

At the end of June he was awarded his B.A. degree. On 1 July 1913 he wrote to his father from Trinity College: 'I think that I shall apply for the African Colonial Service this August (if my chances are thought good enough) and we'll see what comes of it.'[3] He had dined at All Souls with his old Tutor, Brierly; and it was probably on that occasion that he met W. G. S. Adams, Fellow of All Souls and recently elected Professor of Political Theory and Institutions at Oxford. Adams, a Scotsman with an Irish wife, obviously liked this lively young man, and was impressed by his background and recent experience in Montenegro. He suggested that Cary apply for a post in the Irish Agricultural Organization Society (the IAOS), as Sir Horace Plunkett's Irish Co-operative Movement was denominated.

The timing seemed propitious. 1913 was a year of mingled optimism and concern about the future of Ireland. The 1910 British General Election had bitterly disappointed the ruling Liberal Party, reducing their seats to the same number as the Conservatives', and giving the balance of power to the Irish Party and the fledgling Labour Party. The latter parties could therefore ensure that the Home Rule Bill (introduced by Gladstone in 1886, only a few years after the Rents Act that had ruined Cary's grandfather, but blocked by the House of Lords in 1891) was revived and revised.

Meanwhile, in the north of Ireland, Sir Edward Carson had led the Ulster Unionist Party into total rejection of Home Rule, supported by the Conservative Party. Conflict loomed. But in 1913 it looked possible for men of good will to avert disaster and promote a constructive resolution of the 'Irish problem'. And one of the most positive and influential contributions towards such a resolution was Horace Plunkett's Co-operative Movement. The inspiration for his co-operative work had come during Plunkett's student days at Oxford, and throughout his later life he was nostalgically in awe of the Oxford ethos. He had studied Modern History in the 1870s, the culminating decade in England of a period of very extensive social reform that saw the establishment of trade unions as well as co-operative societies. ' . . . I took a strange somewhat vague idealism,' Plunkett recalled. 'That either the English or the Irish social economy, in which I had been brought up, would endure, I did not believe. In some way it all seemed wrong.'[4]

Returning to Ireland in 1878 to manage his father's estate, Plunkett immediately set out to right the wrong; and since Ireland is primarily an agricultural country, he adapted his knowledge of co-operative principles and organisation to help farming and farmers. By 1908 there were 345 co-operative creameries, with a membership of 40,000, producing more than half of one of Ireland's staple exports, butter; and more than 260 credit societies supporting farming ventures with cash loans. By the time Cary was encouraged to apply for a post in the organisation in 1913, the IAOS was becoming respected around the world as a model for agricultural co-operation.[5]

As an undergraduate, Cary may have heard Plunkett speak. He had been a member of the Oxford St Patrick's Club (the menu he kept of a Dinner on 11 June 1910 has, on the back, the pencilled signature 'W. B. Yeats'[6]), and Plunkett had attended Club Dinners of those years – he was always keen to recruit new workers in Oxford.

Cary responded enthusiastically to Adams's suggestion. His 'Irishness' had been strengthened in Montenegro, where he had seen so many similarities to Inishowen. Now, unexpectedly, there was an opportunity to play a constructive role in Ireland, and at the same time to establish himself in a profession. This was much more attractive than colonial service in Africa. He applied to Plunkett for a post in the IAOS. 'My ideas were to do something useful and practical for the Irish peasantry, and perhaps find time and material for writing'.[7]

Cary had been invited to stay with the Ogilvies; when he arrived there on the afternoon of Friday 11 July, he must have been bubbling with optimism.

Most of the weekend he spent playing tennis with Heneage, Freddy and

Gertie. But on the Monday, Gertie's diary records, 'All the others went into town early, except Joyce so we were alone all day.'[8] Here was his opportunity. 'I shall never forget,' Gertie told him later, 'your holding forth to me about schoolmasters at the lunch when we were alone . . . You were pretty withering about them, I remember.' (Flo's husband, the Revd Malcolm Venables, was a schoolteacher, so this was tactless; but Cary was tired of being urged to consider schoolteaching as a profession, and was adamant in rejecting it.)

'That same afternoon,' she continued, 'you asked my advice about W. Africa in the event of your being married, and I wondered who the young woman was. It was only when you made me furious by saying that I would never get to India if you had anything to do with it, that I guessed that I was the woman . . .'[9] But she gave him no indication that she had received his message. Late in the afternoon, after tea, 'Joyce read his Montenegran account aloud to me.' If he had hoped, as he related 'hairbreadth escapes i' the imminent deadly breach', that her response would match Desdemona's – 'She loved me for the dangers I had pass'd' – he was disappointed. 'The others returned home about 8' and the decorous Glade round resumed; 'After dinner we sang partsongs and Gilbert and Sullivan'.[10]

On other occasions Cary tried directness. Finding her sitting at a table sticking photographs into an album, he burst out 'You do care for me, don't you?' She fled. Then, while she was playing the piano in the drawing-room, he 'stood by the fireplace and calmly remarked "I am afraid you are not as much in love with me, as I am with you." What a bold mon – and I couldn't say anything – I think I got out of the drawing-room as quickly as possible in a great fright.'[11]

His tension exploded in another fierce quarrel with her. He must have been almost relieved when he received a warm note from Plunkett written at 'Kilteragh, Foxrock, Co. Dublin', confirming arrangements for his visit.[12] Before he left The Glade, he was invited to join the Ogilvies later in the summer, at Balmacara in Scotland; so, after all, there would soon be another opportunity to woo Gertie. From Gunnersbury, about to leave for Ireland, he telephoned to thank the Ogilvies for their hospitality; Gertie happened to answer, and afterwards insisted she heard him say 'Oh my darling.'[13]

'The Irish job was closed to me'

Kilteragh, a large country house overlooking Dublin Bay, had been built to Plunkett's careful plans in 1906. It was intended to provide a convenient centre for conducting IAOS business and for bringing 'Irishmen together to discuss Irish problems'. Until the house was destroyed by Republican extremists in 1923, a stream of guests passed through it – 'Irishmen and Englishmen of all politics or none, the die-hard business men of Belfast and the young revolutionaries of Sinn Fein', as well as celebrities like George Bernard Shaw whose support Plunkett solicited or whose ideas he found stimulating.[14]

Cary was a guest at Kilteragh for over two weeks. He arrived on Friday 25

July, and seems to have impressed Plunkett immediately: 'a young Oxonian who has been serving with the Montenegrin Army – as cook, hospital nurse . . . Adams recommended him as a possible worker in Ireland.'

Cary was to be taught the essentials of co-operative organisation and principles, and to be tested for his suitability for appointment as an assistant organiser. On 26 July Plunkett 'Spent the day mostly in instructing Cary and Smith Gordon [another young Oxford graduate] in the "Movement". I am treating this in its "English Speaking Countries" aspect rather than in its Irish. It will take University-trained men to run it. Besides *I want successors*.'[15]

Cary's own detailed account of what happened is contained in the draft of a biographical outline written in the 1940s: 'Plunkett's idea was to use members of the old Anglo-Irish families . . . because of their supposed special sympathy and influence with the people'; but other senior members of the Co-operative 'wanted agricultural specialists; and probably they were right'.[16]

Writing in 1919 to his wife, Cary identified R. A. Anderson, Plunkett's 'lieutenant', as the leader of the group opposed to Plunkett's views: 'The Irish job was closed to me . . . Plunkett was pleased with my work, but Anderson fought his battle while I was at Balmacara, and won.'[17] It is possible that Anderson, sedulous son of a Scottish minister, rejected Cary for additional reasons. His memoir implies a complex personality locked in an intricate relationship with his leader.[18] He may have resented Cary's rapport with Plunkett, or judged Cary's personality too ebullient.

One senses in all Cary's statements about the affair a deep disappointment. He had been so close to landing a post that seemed well suited to his abilities, recent experience, and family circumstances. Plunkett was also upset, as he showed in a letter to Adams on 29 September: 'I am sorry to tell you that Cary, after full trial, proved not to have had the gift of agricultural organisation, and to my great grief will have to seek some other outlet for his energies.'[19]

Plunkett was a man of extreme complexity who puzzled and sometimes offended his own disciples. Gerald Heard, stressing Plunkett's extraordinary courage through much physical pain and public villification, argued that stoicism was 'the real basis of his life'; he 'hated sentimentality but admired deeply heroism, courage and self-sacrifice'. Although continuously turning over in his mind 'the basic problem of the meaning of life, he kept on questioning but never really enquiring. His mind was in some ways closed . . .'[20] Plunkett was in constant tension between patrician and populist aspirations: 'The thought of treating someone as an inferior was repulsive to him, but the idea of feeling that someone "of a lower class" was one's equal, that was really impossible for him.' 'No one quite knew where they were with Plunkett.'[21]

Strikingly similar comments were made of Cary, and there is a teasing resemblance between the two men, even in appearance. Like Cary, Plunkett was 'a thin spare man . . . with a prominent nose and kindly eyes', about five feet ten inches tall. Both were men of 'remarkable energy' who 'loved horses and the rough outdoor life',[22] but who forced themselves to the lonely indoor pursuit of writing.

Cary must have recognised his affinities with Plunkett. But their very similarities – and Cary's failure to find final acceptance at Kilteragh – would have thrown into relief some of their profound differences. A character sketch made many years later shows that Plunkett remained vivid in his memory, to contribute to the evolution of at least one of his major characters: 'Plunket, attentive, lisping, eager . . . full of schemes. watchful to pounce. forgetting all but his aim. A monomaniac.'[23]

'universal hostility'

Cary joined the Ogilvie family at their holiday house near Balmacara, on the west coast of Scotland, opposite the Isle of Skye, on 14 August. He was of course anxious to restore good relations with Gertie and also to persuade her and her family to accept him as her suitor.

During the weekend after his arrival, the young people went across to Skye on a painting expedition. Cary's first attempt to renew personal contact resulted in Gertie's jumping over a stream to escape him: 'you . . . sat down with Freddy in the grass and glared at me', full of 'outraged virtue . . . indignation and repulsion . . . But I ought not to have put my hand on your shoulder or said anything about your perspective – I tried to be friends again too soon. And tactful Freddy took me away by myself – poor Freddy in the difficult position of protecting his sister from his friend.' Freddy went further. He 'spent an evening explaining carefully how all the family were convinced I was torturing you on purpose, and that the sooner I cleared out the better.'[24] The night after the Skye incident Gertie told her mother 'No, I can never marry him!'[25]

The Monday was very hot. Gertie recorded that 'Flo, Malcolm, Joyce and I started off walking to Killilan at the head of Loch Long, and the others followed in the brake.'[26] Once again Cary offended: 'Do you remember how annoyed I was that day at Loch Long, when you showed Flo and me how to scrub out a saucepan.'[27] Even the fruits of his Montenegrin labours withered when exposed to Gertie.

It was hopeless. All Cary's efforts to convey his love merely increased Gertie's nervous hostility. They were both, she revealed later, prisoners of the female Ogilvies' conviction that, all the more since his Montenegrin exploit, he was hopelessly feckless. Heneage (who had not returned with Cary for a second dose of war) was safely settled back into his medical career at Guy's. But here was his scruffy friend, the 'unreformed bohemian', 'the mon with no waistcoat, and who used to leave all his things about the house,' tormenting defenceless Gertie. In fact he was utterly 're' (an expressive Ogilvie compound-abbrevation of such terms as repellent, repulsive, revolting). Later Gertie told Cary of a family discussion about him at the dinner table after her parents said someone they had 'seen at the Coliseum had reminded them of you – some man dressed as a vagabond'.[28]

Cary felt surrounded by 'universal hostility' at Balmacara – although he had enjoyed some sailing with Heneage. Hurt and deeply disappointed, he left on 20 August – to face disappointment in Kilteragh. This was one of the lowest periods of his life. He admitted years afterwards that 'the Gertie of Balmacara . . . nearly made me hate her'.[29] She, shaking hands with him and watching him go, suddenly thought with a pang that she might never see him again: 'it was a great shock to find there was no chance of making things better – though I doubt of course if I had had the chance I would have attempted to make you understand things. My appallingly stilted letter was a ghastly fiasco in that line in any case.'

He replied to it (only the second letter she had ever received from him). What she read 'made me presume you didn't mean to have any more to do with me. I tore up the letter and then felt miserable'. After that –

> I would have run away if you had called. When I thought you didn't care for me any longer as I did at that time – how could I make the slightest advances as a friend – and I can't understand how any girl could. Though I loved you all the time (at least I think I hated you intermittently!) I would sooner have bitten out my tongue than mention you to Freddie or ask after news of you.[30]

They were not to see each other again, or even write to each other, for three years.

In September 1913 Cary submitted an application to be considered for appointment as an Assistant District Officer in the Northern Nigerian Political Service. He was still attracted by 'what seemed to me important and valuable, constructive political work'.[31]

His association with Plunkett and the Irish Co-operative Movement, brief and finally painful as it was, would help him become an exceptionally successful junior administrator in Northern Nigeria. But the failed attempt to return to Ireland closed a psychological door. Although, in later years, he occasionally mooted the possibility of going to live in Ireland (and even, late in life, considered buying the Castle Cary property in Inishowen[32]), his future was committed to England. From now on, the lines of experience would draw his personality inexorably towards the 'Englishness' implicit in his Anglo-Irishness, and away from its 'Irishness'. While in early years he always called himself an Irishman, in middle age he defined himself as an Englishman whose forebears had happened to live in Ireland. But a tension would remain to the end – a tension all the more forceful and creative because his 'Irishness' was fundamental, woven into the potent memories of childhood, and would constantly struggle to reassert itself.

CHAPTER TWELVE

BAUCHI

1914

'an enthusiast for indirect rule'

The Northern Nigerian Political Service was, by 1913, the elite colonial administration of Britain's African territories, and Cary was always proud of his membership and contribution. After he had been selected as a probationary Assistant District Officer, Cary and his fellow recruits were required to attend a three-month training course of lectures at the Imperial Institute in London. The course ran from 12 January to 10 April 1914, and left him 'extremely ignorant of the whole work of government, and very ready to believe all that I was told'. He complained that he was 'taught nothing of political economy; I did not know how to carry out a field survey; and my long and elaborate notes on native customs were completely useless'.[1] The many drawings among his notes certainly suggest that his attention was rarely rivetted by lectures on accountancy, law and tropical hygiene.[2] But he did learn something about the recent history of Northern Nigeria, and the administrative policy in force there; that

> Nigeria was governed by indirect rule; an old invention adapted by Lugard for Nigerian conditions. He left the native chiefs in power and governed through them.
>
> I saw the advantage of such a system. I was an Irishman. I understood nationalist feeling from both ends. I knew its power and I knew too, after some experience with Sir Horace Plunkett and the Irish Co-operative Society that it could be a power for good as well as evil. I saw in Lugard's plan a means of ruling people for their advantage, while leaving them to think that they ruled themselves.[3]

Just as he had been converted to Impressionism a decade earlier, he now became 'an enthusiast for indirect rule'.[4]

'When Lugard was made first High Commissioner of Northern Nigeria in 1900,' Cary explained, 'he had not only to bring this vast region to order, but to devise for it an administration. Some of the great slave-raiding emirs proposed to fight. But they were not popular with their own subjects. Lugard's campaigns were short and almost bloodless, and by 1903 the whole of Northern Nigeria, except for the remoter pagan areas, was at peace.'[5] Indirect Rule was at least partly pragmatic – Lugard himself pointed out, in his apologia *The Dual Mandate* (1922), that 'The staff of a tropical dependency must necessarily be small in comparison with its area and population'.[6] To try to dismantle the Emirates, with their established, autonomous administrations, and replace them with a handful of British officials, would have been risky – but not, Cary argued, impossible; and he always believed that Lugard had chosen Indirect Rule largely 'for ideal reasons'. 'By maintaining the power and prestige of native chiefs, and the continuity of native rule, as a system familiar to the people', the British would avoid causing confusion, despondency and corruption; and 'Native Africans . . . would learn better how to govern themselves in the traditional setting than in one imposed from above and strange to local experience'.[7]

'The rule by which I was to be guided,' Cary recalled in 1936, 'was laid down in *Political Memoranda*, a book by Lugard himself, which is found in every Nigerian office . . . I mayn't quote it; but I can risk a paraphrase; for the honour of my old chief and my old service. "The object of the political officer is the regeneration of Nigeria through its own indigenous government. Unnecessary interference with a native ruler humiliates him and destroys his prestige and his interest in his work."'[8] The 'unnecessary' clearly begs a question. And Cary also found in *Political Memoranda* statements that Indirect Rule 'was not intended to stereotype native autocracy, and that political officers were not to regard themselves only as maintainers of the native institutions, but also as critics and improvers'.[9] Lugard's policy in fact balanced on a razor edge between two cultures, with their different religions, mores, languages. Sir Alan Burns draws attention to this in a definition of Indirect Rule which recognises that the customs and traditions of Nigerian rulers were to be endorsed only 'so long as they were not repugnant to British standards of humanity and justice'.[10]

In practice, Cary was to find, 'it was often very hard to make any distinction between indirect rule and direct rule'; and the crucial question was always 'how much authority is delegated to the chief'.[11] Indigenous peoples not under Emirate control when the British arrived were in fact governed directly (they were called 'pagan tribes' since their religions, known pejoratively as 'juju', differentiated them from the rest of the population). As always, administrative principles and methods had to be adjusted to the exigencies of the particular situation.

'Too Good to Be True'

When Cary and his five fellow recruits sailed for Nigeria, in April 1914, they were armed with a pamphlet which informed them that, on disembarking at Lagos, they should employ two servants, a cook and a steward boy, and travel by rail to Zungeru (Headquarters of the Northern Nigerian Political Service) where they would receive further orders. It was their duty to become familiar with 'the laws and standing orders of the Protectorate' and to study *Political Memoranda* as soon as possible.[12]

At Zungeru, on 14 May, Cary and two of his companions, Cadell and Smyth, were ordered to travel on to Naraguta and report at the Provincial Office there. This must have pleased and excited them. Bauchi, a large province towards the eastern border and south of Kano, was known as one of Nigeria's most beautiful, varied and challenging areas. Its Resident was stationed at Naraguta; under him three District Officers administered the Province's three Divisions – Bauchi, Naraguta and Gombe. A 4,000-foot plateau (with an attractively temperate climate) dominated Naraguta, the western Division. Naraguta town had become the centre of a rapidly growing tin-mining industry that was threatening the immemorial ways of a large population of pagan tribes, some of them still unpredictably warlike.

The main railway line took the three young men as far as Zaria, from where a light miners' railway, still under construction, branched off for Naraguta. Cary's largely autobiographical short story 'The Railway Camp' begins with Corner being informed that 'There would be a special train for him at half past seven. He hurried to the station. The train did not arrive and no one knew when it would arrive, except that it would not be to-day.' Corner's two servants – Tom, the cook, and the houseboy Jamesu, 'fresh from a catholic mission' – set up camp for their master on the platform – where he watches the passing scene for three days. On the fourth morning Corner is woken up before five o'clock in the morning – 'Your special train is here sir, and it ought to go in ten minutes . . .' As dawn breaks over a landscape 'which looked like scientific plates of the moon' the train crawls up the Guta Mountains. 'Then the sun came up and the hills were brown, rusty, barren, not at all like any romantic idea of Africa, but much better, of course, because they were real.' Then suddenly the train stops. 'Nothing could be seen but the tumbled hillside and jagged crests. This couldn't be the end of the journey. But he saw all at once that it was the end of the rails.' Bemused, Corner climbs down from the truck.

> Suddenly about a hundred natives, some in turbans, some naked, some carrying spears, some swords, sprang up from a hollow and rushed at him. He was too stupefied to feel alarm . . . The chargers, having reached about two yards range, uttered loud yells and fell on their faces. Cook Tom, above on the truck, said with impatience . . . 'Dey salute you, sah.'[13]

The reception party has brought horses, and soon (according to the sketch 'Life is a Melon') Corner is 'Cantering all alone through the desert . . . A dirty little boy appears and takes him to the tent – and a voice says behind the net. How are you – had a good trip.' A District Officer, H. S. W. Edwardes, had come to meet the three young men at Gurrum and conduct them to Naraguta.

'Too Good to be True', an unpublished short story, adjusts reality to set Corner's first encounter with Edwardes in the Provincial Office at Naraguta. Soon after his arrival, Corner is in the Naraguta rest-house, his temporary lodging. A police orderly appears at the door, salutes, and delivers a message from the Resident, F. B. Gall, instructing him to report to the District Officer.

Astonished, Corner hastily dresses himself in his new khaki uniform and helmet, and sets off for the Provincial Office. It is empty. He waits. Three men come in, 'talking with animation. One was a square shouldered fair man, strongly built with the head of a pugilist. He was wearing a light tweed suit with the largest checks Corner had ever seen.' As the conversation ends, this man notices Corner and makes 'a kind of lunge like a boxer about to give a knockdown blow, and seized his hand and said "You're Corner, aren't you. I hear you're coming with me. Very pleased to have you. Have you got a cook, and a boy and a horse. You'll want a house boy, and I suppose you'd better have an interpreter at first . . ."'[14]

In fact, Edwardes had himself only recently 'Found orders awaiting me to go to Bauchi and take over'.[15] Cary's fellow recruits, Cadell and Smyth, were to remain in Naraguta while Cary travelled the 70 miles between Naraguta and Bauchi town – a four-day trek over rough terrain. As Cary recalled it in 'Too Good to be True', the journey was a series of epiphanies, revelations of Edwardes's personality – beginning with his unusual bush kit.

> He was wearing a pair of buccaneers boots, in soft brown leather; turned over from the knee in a flap about eight inches deep. His shirt also, as Corner noticed, was peculiar. It was not a shirt at all, but a cape, made very loose, with no attachment at the waist, and two little capes for sleeves. Moreover, on one enormous arm, covered with short yellow hairs which glowed in the evening sun, E wore two gold bangles [each] as thick as a little finger.

They camp that night on the edge of a gorge. Next morning, after a gargantuan breakfast, Edwardes produces a pair of gold-rimmed glasses and a volume of *The Decline and Fall of the Roman Empire*. 'MAG-nificent – what a style. But tell me, you were at Oxford, weren't you, what do you think of Gibbon . . .?' Corner, who has read no Gibbon, recollects hearing a vulgar parody ending 'the ponderous ballocks of the Roman proconsul', and smiles derisively. Then notices that Edwardes is also smiling – a smile 'full of an artist's delight and an artist's sympathy. "Out of date, I suppose," he said gaily but with a pugnacious jut of his chin.'

They descend from the plateau and come to 'a small river, with a swift-running yellow current which poured through its deep channel with force. While Edwardes watches from the far bank, Corner begins to ride across the ford. Suddenly his horse steps into a deep hole, Corner flounders down with it, and splutters sodden to safety. Proffering a flask of whisky, Edwardes asks Corner what he was laughing at as he went under. 'The young man was surprised. Had he been laughing? Suddenly he felt [himself] beginning to smile. Do what he could, a broad grin broke out. It was as though everything that had happened for days past was urging him to this senseless grin.' Then he sees that Edwardes is smiling too; and knows that this smile 'had exactly the same cause, whatever that was, as his own . . . As they looked at each other, something flooded between them; they both gave a loud laugh.'[16]

The rapport that grew between Cary and Edwardes during their four-day trek to Bauchi was never broken. Although he had already noticed that Edwardes' servants 'never moved quickly . . . he was one of those masters who are too easy going for good service,' Cary's initially favourable impression was succeeded by respect for Edwardes's administrative work, and throughout his own career in Northern Nigeria the older man was his mentor and inspiration. In later life, Cary noted two fundamental traits of Edwardes as 'His democratic hatred of government and furious energy'. [17]

'my people'

They reached Bauchi town on 30 May, and Cary's first month in the Service was spent under Edwardes's tutelage; learning office routine and the elements of administration.

Bauchi Division had an administrative organisation typical of Northern Nigeria. The Emir– 'autocratic and quarrelsome', 'an old man, who had fought against us in 1903' – 'had his own Council, his Treasurer, Chief Justice, Chief of Police, and Vizier, or confidential chief minister. He had his own police organisation, treasure, prison, etc.' The Divisional Office, 'about a mile from the Emir's capital town, in the European station', had a staff (in addition to Edwardes and Cary) of 'a doctor, two African clerks, and a detachment of infantry under European officers in charge of a ruined fort'. Taxes were assessed 'in bulk' by the Divisional Office, in co-operation with the Native Administration (which was responsible for 'the final assessment on each household'), and on collection divided between the two treasuries. The Emir's Court 'tried all cases concerning natives of the emirate' according to Muslim law; the D.O.'s court, using English law, handled appeals and cases concerning 'Europeans or Africans not native to the emirate'. The D.O. and Emir 'met at intervals to discuss public affairs', and the Waziri (Vizier, or first minister) met every morning with the D.O. 'to bring reports, and to receive news or orders'. After the Waziri's departure, the rest of the morning was spent hearing cases or in office work (the Native Treasury's books were checked regularly, for instance); and in the late afternoon, public works (like 'a new market, or a new sanitation ditch') were inspected. Edwardes spent at least half his time 'on tour through the villages' to 'know the people' and 'what's going on in his division'. Much less typically, he also 'kept open house night and day to complaints' in an effort to prevent repression, corruption and injustice. 'He made it a rule and he taught me the rule to receive anyone who approached him anywhere, and not to allow any junior official, clerk, orderly, or court messenger to stand between him and the people.' [18]

Soon after his arrival, Cary had his first lesson in how problematic Indirect Rule could be in practice.

Some women had been flogged for theft and prostitution and the case was reported in a coast paper. It had reached the London press and there was an outcry. Orders came down for an enquiry.

This demand, telegraphed from H.Q., was the first we had heard of the floggings. They had been ordered, as routine, by the Mahommedan Court, under Mahommedan law. And we had guaranteed that there would be no interference with religion and native law, in this case Mahommedan law.

We sent for the Chief Justice, a learned and distinguished Mahommedan lawyer. He was astonished to hear of our objection. He said, 'Quite apart from our laws, what am I to do with these very bad women?' 'In Britain,' we said, 'they would go to prison.' But now he was really horrified. 'You can't send women to prison,' he said. 'That would be an abominable cruelty as well as a wicked act. A woman sent to prison would die of shame and grief. And what prison? We have no prison for women here.'

A long argument followed. In the end we compromised. Women sentenced for theft would not be flogged; but they would have their heads shaved. In bad cases, they should be put in the stocks.[19]

Edwardes had such a driving concern for the wellbeing of the people, especially the poor, that he was constantly at work devising improvements, some of which, together with his impatience and tactlessness, brought him into conflict with his superiors. One of Cary's sketches centres on a typical outburst, after Edwardes had shown him a missive just composed to complain to Headquarters about the mistreatment of railway labourers in the Division: 'Bauchi. My people, report to the Governor. What do you think of the style. But sir, I don't think he'll like it. Gulard [Lugard] is a bit of an autocrat. E blows up. Killing my people . . . *my* people.'[20]

Edwardes believed strongly in the importance of formal education – the year after Cary's arrival, he started the first school in Bauchi Province. He was also passionately convinced of the need to improve communications, especially by building roads and bridges; and just before Cary's arrival had published, anonymously, a pamphlet entitled 'On the Improvement of Native Paths in Northern Nigeria'. Young administrators like Cary enthusiastically accepted Edwardes's basic argument that 'An enormous amount can be done at an almost nominal cost to make . . . tracks good and comfortable going, and the return in human happiness as well as material prosperity is simply incalculable'.[21]

Although Cary would not have seen any road making at Bauchi (he had arrived too late in the year), he would have heard much on the subject, for road making was then one of Edwardes's priorities. In September 1915 he wrote to tell Cary 'I am going to get some roads made this dry weather if it lands me in Stellenbosch. There is humour in the fact that the opposition to and distrust of any beneficent measure always comes from above. One has to fight the Government all the time. The man who is discouraged by rebuffs never gets anything done. I enjoy the battle and in the end they usually let me do it to shut me up.'[22]

Ultimately Edwardes was to pay a high price for his victories over resentful and jealous superiors. In April 1916, he learned that Gall had 'reported on me very badly', and the consequence was a 'Solemn carpeting'[23] by the new Governor of Northern Nigeria, Sir Charles Temple (who succeeded Lugard in 1914 when the latter became Governor General of Nigeria). Gall had complained that 'Mr Edwardes reminds me of a newly joined enthusiastic officer, very energetic and interested in his duties, who has not however matured, and who does not sufficiently study a matter before pronouncing opinions on it.'[24]

But no sooner was Edwardes transferred to parched Sokoto Province (in the extreme north-west) than he was directing his formidable energy and practical skills to improving the lot of his people. This time it was an irrigation canal at Gande, some 25 miles west of Sokoto city.[25] But again Edwardes ran into problems with his superiors, and this time with severe consequences. In 1921 he was Acting Resident of Sokoto Province while the Resident, Webster, was on leave. He had been concerned about the Sultan's 'oppression of the people', so, 'Encouraged by a liberal and vigorous policy statement from the Governor, he urged that the Sultan be deposed and he left no doubt in the minds of his superiors that in his opinion the trouble was all due to the laxity of the substantive Resident . . . Swiftly the higher-ups closed ranks . . .' The official investigation deliberately avoided the central issue.

Edwardes's charges were later borne out when, in 1930, serious disturbances resulted from the unchecked corruption of the Sultan's Administration. But that was too late for Edwardes. He had been 'abruptly transferred'. 'His final years were spent in the dustbin posts of Kabba and Munshi and he retired in the mid-1920s, well short of his fiftieth birthday. He had committed not one but two sins, either of which would have been enough to ruin him: he had dared to criticize his superior in an official document; and he had violated a cardinal rule of those years: "Do not become known as a friend of the peasants".'[26]

CHAPTER THIRTEEN

GOMBE

1914–1915

'a very bad station'

Cary was beginning his career as an A.D.O. at a difficult time. While the outbreak of war in Europe was still two months away when Cary started work under Edwardes, the famine, caused by a long drought, was an urgent part of his daily round. Corn had to be gathered and distributed to the starving. Cary probably accompanied Edwardes when he 'Visited Emir re corn' on 9 June. On 17 July '100 loads corn arrived' from the Emir. 'The eagerness of the people to get it was rather pathetic. Sent urgent letters to the Emir to hurry up the remainder.' 29 July: 'People very hungry.'[1]

Cary never forgot seeing 'old men dying by the roadside, with dying children in their arms' – all of them resigned to 'the mysterious injustice of nature'.[2] Probably he saw those results of the famine on his way to Gombe Division, the most easterly and topographically varied of the three Divisions of Bauchi Province, with its rocky mountains in the south, inhabited by pagan tribes, its scrubby plains supporting Hausa farmers and their cattle, and its extensive swamps. The Divisional Office was at Nafada, well over 100 miles north-west of Bauchi town, on the Gongola River. The D.O., J. F. J. Fitzpatrick, needed help, and Cary was transferred there on 28 June.

Before he left, however, he was given the task of settling a disputed stretch of the boundary between Bauchi and Gombe Divisions, at Buri Buri. As Cary explained to his father, 'They gave me authority to change the boundary if I liked, and since it appeared the best thing, I did change it over a ten miles line. More than a hundred farms are affected, and I don't know whether my report will be well received – but I am protected from revision by my authority which I took care to get in writing and as explicit as possible.' The task was complicated by a furious encounter with Fitzpatrick and the vociferous presence of the farmers whose land was affected. When the decision was at last made, predictably it pleased nobody.[3]

After reporting his settlement to Edwardes in Bauchi, Cary hurried on to

Nafada in late July, spending altogether 'ten days in the saddle'. He was not impressed by Nafada:

> a very bad station among river swamps, and full of mosquitoes which bite morning and noon as well as night. My house is leaky and literally an ant-heap. I hung a strap on the wall the day I came, and it was eaten through by the next morning. They eat all my chop-boxes [food-containers] and would eat my boots if I did not keep a close watch on them. They have eaten also nearly all the supports of the house and a big tornado might bring it down . . . There is no money here allowed for buildings because they have spent so much on the houses at the central station at Naraguta, that the vote for the Province is already exhausted. I shall probably have to do some roofing out of my own pocket for at present I sleep in my oil-skins and my kit is ruined between the rain and the ants, and the rivers it has been dragged through on my travels.

He expected to 'be alone here, and continue alone for a month, which means (for a district bigger than Wales) that I shall be very busy. The D.O. is going off with some soldiers to tackle some rebellious villages in the south'.[4]

But all plans were about to be disrupted – he was writing on 3 August. The following day, Edwardes, in Bauchi, received an urgent wire in the evening 'saying that A Co. would proceed to Nafada at once'. Next morning, the explanation: 'a wire came through that war with Germany was declared. So now we are in for it . . . Nigeria is rushing troops to the Cameroons border'.[5]

Meanwhile, at Nafada – through which troops would pass on their way to Yola, a town near the Cameroons border – life was yet unchanged. The heavy rains that had forced Cary to sleep under oilskins had also brought down the telegraph line from Bauchi. An unfinished short-story draft entitled 'Marching as to War' dramatises Cary's memories of those few days. His fictional self is the A.D.O. Cole, 'a very young man lately joined from Oxford, with an eyeglass and some very smart bush-shirts of a new and dashing pattern'. On 6 August,

> an exhausted horseman, on a dying horse, reeled into the station with a huge bundle of telegrams dated at a fort two hundred miles away [Naraguta] two days before. The telegrams full of abuse of Rairai [Gombe Division] and the movements of troops, threw the station, all except the D.O., into panic and confusion. It seemed that all the troops in the country were moving on Rairai. Something had happened at last. But what.[6]

'my own bit of trouble'

The rest of Cary's first tour of duty in Northern Nigeria was dominated by the Great War. Fitzpatrick later summarised the situation he and Cary faced by mid August. An assault on the Cameroons (a German colony) was to be launched from Yola, a large town close to the border. To get there, most of the Northern Nigerian army would have to travel through Gombe Division; so, within days,

> Troops came streaming into Nafada . . . horse soldiers and foot soldiers, signallers, and doctors, machine guns and carriers, black soldiers, white officers, and small parties of Europeans – miners, traders, officials, – volunteers for the Cameroons Expeditionary Force . . . The two notable

things in Nafada at the time were a famine and an unfordable river, half a mile wide, full of brown, rushing, ugly-looking water. All arrivals had to be fed, and had to be got across the river . . .[7]

Cary was sent to Jamari, up the Gongola River, to make roads and organise a depot for troops approaching from the north, while Fitzpatrick remained in charge at Nafada. 'Hope you are comfortable where you are, and finding things not too stiff,' Fitzpatrick wrote on 9 August. 'Wire just in to say the Gold Coast Regt has occupied Southern part of Togoland . . . Get as much of the grain turned in to Gari as possible, and issue it in bulk to the people as they come along.'

There were many problems. Villagers threatened with starvation were naturally reluctant to sell their corn and cattle. Frequently there was uncertainty about the numbers and routes of the approaching troops. Ferries and canoes needed constant supervision.

Cary was upset when informed by Fitzpatrick that Edwardes had addressed a broadside to the 'political officers in Gombe, who are unable to protect his carriers and people at Gabarin [across the Gongola in Bauchi Division] from high handed action by troops'.[8] Fitzpatrick gave Cary permission to try to sort out the problem, and Edwardes responded warmly to a letter of concern and apology: 'My dear Cary, Your fears re Gabarin pain me. Am I the sort of fellow who would trouble his head over a point of punctilio? Are you the sort of fellow who couldn't be trusted to do the job well? Go ahead my dear fellow and compensate any of my people oppressed by the military.'[9]

Within three weeks the crisis was over. On 27 August, Fitzpatrick sent a perky note to Cary: 'All troops leave here to-day. So no supplies wanted, nothing more at all at all! Come along in . . . Glad to see you again. Cheerio.'[10]

Cary's strenuous efforts at Jamari received recognition from his superiors. As Cary told his father, 'I have made a sort of reputation out of the work I did in August – I made a Depot in the bush and fed the troops passing up the road – during famine time . . .'[11] Fitzpatrick had then written 'You're doing fine, and everything at your end has gone swimmingly, as M. I. [Mounted Infantry] and all others testify'; and Gall had even proposed to send a wire to the Governor praising Cary for 'doing excellent work getting supplies'. But the wire was not sent, and Fitzpatrick's tortuous explanation suggests complexity in his relationship with Cary.[12]

Unlike the generous and straightforward Edwardes, Fitzpatrick – volatile, peppery; like Cary, of Irish descent but educated in England – was a touchy and unpredictable superior. He was a scathingly outspoken critic of Indirect Rule, but his practical work was less effective and consistent than Edwardes's. The latter admired Fitzpatrick ('a man to love. Full of good sense in spite of his fads. A deadly foe to humbug and snobbery of any kind, utterly sincere'). But Edwardes could not avoid noticing Fitzpatrick's administrative deficiencies; he once came across a 'hospital for syphilitic women started, – and apparently forgotten, – by Fp. They had not been vetted or had any medicine or regular food.'[13]

Fitzpatrick's earlier career in the Service had involved him in frequent administrative conflict. After the war, suffering from anxiety and poor health, he was put in charge of the insalubrious Kebba Division bordering the lower Benue River ('a very rough, hilly district involving much travelling'), suffered from insomnia and attacks of breathlessness, and was then transferred to another undesirable post, in Muri Province.[14] (The customary Headquarters strategy for disposing of a troublesome official, Cary wrote, was to 'send him to an unhealthy place, and kill him with overwork, refuse his increments, and pass him over for promotion'.[15])

Finally, in 1922, Fitzpatrick was accused of 'grossly irregular methods of dealing both with Government and Native Administration money' and in 1925, he moved from Northern Nigeria to another colony, Nyasaland [Malawi].[16] Shortly before that he fired a farewell broadside in an article he entitled 'Nigeria's Curse – the Native Administration': 'Before the British took over the country an Emir was an Emir just so long as his hands could guard his head. The system was one of autocracy, tempered by assassination . . . The tempering by assassination has been abolished, the autonomy, tyranny, remain, reinforced.'[17]

The sad end of Fitzpatrick's career in Northern Nigeria was apparently prompted, like Edwardes's, by an accretion of official hostility caused by his open criticism and rebellious behaviour. But, unlike Edwardes, Fitzpatrick was embittered, obsessed by a sense of injustice, even at the time Cary worked under him. Their relationship was never as warm and secure as that between Cary and Edwardes.

Nevertheless, Cary became uncomfortably involved with Fitzpatrick. Two references in Fitzpatrick's letters to Cary indicate that he had received painful news early in the war: 'a soldier here . . . got a cable last night . . . to tell him that one of his Brothers was killed in action in France. It hit the poor chap very hard, and I was forced to think of my own bit of trouble, when you were so friendly and helpful'; and again, 'I am very much in your debt for a lot of kindness and sympathy, which I do not forget'.[18] Cary seems to have been referring to the same episode when he wrote in 1916 'I've seen most unexpected hardened old men even in tears – one here [Nafada] last year, when he heard his brother was killed, I had to nurse him like a child and comfort him – he's quite bald, 35 years old, and one of the best hated men in the country for his malicious tongue . . .'[19] Whatever the circumstances, it is clear that Cary's brief relationship with Fitzpatrick was complex and disturbing.

When the last of the troops left Nafada for Yola in late August, administrative life began to return to something like normal. But soon Fitzpatrick, who had been a professional soldier, was seconded as a Captain to the Cameroons Expeditionary Force, and by the end of September had set out for Yola. Cary had volunteered too, and hoped he might yet be permitted to go. 'Two men now in Nafada are going tomorrow,' he told his father on 1 October; 'both want me and are going to ask for me . . . but it is very difficult to persuade Headquarters to let any Political Officer move. There are now no troops left in the Protectorate – and though the natives are perfectly quiet they [Headquarters] don't want to leave anything to chance. Fifteen million blacks who have all been accustomed to fighting and have only been stopped in the last ten or twelve years need to be watched.'[20]

From Yola he received two breezy letters from Fitzpatrick – who had taken with him a boy called Mister Johnson. 'We are all very warlike, there are forts and redoubts and trenches and pickets and things all over the place . . . I wish you were here with us. You'd be very happy, and I should be glad of your company.' An attack had been launched in the north on one of the main German strongholds in the Cameroons, Mora Mountain; and troops from Yola were advancing against the garrison of Garua immediately to the east – it was 'very strongly fortified', Fitzpatrick wrote, 'But I think we shall soon finish this local war now. I give it another three months at the outside.'[21]

'damaging contradictions'

Meanwhile, Cary was working hard under the D.O. who had replaced Fitzpatrick in Gombe Division, T. F. Carlyle. The two of them were, Cary told his father on 1 October, 'now alone here . . . no other white man for 150 miles – no doctor and no possibility of help coming in case of a row in less than seven days.' By 19 October, he had accepted that 'I have no hope now of getting to the front [in the Cameroons] and everyone agrees that I have had very bad luck since I actually started with the soldiers and made a good job of it.'

Cary was now in charge of the day-to-day running of the Divisional Office. 'The D.O. is settling some bigger questions of policy and clearing the ground for a new assessment of the Division, which we'll do together. A quarter of a million people (and this is a very moderate count) take a good deal of counting and sorting and assessing.' He described his responsibilities in some detail:

> Just now I am receiving the taxes and very busy: I write this only while I have time till the Mallams and scribes sitting on the floor have finished counting – then I must check and give receipts and record and sign the bags. I can write their language by now and talk a certain amount. I think I shall be [ready] for the exam. at the end of the tour.
>
> There is no news here. Our own little campaign I daresay you have read about and if you haven't I mustn't tell you for I am actually a censor as well as Builder, Surveyor, Road Constructor, Police Inspector, Assessor and Collector of Taxes, Magistrate, Metereologist, and Doctor.

He was also teaching thirteen mallams how to write in English so they could 'act as secretaries to the small chiefs'.[22]

Two incidents of this period showed up 'damaging contradictions' in administrative practice. 'When I was at Nafada in the Gombe [Division] of Nigeria, my chief had a letter from the forestry officer asking for a durbar of chiefs at which he could give them instruction.' In his speech to the assembled chiefs, the official said 'If you get no rain, you and your people will starve. But the trees draw down the rain and hold it with their roots so that it does not run away too quickly . . . Burn no more grass, even for the hunting. Your lives depend on it.' But the following month brought a visit from the veterinary officer, who also requested a durbar. 'He too gave an eloquent address, on the care of cattle, and he ended "But the chief means of preserving your cattle from these terrible pests, especially the rinderpest, is grass burning."' To both experts the chiefs 'bowed down and cried "To, Zaki" which means "We agree, O Lion"'.

The contradiction remained unresolved. 'In fact, I myself,' Cary confessed, 'in all my period of service never knew and could never find out what was to be done on this very matter.' This was a straightforward case of conflicting advice – perhaps irreconcilable truths; and Cary was to become aware that 'more subtle but not less damaging contradictions exist throughout the African service; altogether apart from conflicts of policy . . .'[23]

In November, while Carlyle was off pacifying a rebellious tribe and about four months after he had been ordered to Gombe Division, Cary told his father that he was

> quite alone here now – no Doctor or Soldier, or anyone else, so that I have a great many different things to look after . . . We are really bluffing the whole country now as all the troops are in the Cameroons, but everything has gone very well indeed up to now and there's no sign of internal trouble anywhere.[24]

Towards the end of 1914, Cary saved the life of a colleague. The Resident of neighbouring Bornu Province later stated: 'Mr Slingsby having been reported as fit to travel in a hammock, he left here on November 26th in charge of a convoy of specie for Nafada. As he arrived there he went down with blackwater fever and I think it may fairly be said that it was only through the unremitting care and general efficiency of Mr Cary, Assistant D.O., acting on instructions telegraphically communicated by Dr Moiser, that his life was saved.'[25]

After Dr Moiser's arrival, an incident occurred that Cary remembered as an illustration of the power of superstition:

> In Africa I nursed a man with blackwater. Afterwards he suffered acute pains and could not sleep. The doctor gave him injections, but he did not wish to continue them every night. One night, Christmas night I think it was, we were called to see the patient, who was in great pain, and the doctor gave him an injection. The man sighed, thanked him and in a moment or two fell asleep. But afterwards [the doctor] shewed me the two morphine pellets in the palm of his hand . . . The injection had been plain water.[26]

Another, very distressing, illustration of the mind's vulnerability came only a few weeks later. Early in 1915, the people of Gombe, weakened by the famine, were afflicted by further misery, an outbreak of smallpox. Cary did all he could to help them. In A House of Children he recalled 'the smallpox camps, where whole families sat all day, with their enormously swollen faces, waiting upon fate with a submission so complete that I had to have some of them spoon-fed. They had lost all confidence in remedy and even in food.'[27] One of his sketches centres on 'The Mothers' in the camps, who became indifferent even to the fate of their babies.[28]

For more than three months, Cary had had to administer Gombe on his own – for, after dealing with the restive pagans of the south, Carlyle was summoned to help put down a serious revolt in the north of Bauchi Division. And, like a Conradian hero, Cary faced a severe test when in his isolation. This is indicated in a largely autobiographical short story, 'Adamu'.

'Corner had been left alone, for the first time, in charge of the division . . . He didn't want to [do] anything wrong and yet he was quite sure that he would do so. He knew nothing about the pagan district for instance; and treasury notes were still mysterious to him.' The test comes with his discovery that a member of the Native Administration has been accepting bribes. Corner is outraged. 'For one thing, he has rather fancied himself as the father of the Fada people, especially the poor' (the influence of Edwardes's paternalism is as clear as Cary's irony at the expense of his tenderfoot self). Corner decides that he will sentence Adamu to a year in gaol.

Fortunately Carlyle arrived just in time to initiate Cary into a higher awareness: 'I know an old Alkali down at Guta who got jug for taking bribes and he was the honestest old man in Guta. He took presents but he never allowed it to affect his judgement. That of course, was why he got run in. He offended some chief or other.' In fact, Corner learns, 'African justices were used to accepting presents from litigants – corruption did not arise unless the presents affected their judgments'. So, initiated into the complicated context of political morality (especially under Indirect Rule), he 'felt a kind of panic at the nearness of his escape . . . He had always respected the old man. He knew that he was the honoured father and grandfather of the family household, and yet he had nearly wrecked and broken that honest good life.'[29]

'a pagan man'

Edwardes told Cary 'you will find Carlyle a fine great-hearted fellow'[30]; and so he did. Carlyle influenced him as strongly as had Edwardes and Fitzpatrick. He was one of the most successful and respected of Northern Nigeria's 'pagan men' – administrators whose main work was pacifying and ruling pagan tribes who, in the remote mountain fastnesses to which the Muslim invasions from the north had driven them, were feared for their ferocity, cannibalism and unpredictable responses – friendliness, tolerance, or poison arrows, depending on the personality, reputation and perceived intentions of the visitors.

Carlyle was 'a huge man, with large ideas – Everything about him was big. He built enormous mud houses, made prodigious journeys in his district, and was in every way a forceful character.'[31] His courage and diplomacy had earned the trust of the two tribes 'in the pagan part of Gombe', to the south. 'The Tangales are cannibals like the Tulas,' Cary wrote, 'but whereas the Tulas are a good natured pleasant set of people – the Tangales are low scoundrels.'[32] But Carlyle had as deep an affection for the Tangales as Edwardes had for 'my people', enjoyed being with them, and was admired by his superiors for his administrative expertise.[33] When he had settled the troubles of November 1914, he wrote to Cary from 'a jolly camp on a button over the twin towns of Biri Ful and Biri Habe', where he was relishing 'a real

Sunday's laze' and 'a delightful sense of seclusion foreign to every other camp I know'.[34]

Cary admired Carlyle personally (a colleague remembered, many years later, how in 1917 he spoke of 'the inspiring examples and personality' of his superior[35]), but he was ambivalent about changes for which Carlyle's success was responsible:

> In a very short time the Tangales were bringing produce to the Nafada market and taking back Manchester cotton and Birmingham knives. I remember our long fight with the trading firms to have them paid in cash. Yet all the time, whenever I saw a Tangale, still naked and as I thought unspoilt, going back to his own country with a bale of cloth on his head, from which to make clothes for himself and his wife, I felt guilty and ashamed, as if I was furthering a stupid crime.
>
> I far preferred the wild cannibal Tangale . . . to my own Christian South Coast servants, clean, devoted and responsible.[36]

Although Carlyle enjoyed his bouts of solitude, and hobnobbing with pagan tribes, he was also a renowned conversationalist. Cary, who had so delighted in Fergusson's talk in Paris, looked forward to his superior's every appearance in Nafada. 'He is a wild kind of talker – he sees a notion like a butterfly – you can even notice his first glimpse of it fluttering, his eye lights up, and he is off at once and doesn't in the least mind where the chase ends.' At his best, Carlyle 'poured out a stream of stories and jokes and doggerel verse' that would keep his companions merry for hours – 'he has an astonishing energy in whatever he does'.[37]

Cary's final comment on Carlyle is true of all three of the District Officers he worked under during his first year as an A.D.O. All three were forceful, individualistic.

Edwardes and Fitzpatrick were outspoken rebels ultimately defeated by the jealous, unimaginative vindictiveness of superiors. But their personalities contrasted significantly: Edwardes creative, generous, self-forgetful, dedicated to the service of 'my people'; Fitzpatrick erratic, malicious, obsessive, a man with a grievance. The contrast epitomised by their respective responses to injustice helped to define Cary's treatment of a fundamental theme in his writing.

Carlyle, whose ebullient personality resembled Edwardes's, was also a rebel, but a licensed one. His pacification of the Tulas and Tangales made him valuable to the authorities; independence and eccentricity were tolerable, even necessary, foibles in a 'pagan man'.

Cary's lasting respect and affection for Edwardes and Carlyle are clearly expressed in the 1944 dedication of *The Case for African Freedom* to them, 'from a grateful junior'. But while he had reservations about Carlyle's work among 'pagan tribes', his admiration for Edwardes's work was never less than wholehearted.

Both men are to be found in his fiction. Carlyle was the prototype of Monkey Bewsher, central character of *An American Visitor*; the very name of Brewsher's pagan tribe, the Birri, recalls Carlyle's letter of November 1914 from the 'twin towns of Biri Ful and Biri Habe'; and no doubt the novel is indebted not only to Carlyle's exploits but also his yarns. He also contributed to the characterisation of Jim Latter, in the Second Trilogy; and, before it was removed at the publisher's request, Carlyle's name was included (as a compliment, Cary explained) in *The African Witch*.[38] Similarly, Edwardes is complimented in *Mister Johnson* as 'Sturdee', a Resident 'well known for his enthusiasm in road-building'; from him, Rudbeck, the A.D.O., 'has caught the belief that to build a road, any road anywhere, is the noblest work a man can do . . . As Sturdee is fond of saying "When you make a road you know you've done something . . . you can see it!"'[38] And in *Aissa Saved*, Bradgate, the Assistant Resident, significantly amalgamates traits of Edwardes and Cary himself.

Fitzpatrick was the main influence on Cock Jarvis, eponymous protagonist of a seminal novel which subsequently contributed Jarvis to *Castle Corner* and strongly influenced the characterisation of Jim Latter in *Not Honour More*. Although Cary rejected Fitzpatrick's negative, self-destructive response to injustice, he sympathised with it; and, ironically perhaps, it was Fitzpatrick who was to dominate near the beginning and end of Cary's career as a novelist. But Carlyle and Edwardes dominated its centre.

CHAPTER FOURTEEN

BUSH FIGHTING

1915–1916

'a special distinction'

Cary was wrong when, in October 1914, he asserted that he had no hope of fighting in the Cameroons. As in East Africa, that campaign against the German colonial forces had bogged down. The other German colony in West Africa, Togoland, had surrendered within weeks of the war's outbreak, but in the Cameroons there had been serious reverses.

The assault on Mora Mountain in the north had failed. Then a Mounted Infantry detachment of the West African Frontier Force (which had passed through Nafada in mid August) crossed the frontier from Yola, where the British troops had assembled; and, after occupying a German outpost, advanced up the Benue to attack the mountain fortress of Garua on 29 August 1914. But, in the haste to strike first, preparations had been minimal, and the men were exhausted after long marches in the rain. The Germans counter-attacked, killing the commander and several officers; and the survivors, only about half of the detachment, struggled back to Yola. One said 'it was a terrible loss, and there was absolutely no glory in the whole fighting, taking place as it did in a little out-of-the-way spot 5,000 miles from England, that not one person in a thousand had ever heard of.'[1] Two other expeditions had crossed the border further south, with similarly disastrous results.

The British had then called on their Navy for help. Duala, the capital and main port, was bombarded into surrender on 27 September. The German forces retreated northwards to Yaoundé and the thickly wooded, mountainous wilderness of the interior; where, around strongholds like Mora, Garua and Bayo, the fighting evolved into something close to guerrilla warfare. As Cary put it,

> The Cameroons campaign of 1914–16, against the German army of occupation, was a war of raids, ambushes, sieges, enormous marches, and especially surprises. There was no reconnaissance by air, no radio, and intelligence could only be got by scouts and spies. Whole columns would disappear for weeks together, to burst out, a thousand miles away, upon a

panic-stricken capital. Two patrols would stumble upon each other by accident in high jungle and stare with amazement for a few seconds before grabbing their rifles.[2]

Even more graphically, in a short story entitled 'Guda': 'Bush fighting is one ambush after another. Men are shot from ten yards range when lighting their pipes, or calling out "We'll camp here".'[3]

Cary was plunged into this fighting during April 1915. 'When war broke out, I volunteered all round and wrote and wired and got snubbed, and then was sent off at 12 hours notice after I had lost hope.'[4] Officers were urgently needed to replace those lost at Garua, and he had some military experience.

He was stationed at Yola for two months, on the staff of the Commandant. One of his duties was overseeing the horse lines. A memory of this period is preserved in a sketch: 'The mares at Yola – the foals walking after you and nuzzling in your pocket. the service – the surprised and as it were awakened look of the stallion after receiving a kick in the stomach and [the] sort of broken swagger of his retreat.'[5]

The tale of how one of the stallions, black Satan, came into Cary's life is told in the short story 'Buying a Horse'. Corner has come across a group of tethered ponies brought back from Garua the previous August ('The Horse marines . . . were killed or wounded and their ponies were left in a bush station where two or three of them died every week . . .') One, 'a tottering skeleton covered with dirt', nibbles his shirt, and 'Corner was touched. He had a weakness for good-natured horses of which he was quite aware'. It is an Asben, 'a type of small Arab . . . much prized in Africa', and is owned, it turns out, by a wounded Scottish Major soon to be invalided home. Extensive negotiations are necessary (the episode becomes almost farcical, in the style of Surtees, one of Cary's favourite writers) before Satan is 'yielded for thirty shillings'.[6]

Equipped with pony, Cary was ordered at the beginning of July to proceed to Garua, which had been in British hands since 10 June, when its German defenders had suddenly fled. There he received a letter from Carlyle: 'Splendid fellow. I paint you in Garua arms akimbo standing on dead men's bones . . . I am always hoping you will come back here.'[7] Cary was a lieutenant in H Company of the Nigerian Regiment (made up largely of the WAFF), part of a column of about 1,500 infantrymen commanded by Brigadier General F. H. G. Cunliffe. They were preparing for a further attack on Mora Mountain. The Mountain 'covered a rough circle about thirty miles in circumference and rose in cliffs to a height of 1,700 feet. In only a few places could the top be reached by men using both hands and feet in climbing, and in the rare breaks in the cliffs where this could be done, the slopes were covered with huge boulders that gave magnificent shelter for a defending force.'[8] Although cut off after the fall of Garua, the German stronghold, well supplied with food and water, seemed all but impregnable.

Cary was given a vitally important task in the preparations for the attack. His memories of it are preserved in three short stories, 'Bush River', 'Umaru', and 'The Raft'; all of which, like 'Buying a Horse', were 'autobiographical'.[9]

'Bush River' presents Corner as, 'at twenty-six, an extremely conventional young officer, a little bit of a dandy, a good deal of a coxcomb'. With his 'eyeglass in his right eye', 'his clipped hair which left him almost bald, his clipped moustache', he has an 'air of severity, of an austere and critical aloofness'.[10] This portrait is not at odds with the memory of a fellow officer that Cary was 'very difficult to get on with he being exceedingly cynical and superior in his attitude towards most others but I had a respect for his soldierly qualities being full of courage and initiative . . .'[11]

Clearly it was his courage and initiative that resulted in

a command regarded by himself and most of his brother officers as a special distinction, a step to promotion. He was to take charge of a sticky and dangerous operation, the planning of a route through the heart of enemy country, by which a heavy gun could be dragged, in secret, to Mora mountain, a German stronghold that had held out against two assaults. It was thought that the fire of this gun, taking the Germans by surprise, would not only smash their defences on the mountain-top but break the morale of their local troops, who could have no experience of high explosive . . .

Corner's instructions were to avoid anything like a road or even a made track. They were likely to be watched. He was not even to cross a road by daylight. He was to plot his line as far as possible through untouched bush, to avoid any indications that might put the enemy patrols on the alert, and to hide by night.

His fondness for Satan causes danger for Corner and his men when he decides to take the pony. Satan has neighed loudly, twice, alerting any nearby Germans. Now the nervous detachment – Corner, Sergeant Umaru, eighteen soldiers – face a wide, turbulent river. Corner decides to swim Satan across – partly as an example to his men, but mainly out of sheer exhilaration. 'He had been carried far away from any notion of Germans, of crocodiles. He had no mind for anything but the river and Satan beneath him . . .' As Satan threshes against the strong current, Corner feels 'an affection for the little horse, an exultant pride in his courage . . . a feeling so strong that it seemed to have its own life, full of delight and worship . . . rejoicing in all devotion and courage; the mysterious greatness of the spirit.'

They reach the far bank. Corner dismounts, and lies down beside Satan, exhausted. 'Suddenly he heard a click and turned his head towards it. Over a bush not ten yards away, he saw the outline of a head in German soldier's cap and a rifle barrel . . . He was stupefied again by the spectacle of his own enormous folly, but also by something incomprehensible behind it and about it.' In 'a kind of despair' he lies 'holding his breath for the shot. He had a queer sensation so vivid that he still remembered it twenty years after, of floating lightly off the ground. Nothing happened. There was a deep silence.'

Was the German soldier real? The reader is left uncertain. But Corner has no doubt: 'Why had the German not fired – orders to give no alarms? – panic at the sudden appearance of his own men coming up the bank in force?' As so often in the stories focused on Cary's experience of Africa, Corner feels like 'one appointed to a special fate, to gratitude'.[12]

The expedition also gives Corner an opportunity to get close to the men he is leading – especially Sergeant Umaru, for whose honesty and courage he has great respect. Umaru is 'a little man with a strangely wrinkled face' who 'had served in the old Niger Company police twenty years before. He limped on the right leg and one shoulder was much lower than the other. He was neither a smart soldier, nor a very reliable Sergeant. But he was a first class fighting man and extremely intelligent.'[13]

They are forbidden to light fires and 'No tents were carried'. On the second night of 'drizzling mountain rain', Corner, sorry for the sodden men 'huddled in their cloaks while they ate their cold porridge', suggests that they all sleep under an old tent-fly he has 'looted from some German camp'. As he listens to their drowsy conversation, Corner's understanding and affection are deepened. The men fall asleep; but he remains 'feverishly awake', intensely aware of the clouds' 'commotion' across the moon. Then he realises that Umaru, beside him, is also awake, and the two talk quietly. Umaru has no home; he was born, he says, 'On war'; he has no friends – 'Friends are no good.' Despite the cultural and personal chasm between them, 'a warmth of sympathy' springs in Corner, 'especially at the point where his elbow touched the old man's back', and expands into 'an affectionate concern', a 'serene enjoyment'. 'But Umaru, it isn't good for a man to be lonely,' Corner has protested. '"Yes, it is very good . . . That's the way to live – like a Haji." (A Haji is a pilgrim.)'[14]

This magnificent, moving story – one of Cary's best – distils again the hard, joyous wisdom of another servant, Barney Magonegal, expressing a theme recurrent in Cary's novels, the human mandate to be a pilgrim.

'a beautiful shot'

Cary's mission was a success, and the big French gun was duly hauled the 150 miles to Mora – a long, hard march. Cunliffe reconnoitred carefully, and decided to launch the assault from a hill north of Mora Mountain. The gun was hauled up it. An attack was ordered 'to commence during the night of September 2nd/3rd'.[15] In fact, three attacks had to be made, across the valley and up the precipitous mountain. Cary was flattered and moved to find that, in a charge, half a dozen of his soldiers 'closed round me, placing their bodies between me and the bullets. I spoke of this to an old officer who answered, "Yes, you're the latest juju, but don't get hit or they'll say 'This juju is a dud' and leave you in the bush".'[16]

Cary was in the final attack, which reached the summit but was then 'stopped by machine-gun fire fifty yards from the German redoubt. For forty-eight hours the native troops clung to the Mora summit . . . No food or water reached the men, for the German machine-guns swept all the slopes . . . On the second night Brigadier-General Cunliffe had to order them to retire as best they could.'[17]

But Cary was already dead. Or rather, 'I thought I was killed when I was shot, and in the few seconds' consciousness I had, had no unhappy thoughts or pain or fear – only a sort of surprise that such a terrible thing as death should happen so easily and suddenly . . .'[18] Again his luck held. He had been 'ordered to lead his 25 men in a charge up a hill. He got his objective, but lost half his men in the first minute and a half. It was there that he was wounded – 'a beautiful shot' that pierced his helmet, chipped the mastoid bone and went right through his ear.[19]

Although clearly a dud juju, he was not abandoned in the bush. And his wound was in itself minor. After the failure of this second offensive against the Mora fortress, Cunliffe led most of his column south to join a concerted attempt by British and French forces to conquer the main German fortresses to the south, Banyo and Yaoundé. They reached Yola on 26 September, and Cary was able to recuperate there.

Meanwhile Arthur Cary had received a letter from the Colonial Office on 17 September informing him that his son had been 'wounded in the attack on Mora – it says "Mr Bonar Law infers that it is not of a serious character" – but of course I know that all wounds out there are more serious that those in temperate places and I am anxious for more news. Mora is such a long way up that I'm afraid you cannot get to the Coast until you are pretty fit again. I have quite cheerful news from Jack' (who was now a Turkish prisoner-of-war at a camp some 150 miles from Constantinople; he had been in an Australian submarine captured in the Dardanelles in April). 'On the day you were wounded, the Zeppelins paid us a visit and made an awful row . . . I stood on the flat roof of the bathroom, and listened to the roar of the bombs . . . All send love and sympathy.'[20]

Freddy Ogilvie wrote at the end of October: 'I do hope you're not too bad, Joyce, and that you will be in England soon . . . I also was wounded, in April: one lung is a bit damaged, and my left hand is in a waste-paper basket.' Freddy Ogilvie had, in fact, nearly died.[21]

In August, Heneage Ogilvie (married six months earlier) and Elsie were posted to France, he as a surgeon, she as a VAD nurse. He wrote to Cary from an Urgency Cases Hospital on the Meuse in November:

> I can't tell you how glad I am to . . . hear that you are alive and pretty fit . . . the world would not be quite the same place if it didn't contain you in some corner of it, liable to turn up with your messy habits and your warm heart – your gabble of talk, at any time when you were most forgotten. All the bits of recent years that stand up off the flat bring memories of you – those fine strenuous days of punting up the Cher, the fire in the outer court of the Mosque at Vilgar with the smoke going up through the beams to the bright stars, and the wild tales that went round . . .[22]

'they said I had killed someone'

The rest of Cary's fighting in the Cameroons was often nightmarish. 'I was wounded at Mora Mountain, but suffered much worse from starvation, dysentery and bronchitis which brought on asthma';[23] and he also suffered from a 'fever, which refused to be cured'.[24] He was badly run-down, emaciated – as a photograph taken around this time shows. Because his condition was not obviously serious, he was allowed to rejoin his company after treatment, for the long march south from Garua to Banyo.

They reached that objective at the end of October, having covered 450 miles in five weeks. Cary's company was first into Banyo town, below the 1,000-foot mountain crowned by a German fortress. Banyo 'had been selected by the Germans as a rallying-point for their garrison of the central plateau and equipped and provisioned to withstand a prolonged siege'.[25] After bombardment, after arduous climbing through thick fog and heavy rain and finally a ferocious thunderstorm, after the loss of the officer and many soldiers in one of the five companies, Cunliffe's men finally struggled over slippery precipices to the fortress – and found it deserted; the German defenders had escaped during the storm.

Cary's memories of the battle are hazily preserved in a sketch: 'Battle of Banyo, in the cave; don't like to shoot . . . The ambush and the man saying, in English, Dey better look out . . . The doki boy after the noisy battle – his astonishment, and dismay.'[26]

Now Cary was diagnosed as having bronchitis, and sent back to Yola while the combined British and French forces advanced south. After taking Yaoundé, Cunliffe's column then marched north again to deal with the unfinished business at Mora; but no further fighting was necessary; the Germans there surrendered on 18 February 1916.

Cary lost his 'beloved Satan'. The black pony, that had 'carried me over about 800 miles of rough country in that war', died in Yola after being bitten by tsetse fly.[27]

Even more distressing was the death of a friend and fellow officer. Two years afterwards, Cary's grief was still sharp when he mentioned how all who had fought in the Cameroons

> knew well no one cared a dump what happened to us. Neither for praise or blame. I remember a friend of mine, Charles Marwood, saying as much, when someone had remarked it didn't much matter where one fought, it was just the same if one was killed. Marwood said half and more of his Regiment was dead in France, and he would have wished to be with them, but he didn't want to be killed in the Cameroons, it was too lonely. And poor Marwood *was* killed – shot at ten yards out of the forest – he died in two hours – and is buried in a desolate waste of scrub and stones – a thousand miles from anywhere under a pile of stones to keep the hyenas from him – a lonelier place could not be found.[28]

Cary was now at the end of his tether. During February, in Yola, he suddenly lost his self-control and lashed out violently. Then blacked out. When he came round, 'they said I had killed someone. It was a stupid lie, and no one had been hurt. I knew I had knocked and kicked about freely. But I was in a bad way at that time and a nervous wreck, and so I couldn't keep my temper.'[29] Cary was devastated by the thought that he had committed murder. The frequency of violence and killing in his novels may have a subterranean link with that incident.

Clearly it was essential that he rest and recuperate. At the end of March

1916, a medical examination found him physically unfit for further combat, and he was given permission to go home on a three-month leave. He arrived in England on 15 April. He was engaged on 2 May. On 1 June he was married.

'a sunshiny day'
It happened like this.

Cary had often thought about Gertie on the boat going out to Nigeria, he later confessed; but during his two years in West Africa 'Just now and then I had a recollection of you which generally caused me to say "D**n girls". I fancy I had rather a reputation as a misogynist in those days. I know I used to scorn a fellow . . . who was on the column with me, and who was engaged. While he sat with his nose buried in letters, I drank my drink and smoked my pipe like a free man, and thoroughly despised both love and women.' On the other hand, some nights, 'when I sat alone in my chair and smoked an after-dinner pipe, and remembered you, I wondered what you were doing or thinking, and if I should ever have the courage to see you again, even if it would be wise or kind to see you again. Do you know that coming home on the boat, I determined not to go to The Glade at all unless you were away, and I called up on the telephone partly to know if you were there.' But Freddy answered and 'That brought back all the old happy times and friendships to me, and I wanted to see you then, even though I still thought it unwise.'[30]

And Gertie? Convinced that Cary wanted no more to do with her, 'She made up her mind she would think no more of the mon, and tried to put her foot down on herself whenever she wondered about him in all the time he was away . . .' But she found herself thinking about him nevertheless – 'In fact darling you gave me a bad time – as I used to get so nervous when I heard inadvertently that you were chasing murderers or working in small pox villages – and when I knew you were fighting it was still worse – and I only by chance heard you were wounded – and of course I pretended I didn't care 2d.' She thought that his ear had been shot off and 'nearly broke her heart – and discovered that after all she loved him very badly, and had loved him ever since he went away'.

But neither could speak about their relationship. The first evening of Cary's stay at The Glade was uncomfortable. Before she went in to shake his hand, Gertie nervously 'tried to get glimpses . . . through the drawing-room door to see if you had altered'.[31] Cary: 'You started up from the dinner table at dessert from beside me, and went to your Mother, and then hid behind Freddy's chair from where I could catch glimpses now and then of very ambiguous glances.' He was fearful of 'being within ten yards' of her lest she run away offended. One night he sat out in the hall on the couch with Freddy, smoking, while she sang 'that folk song about the cloudy morning that may be a sunshiny day – I had a very great lump in my throat . . . I thought of our own cloudy morning and wondered if the sun would ever break through.'

In the end it was Freddy, beloved wounded brother who would not play the piano again, benevolent and critical friend, who banged their hearts together. 'Freddy married us – we wouldn't be married now but for Freddy,'

Cary wrote in 1917, 'for I was going the day after, and once I had gone I wouldn't have gone back unless Fred was there to keep me in countenance, and Fred was going too.'[32] Having convinced Gertie that Cary loved her, having persuaded Cary to stay longer than he had intended, having urged him to propose immediately, Freddy engineered 'the final agonizing hour in the dining-room when,' she insisted, 'you DID NOT propose. Your exact words in the dining-room were, "It will always be the same with me" – now darling do you call that telling a poor young woman that you (think) you want her to marry you.'[33]

She put a hand on his arm. He tried to kiss her. 'What a failure, my first attempt at a kiss, I don't think it even reached your cheek, and if you kissed me at all, you kissed the air. Then we hurried off at once to tell Mother as if we couldn't face each other another moment.'[34]

She had accepted him – the 're' Bohemian 'who I said was the last person in the world I could ever marry'.[35] Relief. Rejoicings. Their mutual shyness made the short engagement tense. Gertie found him 'frightening and rather chilling . . . I didn't truly know you at all till we were married and I expect you didn't know me either.'[36] He conceded that his behaviour had been very restrained; but 'My darling sweetheart, if I never made love to you when we were engaged, you must not think I was cold.' He was frightened still that she 'would fly away again, and I was very much concerned about my responsibilities and nervous of the near future.' Also 'I wasn't well. I don't think I was ever very fit . . . I hadn't recovered from the Cameroons. And so I was irritable over trifles.'[37]

Both families tried to help – although Gertie found her first meeting with Arthur Cary an ordeal: 'Dad walked very solemnly and slowly across the room without saying a word – and I haven't often felt so frightened of anyone – but once one knows him, I think he is one of the easiest people to talk to.'[38] Mr Ogilvie gave Cary advice on how to manage Gertie: 'He seemed to think you were decidedly a difficult proposition, while at the same time he assured me it was worth tackling. The picture left in my mind was rather of a golden hearted porcupine . . .'[39] Mrs Ogilvie was reconciled to the idea of Cary as son-in-law; she and Flo agreed that he was much improved in manner and dress, and no longer to be dismissed as 're and shams and untidy and careless, and contemptuous of women, and forward, and rude'.[40] Heneage wrote delightedly from France:

> Joyce my old dear,
>   What a thing to do. I can't pretend to be surprised either, for I have known all the time since the Balmacara days and I know what it meant to you then, and I felt pretty sure it meant a lot to Gertie too. But what a thing love is. When you first told me of it on the tennis lawn I was really absolutely taken aback – I could never imagine anything in common between you two; but I am sure there is a lot of undeveloped ruffian in Gertie and in you much concealed domesticity . . .[41]

After the hastily arranged wedding on 1 June 1916, they spent a night at the Langham Hotel in London. Cary: 'It was a strange wedding-night. We were both very calm and grave.' But he was also feeling sick – possibly, he feared, with blackwater fever. When he came out of the dressing-room, he suggested that she go to the theatre with an aunt who was living in the hotel! Then they went to bed, 'sleeping miles apart in that big room'.[42] Gertie: 'I remember I didn't sleep a wink all the first night, while you slept like a log, and I felt very indignant. You patted my hand in a fatherly way the first evening, and I think got as far as kissing me in the morning.'[43]

Later that day, they travelled by train to Cornwall, where, in a cottage at Trebarwith (a village near Boscastle and Tintagel Castle), they spent their honeymoon.

Cary's orders were to return to Northern Nigeria 'at the expiration of three months from the date of arrival at Plymouth'.[44] He booked his passage on the S.S. *Abasso*, leaving Liverpool on 9 August. There was much to do in their few weeks of married life, including buying new kit and provisions.

Then there was the matter of Gertie's accommodation during his year and more away. By their marriage settlement, Gertie was to receive an annuity of £300 from her father; together with Cary's annuity of almost the same sum, his small income from shares and Irish rents, and his salary of £315, this would give them an annual income of around £1,000 – which seemed to make possible Gertie's wish to buy a small house not far from The Glade. But Cary was unenthusiastic about living in a London suburb, and already the war was raising house prices. They had a row while looking over a house in Maida Vale. Then, on 23 July, Gertie discovered that she was pregnant. It was decided immediately that she should remain at The Glade, where she could be cared for by her mother and the servants.

Cary's departure loomed. For her twenty-fifth birthday, on 26 August, he left a letter to accompany his gift of a jade necklace:

Darling Gertie,   Sunday Aug. 6th
    This is for your birthday xxx, and I will give you these three kisses in a few minutes myself, for I'm going after you as soon as this is written, to lay my head where it is most comforted, and I am happiest. But when you get this, I won't be able to, and every time I put my head on the pillow will remind me of what I lost when I went away . . .
    But darling, it can't be helped, and you must be brave not only for yours and my sake, but for someone else's as well – as a brave woman would have brave children – and so my love, I wish you many happy returns, and especially I wish myself many happy returns – for it will be the happiest return of all to come back to you.
                                      Your loving Joyce[45]

CHAPTER FIFTEEN

OFFICER IN CHARGE

1916

'a fellow killed by pagans'

When Cary returned to Northern Nigeria he made two promises. The first – to write to Gertie every day – he carried out faithfully; he would write several pages of a journal letter, then post it to her, crammed into a small envelope, after four or five days. Gertie kept all these letters; embellished with lively sketches, they compose 'one of the fullest . . . and most vivid accounts ever written of a district officer's life'.[1]

His second promise turned out to be more difficult to keep. During the unsettled two years of his first tour of duty, he had found neither time nor energy for his 'work', as he termed his imaginative writing, underlining its importance in his life. During the three-month leave he had tried to make a new start. At The Glade he had often retired to a dressing-room to work and on honeymoon at Trebarwith had written some poems. Gertie fully supported those efforts to revive his vocation; he showed her a plot he had devised for a novel, and promised to send her the chapters, for her criticism, as they were completed. He was determined to make good progress during this second tour of duty.

He was nearly twenty-eight. In her letters to him after the parting, Gertie dwelled lovingly on his appearance and personality, 'brown eyes, a nice straight nose, a very determined chin, and a small bald patch on the back of his head. He can talk very well when he wants to and can tell stories, risky and otherwise by the dozen – he can also blog [behave moodily] when he wants to with a vengeance. He has the truest most loving heart in the world . . .' His conversational abilities had always impressed, and intimidated, her – 'I remember when you were holding forth to Mother about Nigeria . . . I used to listen spellbound . . .' Above all, she admired his courage and optimism: 'You really are a plucky mon' with 'equanimity [and] determination to look at everything on the bright side'. 'You are like Elsie, and take people as you find them, and like them for what you see is good in them'.[2]

At Euston Station to catch the boat train to Liverpool, Cary encountered

Brigadier-General Cunliffe, under whom he had fought in the Cameroons, 'and when I got on board I found that, although I had myself arranged to sit modestly with modest people, I was put down to sit with the General'. Cunliffe was going out to raise an Expeditionary Force for service against the Germans in East Africa, and he promised to include Cary. Their table companions were military or political officers, all considerably senior to Cary; but he managed to keep his end up with yarns and jokes, and the General entertained them with a flow of reminiscences. Particularly interesting were 'queer stories of Nigeria ten years ago and the old times', one about a Resident who had tried to educate his two sons – 'starved himself to keep them at Oxford, but starved himself too much and died; so I suppose they had to go down and the poor old man had defeated himself with his own unselfishness.' Cary's completion of the narrative indicates his alert response to any incident illustrating the injustice of life. The Resident's destruction by his own unselfishness, and the sons' deprivation, echoes the fate of the Inishowen Carys.

On 25 August, they reached Lagos. 'I have my orders now, and find I am still a soldier – I am to go to Yola at first but perhaps shall go afterwards to East Africa or Egypt.'

After two racketting days on the train, he parted from the General ('who patted me on the shoulder . . . and promised I would not be forgotten in Yola'); and on 28 August was on the Niger, aboard the *Black Swan*.

He was disappointed to learn next day that 'I am *not* to go to Yola – so I don't know what to do. I should hate to be left here in Lokoja – expensive and dull, and no allowance . . . I shall be here till I get other orders . . . I've not done any *work* (you know what I mean by *work*) since I left the *Abasso*.'

He was stuck at Lokoja for three weeks, attached to a company of the WAFF. There was time for meditation, and some depression:

> I wish I had had the courage years ago to defy all conventional notions of respectable livings and write, write, write, for whatever I could make by it, even nothing. This tour I had promised to try my hand and see if I could make MONEY, the magic stuff that I must get for my wife and family or stay in this exile for 12 years of my life and yours, the best of both of us – but nothing is possible now and I doubt if I will be able to do anything at all. The day is cut up in small jobs – there is no privacy (I share a bungalow with another fellow) and you know how necessary that is to me to *work*.

He quickly overcame his depression, however, and buckled down to making the best of his situation. He began a debate with Gertie about literary standards. 'I read a book on board coming out by Zola, or an extract rather, and I liked it . . . I hate hypocrisy anywhere and would rather have honest wickedness honestly written about, than the hypocrisy of a writer who pretends the world and the people in it are better than they are.'

The next afternoon he began writing again. 'The day has gone quickly enough – two parades in the morning, turned out the guards after lunch, then read a book, and did two hours' *work* – very successful, so very pleased.' And for the next two weeks he found time and energy to write about 2,000 words most afternoons. 'I'm not writing the thing we went through together – that was too artificial a plot and unworkable when I got to practice – this is more natural and less confused, and deals more with the doings of ordinary people neither good nor bad.'

Happier, he found his colleagues and military duties more interesting. Bales, 'quite a good solid dull fat sort of man,' came for a drink, 'got slightly drunk and I managed to make him talk about himself (everybody is quite willing to do this) and he was very interesting.' The Adjutant turned out to be 'a very good fellow', and Feasey was 'fourteen stone of good nature'. He joined them in the Mess for drinks, and even (to Mrs Ogilvie's horror) played cards for money occasionally.

On 13 September an order was received in Lokoja extending tours of duty, while the war lasted, from one year to fifteen months; 'I shall not be coming home at soonest till the end of December 1917, allowing for the journey. It can't be helped . . . War is war, the worst and wickedest thing there is, the cruellest and most unmeaning, but I suppose it can't be avoided any more than pain, which is often cruel and senseless, and seeming to make those suffer who least deserve it.'

On the same day came a further piece of information, which was to yield the protagonist and plot of his first extended fiction on a Nigerian theme, *Daventry*:

> This morning I went to Orderly Room to find the Adjutant. I am now O.C. Company and a fearful swell by the way. The adjutant wasn't there but the Major was. 'Hullo! Cary,' says he while I saluted like blazes. 'I want you. Can you leave at short notice?' And he said I was to go on the Montal patrol. You remember I told you of a rumour about a fellow killed by pagans. The fellow was Maltby and the Montals [the Tel] did him in. West found his skull wrapped up in his burberry in the Montal Juju house. Poor Maltby ought never to have been in Montal [just south of Bauchi Province] without an escort . . . Four tribes ate him, and they are all for it. I was very glad about the chance of getting out and making some allowances and avenging M. all at once, but this afternoon I hear Feasey is to go, since I have a company and Feasey hasn't. It's between the two of us because we are the only two here that know the country.

Five days later: 'News for you. I'm ordered to Nafada . . . I shall have a company there and draw command pay, but I shall be out of everything at the same time, lost and forgotten. My *work* will go on though. It goes on every day now, and is a great consolation for every reverse.' He faced a three-week journey, and was worried about her letters going astray.

His final Mess was a 'strange' one. 'I was in one of those moody states which sometimes worry you and myself.' He had already drunk 'a stiff whisky or so before, at a parting small chop [informal evening meal] and knew I should begin to be shaky if I went on, so I refused'. The adjutant was not offended by his unsociability. 'Cary, you know, I'm awful blind, and if I thought you were a shit, I'd shay sho, because I'm blind. But I like you, Cary, you're a good feller . . .'[3]

'the work goes famously'

Two days later, on 21 September, he was on the *Woodcock*, going up the
Niger as far as Baro, from where he could travel by train to Naraguta. Again he
enjoyed the boat journey:

> We are hopelessly stuck in the middle of the bush all among the tree
> tops . . . The Niger is higher than it's been for years . . . This morning
> when I was exercising, in nothing at all, I was startled by loud feminine
> squeals and turned to see a whole small population, mostly ladies, watching
> me from ten yards' distance. I expect they thought my movements were
> religious. These little villages are so hidden away among the trees we come
> on them in a minute as we wander along over the floods. We are taking a
> cross-country course to avoid the strong current in the big stream, and have
> been aground several times . . .
>
> I love this river-journeying.

Because the boat was delayed by a thunderstorm, he missed his train and
had to wait three days for the next. But his spirits were high – as usual when he
was travelling and writing. From the Baro rest-house he announced that 'the
first draft is finished and I am doing the first revision' –

> That is I read the whole thing through this morning and considered it from
> every point of view – what parts were too short, what too confusing and
> needing more explanation, where I had missed chances and where I had too
> many incidents crowded together – then I made notes and have started to
> add. First of all I add roughly, whole pages at a time – bringing in a
> character that does not appear often enough in other places, or explaining
> the plot. For instance if a person only appears once or twice at either the very
> beginning or end, the character is almost wasted, and also gives an
> appearance of only being dragged in to carry on the plan. When I write a
> first draft I don't worry about this but bring in a character only when wanted.
> Now I must weave them into the texture of the work. This is not difficult in
> the early stages as now. The first draft runs to about 40,000 words. And this
> book will have to be 100,000 or more so there's lots of room for
> expansion . . .

That evening he was sitting 'on the verandah at my table with a whiskey soda
at my elbow, a pile of lovely foolscap, a pipe and baccy, and I'm whistling like
a bird all for good spirits and gratitude for the lovely world'.

He was glad now to be 'already getting into my own well-loved bush
country', and looked forward to '10 days or so riding, marching – breakfasts
under the trees and dinner in camp. The rains should be nearly over as far
north as this . . .' But before his trek began, there were the pleasures of
Naraguta, with old friends to welcome him – Dr Pollard, 'bursting with
kindness', and Cadell, the A.D.O. with whom he had first travelled to
Nigeria. Above all, there was the joy of finding four letters from Gertie at the
Post Office: 'Oh darling how I love you and long for you . . . I'm afraid all my
letters are rather headlong and I tell you more than Mother might approve,
but I can only write one way and if I begin to hold in on one side I shall fail
somewhere else too . . . if I was parsonical I doubt if I should love so much.'

He bought a horse from Pollard for £8, a worthy successor to Satan, 'strong and . . . trained for polo'; and, while waiting for his carriers to assemble, he continued to work on the second draft of his novel, 'writing slowly and carefully, and expanding all the way along'.[4]

On 4 October, he set off for Nafada: 'I am really in the bush at last, away from civilization and cold drinks and dinner parties.' The 250-mile trek, with a daily journey of around 20 miles (varying from 15 over rough country to 25 along good level paths) took two weeks. For most of it, Cary was 'a scandalously happy grass-widower'.[5] An early-morning march, a big breakfast on arrival at the next overnight camp, a siesta, lunch, an afternoon of work, an evening of letter-writing and relaxation (he often played his accordion), an early night in preparation for the next morning's early rising: this routine so pleased him, with its regular alternation of physical action and literary creativity, that he sought to recreate it in later life.

At Bauchi town he was delighted to find six letters from Gertie, and was relieved to know that, four months into her pregnancy, she was in good health. About his absence in Nigeria she commented 'I could never bear to think that you might think of giving up the service because of me – but I know that if your writing was successful, it was always what your heart was in – I feel you are doing such splendid work in Nigeria that it would be awful for you to give it up – though it is hard for both of us to miss so much of our life together while we are still young.' Not all her family shared that view. On 10 September Gertie wrote 'I know you didn't want your writing talked about in the family darling, but Mother of her own accord said the other day, she thought after all you might have to give up Nigeria, because the separation was so bad for us, and spoke of your writing as the alternative. You had evidently spoken to her about it.'[6]

His work was going as well as the trek. 13 October: 'The work goes famously, about 15,000 words of the new version – all the characters blossoming and getting flesh on their skeletons. I shall have 20,000 by the time I reach Nafada, and be done by January or February.' On 15 October he 'got over a difficult place. I'm learning a great deal as I go along, for instance about the proper alternation of dialogue and solid reading – and light and heavy. I have a method of my own at any rate – good or bad, I don't know, but it's individual. I read some Tolstoi – fables . . . *Master and Man and Other Stories* . . .'

He would be glad to reach Nafada – 'I'm tired of short nights and long days for the present – the milk was sour to-day too, and there's only goat's milk here – and the cook is sick and two of the labourers have sore feet. 15 days' march is enough for one journey, though I'm very fit and hard.'[7]

'the best game I ever played'

On 19 October Cary reached Nafada, after a 28-day trek. As in Lokoja, he was not happy at first. 'The Political seem to be at loggerheads with the soldiers . . . and trouble of all sorts is promised. I have a pain in my stomach and am feeling depressed – the company consists of the sick, halt and maimed and a row of very unpromising recruits.'

133

But again his spirits quickly rose as he settled in, and his five months at Nafada were mostly enjoyable. On 20 October, 'The whole Station has been dining with me as O.C. Troops (do you know they present arms to me once a day when I go into the Fort!!!)'. On acquaintance, his colleagues were 'good fellows all': the Likita (doctor), Rolleston, 'fat, fair, and a great horse-coper but a very good doctor too'; the A.D.O. in charge, Falconer, 'a war volunteer, late Professor somewhere, about 40, very quiet and official'; a second A.D.O., de Putron, 'a tall Etonian', about to go on leave; the Subaltern, Phillips, 'not at all a bad bird really, only rather a chump'.

Just over a week after his arrival, he decided that, although they were 'a long way out of the world', and received little news, 'I'm much more alive than I was in Lokoja all the same'.

One of the reasons for his sense of wellbeing was a decision taken during conversation over drinks on 20 October: 'We are going to start a Polo Club here, and I hope to learn something of the game at last . . .' They wasted no time. 22 October: 'Started polo to-day and knocked a ball about. I can't help seeing that a special luck follows me everywhere – first the shot that didn't kill me, then you darling, then a pony that knows how to play polo tho' I never knew I should be able to play when I got him.' A polo ground was cleared: bare earth, but 'not nearly so dangerous as it looked'.

Games were arranged whenever teams could be mustered; they often played three a side. Elder arrived – a D.O. from Maiduguri, 'a little fierce dried-up man who has bush-whacked all over the world in his time' – and was summarily pressed into play. Afterwards, Cary felt 'most gorgeously tired and well. All my muscles ready for sleep, but no stiffness. Polo is the best game I ever played – for excitement and speed and interest – the scrimmage sometimes with ponies and sticks and men all in a confused mass of dust, from which issued bursts of cusses, was delightful'.[8]

The horses were a formidable hazard. 'In West Africa ponies are stallions', and would 'stand up and fight' during a game 'if they weren't kept on the move, and pretty fast'. Given the opportunity, they would also bite human beings. In one game, Cary was pursuing Rolleston, who had the ball.

> My black gradually came up to him until I, by leaning forward, could hope to hook his stick when he swung it back for a drive. But just then, my pony, wildly excited by the chase, made a tremendous spring forward, stretched out his long neck and bit the Doctor in the behind. He stood up in his stirrups with a yell of pain, I got the ball, and sent it to one of my forwards, who scored.

Polo games also had serious professional implications. After a bad fall, Cary climbed straight back on to his pony and the game continued – for he could never forget that he was 'Officer Commanding Company and most of my company were looking on. My men would have bitterly resented their loss of face before the civilian population if their O.C. had failed to go on with the game, after any number of crashes. A broken collarbone or leg would have ruined my prestige with these pagan fighting-men. O.C. of troops among pagans has to be unbreakable and unkillable, he has to have the most powerful kind of juju or some local juju-man will run his company'.[9]

He found his office duties increasingly tiresome: 'Blow Returns, Parade States, Minor Office Reports, Casualties among Govt Horses, Description Roles, Daily Orders No. II, Monetary Reports and all the rest of 'em. I am irked and angry from top to toe and when I asked a fellow just now if he were a Mahommedan or a pagan and he said he didn't know, which would I prefer, I cussed him most horrid, when I ought to have laughed. Thank goodness the doki [horse] is being saddled this minute and I'll go and gallop off the cares of this world and knock the ball about instead of myself.' In fact, he took great pride in doing all his duties well, and had set out to 'get things properly systematised' after the disorder bequeathed by his predecessor.

One of Cary's duties was to recruit soldiers for Cunliffe's Expeditionary Force. 'Old soldiers are rolling up every day to enlist, which pleases me as other people aren't so flourishing . . . It's quite delightful to see the thoughtful villainy of their war-torn countenances on parade and they know their work too – anything from six to eight years' service.' His success was largely due to the good relations he had quickly established with the Political Officers, especially Falconer; as a spoof-letter to Gertie indicates:

Dear Mrs Cary,
I have just come from small chop at Lieut. Phillips' house – Phillips always has a good fire and I enjoy sitting over it and keeping my legs warm. Your husband was there in his usual black top-boots, pyjamas, sweater and khaki scarf, smoking a curly pipe, with his glass and tobacco on the ground beside him and a very rickety old chair. I can't quite make him out – when we talked about Home Rule, really at one time I thought he was a Home Ruler (allowing that Ulster should be independent) and he gave us a long speech on Agricultural Co-operation which made me very sleepy. However he was most polite to me since I sent him those 24 Gwani recruits this morning and I think I shall get on with him quite well – he is certainly taking great pains to smooth out the late difficulties between our Departments, and takes trouble about the Polo ground. In fact I saw him breaking up ants' nests for an hour this evening, and his company tailor has made us some excellent red jumpers to play in. He has had his disreputable grain store in the Fort repaired too this week, and will be able to take over the corn from the Emir, thank goodness – the soldiers seemed to think we were going to look after it for them for ever. I trust you are well, and have the honour to remain, your very sincere well-wisher

F.D. Falconer, Professor, A.D.O.

There were other military matters to arrange. Carlyle had come in for Christmas, 'as usual in bursting spirits'; had played polo and entertained the whole station with his conversation. Their official relationship was changed (Cary was now 'a twin in authority – he chief in his way – I in mine') but not their mutual respect and affection. So, when violent unrest broke out among the Tangales in February 1917, Cary must have been pleased to be able to despatch a detachment of ten soldiers, under a white officer, to support Carlyle. 'I should have liked to go myself – but O.C.s don't usually go unless with the whole company . . . and Headquarters wouldn't allow it.'

Other decisions had to be taken rather more rapidly. One day 'a man ran amuck and arrived in my house all at once waving a spade – he was so crazy with excitement and rage he wouldn't listen to me – the orderly Corporal arrived and explained that the man had been refusing work, and disobeying the Sergeant Major'. While the man raved, Cary calmly ordered the Corporal to fetch reinforcements. 'Meanwhile I sat and read a book and pretended the man did not exist – rather difficult as he was waving the spade and yelling a yard from me. You see I couldn't hit him, because that's against the rules and a bad thing in any case . . . He laid all the guard out when they arrived and broke the Corporal's head, and he's now in clink with hand-cuffs and leg-irons.'

Recurrent administrative problems were caused by the anarchical presence of women in the barracks, so he embarked on 'a great feminist experiment':

> The women in the barracks – 54 of them without their husbands – have been behaving in a very rowdy and worse than rowdy way. Last week I appointed a Serikin Mata, or queen of the women, to look after them. Yesterday, after the ordinary orderly room was over, and defaulters marched off – in came the Ser. Mata – a tall stately lady in a blue robe, followed by a fierce little woman carrying a large stick [and] scowling ferociously – then two prisoners looking highly pleased with themselves – and then another police-woman with a stick and a scowl. The case was conducted with great solemnity – and the police were exceedingly officious about the etiquette of the court – wanting to knock the prisoners down whenever they opened their mouths. One lady was convicted of fighting, the other of loose behaviour in town, and they were both admonished – and warned that they will sit in the stocks at the next offence. The Serikin Mata has really shewn herself most capable – chose her own police – states a case clearly, and is keeping a very unruly crowd of exceedingly unscrupulous women in excellent order.

(But among the women, as among the men, there were irrepressible rogues who delighted Cary: 'One lady this morning calmly undressed herself during the case – I suppose to shew her indifference to the proceedings – she was up for violent assault and battery – and then put on her robe again with the most affected care – to the scandal of the whole court – I didn't laugh till they were outside again – one must look solemn on these occasions – then I laughed so much I dropped my eye-glass.')[10]

CHAPTER SIXTEEN

TRANSITION

1916–1917

'*ups and downs*'

Before the end of 1916, Cary's life at Nafada had settled into a pleasant routine, with occasional surprises. He was at ease in yet another masculine community. Domestic arrangements were comfortable: his house was a large, long, three-roomed hut surrounded by a verandah, on which he slept inside a mosquito-house ('It's a breezy place . . . and cool at night'). For three weeks he even had a pet, a baby antelope – 'she stands on her long tottery legs and wags her tail and looks at you with a round pair of dark eyes as if she thought you were her mother . . . I never saw so pretty and trustful and gentle a little thing . . .' But she died suddenly, just before Cary fell ill himself.

Dengue Fever kept him in bed for a day, then left him very weak for a fortnight – 'all my joints are rheumatic, my back creaks, my hands feel as if they were swollen and my head is splitters.' It also contributed to a depression that reached its climax on 7 December, his birthday. In late November, under the weight of his illness, he was in despair about his writing. 'The truth is it is very hard to work in uncongenial surroundings . . .' He also lamented the lack of good reading. 'I never brought a worse selection in my life, all poetry and essays and I abominate poets and essayists. I long for some good novels, a Compton Mackenzie or two, a Gilbert Cannan or so, a William de Morgan, a good Arnold Bennett (not one of his pot-boilers), some Thackerays, a Meredith, and a Hardy.'

His depression was exacerbated, he confessed, by a conversation at small chop. There had been

> bad news of the war – and the Doctor asked me if I wasn't 28 to-day. I said, 'yes I am.' 'And how long have you been out?' he said. '3 years,' I said, 'all but a bit.' 'Then you're 31,' said he. 'Years in Nigeria count double . . . .'. Of course this is absurd of the doctor, but it depressed me because I thought how shall I ever be able to say 'I'll go now or I'll go next year' unless I can retire to do some other work? And there's nothing I can do but this d***d writing . . .

And he added 'What ups and downs I have – I suppose it's Irish blood. I was as happy as a sandboy at polo and as blue before dinner. I let my bath get cold while I brooded over my past, present and future . . .'[1]

Ups and downs continued into the New Year. Carlyle, polo, conversation at small chop, were all invigorating pleasures. There was a small chop gathering every evening, from about 6.30. He painted the scene for Gertie: 'the dark, trees and huts, the moon low down, some stars, a camp-fire, the table covered with bottles and glasses, and four men in shirts, slacks and long boots are lying in deck-chairs with pipes in their mouths, four or five mongrel dogs lying around, and a horse or two standing behind, and the river in front . . .' Sometimes the talk was 'nothing but shop – laws, taxes, patrols, murderers, cattle, horses, small wars, chiefs – the best weapons for native police – the best way of tackling native enemies – the relative characteristics of different tribes and so on'. Sometimes it meandered round the world: 'cat-fish and why they have skins instead of scales, and pearls, why they can be bought cheap at Colombo (because they are stolen from Government preserves) . . . how far apart coconut trees should be planted, the difference between *bêche de mer* as spoken in the Pacific and the Pidgin English of the Coast'. Sometimes the talk would shift from discussion of 'why men were bigger than they used to be, as one can see by the small size of the old armour, which subject came from the remark that heavy horses were needed to carry knights, and where did they come from – as in Ireland, the original stock were all thoroughbred till some ass introduced Shire-horse blood' – to literature: 'I talked of my precious Chaucer'.

A prototype of Gollop, the store-keeper of *Mister Johnson*, was one of Cary's favourite companions: 'Hall of the Niger Coy . . . with a big voice, who tells very long and pointless stories'. He was 'an old sailing mate, a little wizened man with no chest and very little body but a very large courage' and 'so much energy and pluck in him you wonder where he packs it away'.

Cary's sympathy deepened during this period in Nafada. A District Officer called Benton

> passed through yesterday on his way to Bornu. He is ill with asthma and has been in hospital at Kano since June with it. To-night I have been sitting with him and we talked books while he sniffed his remedies. I expect they will invalid him next tour – he has done ten years, his pension will be about £130 a year. He hardly ever gets any sleep and is wasted to skin and bone. All he wants to do is to get to Maiduguri in Bornu and start his work . . . He is a brave man, and many stories are told of his personal courage – but all his life is courage – and he is perfectly uncomplaining . . . a man I suppose of forty, an invalid with the most miserable of illnesses (I can speak from a little experience) who has worked hard and taken many risks at that work, and what has he to look forward to?

Of Nigerians, too, Cary's understanding was growing. At small chop he heard many derogatory comments about pagans. But some Tula tribesmen impressed him: 'the station is full of their music and singing all day. I have a gang working for me in the barracks digging a new drain, and they always escort me up to morning parade with a band of flutes and strings . . .' He perceived that 'The pagans . . . for all their cannibalism, and dog-eating (they dug up two dead horses here the other day – buried some time – and ate 'em) and nakedness, are most moral men and husbands . . . '[2] In fact, he responded to these Tula tribesmen neither as noble savages nor as some lower form of life but as human beings.

Clearly he enjoyed the harmony of Nafada station – for which his sensitivity, straightforwardness, good humour and efficiency were largely responsible.

On 3 January, Cary received 'a wire from Lokoja with orders from the Governor to return to civil duties – so I'll be an A.D.O. again in a day or two'. Since Carlyle was due for leave, he had good reason to hope that he would be ordered to take over Gombe Division: 'I daresay I shall be busy too if left single-handed to carry on the whole shew – the tax is £15,000 a year for instance and the population pretty large . . . Of course,' he continued with unconscious prescience, 'they may pack me off to Borgu or Bussa or Sokoto or somewhere else six weeks' journey from here – it is exactly the notion that would strike them . . . ' On 5 January another wire arrived: 'Priority, you will remain in command until further orders'.

Meanwhile, although he was still not writing much, he was again reading, for Gertie had sent some novels he had suggested: *Pendennis* ('I'm bound to say I like Thackeray always – and don't find him prosy'), H. G. Wells's just-published *Mr Britling Sees It Through* ('there is a certain hard material test-tube sort of outlook about the man I don't like . . . his very style is coarse in the grain'). And he was deeply moved by a book Dr Rolleston lent him, *The Thief on the Cross* by Mrs Harold Gorst: a realistic novel about injustice ('the story of a low-class family in London . . . the heroine is a girl – a girl with . . . the badness of her class which seems very gross to ours, but her goodness the only sort of goodness there is, love, unselfishness, self-sacrifice. She struggles with a hopeless situation . . . a very fine woman finely shewn . . . I don't like it for its grossness, or even its truth to life – the life that Heneage knew about [at] Guy's – but for its tragic picture of fine instincts and a sound heart fighting their way through hopeless difficulties to a hopeless end').

Unsettled by the countermanded order, he was also increasingly concerned, by mid February, about Gertie: 'this is the eighth month and I'm afraid you're very uncomfortable – it will be close to your time when you get this letter'. 'I think of you in your small bed all by yourself perhaps not sleeping and probably anxious and troubled.'

Then, on 8 March, new orders ended Cary's two months of suspense. 'I am to hand over to a Captain Silver as soon as he arrives which should be soon now, and return to Political duties.' He was to be stationed in Kontagora, a large Province to the west.[3]

'to Bush again'

Leaving Nafada, 'where every soul is a friend', on 24 March, Cary's emotions ran high. 'I was very much touched by the kindness of everyone to-day – Silver especially and the Likita – the guard turned out and the bugles played the Hausa Farewell as I came down the road'. Before him was the two-week trek to Naraguta, the train journey to Zungeru, then a further trek to Kontagora.

Writing to Gertie from 'the first rest-house on my road', Cary confessed that he was 'very unhappy . . . I feel very small and forgotten and lonely, and am very homesick too – not for home, for I haven't one yet, but for you and love.' The baby was expected on 28 March, when he would be somewhere between Nafada and Bauchi town. 'I shall be in a fever long before I get to Bauchi if no runner has come, and if there is nothing at Bauchi I shall have to go to Bush again without news. I only hope you will not worry if you get no answer at once, but put it down to the war . . .'

It was a bad time of the year for trekking. 'This is the hottest, dustiest and worst trek I ever did – worse than anything in all those months of Cameroons. Last night I had to sleep out because the house was so hot I sweated even naked (the walls were hot to touch) and a gale got up and blew away the net, and covered me an inch in sand and cinders from bush fires, and bits of branches off the trees.' Further reading of novels Gertie had sent gave some consolation. Gilbert Cannan's *Mendel*, a novel about an artist (based on the *avant-garde* painter Mark Gertler), excited him ('It has left me disturbed as all good books do, and should do, with a mass of new impressions and suggestions to digest'); but he thought it inferior to *These Twain* ('Cannan has not the fine delicate skill of Bennett, nor his clear perceptions').

On 28 March he wrote a feverish letter to Gertie: 'Whether this is the day or not, I know you are suffering, my dearest, and I wish I was with you. Apart from your sickness, I am hungry and thirsty for you . . . Motherhood must not swallow you up, as it does so many women. Men and women are different, physically, mentally, morally, and it is a good thing, for a world all feminine would be a nightmare, and a world all masculine would be a desert – and either sterile . . .'

He reached Naraguta on 10 April and – 'Darling, I had the Great News this morning . . . I am awfully glad the wee mon is a son . . . Perhaps there will be a girl another time – I would like awfully to have a daughter. Everyone here, and the place is full of people, knows the news and I have been congratulated all day . . .'

Relief and exhilaration did not, however, improve his railway journeys, or Zungeru, Headquarters of Northern Nigeria – 'the most decayed of stations – everything seems to be at sixes and sevens – and it is doubtful whether I shall get carriers to take me on'. Kontagora town was 75 miles north-west, a six-day trek, and 'They seem to think here I may be going to the pagan division of Kontagora, which is a long way from civilisation and rails'.[4]

'the loneliest station of all'
'In Africa I was on the list of men who could be sent to the loneliest place without the risk of sending them off their heads,' Cary confided to a friend nearly forty years later, 'and I did go to the loneliest station of all in Borgu.'[5] However, official recognition of his psychological toughness was not the only

reason that Cary was chosen for a difficult and potentially dangerous task. There had been an uprising in Borgu during 1915. Uncertain calm had been restored, but the British Administration there was in ruins. The man capable of rebuilding it would have to be courageous, industrious, self-reliant, sensible and sensitive; and adequately experienced both politically and militarily.

Soon after welcoming Cary at the end of April 1917, the Resident of Kontagora Province, Major W. Hamilton-Browne, began to explain the situation. Cary wrote to Gertie a few days later:

> My dear, this Province is not Gombe, by no means. It is the most backward and desert province in Nigeria with an average population of 4 to the square mile. I am going to start a new Division, a new office, new everything, with two new Chiefs, and foresee massamoras as thick as bones in a gravy. The last man made a mess of the place, and one morning they all started cutting each others' throats, making such a clean sweep that a new start must be made. The people are not against the white man, so don't be afraid for me, darling, they were against the bad officials of their own chiefs, who were not properly looked after by an incompetent D.O. H.B., who is the best of fellows, has made new arrangements all round, and is making things as favourable as possible for me, but I shall have the toughest time yet without a doubt. Mails will be most irregular, I fear, darling, as it is an enormous division and I shall have to try and tour it all. There is no telegraph, and I may be as far as three weeks from the railway – so letters may take up to two months.

The 'new Division' was 'some 10,000 square miles, mostly deserted bush, with a large population of lions, snakes, crocodiles and mosquitoes . . . and the people backward. Hundreds of miles are swamp.'[6]

As Cary wrote later, the Borgu Rebellion of 1915 was 'quite a thing at the time';[7] and behind it lay complex social, political and historical facts that continued to disrupt the British governance of Borgu long after Cary's time there. One of the fundamental problems facing Cary in a situation where there was still widespread unrest was the necessity of administering through two 'quite separate and independent' Emirates (Bussa and Kaiama) which, although 'superficially alike', were 'in fact widely different in their history, racial affinities, language, political situation, and economic life'.[8] Moreover, the two Emirs and their administrations were in constant rivalry and tension, a problem that had been largely caused by Lugard.

The ruler of Kaiama 'at the arrival of the British' was Morata Sudi. He was 'the eighth chief of Kaiama, and a man, by all accounts, of strong character and high intelligence'. He was also ambitious 'and desired early to emphasise the independence of Kaiama, and the dignity of his position'.[9] When Lugard marched through Kaiama in 1894 on his 'Nikki Steeplechase', he was befriended and helped by Morata Sudi; so Lugard rewarded him in 1904 by recognising him as a 'first-class chief' equal in status to the Emir of Bussa.

But this was not acceptable to the Emir of Bussa. He and the Emir of Nikki, 'both by the antiquity of their families, and the legendary descent attributed to them, possess great spiritual influence. They are rulers by divine right.'[10] In their eyes, and the eyes of their subjects, the Emir of Kaiama was an upstart whose eminence was entirely a British invention. Although the Emirs of Kaiama who succeeded Morata Sudi were denominated 'second-class chiefs' by the British, the insult continued to rankle until as recently as 1955, when the Bussa Emirate was redefined as the Borgu Emirate, and the chief of Kaiama became clearly subordinate to the Emir of Borgu.

Even before Cary's main immediate predecessor in Borgu exacerbated the tension between Bussa and Kaiama, general resentment had been caused by Borgu's loss of status – it had been demoted in 1907 to a Division of the new Kontagora Province across the Niger – and lost territory in the north to Sokoto Province. After his initial enthusiasm for Borgu, Lugard had concluded that the region's 'economic prospects are very poor, owing to the extreme paucity of the population and their apathy'.[11] It looked insignificant in comparison to the huge, powerful, newly conquered northern Provinces (Kano, Sokoto, Katsina, Gwandu). In Cary's day, there were only about 35,000 Borgawa in the region's 11,000 square miles. At least half the population was settled along the Niger in the east, on the major north-west trade route running near the western border with French Dahomey (Niger), and in the south. The centre was thick, uninhabited bush.

At the end of 1912, the authoritarian D.O. in charge of Borgu Division, J. C. O. Clarke, had embarked on a reorganisation of Native Administration in Borgu. He deposed the Emir of Bussa, Kitoro Gani, in early 1915, replacing him with an ex-slave, Turak; and, in Kaiama Emirate, he replaced the important Sarkin (Chief of) Yashikera with an old soldier, Mashi, who was not even a native of Borgu. Then, insulting both Emirates simultaneously, he amalgamated Borgu, as junior partner, with Yauri, the Emirate and Division across the Niger. Unrest spread through Borgu, and was sparked into open revolt when Clarke attempted to extend and increase taxation.

In June 1915, Sabukki, younger half-brother of the exiled Kitoro Gani, led about six hundred men, armed with bows and arrows, into Bussa town, and some sixty members of the new Bussa Native Administration were killed, This was the Borgu Rebellion. 'A patrol was sent out to suppress the rebels and succeeded in dispersing them . . . '[12] Sabukki was arrested and gaoled, but escaped into the bush.

Clarke took advantage of the patrol's presence to make further high-handed and provocative administrative changes. He deposed the Emir of Kaiama, Sabijima, and put in his place Mashi, the unpopular newly imposed Sarkin Yashikera (endorsing this, Hamilton-Browne stated that 'the Borgawa are an indolent, drink-sodden people and need a strong man to rule them'[13]).

After an uneasy calm had been achieved under the guns of a second and third patrol, an official enquiry into the disturbances was held, and Clarke was blamed almost entirely, although all his 'reforms' had been endorsed by his Resident, Hamilton-Browne, and authorised by Headquarters. (This fact alone, assuming he learned it in Kontagora, must have given Cary pause for reflection.)

*　*

Cary spent ten days in Kontagora town. During this time, while he was learning about the Province and his responsibilities in Borgu, he had all his meals with Hamilton-Browne and his wife. He liked H.B., a charming, easy-going man with an impressive military record. Edwardes, meeting him in 1914, had found H.B. 'most interesting', with his yarns about exploits during Lugard's 1903 expedition against the northern Emirs. 'He has done 12 yrs service in West Africa, and has seen enough for one man.'[14]

But it is unlikely that H.B. told Cary many yarns – at least while his wife was present. Mrs H.B. was a shock for Cary. He left his first meal

> absolutely stunned by the most astonishing stream of talk I ever heard come out of a human creature . . . I have had long quotations from her children's letters, eulogies of her husband, floods and floods of tangled talk – the most intimate confidences. She calls all the juniors in the province by their christian names (she will be calling me by mine in no time) and says she is a terrible one for the boys. Yet she is obviously a devoted wife and mother. Of course I'd heard of her – she is famous – but she exceeds all my wildest dreams.

His patience dwindled with further exposure to her 'senseless chatter' and 'rather impertinent questions'. She asked 'if I was married, when, any children, what colour hair you had, how old you were, how I did it on my pay'. But he was disconcerted by her equally persistent generosity and kindness.[15]

Humorous though it is, this episode exposes limits to Cary's sympathy and understanding. Gertie responded to his accounts with 'poor Mrs H.B. – you have left the lady with no legs to stand on, certainly no intelligence and very little character . . . perhaps her two kindnesses in darning your sweater and making you a cake, made up for some of her failings . . .'[16] It does not seem to have occurred to him that, cut off from her family and friends in a strange country and a masculine environment, his superior's wife might be lonely and ill at ease. He had responded with notable sympathy, patience, even tenderness, to men in distress. But, in seeking to penetrate his reticence and force him into confidences, Mrs H.B. had obviously offended not only his personal code of conduct but the mores of the masculine communities that had helped to form it. Above all, in arrogating a maternal role, she seems to have intruded on the sacred ground surrounding the loss of his mother. His deepest uncertainties aroused, he found he could never 'make the right remark, and I suspect my solemn dullness only makes [her] worse' – 'I think H.B. thinks I am very reserved and cold – so do plenty of other people and you once upon a time.'[17]

Although the disastrous amalgamation of Yauri and Borgu was now to be abandoned, H. W. Cowper, the D.O. in charge of Yauri Division, who had been in charge of Borgu since Clarke's exit, would for the present retain control of north-east Borgu, just across the Niger from his station at Yelwa. Co-operation would be essential, and Cowper had important documents and advice to contribute. He and Cary were to travel together to Yelwa, where Cowper would officially hand over administrative responsibility for Borgu.

On first acquaintance, Cary found Cowper unprepossessing: 'a long ghost of a man, quite bald tho he is very little older than me, full of fever'.[18] But his opinion rose steadily as he found Cowper 'conscientious and methodical'; much later, he defined Cowper's personality as that of 'the banished earl, the diplomat'.[19] Cowper was to remember Cary as 'not an easy man to get on with' but 'very straight in all his dealings, highly intelligent and very critical of men and things'.[20]

They reached Yelwa on 11 May after 'a pleasant journey'. Cary quickly encountered problems. 'I find that whereas H.B. gave me [to] understand everything I wanted was at Yelwa, including records and papers I can't do without, these are not at Yelwa. So I am staying here worrying H.B. on the wire till I get 'em. Bussa has no wire, so I am not going away from the telegraph-line till I have what I want.'

As the days passed without remedy, Cary's confidence in Hamilton-Browne plummetted. 'Every day reveals deficiencies in my equipment and more wires go to H.B. Cowper says H.B. is one of those easy-going do-it-to-morrow men who leaves all his subordinate officers to make bricks without straw, unless the officers demand the straw frequently and urgently.' Which is what Cary did. He was obviously determined not to emulate the ill-fated Maltby by going into Borgu without the maximum preparation and protection available.

Nearly a week later, when there was still no response from Kontagora, he was becoming angry and worried. On 16 May he wrote 'I can't go without police so I must wait till I hear if I wait another week.'

But there were diversions. 'Cowper and I went shooting to-day over the Niger . . . and now I am delightfully tired and lazy after dinner and a cigar. I am going to one of the best places in Nigeria for big game – full of lion, elephant, buffalo and all the rest – it's a pity I can't see well enough to shoot – and at any rate I haven't a rifle.'[21]

Comments of this sort brought a rebuke from Freddy Ogilvie: 'I hear from Gertie that you are in the wildest of wild country. You, she says, are very cheerful; but she, poor child, is not: you must not paint the crocodiles and the ticks too big, old boy, whatever their size.'[22]

Other family letters, however, were a source of deep happiness during this pause at Yelwa. He read and re-read them, relishing each detail about his baby son. Arthur Cary wrote to say that Michael was 'a lusty specimen, and sound in every way.'[23] Mrs Ogilvie assured him that Michael was 'a splendid little fellow . . . he gazes about him in the perkiest way as if he was taking everything in, and criticizing his surroundings – like you!! . . .'[24]

Missing his own child, Cary began to look closely and sympathetically at the children all round him. 'There are twenty-five ladies from the bush here white-washing the office. Nearly all of them have babies, and I always go to have a look at them, as I pass. The baby is always slung on behind, in which position he sleeps most of the time – but you find 'em lying about all over the place at the same time, always very good and sound asleep . . . '. He even 'dared to make friends with one of the small black babies on her mother's back – when I held out my hand she accepted it quite gravely – these babies never smile – but are the quietest, stoutest little children imaginable.'

Another interest was the progress of the war. The previous year, at Nafada, there had been occasional euphoria, despite the huge losses at the Somme. Now Cowper received 'a bad Reuter about Russia, a candid Reuter for once, saying how near they are to anarchy over there'.[25] Heneage wrote a few months later, in near despair, from his hospital in France: 'It is a bloody war. One felt it might be doing some good while the wreck of cathedrals, starving of women and children, and the carnage of young men, was the worst. But it seems that tolerance and sincerity are fast disappearing: there is a kind of conscription of soul and intellect following on that of the body, which seems to be undoing all the work of civilisation . . . '[26]

Worried though he was by the war news, Cary, in remote Kontagora Province, was largely isolated from the cynicism now sweeping through his contemporaries in Europe as they recoiled from the seemingly endless spiral of suffering and destruction. The comic liveliness and comparative optimism of his mature writing, contradicting the general literary mood in Europe, surely owe something to this fact.

CHAPTER SEVENTEEN

A. D. O. BORGU

1917

'an immense black brain'

Cowper had told Cary that he would 'have to go down the Niger as far as Bussa (near where Mungo Park lost his life in the rapids)'.[1] On 3 June, Cary was established there and beginning to enforce his authority by reviewing the administrative situation. He was anxious to visit Kaiama as soon as possible, although he arrived in Borgu during the wet season, when there are frequent fierce thunderstorms. His annoyance at discovering one delaying administrative deficiency after another in Bussa provoked an outburst on 26 June, as he was finally about to leave for Kaiama after more than three weeks in Bussa:

> The state of this Province is rotten all through . . . and it won't wake up till we change the Resident . . . It's a bad province anyhow, with a wretched small population . . . so of course it is neglected, understaffed. 4 white men in a country as big as Wales. I believe I have a filthy trek tomorrow, with three rivers to cross, and no canoes, which means getting soaked to the neck, and the Emir insists on coming with me, so I will have a lot of fools prancing round me on half-broke horses all the way, and the drums and trumpets going for five hours.

His temper was little better the following night. Departure from Bussa had been attended by 'the wildest confusion – two policemen fighting with their wives [who did not want to travel 'on account of the wet'], about half-a-dozen people to see me on important matters which they had put off till the very day I was starting, and all the Emir's men rushing about on horseback and shouting.'[2]

Kaiama, however, was better in every way than he had expected, and he quickly decided it was preferable to Bussa. Not only was the town's situation infinitely more salubrious than humid, pestiferous Bussa, but Cary was impressed by its Emir, Yerima Kura, who had been appointed just months before Cary's arrival after Mashi had been found guilty of extortion and deposed. Yerima Kura also had good men in his Administration, like his Waziri, 'an intelligent and useful official'; in fact, the whole Native Administration of Kaiama was 'much better than Bussa'.[3]

Cary planned to set out as soon as possible on a tour of Kaiama Emirate (the most populous part of Borgu): 'trouble is apt to brew where the people are left alone too long. It is besides on the Dahomey border, and Dahomey is not so well administered as Nigeria . . . Our criminals all run over to Dahomey, and theirs come to us . . . The bungalow here is rather pleasant, though the floors are rotten and my foot has gone through in two places already . . . ' (As it was a two-storey bungalow, with Cary's living-quarters upstairs, this deficiency was not negligible!)

There was much to do in Kaiama itself. A priority was to rebuild the legal system. Every day Cary's precious time was largely taken up with adjudicating a backlog of minor domestic disputes. On 7 July, after 'another perfectly beastly morning in Court with case after case, all complicated to an extraordinary degree – no one telling the truth – no one telling a plain story – everybody convinced the right way and the only way to get a verdict is to flatter the judge as much as posible and lie like the devil,' he wrote that he was 'hurrying forward the establishment of native courts as fast as I can'.[4]

At this point, only six weeks after he had left Yelwa, he was fighting off depression. To judge by his letters to Gertie (although he may well have suppressed comment on this topic), he had not faced any outright opposition or threat of violence in either Bussa or Kaiama; and both Native Administrations were ready and even eager to co-operate in re-establishing order. But, only a few days after his arrival in Bussa, he had suffered a sharp reminder of his vulnerability and isolation. The account in his letter of 9 June gives some indication of the intensity of his reaction after he had 'nearly got bushed. Certainly I am the luckiest beggar on earth, I've always thought so, and have proved it again and again. I went for a walk and managed to lose my way . . . Most of the bush is pathless. You might walk 100 miles and never meet a soul. You dare not lie down at night, or some beast would eat you . . . I shall not lose my way again in a hurry . . . The last man I heard of who was bushed, was found eaten by ants . . . '[5]

But he *did* lose his way again, even more frighteningly, some months later. On this second occasion (he did not tell Gertie about it), he was 'hopelessly bushed', and even more fortunate to survive. In a draft of an autobiographical essay written in late middle age, he linked it with the traumatic childhood experience of losing himself in the woods at Tugwood soon after his mother's death.

I had walked out nearly due East into the jungle where I meant to look for a possible road-line. I came back, at dark, due West, and ran into a deep swamp . . . I had seen no sign of this enormous swamp on my outward journey, but now it seemed to enclose me. I was barred not only to the West but in every direction. When I tried to make my way back, I sank up to the waist, and when I probed the ground beyond with a polo stick I carried on such walks for just such a purpose, it could not find bottom. I stood helpless, and it was then that I had the feeling that I had been trapped by some power which was deliberately playing tricks on me, and that it was perfectly hopeless for me to struggle against its malice. It was not only able to change the landscape as it chose, putting swamps where dry ground was, and impenetrable jungle where the trees had stood open, but it meant to kill me.[6]

Such intuition of lurking menace gave expression to the potentially dangerous uncertainties of his social and political isolation. Supreme authority in a huge territory recently in turmoil, he was reliant on a staff of 'twelve police with single-shot carbines and ten rounds apiece; a Political Agent . . . who spoke the local languages and was supposed to be an expert on local affairs; and a couple of office messengers . . .'

> No one not placed in such a position can fully realise the sense of blindness and distrust which took possession of me in those first moments of solitude in Borgu. I say 'took possession' because it was at once like a foreign invader seizing my mind, and a kind of demon. I would wake up at night and feel as if the dark itself was an immense black brain, meditating, behind its formless countenance, some deep plan for a new and still more surprising outbreak.
> I could not forget that the last rising had been caused by nothing but the failure of the District Officer, in exactly my position, to know what was going on under his very nose . . .[7]

Not surprisingly, Cary was tense, watchful, uneasy. Soon after reaching Kaiama, loneliness began to afflict him. 'I would like to have someone to talk to for an hour or so,' he wrote on 3 July. 'I began to feel this to-day, when I came up from lunch, very tired, and passed an afternoon with nothing to do in it but more work and an evening with nothing to do but go for a walk by myself.' People who complain of loneliness in England, he continued, 'should be sent to Borgu for a few months, to read the same books over and over again, to get papers 6 weeks old, to eat chicken at every meal and yam, to play the same tunes on a degenerate acccordion, and never see a friendly face at all . . .' A few days later: 'I got so bored with myself at dinner I felt like throwing the lamp over the balcony.'

He was now struggling to avoid debilitating 'bush hates'. 'A bush hate,' he explained to Gertie, 'is one of those unreasoning fancies which seize you when you are alone in the bush. Everyone knows 'em out here. They lead sometimes to strange and even tragic results. I am always on my guard against them, and try and keep a balanced attitude.' And insomnia was another problem.

He was careful about his health, doing exercises every morning, walking every evening, taking quinine pills every day. He often entertained himself at night, and in one letter celebrated the visit of 'a famous accordion soloist' whose repertoire was rewarded by 'tremendous applause. Refreshments were served during the evening, and smoking was allowed . . .'

He had been writing, but spasmodically: 'I can't work with this unsettled bucketing life, here to-day and off to-morrow, and all my papers anyhow – since I'm not happy when I can't work I admit I'm depressed about it.' But reading was a consolation. At Bussa he had enjoyed 'reading the life of that admirable Benvenuto Cellini . . . I do delight in that rascal. He must have been a horrible brute to have any dealings whatever with, but what a man!'[8]

'the draft animal of the country'

After two weeks in Kaiama, Cary was satisfied that basic administration was functioning adequately. 'I'm off to-morrow early,' he wrote on 14 July, 'for what will prove I should fancy a very wet and uncomfortable journey of a fortnight or so through the neighbouring bush.' He would be touring a wide sweep of the towns and villages south-east of Kaiama town that held much of Borgu's population.

Often he found himself a cause of wonderment: 'two Fulani women came twenty miles especially to see me. They had never seen a white man before. They knelt modestly among their men folk, and peeped at me just out of one eye, then the other, topways, sideways, roundways, while their small babies gazed round wildly from behind their backs.' One village was completely empty. A lion had killed some of its inhabitants.

> The big chief then came and cast a spell on all the lions and three of them died. The village had however no sooner settled down than a Spirit came and played the drum all night in the top of a tree. This was too much for the villagers and they ran. But one does not laugh so easily at these things when one has spent some time in the middle of Africa. There is no place where the night is so full of strange noises, or where trees, hills, clouds and rocks take stranger shapes . . . I think I should try a scatter-gun on this ghost, but it is risky here to interfere with superstitions. You never know what you are up against, natural phenomena, a madman, a swindler, or a powerful secret organisation.

He remained at Ilesha, a large town near the southern border, for six days. Here a major trade route from the south entered Borgu, then passed through two other large towns, Okuta and Yashikera, and skirted the Dahomey border in running north towards the great distant city of Sokoto. At Ilesha, Cary concentrated on evaluating the tax on cattle, and quickly recognised that the local Kaiama officials had allowed evasion to flourish. He wrote excitedly to Gertie:

> Last year the Cow Tax brought in £200. And as the place has now been administered 15 years, it might be supposed the cows were well counted. With any luck I shall double this tax. I've put the fear of God in the mallams somehow, I don't know how, for I'm very polite, and already 2,000 cows have been miraculously discovered that weren't last year . . . I am beginning to know how to manage the black man . . . or think I do – the first thing is politeness, never be rude or violent – the second is patience, let 'em go slow if they want to as long as they are trying – the third is rigid justice, where a man wilfully does wrong and you're sure it's wilful, jump with both feet – the fourth is, explain to them carefully and exactly their work, and *why* it is important, why you want it done this way – then all you've got to do is watch, watch, watch, distrust everything you don't see yourself, check everything yourself . . . Of course there are a thousand cheateries going on I know nothing about, I daresay I shall still be defrauded of hundreds of cows

– but things promise better. I have no illusions about my own actual wisdom. I know the old rascals in the market-place could tell me a thing or two. Even if I knew my real nickname I daresay I should get a shock. My polite one for general use is Glass-eye, and all white men have two or three.[9]

From Ilesha he sent off a letter of information and queries to Hamilton-Browne. The reply was supportive: 'far from objecting to your touring I strongly approve of it – this Division cannot get too much touring'.[10]

Travelling on beyond Okuta, Cary noted 'dozens of family parties on this road, which is a great caravan route. First of all come the small boys and girls, then the wives, two or three, then a servant or two, all carrying loads, even the children, who carry one pot each, and lastly Papa with a large sword, and bow and arrows, very dignified, and *not* carrying a load. Why should he, is he not a *man*, a *married* man, and a *father*?'

As he turned east to return to Kaiama town at the beginning of August, Cary was pleased with himself. 'I can now see the end of my first Political operation of importance – the Cow Tax or Jangali . . . I've rather more than doubled this tax, without any fuss or nastiness whatever.' He would return to Kaiama for a few days, then go on to Bussa – but 'I shall have to go off pretty soon even when I get to Bussa, as there are . . . murderers to catch. But I hope to be able to sit down for the latter part of September and some [of] October too.'

He spoke too soon. The next day brought several official letters requesting detailed information about the Division – 'work like making bricks without straw,' Cary commented wryly, 'as returns are wasted when no statistics have been kept and reports where there is no material for a report. The A.D.O. is the draft animal of the country, he beareth the burdens. I have 7 districts to report on, and each town in each district, Forestry, Agriculture, Geology, History, Flora and Fauna, Genealogies and titles of chiefs as well as population, local industries, and crops and average income. However as Dad says it's a poor heart that never rejoiceth, I might be dead.'

His first tour of inspection gave Cary confidence and pleasure. He had learnt much about his domain and its peoples. He had applied Edwardes's administrative method, and the results were good – particularly among the Fulani whose cattle he had been enumerating. He had also enjoyed surmounting the physical challenge of trekking in the wet season.[11] 'My dear, I think I am cured of false modesty. I had to take off all my clothes to-day before 40 men and 20 women in order to swim a river, which I did in a helmet.' The pleasure he took in trekking is well expressed in a poem written, probably, much later:

Dawn comes like a ray through the sea
The trees stand up dark and still as memories
I tread out the memories of the present and look ahead
Far ahead is the cook with the kitchen-box
Far behind the flute of the carriers
When the sun climbs, I shall call for my pony
And when I reach camp, breakfast will be ready
Then under the thatch I shall smoke and feel satisfaction[12]

CHAPTER 18

PROBLEMS

1917–1918

'I have made great efforts'
On arrival in Kaiama, Cary faced a more intractable problem, Gertie:

> I see you have inwardly made up your mind about remaining in Nigers for good . . . I am not going to try and dissuade you dearest if you feel it is the best and only way for us both . . . but dear apart from having you away from me, it is so awful to have you in such a ghastly country, risking your health and perhaps your life every day . . . I know the work you do is splendid, and that it should be done by someone keen and capable, but I think you mean to stick to it merely for financial reasons and because you think there is nothing else you can do . . .[1]

Deeply disturbed by her letter, he replied at length on 10 August:

> My dearest, I was made awfully unhappy by some things in your letter, where you say I have decided irrevocably to stay in Nigeria, and that I am wasting both our lives. My darling I have decided nothing . . . I would give anything to be with you always, surely my dearest you know how miserable I am to leave you. But have you considered what educating children costs? I would be a selfish beast to give up a sure income merely to gratify myself, at your and your children's expense. Do you not suppose life is dear to me? Do you not think I feel this exile from all I hold most dear, and the only things I like in material life, letters and books and pictures? I dare not look forward to all the years, or think that this climate may shorten my life . . . This is the only alternative, that I find some other way of making an income . . . The only aptitude I seem to have is writing. It is a poor enough hope in these days of specialists and competition, for an amateur, in a harassing occupation and cut off from all human intercourse, to make a name for himself sufficient to allow him to throw up a certain income and a pension, when he has a wife and children, for such a business as writing. But it's the only chance. I have made great efforts this tour already and written as much as would make three novels, but never finished anything. You may call me all the bad names you like, I deserve them. Here is my only chance, and I

151

haven't the application to carry it through. But remember, or try to imagine, my difficulties . . . Give me only two months of peace, I might do something . . . I mean two months under decent conditions. I may sit down to work to-day. To-morrow will be spent on horseback, and I could not think of a word if I tried when I get in. The day after I am all day at rotten petty cases, and then another afternoon in which I can work. But I have forgotten all about my intentions. The bit I wrote yesterday won't hook on. I don't get even Sundays to myself at work like this. Yet I know how much depends on this, and I am still making valiant efforts.

Gertie had responded to his request for novels by Hardy. He enjoyed and admired *The Woodlanders,* but *Jude the Obscure* 'reduced [me] to such a condition, I had to go and hide in case the boys would see me', and a night later he could not sleep because 'the story of those hopeless lovers and the frightful cruelty their love suffered and caused them, made me nervous and panic-stricken about us.' Depressed and angry he then exploded into a tirade about colonial mismanagement.

The problem of his continuance in Northern Nigeria was to return, and exacerbate the tension within him. But the next day, as he was preparng to leave for Bussa, the psychological crisis set off by Gertie's letter was over. 'I see that I was in a bush hate . . . Really I've not any reason to complain about the poor old Government. I seem to carry on all right, and even save money.'[2] But that depressive episode, and others he endured in Nigeria, disturbed him deeply: destroying a self-control that he knew to be precarious, they drove his personality and opinions from calm rationality to frenzied emotion. As in the traumatic act of violence at Yola, he then surprised in himself a destructive personality, the opposite of his usual creative self, and immune to his will. His mature writing would explore that duality.

'a new masterpiece'
Back in Bussa, Cary found he had 'two months' arrears of Bussa work to make up – I have to report on the Value of Oysters for Lime-producing, how much does it cost to collect 'em, the Cow Tax, with names of all the herdsmen, Markets and Ferries, Trade, Police, Courts, General Politics, and the Chiefs. When I'm not writing, I'm dashing round looking at piles of oyster shells, which are always in the middle of a damn swamp, I find. They're going to make cement of 'em, and various bigwigs are presently excited about 'em, and can hardly sleep at night till I report.'

He was cheerful again, finding constant interest and pleasure in his surroundings. Children continued to divert him, and he wrote with great warmth and affection after some of them had visited him while he was 'lounging in a chair after lunch reading an ancient paper and smoking'.

He delighted, too, in Borgu's fauna:

When I peeped under an old bed I use for papers, to-day, I saw five toads sitting in a group on the pile of stationery as calm as you please. They didn't move even when my face was only a few inches from them. I rather like all these beasts in the house, they make it more cheerful – birds fly in and out of the place all day, and at night they have arguments in the roofs sometimes, or wake up for a moment and chirrup. There are not so many lizards now, or perhaps it's the wet that keeps them away.

The toad family took up residence on the stationery. 'Old mother toad (I think she is) simply never moves at all. The others wink sometimes but she doesn't even wink. She is rather squarer than the rest poor dear, and has quite lost her figure. In fact she is shaped just like a pat of butter that has been dropped out of a fourth-story window on to the pavement.'

And he conducted long-distance debates with Gertie on topics of the day. For instance:

> You are quite bitter against anyone who thinks we are winning the war, and give poor Lloyd George some cruel backhanders for not agreeing with you . . . So far from it being the case that braggarts are generally liars, and accomplish nothing at all, my experience is that they often have a great deal more to brag about than the silent strong man so popular in the bookstall. A man who thinks himself big, frequently does big things because his self-confidence allows him to tackle big problems . . .

As he continued his daily stint at 'The Episode' (as he called the novel), he meditated on literary issues too.

> Did you notice that Hardy has separate ideals for men and women, his men passionate or at least normal males, his women tending to cold-bloodedness? But I'm not sure if he doesn't choose these women to assist him in the exposition of his bitter humour. Because a cold-blooded woman can play the devil in the world, while fancying herself all the virtues. I don't mean a prude, for Hardy is too much of an artist to use such a vile coarse instrument as a prude to point his moral. A prude is a moral eunuch and just as nasty on the moral plane as the physical eunuch in its.[3]

Towards the end of September, after six weeks of sustained effort, Cary again ran into difficulties with his writing:

> I've had one of my bad days to-day about my work and done nothing . . . I have been worried as usual as to its purposes. I don't mean moral or material purpose, that is no concern of mine unless I want to confuse the issue hopelessly. What I want to do is to say what I have to say in the simplest possible manner, about everything that interests me anywhere. This 'manner' is the difficulty. I seem sometimes to be too florid, sometimes too narrow, sometimes I have too large and full a canvas with too many figures, sometimes too bare and small with too few. You see, my characters are me, but I can just as easily put forty me's in a book as one or two – there are more than enough to go around. But 40 would not have room in which to deploy . . . In my book now I have no great number, but to-day I began to fear they were yet too many, and all too important.

A few days later he abandoned 'The Episode', as he had abandoned its predecessor in Nafada. He began another 'story' – 'at least the 20th of this tour,' he told Gertie, 'and none finished'. But this time he was philosophical about the failure. 'Aren't I an extraordinary bird, at 28 1/2 years of age, to go on in this hopeless way, always beginning with the firmest vows, never finishing, and starting again at once on a new masterpiece generally with an entirely new plan of campaign. Yes, I am, but I suppose I was built hopeful, and despairing too. I go up and down like a seesaw.'[4]

'I am really coming home'

As September ended, Cary knew that his tour of duty would soon be over, even though all tours had been lengthened by the war and leaves were granted only on medical recommendation. His life in Borgu, though unsettled, had achieved some order. He had now been on his own for four months, and, he told Gertie, 'I've done really a good deal of work of all sorts, official and otherwise, and I've found out a good deal about myself. One does in solitude. I often wondered how I would stand being alone.'

He was very busy in the office. On 2 October he proudly 'fired off a mass of returns and reports', only to receive, two days later, 'orders to get all the Land Tax in before I return even to the civilisation of Kontagora for a day or so – that means at the very least another month and probably two in Borgu. But unless I am so absurdly well in two months that I daren't go before the doctors, I shall then try for leave, or at the latest at the end of the year. I may stay if fit to the end of the year, if only to round off my work.'

In fact, he was far from 'absurdly well'. He had been suffering from 'a back ache, an eye-ache, a headache, a wrist-ache, an ache all over'. He recovered quickly, but within a month had a bad cold, and at the end of October had neuralgia and tooth-ache. The wet season was almost over, but Bussa was, if anything, more unpleasant as the heat increased. 'I am sweating profusely now, and can hardly see through my glasses for steam. This place will be like a Turkish bath soon . . . My clothes are nearly all rotten already . . .'[5] He longed to 'fly off to Kaiama'.

His first tour of duty in Borgu ended by keeping him in the office – and, after all, in Bussa. Late in October he was busy 'clearing up for Diggle', the A.D.O. who would, so H.B. said, soon arrive to take over. 'I shall have to write special reports for him and so on,' Cary explained, 'because he is taking over in the middle of things and must be told what's going on . . .' And on 6 November the last of the Land Tax arrived in Bussa. The total was £1,800, 'in shillings, sixpences, threepennies, pence, halfpence and even tenths'! 'I have had my nose in paper all day writing out summaries and working out percentages of incidences – shewing what percent a man pays or a woman pays or the whole population pays. All these returns are on huge sheets of paper which are a great nuisance on a breezy day. I work in nothing but a vest and slacks but it is dashed hot even then.'

He was trying to restrain his excitement at the prospect of setting out to rejoin Gertie and meet his year-old son. There were frustrating delays and changes of plan. Diggle was not coming – Cowper would relieve him 'as soon as some old dug-out called Captain Blake arrives' – no, 'Diggle is coming after all. Someone has made a muddle. So I don't know when I will get away.'

Then came news that Diggle was on his way. 23 November: 'I have canoes arranged to bring him right down the river just below the house. I am quite excited at the notion of meeting him. It's more than six months now since I saw a white man. I daresay I am more shy than I was.' 24 November: 'DARLING, I really do think now that I am really coming home. Diggle wrote to me to-night from a day's march away, to say he will arrive to-morrow morning.' 25 November: 'Diggle came to-day. This is awfully late and we have been talking 10,000 words a minute ever since he came, he is a good bird . . . I shall want to sleep most of the leave and you must not keep me awake as you used to do with kicking me to pieces and snoring like a grampus, or leaving hairs lying about.'[6]

That his first tour of duty in Borgu was administratively successful is attested not only by his own satisfaction but also by his Resident's comment on it for the Governor: 'The task of organising the Native Administration of Bussa and Kaiama fell to Mr Cary . . . and he has done remarkably well – I have the highest opinion of his ability.'[7]

'doubts and misgivings'

Cary's journey home on a six-month leave was uncomfortable and perilous. Several ships plying between Britain and West Africa had been sunk by German mines and submarines, so there was tension and crowding on the remnant – Cary remembered sleeping in passageways to escape 'stifling cabins with the ports closed'.[8] But even in wartime conditions Elder Dempster mailboats offered some attractions after Borgu: he remarked to a friend much later that he had 'adored the boat in the old days from West Africa when we had been living for months in a mud hut and eating nothing but African chickens, which taste of sand and burnt feathers, and no butter and milk or potatoes, and baths in a thing like a saucer lid. I simply ate and slept all day and talked Service gossip . . .'[9]

He reached England on 5 February 1918.

> A miserable cold misty morning in the estuary. We steamed up slowly at dawn, and were promptly ordered to go back again. Then recalled – and expecting to get ashore after breakfast. Then the long day with Alien officers, custom officials, stevedores and porters. The rush up to town – I just caught the Harrow train – and the two other men in the carriage, returning from business, looked at me casually as if I was not returning to a wife and son from 18 months in countries they have probably never heard of. Then the hopelessness of the wait at the station – no cabs – thick fog. The walk –

And suddenly, when least expected, a brush with death as he was hurrying on foot up to The Glade. Out of the thick fog came a 'runaway horse, which sent me flying'. Shaken and confused, he then lost his way. 'What a pretty tragedy it would have been if the shaft had hit me instead of missing me by two inches. "Poor young man killed within a mile of home" . . . But I was born to escape this sort of thing – I shall not die a violent death.'[10]

He and Gertie went on a week's holiday together at an inn on the Somerset coast, and walked the twenty miles between Porlock and Countisbury, and were happy. Back at The Glade, he was to be found 'sitting in the schoolroom smoking a pipe and engrossed in a book – talking with father in the dining room over another pipe – arguing with Mother at dinner with one arm over the back of your chair – going a walk with me round the common – or coming into my room in the evening to do me up for dinner'. After dinner he made a fourth for games of Bridge. But he would escape up to the attic in the morning to write, 'sitting at the little table in the attic in your old tweed coat.'

There was Michael to be cherished and admired, and coped with. Gertie wrote 'I always think of the mornings in our room – when the wee mon climbed on you – was deposited on the floor – and then we used to listen in fear [for] the expected sounds of escaping gas, or upset water.' There were discussions, some of which turned into arguments. One was about 'the respective "business" of men and women . . . I remember you mentioned that women's so-called duties at home – housekeeping, looking after children, daily housework of servants . . . are quite unnecessary, and that husbands would get on just as well if their wives didn't order the dinner for them but read *The Times* instead.'[11]

In March they had a massamora after she refused twice to kiss him; and when they quarrelled at a play ironically entitled *The Naughty Wife*, he sat in misery, watching her 'lips tremble, and the tears run down (in spite of the chocolate)'.[12]

The tension had several causes. Although his health was far better than during the summer of 1916, he had to have an operation on his nose in April (a consequence of the old schoolboy injury) and was 'pulled down by it'.[13] More importantly, there was the ever-advancing shadow of his return to Nigeria, and the disagreement between them that it focused. Her 'pesterings' on the subject, and the Ogilvie conviction that he should remain in England with his wife and son, provoked irritation and guilt that he struggled to suppress.

Linked to this was the problem of their accommodation. The small house in London that Gertie longed for seemed now to be out of their financial reach. Moreover, Mrs Ogilvie had written to Cary some months earlier to say she would like Gertie to remain at The Glade. His response had been ambiguous: 'Of course it is always better for you to be with them,' he had told Gertie, 'especially when I am away, but it seemed to me I would be shirking my responsibilities if I didn't take you off their hands sometime.'[14] Mrs Ogilvie's health was deteriorating, and there was ever-increasing difficulty in finding servants to keep the large house running to her standards. Should Cary now make another attempt to find a house for Gertie?

Again the question became academic, and for the same reason. Two months before Cary's departure, Gertie learned she was pregnant. For the second time he would be away for the birth of a child. For the second time she would have to cope on her own until the child was over a year old. She must remain at The Glade.

That the pregnancy was unintentional and ill-timed was the outcome of another cause of marital tension. Gertie, like most young women of her class and generation, had married in sexual ignorance. 'You say you had help from men who had talked to you but you see I had no one to consult, or to help and advise me – no woman had ever spoken to me about marriage . . . I must have disappointed you the very first day of our marriage . . .'[15]

In the letters they exchanged during Cary's next tour of duty, they faced the problem with mutual courage and sympathy. When, several months, after the birth of their second son, Peter, Cary wrote openly of his suspicion that 'you only consented to bodily love, because you knew it was your duty, or because you wished to for my sake,'[16] she responded eagerly: 'Your letter was a relief to me. I have had awful doubts and misgivings all the time too – I realised the disappointment of last leave – and if you hadn't spoken about it I should have dreaded what might happen next leave. The whole sky was clouded . . .' And she explained that she had been longing for him to speak all through the leave, 'but I know how difficult it was for you', and

> From the beginning I seemed tongue tied. I thought, you were putting all the responsibility on me, and I tried to find out what you really wanted – and then everything seemed to get worse . . . Dearest it was because I loved you and wanted you that I felt there was something between us which we couldn't break down. And which made me think you were not happy with me as you had been, and this made me doubly shy and sensitive – and perhaps it was this which made me appear cold to you sometimes.[17]

Because he had come to fear that they 'could not live together in marriage' he had 'suggested ways of living apart – and I thought you wished that and was unhappy about it.' He admitted his own failings of ignorance, reticence and evasion, and advised her to read books by Marie Stopes, especially *Wise Parenthood*. 'When I came home . . . I suggested that we ought not to have another baby too soon. I see now that I seemed to throw the responsibility at you, as you say, and I should not have done that. But that is the strong point Mrs Stopes makes – that babies ought not to be born too near together. She says at least 3 years should elapse between . . .'

Writing openly about the problem was as much a relief for him as for her.

> My dear dear Gertie, I love you so much that it is impossible to speak of failure, or anything like failure. I have been happier than I thought possible, and every day since I married has proved to me more surely the difference of my life now, and before, when I was really alone. I cannot tell you how deeply I feel – it is much love, but much gratitude too – for all you are to me. It is impossible to think of life without you.

And he assured her that during the leave 'I was never disappointed – I was afraid. I thought sometimes I might be doing wrong – offending you or hurting you, and I could not make out how you really felt. But I loved you passionately as I love you now, and I was not disappointed.'[18]

In the summer of 1918, however, their marital problem was still stoically repressed. When he went aboard the S.S. *Burutu* at Liverpool on 29 July 1918, they endured a parting darkened by a war still grinding out its detritus of suffering and death; and by their deep personal anxieties.

CHAPTER NINETEEN

TRIALS & REPORTS

1918–1919

'my own master again'

The voyage to Lagos was unpleasant. Cary was not only depressed by his parting from Gertie, he also had a bad cold that, by the third night out, had brought on an attack of asthma. His inside cabin, shared with two other men (one of them frequently drunk), was stifling. His table companions, unlike those of his previous voyage out, were unimpressive; and he was so angered when one of them said with apparent sarcasm 'What I like is your sparkling wit!' that 'I turned on him, and said "Are you trying to be rude to me, Pearce," and then lost my temper and said more than I meant. My exact words were "because if you are, I'll push your face through your neck and bloody quick too".' He was 'shaking with rage', and afterwards commented 'One reason why I am usually so careful of my tongue, is that if I do let it go, my temper goes too . . . I've not done such a thing for a long time now, and thought I had better control of myself.'[1]

Wartime conditions – travelling in convoy, mine-sweeping – not only created tension but lengthened the voyage to over three weeks. The *Burutu* reached Lagos safely; but two months later went down with the loss of 150 lives. Gertie wrote at that time 'Isn't it extraordinary that the "Abasso" and the "Burutu", and I believe the steamer you first went out in should all have been sunk – God has kept you safe for me.'

Cary had told Gertie that he wanted to go back to Borgu Division because he 'already knew it and the people know me'; and he was 'keen on being my own master again'.[2] He got his wish, but was anxious for news of Gertie before 'going further and further from mails every day'. From Kontagora town he would 'have a long 10 or 12 days ride to Kaiama (Borgu headquarters are now at Kaiama) and pass no post office . . . I hear I am to get Duty Pay this tour, £80 a year. This is partly because the revenue went up a good deal last year . . .'[3]

Cary set off for Borgu worried about the news from home. The baby was due in November. Gertie had been feeling tired, ill and depressed; 'I sometimes feel I cannot bear all the years of separation that lie in front of us,' she added. Her parents had just decided to sell The Glade and buy a smaller house; Mr Ogilvie, distressed both by the decision and its main cause, his wife's poor health, wanted to move as quickly as possible; already furniture was being sold.[4]

Cary reached Bussa on 8 October. 'Here I am in the old house. The walls are a year more ruinous, and the roof is new. Otherwise it is the same, and I wish I were somewhere else. I shall be glad to leave it. I remember too many lonely weeks in this place.' He had just heard that a murderer had been caught in Kaiama. 'Rather a nuisance if I have to hang a man. I shouldn't like that at all. I haven't a notion how it is done, and I don't know how I should feel either. It is rather hard to have to try a man and hang him too. I would much rather have him shot.'[5]

'Now hang me, judge'

Cary conducted the case of Rex v. Jarimi, on 2 December 1918 in Kaiama. It is significant not only for provoking the deep apprehension about hanging a man which became a germ of *Mister Johnson*, but also for the lasting impression made on him by the murderer, Jarimi:

> a leper was brought before me for the murder of his wife's lover. He admitted the murder and said, laughing, 'Now hang me, judge.' I explained that no murderer was allowed to plead guilty, and the case went on. It was proved that he had loved his young wife but that she revolted from his leprous hands . . . All the time the prisoner kept laughing and saying 'Now hang me, judge'.
>
> I had no intention of hanging him, if I could possibly help it, and as, by Nigerian custom, I was in the position of counsel for defence, as well as judge, I took the first occasion, during an interval, to explain to the prisoner that even though he had killed a man, he might not be guilty of murder. Provocation could reduce the charge to manslaughter . . . The man, young, well built, still handsome and marked only in his hands by the pink patches of the disease, turned his smiling face to me and suddenly became furious. He struck both fists against his chest with the gesture of one in unendurable pain and said 'What else can I do – what else can I do.'[6]

In his summing-up, Cary noted that there *had* been provocation, in that Jarimi had had reason to believe that his wife's lover intended to take away his child as well as his wife. Cary's verdict was, unavoidably, Guilty; his sentence was Death with a recommendation to mercy; and, after the requisite review of the case by the Chief Justice of Northern Nigeria, the sentence was reduced to fifteen years' imprisonment.[7]

Told that he had been reprieved, Jarimi looked at Cary 'with an expression of stupid astonishment as if I had hit him on the head with a club,' then 'inclined his head towards my shoulder and smiled to himself . . . I have seen that same smile, neither derisory nor spiteful, on an Irish peasant's face, when I asked him why he was in debt; and on the face of a child when suddenly accused by the school bully of insolence . . .'[8] The smile of a human being in the face of life's remorseless injustice, a smile of helplessness. For Cary that smile was emblematic.

Two other killings involved witchcraft. Cary had already tried several minor witchcraft cases, and had found them problematic because of the sharp cultural contradictions they raised. In August 1917 he had wrestled with an old man's complaint that all his children had been killed by his brother through witchcraft; the cause of death was smallpox, but the old man refused to listen to this explanation, and Cary had been forced to handle him with great care because 'Dozens of people came up to hear the case, and feeling might easily run to bloodshed'.

The first of the two major cases was tried on 5 July 1919, and resulted from information, Cary told Gertie, about 'A man and two women killing a baby – because it was a witch!!'[9] Bio, the dead child's grandfather, had given her to an old woman called Kokode. In his summing-up, Cary stated

> It should I think be remembered that Bio acted under the very real fear of a witch-child, that Kokode obeyed what she thought a very simple request . . . The evidence of Farji is typical of the local attitude – that under the circumstances Bio had every reason to want to get rid of his granddaughter. Nevertheless, the evidence of the Sarkin Kudu shows a more enlightened view which is already widely held, and will increase rapidly in the future. Already among most of this tribe and their cognates it is usual to give some harmless medicine to babies born with teeth or on their face, instead of killing them . . .[10]

Again Cary recommended mercy, and again the Chief Justice concurred. In his unpublished 1936 Preface for *The African Witch*, Cary gave further information about the old woman Kokode

> whose profession was finding out witch babies and burying them alive at a fee of one to three shillings a time. Any child might be judged a witch. This old woman had been killing children for at least thirty years. During the last twenty she had practised within half a mile of the successive British district officers in charge of the division . . .
>
> To punish this old woman would have been stupid as well as unjust. It could have done no good. It would only have proved the power of the witches who had finally destroyed her. I was obliged to sentence her. But her punishment, in actual fact, was a government job with good pay. I made her cook to the native prison where she could be watched . . .[11]

The only cure for witchcraft, he insisted, was education.

The death that resulted in the second witchcraft case occurred near Agwarra. Four men were accused of responsibility for the death of a young woman. Cary's summing-up:

> Yigbani, the wife of a younger brother Dogo, was accused of witchcraft and immediately beaten and tied up. In her terror she promised to reveal the real witch, but was even unable to invent a name for her. She then took the opportunity to escape into the bush, and having her arms tied, either died of starvation or was killed by beasts . . .
>
> It should be remembered that the prisoners tho' guilty of a cruel injustice,

did not intend the result, that this is the first prosecution of the kind in this neighbourhood, and a long sentence to these bush-pagans, involving transfer to a central gaol, would be certainly a sentence of death, as they would pine away.[12]

Cary drew on those witchcraft cases in the first and third novels he published, *Aissa Saved* and *The African Witch*.

The fourth major case did not concern pagan Borgawa tribemen, as the first three had, but a Muslim member of Cary's own staff. From the beginning of his mandate in Borgu, he had depended heavily on Musa, the Political Agent, as adviser and interpreter. Musa was 'my professional diplomat and agent . . . He offered his gifts, as negotiator and adviser on local affairs, as a soothsayer of local feeling, to the highest bidder. He had belonged to two Emir's courts before he came to me.'[13] A cordial relationship had developed between the two men. So it was a very unpleasant shock for Cary when Musa was accused of corruption.

Cary tried the case on 4 November 1919.

Musa sweated, literally poured with sweat, in his indignation and outraged virtue; the Chief of Ilesha, a witness said to have bribed Musa, who is over six feet high, of frightful emaciation, and a hideous cold protruding eye, with every line of his debauched countenance speaking his guile, treachery and folly, fluted in a high voice one contradiction after another, the Mallam rolled his white eye in the background with a look of concentrated malice and venom difficult to imagine, and the Emir in the middle sat unmoved and calm, and probably half asleep. Musa got off for lack of evidence. It's impossible to say whether he took the money. There's no doubt he combined with S[arkin] Ilesha, who is the worst ruling chief in Borgu, and a dangerous knave . . .[14]

To some extent this case repeated the situation near the beginning of Cary's first tour, when, alone in Nafada, he had been faced with the 'corruption' of a respected official. In the three earlier major Borgu cases Cary had shown sensitive consideration of cultural differences and their ethical implications. Of Musa, however, he believed the worst, even when deeply suspicious of the complainants' motives.

But the public humiliation and suffering of his Political Agent taught Cary again how easily, and unjustly, loyalty and generosity of spirit could be discarded by the powerful; and his ultimate assessment of Musa, as implied by the dedication of *Mister Johnson*, with its accompanying quotation 'Remembered goodness is a benediction', is surely a retrospective acknowledgement that he had not sufficiently valued Musa's good heart when in Borgu, had allowed wariness and legalism to obscure the much more important personal qualities of a man who did a difficult job as honourably as possible.

Apart from those major cases, Cary had to try many minor cases. Even when he was the sole judge, there were often severe problems. 'I loathe cases as a rule because it is so difficult to discover the real truth,' he confessed to Gertie, 'and so easy to be unjust.'

When both Administrations were involved, however, political factors complicated judgement, as the principles of Indirect Rule became relevant. Just after trying the case against Musa, for instance, Cary and the Emir of Kaiama together

> tried the Chief of Okuta for an extraordinary piece of injustice. I said I wanted to turn him out. The Emir wants to give him another chance. I shall submit it to Hammy, and suggest that we take the Emir's advice, as tho' the fellow is useless, I want the people to see that the Emir is not a cypher. Neither do I want the Emir to feel that his advice is only a matter of form. The only way to make men do their work well is to give them responsibility, and take the risk of a few failures by the way. And that is exactly our plan out here. To teach these people to rule, by letting them practise the art.[15]

Cary had also learnt the value of judiciously circumventing the strict letter of the law if the result was likely to be beneficial. Sabukki, the leader of the 1915 Borgu Rebellion, was still at large, a potential cause of unrest. During Cary's six-month absence, Diggle had recommended that Sabukki and his supporters should be pardoned. E. C. Duff, while Acting Resident of Kontagora had supported Diggle's opinion: 'The application for the amnesty is based on the fact that all efforts to capture him have proved fruitless, that his presence in the country as an outlaw is a latent cause of disaffection; that his pardon would be a most popular event; and that his crimes were the outcome of harsh and injudicious treatment by the Administration.' But Headquarters had seen the recommendation as 'A confession of weakness on the part of Govt', and turned it down.[16]

Cary's attempted to resolve the problem by 'letting it be known that if [Sabukki] surrenders himself I'll give him a short sentence.'[17] His plan did not succeed; but it helped his authority and reputation; Cary is remembered to this day in Borgu for his refusal to persecute a man now revered as a nationalist leader.[18]

As he proved during his second period in Borgu, Cary was an able magistrate, sensible and sensitive, aware of the complexities of cultural diversity; able to work amicably and creatively within the constraints of Indirect Rule. Yet he was never content merely to endorse the status quo, if he was convinced reform was important and practicable. On 29 January 1919, for instance, he wrote from Bussa to tell Gertie, with his usual self-deflating humour,

> I spent the morning making a code of Criminal Law – Justinian was left at the post. You see the pagan courts administer pagan law – as far as it is compatible with more modern ideas of justice. In marriage and divorces especially improvements are required.[19]

Apart from giving him material he later used in novels, the cases Cary tried in Borgu sharpened his understanding of human nature and the problematic nature of truth and justice.

'interesting and practical work'

Diggle's decision to move the Borgu Divisional Office from Bussa to Kaiama, although it exacerbated Borgu's political problems in the long term, added greatly to the pleasure and achievement of Cary's second tour of duty there. When he arrived on 16 October 1918, he was immediately impressed by the vegetable garden Diggle had established near the bungalow. There were even thirty mango trees, 'but they are very small just yet. I shall watch them grow all the year. I feel quite a gardener already. Do you think you could get any seeds?'

Only worry about Gertie seriously disturbed his equilibrium, and he succumbed to a brief bush hate when, yet again, no letters arrived. But by the next day he had retrieved his balance: 'I was so busy all day that I had hardly time to be troubled about mails, and now I am resigned to what cannot be helped or avoided. All morning tax was coming in and I was entering and answering official letters, and this afternoon I had not yet finished the mail. I can't go off for a day or two yet as I have all the monthly accounts yet to do, and reports on the Native Courts and so on – Prison Returns and Police Returns.'[20]

Apart from the routine office work now familiar to him, he was to compose a full Assessment Report of the Kaiama District and, until it was completed, would not be able to go further afield. This suited him well while he was anxiously awaiting news about Gertie. He made a series of short excursions to villages around the town, collecting information for the Report. By early November it was taking shape and he was busy 'describing the different processes of beer-brewing, mat-making, dyeing, weaving, spinning, and the intricacies of the butcher's trade, and working out the average profits of each, to find out what taxes they ought to pay.' As he travelled around Kaiama District Cary gained not only information but an increasingly sympathetic understanding of the people and their circumstances. He was also reinforcing his conviction that, although truth and justice were relative, although cultural differences might be profound, there were fundamental values and modes of behaviour common to all humanity.

The Assessment had pushed him into map making, which gave him as much pleasure as the rest of his assessment work, and when, some months later, he discovered that a 'large beautifully printed map – by the War Office' had placed the Niger River ten miles off course, he crowed with delight. His own maps were meticulously researched, and he found the final penmanship particularly absorbing – 'I suppose it's the old love of drawing redivivus.'

His method of gathering the requisite information had to be 'the simplest kind – where one goes along a road taking bearings all the way – and judging the distance from bearing to bearing. Thus the work is checked when one puts it down because when one comes back by another road to the place one started from, the last bearing and the last distance should be correct on the map. So far mine seems to be right.' (In fact, Cary's maps of Borgu were so accurate that they were in official use decades later.)

He enlisted the help of his office scribe, 'a weedy and weakly youth of 18' called Lafia. From a village over thirty miles from Kaiama, Cary sent him 'to measure a road with the help of the kitchen clock – i.e., to write down the time he took to reach various points'. Unfortunately, Lafia 'had picked up the notion that he ought to do the whole road in one day'. He reached Kaiama in extreme exhaustion.[21]

Cary did not forget Lafia, or his feat. As he revealed in his Prefatory Essay for *Aissa Saved*, the character Ali, on whom the book originally centred, was largely based on him. Lafia was 'a chief's son from the Government school . . . I still remember . . . his efficiency and exact devotion to the job. He was a new kind of helper; he had quite different standards of conduct from anyone else in the administration.'[22]

While praising Lafia's courage and endurance, and the strong sense of duty inculcated by his 'English' education, Cary also recognised how vulnerable these qualities made him, differentiating him from his fellows by subjecting him to the mores of a different culture. There is something of Lafia in Mister Johnson.

On 3 January 1919, after more than two months of hard work, the Report was ready for submission: '108 pages of close-written foolscap – about 20 statistical tables – a map as big as this table – and a separate double sheet, apart from the report, for every village. This is only for one district out of the seven in my dominions. I feel very lordly sometimes . . . Unfortunately most of the inhabitants are leopards, antelopes, snakes and monkeys. But the Revenue is about £4,000 and that's not bad.'[23]

Cary completed two Assessment Reports during this tour of duty – the second, of Yashikera District to the west, was submitted eight months later. Both were cogent, carefully organised, clearly written. The Kaiama Report was received with 'approval' by Kaduna. The Yashikera Report was hailed by the Secretary of the Northern Provinces as 'excellent . . . one of the best submitted to Headquarters recently. I am sending this report to His Excellency to note the good work being done by Mr Cary.' The new Governor, Clifford, was equally complimentary: 'A very interesting and informative Report for which, in my opinion, Mr Cary and the Resident deserve great credit. It is particularly satisfactory to note the very close scrutiny which has been brought to bear upon local conditions etc.'[24] In his *Revolt in Bussa*, Michael Crowder commented that 'From the historian's point of view it is only a pity that the painstaking Cary did not carry out a re-assessment of Bussa'.[25] Comparing Cary's two Assessment Reports with others of the period, one is struck by their wealth of detail based on careful observation and questioning, by his interest in the Borgawa as individuals, and by his emphasis on crafts, manufacturing and small trading (which are clearly seen, and welcomed, as a nascent co-operative network).

Cary argued, in both Reports, for administrative reform. He regarded the existing poll tax as 'an antiquated and unequal system' because rich and poor paid the same sum; and in the Kaiama Report claimed that, with the support of the Emir, he had successfully introduced a modified form of income tax.[26] One of his successors, Hoskyns-Abrahall, disagreed totally with Cary in 1922, arguing that 'The village heads, almost without exception, are quite incapable of anything but collecting from each individual an exact amount that he and the individual both know to be the sum wanted . . . To introduce an income tax is simply to ask for trouble and peculation . . .'[27] Cary's concern for equity, and especially the wellbeing of the poor, was, no doubt, a further expression of Edwardes's influence; but it also indicates his fundamentally economic perspective as an administrator, his democratic meliorism, and his readiness to risk a premature devolution of responsibility in the interest of fairness.

While he was working on the Kaiama Assessment Report, Cary decided that the Native Administration needed a new Treasury. The building went up quickly: 'It is rather pleasant to be able to design a house on Thursday, and see the walls already five feet high on Sunday.' A mud structure 'in the Moorish style', it was to have windows 'like the windows of Stamboul', he told Gertie – 'Stamboul is for them the legendary capital of the world.'[28] In this way Cary adapted his experience of nationalistic art in Edinburgh and Montenegro, and left an aesthetic mark on Kaiama's architecture (the present Chief's Palace incorporates doorways that imitate the windows of the Treasury Cary designed).[29]

As his birthday approached, Cary fell into a short gloom: 'My work is hopeless – I can't do anything. I don't believe – sometimes I don't believe that I ever will do anything. I am 30 in three days, and someday will be 60 if I live so long, and then perhaps I will say what I say now – what have I done with the years?' But he knew that his depression had more immediate causes, 'the strain of waiting for, and never getting, any news'; and a cold he could not shake off, 'this wretched slow illness, which leaves me still a rat for weakness'.

On 18 December the long-hoped-for wire arrived and he burst into a paean of relief and joy: 'Darling love, I've just had the GLORIOUS NEWS – this minute. I can hardly write straight I feel so excited . . . So you send me your love my darling – I send you all mine – and have been sending it every day. Dear sweetheart – I hope you are glad it is a boy . . . I thought up to five minutes ago I wanted a daughter very badly – but when I think of that great fellow Michael – I'm glad there'll be another like him. Think of the pair of 'em – the rascals – in a bath together.'[30]

Christmas Day 1918 was, despite his loneliness, profoundly happy. The birth of his second son, Peter; the end of the war; steady administrative achievement; Kaiama, and his rapport with its people – there was much to be thankful for.

'Just after sundown . . .I took my bath in my top storey as a file of women in their bold, flowered prints, and in separate groups their men in their best, but still dusky, white gowns, streamed past the corner of the office below with that continuous babel of African talk and laughter which always seems more gay than any other in the world – and with a special kind of gaiety . . .' Later, 'dressed formally in clean pyjamas and mosquito boots', he sat down to dinner on his balcony – mutton (a luxury in a world of scrawny chicken), tinned peas, tinned fruit – while the policemen and their families drank and ate and danced in the barracks. By now he had become, 'for the first time in my life, punctilious, tidy; I kept up all the ceremonies of parade, drill and court-room . . . and I dined by candlelight.'

As the drumming reached 'a high point of virtuosity', he remembered how he had 'hated' Borgu at first as 'a solitary and desolate land where the very night seems to have a special quality of threat . . . I had left an Emirate of the North with its desert traders, its pageants of horsemen, and got in exchange twelve thousand miles of waste . . .' Now he counted his blessings: 'Just because Borgu was remote and cut off, just because I had no wire, I had been given free leave to make quick decisions, in fact to do what I liked. And there was always interesting and practical work at hand.[31]

CHAPTER TWENTY

BRIDGES & ROADS

1919

'I love making things'
In 1919 Cary evolved a plan to develop trade routes from the east, through Bussa and Kaiama, to link with the main route along the western border of Borgu. This would, he hoped, increase prosperity in the Kaiama and Bussa Districts by drawing them into the established pattern of trade in and through Borgu. But the new routes would have to 'pass through stretches of uninhabited bush, too long for a day's journey. Small parties of travellers could not sleep in the bush in danger from leopards and lions, in fear of ghosts and werewolves, and we wanted the small parties. It is the solitary pedlar, or one who travels with only his family, who makes trade flow in the remote bush.'

With difficulty (since Headquarters would not allocate funds) he had two small zungos (rudimentary inns) built on the route from Kaiama, and at the same time founded several new markets. Results were spectacular.

> The flow of traders doubled in less than a month; in a single year the new markets had become too small. Money and goods began to flow into the villages with immediate effects on their local economy. Demand for products, such as shea butter, dried fish and hides, went up, and poverty visibly went back a little. There were not so many appeals, at the end of the dry season, for remission of tax; not so many children with swollen bellies and skeleton faces; and casual labour was very difficult to hire. [1]

By the time he composed his Yashikera Assessment Report in mid-1919, Cary was able to claim that great improvements had been made to the trade routes, so that 'The trade of the whole country is increasing very rapidly, and every year finds the people of all parts richer, and more enterprising'. [2]

But the rapid increase of trade demonstrated that 'every reform we brought also caused dislocations or evil of some kind; and this was inevitable'. The chief of a town

> hated the whole development and blamed me, fairly enough for, the trouble it had caused. His people were better off but increased incomes and security only made them insubordinate. Alien traders did not salute him, and spread

revolutionary ideas. He did not want change. What I called progress, he saw, again quite fairly, as a backward step into social confusion, crime, political strife . . .

His opposition did not surprise me; but I was startled to find that my trade representatives were even more unmanageable. They were all making money out of the new prosperity, but they complained bitterly of the foreign traders; they wanted to keep them out of the markets, to raise taxes on them. As for village chiefs, several of them complained that I was breaking up family life because the women could now sell food at good prices to the traders, and were neglecting their home duties. What is more, as my Political Agent informed me, the Emir and chiefs imputed the whole new economic policy simply to an anxiety on my part to get in the taxes. Nothing would presuade them that a large proportion of tax did not go into my own pocket. [3]

This contest between conservatism and innovation repeated the pattern he had earlier observed in Ireland and in art. As expressed in Borgu, that conflict would become a central theme in his Nigerian novels, especially *Mister Johnson*.

In February Cary set out on an arduous trek that took him south to join the great trade route where it entered Borgu, then north along it beyond Yashikera to Babanna, across the centre of the Division, and so back to Kaiama via Bussa. This journey of about two hundred miles took him three weeks. It was the dry season – the best time of the year for trekking – and he enjoyed himself thoroughly. 'I have plenty of time to think of you and Peter as I ride along the roads in the morning,' he told Gertie.

Kennu, reputed to be 'the thieves kitchen of all Borgu', he approached with some apprehension: 'They are a happy collection of scoundrels in a very strong position among the hills. I hope I won't be looted. But I have four police, with ten rounds apiece – and I have four cartridges in my revolver . . .' But Kennu turned out to be 'very peaceful. A large deputation of brigands met me on the road and escorted me in. The old chief is blind – and came to me led by a small boy. He looked like Lear.'

And as Cary journeyed on, he found pleasure everywhere – above all in his meetings with villagers:

At each place the chief and principal men come up and I ask them if they have any complaints or want any information . . . They are pleased afterwards with their few minutes of honourable distinction, but at the time they are slightly incoherent. It isn't me they are nervous of – or not so much – as their own chief, who is really a big man – of a royal house which rules half Dahomey as well as Borgu . . . [4]

Most of his stops were much less formal:

When I visited villages in West Africa, the people used to come together and we all sat down under a tree to discuss our common difficulties. There was no ceremony about the proceedings. Children and goats wandered about as they liked, the elders had long arguments among themselves and it was only difficult to keep anyone to the point. It was very hard to persuade the elders that they had the power to organise anything at all . . . this very easy going kind of life was only an appearance. The people were in fact strictly controlled by tradition and religion or social rules. [5]

He found the trade route endlessly interesting, with its traders 'passing up and down all day long. Men coming North with huge loads of kola nuts, and men going South with cages of pigeons, cattle, and sheep.'

And all the way he was paying particular attention to the state of the bridges and roads. He had sent orders ahead for wood to be gathered where the road crossed the big Oli River half-way between Bussa and Kaiama. There he would 'stop two days at least to build a bridge – as it is to be a model for construction elsewhere. It will be a joke if it falls down . . . But I love making things, and I expect I shall enjoy the construction. It will have to be built without nails or rope – though I hope to get a blacksmith to make some sort of a metal rivet for the crucial parts.'[6]

This was the first of many bridges made according to Cary's specifications during the next few months. His Yashikera Assessment Report, noting that in the wet season several large rivers in that District 'entirely stop all traffic, sometimes for four or five days', recorded the completion of six bridges between Kaiama and Yashikera. His bridge design he described as 'a modified trestle,' and he claimed with pride that the largest so far built, 'seventy yards in length, and twenty-six feet high in the middle of the bed', had cost less than £7. [7]

On 26 February, he erected his prototype over the Oli River. Cary's foreman was 'a little pagan called Tasuki, about four feet high . . . ragged and dirty, usually in pain from a complication of disease including syphilis, and always laughing'. Cary had first seen him as 'an umemployed waster . . . covered with bruises. He had been flogged by at least one court'. Yet, to Cary's amazement, Tasuki erected the trestle of a bridge by extemporising 'all by himself and for this one job, the compound lever, the multiple pulley and several other devices never seen before and probably never used again'. Tasuki had 'brains, guts, and powers of leadership'. Like Edwardes, he came to epitomise for Cary the creator, who delights in doing 'that for which he had been fitted by nature'. [8]

After the 1919 wet season, Cary was able to evaluate what he, Tasuki and a multitude of labourers had achieved: 'All my bridges are standing, and are in so much use, that in some cases the traffic has deviated fifty miles to use them. I haven't done anything here I am so proud of . . . I only wish I could get a few steel girders, a pair of iron wheels, some good tackle, and a carpenter able to saw planks. But these are for the future. We must crawl before we can run – especially in this poor place.'[9]

'a wave of industry'

Back in Kaiama early in March, his satisfaction was dented by the discovery of 'a grand system of corruption and rascality'. Although it involved the Emir, whom he liked and admired, he acted quickly, firmly and confidently. This was institutionalised fraud at the expense of the poor, and must be stopped as soon as possible. [10]

Even more distressing was a letter from Gertie. Before the birth of Peter, upset by her parents' decision to sell The Glade, she had again raised the sore point of his absence in Nigeria: 'You have told me often not to build my hopes on your ever giving up Nigers, but I *can't* help hoping sometimes dearest!'; and 'What I feel is that if you were not married to me, you would have given up Nigers now and done the work you really like best.' Now she was 'worrying about the perplexities of the future. Mother and Father had a serious talk with me about the house question, and they wanted to know what I was going to do, and when I was going to look.'

It was tentatively decided that, when The Glade was sold, Gertie would move with her parents to their next, smaller house, and that she and Cary would try to rent or buy a house of their own during his leave. However, as the time approached for them to vacate The Glade, Mrs Ogilvie lapsed into depression; she clung to Gertie, telling her that 'what she was dreading more than anything was my leaving her later on'.

At this anxious time, Jack Cary, who had been a prisoner of war in Turkey for several years, suddenly appeared at The Glade, with his proud father, to meet his sister-in-law and two nephews. Gertie wrote: 'He is much bigger and taller than I had imagined from his photographs – also I have been trying to find some resemblance to you – but can't find any except the nose!' She thought him 'very silent'.[11] Two months later, he was ordered to Australia, where he would be surveying coastal seas for two years. (He discovered a small island there, named it 'Cary Island', and years later informed Cary with mock dismay, that it had been renamed Kareng si Ajar – 'considering that I buckled the rudder off a motor boat on it, I think it is most unfair.'[12])

Arthur Cary wrote that 'G.M. was looking in radiant health – never saw her look so sweet – and pretty – and Michael was in good form . . . I never saw a finer kiddy, and he and his other grandfather are great pals'.[13] But the Ogilvie turmoil over the sale of The Glade continued. Mrs Ogilvie seemed to be close to a breakdown: Mr Ogilvie was depressed now too. Fortunately for Gertie during these travails, Peter was 'the most wonderful baby – he scarcely cries all day long – and when he isn't sleeping is generally grinning or gurgling'.[14]

Cary was deeply concerned about Gertie's situation. 'Dearest, of course I would like to be with you at home,' he wrote on 27 February – and went on to repeat all his arguments against giving up his administrative career. 'Ours is a hard fortune, but incomparably better than hundreds of thousands of others. And remember that I am writing and might possibly be successful . . . If I followed my feelings, I would leave Nigeria at once, and thus imperil your happiness, and the children's whole lives.'

On 10 March, he had to set off on another trek. This time he was away from Kaiama for over a month. As he journeyed east 'a wave of industry' preceded him. 'I hear the Emir of Bussa is frantically building the bridge which should have been finished a month ago – he started the day before yesterday. The work at the Woko bridge had only just been accomplished when I arrived.'[15]

At Agwarra, he met Ryan, the A.D.O. now in charge of Yauri Division, a sketch of whom shows Cary's interest in his personality: 'Ryan, red-haired, gay manner, stories about his own stupidity, and drinking, his compliments . . . Neat dress and disorderly household. Admiration of his wife whom he didn't live with.'[16] Something of Ryan was distilled into the characters Cock Jarvis and Jim Latter; and a story he told Cary about the aftermath of an argument with his wife at Lokoja in 1907 (he found her walking fast towards the Niger at night, took her by the arm, and they walked back in silence) became the seed of fictional incidents relating to the two characters.

After nearly six months of loneliness, Cary was at first 'strangely shy and awkward' with Ryan. But soon he was 'making pretty maps all day – while Ryan read a book'. The maps were of the 144-square-mile Agwarra District, whose return to Bussa jurisdiction Cary was negotiating: its nearly 3,000 inhabitants would bring a useful increase in Borgu's revenue, as well as boosting pride and morale in Bussa.

Then he travelled down the Niger in a fleet of canoes towards the end of March, and, after a few days in and near Bussa, trekked on to Kontagora, where he took and passed his Hausa examination. A few days as Mrs H.B.'s guest made him yearn for the silences of Borgu ('She talked so much to-night that I could have got up and shouted . . . Yet she wants to darn my socks and is going to give me a cake and a bottle of whisky to take away').[17]

Back in Kaiama, he noted some pleasing changes:

> For 80 years ever since it was built Kaiama has had a water famine every year. Moreover 50% of the population get guinea-worm – a beast which lives in the legs and makes a temporary complete cripple of its victim. Then when he washes his sores, it lays its eggs in the water, which someone else drinks. So that in the farming season half the farmers are laid up. So I have had four wells dug – people can't put their feet in a well – and we have found water in every one. Moreover the people are digging 5 more wells for themselves . . . Next year I hope there will be no guinea-worm. To-morrow or next day, I start the new prison buildings and a man went off this morning to build another bridge. Borgu is really waking up.

He was perturbed, however, to hear that a missionary had 'popped into Kaiama' during his absence. 'The Emir asked him to wait and see me, but he said he preferred to write, and hastened away. It seems unfair to impute design, but the ways of the missionary are sometimes Machiavellian to an extraordinary degree . . . many of them seem to look upon the Service as their natural enemies – and many more are completely ignorant of our principles of government, which they do not understand and try to thwart . . .' 'Religion is of course a great difficulty . . . we don't want any more bloodshed here. I have no intention of getting scuppered in a religious war.'[18] These concerns led him towards the theme of *Aissa Saved*, and also influenced *The African Witch*.

'a grave enough matter'

Now at ease in his large domain, confident that his administration was beneficial in the eyes of his superiors and of many of his subjects, Cary was careful not to allow success to go to his head. After a long walk to a village during which 'women I passed went down on one knee, and the men bowed their heads literally to the dust, and cried out "Lord"', and 'even farmers a quarter of a mile away in the fields hailed me, and salaamed,' he meditated lever-headedly on his role as ruler:

> how strange it would look in democratic Europe – and what a little person I am in reality. Who knows me at home – but 25,000 people here call me 'Baba' or Father. Of course they call Diggle 'Baba' too, or anyone else who is sent. And they don't care twopence for me really – there's no affection, or loyalty – only respect . . . Yet they run to me when they are in trouble, and they depend on me for much – for protection from tyranny, and exploitation, and injustice. I could do more for them if I was allowed to spend a little more money – I want a vaccinator and a vet – I want an engineer and some bigger bridges than can be made with bush-timber – I want some better roads – and a larger staff. But the policy is to go slowly, and on the whole it is a wise one.[19]

If, as he wrote in his article 'Africa Yesterday: One Ruler's Burden', he was a dictator in Borgu,[20] his power was used responsibly and with a steady determination to improve the lot of the people.

While he continued to trek from village to village in the Yashikera District, gathering information for his Assessment Report, Cary was still worrying about Gertie, and their future. She had now suggested that it might be better if she did not accompany her parents to their next, smaller house, but use the move as an appropriate occasion for the inevitable break. He agreed, but still disliked the idea of living in a London suburb, and now mooted the possibility of buying a house in Oxford. There, he argued, 'we will both have friends, many lovely gardens for the children, the country, the river, books and music . . . Society is good, the town is charming . . . Moreover Oxford will always be a mecca to Heneage, Freddy and Elsie – they will love to come and see us there.'[21]

Then, on 29 May, when he reached Bussa on his way back to Kaiama, he received the letter he must have been dreading:

> I am going to be selfish and say exactly what I think, and please don't say, even to yourself – Oh women don't understand the facts of life – they just want to follow the feelings of the moment, wherever it may lead them – because I do see your points about money . . .
>
> Darling I know if you gave up Nigeria to please me – and against your own inclination and what you thought was right – we might run a great risk of having big massamoras to last our lives. If you didn't like your work – if you don't make much money, if the pinch came when the question of education arose – I know our lives might be spoilt. I should of course be to blame for having persuaded you to leave . . .

And firmly, cogently, she presented the case against his continuing his career in Nigeria, stressing her conviction that if he 'knew what it was to be a woman with a husband away, and with children whom she wanted to bring up with him . . . you would think a bit differently about our lives' – 'If you were in my place you would see things as I do . . .'[22]

He was deeply disturbed, and impressed, by her long, eloquent statement.

After two days and a night of reflection he replied carefully, confronting her arguments one by one. If he continued in his administrative career, he would be home at regular intervals – the children would not forget him; and 'I hope that both of them will get this from me at least – the tradition of service, and duty – the honourable traditions of their class, which will make them worthy men whatever their profession'. He had no 'special qualifications' beyond 'the knowledge of my work here . . . it would be impossible to hope for work [in England] – even clerical work of the poorest sort.' And he had already completed 'nearly a third of my time. In 18 years service, I have to spend 12 years in Africa. In 3 months now I will have completed 4 years in the country.' Finally, it was unfair to suggest that he was inured to solitude:

> I doubt if you would think so if you had known how I felt last night – how strong the temptation was to take advantage of you, and throw it all up . . . You know how I do succumb to temptation. How I left school for France, France for Edinburgh, the Art School for writing, writing for Oxford, Oxford for Store Street, Store Street for Montenegro, [Montenegro] for Ireland, and then Ireland for Nigeria. Nothing has steadied me but you and the children. I believe I might have made a failure of my life without you. And Dad's affection for you is not a little based on the belief that you have steadied me. Now even if I never write a book worth reading, I know that I have done something in the world – work which can be respected, which is good, and has been good for others.

He knew she would find his reply painful; he regretted her predicament; he loved her. 'But I must carry on . . . and take the risk of alienating some of your affection. I believe from my heart – as strongly as anyone could believe anything – that I am doing right – right for you – right as a husband – right for my children – and that I would be selfish to do anything else, and deserve the punishment I should probably suffer – to see you suffer for me.'[23]

'hundreds of thousands of words'

The crisis turned on his writing, their common hope for a solution. On 4 April he had confessed to Gertie that he had 'done none for a long time now – I am much too busy. Yet what I have done this tour is a little better, I think. And I may have more time in August and September to write . . .' Even his reading had dwindled. At the end of January he had been savouring *Wild Life in a Southern County* by Richard Jefferies. But he had not read a book for nearly three months after that. On 20 April he had read *Pride and Prejudice* 'for the 3rd or 4th time'; at first 'with much pleasure', but then with mounting depression: 'How wretched seemed my own work – when I am doing it. Writing is hard work – and wearing work . . .' He had now returned to one of his 'stories' and was working at it desultorily. 'I may be one of those who mature slowly', he wrote.

In mid May he had read several books sent by Gertie. Hugh Walpole's recently published *The Secret City* he thought inauthentic ('he deceives himself if he says he writes as an Englishman looking at Russia. Let us say rather a milk and water Russian novelist looking at Russia'). But two further books by Richard Jefferies were 'delightful – so plain – so unaffected. What a secret it is to observe carefully, patiently, to write down faithfully – careless of whether the reader likes it or not, whether he is bored or indifferent. This is originality, to look for oneself'. And he had praised Conrad as a truly original writer who 'looked out of his own eyes, and saw a new world – as anyone does who trusts his own vision'.

A few days later, leaving Yashikera, he had commented again on his own writing, after carefully reviewing it:

> Do you know I have written hundreds of thousands of words – as much as would make two novels and a half this tour. But you say – nothing finished. No. But I am learning. I refuse to be depressed. Writing is not like painting. The best way of learning painting is notoriously to go and watch a big man paint. An hour of that is worth a week or a year of the art-schools. But one cannot see the novelist at work. Most of it is done in his head. Of course method one can learn. But where. No novelist has given a description of his method worth twopence. Each has to learn for himself. I am learning now. I am evolving a method. And four days ago I started a new story on a new method. I am going to spend much more care on the planning and scheming. In fact have a whole skeleton novel written before I start. The first skeleton is nearly done (I put in three whole 3-hour days at it at Yashikera and four to-day). And already I find an advantage. I see weak points. I perceive the danger spots. A novel should have a plot, but that plot should be told or rather tell itself through character. And that is where I fail so often. I make a plot – get the characters moving – get to know them – and then I find they are not evolving the plot – rather struggling with it. But this time (how many times now) I hope to avoid this. I shall not plunge as usual into my tale before I see the end of it. I am going to work on that plan – pull it about – rewrite it – for a week yet at least . . .) I shall have to walk this time before I can dance . . . I have finished four or five short stories, and a short novel – or rather sketch of a short novel – but the latter will have to be rewritten, and the short stories are meant to be pot-boilers.

As he travelled on, now back towards Kaiama, he was rewriting the 'short novel' (possibly *Daventry*). He quickly found himself 'fairly over ears' in it, and had written more than a hundred pages of it by the time Gertie's letter reached him.

After many weeks of concentrated and increasingly optimistic work on his writing, Gertie's ultimatum might well have been a disabling blow. It was not. He did not abandon the new novel – even during his emotional turmoil, long consideration, and careful writing of his response to her.

He now sent off to a literary agent in London (A.P. Watt, an Oxford acquaintance) some of the short stories 'meant to be pot-boilers'. Then he continued working on the novel. By 4 June, he could report equably that it was 'not going so badly. I am at page 171, and sticking close to that famous scheme', the 'skeleton novel'. 'Formerly with my much rougher schemes – I used to allow myself to put in improvements and small changes as they suggested themselves'; then, after 'an enforced break of a week', he 'would discover a hideous gap or inconsistency'. 'It is surprising how interdependent are all the parts of a story. One conversation may affect the whole – and one change may affect every second page all through.'[24]

If there was one action in Cary's life that decided he would be a novelist, it may well have been when, in Bussa, he picked up his pen to continue writing that 'short novel'.

CHAPTER TWENTY-ONE

DEPARTURES

1919

'abandoning everything'

Back in Kaiama after his long trek, Cary settled into a productive routine. On 11 June he finished his Yashikera District map ('It really looks very imposing in different inks, and my best mapping hand. That makes two big maps.') He was 'doing a fair amount of writing again, and the thing seems to go well.' Even the garden was thriving: 'my mangoes are putting on new leaves every day. And I had my first tomato of the new crop (your seeds) for dinner'.

So he was bitterly angry when disruption struck. On 22 June he received instructions to proceed to Zuru. 'I am abandoning everything, my work here, my garden, my mangoes, and my well-earned peace during the wet season. Think of the garden alone. The gardener nearly wept when I went down this evening . . . No one relieves me here. Borgu is to be abandoned for any length of time.' The Emir arrived at Cary's office 'to say he was afraid he would have trouble with his chiefs and people if I went – the former being insubordinate, and the latter truculent. But I explained I could not help it.'

He reached Kontagora, on 8 July, with a bad cold, after 'a most miserable trek in the rain'. Only to find that 'I shall go *back* to Borgu next week – and all my trek was for nothing'! Arrangements had been changed while he was on his way. Mrs H.B. gave him a 'huge lump of cake' and seeds for his garden, and told him when he left that 'she would miss him very much'.[1]

He was still suffering from his cold when he started back to Kaiama on 22 July, but his spirits were high. Despite the disruption and uncertainty, he was pleased that, after all, he would be spending the final months of his tour of duty in Borgu.

And he had also received several letters from Gertie that eased his mind; her warm response to his letter of concern about their sexual problems infused the correspondence of the following months with loving reminiscence and reassurance. At the same time, their worry about her immediate future had been lifted. Mr Ogilvie had revoked his sale of The Glade at the last moment. The consequent penalty, and the resale of the small house he had bought, eventually resulted in a loss of about £3,000. For Cary, his father-in-law's change of mind was a relief. Gertie was back at The Glade with her children and her parents; there was no need for her to buy a house before his return.

Gertie also fully agreed that they should look for a house in Oxford ('I have always loved Oxford'). And their mutual enthusiasm was strengthened when Duncan MacGregor won a Fellowship at Balliol, and it became clear that Freddy Ogilvie was also likely to be in Oxford. After thinking seriously about becoming a priest, Freddy had returned to Balliol, taken a first in Greats and was now studying Economics and being considered for various academic positions. (In September he accepted a post as Lecturer at Trinity College and was allocated Newman's rooms.) Meanwhile Heneage was establishing himself as a London surgeon (he had just completed his FRCS at Guy's) and might be a frequent visitor to Oxford. Gertie went to Oxford with her mother to look at houses, and even made an offer for one – Cary had made it clear that she should feel free to buy a house there before his return; but in the end the decision was postponed.[2]

Unfortunately the calm of this situation was seriously disturbed when Mr Ogilvie, distressed by his wife's continuing poor health, wrote impulsively to Cary at the end of August. He and Arthur Cary had found themselves in disagreement over the plan to buy a house in Oxford: while Mr Ogilvie was in favour, Cary's father, apparently because of his rooted fear of 'Cary extravagance', offended Gertie by voicing opposition. Mr Ogilvie's letter attacked Cary for failing to arrange accommodation for Gertie and the children, and accused him of unrealistic expectations: 'it is getting too much for Mother, and I am afraid of a breakdown at any time. We are both 67 now and have only a few more years . . . Gerty must have her own house somewhere . . . I daresay I shall always be able to help her, as I have been doing . . . We have lost several good servants, because they won't come where there are children.'[3]

Cary, stung particularly by his father-in-law's reference to financial help, told Gertie that, in future, they must 'be absolutely *independent*' of Ogilvie money apart from her annuity; 'we must go house-hunting as soon as I come, and if we can't get a place in Oxford, try elsewhere'.[4] Mrs Ogilvie, when she learned from Gertie what had happened, wrote to try to repair the damage: 'we love having Gertie and the children . . . I can't tell you how sad it would make me if any real difference were to come between us and you ceased to look on The Glade as a home . . .'[5] But Cary's relationship with his father-in-law had been hurt.

Meanwhile Gertie had reconsidered her opinion that Cary should give up his Nigerian career. After reading a book about Nigeria that he had recommended, she commented 'I feel I understand much more about your work . . . and I really want to see the country one day, if I could only be sure I wasn't a hindrance to you'. And at the end of July, she softened still further, worrying that he might 'throw up Nigers because of an impetuous and selfish letter' from her, and agreeing now with all of his arguments for continuance: 'I am with you in heart and soul . . .'[6]

'a new grand trunk road'

The final months of Cary's second tour of duty were a joyful coda to his life and achievements in Borgu.

First the Yashikera Assessment Report must be copied out neatly for submission (there was no typewriter in the office). But at last he had some substantial help. On 12 August he told Gertie that 'my clerk came yesterday – a long lanky youth in gold spectacles – Mr Graves by name and look. He knows nothing, and I shall have to teach him, as well as do my own work. But he will save me some copying.' Next day, Cary gave Graves the Report and was amused by his answer when asked after two hours how much he had copied: Graves 'had spent every minute with his nose to the paper, and he replied cheerfully "Two pages, sah." There are 100 pages, so he has plenty before him.'[7] In fact, Graves ultimately

> sat up all night to copy [the] report in time for the mail. I did not ask him to work for twenty hours on end, at the dullest possible job; I had given up all hope of catching the mail . . .
>
> No doubt when he appeared in the morning, with bloodshot eyes and a triumphant smile, to show me his copy, he was taking pleasure in giving me a surprise. But I know from other instances that he had also the strongest sense of duty; a zeal which sometimes got him into danger, as when he tried to stop a fight in the town, single-handed, and was nearly killed.[8]

George Graves's sense of duty was very like Lafia's; but he was not a local man. He was from the Gold Coast [Ghana], and had been in Nigeria only since 1914. Educated at King's College, Lagos, he was twenty-one when sent to Borgu on his first posting as a Divisional Clerk. He felt uneasy there, a stranger: 'There were no Mission Schools and Churches. The inhabitants are pagans and Mahomedans.' Cary he remembered as 'very hard-working. A polite and unassuming officer. A good Administrator and an impartial Magistrate, kind and sympathetic.'[9]

Cary was impressed by Graves's neat, curlecued script in which the capital S, when standing alone as abbreviation for 'Sarkin', asserted itself in sinuous simplicity. He was also impressed by Graves's neat table – so impressed that he set about tidying his own part of the office, including 'some piles of papers which have been lumbering the room since January. And you should see my pigeon-holes – all labelled, and full of sorted papers, with indexes'.

He found Graves's personality and situation interesting; and in his expression of that interest one can discern the origin of the character first called Mister Montagu and then Mister Johnson: 'The world of a clerk is strange. Here he is as much a foreigner as I am.'[10]

Cary was clearly thinking of Graves when he wrote of the 'educated African': 'If he knows that you like him and that you appreciate his help, he is the best colleague you could find; he enters into things with an eagerness, a freshness of mind, that makes him a perpetual source of encouragement even in dull routine work . . .'[11] He would have valued Graves's opinion of him.

Graves's presence in the Divisional Ofiice at Kaiama gave Cary more time for the outdoor activities he so much enjoyed, and as the wet season drew to a close he announced to Gertie his last major project: 'I am starting a new grand trunk road.'[12]

In his Handing-Over Notes at the end of this tour of duty, he noted that 'A new road policy has been started . . . Briefly it is proposed to make a few miles of properly surveyed, ditched and cambered road every year, in place of the old wasteful method of clearing annually bad and crooked paths.' The stretch he supervised during the last quarter of 1919 replaced the first six miles of the track between Kaiama and Bussa – which now had adequate bridges over the rivers it crossed. It was to be part of 'a great connecting highway' running across Borgu from Bussa and Kaiama to the main trade route of the western border.[13]

In 1921 his successor Hoskyns-Abrahall disagreed firmly with Cary's policy in regard to both roads and bridges: 'Road is in excellent condition, and would take a Rolls-Royce or tractor most places . . . [but] it appears to me to be rather a waste of time and expenditure to make such a wide road . . . only a very narrow track 2 [feet] wide is ever used by anyone . . .'[14] Again Cary was looking as much to the future as to the present.

The road's successful progress owed much to Tasuki, bridge builder and now road maker, whose exceptional abilities again became immediately obvious. By 23 September Cary acknowledged that Tasuki 'is really a treasure. The road would have been impossible without him.'[15] Tasuki, too, was to contribute to *Mister Johnson*.

By the time Cary left Borgu, Tasuki was established as the Division's road maker; and so he continued for many decades. He is remembered in Borgu, with affectionate respect.[16] In recognising and exploiting his creativity, in training him to make roads and bridges, Cary made one of his finest contributions to the future of Borgu.

Daventry

There were further ups and downs for Cary as his tour drew towards a close. At the beginning of October he feared that his lamp, on which he depended for reading and writing at night, was about to break; and this provoked a brief bush hate: 'I loathe Borgu. I am wearied to death of living worse than a navvy. I hate my meals. And when my lamp goes . . . it will really be about the last straw . . . If I died to-morrow I should only be a name in the Gazette. They wouldn't even know for a week. I'd be buried before they knew.'

Both his anxiety about the lamp and his deep sense of isolation were connected with *Daventry*, now close to completion. It had been going well, and on 6 October he had been 'cheerfully writing away again . . . I trot about all day when I'm not doing official work, chuckling over the situations I invent . . .' A few weeks after his bush hate, with the lamp still holding together, he was 'cleaning up' the novel: 'It is the first time I have a finished book to work on, and I find it very interesting and instructive'. After that, he wrote short stories again, feeling unable to concentrate on anything demanding.[17]

George Graves remembered that Cary 'wrote and re-wrote' his fiction, and that 'many sheets of his manuscripts . . . were burned'.[18] In fact, apart from the short stories and *Daventry*, hardly a scrap of paper remains to represent all the fiction Cary wrote during his time in Nigeria.

But *Daventry* he valued. In 1956 he mentioned it in an interview as 'a novel I wrote forty years ago in Africa under [Conrad's] influence'.[19] Its plot is based on the Maltby incident of 1916. Cary had been deeply moved by the murder of the young, unarmed A.D.O. and 58 members of his party by a pagan tribe. His response to Maltby's fate seems to have been strengthened by his near involvement in the aftermath, and later linked to the prior death of his friend Marwood in the Cameroons, and his own experience of intense isolation and vulnerability in Borgu (especially when, in August, he was prostrated by flu and knew he was at the mercy of his servants). The novel also incorporates many aspects of Cary's life and thought as an A.D.O. in Bauchi and Borgu.

Daventry, like Corner a tenderfoot, is overjoyed when his superior, Crampton, requests him to 'make a road through the pagan division, not only for the sake of the road, but as an excuse for getting into touch with the people'. Hero-worshipping the idealistic Crampton, Daventry decides to make his preliminary expedition without an escort.

The party is attacked. 'A dark flash seemed to cross before his eyes.' After two of his servants have died, in rage and madness respectively, Daventry, now himself dying from a poisoned-arrow wound, is abandoned by his last companion, the horse-boy Ibrahim. Before leaving, Ibrahim demands a letter of reference, and steals the contents of his master's pockets. 'Daventry was quite aware of the theft, and . . . smiled to himself. His education was complete.'[20]

The central theme of this short novel is betrayal, rather than injustice. Crampton's idealism betrays Daventry; Daventry's ignorant romanticism betrays him and his followers. Reality, all too late, educates Daventry. Cary's attack on culpable innocence, like other aspects of the novel, surely owes something to Conrad's portraits of Kurtz and the Harlequin in *Heart of Darkness*. But it also indicates, in his determination neither to romanticise nor to villify the pagan tribe, in his refusal to exculpate or sentimentalise his hero, Cary's commitment to irony and objectivity.

Daventry is not in a final state. Cary's manuscript shows considerable but incomplete revision. But the body of the narrative is briskly and effectively handled. *Daventry* is important in indicating the strength of Conrad's influence near the beginning of Cary's career, and as an impressive prelude to the group of novels which successfully drew on his Nigerian experience and established his name as a serious novelist.

Cary was reading avidly again. All through his writing career he drew encouragement and sustenance for his fiction from the books he read – one of the creative habits established in the loneliness of Borgu. During four weeks from the end of September to the end of October, he read at least seven books, a characteristically catholic selection of novels and memoirs. Daisy Ashford's recently-published *The Young Visiters*, and the controversy surrounding it, intrigued and pleased him. 'Daisy Ashford may not have written *The Young Visiters* but it is a perfectly possible and likely feat for a clever child of her age.'

Conrad's *Arrow of Gold* was disappointing. 'One expects so much of Conrad', and this novel was weak: 'I suspect he is playing off some allegory on me, as he did in *Victory* – a sort of World, Flesh and Devil again, at enmity with Good . . . and I don't like any powder in my jam'. After Conrad he dipped into one of his old favourites, Arnold Bennett's *The Old Wives' Tale*, 'an incomparable story'; and then indulged himself with one of William de Morgan's rambling, old-fashioned novels.

On 23 November he finished A *Portrait of the Artist as a Young Man*, which he had specifically requested Gertie to send, and proclaimed it 'a little masterpiece. Wells I see says it is like Sterne, but I call that inept. It is not at all like Sterne. Sterne enjoys an equivocal word or phrase for its own sake . . . Joyce is honest, sincere, and so all that in Sterne which must always be half-contemptible, is in him artistic truth – and plainness. Sterne is the servant of a bad, or at least shallow purpose, but Joyce aims high, and takes all between.' After reading another book he returned to Joyce's novel, fascinated.

> I don't know why I can read bits of it again and again, though it is true I have a special interest in it, for its being about Irish people, and also for its style. It is a very novel and interesting style – much more so than one would think at a first glance. I am very curious to see this man's other books, and see what he will write next . . . I once began a book a little like *The Portrait* – though it was not a Portrait of one person, but of a family – I came across the beginnings of it the other day when I was sorting my MSS. It will have to wait for a long time. I have three or four books to write before I come to it. [21]

CHAPTER TWENTY-TWO

DELIGHT

1919

'what I am, I cannot hide'
In the months after his marriage Cary had lamented his 'wasted years' of feckless 'idleness', and recalled the 'very black fits of depression' that he had endured, a 'hopeless depression – which . . . seemed to be quite causeless' – 'I used to make myself ill with nothing but brooding'. Marriage, and his career in Northern Nigeria, had 'steadied' him. He had never had a home, he told Gertie, never been truly happy in any house except Clare Cottage.

Now he recognised that his volatile personality, his frequent 'ups and downs', were not merely a burden: they expressed 'an elastic kind of spirit very hard to break'. His initial shyness on meeting people, his independence, and his insistence on preserving his privacy led some to think him 'reserved and cold', but, once he was at ease, his lively, enthusiastic conversation and story-telling ability made him a popular companion. Although deeply aware of 'life's injustice', he was an optimist, with a well-developed sense of humour. And ebullient: 'For many a long year I have been pretty well aware that what I am, I cannot hide. I am sure to open my mouth, and blab my character.' But he was also a good listener, with 'a design, and perhaps a flair, for receiving confidences. I like to hear about people's lives.'

His ability to endure long periods of loneliness indicates psychological resilience and physical stamina. He took care of mind and body through regular relaxation and exercise; reading and writing were valuable aids – not least the long nightly letters to Gertie in which he could conduct quasi-conversations and express his emotions.

He believed that he had had a 'poor education' ('I know for instance no Greek at all') and, like Thomas Hardy, was endlessly curious, avid for knowledge. Like his father, he continued to enjoy not only physical exercise but a wide range of practical activities. Increasingly, he aspired to the highest standards of personal and professional conduct, abhorring laziness and self-indulgence: both as soldier and A.D.O., he was responsible, diligent and energetic. Decisive, assertive and sometimes impatient, he was also notably sensitive, generous and respectful in all his relationships.

Although Cary was essentially conservative in his conduct and values, his intellectual acuity, scepticism and openness of response – encouraged by the principles and practice of Indirect Rule – steadily strengthened his sympathy for other points of view, even those radically different from his own; and by the end of 1919 he had come close to espousing a form of relativism. 'Realise that anyone's conduct is what you think it is,' he told Gertie; 'it depends for the observer on his own knowledge.'[1]

'I want my policy to go on'

As the end of Cary's tour approached, he was still, deep in his mind and emotions, a divided man. He wanted to continue a job that he enjoyed and was good at, in a country he found fascinating: yet he wanted to be with his wife, at home, a full-time writer.

He was growing more and more restless. On 6 November he heard that 'Cowper is to relieve me at the end of the month . . . so that I will be in Kontagora early in December. I am to build a bridge there which may take a day or two, but I should be able to catch a boat about the middle of December and be home early in January.' Even at this late date, however, he was initiating a new project – a road running south from Kaiama towards the southern border. ' . . . I shall send for a gang and start the work. That is my cunning. I want my policy to go on. Therefore I leave a piece of work – a big piece – half done and the next man must carry on with it even if he swears.'

In mid November, when Cowper was due to leave Kontagora, Cary started writing his Handing-Over Notes. But by 29 November Cowper had still not appeared, and he was occupying himself with small practicalities, like 'cutting up chop-boxes and making pigeon-holes'. 'I had hoped to be half-way to Kontagora by now and started towards the sea and you, but here I am still to wait I don't know how much longer. I look down the road from the balcony a dozen times a day – every time some bird makes a call which might be a carrier's shout, or a voice, but no one comes.'

He was suffering again from asthma, and, as his impatience grew towards a bush hate, he distracted himself with a self-analysis that unconsciously outlined his future. In replying to Gertie's comments on an acquaintance who had proclaimed a 'determination to make a fortune', Cary, characteristically, admired the man's 'confidence and energy', the 'dash of adventure in his plan'; then commented ' . . . I have no notion of money making, and . . . want other things so much more than money that I should not get money. What anyone greatly desires, and seeks, is very likely to be attained soon or late. I could never keep my mind solely for money-making. I am steeped in letters. I pass not a day without thoughts of writings of my own or others.'[2]

In 1981, His Highness Alhaji Musa Muhammadu Kigera III, Emir of Borgu, expressed a high opinion of Joyce Cary's work as an A.D.O., noting four major achievements: Cary was a good administrator, especially in his building of roads and bridges, and had trained Tasuki to continue that work; he had refused to pursue and arrest the rebel Sabukki, half-brother of the rightful Emir of Bussa; he had acknowledged the traditional pre-eminence of Bussa over Kaiama, and made efforts to re-establish it; he had returned the administration of the Division to Borgu in July 1919 after being ordered to transfer it to Kontagora.[3] Only for the last of these does Cary not deserve credit. His legacy in Borgu was positive and lasting.

Cary's first two successors approved and continued his policies. The first, Campbell-Irons, reported that 'Mr Cary started a new road policy . . . I have carried on the policy as laid down . . .'[4] In fact, Cary's strategy of initiating projects that his succesors would be bound to continue was strikingly successful. In his Handing-Over Notes, signed on 18 December 1919, he had referred to the road south of Kaiama, just started, as 'intended to form part of a great connecting highway with Kifi [Kishi], and the Southern road system [linking Kaiama to Ilorin and Lagos].'[5] Over a decade later, in September 1931, the D.O. then in charge of Borgu reported that 'The most important item of road work in this Emirate [Kaiama] is to complete the metalling of the Kaiama–Ilorin road. Tasuki is still head road maker.'[6]

Undoubtedly Cary's administrative successors in Borgu during the decade after his departure respected his work – even if the most critical of them, Hoskyns-Abrahall, disagreed with some of his policies. None of them disagreed with his assessments of the administrative personnel of the two Emirates, and all profited from his shrewd comments and excellent appointments. Hoskyns-Abrahall admired Tasuki, and rated Lafia highly enough to wish he was Treasurer of Bussa.[7]

Although Cary was impressed by assertive and flamboyant men, he was also sympathetically appreciative of the shy. In his Handing-Over Notes (which, while firmly critical, were strikingly positive) he made a point of praising the young Treasurer of Kaiama Emirate, Sulé: 'He is very trustworthy, but always very nervous . . . He has worked hard this year to improve himself, and deserves encouragement . . . Sulé will slowly efface himself out of pure diffidence, if he is allowed to. He has kept all the road accounts with care and accuracy, and will be a valuable officer when he acquires more confidence, and a little more arithmetic.'[8] In 1981 Suleiman dan Galadima, in respected old age, still remembered Joyce Cary with affection.[9]

'worthy of delight'

Karen Blixen (Isak Dinesen) noted that in colonial Kenya 'white people to whom the past was still a reality – in whose minds the past of their country, their name and blood or their home was naturally alive – would get on easier with the Africans and would come closer to them than others, to whom the world was created yesterday . . .'[10] Cary's aristocratic Anglo-Irishness, his engrained love of his family's and his people's history, certainly seem to have helped him become, like Saxby in the short story 'Government Baby', 'an excellent district officer, hard-working, conscientious, with a strong natural sympathy for the natives, and he had never stood on his official dignity'.[11]

But more: as Molly Mahood recognised, Cary was also 'fired by his vision of a healthy and prosperous Borgu'. When he retired from the Northern Nigerian Colonial Service, an excellent administrative officer was lost. If he had returned? It is unlikely that he would have been sent back to Borgu, regarded at Headquarters as a backwater; he had proved himself. But would he have been happy in higher, less active bureaucratic reaches? Would he (any more than Edwardes, Carlyle and Fitzpatrick) have patiently climbed the ladder, shouldered by die-hard conservatives clinging to power and careerists reaching for it? Possibly. But writing was his vocation.

Cary's experience of Africa, wrote Molly Mahood, 'is in sharp contrast to Conrad's. Both novelists made a journey to the interior, but Cary found no horror. Rather, he discovered with delight his own creative freedom . . .'[12] Cary's optimism, his positive achievements as administrator, meant that Conrad's influence on his thought and writing would not be pervasive. Cary's genius was primarily comic, like Chaucer's or Joyce's – even if his lifelong concern with the problem of injustice drew him to Conrad and Hardy, Tolstoy and Dostoevsky.

Two literary contemporaries shared with him early experience of colonial administration: George Orwell and Leonard Woolf. All three became notable for their plain, direct styles, and for persistent concern with political analysis (Woolf claimed that 'seven years as a civil servant in Ceylon had made me very much a political animal, and I have remained one ever since'.)[13] They were younger than Cary, and less travelled, when they began their careers in colonial administration, Woolf in the Civil Service of Ceylon [Sri Lanka] (1904–11), Orwell in the Burmese Imperial Police (1922–7).

Cary's colonial experiences and views were closer to Woolf's than Orwell's, and in *The Village in the Jungle* (1913) Woolf wrote a novel that, in its irony and objectivity, resembles Cary's Nigerian novels, and is similarly admired for its integrity and power in representing an alien culture.[14]

Woolf's account of his Ceylon years closely parallels Cary's letters from Nigeria. Like Cary, he quickly became deeply and imaginatively interested in the lives of his subjects, seeking to understand their thought and behaviour. Also like Cary, he was given responsibility for a large, remote district where he 'learnt the profound happiness of complete solitude' and spent much of his time travelling about 'acquainting himself with the characters and work of his headmen and the conditions of the people, considering possibilities of improvements and development, enquiring into requests and complaints, and settling the interminable disputes and feuds of village life'. But, unlike Cary, he 'had to see six or seven men hanged', and was left shaken and disgusted. By the time Woolf left Ceylon, he had, unlike Cary, 'come to dislike imperialism'; and committed himself to Socialism while Cary remained a Liberal.

Cary, who had his writing and reading, his family worries, his exercises and walking, his accordion, did not narrow himself to Woolf's 'obsession with work'[15] (although he came close to this, as he recognised, during his final months in Borgu). That is surely one reason why his memories of Nigeria are suffused with a joy almost ecstatic in its intensity: 'I delighted . . . in experience, in the sense "This is the middle of Africa – this ground is a road now trodden by boots". My whole existence apart from my work, was a stream of feeling, and even in my work, I was always aware of Africa, of my friends in Africa and their work which seemed to me magnificent in a peculiar sense: I mean not only valuable in itself, but distinguished and worthy of delight.'[16]

On 7 December 1919, Cary celebrated his thirty-first birthday. He had just heard from his agent in London, A. P. Watt, that three of his short stories had been accepted by the *Saturday Evening Post*. Cowper remembered him saying that the stories had earned him £240 – 'If you could make that much money, he said, after 6 weeks work, he could do far better as a writer than in the Nigerian Service'.[17]

Cary left Kaiama a few days before Christmas. On 8 January 1920 he sailed for England. Some thirty years later he was to comment 'People think of me as a writer but my years in Africa . . . are richer to my memories than any of my books'.[18]

PART TWO

Writer/Man of Action

'A man is integrated by a coherent idea of life . . . By means of the idea he organises a world in idea and in fact.'   (C 271/N82)

'Roughly, for me, the principal fact of life is the free mind. For good and evil, man is a free creative spirit. This produces the very queer world we live in, a world in continuous creation and therefore continuous change and insecurity. A perpetually new and lively world, but a dangerous one, full of tragedy and injustice. A world in everlasting conflict between the new idea and the old allegiances . . .'   ('An Interview with Joyce Cary')

' . . . I believe in God . . . with an absolute confidence. It is by His grace that we know beauty and love, that we have all that makes life worth living . . .'
                             ('An Interview with Joyce Cary')

'All novels are concerned from first to last with morality.'   (*Art and Reality*)

'I should like to think I shall be remembered. I should like to think I'll be read, because every writer is an evangelist . . . I think my view of life is true. Otherwise I wouldn't be writing about it. And I want it to be understood.'   ('A Conversation with Joyce Cary')

CHAPTER TWENTY-THREE

A NEW START

1920–1921

'a characteristically North Oxford house'
In 1920 Cary decided, finally, to become a professional writer, a decision so momentous it was still unmade a few weeks before his impending return to Nigeria. Once made, it was to cause deep unhappiness in the next two decades.

The year itself was, on the whole, happy and purposeful. Soon after he and Gertie were reunited, towards the end of January, they began househunting; and in April took 12 Parks Road, Oxford, on a 99 year lease – a high, narrow, brick, semi-detached house with four floors (including basement and attic), just north of Keble College and opposite the University Parks. Its situation was its main attraction: Carfax, at the centre of Oxford, was about half a mile away; the colleges, Bodleian Library, Dragon School, Radcliffe Infirmary and shopping were all within easy reach by foot or bicycle; yet across the road were many acres of pleasant parkland, offering exercise and relaxation – and especially the long walks Cary had made part of his daily routine in Borgu.

The house itself, though big enough for a large family with servants, was unimpressive. Two visitors in the mid 1950s thought it 'rather gloomy' – 'a Victorian building with pointed Gothic windows and dark prominent gables . . . a characteristically North Oxford house, contriving to form part of a row without any appearance of being aware of its neighbours. It lies only a little back from the road, behind a small overgrown garden, thick with bushes. The house and garden have all the air of being obstinately "property", self-contained and a little severe.' Inside, 'the atmosphere is a little Edwardian, solid, comfortable, unpretentious, with no obtrusive bric-à-brac.'[1] In 1920 as in 1955 this description of 12 Parks Road would have sufficed.

Before moving into Parkers (as they were soon calling it), at the end of April, Cary introduced Gertie to his only close relations left in Ireland. His Aunt Netta, now Mrs Peter Clark, had two lively teen-aged children, Cary and Toni (Antoinette), and lived in a large house, The Bungalow, at Castledawson (about half-way between Londonderry and Belfast). Although Gertie felt rather constrained by Irish ebullience, they all got on well, playing tennis, walking and picnicking, talking, on this the first of many visits Cary made to The Bungalow in the 1920s and 1930s. It became his Irish 'second home', where he always felt welcome and at ease.

In early May, soon after their return to Oxford, Mrs Ogilvie wrote to Gertie. She was worried – 'wondering if it will be possible, with your utmost endeavours, to be really quite "settled" before Joyce leaves.' The Carys had planned a short holiday for later in the summer, 'and then I suppose Joyce would have to get ready. Only try to avoid the ceaseless rush and whirl . . . during Joyce's last weeks.'[2] Cary's decision to resign from the Northern Nigerian Political Service was probably made in early July. A letter from the Colonial Office dated 24 July informed him that his resignation had been accepted 'with effect from the 3rd of August next inclusive'.[3]

A visit to the doctor (probably for a general check-up before departure) had brought a warning that, if he returned to the tropics, his health would deteriorate rapidly; and in particular that his occasional attacks of asthma would probably become a permanent affliction. The reiterated arguments of his wife and her family were also, of course, influential. And he had recently earned an encouragingly large sum for his writing, making it difficult to contend that becoming a professional writer would condemn his wife and children to poverty. Whatever difficulties and uncertainties he would face at the outset of a writing career, it looked feasible for him to supplement their joint income of about £1,000 to an extent that would sustain a secure upper-middle-class life in Oxford.

Now, in the spirit of their new beginning, the Carys decided to replace 'Gertie' with 'Trudy'. Sensitive from an early age to the implications of names, Cary had always felt that 'Gertie' was embarrassingly inappropriate. In May 1917, after seeing an announcement of Michael's birth, he had commented 'I see you are Gertie Cary in the *Morning Post*. Mrs Hamilton Browne sent it to me. Gertie looks rather cold and lonely in the print – reminds me of Gertie Gitanja and other favourites of the Music Halls. I wonder why the name is so popular among the worst sort of women – it gives me a queer sensation now to hear a doubtful story with a heroine called Gertie – or to listen to a man talk of "the Gerties and Flossies of Leicester Square".'[4] And she had replied 'I agree with every word you say about Gertie – of all ghastly names, I think it takes first prize, but do what I will it has been stuck on to me to the end of my days . . .'[5] The move to Oxford, and their changed lives, gave opportunity to underline their optimism by proving her expectation wrong.

'pot-boilers'

Seven of Cary's short stories had already appeared in the *Saturday Evening Post*. In all, ten were published that year, bringing in well over £1,000 – at least three times his final annual salary in Northern Nigeria. All were published under the *nom de plume* he had adopted in 1909, Thomas Joyce. And like the short story of that year, 'The Crime is Punished', they were written primarily as popular entertainment. Cary himself called them 'pot-boilers'. After writing the first few of them in Borgu during November 1919, he commented that he would not 'waste time and thought on them unless they pay. So far from being good practice for novel-writing I believe they are bad . . . I can turn out the sort of plot required without much difficulty . . . The essentials are a little senti-ment, a little incident and a Surprise. The latter must come at the end. But the end itself must be happy. Commercial art if you like, but it need not be bad, if it is honestly done.'[6] A passing reference to O. Henry (then amassing fame and fortune) identifies one of his models for these stories. But they are not as negligible as Cary thought, and never less than well-crafted examples of the 'commercial' short story so prolifically published between the wars. Mostly third-person narratives, their mode is, with one exception, comic rather than tragic, and they are distinguished by a pervasive and often complex irony – an indication that the author was essentially serious and ambitious, and would not long be willing to churn out 'pot-boilers'.

Elton in 'The Springs of Youth' is perhaps the first of those Cary characters who triumph in the face of adversity. The coiling ironies of this subtle short story – are finely meshed in its simple reversal plot, and its social comedy is both urbane and serious ('William was learned in the ways of woman. He belonged to three clubs, one of them exclusively of bachelors or men who had been bachelors long enough to know a great deal about women').[7]

Much that is characteristic of Cary's mature writing is foreshadowed in these 1920 short stories. The theme of injustice recurs. Brant, the crafty protagonist of 'Salute to Propriety', is one of several ebullient rascals – 'a pug-faced man, prematurely bald, with a cock nose', he has 'at times something of pleasant wickedness in his eye, which had a very invigorating effect'.[8] And like many of Cary's later female protagonists, the malleable Sylvia of 'The Reformation' allows her generosity to be exploited, and ends excoriated by those she has tried to help.[9]

The plots of six of the stories are built on love triangles. In two, competition for the heroine is between a young man who is clearly a version of Cary, and an older man with the advantages of experience and achievement. Young Anderson, in 'The Springs of Youth', has deteriorated physically in West Africa. 'I do wish, Johnny, that you would give up the Service!' pleads Nelly. 'Why do you stay out there?' 'Nowhere else to go. You see, Nelly, I've no special knowledge, except general office work and correspondence. Of course I know some law.'[10]

'A Piece of Honesty' is the story that Andrew Wright had in mind when he commented that one of the group 'is pure Conrad'.[11] Were it less sombre, one could read it as parody of *Heart of Darkness*. Narrative strategy and style are closely imitative, with the narrator listening, 'on the narrow deck of a stern-wheeler on the River Benue in Nigeria', 'under a blackness which no stars could pierce', to one Andrew Bell – 'a voice, and a strangely uninforma-tive voice at that'. The story is about a wealthy diamond dealer whose life of deceit destroys him when he tells the truth and his wife cannot believe him. It accumulates a convincing, painful intensity. While clearly indicating Cary's sympathetic response to Conrad's writing, 'A Piece of Honesty' also suggests, in so sharply contrasting with all the other stories, that the Conradian influence on Cary was far from pervasive.[12]

It was probably Conrad's example, however, that encouraged Cary, in 'A Consistent Woman', to attempt a sophisticated narrative device. For most of its length, this story appears to be told by an omniscient narrator; but towards the end he is revealed to be an interested bystander.[13] In other stories, the narrator's authority is also undermined. Towards the end of 'Salute to Propriety': 'Brant was still struggling with his feelings, whatever they were . . .'[14] And in 'The Reformation' the omniscient narrator is abruptly shouldered aside: 'An experienced writer would put a row of asterisks at this point. Asterisks are highly exciting and they do not involve any banal explanations.'[15] Cary's early interest in point of view, and in questioning omniscient veracity, accord with the prominent role of irony in these stories and, associated with love-triangle plots, point towards the evolution of his relativistic first-person trilogy form.

Indeed, when one scrutinises these ten 'pot-boilers', they yield many instances of quiet experimentation by a sceptical intelligence. Even the consistent tone appropriate to a 'commercial' short story may be attacked from within. The necessary happy ending of 'A Consistent Woman', for instance, is teased into ambiguity when James admits to Sara, who has just agreed to marry him, that he has not in fact been in love with her all the time.[16]

In the last of the stories, 'Salute to Propriety', neither Brant, the hero, nor his wife Fenella, behaves virtuously. In a contest of wits suggestive of Beatrice and Benedick, their triumphant reunion is achieved by trickery on both sides; so that their laughter, as the story ends, has a note of mockery that seems to direct some of the title's irony towards the reader and the mores of the 'commercial' short story.[17]

During 1921, three further Thomas Joyce short stories were published – not in the *Saturday Evening Post*, which turned them down, but in English magazines, which paid at a very much lower rate (one of the larger stories earned only 18 guineas). Cary probably wrote all three in Oxford, and took little pride or pleasure in them: 'Dad says he saw a story of mine in Hutchinson's. I suppose thats the Uncle – a bad yarn. I still wonder why they bought it.'[18] Cary's heart was not in these stories. He had already embarked on more ambitious projects.

One of the obvious strengths of his better short stories is their dialogue; so, with Trudy's encouragement, Cary decided to write a play during the summer of 1921. 'Prue' was sandwiched between two attempts to write novels, 'William' and 'Georgy'.

By the end of May, he was close to finishing 'William', which Trudy later typed for him. But 'William' has not survived. Notes connected with it suggest that its plot (perhaps developed from a 1920 short story) is built on the love triangle later used in *Cock Jarvis* and the two trilogies. 'The woman hesitates between the two lovers one she loves one who loves her. Marries the one who loves her, and is unhappy. Runs off with the one she loves, and is still more unhappy . . .' William was apparently the young unmarried lover – though Cary also considered making his narrator the older *married* lover, as if unable to decide which of the two had better claim to interest or sympathy. [19]

As he was finishing 'William', he wrote to Trudy 'Georgy must be much better than William'. Perhaps he began to make notes for 'Georgy' in June – for already it was becoming a habit to compose more than one work at a time; but he did not start writing it for a few months, and never completed it. The surviving typescript of its opening shows 'Georgy' to have been planned as a popular love story with international politics as one of its themes, an aspect of the putative novel which may have been contrived for popular appeal; in the aftermath of the Russian Revolution, 'the threat of Communism' was being widely debated. [20]

In the summer of 1921, most of Cary's effort was given to writing 'Prue'. At first he enjoyed it, but by the end of July confessed that 'Prue isn't by any means finished, and I'm having a hard struggle with her.' Then she expired; and only fragments remain. When he had first shown interest in writing plays, during 1918, Cary had requested his wife to send him a popular book on play writing and some collections of plays (including West End 'hits' by Hubert Henry Davies, best known for the light romantic comedy *Cousin Kate* – which E. M. Forster was to ridicule in *A Passage to India*[21].) 'Prue' seems to have been a play of that type – a light comedy of no intrinsic originality. [22] Perhaps Cary's lack of artistic commitment doomed the enterprise. If so, this was one reason among several, for during this summer serious personal problems destroyed the optimism with which his career as a professional writer had begun only eighteen months earlier.

'an awful strain'

Cary's 1921 crisis began when Mrs Ogilvie, who had been in poor health for several years, had a heart attack towards the end of May. Trudy rushed to London to look after her, and then spent most of the summer at the West End flat to which her parents had recently moved, or at Blair Atholl in Scotland when they went on holiday.

For part of the time, the children were at home with Cary and their nurse, and his half-sister Shiela soon arrived to help in running the home. He enjoyed his temporarily more prominent role in his young sons' lives. His friends and Freddy rallied to him, visiting and inviting him out; Heneage came to Oxford to write some examinations, and they went punting together. But Cary often felt lonely and unhappy. He was sleeping badly, and, he said half-jokingly, he was missing his 'secretary . . . I believe my mind works better to the accompaniment of "bother" and "dash", on the other side of the table'. Trudy's involvement in his literary work, as typist and critic, was becoming important to him.

Exacerbating his uneasiness in Trudy's absence was an accumulation of worry centred on their precarious, and rapidly deteriorating, financial situation. The 1920 windfall from the *Saturday Evening Post* had been quickly swallowed by housekeeping costs; and it was becoming obvious that, on their joint income from annuities, investments and Irish rents (all of which had been reduced in value by the recession, political turmoil, or the post-war rise in the cost of living), they could not afford to maintain Parkers much longer. Already they were living hand to mouth: 'A bill for rates has come in,' he wrote on 20 July, 'but I think my Derry [rents] should be paid next week and then I can meet it. At present my balance is nine pounds'. Needed new clothes could not be bought; hiring Trudy's typewriter was a burden.

There were, it seemed, only two viable plans of action: to rent out part of the house, and, if that proved insufficient, to move into cheaper accommodation; or to approach Mr Ogilvie for financial help. Cary favoured the first course. To the second course he was strongly opposed; his pride (and no doubt his memories of past Ogilivie scepticism and the 1919 contretemps) rejected any cap-in-hand appeal to his father-in-law.

Both he and Trudy had become sensitive about family references to his writing, interpreting enquiries as hostile criticism. When Trudy reported one such incident, Cary responded 'The family interest in my work is rather sinister (except dear Mum's) – they're all waiting for the smash. I don't mean there's no sympathy, but I've no doubt some of 'em say to themselves "Well – it was obviously madness for him to leave Africa – and this result is not surprising." True enough too.' Trudy must have recognised, in his final comment, the danger that worry over money could precipitate severe marital tension if it reopened the Nigerian debate. Perhaps it was then that she decided to risk taking action herself. She told her parents about the financial problem. Immediately Mr Ogilvie offered Cary £1,000.

Reluctant to accept, and no doubt hurt that Trudy had intervened, Cary decided to go to London to discuss the matter. 'I have been worrying over dear Father's proposal all day,' he wrote to Trudy. 'I need not say how grateful I am', but 'Suppose the position at the end of 2½ years if I have swallowed all this money and failed, as I easily may have failed in two years, or ten years. A situation not desperate would have been converted into something like disgrace. Because the money would have gone to maintain a standard of living to which I was not entitled by success.'

Having put the case for refusal, he went on to assess the advantages of accepting: 'my original purpose was to hold on here for a year at least – living if necessary on securities which have now depreciated so much that it would be a serious loss to sell them. I would still like to hold on for a while if I could . . .' Although he would prefer Mr Ogilvie's help to be in the form of a loan, he conceded that to move from Parkers would involve 'much difficulty, discomfort, and interruption of work – and a harassing six months for you and perhaps the poor children'. So he would consider accepting the offer. But he warned her that 'If at the end of the year we are tottering again, we must go into a littler house or rooms, and let this . . .'

He pocketed his pride, but the ensuing discussions in London caused further tension in the marriage. Trudy complained, on his arrival, that he had not discussed the issues frankly with her before the crisis. Writing to her after his return to Oxford, he accepted this criticism; but went on to complain 'I did not feel when I came up [to London] that you were with me.'

I gave way [in accepting Mr Ogilvie's money as a gift rather than a loan], and immediately afterwards you said you did not understand what all the trouble was about. I should have explained again, but I had had an exhausting and difficult session with father already, had written a full account, had heard your own opinion when you replied, and wanted to drop the subject . . . I think you do understand . . . why dependance is hard for me, and vitally affects my situation. But the matter is now finished, and it is a relief to know that we are secure – for this year . . .[23]

But the matter was *not* finished. Writing from Blair Atholl at the end of July, Trudy tried to cheer him up: 'It is no good saying "don't worry" dearest, but try and not get too low about things – we have a lot to make us happier than plenty of people who are not in such low water – and you are very plucky – the perpetual bad luck is enough to make anyone chronically gloomy, and I know I should have more fits of depression than you have – especially when you feel your work is good – and we both know it is much better than plenty of the stuff which sells by the million.'

The early 1920s were also difficult for some of their relatives. His father was unsettled, having had to move to another engineering company as a result of the post-war recession; Jack was unhappy in his naval posting. In the Ogilvie family, some cheer came with Freddy's engagement to Mary Macaulay, a Scottish girl who, as an undergraduate at Somerville College, had become one of his students. Trudy met her at Blair Atholl and liked her;[24] so did Cary when he got to know her; and she quickly become a close friend. Because she was only twenty and 'nobody could be good enough for Freddy', she had to endure hostility from Mrs Ogilvie, and remembered with gratitude Cary's support during the two years before her marriage.[25] Cary's affectionate admiration for her is indicated by a much later character description ('Mary . . . with her courage and matter of fact cheerfulness; her rather detached and critical air'[26]); by her influence on one of his sympathetic major characters, the limping, scholarly Judy Coote of *The African Witch*; and by his dedicating *Herself Surprised* to her.

Cary received an unexpected visit in the summer of 1921: 'Murry called on me yesterday, he is off to live at Mentone. I believe his wife [Katherine Mansfield] has consumption, poor thing. He is writing for the Supplement as well as the Athenaeum.' No doubt Cary was left feeling more desperately than ever that he must struggle on; in his financial difficulty, Murry's success must have seemed a rebuke. This was their last meeting for thirty-five years.

Bouts of depression recurred, but there were some enjoyable days. In mid August, he told Trudy that, though depressed the previous day ('I was moody because I had not slept . . . and had L.S.D. [money] on my mind as usual'), he had just 'done a fair day's work . . . and had some glorious tennis this afternoon . . . Then Elliott came on to tea, and we talked books for an hour and now I feel in excellent spirits.'

But financial worry continued after Trudy and the children returned at the end of the summer. Although plans to rent part of Parkers as a flat had been shelved, the Carys took in an undergraduate lodger. In November, Mrs Ogilvie had another heart attack and Trudy again had to spend time in London. Cary wrote to her 'I'm afraid Father doesn't like his presents going on housekeeping. God knows how we spend so much or rather how our actual income seems so small when we have to spend it.'

And he now put it to Trudy that they would have to rent out Parkers and move into cheap lodgings – as he had warned her they might have to do. When she agreed, he launched into a relieved, guilty, loving, anguished response, telling her how close he believed he had come to a complete breakdown:

> I shall be as sad as you to leave our first home even tho' we have never been able to enjoy it. But this has been a wretched year for both of us . . .
>
> It makes it worse for me at least that I see how we miss happiness. I love you and need you and bless my luck for marrying you more than you think. I know you better since I have seen you in difficulty, and I love what I know now of your courage and patience. But we needn't live so uneasy a life. Thousands would be astonished or contemptuous to know that we fail to live happily on our income . . .
>
> I am confident, as far as any man can be confident, of my ability to write well. Success is another thing, but sooner or later, if I can wait, I ought to succeed. This isn't an unsupported notion, for I have had beginnings of success – I mean, a public success. But I cannot go on at this pressure. The fact is that I have been overwriting already. My output for these two years has been enormous. And this last week has given me a warning. You know how I got stuck when I got back from town [after accepting Mr Ogilvie's offer]. In those efforts to begin again I felt myself losing grasp – and this last week I haven't been able to keep my head or my legs still . . . I am too tired to control my muscles, or thats how I feel. [27]

He now discussed the financial problems, and their proposed solution, with Freddy, who was helpful and sympathetic; but the same day a depressing parcel arrived from his literary agent: 'Watt sends back two stories, which have been on a round of 20 magazines or so. I shan't begin to do anything until I have published a novel or two.' [28]

Trudy wrote to say she had told her parents about the coming move; and, after suggesting she and Cary should try to get away for a short holiday together, delicately referred to their increasing estrangement: 'I am afraid you haven't felt much like honeymooning lately have you?' [28] The euphoria of 1920 was no more than a taunting memory. His situation at the end of 1921 could hardly have looked bleaker.

CHAPTER TWENTY-FOUR

SETTLING DOWN

1922–1926

'I had to re-educate myself'

The Carys did not, after all, move out of Parkers. They divided the house into two flats, occupying the two upper floors themselves and letting the lower two. While this certainly alleviated Cary's financial worry, it increased other tensions. In July 1921 Cary had commented to Trudy that 'The children are of course a steady strain . . . they are noisy, and ought to be noisy'.[1] Now they would be living at closer quarters, with the added strain of a second family in the house (a situation that continued, with intervals, until after the Second World War).

It was during this period of readjustment, in 1922, that Cary set himself to a regime of methodical reading and careful thought, now seeing them as essential to success as a writer. His intentions and practice had so far been erratic. Did he really know what he wanted to write? Was he intellectually equipped to fulfil his ambition to be more than a composer of 'potboilers'? Such questions underlie his much later statement that, 'after ten years of active, thoughtless, and various experience in the world', he had begun, 'rather late in youth, to ask what it amounted to; to dig up all his foundations, to find out exactly what they were'; and then, finding that those foundations were deficient, 'slowly and painfully rebuilt them . . . as a coherent whole, on which to found a new life and a new mind'.[2]

Having survived the crisis of 1921 with his chosen profession tenuously intact, he must now steady himself for a long haul; to accumulate the knowledge and expertise that would enable him to become the writer – popular but serious – that he wanted to be. 'I had to re-educate myself as a novelist and it took me over ten years. Nothing I wrote during nine of those years was published – most of it was unfinished.'[3] Indeed, apart from one story at the end of 1923, he published nothing between October 1921 and January 1932. And among the vast collection of his manuscripts, very few seem to have been written during 1922 and 1923. Only in 1924 did a substantial, ambitious novel begin to emerge. Before that he probably wrote little and concentrated on his informal programme of reading, trying (in the words of his countryman W.B. Yeats) to 'hammer his thoughts into unity'.[4]

Two abortive novels may have been written before 1924 – 'The Memoirs of Maurice Moody' and 'Whick MacArthur'. In the first, political satire surges round Maurice Moody, an innocent whose name and behaviour link him loosely with Middleton Murry. 'Whick MacArthur', on the other hand, is in realistic mode, with autobiographical elements; in an early episode, the eponymous hero is abandoned by his flighty mother when he is six years old and left in his father's care.[5] Taken together, these two radically different attempts suggest that Cary was feeling for direction; but they also define the poles of his later fiction.

Regular use of notebooks (larger ones for home use, small ones to carry with him), as well as folders or files to hold sheets of notes, became habitual. Notes in a particular notebook might include sketches (of situations), plot outlines, character descriptions, lists of names and places, occasional diary entries, passing observations, and cryptic philosophical meditations, as well as notes from his reading. Some notebooks were filled and discarded quickly, others used frequently over many years. No doubt several, particularly of the 1920s, were lost. The scribbled contents of the over 350 extant notebooks are sometimes illegible, and often difficult to date (although Cary's handwriting changed notably – even sharply at some points – over his lifetime). They compose a rich, but often confusing and infuriating, subtext to Cary's development as a writer.

Some of the earliest jotted ideas of his own during the 1920s are reiterations: 'No rules of thumb they are all the devil's', for instance, repeats a conviction first recorded in his Borgu Notebook. Others show him mulling over fundamental ethical and religious issues: 'Good is absolute and eternal, so is evil, and they are parts of one thing like day and night – the climate in which the spirit breathes and can breathe nowhere else.'[6] As implied in those two notes, dualism and relativism, with a desire to achieve a unified, absolute understanding, seem to have haunted his thinking in the early 1920s, as his 're-education' began.

'Not Wholly Matrimony'

The summer of 1922 brought an unexpected escape from routine in the form of a fact finding visit to Hungary, not far from Cary's fondly remembered Montenegro.

At the end of the First World War, the ramshackle Austro-Hungarian Empire had disintegrated, dethroning Karl, who had succeeded Franz-Joseph as Emperor of Austria and King of Hungary after the latter's death in 1916. In Hungary there was turmoil, as the government of the republic established in 1918 was rapidly replaced by a Communist regime and then, in 1919, by a restored Kingdom under a Regent who refused to accept Karl's claim to the throne. Twice in 1921 Karl and his supporters attempted to overthrow the Regency. Sympathy for his cause in Western Europe included demonstrations and a visit by Oxford undergraduates which resulted in plans for a tour of

Hungary by a group of Oxford dons and students. Cary's old friend Tommy Higham, a don at Trinity College, was invited, and suggested Cary as a member of the group – which also included Julian Huxley.

Cary's letters to Trudy express vigorous enjoyment. On the way to Hungary the party spent some time in Vienna. Cary saw 'no signs of destruction in the streets, but many of a rapid disintegration of the polity. The police, officials etc seem dejected and spiritless.' In Budapest, a strenuous round of official engagements awaited them. 'It is too much of a rush. Our hosts are too anxious to entertain us. But I have never had so interesting and enjoyable a holiday.' At a 'huge official lunch', Cary 'made a speech and gave a toast. Royal Hungary and its people . . . I *was kissed* by a gentleman who had not shaved very well.'

Of little direct importance in Cary's life and work, the episode does indicate the persistence of the conservative in his personality. He identified easily with the Hungarian aristocrats, and seems to have shrugged off social ills for which they held much responsibility. He spent one morning reading 'while the others [went] to see the slums. I know what slums are. This afternoon we have tea with Count Andrasty . . .'[7]

Thereafter Cary's sober, steady efforts resumed, and continued through 1923. His short story 'Not Wholly Matrimony' appeared in the Christmas issue of *Strand Magazine*. It was published under the authorship of Thomas Joyce, as if signalling that the process of his literary regeneration was far from complete. Although still in a 'commercial' mode, and reminiscent of 'Salute to Propriety', it is better than the three 1921 short stories – alert and cheerful, even if it fails to sustain its strong start. This neatly ambivalent story about marriage contains references suggesting that Cary was beginning to read the great Russian novelists extensively during 1923; behind his story's dialogue is an inward debate about their importance, and perhaps a resolution to tackle 'fundamentals' as they had done – but without their 'monotony'.[8]

'Not Wholly Matrimony' seems also to reflect the tension increasingly disturbing Cary's own marriage at this time. Trudy felt excluded by his immersion in reading, and there was little for her to type. Retreating into housework, she characteristically blamed herself for their mutual unhappiness. She was also deeply distressed by Mrs Ogilvie's continuing decline.

On a short walking holiday with Tommy Higham in the Cotswolds during April, Cary wrote urgently to her, with a forthrightness that neither found easy in speech:

Will you believe darling that I love you, that I never forget that even when you are dejected and apparently willing to make me suffer for it, that your very indignation springs from your love. You have a heart like Mother's, feeling so much for others that you torture yourself for them. But I feel too, much more keenly and nervously than Father, while, to tell the truth, in these last three years I have been living on the edge of nervous exhaustion. I don't like writing of it, and I don't speak of it. To think of it is stupid for it only increases the strain. But I think that I should have been more frank even at the risk of your contempt. You are much stronger nervously, or so it seems to me, and cannot perhaps understand my inability to bear the company of other people, or anyone at all, for more than a short time; my need of solitude; my ridiculous fear of small worries, of the smallest exaggeration of passing anxieties, my dislike of looking forward . . . Your life has been hard and difficult but you must not think I can't appreciate your loyalty and unselfishness with a husband who seemed to you selfish and careless. I can't tell you how hard it has been to me, often, to leave you after dinner, when you have played and sung to please me (choosing often the pieces you know I like) to work or sometimes only to read. When you catch me reading alone, I feel guilty, and I am annoyed to find myself with such an emotion, tho' I honourably resist the temptation to hide the book and pretend to be at work. But reading with me is a form of work, and absolutely essential. I have read too little. I must read alone, for the small fear of interruption, resting in my mind, is sufficient to break the necessary force of attention . . .

I know I am an erratic moody fellow, not a suitable husband for anyone. But I love you and enjoy my greatest happiness in your love and happiness. It is a paradox that I do nothing to make you happy and ask you to be happy to make me happy, but the secret of happiness is to look at truth without fear or prejudice and acknowledge it.[8]

'the disappointment of these five years'

In the mid 1920s, the Carys' life in Oxford was very quiet – partly by inclination, partly because of their financial difficulties. They saw Freddy and Mary Ogilvie quite frequently, and their close friends Duncan and Dolly MacGregor and Tommy Higham. They had also made a few new friends – like the don G. Hope Stevenson (author of books on ancient Greek history) and his wife Phoebe. Cary dined occasionally at Trinity or Balliol College, and read in the Bodleian Library. Each summer they went to at least one Commem. Ball with their friends. But there was little other relaxation. They played occasional tennis on golden days, or punted on the Cherwell; and went on short skiing holidays in Switzerland in 1922 and 1923. Early in the 1920s, he had sometimes gone horse-riding, but that had stopped, presumably because of the cost. Otherwise his daily regime kept him in or near Parkers. Most days he worked for periods of one to three hours – in the late morning, mid afternoon and early evening – with brisk walks in between for exercise and contemplation (self-communing became so habitual as he strode rapidly and jerkily along the paths that in later years he would pass friends without noticing them).

Mrs Ogilvie's death in July 1923, after a third heart attack, brought an unexpected change in their family life; for her husband remarried just over a year later. Elsie wrote to Trudy from her home in Cheshire expressing consternation: 'This has been a most awful shock and sorrow to us all I know; my heart *aches* for Father . . . Mother's love for him was such a tremendous and fine thing . . . If he has made a great mistake, he will need our love and help all the more.[10] However, Mr Ogilvie's second marriage brought great happiness to the last five years of his life. Rotha Thomas was his 'old love'; as a young man in Bristol, before he went out to Chile, he had proposed to her,

Left Charlotte Louisa Joyce   *Right* Arthur Pitt Chambers Cary

Arthur Cary with his sister Mab, and Bay Joyce outside the back door of
Castle Cary, about 1883

Left Jack Cary as naval cadet, about 1904   *Right* Joyce Cary, about 1904

The Gryphon Club, Trinity College, 1911: Thomas Higham (back row, 7th from left); Dr Blakiston (President of Trinity), the Rev. Ronald Knox, and Duncan MacGregor (middle row, 2nd, 3rd and 4th from left); Joyce Cary (front row, 6th from left)

Joyce Cary, about 1912

Gertie Ogilvie, about 1912

Above Joyce Cary (left) in Montenegro, 1913

Joyce Cary (front) sailing with Todd (centre), 1914

Right Joyce Cary, Second Lieutenant in the West Africa Frontier Force, after being wounded in the Cameroons, 1915

A bridge built by Cary (with his messenger Garuba crossing it)

Christmas 1919: Cary dining on the balcony of his 'bungalow'
at Kaiama

The Ogilvie family in 1929, shortly before Mr Ogilvie's death. The adults are (standing left to right) Elsie Carlisle, Frederick Ogilvie and his wife Mary, Heneage Ogilvie, Re... Malcolm Venables; and (sitting) Magdalen Ogilvie (Heneage's wife), Trudy Cary, Rot... and William Maxwell Ogilvie, Flo Venables, and Joyce Cary. Among the children ar... Peter (back, right of Heneage Ogilvie), Michael (left, below Elsie Carlisle), George an... Tristram Cary (held by their parents), and Antonia Carlisle (front, second from left)

On the set of *Men of Two Worlds*, 1945. Joyce Cary and Thorold Dickinson are in the centre

yce Cary beside his painting of
rudy playing her cello to Peter's
companiment, early 1950s

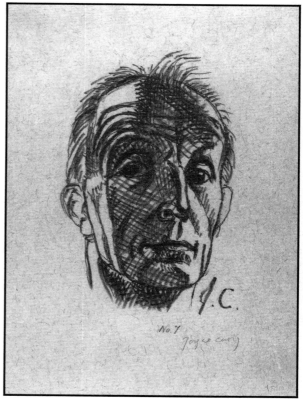

yce Cary's final self-portrait

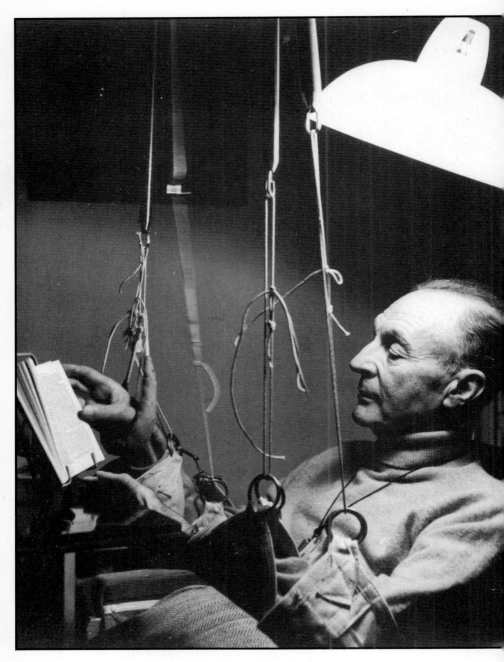

At work, December 1956
(photograph by Douglas Glass)

and now 'she had consented to marry me after all these years'.[11] They moved to Oxford, just a short walk from the Carys'. Her father's arrival was particularly welcome to Trudy but Cary liked Rotha Ogilvie very much, responding to her warmth and generosity (he dedicated one of his novels to her). He also became very close to his father-in-law, who was generous in offering unobtrusive financial help. And it seems that the kindly presence of the elderly couple, seizing happiness together in the face of death (Mr Ogilvie had already had one heart attack) was altogether a beneficent example for the younger couple.

The Carys' financial worry, though now less pressing, persisted. In July 1924, Cary spent a few days in London visiting Heneage (now a house surgeon at Guy's Hospital) and Jack (recently returned from Australia and working as a cartographer in the Admiralty). Worry about his work was frequent and insistent, even in London: 'I *must* get a piece of work finished or I'm afraid of what might happen to me. I'm getting desperate . . . we must start the typewriter again.'[12]

In August and September 1925, he went on holiday to Wales and then Ireland, taking Michael and Peter with him; and in the long letters he and Trudy exchanged, they again anatomised the causes of tension in their marriage, apologising to each other, reassuring each other about the love they always found it difficult to express orally. Although these letters show how serious were the strains, they also show confidence in the fundamental strength of their relationship.

'I don't like to see you write that we have drifted apart,' he wrote. 'What people think for a long time and especially about human relationships comes to be true because they think it, and the thought affects their actions.'

> I am not a good husband simply because I can't give enough time to you any more than to the children . . . No one could be a better wife or mother than you . . . You must believe that I do understand your position. You have no friends in Oxford, and not enough leisure to make any. You spend all your life at dull tasks which must be done again and again without progress, and you have almost no amusements, and apparently very little sympathy . . . I only don't say every day how sorry I am to see you bothered and overdriven because the mere verbal repetition would make it worthless to you. Personally I could not live with anyone who sympathised with me frequently, as if I did, I should know I was going to pieces . . .[13]

He had not, however, responded to her comments about 'the forbidden topic' and she felt driven to return to this issue while he was at Castledawson in September:

> Dearest Joyce – I know you hate me referring to your work – and trying to give you any sympathy – and I know I should hate it in your place – but I only want to say this now – that I have so often spoken as if I didn't understand or realize what a big thing this is for you – I was miserable last night in thinking about it – and what the disappointment of these five years must have meant to you. Darling I *do* understand – and there is nothing I long for more than for you to succeed – and I do think you will. My heart

just aches for you sometimes – when I think how hard you have worked – against awful difficulties – and under the most impossible conditions in the house . . . we must somehow manage to make things easier for you. You have been awfully patient with the difficulties at home . . . perhaps you should have a room out – where I *cant* come and pester you. I am afraid I cant say what I want to – but I do understand about Nigers too – and you have been a darling (more than that – but I cant think of the word) never to have referred to it during these years – I know what you have missed – and whatever you may say – I know I was responsible for your leaving – if we made a mistake then – If your work had succeeded at once – we wouldn't have thought it mistaken – and I think we must believe it was for the best . . .[14]

He returned from Ireland in good spirits after an exhilarating holiday at The Bungalow. He had visited Londonderry, too, hoping to arrange the sale of the inherited houses in which he and Jack had shares – 'It would be a perfect blessing to sell the property. I should get probably a larger income, and be relieved of a great deal of anxiety. The tenants would be better off as owners.' Although that had not proved possible, the effort had necessitated a meeting with his Aunt Bay and his cousin Helen, now the mother of three children and living in Limavady. 'Helen and I who have not met for years exchanged a great many recollections of old times.'[15]

Soon after his return to Oxford, the Carys rented an upper room in a large house belonging to an Anglican clergyman and his wife, the Campbells. Rawlinson Road, near the Dragon School where Michael and Peter were day boys, was a short cycle ride up the Banbury Road. Cary now had an office to work in every day. Trudy's wise suggestion not only removed further cause of tension in their marriage, but helped him to focus his efforts; from that time he wrote more, and to better effect.

'Would you sing a whistle, Daddy'

In May 1925, when Michael was just eight and Peter six and a half, a third son, Tristram, was born; to be followed two years later by a fourth, George. The Carys' increased security, partly owing to Mr Ogilvie's benevolent presence, undoubtedly encouraged their decision to have more children. But, though they had wanted a daughter badly (even consulting a medical 'expert' who gave advice on how to conceive a girl[16]), they ended with a family composed of two pairs of boys.

Cary's relationship with his first two sons had not been close during their early years. Not only had both had been born during his absences in Nigeria; since he had been home, his life had been filled with anxiety. In sad contrast to Arthur Cary's role in his sons' lives, Cary's two elder sons knew him mainly as a distant, preoccupied figure who, though he would tell them entertaining serial stories at bedtime, was often irritated by their noise. Particularly for Peter, who had experienced so much turmoil in his earliest years, this was unfortunate; he drew close to his mother, and felt some hostility towards his father.

With his second pair of sons Cary was to develop a much closer bond. This can be inferred from tender paintings of them as small children, and a series of brief entries in various notebooks where observation and speculation are complemented by emotional warmth. This one is dated 13 September 1927, when Tristram was two years old:

> The other night when I went up to say good-night to T. at seven, I found him asleep with one hand under his cheek, the other lying on the coverlet. The left cheek pressed upwards by the hand crumpled and sharpened the curves of his mouth, and for some reason made more charming and tender the spectacle of the child sleeping. I could not go away or take my eyes off him tho' I was afraid the light might wake [him]. But it did not, and even while I was pulling the clothes over him he continued to breathe so easily that he seemed not to be breathing at all. [17]

And the following notebook entries were made in 1928:

> Jan 2nd
> G., when the bottle was done, wanted more, and was bitterly offended that he did not get more. He buried his head down on his chest, and doubled himself up as his mother held him between her hands, and howled with indignant rage. In the same way, when T. at two was attacked and worried by a playful dog, he, when rescued, bowed down his yellow hair, almost touched the ground and wept with fury and astonishment.

> Feb 11th
> Tristram asks me, Would you sing a whistle, Daddy, and yesterday Could he shoot the typewriter. [18]

Circumstances and, one suspects, his acceptance of English and Scottish upper-middle-class values (instilled by his public-school education, and endorsed by the Ogilvie ethos) made Cary a much severer parent than his own father had been. But the birth of his third and fourth sons revived the deep affection he had felt for children in Nigeria, and strengthened the general interest in childhood that originated in vivid memories of his own early years. At about this time he scribbled in a notebook 'The difference bet. children and grown ups is that the latter have less vigour in all their senses and nerves, and more hypocrisy. They are more skilful in hiding their feeling and motives. Among children even of four and five you will find saints, heroes . . . and philosophers, little beings not so tall as your thigh who will bear atrocious pain in silence, out of pride, or out of unselfish goodness, not to annoy some busy nurse or disturb some other child's sleep . . .'[19] His renewed interest in children and childhood found quick expression in his writing and was to remain influential through most of his career. Some of the finest short stories of his maturity are rooted in these responses to Tristram and George; and his two novels about children are enriched by them.

'piling pigs' carcasses'
In the summer of 1926 came an opportunity to escape routine that had similarities to the Hungarian trip four years earlier. This time, however, he

did not travel far. 'The cloistral calm of Oxford was disrupted by the General Strike,' wrote A. J. P. Taylor. 'No one in Oxford had discussed it beforehand . . . But when the General Strike started most undergraduates responded to the call of duty and went off as strikebreakers.'[20] One who did not was A. L. Rowse, a committed Labour Party supporter. On 1 May 1926 he had written in his diary 'What is impressive is the solidarity that exists in the trade union ranks; but the Government seems equally determined; the preparations made for running essential services and for drafting soldiers into South Wales look ugly to us . . .'[21]

Less than eight years earlier, Cary had written sympathising with the strikers who disrupted the English railways as the First World War ended. Now, whatever sympathy he felt for the strikers of 1926, threatened with lower wages and longer hours at a time of rising unemployment, and whatever antipathy towards Stanley Baldwin's Conservative Government, he decided to respond to the Government's call for support. Again he was giving primacy to the conservative in his personality. His reasoning was probably similar to Sir Philip Gibbs's: 'My sympathies have always been on the side of the underdogs and the underpaid, but they were not in favour of this general strike which was an attempt by the T.U.C. to coerce the Government of the country and take over its power. It was an attack on our Parliamentary system and tradition, and, if successful, would have been the tyranny of a minority over the commonweal.'[22]

For about a week Cary worked as a volunteer docker at Hay's Wharf, Southwark: 'This place is between Tower Bridge and London Bridge,' he wrote the day after his arrival. Accommodation was free, and 'pay I believe 12/- a day'. He spent his first two days 'carrying and piling pigs' carcasses', then was put to 'slinging butter or cheese from a door in the side of a warehouse into vans beneath'. Although he had caught a cold, and the food was poor, 'The work itself I like in all the varieties I've tried, and my companions are usually charming whenever I find myself on the wharves.'[23]

Then the strike was over. For Cary the General Strike seems to have remained a disquieting concern, in the political and moral issues it focused; and thirty years later, he recreated it at the centre of the last novel he completed, *Not Honour More*. Another literary effect of that week in May 1926 came from his observation of the Thames at Southwark: Gulley Jimson's evocation of his surroundings in the early part of *The Horse's Mouth* ('I was walking by the Thames . . . Low tide, dusty water and a crooked bar of straw, chicken-boxes, dirt and oil from mud to mud . . .')[24]

Before 1926 ended, there was a treat for Cary. Heneage Ogilvie had bought a tiny fisherman's cottage, one of a row, at Bosham, a sailing haunt on the Sussex coast. 'It was the smallest cottage we had ever seen,' he wrote, 'covering a floor space of five yards by four. The two tiny rooms were panelled in pine planks . . . Over the door was the name "Bosham Castle" . . .'[25] When Cary joined him there, for the first of several sailing holidays, he was seized with joy at this renewal of his boyhood enthusiasm. 'To-day I have spent all day sailing,' he wrote to Trudy, 'and I haven't enjoyed any day so much in some years . . . It has been the best weather possible for a day in boats – plenty of wind – running small clouds and spells of sunlight between . . . I have always liked this kind of place full of boats and boatmen where even the visitors are practical sailors.'[26] This, too, was to have positive literary results – notably the sailing scenes of his Second Trilogy.

Cary had several times thought he had turned the corner, only to find himself in an apparently endless gully of toil and worry. But as 1926 ended, it really did seem that his life was becoming happier and more productive. Could he now begin to achieve success in his vocation?

CHAPTER TWENTY-FIVE

INJUSTICE & GOD

1922–1928

Cock Jarvis

Before the end of 1924, Cary had embarked on a major writing project: a novel that was to absorb much of his energy and time for the next decade. 'I wrote an enormous book in the twenties which I was never able to finish.' Although abandoned in 'massive ruins',[1] it was, he said late in his life, 'The best novel I ever wrote – at least it contained some of my best stuff – there's about a million words of it upstairs . . .'[2] Jarvis, his protagonist ('probably the best character that ever came to me'[3]), was 'alive, my God he was alive'.[4] But Cary had not been able to control the novel: 'Neither my ideas of life, nor my technical experience were well enough established to handle even a small and simple tale. I wasn't yet sure of what I thought about a lot of things and so I had difficulty in character and dialogue . . .' Cock Jarvis was therefore 'far too ambitious. It took on too big a subject. It went on raising fundamental questions about religion and politics, to which, very much to my surprise, I found I hadn't got the answers . . . I tried to find the answers while I was writing, and the result was a most tremendous muddle. But I was so interested in my chief character and my problem that I went on struggling . . .'[5] In fact, he struggled on for over twelve years. After many preliminary attempts between 1924 and 1926, his most intense efforts were made during 1927 and 1928; then there were several intermittent attempts to revise and complete it up to 1935, when Cock Jarvis was absorbed into a projected novel sequence of which only the first novel, Castle Corner, was completed.

The central theme of Cock Jarvis is injustice, a topic that had been at the centre of his mind since childhood; and this first sustained attempt to grapple with it became crucially important to Cary's development as a serious writer. 'No Justice in world', one note begins. 'Only secret of happiness is to forget oneself. Like J. get on with ones job and not give a damn for anyone . . . In point of fact, everyone must give way to circumstances or other people; or be unhappy. All must learn to conform.'[6] However, Jarvis, like his creator, found it difficult to conform; his struggle to come to terms with injustice could not be resolved so easily.

For the critic Walter Allen, Jarvis is the first appearance of 'the Cary man': 'Jarvis is the indomitable nonconformist who is at the centre of all Cary's work, nonconformist in the literal sense of being incapable of conforming to the Establishment, to authority, and beyond that in the religious sense . . .'[7] Perpetual odd man out, constant victim of injustice, Jarvis is destined for failure and despair if he cannot find a way of overcoming resentment and hatred.

Cock Jarvis, with its mountain of notes and drafts, demonstrates the complex – almost Byzantine – process of composition that characteristically lies behind all Cary's novels. ' . . . a finished book of mine,' he said, 'starts usually, perhaps ten years before, as a character sketch and a bit of description; it goes on to an incident or so, it gathers subsidiary characters, and then perhaps I grow interested in it, and set out to give it form as a book.'[8]

The first phase of this process (he once called it 'the approach') is essentially 'exploration of the theme' in relation to the protagonist, who is 'in a jam' – a situation that tests and reveals personality and generates the novel's central theme. Cary would both 'feel the character' and 'feel what the character feels in that situation'.[9] And 'if you can hold on to that feeling, and somehow record it, so that you can get it again, you have the beginning of your theme, and possibly a book.' Then the second phase ('the formal construction') can evolve.[10]

At no point was plot of great importance: 'A plot is the last thing I think about, and it is never fixed until the story is finished. I may make fundamental changes in my last draft.' Nor was form, in itself, of consequence: 'The form of a book . . . is not in some artificial pattern . . . but in its relation to ultimate truth.'[11] Only 'the whole presentation' need be considered carefully: 'are you going to do it in the first person or the third person? and, if it's in the first person, what style? what sort of person is going to tell the story?'[12]

Throughout the process of composition, one thing mattered utterly: 'The theme is the important point . . . I suspect that the theme, for me, and for most writers, is actually the vital element. And that it is active at both ends of the writer's work, both in the first germ and the development.'[13] Indeed, the theme, intrinsic to the original 'feeling of a character and a situation', 'is the whole reason for the book'.[14]

So Cary's writing during 'the formal construction' of a novel concentrated on particular episodes that seemed to express the theme: 'I write the big scenes first, that is, the scenes that carry the meaning of the book, the emotional experience'. These would then be fitted into a plot, and some might have to be excluded during the extensive cutting and shaping that his novels underwent after the first draft was completed (but even then, 'they have defined my meaning, given form to the book').[15]

This was a writing method that, for all the advantages Cary found in it, often caused disruption and confusion as he wrote version after version of key episodes, transferring them from one part of the plot to another, or from an earlier writing of a whole section of the novel to a later. Moreover, 'The book is composed over the whole surface at once, like a painting, and may start anywhere, in the middle or at the end.'[16] Characteristically, too, he wrote drafts of key episodes with great rapidity, on sheets of foolscap; this encouraged both the proliferation of versions and, as he incorporated passages from earlier versions, muddle.

In time, Cary would facilitate his idiosyncratic process of composition by using envelopes, folders or files for sections of a novel, and by designing a special desk with shelves to keep them separate. In the 1920s and 1930s, however, there was little organisation. Cary's problems with *Cork Jarvis* were certainly increased by his writing method.

A further complication was his habit of working on several different novels in the same period. 'You ask me how I write a novel. But I do not in fact write one novel at a time. The process is more like collecting';[17] 'I have a great many books at any time in various stages of construction'.[18] (In 1933 he even worked on two different novels on alternate days, cheerfully claiming that 'A good idea about No. 1 occurs apropos of something in No. 2 and vice-versa.'[19])

Cock Jarvis, written over an exceptionally long period, is closely connected with several contemporaneous works: notably the unfinished novel 'Cynthia' (the story of a 'spoilt beauty, loves the old man, engaged to the rich one');[20] and the completed but unpublished *Tottenham*. In the first two, Jarvis appears as a minor character; in the second, Jarvis's 'jam', injustice, is worked out with a victimised schoolboy, who commits suicide, as protagonist. But the influence of *Cock Jarvis* extends far beyond those minor works, to at least three major novels – *An American Visitor*, *Castle Corner* and *Not Honour More*. Indeed, it is arguable that *Cock Jarvis*, in its effects on his development and his achievement as a novelist, is the most important single work Cary wrote.

Jarvis (then spelt Jervis) originated in sketches Cary made in 1924. Moving away from the light social comedy of 'Prue' and the majority of his early short stories, he had been considering various African subjects, some clearly based on his own experience, others on imagined situations, or yarns he had heard.[21] Daji (Hausa for 'thick bush') is obviously a fictional representation of Borgu, and Cary drew extensively on his memories as well as his historical knowledge of the area. Vivid incidents fictionalise events described in letters from Borgu.

In 1932 Cary described Jarvis as 'one of the Victorian School . . . with his Elizabethan culture of romantic chivalry, fierce pride, and naif Bible religion'.[22] This omits some of his most prominent characteristics, such as self-pity and a proclivity to violence, to present Jarvis as a type. But he is also strongly individualised. In fact, like all Cary's most effective protagonists, he convinces as both type and individual. That he does so is at least partly because he was drawn from many disparate sources.

As an individual, he is composed primarily of characteristics drawn from Cary's first three superiors in Nigeria. Like Edwardes, Jarvis is 'too easy going to get good service', is concerned about 'my people', and comes into conflict with superiors. From Carlyle, the 'pagan man', have come Jarvis's emotional involvement with his Dajawa, and his genius for talk. But it was Fitzpatrick, the man obsessed by a sense of injustice, who contributed most. Jarvis's troubles with his colleagues and superiors, his grudges, his malicious tricks, his self-pity and sufferings, suggest Fitzpatrick. Then there was the story of a Resident of Bauchi, the Hon. Oliver Howard, who had committed suicide there a few years before Cary's arrival. [23]

Also contributing to the portrait of Jarvis, it seems, were Cary's own father, and Cary himself; both victims of injustice in being deprived of their Irish heritage. When Jarvis performs the act of a sportsman (as he does in his crossing of the Dorina River, 'famous even among the natives, who like all pagans delighting in skilful and dangerous feats, used to come from a distance to watch it'[24]), Arthur Cary was surely in his son's mind. And Jarvis's proclivity for violence? Like other qualities of the man (including his name, with its inversion of Cary's initials), there seems to be a subterranean link with his creator.

Moreover, by the early 1920s British colonial policy was under fierce attack from the Labour Party, which won the 1924 General Election just when *Cock Jarvis* began to preoccupy Cary. His political allegiance was to the Liberal Party, already split, and so badly mauled in that election that, like Jarvis, it seemed 'done for'. Cary valued Liberalism as a democratic force for controlled social melioration, and saw Indirect Rule as a quintessentially Liberal compromise. As one who had administered Indirect Rule, he felt that not only respected ex-colleagues but he himself were among those repudiated by an 'efficiency brigade' of doctrinaire socialists. His sympathy for Jarvis quickly reached towards identification.

As a type, Jarvis owes much to Cary's knowledge of Victorian military and administrative imperialists, notably General Gordon and Lord Lugard. Cary owned a copy of *The Journals of Major-Gen. C.G. Gordon, C.B., at Kartoum*, and wrote of the effect of Gordon's death in 1885 in terms that echo his description of Jarvis.[25] Like Gordon, and Lugard, Jarvis is a military man. The exploit that made Jarvis's name – his 'celebrated march to Daji' in 1902 – is directly based on the exploits that made Lugard famous, the 'Nikki steeplechase' of 1894-95 and his defeat of the Northern Emirs in 1903. Just as Gordon and Lugard were being attacked by a new generation critical of their values, so is Jarvis attacked.

Like Lugard, he is a peppery little man; and his 'naif Bible religion' is Gordon's, as recorded in *The Journals*. Like both imperialists, Jarvis is authoritarian, yet insubordinate towards those in authority; and loathes politicians. These qualities were revived forcefully in Jim Latter, whose very style in *Not Honour More* renews Jarvis's clipped fury. But while Latter was presented as a fascist, Cary felt a large measure of positive sympathy for Jarvis, and struggled to save him from himself.

What Cary could not resolve, ultimately, was the all-important theme. His notes in fact show a long, painful struggle to establish it, a difficulty exacerbated by his early uncertainty about whether Jarvis should end the novel by committing murder or suicide. Either response to injustice seemed appropriate since Jarvis had in him the extremities of both violence and self-pity. But Cary was radically dissatisfied with both conclusions.

As he tried to complete the main version, in 1928, Cary oscillated between the two conclusions, writing urgent notes ('Does J. want sympathy or justice') and even trying out a compromise in which Jarvis attempts murder and fails, then commits suicide ('He sees her in the moonlight . . . and fires . . . ponders – it's too much Cuts his throat and leaves a letter.')[26] This, too, did not satisfy him. But he would in time achieve a resolution – 'Only a man of imagination can overcome the injustice of life'[27] – through further wrestlings with Cock Jarvis.

'the nature of experience'

The wide-ranging speculative cast of Cary's mind is well illustrated by his analytical and theoretical reading in the 1920s. He had begun by concentrating on political theory (one of his two copies of J. S. Mill's *On Liberty* was acquired in 1920), so continuing an interest that his practical experience as an administrator had inaugurated, and establishing it as a lifelong focus of thought. 'Maurice Moody', and before that 'Georgy', had emerged from that interest.

When, however, Cary embarked on his long 're-education' in 1922, his reading shifted sharply to philosophy, and over the following five years ranged also through anthropology, psychology and, especially, theology. ' . . . I began to read philosophy, I seized hold first of aesthetic philosophy, I greedily read Croce, Carritt, Hegel, Schopenhauer.'[28] As well as primary texts, he bought critical commentaries (often in cheap second-hand copies) like *Hegel's Philosophy of Mind* by William Wallace, and *Schopenhauer* by Thomas Whittaker. The closeness of his reading is attested by extensive pencil annotations on fly-leaves and margins; for instance, in Carritt's *Theory of Beauty* 'All beauty the expression of emotion and all such expression beautiful.'[29]

Seeking fundamentals, Cary had obviously decided in 1922 to return to the domain of thought that had most interested, provoked and confused him during his undergraduate years at Oxford. In particular he had taken up again the task of finding an answer to Prichard's challenge of 1909. Carefully, and as methodically as he could manage, he set out to explore the thinking of authoritative aesthetic philosophers in order to evolve his own conclusions. But 'Of course, I was led on at once into the study of general philosophy. For philosophy is like a box of string, one cannot pull at one end without bringing others with it, and at last the whole thing is on the floor.'

By the mid 1920s he was devouring major works like Freud's *Totem and Taboo* and Jung's *Psychology of the Unconscious* (both in translation), Frazer's *The Golden Bough* (the abridged edition of 1922), D. H. Lawrence's *Fantasia of the Unconscious* (1923); commentaries like Eduard Hitschmann's on *Freud's Theories of the Neuroses*; textbooks like William McDougall's *Psychology: The Study of Behaviour*. All had some influence on his thinking. But the main path of his intellectual odyssey led him inexorably from aesthetic philosophy to theology. 'I perceived [that] the nature of experience was for me a key question, because I said "It is through experience that I know the world". And my answer to my question, What exactly is the experience of colour, was at once "A personal experience".'[30]

While he was struggling with *Cock Jarvis*, he began to read such books as R. R. Marett's *Threshold of Religion*, C. E. M. Joad's *Common-Sense Theology*, Rudolf Otto's *The Idea of the Holy*.

It was an Oxford acquaintance, however, who led him towards a solution of his central problem. Through Duncan MacGregor, Cary had come to know two Balliol philosophers. A. D. Lindsay, Master of the College from 1924 to 1949, had published books on Plato and Bergson; in 1927 *The Nature of Religious Truth: Sermons preached in Balliol College Chapel* came out – Cary may well have heard the original sermons, and probably knew the book. John MacMurray, later Professor of Philosophy at London and Edinburgh Universities, was a tutor and lecturer at Oxford between 1922 and 1928. Cary enjoyed discussing philosophical issues with both acquaintances and must have profited from their suggestions for his reading.

In 1927 MacMurray gave Cary a copy of *Adventure: The Faith of Science and the Science of Faith*, edited by Burnett H. Streeter and others. MacMurray's own contributions to this collection of essays comprise Parts II and V of the book, 'Beyond Knowledge' and 'Objectivity in Religion'. In the latter Cary marked several passages heavily, including: 'God is . . . necessarily personal. On no other terms can the demands of the religious experience be satisfied, since the relations which are the stuff of religious life are personal relations. God must be judge, confidant and helper. Can prayer be addressed to the impersonal?'[31]

In later years, Cary repeatedly asserted a view of the nature of God very similar to MacMurray's. For example: ' . . . I believe absolutely in God as the ground of love, beauty and goodness. These are general things which can only exist in personality; that is why we think of God as a person.'[32] And again: 'Can you imagine a feeling floating about by itself, without anyone to feel it? Love without a lover? The goodness, the love we find in the world is personal. That's why we know God as a person, and only as a person.'[33]

MacMurray may also have helped Cary towards a reconciliation of his relativist–absolutist dilemma. He claimed that 'the more universal a person becomes in his self transcendence, the more unique does he become in his individuality. The transcendence of God is His unique individuality; His immanence is His absolute universality.'[34] Although Cary might have jibbed at so paradoxical a statement, his ultimate view that human experience is composed simultaneously of the contingent and the permanent, the relative subsumed by the absolute, is not essentially dissimilar from MacMurray's reconciliation of the universal and the individual. 'The world is not merely a flux of senseless change,' Cary wrote. 'Underneath all the turmoil there are certain fixed and permanent things too. In daily life there is always affection, family love and responsibility, ambition . . . and on the other hand anxiety, loss, bitterness and danger . . .'[35] Another statement of this belief opens with a significant reference to painting: 'There are only three primary colours from which painters have built up the whole of their art, but those primary colours are constant and reliable . . . we are all of us every day dealing with the permanent elements of life as well as the transitory.'[36]

In 1927 Cary had not yet arrived at the basic tenets on which his later, holistic thought depended; but he was moving towards them. At about the same time as he read MacMurray's argument for a personal God, he was also reading A. N. Whitehead's argument for an *impersonal* God, in *Religion in the Making* (1927). His first response was positive. He found himself strongly 'attracted to the philosophy of Whitehead, who seems to explain the existence of pure experience in the human mind, without committing himself to a personal being in the universe'. Extensive annotations in his copy of Whitehead's book indicate one aspect of the philosopher's thought that was particularly congenial, and provided an answer to Prichard: its apparently seamless integration of the aesthetic and the religious. As summarised by Cary, 'God is self-consistent among change – he is measure of aesthetic consistency in world. His immanence gives consistency to creativity . . . Aesthetic experience = an actual fact . . .' This had attractive similarities to Cary's own intuition.

But Whitehead's insistence on the impersonality of God troubled Cary because it implied a conception 'of the world as an immensely complex psycho-physical machine; a real of real forms, like Plato's world, but still, even in the spirit, rigid and restrictive . . .' Cary found this impossible to accept, and continued 'believing in freedom in spite of my reason'. Who was right about the nature of God: Whitehead or MacMurray?

Resolution of this dilemma came to Cary as an epiphany, a moment of grace tantamount to a religious conversion. Describing it long afterwards, he could not date the experience; but it may have occurred in the spring of 1928, when he had temporarily abandoned *Cock Jarvis*, had written *Tottenham*; and was urgently seeking some acceptable explanation for pervasive injustice in human experience. Jarvis, after all, could respond to injustice, however repugnantly, by murder or suicide; but a small boy tormented by his fellows until only suicide offers relief? For Cary, the suffering and death of innocent children was the ultimate test of religious belief; and that was the very theme he was exploring in 1927, even while he was debating the conflicting theoretical positions of Whitehead and Mac-Murray. If God was personal, how could He allow the innocent to suffer? If He was impersonal, how could there be any freedom in a mechanical world?

> . . .one day, when I was walking in the Parks, looking with pleasure at the trees by the Cherwell, . . . I had a very sting of that personal quality in experience, which had been present to me before . . . it struck me with force that it is impossible in fact [to] conceive of personality in the terms that I had used, as a diffuse psychological character.
>
> I had said, the psyche or spirit which is the centre of experience no doubt is a realm of experience or intuition peculiar to itself; but it depends upon the body, the body upon . . . space-time . . .

But now . . . I perceived that by a personal experience one means something quite different from a psychological experience, one means something in short that happens not to the mind but to the self. When I had said before that the experience of colour was a personal experience I had failed to comprehend my own meaning which was simply that colour could only be felt by a self and communicated by a self. So . . . as it were, in the middle of the parks, I stood in the presence of God, not indeed the God of religion and theology, but a God so close and present, since he spoke to me through my very eyes, that I felt in a real sense, my being as part of his being. And so far from this impression becoming weaker, it strengthened. So that I could not conceive how I had ever failed to mistake it. It was as obvious to me as the earth and the sky that all experience took place in the self, in the person of the universe, and could not take place in any other way. [37]

That epiphany, finally meshing his artistic intuition and intellectual speculation, gave Cary the metaphysical foundation that he craved. On it he was to build an interpretation of human experience which answered the question that had tormented him, satisfied his urge for unity of thought, and allowed him to become a confident writer.

Cary's intellectual struggle was far from over, and there would be many uncertainties – even after the publication of his first novel in 1932 – as he gradually forged his 'philosophy of life'. But as the 1920s ended he could feel that his thought was at last consolidating, reaching towards coherence.

CHAPTER TWENTY-SIX

PUBLISHED NOVELIST

1928–1932

'a family man'

By the late 1920s the Carys' personal life was much improved, after the severe strains that had harmed their early years in Oxford. But financial worry did not evaporate.

Mr Ogilvie's death in 1929 both removed his generous informal subsidy (especially of the boys' education) and provoked a family disagreement that marred Cary's relations with Freddy Ogilvie during the rest of their lives. Mr Ogilvie's will established a trust fund from which annual stipends were to be paid to Rotha and his five children. Heneage and Freddy were appointed trustees. For the Carys, at a time when school fees were an increasing burden and share prices were falling, this arrangement was much less helpful than a large lump sum that could be invested and drawn upon at need. Cary asked Heneage and Freddy to break the trust and pay out Trudy's share of the estate. Heneage was reluctantly amenable; probably Rotha and Elsie supported him; Flo and her husband the Reverend Malcolm Venables may have had reservations. But the deciding voice was Freddy's, and he refused outright.

Although the Carys' financial state was never as bad as during the early 1920s, it steadily deteriorated for several years after Mr Ogilvie's death, especially when, from 1931, the Depression took hold. But this worry interfered less seriously with Cary's writing.

Not did he allow family tensions to distract him. In July and August 1929, he was working hard on a novel, so had refused to go away on holiday near Plymouth with Trudy and the boys. He remained in Oxford, first with Rotha Ogilvie in Charlbury Road and then at the Campbells' in Rawlinson Road (where he still had his office), having promised Trudy that he would join her as soon as possible. When she became importunate, he tried to be patient. When she persisted, he became angry: 'Please dear for my sake try to think of it as a job to be done with as little waste of nervous energy as possible – or a pain if you like – like toothache – and do not let it make you old before your time.'[1]

There were other family worries. At birth George had been very weak; as he grew older, his health gave cause for further concern. A brief description of him as a baby, probably made in 1929, in hindsight suggests one of his disabilities: 'When I came into the night nursery at eight, it was not yet dusk, and I saw a round dark object rising from the head of the baby's cot. He scrambled hastily but in silence to his feet, and grasping the top bar of the cot, peered at me, sidelong. My face was not a foot from his, and I could feel [see] the dark circles of his eyes, wide-opened, not frightened but wondering. He did not know who this was.' A year or so later it had become clear that George's eyesight was seriously defective, though he was growing into a fearless and high-spirited little boy. In October 1930 he had the first of several eye operations in London.

Meanwhile Tristram was showing early signs of a creative temperament and his liveliness got him into constant scrapes; together the two little boys were more than a handful. Cary was, he often said, 'a family man'. And never more so than after the births of his two younger sons. His greater involvement in family life during that period absorbed time and energy. But this, too, did not greatly distract him from his work. He was mounted now, and riding with greater assurance.

An optimistic, determined tone is characteristic of Cary's letters during the years between 1927 and 1932. After the publication of his first novel, a temporary loss of confidence revealed how firmly he had had to exercise self-control to leap the first fence: 'I hope you won't allow yourself to worry for a more unprofitable and disastrous occupation couldn't be found,' he told Trudy.

> As you know I simply cant afford to do it. I have very little confidence in myself and most of my life is a struggle to assure myself that I shall not be a failure. Events do not support me in this struggle up to the present. Ten years to produce one book shows what lack of faith can do . . . Books are a compound of magnetism and hard work (which I give them, God knows) and sublime self-confidence which I haven't got. I only have a kind of artificial pumped up kind, wound out of my own belly and leaving me little appetite for the ordinary pleasures of life. [3]

Aissa Saved

Cary's first two published novels were rooted, according to a draft Preface, in a single experience that 'stuck deeply in my memory, and wld. not let itself be forgotten'.

On a Nigerian river steamer, 'sometime about 1915', he had met an American missionary, 'a gentle sad man, with a wife and baby'. 'The baby looked as if it were dying; it was too feeble even to cry. The mother, worn by fever, held it in her arms the whole time and never took her eyes off its face . . .' Cary spoke to the missionary,

> And what struck me (I was very young in the Service) was his remoteness. He was aloof; not so much hostile to us as British officers, and servants of the Empire; as calmly assured of our damnation. We were wicked men. Also we

were blood-guilty men, for we were fighting a war. We were anti-Christ. For him . . . God literally settled everything . . .

I have never forgotten that man and his family, or seeing them going over the side later that day into a dugout. We had supposed that they were going down river to hospital. We found now that they were on their way to duty, to a bush station among fever swamps . . . I watched the woman . . . holding a topee over the baby's shaken face and head. Her yellow hollow face had no expression at all . . . The man, crumpling his big legs in the narrow dugout, did not speak to her or to us . . .

. . .I still remember the strong emotion of frustration with which I looked at the woman and baby . . . One could not help pity and yet . . . the pity was not wanted . . . And again with the man, baffled exasperation at his intolerance, his enormous self-assurance, was mixed with admiration for his courage and self-sacrifice.

Above all, I had felt, in [that] experience, the immense power and dangerous potential of religious conviction . . .

From these impressions came several notes, little pieces of dialogue and description. One of these gave birth to a quite different missionary in *Aissa Saved*. Another, combined with recollections of a lady, a very charming American lady, helped to produce Marie Hasluck [of *An American Visitor*] . . .[4]

Cary's 'approach' to *Aissa Saved*, in notes and 'pieces of dialogue and description', probably began in the mid 1920s. By the end of 1927 he was working on a story apparently called 'The Ass' (a reference to its missionary protagonist?). Early in 1928 (perhaps in the aftermath of his 'Cherwell epiphany') this seems to have expanded rapidly into a potential novel that he called 'Christians' or 'Juju Christ'; whose plot centred on religious conflict precipitated by a missionary couple who 'must be orthodox but not realising force of their words'.[5] Among its minor characters was a girl called Baju who would grow into the eponymous heroine, as Cary focused on the implications of the 'jam' she was in. 'The essence of this present book,' he told his publisher, Ernest Benn, 'is . . . struggle, conflict.'

Cary also focused on a cause of cultural conflict beyond the religious and social: education. In drafts of a letter to Benn, he explained that 'The general background of the book is humanity in a time of rapid transition; and especially children eager to know what they ought to do' and who can be 'as easily turned into heroic saints as heroic gunmen'. The 'finished products' of their various educations are 'Ali, from the Government school, a mahomedan in name, in ethics a public-school boy, Jacob formed by coast traders, the [missionary couple] and Ojo by the church, Tanawe by the local tradition; and Aissa in process of religious education. Each . . . is convinced that his religion or philosophy of life is the only right one, and the cultures are therefore at war . . .'[6]

When *Aissa Saved* began to emerge and dominate his thought, Cary was still anxious to complete *Cock Jarvis*, and had recently written *Tottenham*; moreover, he had reconsidered *Daventry* (the nearly complete novel written in Borgu), with the intention of revising and completing it for publication. All three works strongly influenced *Aissa Saved*. (Indeed, he linked them to *Aissa Saved*: 'I meant at one time to call this series of books of which several are in construction "There's a War On", as a general title . . . since they all deal with [the] theme of war between incompatible ideals . . .'[7])'The novel's conclusion – Aissa's death, a consequence (like the earlier sacrifice of her baby) of the 'war' – is essentially that of *Daventry*, her role as victim intensified by Cary's recent work on *Cock Jarvis* and *Tottenham*. He had specifically connected the latter two protagonists with Christ: 'He is a Christ and grasps wisdom – no good resenting anything' ran one note about Jarvis;[8] and another saw him as '*a Christian* – full of noble sentiments, patriotism and prayers' who, ironically, '*doesn't understand essence of Xtianity*'.[9]

Cary was also probing Christianity more generally at about this time, as notes like the following indicate: 'Christ's message of love good very good – it *creates* the keenest happiness and also serves internationalism (politically good). But his godship bad because of theological implications and complications. The idea of God derived from Christianity very bad – i.e. the cruel legal[istic] god. The idea of world as waiting or testing place bad . . .'[10] His scrutiny of Christianity may have been stimulated in part by a recently published Middleton Murry book, *The Life of Jesus* (1926); and he had also been reading with keen interest William James's *Varieties of Religious Experience*. It is also possible that a series of impressive, deeply moving small paintings, which linked the Crucifixion to the suffering of children, was begun in the late 1920s.[11]

At an early stage in the evolution of *Aissa Saved*, before Aissa emerged as a major character, the 'Christians' story became entangled with another, the 'Ali story', drawing on the personality and situation of Lafia, the young scribe whose sense of duty had so impressed and disturbed Cary in 1918. The 'Ali story', Cary remembered, developed from an earlier story 'written at a time when I, having just left the Nigerian Service, was a good deal disgusted by what seemed to me the enormous folly and meanness of a great many who were attacking what they called Imperialism'. In that story – 'I don't think it had even a name' – 'Ali', whose 'sense of duty' had made him unpopular with his own people, was 'destroyed by some popular demagogue, some bumsuck of the crowd . . .'[12]

Cary was surely referring to an untitled 'fable' (in one of his notebooks) that begins 'A negro from a cannibal village, going for a soldier to white men, learnt to write and read and figure. Taking his leave after the war, he went back to his village and shewed off his accomplishments' – which do not impress the villagers since they appear to have no practical value. 'However, when the Emir's tax collector came, he was able to reckon each man's tax in a moment, and even to write down his name in the receipt list. Thus no man had to pay twice over. But the chiefs and heads of houses when they saw he had power seized him on a charge of sorcery, and beat him to death. The poor people also were pleased to see him punished . . .'[13] This fable of injustice seems to have influenced not only *Aissa Saved*, with the incorporation of Ali's story, but also *The African Witch* and *Mister Johnson*. In *Aissa Saved*, the 'Ali story' essentially parallels Aissa's – an early example of Cary's 'doubling'.

For all her vigour and resilience – much greater than Daventry's and Johnny

Brant's in Tottenham – Aissa could not escape the role of victim assigned to her by the novel's theme of injustice. But her death is less defeat than triumph, primarily because the force of her imagination, when the narrator enters her dying mind, allows her final vision to insist on authenticity. 'Jesus had taken her, he was carrying her away in his arms, she was going to heaven at last . . .' Aissa's heaven is what her imagination has created out of three cultures, 'the great hall of God with pillars of mud painted white and red. God, in a white riga and a new indigo turban, his hands heavy with thick silver rings, stood in the middle and beside him the spirit like a goat with white horns. Abba was sitting on its back looking frightened and almost ready to cry. One of the angels was holding him and putting his cap straight. The others were laughing at him and clapping their hands.'[14]

This conclusion all but explodes the novel's main theme. Cary was already, intuitively, feeling towards what would become a dominant theme of his mature writing: the power and significance of creativity. By enveloping *Aissa Saved* in a complex irony (beginning with its title), and linking all its many characters to the consequences of cultural misunderstanding, he sustained a fragile thematic unity. That irony so defeated some of his critics, however, that Cary felt it necessary to draw explicit attention to his main theme two decades later: 'Some correspondents took the book for an attack on the Missions. It is not so . . . But it does try to show what can happen to the religious ideas of one region when they are imported into another.'[15]

To Ernest Benn he had written that the novel was 'in one sense an attack on one kind of sacrifice. It seeks to shew that one idea of sacrifice, where removed from that of utility, of service becomes pure juju and also self-indulgence. Thus Carrs conversion in the second chapter . . . and Ojo's and Aissa's discovery in the last that to be happy it is only necessary to abandon responsibility and give up all to Christ are critical points. These are in fact surrenders . . .'[16] Cary was distressed that reviewers utterly failed to recognise that. But the fault was largely his. The power of *Aissa Saved* flows from Cary's intuition and empathy; and these were still, as with *Cock Jarvis*, insistently at odds with his intellect.

For a first novel, however, *Aissa Saved* is remarkably assured and distinctive, as several reviewers noted; even if it suffered from thematic incoherence and a superabundance of characters (some given in authentic names) jostled into a narrow space. In structure and tone, even in its ironically thematic title, *Aissa Saved* predicted – more accurately, in many respects, than its three immediate successors – the novels of Cary's maturity: short, numbered chapters; persuasive realism; rapid and apparently random action; occasional humour (as in the hilarious bridge-making episode); violent incident narrated with succinct objectivity; intensity; a matter-of-fact style; an essentially episodic structure.

An American Visitor

In February and March 1928, after abandoning his effort to revise *Daventry* and before he immersed himself in *Aissa Saved*, Cary had worked hard on the first part of *Cock Jarvis*. After completing *Aissa Saved*, he may again have worked on *Cock Jarvis* before turning to a story with obvious similarities and, as hero, a District Officer who has many of Jarvis's qualities and is similarly a victim of injustice.

Monkey Bewsher is simpler and more positive than Jarvis, however; the Fitzpatrick-like qualities so prominent in Jarvis have given way to a Carlyle-like exuberance. He is first seen performing the daring act of a sportsman, then described authorially as enthusiastic, reckless, nonchalant, and compared to 'a boxer or steeplechase jockey'; his colleague and fellow conservative Gore thinks of him as 'one of the happiest men he had ever known'.[17] Bewsher's political role, too, as a 'pagan man' opposing the forces of 'progress', is Carlyle's, his death at the hands of a rebellious tribe one that Carlyle routinely risked. As presented in the novel, that fate has the ironic ambience of Aissa's. And the role of Bewsher's main antagonist is similarly ironic – for Marie Hasluck, the American visitor who becomes his wife, loves and admires him. Or does she?

This novel, arguably one of Cary's best, grounds its ironies in the personalities and relationships of its main characters as well as in its events. In *Aissa Saved*, Cary's characterisation was far from simplistic (the Carrs, for example, have a convincingly complex relationship, and even minor African characters, like the small girl Tanawe, are vividly realised). But in the second novel he published, Cary reduced the number of minor characters, allowing himself more space to explore the central characters and their conflict, which is rendered inevitable by the clash of ideology caused by political and, again, cultural conflict.

Reviews were impressed: 'a first-rate novel . . . it drives home the mistaken zeal of the idealist endeavouring to plant his ideas in unprepared soil' (*John O'London's*); 'an ironical political parable, which at the same time is a realistic picture of life in British Nigeria' (*TLS*).[18] One fellow novelist who deeply admired *An American Visitor* was Graham Greene. In 1954 he told Cary he was reading it for the third time: 'What a really great book it is – it seems as fresh, as moving, as sad as when I first read it.'[19]

When the novel was nearly finished, Cary told Ernest Benn that it was not only 'more important and elaborate' but also 'a decidedly more popular kind of book than the last'.[20] To Edwardes, his old superior, he confessed that, although the critics had been 'extremely kind', *Aissa Saved* had sold badly (less than 1,000 copies in fact). His new novel, Cary told him, 'deals with a pagan tribe attacked by civilisation in its most insidious forms: social and religious . . . But my interest is not so much in the black man's mind as in everybody's mind . . .'[21]

By his own account, he wrote *An American Visitor* quickly (in eighteen months, he later estimated) – although again drafts proliferated and the total number of surviving manuscripts is far greater than for *Aissa Saved*. No doubt the common origin of the two novels eased his writing of the second, and the central situation, of the pioneer administrator attacked and ultimately betrayed by his wife and a young man she has loved, is of course *Cock Jarvis's*.

Moreover, a central theme of *An American Visitor* – the destructive consequences of political naïveté – had been reinforced by recent experience in
Oxford.

The 'very charming American lady' who reminded Cary of the American
missionary he had met years before on the Niger may in fact have been neither
American nor female. In the draft of a philosophical essay, Cary recalled being
asked by the Headmaster of the Dragon School to attend a lecture 'by a well-
known doctor, a specialist in the nervous diseases of children. The subject was
the psychology of the child.'[22] After 'a great many contemptuous and facetious
remarks about the stupidity of parents and especially mothers', the doctor had
'committed himself to the policy of laissez-faire'. Cary may have known an
American woman of similiar views, but equally he may have invented her, to
avoid identifying the 'well-known doctor'. Perhaps he remembered an anecdote
he had mentioned in the draft of a letter to his publisher: 'Aissa's sacrifice of her
child has had its prototypes in Christianity as well as paganism – I believe a
woman in America sacrificed her child in the same way at a camp-meeting.'[23]

The woman of his Preface to *An American Visitor* is described as arguing that
'children should get their own ideas of right and wrong' without interference
from adults. Cary, convinced that adequate education was essential for moral
and psychological health, did not take her seriously at first. Then was appalled
'when I found that she meant just that'. Despite a 'strong sense of duty towards
the children and society', 'it was her practice to leave children of five and six to
decide all moral issues for themselves . . .' 'She was, in short,' Cary concluded,
'an anarchist of the most extreme kind . . .'[24]

Her opinion allied her to Tolstoy, whom Cary was already criticising as
muddled and culpably simplistic in the writings of his later years. 'Tolstoi says
resist not evil, but his teaching is an attack upon evil . . . It is not possible to
solve the great problem of what is good and what is bad by [any] rule of
thumb . . . One must be prepared to take responsibility every day and always,
and judge each [case] on its merits.'[25] His indictment of Tolstoy's and all 'inner
light' doctrines (as he was soon calling them, after the title of G. K. Hibbert's
book[26]) is perhaps most powerfully stated in a later essay draft: 'How many millions have died in every kind of wretchedness because Tolstoy, in the arrogance
of his power over men's minds, taught them to hate their state or their church,
and to dream of a world without government, without authority . . .'[27] That is
Marie Hasluck's dream. Irradiated by her 'inner light', she can smile welcome
to anarchism, pacifism, communism – the gods to whom she ultimately, and
ambiguously, sacrifices Bewsher.

An American Visitor is more carefully crafted than *Aissa Saved*, its pace
better controlled and varied; and it gains depth from Cary's research into Nigeria's 'pagan tribes' and his reading of Freud and Jung (especially the former's
Totem and Taboo). It is a very 'adult' novel, not only in the unusual absence of
children among the prominent characters, but in its comparatively sombre tone
and emphatic concern with philosophical and political issues. Its main fault,
perhaps, is uncertainty in defining the personalities and roles of some of the
minor characters; even Cottee seems not fully articulated.

The concluding chapter is particularly impressive. Cary's tentative questioning of T. F. Carlyle's conservative ideals, put with some subtlety into Cottee's mind, predicts the emergence of a major theme of Cary's later writing, creativity. But in its elegiac final pages, An American Visitor gives full emphasis to the pain of those (one is aware of the hovering ghost of the painter at Étaples) who, enmeshed in 'sentiments and attachments and associations', must 'see everything they valued, and rightly valued, suddenly overwhelmed and trampled into rubbish . . .' Mutedly present also is the consolation Cary had discovered through MacMurray: 'the roots of beauty [are] as indestructable and as fertile as life itself'.[28] In this controlled complexity and tension the novel's power is rooted.

'The inner light'

Around 1931, in the same period as he was writing An American Visitor, Cary also began to consider writing a story entitled 'The Buchmanite', and did write a wild novel of political satire, Arabella, which attacks Communism and Fascism as destructive 'inner light' creeds. Both works have obvious thematic links with An American Visitor.

Buchmanism, the evangelical movement called after its charismatic American founder Frank D. Buchman, and later known also as 'The Oxford Group' and 'Moral Rearmament', had become notorious in Oxford during the late 1920s. From the first, the movement was criticised for its emphasis on the subjective, its amorphous and superficial doctrines, its often destructive effects on converts. One of those who ridiculed Buchman publicly was Cary's friend A. P. Herbert, who asked Cary to nominate him as Independent candidate for the (since abolished) Oxford University parliamentary seat in the 1935 General Election. Cary watched the campaign with great interest, and after the election kept in touch by visiting Herbert at Westminster, so gaining extensive inside knowledge about political affairs. Herbert attacked Buchmanism in a House of Commons speech;[29] Cary, who knew a promising undergraduate who had given up his studies under its influence, had long been hostile to the movement. A plot outline for 'The Buchmanite' centres on a girl convert; 'Shew Buchmanite hunting for prey and catching it in an unsuspected place'.[30]

While 'The Buchmanite' would have confronted a particular 'inner light' movement, Arabella, which probably originated in 'Memoirs of Maurice Moody', set out to satirise the whole 'inner light' phenomenon, especially as manifested in international political movements of the time. The novel throws aside realism for black humour, flat characters, and a frenetically episodic plot. By absorbing Cary's penchant for the wild and bizarre, it may have purged An American Visitor of such qualities.

In May 1933, Cary lamented abandoning Arabella 'within a fortnight of completion. Simply because I lost faith in it – a natural result of physical tiredness. It seemed to me stupid stuff and I dropped it because I had lots of ideas for other books'.[31] (He completed it later.)

In Professor Hoopey (one of its main characters, Arabella presents a hostile portrait of Bertrand Russell. For Cary – he had recently been reading What I

Believe (1925) – Russell's thought epitomised the 'inner light' mentality, and his copy of the book is embellished with such critical comments as 'Ethics a matter of popular approval. So torture was right in the Middle Ages' and 'No moral standard outside human desires'.[32]

As the novel rampages from one farcical situation, one country and political system, to another, Cary's political and social criticism loses focus. There are certainly fine moments – as when, for instance, Hoopey amiably condones the execution by communist soldiers of two captives (unrecognised by him, they are, of course, Arabella and her companion): 'Oh! if you are shooting bourgeois, that's another thing. So long as you do it with reasonable humanity.' But *Arabella* is generally too flatulent, too repetitively knockabout, too carelessly written, to be effective satire.

It contains a clear expression of Blakean influence, however – a decade before *The Horse's Mouth* – when Hoopey asks 'Did you realise Arabella, what Blake meant when he wrote "A mighty spirit leaped from the land of Albion / Named Newton, he seized the trump and blowed the enormous blast . . ."'[33] The theme of creativity was summoning Cary.

CHAPTER TWENTY SEVEN

FAILURE & SUCCESS

1932–1935

'our bad times are nearly over'

After *An American Visitor* Cary was at first unsure what to write next. He had told Edwardes that, 'tho' I have several other African books in various stages, my next will probably deal with English tribes, pagans and witch-doctors';[1] and he later recalled deciding 'to write no more books about Africa',[2] perhaps because he wanted now to establish himself in the mainstream of the British novel as well as improve his sales. *An American Visitor* would not be published until August 1933 and meanwhile his financial situation was deteriorating as a result of the Depression. He embarked on not one but two stories, both set in England.

The first he referred to as the 'Jew story'. Again his protagonist was to be a victim. 'Levy suffers the most outrageous blows and misfortunes simply from his power of enjoying beauty, goodness . . . His enemy should be another Jew . . .'[3] One scene depicts Levy as the millionaire Chairman of the 'Anglo-Zimbabwe' Company (a situation that would contribute to the creation of Nussbaum and the imperialist theme in *Castle Corner*). No doubt the 'Jew story' was influenced both by Hitler's increasing attacks on the Jews in Germany and by memories of Jewish boys at Clifton College (where they had their own House, during Cary's time, and suffered some persecution; his protagonist has the same name as a Cliftonian contemporary). But the 'Jew story' was soon dead.

'Tod' was largely autobiographical. It expanded into Cary's first projected trilogy. The muddled state of the notes and drafts makes it hard to discern the intended final state of the novels, but they certainly foreshadow aspects of both *Castle Corner* and Cary's two published Trilogies. Although narrated in the third person, each novel was, apparently, to focus on one of three major characters: Tod himself, Moore, and a girl, Catherine Foley. Family history was to be prominent ('Rise of Rankins and fall of Basketts'). Moreover, according to various 'schemes', the trilogy was to reflect English history from about 1885 to about 1930, beginning with the 'Victorian age. Shew its *enormous underlying self-confidence based on material progress* its immense belief in automatic progress and slogans.'⁴

The main theme of the trilogy's first novel Cary defined in relation to *Cock Jarvis*: 'Greatness of Cocky is fundamental problem formed of forgiveness. and resignation. Fundamental problem in Tod. to find something worthwhile.'⁵ Tod, though he may also owe something to his namesake of Montenegrin days (Cary had mourned the loss of a pipe given him by Todd, and had gone sailing with him in 1914), seems to be largely a version of the young Joyce Cary as seen through Ogilvie eyes: 'There was something flamboyant about Tod; his gestures, his dramatic stories, his brag; and when he took off his overall and showed himself in a bright green suit with enormous checks, a purple shirt, a dark crimson tie . . . Ollier almost burst out laughing, and looked round him to see what the Foleys thought of this extraordinary bounder.'⁶ Tod's projected fate was gloomy, however: his 'vitality can't find exit *with art or girls* – on account of his upbringing – and so he tires himself and finally succeeds in killing himself . . . Tods vast power and pride turns into self-contempt and boredom because he can't believe that anything is worthwhile.'⁷

Moore, like Tod, has obvious autobiographical elements, but qualities of his personality (as well as his name) probably also derive from the flamboyant Anglo-Irish novelist George Moore; who, like Cary, lived a Bohemian life in Paris during his youth, and whose *Confessions of a Young Man* Cary owned. 'Young Moore, down from Oxford, running amuck in the joy of life, living in the two worlds of art and fashion . . .'⁸

One weakness that Cary probably perceived in this trilogy is that its two male protagonists are insufficiently differentiated, even if Moore (who has affinities with the young Cock Jarvis) becomes a soldier, while Tod is an aesthete. (Tod and Moore, as extrapolations of Cary's youthful self, are further examples of a 'doubling' tendency later emphatic in *Castle Corner*, *A House of Children* and both Trilogies.) All three novels were to have fictionalised characters and incidents draw from Cary's early experience, with strong emphasis on family life – qualities that indicate their importance as forerunners of *Castle Corner*.

Perhaps trying to make a virtue of the confusion that rapidly overtook the 'Tod' project, one of Cary's notes reads 'General theory of *rambling story* is *the details* by the way . . . *Whole point of book is* to avoid composition of plot. Its the details that matter . . . *Anything may happen at any time* as in life.'⁹

Much of Cary's work on 'Tod' was done during a long visit to The Bungalow, Castledawson, in the summer of 1933: a circumstance that, although initially very attractive to him, seems to have compounded his problems and led to the work's demise.

Earlier that year, he had been forced to write a begging letter to Michael's Housemaster at Eton: 'I'm sorry to say my income has collapsed in the last year and the bank now says I must not overdraw beyond a sum necessary to cover a period of readjustment.' He explained that out of his income, which would 'probably be under £600 for this year', he would have to pay '£150 to Rugby for my second boy' (Peter), £36 to the Dragon School for Tristram, and £15 for George, who was just starting school. 'I am very sorry to bother you. Carter [the Bursar] has been generous to Michael already – but I am at the moment in a very bad position.'[10] As their financial state worsened, the Carys decided to rent out the whole of Parkers for the summer of 1933 and take up invitations to visit relations. Arthur Cary, after retiring from his civil engineering job in 1929, had bought a house in Wadeford, a village near Chard, Somerset, where Shiela and later Jack joined him (Tony, Cary's half-brother, emigrated to South Africa). Burnside was a beautiful rambling old house behind a fast-flowing trout stream and large garden, very close to open countryside. Cary was soon spending more and more time there, and it gradually replaced The Bungalow as his 'holiday home'. But in 1933 it was Michael and Peter who spent most of their summer at Burnside, while Cary went on his own to Ireland, and Trudy, with the two younger boys, visited Ogilvie relations, including Freddy and Mary in Edinburgh.

Cary's long letters to Trudy from Castledawson were, mostly, elated. Life in The Bungalow recalled happy long-ago days at Clare Cottage. ' . . .I love this place and all the people round – I've got Ireland in my blood . . .' He was writing both 'Tod' and the 'Jew story'. 'Tod' was soon 'going like a train and I am now very confident about it. Also it is teaching me something about technique . . . I have been worried a little by the feeling that the story was thin, not in material or quantity but in something I could not define. Then by chance I found an old copy of Gogol in the school room and read Dead Souls . . . it struck me that what was wrong with Tod was its bareness.' For a while he enjoyed himself 'enriching the story' – 'for some reason the irrelevant parts of the character, I mean irrelevant to the plot, or theme of the book, give that plot and theme solidity . . .' When he became discontented with progress on 'Tod', he would switch to the 'Jew story'. Not surprisingly, both rapidly became diffuse, and the holiday atmosphere of the household did not help his concentration.

But at least the financial clouds seemed to be lifting. He had hopes for *An America Visitor* and the Depression seemed to be moderating rapidly in the wake of Chamberlain's protectionist trade policy. Soon he was urging Trudy to sell some shares that had risen. 'I think our bad times are nearly over.'

He was also hopeful that this time he could arrange for the Irish properties to be sold 'before things in Derry get worse'. A sale *was* arranged, for six months later; unfortunately it 'was a fiasco – only one lot bought'.[11] By then his wider hopes had dwindled too.

'the poet, the artist'

In July 1933, while visiting Elsie and George Carlisle, after leaving The Bungalow, Cary had almost decided to abandon 'Tod'. He was 'completely stuck'; moreover, 'As you say, Tod is dull . . .' In August *An American Visitor* was finally published – and prospered no better than its predecessor. The reviews were better than for *Aissa Saved*, but it sold even fewer copies. A bad blow, especially after his high hopes.

Over the next few months he worked desultorily at several projects. He tried writing a thriller, but soon gave that up, and in December he could not 'make up my mind yet about my next book.'[12] Now that both attempts to write about 'English tribes, pagans and witch-doctors' had collapsed, he seems to have lost direction and confidence.

Once again he reviewed earlier work. His literary agent had 'asked me for another African book'.[13] So, at the beginning of 1934, he had yet another go at *Cock Jarvis*, revising it extensively; but again failed to wrestle it into publishable shape. His notes at the time show, however, a crucial shift in his response to the theme of injustice. 'Cocky 1934. The point is – Cocky is the glorious – the poet, the artist in action and sentiment. and he's destroyed by the efficiency brigade – the young etc. not valuing – but even despising his rich world of sentiment.' As he rewrote key episodes attuned to this new interpretation of his protagonist, he began to recognise that it implied the emergence of a new theme which seemed to conflict with the old. 'For the real situation – injustice – shld. have the gentle honest Christian soldier – knowing himself a little stupid – doing his best – and then freely victimised but it is Je's *ambition which gives force to his sense of failure* – and his eagerness, his excitement of feeling which gives intensity to his despair.'[14]

Cary's 1934 *Cock Jarvis* manuscripts show greater firmness in characterisation, but Jarvis himself, as always, was recalcitrant. The new emphasis on his positive qualities merely intensified Cary's thematic dilemma. After a few months he put the novel aside yet again. Then again picked it up. And, as his notes show clearly, struggled desperately to return to earlier conceptions of protagonist and theme. 'Idea, all through Cocky is (he says it himself) no *good resenting injustice*. Forgiveness is wisdom – it is *necessary. or forgetfulness* [Therefore] Cocky must be done down badly – really done down. And no climax – must have his humiliation and despair – he marvels at his own position – his wretchedness . . . rejects himself.'[15] But this attempt also failed.

Clearly the tension observable in both *Aissa Saved* and *An American Visitor*, between his central characters' insistent vitality and their prescribed role of victim, was now impeding Cary's writing. He yearned for a resolution. The conclusion of this inward battle was the emergence of a second major theme, which would counter and qualify the theme of injustice: the theme of creativity. These two themes thread his mature fiction, in constant friction, now one dominant, now the other; they are the negative and positive polarities of Cary's world.

In the philosophical and religious explorations of his notebooks during the mid 1930s, the emergence of the theme of creativity can be traced. 'To be good it is necessary to be active, to seek *improvement*. To create at least oneself . . .'[16] 'The escape from misery in action–creation . . . This is trite–but relate it to *purpose of creation* – it is yielding oneself *to God*.'[17] 'Unless man lives like a poet, an artist, a priest, philosopher he does not live at all; not security is his first aim, nor anything for himself . . .'[18] A badge of the new theme is the word 'poet'.

The African Witch

While Cary was attempting, during 1934 and 1935, to resolve his *Cock Jarvis* dilemma, he may have experienced another epiphany, which resulted in a permanent, but not orthodox, theistic faith. ('I don't suppose any church would accept me,' he said later, 'but I believe in God and His grace with an absolute confidence.'[19]) In the mid 1930s he may have crowned his Crucifixion paintings with a magnificent series of Resurrection scenes. [20]

Certainly the poet figure of his imagination had accumulated explicitly religious connotations. The development of a sketch 'made sometime in the middle twenties' shows this. Cary remembered it as the story of 'an African nationalist. I called him the Black Prince . . .' He had put the notes and drafts of the story into 'one of the canvas bags which I had used in Africa to carry manuscripts'; later (probably in the early 1930s, when he was anatomising 'inner light' phenomena) he had added notes about 'the watch-tower movement . . . and other primitive sects', including 'a newspaper cutting about a prophet who, when he baptized converts, at night, in a deep river, also drowned them, so that, being cleansed of sin, and having no time to sin again, they went straight to Paradise'. [21]

Soon after putting aside *Cock Jarvis*, and reconsidering the contents of his canvas bag, he embarked on a story he called 'The black Christ'. Its protagonist was a young Nigerian outcast who 'upsets the high church missionaries as well as the pagans', is captured by 'juju men' who 'break his legs and arms' and leave him to die; as he 'waits for the revelation', he shouts 'Come, God, come – why you no come'. Probably by late 1934, this story yielded a variation centred on 'Aladé the poet, more attractive to girl than the whites – she is raped by him at last – having played with fire'; he is killed, but she 'misses Aladé' as the story ends. 'Theme. the poet's rejoicing – living.'[22] A provisional title for this story was 'The Horse's Mouth', and a major character was Stein (later Schlemm), a German missionary inspired by Albert Schweitzer.

Cary now decided that 'Aladé' was to be the basis of his next novel. He was very anxious to achieve success with his third major publication, and no doubt felt that 'Aladé' had popular elements his earlier two novels had lacked. In writing the novel, he exploited melodramatic clichés of the romantic 'African' adventure novel popularised by Rider Haggard: witchdoctors, juju, sacred crocodiles – even its title, *The African Witch*, suggests the ethos of *She* or *King Solomon's Mines*. Cary also exploited popular interest in the topic of racial tension and conflict, incorporating a 'women's war' (based on actual incidents that had attracted wide attention in 1927) and the frisson of sexual relations across the 'colour bar'.

His change of publisher also helped. Cary's agent was now Spencer Curtis Brown, who may have recommended the change; or Ernest Benn may have wished to free himself of a writer whose first two novels had sold badly. At any rate, Curtis Brown sent the typescript of *The African Witch* to a new, lively, innovative publisher, Victor Gollancz. The latter wrote enthusiastically to Cary at the beginning of 1936 that he had not only decided to accept *The African Witch* but had submitted it to the Book Society as one of two recommended choices for its readership. 'I must tell you now how immensely I enjoyed the book – and (speaking as a man and not as a publisher) I enjoy very few novels. There is hardly a sentence in the book which one does not read with pleasure. What are your plans for the future?'[23] Music for Cary's ears. A Reader's report sent to Cary was fulsome: 'a remarkably mature and accomplished performance . . . romantic, sophisticated, ingenious and cynical – some episodes are delicately funny, some are breathtakingly exciting, some are terrible and horrible. Miss Cary holds the complicated pattern of pieces on her chequerboard with really masterly finesse.'[24]

There was some concern about possible libel, especially in view of Cary's use of actual event. He assured Gollancz that he had not been present at 'any of the women's wars in Southern Nigeria, though I've discussed them with officials and read the official reports of the court of enquiry . . . I have not taken any incident directly from the real wars.' He had invented his place names, like Rimi, and only one living individual was mentioned –'Carlyle of Tangale is a real person, an old chief of mine, now retired. But he is complimented . . .' And he insisted that 'I take very great trouble to avoid identification of any described character, even a good one, with a real person. This is a considerable sacrifice, as you would understand if you had known some of my old colleagues in the Service, either political or military, on the old coast.'[25]

The African Witch was published in May 1936. Reviews were generally admiring and its Book Society selection boosted sales to a respectable level. Cary had his first popular success as a novelist. It was also published in the United States, by William Morrow, that same year; but sold few copies.

Compared to its predecessors *The African Witch* is a factitious work. A central theme – much more powerfully projected in both *Aissa Saved* and, a few years later, *Mister Johnson* – was, again, cultural conflict. But, attached to the conventional, wooden figure of Louis Aladai, English-educated heir of the Emir of Rimi, the theme loses subtlety and complexity; Aladai's melodramatic death, after succumbing to the juju bloodlust of Coker (at this point in the novel, character and event flatly embody racist prejudices of Cary's time), is ham for the multitude.

However, as in the 1920 short stories, Cary was incapable of writing merely at the level of cliché. There is convincing characterisation in Judy Coote, the liberal-minded Oxford don; in Schlemm; and, above all, in Elizabeth, Aladai's sister, who contrasts with him and all but seizes his novel. During its composition, her story first intruded, in characteristic fashion, on Aladai's, and then went on, with the expansion of her character and the addition of the women's war episode, to dominate the plot. But not the main theme; and part of the novel's comparative weakness flows from the peripheral thematic relevance of its most forceful and interesting character – a weakness flaunted by the title. *The African Witch* also suffers from an air of contrivance (the plethora of paired, contrasting characters, for instance, and busy plotting). But many of its incidents and minor characters are moving and memorable.

There is also damaging ambiguity, especially in the novel's conclusion. In his later Preface, Cary argued that, although education 'is full of uncertainties and dangers', it must be a priority in Africa. And by the early 1930s, education had become one of his strongest general concerns. In the final pages of *The African Witch*, Akande Tom embodies a voracious desire to learn; he fails; but his failure, sheathed in irony, is open to various interpretations. While Cary rightly repudiated a simplistic resolution, it is not surprising that some readers were puzzled. To Cary's dismay, his novel was interpreted as an attack on British administrative practice and 'as a work on the colour-bar' – 'comments on this book made me say I would never write another like it . . .'[26] Vivid and entertaining as *The African Witch* is, it is one of his least authentic and satisfying novels.

CHAPTER TWENTY EIGHT

CREATIVITY & HAPPINESS

1935–1938

'something deeply known in his own roots'
After completing *The African Witch* in 1935, Cary returned yet again to *Cock Jarvis*. The new Jarvis is eagerly, unendingly creative. Cary's rewritten and expanded episode of the young Jarvis's triumph in Daji presents him as poet, artist. In the great mud palace that he has just seized, he is exhilarated by exotic decorations that are

> like a direct expression of something deeply known in his own roots. He stood laughing at these extraordinary shapes . . . they affected him like the impulse of life itself, throwing up a glory of colour with the same gesture of romantic violence which leads a cavalry charge, for the sake of charging, for the sake of the rich feeling of oneself in the thing . . .
>
> He would spend half the night writing, planning; and during the day he was at work from dawn at six till midnight. During this time he not only made a complete study of Daji native administration, a census, a new map; but planned a new system of roads and markets for the whole country; a new courthouse and treasury building in Daji town; and the station which is still, in its original layout, the finest in Nigeria.[1]

Later in his career, ridiculed by younger colleagues, Jarvis remains a figure of towering importance, and, through his own creativity, a spur to creativity in others.

Jarvis's artistic sensitivity, his intense response to the murals in the palace, probably express the pleasurable and exciting effect on Cary, by 1935, of a man he had first met a decade earlier. Gilbert Spencer's high reputation as a painter dated from his first one-man show, at the Goupil Gallery in London, during 1923. Cary admired Spencer's paintings, especially the well-known 'Cotswold Farm', and by the late 1920s they were friends. At Spencer's wedding in 1930, Tristram was a page. Spencer was by then an instructor at the Ruskin School of Art in Oxford; and had moved from Garsington, where he had lived under the wing of Lady Ottoline Morrell, to the village of Little Milton, so as to be nearer Oxford.

In 1934 Gilbert Spencer was offered an important commission to paint murals illustrating the Legend of Balliol, in an anteroom of Holywell Manor (then being turned into an annexe of Balliol College). Gilbert and Ursula Spencer 'saw much of Joyce and Gerty Cary'[2] during the two years that he was attached to Balliol. Cary was greatly excited by participating in the progress of the murals, and enjoyed actively supporting the controversial Spencer against hostility in academic Oxford. Although Cary found the company of dons stimulating (especially if they taught philosophy), he also often found the Oxford academic world infuriatingly aloof, parochial and complacent – once defining it, Dan Davin recalled, as 'a hotbed of cold feet'.[3] He was, after all, on its fringe and had no academic status to subdue snobs and pedants. So it was both a pleasure and a relief to assail Oxford's establishment as philistine, and to argue fiercely on the side of creativity.

Cary's friendship with Gilbert Spencer renewed his close contact with the life and values of the artist he had once been himself, and inaugurated the influence of both Gilbert and his more famous brother Stanley Spencer on Cary's writing – especially *The Horse's Mouth*. In championing Spencer he was also reinvigorating the innovative in his own personality against the traditional and conservative. This must have endorsed the modulation of his thought away from the protagonist as victim of injustice to the protagonist as poet.

Castle Corner

In the final version of *Cock Jarvis* there are many foreshadowings of later novels – including *Mister Johnson* and the First Trilogy. But its immediate influence was on *Castle Corner*, which, in 1936, was evolving as an infusion into *Cock Jarvis* of Irish characters and events based on Cary's family history and earliest experiences. The precipitant of this development seems to have been Cary's 'doubling' of Jarvis on the lines of Tod and Moore. An early version of *Castle Corner* has two closely linked protagonists: 'Cleeve had a great deal of influence on Jarvis, who, in his turn, had much on Cleeve. They had been brought up together; and so they continued the intimacy of brothers with the mutual tension of cousins and critics. They were often taken for twins.'[4]

Cary's publisher, Victor Gollancz, may have contributed the idea of *Castle Corner* itself – the idea of integrating already established characters and events with those fictionalising Cary family history. 'I see in the little biographical note you sent us,' Gollancz wrote at the beginning of 1936, 'that part of your family lives in Somerset. Is Castle Cary anything to do with you?'[5] Did the enquiry set Cary thinking about the fictional possibilities of his family? He had already written sketches, for possible development as stories, based on his early memories; had used autobiographical material in novels; and in the 'Tod' trilogy had intended to include family history. But he seems not to have considered fictionalising his *own* family history before January 1936. Nine months later he was writing to Gollancz

> I find it difficult to describe my book and so I send you a rough and much shortened plan. I have left out all the minor characters and this makes the book seem plotty, but in fact the characters and their development are more

important than the plot. Political and social ideas are only effective in character.[6]

The plan, neatly typed by Trudy, began with a general statement that 'The history of the last century and especially the last 30 years interests me because I think I see in it a turning point or watershed in all history'. 'Ancient history', 'founded upon the notion of supernatural providence', was ended by the First World War. Even 'Gladstonian liberalism' had been informed by 'that basic faith' now 'being replaced by the notion of man's responsibility for his own fate', which characterised the new 'creeds, whether communist, socialist or fascist'. 'I want to deal in my books with this period in which real people, struggling with their problems of life, according to the ideas of their own time, are involved also in the sudden collapse or change of their ideas . . .'

He had, in fact, transferred to his new project a central aim of the 'Tod' trilogy; which also contributed characters and events, and laid the groundwork for *Castle Corner*'s English episodes. Indeed, *Castle Corner*'s evolution echoes that of 'Tod', its vast expansion eventually dooming the project to a similar fate. That the first volume of the projected sequence was completed and published is a testament to Cary's energy and determination.

The plan Cary submitted in September 1936 takes the plot of the first volume considerably beyond the final pages of the published *Castle Corner*. The second volume, 'Over the Top', 'will deal with the war time. It will be an independent novel, not a sequel; and the chief characters in the former book, when they appear in it, will take a subordinate part. Its political background will be the battle between the idea of the Russian revolution . . . and that of the old liberal parties which led Victorian progress . . .'[7] He did not discuss the third volume, 'Green Jerusalem', and little of that was in the event composed.

Cary's aims were extremely ambitious. He researched with enthusiasm and enjoyment, reading widely in political theory and history. Cary family history from the end of the nineteenth century would be the foundation of central events and characters. So, to achieve verisimilitude, he decided to revisit the Cary houses and haunts, and spent at least two months in Ireland, recording details and impessions.

He also quizzed his father about the past. A letter from Arthur Cary describing the game of 'melts', as he remembered playing it, is the basis of a passage in *Castle Corner*.[8] Soon after he had started work on the project, Cary spent some days at Burnside, entering with zest into country life. It was March, with portents of spring. 'Primroses on banks. Trees bare, rivers full. The walk with Jack and Sam. Sam retrieves the skeleton of a rabbit . . . A Jane Austen day. Little whats her name in Mansfield Park had just such a nature.'

Arthur Cary, who had been very ill, reminisced about life in Inishowen towards the end of the nineteenth century, while his son made notes of even minor details. 'The mail car would pass at ten and 5. 1/6 from Castle Cary to Derry. The mail van twice a week. Four or five a side and two horses.' 'Aunt Rose Kennedy, wife of Pitt, sends loads of turf to Aberfoyle before a visit; and walks up to Castle Cary with a leg of mutton carried by her maid Adelaide.'

'Peggy Elkin goes up to Falmore and asks A.L.C. [Arthur Lunell Cary] as a privilege, to be allowed to lay him out.'⁹

During this visit to Burnside, Cary had a visionary experience. One afternoon he walked

> from the cool stone passages of the old kitchen quarter, suddenly into the dining room. I had made that entry pretty often. The rule was that walkers and shooters, coming from muddy fields should enter by the kitchen and clean their boots there. I had been round the hedges with my brother, while he looked for a pheasant, and while he was drying the feet and belly of Sam the Cocker, in the kitchen, I walked through the back passage to seize a good chair.
>
> But when I opened the door, I entered not the dining room, but the past of more than twenty years at my grandmother's house six hundred miles away in Donegal. The effect was such that I stood where I was, with an indescribable sense of wonder . . .
>
> [It] was as if the coarse hard familiar world had itself turned into an illusion or dream, with a dreamlike dimension of space and time, and as if I were part of it. And this effect did not, like the usual bewilderment of waking from dreams, pass away almost instantly.¹⁰

In September he and Trudy spent a busman's holiday at Inishowen. Their marriage was now equable, companionable and although she still wished she 'could have been a better wife – and could be more of an intellectual companion,' she knew that her contribution to his work, as typist and, increasingly, as critic, was valuable. They worked as a team. The year had already passed when he would have retired from the Northern Nigerian Political Service; 'in spite of the disappointment of your writing', she had written to him then, ' – I hope you haven't altogether regretted it – I hadn't realised how your writing really came first to you even in Nigeria – when you were in the middle of your political work.' She had always believed that his writing would succeed 'and that you will be rewarded for these years of disappointment – and that we will yet be able to enjoy our love and being together (in spite of my not being able to talk to you intelligently) – without this grinding worry . . .'¹¹

Inishowen was now, he noted in summary, 'Scoto-Irish, Catholic, Sinn fein. Dohertys, Gillespies . . . Poor land, boggy. Sea fishing by hand lines and long lines for pollock and cod, mackerel. People go to Scotland for potato harvest in June, live very hard there and come back wrecks for their own harvest.'

He went again and again to the places of his past. 'The shore path to Ravenscliff. Its great Gothic door, stucco yellow front and chocolate drip courses, divided from shore by wire fence only but great walls at the end.' Again and again, with his painter's eye and poet's sensibility, he tried to record every significant natural detail. 'The lough seen from the road was the colour of a wet welsh slate, a dark thick purple, but the hills were pale blue like a baby's ribbons and the sky was white cool brilliance flashing everyway.'

233

And around any corner he might come across someone who would happily talk of the past. 'George Orr . . . tells of the races . . . Grandfather Cary did the distance from Moville to Castle Cary gates in nine minutes going and eight coming. Two and a half miles. He likes to see the ould name, and the stock.'[12]

'They Want to Be Happy'

Cary's early work on *Castle Corner* had gone well. During April 1936, while Trudy was away visiting relations for two weeks, he had lived at Rotha Ogilvie's. 'It is touching to see how thoughtful she is and how anxious to make me comfortable.' He was moved by her lonely life as an elderly widow: 'Its not so much that one day comes after another as that each is full of the knowledge of permanent loneliness . . . I feel very sorry for lonely people; really lonely people. I can understand why old people sometimes cling to the last son or daughter.'[13] That sympathetic insight into Rotha Ogilvie's 'jam' was to inspire one of his most moving characters, old Sozy in *Mister Johnson*; it also entered his characterisation of Mary Corner.

Cary may even have dropped *Castle Corner* briefly to start a novel entitled 'Marta', which began with a lonely old lady collapsing in the street. She is identified as Lady Portlock, and the rest of the novel was to have focused on her earlier life. Again a love triangle was central, this time foreshadowing the Second Trilogy; for Felix Portlock, whom she marries, is an evangelical Liberal like Chester Nimmo, while Dick Hamlin, a soldier who loves her, suggests Jim Latter.[14]

Cary was writing, as usual, in his Rawlinson Road office. 'I did a good day's work,' he soon reported to Trudy, 'and I hope to have some typing for you when you come back.' In August, invigorated by a family holiday, he was still optimistic. But on 1 April 1937 he wrote to Gollancz explaining that delay in submitting the novel was due to the need to revise it, but '500 pages are typed already'. He must think carefully before cutting because the novel was 'the foundation of two more.' Next day he wrote again, revealing the extent of his problem. 'I've had a review of all my M.S.S. to-day and my scheme and what I would like to do is this – cut the book in half. It will then be about 700 pages (typescript), and I have time to give it the polish it needs and finish it, certainly, by the end of June . . .' Cutting the novel and reducing its chronological coverage 'would give us four volumes instead of three', the new second volume to be entitled 'Cleeve Corner'. 'I have already more than enough material planned and much of it written, which would therefore be ready for June next year, possibly sooner. You will get a book a year and I will be able to do justice to the theme which . . . is a big one.'[15]

The main theme of Cary's projected chronicle sequence is summarised by its title, 'They Want to Be Happy'. Following 'There's a War On' (the thematic title he considered for his first three published novels), it suggests a more optimistic response to the human situation. This was promoted by recent success, the positive movement of his philosophical thought since 1927, the effects of the emerging 'poet' protagonist – and also by the happiness he was now finding all round him.

His four sons gave Cary intense pleasure. Michael was now an undergraduate at Balliol, studying Classics, after an illustrious career at Eton; Peter, in his nineteenth year, had just gone up to Queen's College. Tristram had recently written a short play called 'The Ghost of Oxford', which his father had proudly admired. He and George presided over frequent 'fairs', in imitation of the annual St Giles' Fair – 'an enormous event in our lives,' Tristram remembered, 'for which months of pocket money was saved'.[16] Details of such occasions, and their joyful vitality, were absorbed into the Jubilee festivities and similar *Castle Corner* scenes.

The behaviour of small children, no less than of the 'poet', vividly epitomised a 'drive for happiness' that Cary now saw as a fundamental human trait. His notebooks of the period contain many meditations on the topic of happiness. 'Ultimately man cannot live and will not consent to live without a certain kind of happiness.' To 'live for duty' was not in itself a recipe for happiness, and could in fact bring great unhappiness to those 'who have admired themselves for being dutiful, and who have looked for some reward'. He considered the case of a woman he knew, 'a very happy person, surrounded by disorder of all kinds, a squalid neglected house'. She 'dreams away much of her time, reads detective stories over and over again. She is devoted to her children and grandchildren but cannot be greatly bothered with them. It is as tho she had within herself a private source of happiness and serenity. I think this source of happiness is in her imagination. Her dreams are works of art.'[17]

Cary was now very close to a notion that would be the keystone of his mature thought: each human being, separated in mind but not in emotion from others, is condemned to create his own world. This notion would allow him to reconcile his evolving theme of creativity to the prior theme of endemic injustice. What is the ultimate source of happiness for human beings? he asked himself in 1936. 'First of all, a strong sense of the true nature of things, and an acceptance of that nature; of fundamental injustice and insecurity. Secondly, a vigorous enjoyment of life in all its aspects and activities.'[18]

But Cary's very exhilaration, together with the ambitious but rather vague scope of his theme, the sheer volume of his material, and the proliferation of characters and incidents, rapidly caused problems for *Castle Corner*. Much was incorporated, or developed from, the late *Cock Jarvis* manuscripts, with Jarvis as 'eager romantic and positive' young soldier and administrator, poet of imperialism. Cary read books on Nigeria to add realistic detail to new scenes beyond his own experience, like those depicting tribal life during the slave-raiding era.

The Irish sequences, fictionalising Cary history, were composed with patent zest. Characterisation, especially of John Chass and Mary Corner; descriptive passages; incidents like the tandem race – all are magnificently realised. 'As you see,' Cary wrote to Lionel Stevenson, 'its not about Castle Cary but about a compound of C.C. and Whitecastle, and even Clare.'[19] Cary's imagination, fuelled by vivid memory, by his recent return to Inishowen, was afire. Undoubtedly the Irish chapters of *Castle Corner* contain some of his finest writing, by turns frenetic, ecstatic, meditative, poignant.

The English sequences are quite another story. Drawn largely, it seems, from

'Tod' and the 'Jew Story', they are limping and tentative – especially beside the vigour of the Irish and the authority of the Nigerian sequences. Yet they carry the burden of the novel's political critique of the age, especially in expounding the reasons for the decline of Liberalism. Cary tried hard to vivify these sequences with grotesque characters like Helen Pynsant and Nussbaum (the latter drawn from the 'Jew story' and, ultimately, from Edinburgh memories of Raffalovich). The Irish and Nigerian chapters are linked realistically by the colonialist ventures of Felix Corner and Harry Jarvis (giving 'the contrast between dying imperialism in Ireland and rising imperialism in Africa'[20]), but Cary's attempts to plot links for the Irish and English characters merely draw attention to an essential discontinuity.

In April 1937 Cary began to feel depressed about the novel: it 'keeps me awake at night with its slowness.'[21] He was still slogging at it in June, feeling guilty about letting down Gollancz – but 'my doctor has been bullying me about overwork'.[22] By 10 August, after the family had gone off on holiday, he was almost desperate: 'It is the hardest and most thankless job I've done yet to patch and fake like this and feel all the time I'm spoiling some of the best work I ever did.' Apart from the pain of cutting the novel, he continued to worry about 'the goddammed english section . . . But it always was a botch'. He rushed to London to check on details: 'Thank Heaven I went to town – the stairs at St Pauls were quite different from my recollection . . .' When he did finally join the family, towards the end of August, he had with him a text, part manuscript and part typescript, that was still much too long and 'full of mistakes'.[23]

At the beginning of September, after the whole family had helped in the evenings, Cary was able to send *Castle Corner* to Gollancz. 'I have treated you badly in keeping you waiting so long,' he apologised; 'my mistake was in fixing a date for such a long and difficult book . . . If its too long I could cut it, but I have already cut it hard, and further cutting would be difficult. Its a jigsaw in which the parts fill certain spaces and trimming one means trimming all the rest.'[24] The Reader's judgement was unenthusiastic. The writing was often 'careless and hurried'; 'a vigorous pruning' was desirable; there was a serious lack of unity, because the Castle did not remain central and many episodes, 'admirable and vivid in themselves, have nothing to do with the Castle at all – and precious little to do with the characters'. But the novel had 'vitality', and, despite its serious flaws, should be published.[25]

Castle Corner duly appeared in January 1938. Although it was a Book Society Recommendation, many of the reviewers agreed broadly with Gollancz's Reader. 'Less a novel than a phantasmagoria . . . Its faults arise from the author's inability, despite technical skill, to master his material . . .' (*Observer*); 'He is as careless about furnishing explanations and arranging climaxes as life itself,' but there are 'scenes that amaze us by their beauty and pathos' (*News Chronicle*). The *Star*'s critic recognised Cary's 'genius for catching the reactions of young children to the small incidents of their lives' and his ability to make his crowd of characters come to life; *The*

Times' critic sensitively noted a Chekovian 'compound of sadness, absurdity, and a rather desperate gaiety'.[26]

Although the reviews were mixed rather than bad, Cary later claimed that he abandoned the other novels of the sequence because critical miscomprehension had depressed him. But it would have required a superhuman effort to continue a task that had become a debilitating chore; and his mind was seething with other projects. He learned much from the débâcle of 'They Want to Be Happy', and was able to put that knowledge to quick use in the next novel he published.

Like the 'Tod' project before it, 'They Want to Be Happy' had disintegrated, not because his theme and protagonist seemed incompatible (as with *Cock Jarvis*) but because he had not reined in his imaginative power; had let it run away with him. So he set out to bring his writing method under better control. Parkers was quiet now – as undergraduates his two elder sons lived away from home, his two younger sons were both at school most of the day. He no longer needed the Rawlinson Road retreat, much as he had enjoyed and appreciated it; and it would be mutually beneficial to work closer to Trudy as she typed out his drafts. So he established himself in the old nursery on the top floor; and organised his books, notes and old manuscripts around him.

An even more important lesson was that his tendency to write expansively and to evolve big projects must be curbed. From childhood Cary had enjoyed the 'loose, baggy monster' of popular Victorian and Edwardian fiction, responding to their profligate vigour and variety. In Nigeria he had delighted in voluminous novels by William de Morgan, and when, late in life, he was invited to recommend a neglected great writer, chose R.S. Surtees, author of long, episodic, sporting novels.[27] This tendency to value long books was buttressed by his regular reading of memoirs, diaries and letters, and by his increasing admiration of the great Russian novelists.

But there were other novels that he had both enjoyed and admired, among them Joyce's *A Portrait of the Artist as a Young Man*. And, however strong was his love of the traditional, Cary also valued the innovative; especially in the wake of Gilbert Spencer's incursion into staid Oxford. It was time to experiment; to try to write, as he had twenty-five years earlier in *Memoir of the Bobotes*, as a man of his own time.

CHAPTER TWENTY NINE

FREEDOM

1938–1940

'loves and griefs'

By the mid 1930s, when Cary was approaching fifty, his family life had settled into a pattern that included several annual rituals: in Spring, the Oxford and Cambridge Boat Race, watched from the Herberts' house on the Thames; a family holiday during the summer; in September, St Giles' Fair; Christmas, with its family activities and attendance at nearby St Giles' Church; on Boxing Day, a visit to the pantomime. He immensely enjoyed them all. That a new set of family traditions had been created was in itself deeply satisfying.

The Carys lost a close friend in 1937 when Dolly MacGregor died in Glasgow: 'I hope you and Joyce know what a large part you have played in my life,' she wrote in farewell. 'You have been very true friends to me . . .'[1] But they had also gained friends, some of them literary. Robert Lynd and his wife Sylvia lived in Hampstead, he an eminent critic and essayist, she a poet. Lynd was Anglo-Irish, from Belfast, 'the gentlest and least arrogant of men' according to his fellow critic Desmond MacCarthy;[2] J.B. Priestley remembered him as 'an enchanting character' who loved 'good talk'.[3] Cary clearly enjoyed their gregarious company, mixing with other writers at their dinners and parties, and joining in their warm family life (they had two daughters). In 1944 Sylvia Lynd inscribed a copy of her *English Children* 'For Joyce Cary / who knows all there is to know about English children including how to amuse them'.[4]

In fact, the Carys' circle of friends widened steadily during the 1930s. Trudy, with more leisure as the boys grew up, had joined the famous Oxford Bach Choir and begun to play the cello seriously again. Many of the new friends were initially hers. Two of them, James and Anna Boyd, persuaded her to add her cello to their violin and viola, and the three held regular musical evenings. He was a Reader in German (later Professor) who had published a book, on *Goethe's Knowledge of English Literature*, not only in the same year as *Aissa Saved* but with the same publisher. So Cary gained a pleasant acquaintance while Trudy had the deep pleasure of music-making. Other music-lovers of Oxford, like Arthur Norrington (then President of Trinity College, an editor at the Clarendon Press, later) also became friends of the Carys.

All the music in Parkers, as well as Trudy's quiet enthusiasm, influenced her four sons deeply. In his later life Michael made clavichords and harpsichords as a hobby; for Peter a professional career as pianist was possible, and he always enjoyed singing; Tristram became an admired composer, well known for his film and concert music in the 1950s; even George, already showing signs by the late 1930s of linguistic brilliance, was a chorister and occasionally composed music. Cary, although so much closer to his younger sons – and especially close to Tristram, whose ebullient personality and artistic creativity made him a stimulating companion on walks – remained a rather distant father. He was intensely proud of his four sons. But his preoccupation with writing, and their absence most of the year at school (they all became boarders in early adolescence), tended to centre conversation on questions of academic performance and possible careers. All four boys – but especially Peter and George, the younger of each pair – were much closer to their mother.

There were many happy family occasions, however, some recorded in sketches and water-colours – for Cary still kept up his drawing and painting as occasional activities. During the 1930s he painted several fine family portraits; one of Trudy playing her cello accompanied by Peter at the piano. The annual summer holiday gave opportunity for relaxed, informal relations – although Cary often felt driven by the exigencies of his work to limit his participation.

During the summers of 1931 to 1934, the family had gone to Saundersfoot, on the coast of South Wales, to join the Carlisles in a guest-house (the two families had holidayed together since the 1920s). Antonia, Elsie's eldest daughter, remembered Cary talking animatedly during 'walks along the cliffs': 'Joyce was a sort of "Magus" for small children, telling us entrancing facts and stories. How things worked – sailing ships, naval tactics, the steam engine. He had a gift of imparting knowledge as entertainment.' She also remembered a characteristic exploit: Cary drove his new car out onto the beach, then 'put the steering wheel hard over so that the car was turning in a closed circle – he then jumped out and the car went circling on. After a bit he jumped in again'![5]

From 1936 to 1939 the Carys stayed each summer in a farmhouse, Hensfield, at Sherford near Kingsbridge, a few miles inland from the Devon coast. Cary particularly enjoyed those farm holidays. After the first of them, he wrote to Trudy 'I was never so sorry in my life to break off a holiday as when I left Sherford . . . A town house without animals, fields seemed a cut-off place after the farm. You gave me a wonderful holiday, my dearest . . .'[6]

His detailed notes about the rural life were to be useful later for novels. ('The pigs lying in the sun, the hens sitting in the chaff behind the threshing machine.' 'In the barn the whole floor vibrated and also shook in waves. Clouds of dust.'[7])

Family life became even more precious when Arthur Cary died suddenly in November 1937. Although his health had weakened – he was in his seventies

– he had again been very active just before the end. His death was poignantly reminiscent of his first wife's, over forty years before. As Cary told Lionel Stevenson, Arthur Cary had gone out 'in a freezing wind without his zip jacket'; he had died on the golf-course at Lyme Regis with Jack beside him. No one, Cary wrote, should 'be sorry for Dad who died so suddenly at a time when he was enjoying life again'; but 'I cannot get used to the feeling that he is no longer at Wadeford and every now and then I think of something to put in my next Sunday letter to him.'[8]

On 28 November Cary was at Burnside, sorting his father's effects – 'Going through papers, old troubles and disasters, loves and griefs, seventy years of history suddenly wound up and thrown away. The lawyers going through the share certificates, and old exploded companies appearing, forgotten by himself. The I.O.U. throwing a sudden illumination' (– did it reveal that his father had helped him at the cost of going into debt himself?).[9]

Arthur Cary's death came just weeks before the publication of *Castle Corner*, to which he had contributed so much. That fact alone would have disturbed Cary's heart into loving memory of all he owed his father; and quickened the process of intense recall that culminated in his most beautiful and affecting novel, *A House of Children*.

Power in Men

After completing *Castle Corner*, and deciding to shelve the rest of 'They Want to Be Happy', Cary had embarked on two major projects different from each other but creatively complementary. One was a novel, perhaps his finest: *Mister Johnson*. The other was a work of political theory that he had first considered writing in 1931, when the Liberal Party invited him to contribute a political treatise. He had demurred because 'I was deep in other studies, in philosophy, history, and letters'. Now the invitation was repeated and he was 'offered a free hand to write what I liked'.[10] He composed *Power in Men* between the spring and winter of 1938, and it was published for the Liberal Book Club by Nicholson and Watson in May 1939.

Cary's recent work on the troublesome English chapters of *Castle Corner* had involved a reconsideration of the role in British life of the Liberal Party, for which he had felt such affinity. He had also been discussing political theory with a new friend, Jack Gough, whom he had met at musical parties given by Gough's wife. Gough, whose book *The Social Contract: A Critical Study of Its Development* had been published recently, was a Fellow and tutor in politics of Oriel College. Cary was impressed by his insistence that 'political obligation rests on the same basis as moral obligation, or rather that, in the last analysis, political obligation is a special kind of moral obligation'.[11] That was Cary's touchstone too: 'Lies are always lies, evil is always evil; public and private morals are governed by precisely the same law'.[12]

In addition to discussion with Gough, Cary drew on notes from a slew of texts on political theory, ranging from Plato's *Republic* to the anarchist Bakunin's *God and State*, from Bosanquet's *Philosophical Theory of the State* to Ivor Brown's *The Meaning of Democracy*.

Cary believed that the Liberal Party held in trust a liberal tradition extending far back into the Middle Ages; 'as we know it today,' he wrote in 1955, that tradition 'has two main sources: the Protestant tradition, and the Whig revolution of 1688 with its ideals of toleration and individual right.' Unfortunately, the Liberals had 'made one capital error, which still haunts their thought, when they defined freedom as absence of restraint' and so came to believe that 'all interference is wrong'.[13] (In his book Cary did not express that judgement quite so harshly.) But liberty (unfortunately Cary does not maintain a distinction between the words 'freedom' and 'liberty') is in fact 'the power in man to do what he likes so far as his power can reach': far from being an 'absence of restraint', it is 'creation in the act'. Democracy is the political arrangement that allows each person the highest possible degree of liberty. And democracy, 'like liberty, of which it is made, is real and indestructible'. One sees clearly here the radiating force of Cary's conclusion that the fundamental drive of human beings, by which they seek happiness in self-fulfilment, is creativity.

Kathleen Nott, a sympathetic critic of Cary's political thought, commented a decade after his death that, like E.M. Forster, Cary had 'remained in the tradition of liberal-humanistic morality, with its Greek and Christian roots'. Both novelists were 'concerned in all their works with the problem and indeed the meaning of freedom', but Cary understood 'both the realities and the structure of power and responsibility and the environmental effect of action upon character, much better than Forster'. 'If he errs it is on the side of democratic hopefulness. For him freedom is the realization of a man's spontaneous power, and he believes that democracy and its methods will show themselves realizing that power: that men of all complexions, in the long run and perhaps in the short, will not be denied this realization.'

But Cary had not taken into account 'Orwellian techniques of organization' and, because his 'African experiences' had shown him 'power at a cruder point of development', he saw 'the power relation as [a] purely human function'. 'I do not think Cary comes to either an intellectual or a practical solution of the problem of freedom-power, of domination and subjection, deeply rooted as it is in the human psychological structure. But . . . his political and social views are both warmly humane and descriptively truthful . . .'[14]

Power in Men is Cary's first detailed attempt to state, in philosophical as well as political terms, the myth that underpins his mature writing. That myth was built on the two insistent themes that had seemed opposed, but were now reconciled as equally truthful to human experience – a myth now essentially complete. The danger was that it would weaken his imaginative writing, turn him into a preacher and propagandist. So it was helpful that his firmly articulated position yet insists that 'truth is not complete': 'Because final truth is not known and can never be complete, all expressions of it have equal title to be heard'.[15]

The Liberal Party leadership was impressed. Soon after the book's publication, Cary received an official invitation to be considered as a parliamentary candidate. He replied politely 'I had no thought of standing for parliament and

I have no idea of what it would cost in money or time'.[16] He went to the Liberal Party's Head Office in London, attended a few political gatherings, and enjoyed this further opportunity to hear 'how the politicians talk and think',[17] but in June decided to turn down the invitation. It seems unlikely that he was seriously tempted by it. His next novel would be published within two months; his literary career was at last beginning to fulfil the toil of more than two decades.

Mister Johnson

Almost certainly Cary started to write *Mister Johnson* in autumn 1937, after the typescript of *Castle Corner* had been sent off; continued it intermittently while writing *Power in Men* between spring and autumn 1938; then finished it in a six-month surge – its typescript was received by Victor Gollancz in April. He told Lionel Stevenson in February 1939 that he was relieved to be rid of *Power in Men* – whose length he had had to reduce to satisfy the publisher, and on which he had anyway 'Spent too much of last year'; he was 'glad to get back to *real writing*'.[18] Even if he had not composed both books, and more, during those eighteen months, *Mister Johnson* would still seem almost miraculous in the rapidity of its composition – especially after his long struggles with earlier novels.

His abandonment of 'They Want to Be Happy' was in fact succeeded by a creative outpouring that in six years produced six novels (the major works on which his reputation will always rest), two plays and two film-scripts, three books of political theory, a long poem, several short stories – and beyond those, as always, many uncompleted pieces. At the same time he lived a demanding social and family life, and went on a difficult and dangerous expedition. For sheer creative vigour those six years – most of them, ironically, during a war – would be hard to match in the career of any writer.

In *Mister Johnson*, Cary finely harmonised his two major themes, of injustice and creativity. Other themes prominent in his earlier books, especially those of education, cultural conflict and racial tension, became sub-themes filling out the novel's orchestration. All are clearly organic, springing from Johnson, the protagonist, in his 'jam': victim but above all poet; teenager; stranger; Black. Religion is all but absent; inappropriate to Johnson's personality, irrelevant to his fate. And political analysis is subdued, partly, no doubt, because it was the contemporaneous burden of *Power in Men*.

After the progressive complication and inflation that had marked his earlier books, in *Mister Johnson* Cary returned to the mode of *Aissa Saved*, refining it, asserting it as definitive (even the short chapters were re-established – although they are not numbered in *Mister Johnson*, the better to suggest the flow of Johnson's exuberant life). In his decision to cast the novel in the historic present, Cary also showed a renewed willingness to experiment. Some readers and critics jibbed at that emphatic present tense, but in his later Preface Cary defended it cogently. Like Joyce's stylistic mimicry in *Portrait of the Artist*, it is effective in enforcing the protagonist's personality and viewpoint without sacrificing the objectivity implied by third-person narrative.

Cary's lifelong tendency to evolve dual protagonists, obvious in his earlier writing, is tightly controlled in *Mister Johnson*, and the novel gains force from Johnson's centrality. On the other hand, the main relationship, between Johnson and Rudbeck, is justified realistically; where Aissa and Ali were paralleled victims with little other connection, the logic and complexity of the Johnson-Rudbeck relationship, clerk and A.D.O., is even stronger than that between Bewsher and Marie in *An American Visitor*.

Mister Johnson profits both from what Cary had learnt in writing his earlier novels and from the burst of energy that followed his emergence from the vast confusion of 'They Want to Be Happy'. It must have been an exquisite relief and joy to kick free of that huge ruin, and find his creativity lifting him smoothly upwards. ' . . . I abandoned the whole enterprise, and turned to write about the simplest characters in a simple background, with the simplest of themes, Mister Johnson, the artist of his own joyful tale';[19] 'as Johnson swims gaily on the surface of life, so I wanted the reader to swim, as all of us swim, with more or less courage or skill, for our lives.'[20]

But it did not come about quite so simply; nor is the novel simple, though one of its achievements is to seem so. In Johnson, Cary found a protagonist perfectly fitted, by personality and situation, to the task of sustaining the themes of injustice and of creativity. Early notes show this: 'He is lost in the world, wants help and gets bad help.' ' . . . his *creative wish* – to make – to do – to be glorious . . . He is driven by impulse – can't help himself – to *create himself* . . . He makes poems all the time . . . His dances.'[21] Yet Johnson seems to have emerged in the same complex way as Cock Jarvis and other Cary protagonists.

The name Mr Johnson was common among black clerks in colonial Nigeria, but it probably also came from a story of that title by Cary's erstwhile superior J.F.J. Fitzpatrick, published in *Blackwood's Magazine* during the First World War. In it, Fitzpatrick and the small boy he calls Mr Johnson 'adopt' each other. When the political officer is ordered to war, Johnson will not be left behind; and a strange, precarious partnership is formed between the White man and the Black boy. As the story ends, Fitzpatrick shoots his decrepit old dog, Zaki; 'And Mr Johnson? Well, he and I went our ways too. And I came home alone.'[22] It seems likely that Cary was subconsciously influenced by 'Mr Johnson' long after he had forgotten the story itself. Certainly his protagonist's name, and the title of his novel, were firmly fixed from an early stage of composition. And the addition to the original plot of the novel's conclusion, Rudbeck's shooting of Johnson, which recalls Cary's fear that he would be required to hang a Nigerian murderer, may well have been fixed by the conclusion of Fitzpatrick's story.

This 'simple' novel draws from wide and deep experience. Cary's Preface connects Johnson not only with Mr Graves, the main source, but with an 'unknown African clerk' whose letters, 'full of the most wonderful yarns', Cary had to censor during the War; and with two companies of Nigerian soldiers whose affection moved him. [23] His dedication of the novel to Musa, with the quotation 'Remembered goodness is a benediction', adds another reference to Nigerian benevolence, and links the novel's tone, if not its protagonist, to Cary's wily, roguish Political Officer in Borgu. Clearly, writing this novel was an act of joy, and of gratitude for what he had experienced in Nigeria.

However, Cary again successfully drew some of his material from reading rather than experience. The songs which, especially in the final chapters, are so crucial in creating emotion, were clearly modelled on translations in Major A.J.N. Tremearne's *The Ban of the Bori: Demons and Demon-Dancing in West and North Africa*. One song of the Bori (Hausa 'spirits') begins 'O Snake, what do you say? / O Wizard of the Night, what do you say?', and its refrain runs 'The Drawer along of the Stomach is having his day . . . / Hey, Crawler, Hey, Crawler, mounting at night is not for you, / By day we like you to mount so that everyone can see you.' [24]

The novel's criticism of colonialism is subtle but emphatic; good intentions are conceded to Rudbeck and his colleagues, and Cary implies a renewed hopefulness that, on balance, positive effects will outweigh negative; but the trade road, once created, achieves a power that dwarfs human intention and denies final judgement about the value of its creation. This is far from Conrad's bitter repudiation of colonialism in *Heart of Darkness*, but it suggests a steady questioning of thoughtless optimism about the whole imperialist enterprise. Cary does not simplify a complex situation; equally he does not flinch from exposing the destructive as well as the constructive in British colonialism.

Cary's characteristic concentration on writing key episodes, with its tendency to create a loose, picaresque-like plot, becomes in *Mister Johnson* a virtue; primarily because it accords with the protagonist's vigorous, unselfconscious personality; but also because Cary controls it to create four rise-and-fall sequences (realistically determined by the absence or presence of Rudbeck) which culminate in the death of Johnson. Unobtrusively a pattern is created reminiscent of the ballad's incremental repetition – a pattern essentially tragic, endorsing the theme of injustice. But it is contradicted by a second pattern, the steadily rising power of Johnson's creative imagination. So that the final chapters of the novel – as the two patterns, and the two themes, merge, and Johnson goes to his death both victim and creator – are intensely moving. Yeats' 'tragic gaiety' is magnificently realised.

When Cary sent the typescript of *Mister Johnson* to Gollancz in April 1939, he said that he thought it the best novel he had written. [25] The Reader did not completely agree. 'The book has not the variety and complexity of *The African Witch*, nor its narrative strength – indeed, there is hardly any story, in the ordinary sense.' However, 'Johnson is indeed a remarkable piece of characterisation, a symbol as well as very intensely an individual.' [26] Cary was disconcerted to hear that the novel would be published as soon as August, but Gollancz explained that the 'international situation' had been taken into account: 'believing that there will be some sort of crisis of the severest kind in September, we think it best to get some of our books well away before that . . .'[27] In the event it was published even earlier – July. But the crisis arrived on time.

Hugh Walpole wrote to Cary 'I think "Johnson" a little bit of perfection . . . Adolf has obscured him for a moment but Johnson will outlast Adolf'.[28] Distracted by rumours of war, the reviewers were nevertheless complimentary, if inclined to interpret the novel merely as a portrayal of 'the negro mind'.

Two Plays

In January 1939, Cary had received a letter from J.B. Priestley, whom he had recently met, probably at the Lynds': 'I have a very good idea for a play, but I need the collaboration of somebody with a knowledge of the type of people and the background, and you, I think are just the man. Briefly, the idea is to put the Government of some African possession of ours into the same position as Pilate, the disturbing prophet, of course, being a negro . . . If this attracts you, let me know when you are next coming to town . . .'

Cary *was* attracted – not only by the theme, which had so much in common with *The African Witch* and with his religious and political thought, but also by the prospect of working with one of the most successful dramatists of the time (Priestley's reputation was at its peak). Having sent off *Power in Men*, and with *Mister Johnson* close to completion, Cary was free to turn his attention to the suggested project. He went to see Priestley, discussed the play with him, and in February 1939 sent him a synopsis. Priestley, 'desperately busy' with his latest play, replied that

> There are some good ideas in the synopsis but also some things that do not seem to me quite on the right lines. First, I should prefer myself to keep a little nearer to the biblical story [Christ crucified] . . . For a play of atmosphere and character there is really too much action . . . The 'Prophet' should speak decent simple English, perhaps having been educated at a Mission school . . . but should not have been to England and Oxford, because I am quite sure this ruins the whole conception . . . You are liable to fall into the error of supposing that a play is a sort of condensed novel, when actually you set about building it in quite a different way.[29]

Cary took the criticism and advice to heart, then, after finishing *Mister Johnson*, wrote a three-act script and sent it for comment to Priestley in July 1939. *Happy Valley* is set in a British colony of 'tropical Africa', apparently during the mid 1930s and involves a visiting film company.[30]

Priestley did not feel that the 'idea comes off . . . To begin with there is too little about Africa and far too much about the film people, who have been treated this way many times before and always tend to bring a rather unreal element into a story or play. I feel that, when the native prophet comes in it does begin to come to life . . .'[31]

For a year or so, Cary continued to hope that the collaboration would come about. Freddy Ogilvie had recently been appointed Director General of the BBC and he and Mary were anxious for closer contact with the Carys. 'Do come up to town, the two of you, as often as you can manage, won't you?' he wrote.[32] At Cary's suggestion, Freddy invited them to a meal with the Priestleys. Cary also sent a telegram to congratulate Priestley when his play was produced, and rented Parkers to the Priestley family for some months early in 1940. Then, recognising that the collaboration was doomed, he wrote the play himself, and called it *The King is Dead, Long Live the King*.

This time the setting is Nigeria. Isa Dan Seriki of 'the local royal house' (his name means 'Jesus, Son of the King') is 'a tall negro in a dark grey suit' who has been at 'all the universities' and now, returned to Nigeria, is becoming a political threat to the British administration as the focus of nationalist agitation. After he has preached the need for political change and national pride, Isa flees but is soon captured and brought before the Governor. Who says, with all the reasonableness of Pontius Pilate, 'you understand the difficulties on my side . . . I know of your plan for cheap village schools . . . but you see, I'm not independent in the matter.' Isa is beaten up and then tied, dying, to a post. 'A soldier picks up the battered brim of [the District Commissioner's] hat and puts it on Isa's head where it sits like a crooked halo.'[33]

Cary's two related plays are not theatrical masterpieces. If *Happy Valley* is weakened by the film-company element in its plot and characters (as Priestley was surely right to suggest), *The King is Dead, Long Live the King* is weakened by its over-explicit Christian parallelism. Although one can imagine the latter play coming to life in a sympathetic production,[34] in neither play are dialogue and characterisation vivid and complex – Cary was not a natural playwright, and was anyway constrained by Priestley's prescriptions. But the exercise of representing conflict dramatically, with the concomitant necessity of sympathetically embodying the anti-administrative viewpoint, was undoubtedly valuable in extending Cary's critique of colonialism.

CHAPTER THIRTY

WAR & CHILDHOOD

1939–1941

'a series of crises'

The war caused immediate changes in Cary's family life. Just before its outbreak he had written to Edwardes 'My eldest son has just got his first in Greats . . . But family life with 4 sons is a series of crises in these Hitlerian times . . .'[1] Michael, now twenty-two, learned just after war had been declared that he had passed his Civil Service Examinations brilliantly; he was appointed Assistant Private Secretary to Lord Portal, in the Air Ministry, but by the beginning of 1941 was 'on a hush-hush job' in the Navy. Peter was called up by the Army, before finishing his degree in English, and joined the Oxford and Bucks Regiment. Tristram, fourteen at the beginning of the war, was at Westminster School (which was soon evacuated from London). Of the four sons, only George was to be little affected; still at the Dragon School in 1939, he won a scholarship to Eton (like his eldest brother) the following year. Trudy joined the Oxford branch of the WVS (Women's Voluntary Service).

Cary had joined the Oxford City ARP (Air Raid Precautions division of Civil Defence) early in 1939: 'the country is in fighting form,' he had assured Lionel Stevenson that April; 'I am going to an A.R.P. practice to-day – telephoning during a raid – it ought to be rather amusing'.[2] After the war began he became an ARP Post Warden, and also joined the Bomb Reconnaissance Corps of the City of Oxford Civil Defence. Throughout the war, he was kept busy with watch duties, bomb exercises, meetings, record keeping. He even went to Bournemouth on a week's course during April 1942: 'We are simply learning masses of details about different kinds of bombs and how to recognise them by their marks of impact.'[3] But he had little opportunity to apply his expertise. Oxford was fortunate: Birmingham and Coventry to the north, Reading to the east, Bristol to the west, Swindon to the south, all heavily bombed; but only the outskirts of Oxford suffered occasional bombing ('it is said Adolf wants to be Chancellor,' Cary joked[4]).

Cary enjoyed the responsibilities and social contacts that the war brought him; it was like being back in the Service, part-time. He made several new friends, including C.K. Allen, Warden of Rhodes House (which housed ARP Post B27) and jurisprudence expert, from whom he took over as Post Warden; and the Australian don Howard Florey (later Professor of Pathology and winner of the Nobel Prize) was a member of the Post.

1939 also brought a change in Cary's publishing arrangements. Michael Joseph, who had been a member of the Curtis Brown literary agency, had recently set up his own publishing house, and Spencer Curtis Brown suggested that Cary consider publishing with him. Joseph had made a 'good offer', including advances of £150, the literary agent wrote – and Cary's 'last two novels would not have covered an advance of £150'.[5] In fact, Gollancz – who helped the new firm get established (he even allowed it to share his premises) – presented Joseph with the typescript of *Charley is My Darling*: 'I'm just going to turn this down. I've published two or three novels by this man Cary. We can't get anywhere with him. He doesn't sell and I don't think he's going to make the grade. But before I turn him down, it's interesting. I thought you might like to see him, read the book.'[6]

Cary enquired about other publishing possibilities, then met Joseph, liked him, and made the move. A quietly amicable relationship was quickly established, with both Joseph himself and Robert Lusty, who saw most of Cary's novels into print. Although they were not profitable, like novels by such popular writers as H.E. Bates, they gave 'respectability' to the Joseph list, since Cary was known to be a serious, interesting and ambitious novelist. Michael Joseph Ltd would remain his British publisher to the end of his career.

Charley is My Darling

After the publication of *Mister Johnson* in the summer of 1939 , Cary seems to have concentrated on short stories for some months. He had returned to the genre in 1938, presumably after finishing *Power in Men* and while writing *Mister Johnson*. He told his Aunt Mab, late in 1938, that his literary agent was 'always wanting short stories', so he had written some 'and now I like doing them so much I shall do some more. But I doubt if editors will like them.'[7] He was right, for the moment. 'Bush River', the first of these stories to be published, did not appear until 1945 – and the next one, 'Umaru', over five years after that. The short stories he wrote in 1938 and 1939 were not, like the ones he had published during the 1920s, 'commercial'. They were, in the main, brief and concentrated 'epiphanies', like Joyce's of the *Dubliners* cycle, with just enough characterisation and plot to prepare the moment of illumination as the story ended. They were also essentially autobiographical. In both respects they were to influence his novel writing.

Cary's renewed contact with H.S.W. Edwardes must have encouraged him to relive experiences of his Nigerian years. Several of the sketches he made at that time (like the two that combined to form *Mister Johnson*) developed into short stories. One of these, the unpublished 'T.R.', was undoubtedly inspired by Cary's meeting with Edwardes in the mid 1930s – fifteen years after they had last seen each other. Edwardes was now living in the countryside near

Fordingbridge, Hampshire. His financial circumstances were constrained, but he was still the vigorous optimist who had so impressed Cary in 1914. He had survived injustice triumphantly. Indeed, Cary's meeting with him may have contributed to the theme of creativity, which was evolving at that time. Later Cary scribbled in a notebook the observation 'H.S.W.E., working on a tomato farm, writes Time passes quickly and one feels that one is part of a highly organised whole which will produce results.'[8]

'T.R.' was clearly connected with *Charley is My Darling*. For while Cary was writing it he was also writing sketches based on memories of his childhood. One, 'The war on the Bath green', used a memory of gang battles in Moville that also entered 'T.R.' and initiated *Charley is My Darling*. In his Preface to the novel, Cary pointed to his 'good memory' of childhood, and went on to refer to his juvenile delinquencies in Moville; he also noted that the 'wrecking of the house in this story was taken from fact',[9] and, elsewhere, that one of the characters fictionalised someone he had known in Ireland, 'even to the name'.[10] If this was a reference to the protagonist, Charley Brown, that is only one source of his name and personality.

Cary had long known the Scottish folk song 'Charlie is My Darlin'' which gives the novel its title; and must have intended the song's simple narrative about Bonnie Prince Charlie to shed an ironic light. ' . . . Charlie came to our town, / The young chevalier . . . / As he came marchin' up the street, / The pipes played loud and clear, / And all the folk came runnin' out / To meet the chevalier . . .' That welcome is far removed from what Cary's young gentleman rider receives in the English countryside; but his ultimate fate, alienation from his society, has its similarity to the Scottish Pretender's.

In *Charley is My Darling* Cary for the first time created the figure of a painter, who is also a bad teacher, Lommax. This key character seems to have sprung from Fergusson and possibly Mackie, the two Scottish artists who had so profoundly influenced Cary in his youth. Lommax's vigorously assertive personality and unorthodox aesthetic certainly mirror Fergusson's. Lommax also expresses a central conviction of Cary's, and Fergusson's: 'all children have prromise as arrtists, as I said before, everybody is arrtistic.' In his own creativity, in his ideas and intense (if unpredictable) appreciation of the children's creativity, Lommax represents a qualified positive in the novel's dialectic; weak, sweet-natured Lina Allchin supports him; but they are opposed by the ultimately stronger negative forces of social inertia, stupidity and hostility. Charley has his Mort (the name's death connotation is obvious) as Johnson had his Ajali.

Ultimately the children's creativity, because suppressed or untutored by adults, breaks out in destructive violence; the scene in which they take over Longwater House and destroy its valuable Constable painting is pivotal. Charley's imagination and daring leadership make that desecration possible. But earlier his creativity is given the significantly positive endorsement of horse-riding imagery: 'He allowed his imagination to gallop away with himself and his friends; relying, for the solution of all his difficulties, as they arose, on more imagination'.[11] Vividly Cary renders the process and potency, the beneficence, of the creative imagination born into each human. Its repression by the forces of conservatism is all the more painful and shameful.

This novel was the most topical Cary wrote. As the war began, he and his family were again on holiday at Sherford. There, on the farms of the area – as well as in Wadeford when he visited Jack and Shiela, and in Oxford on his return – 'vackies' were a common sight; for, in fear of heavy bombing attacks on London at the outbreak of war, evacuation of its children had begun quickly and informally. Cary seized on a topic that slotted neatly into his current interests, gave him a theme after his heart – and was likely to make a popular novel.

His protagonist was similar to Mister Johnson: a lively, inventive boy who, as a stranger, is beset by constant challenges, hostility, complications. And Cary's early notes recall those he made about Johnson: 'Charley likes to be liked – which leads many astray'; he is 'generous, affectionate and social'; 'Idea. Charley, making himself, needs help . . .'. Protagonist, themes, structure – all are similar. But the additional theme 'Tragedy of children' early added a sombre note[12] – partly, surely, in response to the war and its appallingly destructive effects on children.

Again Cary used the present tense, initially in the same way: a brief opening in the past tense throwing into relief a sudden shift into the present. But, occasionally and unpredictably, the narrative later lurches back into the past tense, sometimes for several pages, as if to suggest a lurking threat to creative imagination; and that oscillation also contributes to the unsettled tone of the novel. *Charley is My Darling* is also much longer than *Mister Johnson*; its slower pace and comparative prolixity intensifying its darker mood.

The novel's conclusion, although less ostensibly destructive than *Mister Johnson*'s, is gloomy: even though Liz Galor, unlike Bamu, has remained faithful, Charley's incarceration implies the continuing erosion of his vitality – while Johnson's death was a paradoxical leap to freedom, an imaginative coup. And there is no Rudbeck to ask 'I couldn't let anyone else do it, could I?' Both novels end with a superbly ironic deflection from the expected conclusive statement (one of Cary's finest devices); but Rudbeck's noble question rises in the freedom of Johnson's inspiration, while the constable's 'That's all right – she can't be too particular, can she?',[13] with its appalling irony, its deathly reflection of society's culpable indifference, thrusts the reader into dejection. The resolution in *Charley is My Darling* is painfully negative.

Cary, who always delighted in the common reader's response, was now beginning to receive a substantial fan-mail. 'I think it's the loveliest book I've ever read' was the verdict of one correspondent, and another hailed it as 'an important influence for good'. I can imagine nothing more eloquent and powerful on behalf of the children . . .'[14] The reviewers were just as positive. Robert Lynd, in the *News Chronicle*, called it 'a brilliant story' (though he also wondered if the conclusion, 'in which a girl of 15 is about to have a baby', were not 'too painful for a novel that begins so light-heartedly'). Other reviewers praised the novel's 'patient and penetrating analysis of children's minds' (*The Times*), described it as 'Splendid entertainment as well as electrifying revelation of the young idea' (*Observer*), hoped that 'all those concerned with Juvenile Crime and Youth Movements would read the book' (*Time and Tide*).[15]

A House of Children

When writing *Castle Corner*, Cary had tried out a first-person version. Now, as he started his next novel, also set in Inishowen, he was quickly confident that first-person narrative was the appropriate mode. He had no wish to stress historical perspective as in *Castle Corner*, no need for the sympathetic objectivity necessary to define simultaneously his protagonist's (Johnson's or Charley's) personality and the dimensions of his situation. 'General idea of book, the delightful quality of life for the children . . . Childrens idea or feeling that life is for truth, beauty and goodness, a rich experience and certainty.'[16] It was as if, reminded while writing *Castle Corner* and *Charley is My Darling* of the glories of his own childhood, he would now follow his moving demonstration of the thwarting of a child's creative imagination with a rapturous evocation of the opposite – the delight that childhood can and should be. *Mister Johnson* balanced injustice and creativity positively, *Charley is My Darling* reasserted the constant pressure of injustice; now the power of creativity would dominate, and irradiate an entire novel.

Cary remembered *A House of Children* as inaugurated in 'an English garden', presumably in the summer of 1940, by recollections 'suddenly called up by a fuchsia with its characteristic movement, stiff and springy, in a brisk wind. I was taken back to Donegal where fuchsia is a hedge plant' – and where, two years before, he had again experienced 'the large skies, and wide sea views, which belong to the vision of my childhood'.[17]

For Cary, even more powerful than sight in mediating recall of the past was smell: 'one day, at the age of fifty . . . I smelt thrift . . . it carried me instantly a thousand miles in space and forty years in time back to a certain spot among rocks at an Irish house called Carrig Cnoc . . .' He was 'actually existing, as a child again, in a certain place among the rocks, a high place on the right side of the bay, with the sea on both sides of me.'[18] Cary's ability to recall childhood, with an intensity that cancels the boundary between past and present, explains the utterly convincing evocation of his rapturous Inishowen holidays in *A House of Children*.

The novel is not based only on Cary's own childhood; he incorporated incidents from his sons'. And the characters, circumstances and events of his own childhood are transformed by the force of imagination. Dunamara is essentially Whitecastle, Crowcliff is recognisably Ravenscliff; but while Grandmother Evelyn is a simple translation of Grandmother Joyce, the more important Aunt Hersey is a complex fictionalising of Grandmother Cary. Other characters are similarly varied in relation to their progenitors. Evelyn's cousin Delia incorporates Cary's memories of his Aunt Netta, while Pinto, the children's holiday tutor, is more likely derived from several sources; and only

Evelyn's father seems intended as a true-to-life portrait, a celebration of all that Arthur Cary, so recently dead, had meant to his son.

Cary himself became two characters, the brothers Evelyn and Harry Corner (as the protagonist of *Castle Corner* was 'divided' into the cousins Cleeve Corner and Harry Jarvis). 'I . . . cut myself in two and took both parts,' he wrote in an early draft of his Preface; 'the two together as a single character would be too complex for the kind of book I needed to write'.[19] But that seems to be in part a rationalisation. Harry, the more practical of the two brothers, must represent Jack Cary to some extent, as well as the extrovert in Cary that life at Ravenscliff encouraged; Evelyn's dreaminess and artistic preoccupations certainly reflect the introverted boy of Clare Cottage. At a deeper level, the dual protagonists of *A House of Children* reflect the persistent duality of Cary's imagination.

In this novel the dominant art is not pictorial but verbal. The artist-figure recurs, in Pinto (whose surname, significantly, is Freeman); but he is not, like Lommax, a painter, and, although he can 'give the power of enjoyment', he hates teaching. The true teacher of the novel is Evelyn's father, whose eighteenth-century nobility shows up Pinto's shabby modernity; and the true artist is Evelyn. This novel is, subtly and magnificently, a *Bildungsroman* like Joyce's *Portrait of the Artist*; and weaves into its texture a moving love story centred on Delia, as well as succinct episodes defining the children's growth towards adulthood (the theme of injustice makes a forceful, but restricted, appearance with Robert's *Tottenham*-like experience of school life). Above all, its apparently fragile unity is firmly based on a structure of epiphanies superbly expressive of Cary's vision of childhood.

In *A House of Children* Cary triumphantly recapitulated his own progress towards becoming the writer who was about to publish this his sixth novel – a novel that would garner not only reviewers' and readers' affectionate admiration but a major literary award. He had now expressed a central aspect of his myth in a novel of magical charm – 'Children are born poets and singers.'[20] Each of the novels of the triumvirate that defines his early maturity – *Mister Johnson, Charley is My Darling, A House of Children* – holds one of the three countries that had formed him: Nigeria, England, Ireland. Now he would rise to a new challenge, and create a new, tripartite form; neither Irish nor Nigerian memories would again dominate his novels; he would become an explicitly English novelist.

CHAPTER THIRTY ONE

CANTERING

1940–1942

The First Trilogy

It was probably in the winter of 1940–1 that Cary thought out his 'scheme' for a trilogy. 'The trilogy was planned before Herself Surprised was written . . . Sara, Wilcher and Gulley were all partly realised characters in different sketches and the trilogy was a separate enterprise . . .'[1]

In 'Tod' and 'They Want to Be Happy' Cary had tried to compose sequences, and failed. This time his scheme was both flexible and tight – ideal for his creative temperament. 'What I set out to do was to show three people, living each in his own world by his own ideas, and relating his life and struggles, his triumphs and miseries in that world. They were to know each other and have some connection in the plot, but they would see completely different aspects of each other's character.'

The scheme accorded with his now completed myth, for the situation of each protagonist is essentially 'that of everyone who is doomed or blessed to be a free soul in the free world . . . Each of us is obliged to construct his own idea, his own map of things by which he is going to find his way, so far as he can, through life.'[2]

The trilogy was also designed 'to shew the same world over the same period of time' – 'the last sixty years' – 'from three different points of view.'[3] But because character, not chronology, was the structural foundation, each novel would stand, to some extent, independently of its companions, and could therefore evolve largely on its own terms; and the characters 'had to reveal themselves . . . therefore they had to use the first person, and write in a distinctive style and have a book each for their stories.'[4]

The characters and their relationships within the trilogy had long been defined, in broad terms. *Cock Jarvis* had expressed the trilogy's root conception of two men, opposed in personality but involved with the same woman. Their conflict potentially resulted in 'two kinds of tragedy', that of 'the conservative whose world is being destroyed' and that of the innovator, 'who desires to create his own new world . . . and is defeated by . . . those whose art and reputations are threatened by his innovation'.[5]

That conception would function as a unifying structure, simultaneously dramatising the eternal conflict between innovative and conservative temperaments, and mediating it through the woman's role and personality. Enfolding duality in trinity, Cary had now devised a formal means of expressing both his dualistic perception of experience (with its pervasive conflict of opposites) and his consuming desire to achieve unity. (He described the trilogy later as a 'triptych', *Herself Surprised* and *The Horse's Mouth* 'each a narrow side panel' flanking the 'central piece', *To Be a Pilgrim*.[6])

He would also be writing out of his greatest strength as a novelist: his empathy, his ability to enter utterly, like Chaucer, individuals who were also types. And he would be minimising his most notable weakness, the shaping of plot and rhythm; for in each novel those qualities would be subordinate to expression of personality and point of view.

Cary's trilogy form was probably influenced by several literary works known to him. *The Canterbury Tales* by his 'precious Chaucer'. Arnold Bennett's *Clayhanger* trilogy, long admired. Joyce's *Ulysses*, which for Cary was 'a great masterpiece, or rather several masterpieces',[7] and which linked two very different men with a woman (Stephen Dedalus and Bloom are 'opposites'; Molly Bloom has qualities similar to Sara Monday's and functions thematically as a reconciling affirmative force). *Finnegans Wake* with its cyclical opposition of the twins Shem and Shawn, its eternally reconciling woman.[8] Herbert Read's *The End of a War*: in that tripartite poem, the 'meditations' of two radically opposed men (a 'Dying German Officer' and a 'Waking English Officer') enclose a woman's thoughts, those of a 'Murdered Girl' (whose perspective is split, a 'Dialogue between the Body and Soul').[9] Robert Browning's *The Ring and the Book*, which not only focuses on two men, and a woman killed by one of them, but also gives to its Pope a speech which states implications of Cary's trilogy form: 'Truth, nowhere, lies yet everywhere in these – / Not absolutely in a portion, yet / Evolvable from the whole . . .'[10]

While planning and writing the trilogy, Cary read various philosophical texts to explore its moral issues. A central work was Kant's *Critique of Pure Reason*, which he annotated extensively ('Ultimate intuition of nature moral' runs a marginal note);[11] and it is very likely that he began to explore Existentialist thought at this time ('Kierkegaard states the uniqueness of the individual and I stand by that,' he said later[12]).

Notebooks used in the early 1940s show him repeating his own established views, drawing ideas from his reading, and working his way towards a philosophical position that would synthesise the relative and absolute, and set out the moral implications of his myth: 'Every man is an artist, as well as practical man . . . A stream of experience . . . passes continually through us. It is from this stream that we pick details, form concepts and create our reality . . . All enquiries about truth are limited and must be limited because there is no whole truth . . . Moral is a relative term . . . Moral act is purposive of an end beyond itself and always unique. It is . . . art-full . . . All moral judgements are immediate, empiric and limited . . . Good is that which serves ultimate freedom, bad is what impedes it.'[13]

Herself Surprised

The actual characters and circumstances of the trilogy seem to have been first explored in 'Song of Lally', a sketch whose heroine gets to know an artist (called first Hansell, and then Mr Gulley). In one writing he is clearly a variant of the rogue established in Cary's earliest fiction: 'He wore holiday clothes like a city man at the sea side and bright yellow shoes. He had rather an impudent look and I could see he was an impudent kind of man . . . He kept laughing and telling stories . . .'

That story evolved into 'A Woman's Confession', which in turn became *Herself Surprised*. It is notable that the most prominent relationship is between woman and rogue – a pattern which was to recur in later novels, like A *Fearful Joy*; and that the role of Wilcher, central in the completed trilogy, was originally subordinate.[14]

Once he started work on *Herself Surprised*, Cary found that his scheme, 'like all a priori schemes for books or anything else, proved to have unexpected flaws', and had to be adjusted. The trilogy was to explore art and politics. But when his first protagonist, Sara Monday, talked about these, 'she became less vivid as a character. She lost immediacy as a family woman. In such a problem, familiar to every writer, my rule is character first, so I sacrificed the politics . . .' (In the same way, he had to leave out of the later novels 'most of Wilcher's ideas of art and Gulley's of politics'.)[15]

Herself Surprised, he explained later, was 'meant to have Sara's character of sensuous domesticity'.[16] Sara, although indebted to a series of earlier characters (like the Sara of *Cock Jarvis*), to memories of the Irish cooks of Cary's youth and his own experience as 'Cookee' in Montenegro, was surely also drawn from women Cary knew well, above all his wife. Trudy had lamented the extent of her domesticity; her husband had criticised and her sons teased her for it; but she was always happiest and most confident in that role, and was loved and respected for her selfless commitment to it. J.R. Harris, who made furniture and did small repairs for the Carys, remembered Trudy as 'such a keen cook – she enjoyed and loved her kitchen'.[17] Sara's similar contentment is stressed in her narrative, and warm domestic images shape her prose.

Cary's view of the nature and role of women had been strongly influenced by his early experiences, especially the trauma of mother loss and the subsequent importance of surrogate mothers. During the last two decades of his life he was notably sympathetic towards women who sought fulfilment outside motherhood and the home, in such professions as university teaching, recognising that some women 'are totally unsuited to be wives and mothers'[18]; but he never became an orthodox feminist, any more than he became an orthodox Christian. The hostility obvious in his early portraits of the 'new woman' of the 1920s was qualified in his later writing (witness Ann Wilcher in

To Be a Pilgrim) by greater understanding of the dilemmas women face in asserting themselves against repressive social values.

He gave qualified praise to the 'Revolution of the Women'. 'A man has always been able to decide between family and career'; now Feminism had achieved greater opportunity for women to seek fulfilment – but at the cost of rendering their lives 'infinitely more complex than any lived by women in the past . . . full of difficult choice, and decisions which cannot look to any convention for support'. And he insisted that 'Nothing can destroy those affections and sympathies which bring about the essential family relation whatever its local form. Father, mother, and children . . . are a natural and primitive unit, a miniature civilisation in which love, tolerance and unselfish duty are reborn from generation to generation.'[19] The assumption throughout his fiction is that women find happiness by fulfilling their instinct to nurture; by establishing a home, by bearing and bringing up children.

Sara, struggling to build or retain her nests, to hold her man and be an adequate mother, is in the woman's 'jam', with its injustice and its opportunities for creativity.

The surviving manuscripts suggest that Cary wrote *Herself Surprised* fluently, with little fundamental revision; the final typescript has many emendations, but most are cuts, and the novel has an impressive coherence in all respects. He began it in the spring of 1941 and finished it some six months later.

The title – like all Cary's titles, and all his protagonists' names – was carefully chosen, then tested against other possibilities. Cary had now moved away decisively from descriptive or summarising titles that referred to a central character or house. The title *Aissa Saved*, partly echoed by *Herself Surprised*, had established one type he continued to favour: a resonantly significant phrase, ironic, as well as appropriate to character and theme.

Indeed, the novel's title is the main clue to Sara's personality and situation, defining her as a woman deeply but intuitively responsive to life – like Mister Johnson, she has neither aptitude nor need to cerebrate. Moving from surprise to surprise, she constantly, and paradoxically, accepts her being and the world's as the ground of her creativity. In her convincing but representative individuality, her complex simplicity, in her self-justifying and self-revealing narrative, Sara can be placed confidently beside Chaucer's Wife of Bath, Defoe's Moll Flanders, Emily Brontë's Nelly Dean.

Spencer Curtis Brown wrote enthusiastically soon after the novel's publication to say how much he had enjoyed it ('far and away the most readable and the best story you have yet written'). Many reviewers agreed with that opinion, and the novel did well (within weeks it had sold 4,000 copies – which, Curtis Brown thought, would enable him to 'get a *substantially* better contract for the next books').[20]

The Case for African Freedom

In January 1941, just before *A House of Children* came out, Cary had been invited to contribute to a series called 'The Searchlight Books', edited by T.R.

Fyvel and George Orwell. Believing that 'We cannot defeat Germany unless we have first freed ourselves from our own weaknesses,' the editors solicited texts 'written in simple language without the rubber-stamp political jargon of the past' which, focusing on 'Britain's international and imperial responsibilities', would show 'what is wrong in Western civilisation and supply constructive ideas for the difficult period ahead of us'. [21]

Cary accepted immediately, although he was then mulling over the projected trilogy and making notes for *Herself Surprised*. Writing a treatise and a novel together had worked so well in relation to *Power in Men* and *Mister Johnson* that, for the rest of his life, Cary welcomed such opportunities. The cross-fertilisation, the channelling of his imaginative and polemical impulses, stimulated and disciplined his creativity.

As its title implies, *The Case for African Freedom* is a passionate but reasoned plea for political change, and a measured repudiation of Indirect Rule. Orwell's Foreword was judicious. Cary, he wrote, had an 'unusually independent mind' and was

> first and foremost a realist. He has no use for either the ignorant settler or businessman who secretly regards the African as a slave, or for the left-wing sentimentalist who imagines that the African peoples can be 'set free' by a stroke of the pen and that their troubles will thereupon be ended. He knows that the exploitation of the coloured peoples by the whites has got to be ended, and as quickly as possible, and he also knows that in the age of the bombing plane a primitive people cannot be genuinely independent. [22]

This praise from one of the foremost political thinkers of the day, a man with similar practical experience, was pleasing.

Perhaps even more pleasing was a letter Cary received after the book's publication from one of Orwell's fellow Socialists, Arthur Creech Jones, soon to become Colonial Secretary: 'May I acknowledge the considerable profit I have obtained from reading your recent book . . . I agree with your general theme and am glad you have contributed so valuably to creating a better appreciation of African and colonial problems. In my judgment you have done a fine piece of work.' [23]

Edwardes, when he thanked Cary for a copy of the book, agreed 'with every line of it. It is full of good sense, wisdom, and understanding of the native point of view', and should be acted on by the Colonial Office. [24] And an influential Nigerian intellectual, Davidson Nicol, commented that *The Case for African Freedom* 'so well expressed what educated Africans were thinking about colonialism that many thought the author must himself be a Nigerian'. [25]

To Be a Pilgrim

The Case for African Freedom was published in July 1941. *Herself Surprised* followed in November. By then Cary had been immersed in the second volume of his trilogy for several months.

The title *To Be a Pilgrim* is of another type that Cary favoured from the 1940s: the pregnant quotation, first used in *Charley is My Darling*. Again irony is an important dimension of meaning. The famous hymn 'He who would valiant be', taken from John Bunyan's *Pilgrim's Progress*, defined for Cary the essence of English Protestantism, as well as implying a human imperative. For Cary believed that the Protestant tradition of the 'middle orders', an 'evangelical strain opposed and intensified by native conservatism', is the root of the Liberalism that dominates English history.[26]

Tom Wilcher, his protagonist, is, however, so deeply conservative, so fearful of change, that his life has been warped by fear and restraint. Yet he has not succeeded in rooting out his natural creativity and is challenged again and again by forces of change so that, ultimately, he accepts the wisdom he has so often rejected (even when embodied by loved members of his own family). In this respect, the novel comes close to a parable and, especially in its flamboyant peroration, also seems to express a wartime nationalistic fervour that inflates its 'state of England' sub-theme.

Cary's notes suggest that he wished the novel's peroration to imply that 'The conservative . . . has to *recreate, to maintain*, his activity is protective and maintaining. He must contrive a flexible dogma of standards and must *believe* in those standards. To lose faith in the standards is to lose motive for creation . . . i.e. you can be passive conservative, a mere parasite or a creative maintainer . . .'

This is an important point: the conflict between conservative and innovator is not between right and wrong; the two temperaments are endemic, and both are socially valuable, one to preserve the past, the other to break into the future. What is at issue is creative imagination; and, though it is naturally more difficult for the conservative than for the innovator, he too, Cary believed, can create, be a pilgrim. The jingoistic passages were intended, then, to signify Wilcher's renewal of faith in his standards; but carry such heavy wartime emotional freight that they compromise Cary's intended meaning.[27]

'The tragedy of old Wilcher', his 'jam' in a world of perpetual change, is of course 'that of the conservative who loves his old home, his old fields, and the old ways. For he has created from them a world of associations in which alone he can achieve his desire, his need for affection. He loves things as well as people, and cannot bear to lose them. But even his trees must go to make way for the tractor.'[28] Cary's extensive notes for *To Be a Pilgrim* reveal the very great care he took to consider and reconsider every aspect of the novel as it progressed; Wilcher's style, for instance, was carefully infused with Biblical echoes.

One of Cary's admirers wondered if his 'attitude towards the modern world is at all the same as Mr Wilcher's which I found most sympathetic'.[29] But that was to miss the point: in this deeply moving novel, Cary was seeking to confront, not endorse, the conservative in himself and others. He had himself only recently rejected as no longer viable the political doctrine that he had admired and served, Indirect Rule, and knew well the strength of the conservative impulse in his own personality.

To Be a Pilgrim weaves together several narrative strands, and 'In all stories the flavour of the pilgrimage of life, change, futility of hopes and *wisdom of pilgrim's view*. 'W. throughout is confusing his love for the old forms, separating him from the roots of the good *pilgrim's life*.'[30] As a lawyer, a member of the profession for which Cary trained at Oxford and which he practised in Nigeria, he is representative of much that Cary felt and valued. It is deeply significant that Wilcher, feeling an intense rapport with his fellow humans as the Great War begins, thinks of Chaucer's lines 'Sundry folk, by adventure y fall, / In fellowship, and pilgrims were they all'.[31]

Cary finished *To Be a Pilgrim* at the end of August 1942. Not surprisingly, Michael Joseph received it 'with delight and admiration . . . Lusty and I are both keen to build up your sales . . . and I may add that we take a considerable pride in publishing you.'[32]

'such a famous husband'

The war was continuing to bring changes for Cary's family. Towards the end of January 1942 Trudy received a letter from Freddy Ogilvie to tell her that he was leaving his post as Director-General of the BBC.

> The reasons don't matter greatly, except in so far as they involve some questions of principle – e.g. the limits which representatives of the Church should be allowed the freedom of the microphone in wartime . . .

Freddy Ogilvie, deeply religious, always the man of honour and principle, had fallen victim to opprobrium directed, by Winston Churchill's war cabinet, at BBC broadcasts of talks by pacifist clergymen like Dick Sheppard, founder of the Peace Pledge Union. It would be 'rather fun, and certainly very salutary, to try to begin life again at 49', Freddy Ogilvie continued – and he hoped that 'you and Joyce will not regard your brother as too, too leprous!'[33] If Cary did not respond with admiration and affection, he should have done – especially if, as is likely, Freddy Ogilvie was a model for Thomas Wilcher in *To Be a Pilgrim*.

Heneage Ogilvie was abroad; he had been appointed Consulting Surgeon to the British Expeditionary Force, and wrote lively letters from the Middle East and Africa. In November 1942 he told Trudy it was a pity Cary could not join him in Jerusalem: 'Joyce would be grand fun . . . and he would love Palestine.'[34]

Michael and Peter were both away from home: Michael, in the Admiralty, was on an aircraft carrier in the Far East; Peter was a Transport Officer in the Oxford and Bucks Regiment. Tristram and George, both still at school, returned only for holidays. Parkers was quiet. Which was just as well, since servants were difficult to find and Trudy had to do all the housework herself.

When home, Tristram, now nearly seventeen, had become a close companion on daily walks in the Parks. 'Joyce at 55,' Tristram wrote later, 'was just beginning to enjoy real success and the reasonable financial returns that go with it.' Cary discussed with him the main characters of *To Be a Pilgrim*, and 'bombarded me with ideas, philosophy, plots, history, reminiscence'.[35]

*

Cary's reputation was now high among critics and fellow novelists. L.P. Hartley, himself soon to become prominent as the author of the 'Eustace and Hilda' trilogy (its first volume appeared in 1944), wrote in March 1941: 'I have the greatest admiration for your work: you are alone among the first novelists of today in being able to find nourishment for your imagination and your thoughts in things as they are. I believe you could even write a novel about the present war without making it too depressing.' He implied some scepticism about Cary's 'point of view', wondering whether it did not depend on the 'special cases' of Nigerian and Irish ebullience. But he envied Cary's 'confidence in life', and his 'art, which is so sound and spontaneous and free'.[36]

Partly through Hartley, Cary gained the closest friend of his later years: Lord David Cecil. An English don and Fellow of New College, over a decade younger than Cary, Cecil had already published several biographies and books of literary criticism. As an aristocrat (he was the youngest son of the fourth Marquess of Salisbury), Cecil moved in high circles; and had been a member of Lady Ottoline Morrell's Garsington circle in the late 1920s. He was also unaffectedly enthusiastic and already well known as an Oxford 'character'. A.L. Rowse described him as 'almost a product of another civilisation', who spoke in such a 'rapid, highly Cecilian manner' that 'only two of every three words he uttered' could be made out[37]; Maurice Bowra valued Cecil's 'eager curiosity about all kinds of human behaviour. Though he had strong convictions on religion and politics, he never forced them on you, and was much too tolerant to make you feel that your opinions were absurd'.[38]

Cecil recalled that he and Cary had met at a sherry party in the Randolph Hotel, probably before the end of 1941; at that time he had not read any of Cary's novels, but knew of them through Hartley's admiration. The two men immediately felt 'some deep affinity' and 'within a fortnight we were close friends'. Cary would then often call in at the Cecils' house in Mansfield Road, not far from Parkers, and the two would go for a walk in the Parks, talking volubly all the time. Lord David Cecil's wife Rachel (daughter of the critic Desmond MacCarthy) also liked Cary; and the two families were soon visiting each other.

For Cary this was a friendship with a fellow spirit whose aristocratic background, social values and wide range of interests were similar to his own. Equally lively in the flow of conversation, Cecil and Cary enjoyed striking sparks off each others' minds – though, Cecil noted, Cary 'didn't give way an inch on his own judgements'.[39]

A few months after he had met Lord David Cecil, a letter arrived at Parkers which inaugurated a second major friendship. 'Dear Mr Cary, A short time ago I read your recent book, To Be a Pilgrim and I meant to write to you immediately . . . It has great beauty and wisdom. It's a sad book . . . It seems to me that your attitude to the craft of fiction is more French than English.'[40] The letter was from Enid Starkie, French don and Fellow of Somerville College, who had recently met Cary.

Her sociable behaviour, her memorable red-and-blue matelot's uniform, had already established Starkie as a local celebrity, and through her Cary was to make many of the friends who would later form his 'circle'. She was Irish, she was a 'character', she had published a book (A *Lady's Child*) about her childhood that had similarities to A *House of Children*. Her biographer describes a personality not unlike Cary's: 'outgoing, impulsive, full of *joie de vivre*', 'funny, warm and shrewd, perpetually alert'. Her behaviour was strikingly dichotomous: 'On some occasions she behaved like an *enfant terrible*', on others she paid reverent respect to protocol. But above all she was 'life-enhancing. She lived intensely, and made [her friends] live more intensely, too'.[41]

Cary was away from Oxford when Enid Starkie's letter arrived. Trudy wrote to explain this, and received a reply full of extravagant praise: 'He ought to be doing nothing but write – I consider him one of the most outstanding English novelists today . . . he talks of his craft most interestingly, unself-consciously . . .'[42] Trudy, impressed, told Cary 'She is a real fan . . . I only wish I were more worthy of such a famous husband – though I don't think you will ever get spoilt darling?'[43]

CHAPTER THIRTY TWO

GALLOPING

1942–1943

'the power of art'

In January 1942, soon after he had started writing *To Be a Pilgrim*, Cary was informed that *A House of Children* had been awarded the prestigious James Tait Black Memorial Prize for 'the best novel' of 1941. Apart from its monetary value, the fact that the award was associated with Edinburgh was pleasing: the Regius Professor of Rhetoric and English at Edinburgh University was Chairman of the selection committee. The incumbent Professor, John Dover Wilson, eminent Shakespearean critic and editor, wrote to congratulate Cary and invite him to visit the University and talk to its students. Cary replied immediately: 'it gave me the keenest pleasure to hear your name, so well known to me, and to know that it was on your recommendation that I was given the prize . . . I should like, if you would like it, to send you a copy of the book with a piece of the M. S. and a drawing.'

Acknowledging Cary's gift, Dover Wilson reminded him about the invitation to lecture. Cary replied cautiously 'I have never lectured, in form, but I talk to university societies here sometimes on theory of freedom (real freedom) which would bore your students . . . I have some notions about the novel but they are probably as useless to others as a painters method to his students. Useless or dangerous, and I have never thrown them into portable form.'[1]

In August Cary wrote 'My book [*To Be a Pilgrim*] is finished at last and I want to forget it. It has, like all my books been both a surprise and a disappointment to me; it turned out quite other than I expected, and very much worse than I had hoped. But having rewritten it, like all the others, several times, I know that there was no improving it except by putting it in the fire and starting again from the beginning . . . ' He had agreed to lecture and was looking forward to being in Edinburgh again: 'I have a very old and sentimental attachment to town and people.'[2]

Meanwhile there was a family holiday to enjoy: on a yawl called the *Skirmish* (moored on the River Dart), with Trudy, Tristram and George. Cary jotted down some observations:

At night, the mist, the white deck, a white darkness, anchor noise like thunder, like someone driving nails, flapping slowly like a wet fish, the change of motion at the change of tide – a free lively movement against the labouring rise and fall, like the breathing of an animal tied down by the nose. the dawn. Chinese landskip. The sleepless night. Fog horns, owls, rocks and seagulls. Swans going by with the noise of rusty hinges creaking.[3]

Those sharply pictorial and sensual images suggest that Cary's psyche was already shaped to Gulley Jimson's. Indeed, that passage could almost be Jimson's. Years later Cary wrote that he had had 'no idea of Gulley's style and didn't want one. If I fixed him to a style he would just become a period piece and not simply *the* original artist.'[4] This was not strictly accurate (notes for the novel include 'Short and agile sentences running gradually into poetry. Ejaculations. Quotations.'[5]); but Cary was undoubtedly dramatising a dimension of his own personality, in a style essentially synthesising qualities remembered from the conversation and writing of artists he had known.

During his holiday on the *Skirmish* he had also been working on his chosen topic for Edinburgh, and at the end of September wrote to inform Dover Wilson that he would 'like to talk about Tolstoy's theory of art and morals; as compared with his technical practice and the general technique of the novel . . . I can't think of a good title. Would "Tolstoy on Art and Morals" do?'[6] That was the lecture's title when delivered on 27 November 1942. The following summer it was published as 'Tolstoy's Theory of Art' in the *University of Edinburgh Journal,* and stands as Cary's first published essay (with the debatable exception of a radio talk, his first, 'Britain's Colonial Record', which was published on 26 August 1942).

'The artist is not a mere recording instrument,' Cary states near the start of this somewhat confusing lecture; 'he is a creator with a definite object.' Tolstoy was wrong to argue that 'Art is entirely formal', thus separating content from form; and to simplify human experience by insisting that 'men could only be happy in loving one another.' But, feeling deeply, Tolstoy had created a 'moral theory of art'. And in this Cary sided with him against 'Croce and the expressionist school'.[7]

Cary was often to express the conviction that, 'In the final resort, all novel-writing is moral. It is impossible to give form to a book without some moral creed'.[8] He felt indebted to Tolstoy for this insight, and his Edinburgh lecture concluded with a flow of compliments to the great novelist whose ideas he had so often attacked: 'It is because Tolstoy was so completely sincere, so utterly scornful, like the aristocrat he was, of popular judgement, that he stands before us as one of the greatest men and greatest artists of the world. His faults were enormous. But he showed them to us.'[9] This reconciliation continues a pattern in Cary's life (the revaluation of Musa was an instance) and in his writing (for example, Jarvis's emergence as imaginatively creative); Cary's optimism was profoundly generous and restorative.

Dover Wilson responded positively to Cary, and later told Helen Gardner about the evening when his guest 'sat up most of the night talking'[10] –

'talking about his novels, written and unwritten. It was an unforgettable experience to be privileged to look into the world of a great imagination – an experience, I need hardly tell you, of much value to one who spends his life writing notes on the products of a still greater imagination.'[11] Since Falstaff was on Dover Wilson's mind as the subject of the Clark Lectures he was preparing for May 1943, that 'succulent old sinner' with his 'joyous and victorious pleasure in the life of the senses'[12] may well have been another topic of conversation, adding to the many influences – above all, Cary's own memories, sharpened by nostalgic walks around the Edinburgh haunts of his art-school days – now shaping Gulley Jimson in Cary's imagination.

When he wrote to Dover Wilson a week after getting back to Oxford, Cary was full of *The Horse's Mouth*:

> . . . I had some ideas about a new book, in the train coming South and since then I have been throwing off scenes, characters and dialogue at thousands of words a day. Most of it will be scrap but meanwhile, like Manet, as he painted his first drafts, I'm learning the forms and necessary conjunctions of my matter, discovering its weaknesses before they are fatally included in some general plan, and getting to know my people by putting the question.
>
> It will be a damn queer book but my agent told me to write what I damned well liked and to hell with the publisher; and then the publisher smiled upon me and told me that whatever I wrote would receive his highest consideration or words to that effect. So I am going to give myself a fling. And then I shall write a classical and slow moving novel, what Trudy calls 'a harvest of the quiet eye'. Both these books have much material gathered.[13]

Meanwhile life was frantic: 'I rush out from a chapter which is almost pure lyric, to decorate a birthday cake [his own] with cochineal; and then the telephone rings to know if I can take a class in bombs on Sunday morning. This exasperates me greatly and keeps my humours properly mixed.'[14] And Christmas, with its family rituals, was less than three weeks off.

Men of Two Worlds
On Christmas Eve an unexpected letter arrived, when Cary

> was thinking much more [about] a Christmas party for the family than any literary work. He put it aside and forgot about it. It was Mrs Cary who, some days after Christmas, said 'Didn't you hear from some film company? What did they want?' Cary however could not remember the address of the Company and he had not read the letter. Neither could it be found. It would, in all probability, never have been found if it had not been typed on a peculiar buff coloured paper. Cary was settling down to work one morning when he noticed a corner of this buff paper sticking out of a pile of discarded M. S. ready for the wastepaper basket. He pulled it out and for the first time read John Sutro's suggestion of a conference. A fortnight later he was on a troopship going to Africa . . .[15]

Sutro, of Two Cities Films, was a producer, and the conference was in connection with a project originally suggested by the novelist E. Arnot Robertson, who was working in the Film Department of the Ministry of Information: to 'portray the native African as he really is, and to fit him into a story which sums up one of the chief present-day problems of our colonial administration'. As director of the film, the Ministry of Information had recommended Thorold Dickinson; and in December 1942, he was given 'three weeks to collect a team before the ship sailed for West Africa. Who was to write the story? His wife searched the libraries for books on Africa, and . . . she found a pamphlet on "African Freedom" by a man named Joyce Cary, a former district officer in West Africa. Dickinson read the pamphlet between 11 p.m. and 2 a.m. the same night and decided that Cary was the right man for the job. His publishers were contacted and a letter sent to him.'[16]

It was a challenge and an opportunity after Cary's heart – a sportsman's challenge and an opportunity to see Africa again. The voyage was risky. Their ship, the *Duchess of Richmond*, transporting some 4,000 soldiers to the Far East, 'sailed in convoy at a time when Hitler's U-boats were sinking about a million tons of Allied shipping a month'. Its escorting destroyers 'sank a U-boat, and another U-boat sank the ship that was carrying our movie camera and stock'; but there were no casualties. The troopship's progress was, however, very slow – 'boredom at seven knots' said Dickinson.[17]

Cary worked hard in his cabin on *The Horse's Mouth* and, meanwhile, the film script was taking shape too. 'Dickinson and I had our usual walk on the top deck and discussed the film. We are getting on fast. And agree very well with each other's suggestions.'[18] For Dickinson, Cary was 'a joy to know',[19] and it must have helped their relationship that they were both Old Cliftonians. The four-man unit was convivial. 'We were a happy party,' wrote Cary. 'I have had to give a lecture on board about the African Native and I sit on a brains trust which answers all sorts of questions for an hour every morning.' Moreover, 'This is a very comfortable ship and the food is almost too good.' The 'first sketch of the film is finished and Dickinson is very pleased with it. I have written about 20,000 words of the Horses Mouth as well, and worked out several new chapters.'[20]

Cary shared a cabin with the unit's cameraman, Desmond Dickinson (who was not related to Thorold). This was another stroke of luck for Cary, since his companion was a lively Cockney who knew London's East End well. Some of the vivid authenticity of background and dialogue in *The Horse's Mouth* is owed to him.

They were to disembark at Lagos, but, Dickinson recalled, 'We were put ashore a thousand miles from Lagos' – at Freetown, capital of Liberia – and 'had to spend two stifling weeks begging for air passages among several hundred competitors'.[21] They were entertained to a party by Graham Greene who loaned Cary a Nissen hut to work in. Did the two writers discuss their current novels? It is piquant to imagine Cary writing *The Horse's Mouth* in the setting of Greene's *The Heart of the Matter*, while Greene – stationed at Freetown as an Information Officer – was writing *The Ministry of Fear*!

Early in March they reached Dar es Salaam, Tanganyika (Tanzania) – 'White houses with pillars, balconies and red tiled roofs . . . tall coconut palms . . . a lagoon where Dhows sail'; and quickly got down to work. Then the unit set off to find a suitable 'sleeping sickness area' (required by the film's plot). They drove north towards Arusha ('the great plain below is full of game'[21]) and everywhere they went, 'Natives watched over them armed with spears, bows and arrows to guard them against wild beasts, especially at sunrise and sunset. The heat was intense, and the dangers of accident and sickness not to be taken lightly.'[22] Arusha was magnificent.'Last night we went up native paths along the streams which can be heard everywhere, as on Exmoor . . . We lost our way and came suddenly to a village in a thicket of acacia thorn . . . In one place we found some girls and young men dancing to the sound of a bunch of cow bells. And always in the background one sees the great peak of Mount Meru.'

The unit pressed on to Moshi, 'right opposite Kilimanjaro. It is a wonderful sight to see the great glacier on the summit glittering in the tropical sun. At night this ice cap seems to hang in the air, and the mountain seems made of sky, when the moon falls on it directly . . . we shall be out all day with the District Commissioner, looking at the area.' Moshi was chosen as the film's location, and the rest of the unit scoured the nearby countryside 'while I write the film play, a new version, but I think a better one, with a star part for a white man, the D. O. We are very happy together as a unit. We chaff each other all day. They call me the Colonel and chaff me on my appetite, which is large; and my passion for fruit.'[23]

Back in Dar es Salaam, Cary resisted Curtis Brown's attempt to secure more money for him from Two Cities. He conceded that he was doing more work than the contract had stipulated – by late April, he had already 'been away more than three months and finished three treatments and finally a complete film play', but 'Dickinson is my friend, we have worked very happily together, I have absolute confidence in his integrity; and I feel a strong personal obligation both to him and his unit that no unnecessary delay shall hold up their work . . .'[24] He was then waiting for transportation back to Britain.

The film would take three years to complete, and suffer many vicissitudes (including the loss of the footage taken on location at Moshi). But Cary's part in it was over. He was home by May, and did not participate in the actual filming, though he watched some of it with great interest at Denham Studios. He enjoyed meeting the cast, and for a while kept up a warm acquaintance with Cathleen Nesbit, who played a minor role.

Cary's screenplay was subsequently revised by 'a new collaborator, Herbert Victor, who knowing nothing about Africa insisted on making the script transparently clear to the uninitiated public'.[25] Cary had not been pleased by this tampering. The main characters, the plot and the dialogue are largely his; and, although revised by Victor, and vitiated by the project's intention ('a war job of propaganda,' Thorold Dickinson conceded[26]), clearly relate to his earlier writing, notably *The African Witch* and *The King is Dead, Long Live the King*. For Cary the episode was an exhilarating holiday whose effects infuse *The Horse's Mouth*. It also again illustrates Cary's anxiety to be both man of action and artist. He was galloping harder and harder, but beginning to let the reins hang loose.

The Horse's Mouth

'The title has been misunderstood by some critics. The horse's mouth is not Gulley, but the voice that commands Gulley to be an artist, and makes him struggle to realise his imagination in spite of all discouragement.'[27] As Cary's notes suggest, the title has also a wider reference. 'Horses mouth. know thyself and make thy world . . . Create. You've got to create or destroy. You've got to use your imagination to know the world because it is only to be understood by imagination . . . *You are the fallen man, free and responsible.* You have to *help yourself.*' 'The forms, the colours, the fundamental aesthetic qualities are *given*. They come from the *Horses mouth.*' 'We create by art our own world out of given materials. We are free men. God is free in us. We are the horseness of his imagination.'[28]

Although all Cary's titles were carefully chosen, this one was especially significant. Like several of his titles – *The Captive and the Free* is another – it was in Cary's mind and notebooks for many years, growing in meaning and power; he had first considered using it in the early 1930s, for the novel that became *An American Visitor.*

And Gulley Jimson's particular 'jam', like Cock Jarvis's, re-enacts the pain of the long-ago artist in Etaples weeping in front of his painting: it is the bitter sense of injustice. But 'freedom which produces injustice . . . gives also to man the power to fight injustice, to battle with his own fate. He can create for himself a life which defies injustice. Beethoven deaf at thirty-five, suffered a fearful injustice, but by his will, his art, made himself greater in music than he had been before. He triumphed over his bad luck, his fate.' That is Gulley Jimson's challenge. He 'is not so successful' as Beethoven.

> But he is quite aware of the nature of his struggle, and tells himself that the original artist can seldom expect appreciation in his life time; simply because he is original, because he upsets people who are already attached to established forms of art. And he understands that this . . . is only one aspect of a universal battle between new ideas and old ideas. For since the spirit of this world is a free creative spirit . . . it is always restless, it is always dissatisfied, it is always seeking new arts, new life for itself . . .

Cary also hoped that the reader would never forget that

> The book is supposed to be written by Gulley . . . Thus the sense of the farcical incidents must be read as Gulley wrote them, enjoying their malice, and making fun even of himself. Even his good natured remarks . . . are full of that malice against which he fights. It is that imaginative malice of the poet, the artist, the genius, a malice turned every way, against himself as well as the world, which can be read in the works and lives of many neglected, and even of many successful artists. For such people, in their furious vitality and especially the liveliness of their imaginations, are capable of living several lives at once; their lives are symphonic . . . Gulley can be malicious, friendly, understanding, mischievous, at the same moment and in the same conversation.[29]

As Cary's comments imply, his protagonist had multitudinous sources, some literary (like Falstaff, and Benvenuto Cellini's *Autobiography*), and many personal (himself, his father, Heneage Ogilvie, and artists he had known – especially Fergusson and Gilbert Spencer).

Perhaps most powerful of all as sources – because they provoked the imagination – were anecdotes about Stanley Spencer. Maurice Bowra remembered encounters with the Spencer brothers at Garsington in the late 1920s, when they were living on Lady Ottoline Morrell's estate – 'Stanley Spencer, torn between apocalyptic visions . . . and domestic duties, such as giving the children their baths'; and Gilbert Spencer, with his 'passionate admiration for his brother'.[30] Even then, Stanley was becoming notorious for his eccentricities, and undoubtedly Cary would have heard many anecdotes about him from Gilbert in the mid 1930s. A small man, with a fiery temper and an intense interest in the personality and thought of William Blake, Stanley Spencer's relationship with his wife Hilda (who was physically bigger and stronger) frequently erupted in violence. Moreover, while painting his fine murals in Burghclere Chapel (not far from Oxford) in the late 1920s, he employed as cook a woman named Elsie Munday who became the subject of a series of domestic paintings and accompanied the Spencers when they moved back to Cookham in 1931.[31]

Cary had also heard anecdotes about the ebullient sculptor Jacob Epstein (whose work he greatly admired) and the wild Welsh poet Dylan Thomas. Thomas did not live in Oxford until just after the war (when the don A. J. P. Taylor and his wife Margaret, acquaintances of the Carys, gave them accommodation). But a few years earlier, he was told about Thomas's mistreatment of a flat lent to him by the painter.Rupert Shepherd.[32] Thomas 'had gradually pawned everything until only the silver was left' – and this he was cleaning 'before taking it to pawn also' when 'His hosts unexpectedly returned. "How thoughtful of you to have cleaned the silver for us. You shouldn't have bothered".'[33] The incident irresistibly recalls Jimson's relations with the Beeders.

Cary insisted that *The Horse's Mouth*, for all its humour, was 'a very heavy piece of metaphysical writing', 'involved and highly complex'.[34] Much of that complexity comes from Gulley Jimson's quotations from, and references to, William Blake, and the debate between Blakean and Spinozan interpretations of the human situation.

Cary had long been attracted to Blake's Prophetic Books, but in the 1930s – stimulated, perhaps, by Middleton Murry's *William Blake* (1933) – he began again to read the poet's work carefully, and in 1936 considered writing a 'Novel about William Blake' on the lines of Irving Stone's recently published *Lust for Life: The Novel of Vincent Van Gogh*.[35] Blake was an obvious point of reference for one of the novel's main themes, 'the creative imagination working in symbols'.[36] (The critic Northrop Frye was one expert who paid tribute to Cary's use of Blakean thought and writing; he sent Cary an inscribed copy of his book *Fearful Symmetry* when it came out in 1947.[37])

By the time Cary wrote *The Horse's Mouth*, he had found in Blake's writing an analysis of human experience that seemed to endorse his own: 'For Blake every individual character had its own nature, its 'particular' shape, rather like a Platonic form. This was its essentiality by which it was eternal and belonged to the realm of the 'infinite' . . . You are you, and nobody else. Anything real or partaking of eternal form, beauty, goodness etc. depends therefore on your individual difference.'[38] He also commented in a note 'Point of Blake is his *depth and adequacy – close to the ground*. His acceptance of *evil as real*. Through creation, *generation to regeneration*. The *stoic* english view. but he *enters into freedom and individuality* through experience *as individual*, fights government and so does Gully . . .'[39] Blake believed 'everything that lives is holy. Life delights in life'; 'The world of Imagination is the world of Eternity', 'There exist in the external world the permanent realities of everything which we see reflected in the vegetable glass of Nature': all these statements, validating Cary's own metaphysic, are quoted by Jimson.[40]

Cary recognised 'The Mental Traveller' as especially 'important in the Blake canon'; for, as he explained to Andrew Wright, 'The conflict – an unavoidable and essential conflict – between the necessary intuition and the necessary art to express it is, of course, fundamental in my idea. It is only one aspect of the everlasting conflict between the spirit and the institution, justice and Old Father Antic, the simple goodness which is the fundamental revelation of Christianity and the dogmatic Churches.'[41] The weaving of key passages from 'The Mental Traveller' into Jimson's narrative helps to universalise the implications of Gulley Jimson's 'jam' as an artist in a world of change, and to explain his love-hate relationship with Sara, the enclosing nestbuilder; and Blake's personality, by parallel, helps to define Jimson's as quintessential artist.

Throughout the novel Blake's personality and thought are contrasted with those of Spinoza, the seventeenth-century German philosopher. And correspondingly Spinoza's disciple, Plantie, who patiently endures injustice after injustice, is contrasted with Jimson. Cary had researched Spinoza's life and thought carefully in September 1942. His respectful dismissal is implied by the futile nobility of Plantie. Spinoza stands on the truth ('What he said was, "Life is a gift, and what right have we to complain that we weren't given it different"'[42]), but preaches passivity. His crucial deficiency is a failure to recognise the creative imagination. And so Jimson 'attacks Spinoza as fatalist and enemy of the individual'.[43] Noble acceptance of injustice was as far beyond Jimson as beyond Jarvis. Plantie and Spinoza, in their sad nobility, or Blake and Jimson in their vulgar creativity? The choice is firmly posited.

Although insistently (and appropriately) episodic, the novel has an overall structure of counterpointed rise and fall reminiscent of *Mister Johnson*, with a similar resolution that wrenches creativity out of death's jaws. It also has an underlying tripartite structure founded on Gulley Jimson's paintings 'The Fall', 'The Raising of Lazarus' and 'The Creation'. The thematic implications of this triad are underlined by the paintings' physical fate; none is secure, but they reach progressively upwards in scale and creative daring – the third, on the huge wall of a church, opened to the world as 'The Creation' is simultaneously completed and destroyed.

Although the plot outline of *The Horse's Mouth* that Cary sent to Robert Lusty is close to the completed novel, it lacked that final, apocalyptic scene. The conclusion then was an obituary notice: 'Mr Jimson's last exhibition in the twenties excited considerable attention and in some quarters high hopes for English painting. His best work at this period of maturity showed strongly the influence of Renoir. In late years, however, Mr Jimson devoted himself to murals . . . We understand that one of his intimates, Mr Robin Alabaster, has written a monograph on the painter's life and work . . .'[44]

Before deciding finally on first-person narration by Jimson, Cary tried out the 'false' first person. One draft, in typescript, begins: 'Last year two books were published mentioning a man called Jimson, an artist who had some distinction about ten to fifteen years ago but is now forgotten. I knew Jimson thirty years ago. We were in Paris together, the old Paris of the Fauves, of 1910 . . .' In the narrator's opinion, this 'noisy, dirty little man, always full of new theories of art and always taking up a new style', is 'a faker' who 'kidded himself, of course, they all do, that he was a genius who worked in close collaboration with the Holy Spirit . . .' Jimson goes on to paint murals – 'which was a take off of Stanley Spencer'. But later the narrator is shown some paintings by Jimson and – 'They were all first class, the real thing; and they all belonged together'; each is 'a real surprise' and the series impressive.[45]

That early version resolved the question of Jimson's talent (which has bothered many of the novel's critics, and which could not be resolved with Jimson as narrator); but Cary must have recognised that for small gain he would be sacrificing immediacy, the force of the creativity and injustice themes, and the trilogy's pattern of narration. A problem of verisimilitude remained. It is credible for Sara and Wilcher to write their stories – but the mercurial Jimson? And when he is to die soon after the end of the novel? So Cary played a Jimsonian confidence trick, dangerously increasing the novel's aura of unreliability and ambiguity. Jimson's narrative must be read as stream of consciousness, but is presented as document (dictated 'to my honorary secretary, who has got the afternoon off from the cheese counter'[46]); and the novel's conclusion, while strongly suggesting that Jimson's death is imminent, must therefore allow the possibility of survival. In this as in other respects, the novel is – critics often used the expression – a *tour de force*; but a price was paid for undermining its realism.

Although *The Horse's Mouth* was admired, and became Cary's most popular novel, from the beginning some of its more thoughtful critics were ambivalent. Edwin Muir, who had assisted Dover Wilson in choosing *A House of Children* for the James Tait Black Prize, praised *The Horse's Mouth* as a 'metaphysical farce' of 'inexhaustible vitality', 'delightfully vigorous and free in its writing'; but he also commented on its 'equivocal impression' and 'monotony of energy', and thought that at times Jimson's 'specialised response to everything' made him seem a humour or caricature – 'an extreme personality logically worked out'.[47] And in 1948, G. W. Stonier, a critic who admired Cary's fiction, suggested that the First Trilogy is 'far too casually tied together to be anything but three novels', and wondered whether, 'Despite the shapeliness of some earlier novels, [Cary] has been brilliantly improvising all along'.[48] Such doubts, though they could be interpreted as compliments, were ultimately damaging to his reputation. It is ironic that they were provoked by the novel which gave Cary an international reputation and, for the first time, financial security.

Again, although the novel was greatly praised for its characterisation, early dissenting voices questioned the authenticity of Jimson as representative artist. Cary gratefully acknowledged Augustus John's favourable response: 'I value the compliment especially because I once meant to be an artist myself';[49] and artists have generally accepted Jimson's authenticity. But critics have tended to be sceptical. J. B. Priestley commented 'my trouble is I don't believe in that great painter of his';[50] Martyn Skinner told R. C. Hutchinson that *The Horse's Mouth* was fatally flawed because 'poor old Cary really believed that Gulley Jimson could have been a great artist. If only he had drawn him as a charlatan who believed he was a great artist . . .'[51] The debate about Gulley Jimson is testimony to the vigour of Cary's characterisation, in part, and in part to the continuing provocation of that romantic stereotype, the artist as rebel. Cary was well aware that Jimson's facetious 'vulgarity, the flash slang of the British', had offended some critics – but the vulgarity was necessary, he argued, to express his protagonist's 'desperation, his rage against the world'.[52]

Younger writers were often impressed and heartened by the novel. Julian Fane came across *The Horse's Mouth* in his early twenties while deeply depressed. 'The story . . . was extravagant and even unlikely', yet the novel struck him as 'a practical guide to conduct'. Its 'courage, humour, and informed optimism and idealism' conveyed the message 'that a man can be more than his circumstances, and . . . that art is tied to life'.[53] Cary might have objected that he was not Gulley Jimson (his novels, he told a critic, reveal no 'subjective centre'[54]), but he would have been pleased by that response to his novel. It accords with the direct advice he gave another young writer who corresponded with him after reading *The Horse's Mouth*:

> You must not be depressed about a novel you have finished nor trouble what anyone on earth thinks of it. You probably won't like it – my books have all disappointed me and they are full of things which disgust me with their stupidity; but I am not interested in them, I am thinking of the work in hand or of the whole vast work which has to be done and never, I suppose, will be done. It is not what people think of your books that ought to matter but how far they put over what you meant to express about the world and people in it.[55]

CHAPTER THIRTY THREE

SOLDIERS & WOMEN

1943–1946

The Process of Real Freedom

Cary got back to Oxford from Africa in May 1943. 'I have had a wonderful journey, in all literalness,' he told Dover Wilson; at '7000 feet somewhere over the Atlantic coast of French Africa' he had consumed 'a four course dinner served in a neat dining room'. 'Night flying over war zones was more macabre than strange; one was merely contained in a dimly lighted chamber among a bombardment of snores, groans; from distorted piles of humanity reminding one of Hopkins' "heaped bones" under God's "darksome devouring eyes"'. He was waiting for his manuscript, 'now in the hands of the censors office – I don't envy his struggles to read it or to find out what its all about – it is full of Blake quotations and all kinds of picaresque.'

While finishing *The Horse's Mouth*, he fitted in two other tasks: writing a short treatise, *The Process of Real Freedom*, and revising *The Case for African Freedom* for a second edition.

The first, published in November 1943, was essentially a popular development of *Power in Men*, stressing (partly as a contribution to wartime morale) the strength of democracy. Because education promotes freedom, the 'extension of literacy' has created a continuing political revolution, transforming 'all modern government'. 'This process must, in the end, in my view, transform any authoritarian regime whatever, including that of Russia. A transformation of power there has hardly begun, but it must continue; all nations must now educate in order to satisfy the demand of their people for a rising standard of living. Thus the choice before an autocracy is either delegation of power or revolution.'[1]

An academic acquaintance to whom he sent the booklet found the argument by turns 'optimistic and idealistic', 'pessimistic and realistic'; so identifying its main defect, a lack of consistency and careful logic. He also questioned Cary's assumptions about democracy: 'I am not sure that representation is the essence of democracy . . . I think that the true mark or measure of a democracy is the degree of its respect for the rights of minorities.

Decisions by majorities, however representatively elected, may be quite despotic . . . '[2]

The euphoria and carelessness of *Process of Real Freedom* may be in part due to its composition while he was writing *The Horse's Mouth*, but they also underlined a potentially destructive element in Cary's personality.

It was probably after finishing these tasks, and *The Horse's Mouth*, that Cary wrote a topical screenplay, utilising the expertise recently gained from his work on *Men of Two Worlds*. *The Battle Axe* is set in the blitzed East End of London and has affinities with several of his novels. Its text, typed by Trudy and perhaps submitted to Thorold Dickinson for comment, clearly needs revision; but it is intrinsically promising, and one wonders why Cary abandoned it.[3]

Marching Soldier

The Horse's Mouth was published in August 1944, a recommended choice of the Book Society, and sold so well that in the 1945-6 tax year Cary's literary income was close to £3,000.[4] For the first time – when all but one of their sons had left school – he and Trudy were comfortably off. And he was also now widely acknowledged to be one of Britain's leading novelists. A few months before that, however, disaster had brushed past the Carys.

At the end of 1943, Cary summarised for Lionel Stevenson his family's situation. He and Trudy were 'very busy as we have our war jobs as well as our ordinary work; and no help. And all services have been cut down . . . ' Trudy had been persuaded, at the beginning of the year, to become the WVS Area Housewife, responsible for running the organisation of '250 women who can't leave their homes for one reason or another, but undertake to receive casualties and give information', and she was also 'fire officer for the street'.[4] Her life was very full.

George, now sixteen – and 6 foot 4 inches tall – was still at Eton. He had passed his School Certificate brilliantly, with six distinctions. Tristram had left Christ Church, Oxford, after two terms studying Medicine, and joined the Navy as a radio mechanic; his first love was still music, but his interest in electronics enabled him to fulfil a boyhood ambition to serve at sea. Michael was 'on shore for the time, at the Admiralty, in a staff job'.

And Peter, an infantry officer, was 'now overseas, we don't know where for we haven't had his first letters.' In fact he was in North Italy, where fierce fighting was gradually driving the German army back. A few months later, a telegram arrived for the Carys: Peter had been wounded. He had always been close to his uncle Freddy (who was also his godfather), and Trudy must have felt anguish as she waited for further news about her son and remembered her brother's suffering in 1916. By the beginning of April 1944, Peter was back in England and in hospital – 'a very good hospital where they let us sit with him the whole afternoon,' Cary wrote to Stevenson. And he went on to comment that 'the men who bear the brunt of this war are the P. B. I. the poor bloody infantry; and especially the English county regiments – their casualties, by percentage, are far the highest and they take all the dirty jobs'.[5]

This was the origin of the first long poem that Cary published. *Marching*

Soldier is dedicated to 'The Infantry' and draws on Peter's experiences in North Italy. Cary had written, in relation to *The Horse's Mouth*, that the appropriate way to face injustice is to live like a soldier. That is the poem's ethic. It is both a paean for the British soldier in wartime and a moral metaphor.

Peter had hoped to rejoin his regiment in Italy, but on discharge from hospital was sent to a camp in Kent, where the monotonous, purposeless existence depressed him deeply. Reading, collecting wild flowers and, when possible, playing the piano were his defences. 'I found a piano down at Folkestone the other day, and started playing the Moonlight. By the time I'd finished I had ten Corporals round me . . . ' 'Work is very hard and life very dull, and I have now been doing a Captain's job for 4 months. My brain is reeling, and I'm about ready for a breakdown.'

Cary tried to help his son by sending books and copies of the *TLS*, writing cheerful, encouraging letters, and asking him to criticise the typescript of *Marching Soldier*. 'It was lovely, daddy, to get the poem today. Thanks very much for sending it. It makes wonderful reading, and the letter inside brought tears to my eyes.' Peter was touched too, by the dedication, with its implied tribute to him.[6]

Marching Soldier – 600 lines, in free verse and a colloquial style – is not a great war poem, but nor is it negligible, and after an awkward beginning presents moving vignettes. Cary received some unexpected praise. Nevill Coghill, a fellow Anglo-Irishman and an English don at Oxford, wrote to praise 'its effortless talk, the imagery, the plain common sense English strength and vision . . . never a line feels wrong or false'. He compared the poem to *Piers Plowman*.[7] Vita Sackville-West wrote to say it was the only poem of the Second World War she had been able to admire.[8] It was published by Michael Joseph in March 1945. In May Germany capitulated; in August atomic bombs were dropped on Hiroshima and Nagasaki. The war was over.

'in love with life'

During 1945 Cary wrote several summaries of family affairs for his Aunt Mab and Lionel Stevenson. Although the war was over, 'Rations here are more difficult than ever but . . . we are promised some extra fats for Christmas. People here say "When the war is over", meaning when we have more food and clothes. We all feel that the war is still on and there is a lot of war feeling about.'

Peter was now stationed in Germany, 'where he has an interesting job as sports officer and also officer in charge of some Polish camps'; he would be demobbed soon and Cary hoped that, having recovered from his wound, he would 'soon be able to begin life after six years interruption'. Tristram, commissioned in the Navy at the end of 1944, was on leave from his ship, HMS *Triumph*, and 'may soon be going East as radar officer in the Navy'; unfortunately he would miss his uncle Jack, who had just been ordered home from Singapore. Michael was now back at the Air Ministry, 'where he has very responsible work'. George had won a major scholarship and 'goes to Trinity,

Cambridge, next term as a classical scholar.' Trudy and he were hoping that all four sons would be back for Christmas. Meanwhile 'Fred Ogilvie (now Sir Frederick) has come to Oxford as Principal of Jesus College, with a most beautiful 16th century house in the Turl. So we have a large family circle in these parts.'[9]

He had also come to know several literary contemporaries – mainly women who admired his writing, like Rebecca West, Rose Macaulay and Jacquetta Hawkes. Pamela Hansford Johnson had met him just as the war was ending: she had suggested they lunch together at the Café Royal.

> Handsome, Roman-headed, smaller than I had expected, alert as a blackbird hopping through a hedge, he started to talk, about painting mostly, all the way to luncheon and halfway through it. He was difficult to pin down – not elusive, not in the least concerned to evade questions, but all on fire to ask questions himself. The first impression he gave me, and it was a true one, was of absolute *niceness* . . . he was so much in love with life that he could not have spoilt it by falsity, meanness or malice.
>
> After that meal we went out and talked for a time. Coming suddenly on a greengrocer's barrow he gave a sudden hop – one step forward, two steps back: 'Look at that! Just look at those lemons and those beetroots! Look at them!' And he saw such colour that it stopped him short, he was filled with delight . . .[10]

Another woman writer Cary met at this time was Ivy Compton-Burnett. He had written to say that he and Helen Gardner ('probably the finest English scholar at Oxford, and one of the most brilliant women I know') considered her one of the 'supreme woman novelists of the country'.[11] He was invited to tea. But then blotted his copybook. 'Joyce Cary,' she told a friend, 'wrote a very kind letter . . . I was quite glad to have it . . . sending a copy of my book to be signed, and saying he would like to have it back quickly because at least a dozen people were waiting to borrow it . . . Such a dreadfully stupid thing for one author to say to another. I always write my friends' books into my Harrods list, even if they give me a copy, and then I keep it out quite a time so that other people can't have it.'[12]

Cary was now 'as busy as I can be with various books and also with film work. I find the latter very interesting and a relaxation after the hard concentration of three dimensional work in a novel. But I am lucky in my directors who pride themselves on treating a writer with consideration.' The 'film work' was a script for a project that would take him to India early the following year. And the 'various books' were again, a novel and a treatise: *The Moonlight* and *Britain and West Africa*, published respectively in May and August 1946.

The Horse's Mouth, he reported at the end of May, was selling so well that 'the Readers Union are bringing out 20,000 copies more in a cheap edition, this winter'. (But American publishers had declined it as 'a "man's book" and therefore difficult to put over in America'.)[13]

The Moonlight
In the early 1930s, Cary had read Tolstoy's *The Kreutzer Sonata*, and

disagreed so violently with its 'message' that he had immediately planned a fictional rebuttal, making notes under the heading 'K. S. Inverted'.[14]

Tolstoy, he complained, 'tells us . . . that women are brought up only for the marriage market, taught from childhood to exploit their sex, that marriage itself is merely a sexual conspiracy or a sexual battle, and that from these causes arise all the evils of society. It is pure propaganda . . .' *The Kreutzer Sonata* was 'penetrated throughout with Tolstoy's obsession with sex which . . . filled him with loathing' so that he 'wanted to abolish sexual attraction . . . But sexual attraction cannot be abolished; it can only be civilized . . .' 'I thought that great novel not merely unfair to women, but stupid about them, and stupid about the world in which they had to create their lives.'[15] His quarrel with Tolstoy intensified and formalised his long-established conception of 'a woman's life'.

As first attempted, Cary's fictional reply to Tolstoy was 'the exact reverse of *The Kreutzer*. An old woman in a railway carriage (instead of Tolstoy's old man) was to tell how she had murdered her sister for preventing her daughter's marriage.'[16] Cary wrote 'A good deal of this story, perhaps fifty thousand words, and then for some reason abandoned it.' Soon afterwards he began a different novel entitled 'The Forgotten Women'. A story of three women, this had orginated in Cary's hearing about an incident of 'bitter injustice': 'three girls were left alone; their mother died and the eldest sister had to look after the other ones . . . her reward was to be . . . hated by one of them.'[17] This, too, he had abandoned. Then, a decade later, probably in the spring of 1942, Cary came across his 'notes on Rose and her sisters, and the two different conceptions ran together and interested me so much that I set out to write *The Moonlight*'.

The novel as it evolved was very different from its two sources. Like 'Anti-Kreutzer', 'The Forgotten Women' was a first-person narrative, told by one of Rose's sisters, 'the equivalent of Ella. I did not dare even to read the old manuscript . . . in case it should overwhelm the new scheme.' His main aim now 'was to give a larger background, to show the woman's special dilemma in different generations. and the means by which, in different social periods, it might be solved. And I wanted also to show the relations between . . . the conventions of a time . . . and the fundamental quality of a woman's life . . .'[18]

As the novel was 'gathering in a drawer', a 'quiet and simple book', he was using the title 'Captive and Free' and relating it to his conception of female life: 'Captive of sex, but free with its *special power* of love and the creation of character'; 'Captive and free. applies to special position of women . . . As background . . . change of *idea* of women's position.' But his novel was *not* to be 'a thesis like the Kreutzer', which is 'a man's view'.[19]

Perhaps as a result of Peter's account of playing Beethoven's 'Moonlight Sonata' to a group of soldiers, the novel's final title, so apt as an implied response to *The Kreutzer Sonata*, then established itself.

An important literary association was with D. H. Lawrence's *The Rainbow*, in which moonlight is a major symbol, ambiguously dominating three generations of sexual relationship. (Cary had been reading Lawrence's novels, and rejecting his view of sexuality as naturally subordinated the feminine to the masculine; seen from the woman's perspective; Lawrence's sexual ethic was just as repressive as Tolstoy's.)

Moonlight, like the 'Moonlight Sonata', is a symbolic motif in Cary's novel. Near the beginning and end, Ella Venn plays the sonata. One draft of the latter scene is notably more positive than the final text, and introduces (somewhat incongruously) horse-riding imagery: 'The old woman began to play. She was happy, exalted. She felt the triumph of the music which she made, and also its own power. She was the artist who is at once the creator and part of her own creation, who feels intensely and rides upon those strong feelings with mastery.'[20] Ella is the novel's artist, her elder sister Rose its conservative.

In the novel's 'present', 1938, Rose is dead; and Ella's mind (like Tom Wilcher's) ranges between past and present, lingering guiltily on her responsibility for Rose's death, counterpointing the lives of two generations. Both Rose and Ella are Victorians, and once again Cary enjoyed depicting that age, now interpreted as both monolithic and riven by conflict. 'Such a system is always under attack from *fundamental anarchism* – the creative, optimistic, reckless drive of the young'.[21]

When writing *The Moonlight*, Cary came dangerously close to determinism. That, perhaps more than the circling plot, the ponderously enclosing interiors (which are only emphasised by that climactic outdoor scene, the Pinmouth Fair sequence), is why this novel is so brutally claustrophobic. Its moonlight is chillingly ironic; far from romantic in implication, it drapes a view of the world no less harsh than Tolstoy's in *The Kreutzer Sonata*.

Cary wrote this novel over about two years. He was correcting its text by October 1945; it was published in May 1946. Trudy thought it one of his richest novels ('Ella is one of your masterpieces'),[22] so did Rachel Cecil ('I think you do all the women extraordinarily well . . . Your imagination and sense of beauty is extraordinary . . . I really do think it is a marvellous book – the theme interested me enormously').[23] Many critics agreed.

Britain and West Africa

The treatise he wrote together with *The Moonlight* gave Cary a further opportunity to assess his own administrative experience in the light of the changing thought about colonial policy which he had helped to focus a few years earlier. But his context here is more historical than political, and his scope severely limited since the text is only half the length of *The Case for African Freedom*. It is his penultimate developed statement of opinion about colonial Africa, the final being his 1955 article 'Policy for Aid'.

Commissioned by Longmans, Green, as one of a series of pamphlets about aspects of the British Commonwealth, *Britain and West Africa* is essentially a sketch of the imposition and consequences of British rule. But it too shows some darkening in Cary's views. The euphoria of *The Process of Real Freedom* is gone, the optimism of *The Case for African Freedom* is qualified.

In his comparison of Indirect Rule and its successor, Britain's 'New Colonial Development Policy', Cary's stance is perceptibly changed. Although he conceded again that 'in Indirect Rule, with its devolution of power, its respect for traditional attachments, there is an easy-going quality of the air' that promoted *laissez faire*, he went on to praise the policy's 'flexibility' and warn that, 'just as it was once too uncritically admired, it may now be too hastily damned'. In fact, for the successful introduction of 'any new government policy', the people's 'sympathy and understanding' is essential – 'And there is more chance of getting that support under Indirect Rule than direct'. Cary's acceptance of the new policy's 'schemes of capital development' as 'the only means in West Africa of keeping the social balance'[24] seems correspondingly less enthusiastic than in *The Case for African Freedom*.

'Policy for Aid', his final critique of colonial policy, nearly a decade later, would similarly find much to regret in the passing of Indirect Rule and the concomitant recession of hope for 'a gradual and therefore safe development . . . to full democratic self-government along the course which history has shown to be natural and rational'. Britain must bend before the wind. Self-government must be granted, and quickly. But Cary's now negative emphasis on the likely consequences is discomforting: 'The democratic machinery – votes, elections, parliaments – except in a developed industrial state with literate workers and responsible middle class, are merely forms. They not only increase confusion and turmoil, they are dangerous to the unity and continued progress of the state.'[25]

CHAPTER THIRTY FOUR

FAITH & MYTH

1946

'an anxious and unhappy country'

Cary was writing *Britain and West Africa* while preparing for his journey to India. There political conflict, which had increased during the war, was rising towards its terrible climax of early 1947, when communal violence would become so frenzied that only rapid independence seemed to offer hope of restoring peace.

The new Labour Government of Britain (which came to power in July 1945) was fully committed to Indian independence and quickly announced a general election; and this was held at the end of the year, amid disturbances. During February the following year, while Cary was in India, a Navy mutiny indicated that disaffection against the Raj was spreading rapidly, so the British Prime Minister, Clement Attlee, sent out a special mission of three cabinet ministers to seek agreement on the constitution of an independent India. No doubt the unrest in India, as well as his increased sympathy for 'the Victorian age', diminished Cary's earlier optimism about the possibility of transferring power peacefully and constructively to Britain's colonies.

There was family tension over Cary's expedition, for it had been expected that Trudy would accompany Cary. As a small girl she had longed to visit the Far East, and this journey with her husband would make up a little for being left alone at home so much since her marriage. But, when the time for departure approached, Cary told her she could not come with him. Presumably the main reason for his decision was the dangerously unpredictable state of India (after the success of *The Horse's Mouth* the cost of her travelling could hardly have been a serious issue). But one must wonder if, underlying that reason, was a reluctance to have his freedom and independence qualified; only recently he had enjoyed an adventurous expedition that partly recreated the conditions of his Nigerian days.

Trudy was deeply hurt. She wrote to him later 'I am afraid I did not feel at all brave when you left me – I expect having had the prospect of India with you on the cards at all – made it harder when in the end I had to be left behind!

Anyhow perhaps I would have been a nuisance with the travelling . . . '¹ It can only have increased her hurt that Thorold Dickinson's wife, Joanna, went with the unit. Did she also remember Cary's saying, before they were married, that he would never allow her to go to India?

Obviously feeling uneasy, Cary wrote regularly and fully to her all the time he was away. His first letter was written. in fact, from the airport as he waited on 3 January to be called for the flight: 'I was very sad at leaving you yesterday in that crowded train, and I could not say how much I felt for you, going back to dull household jobs . . . All my love, my darling – how I wish you were with me – but already I look forward to coming home again. It is like the old days in Africa – but luckily my tour of duty is shorter.'²

The film project had been left deliberately vague; as the *Times of India* reported, the visit was a 'twelve-week study tour to "find a formula which will lend itself to a subject of international interest, with an Indian background sympathetic to the Indian point of view"'.³ That cautious statement clearly took account of India's edgy politics.

Two days after arriving in Calcutta, they went on 'a boat trip down river to see the water front – a possible background', and a couple of days after that visited a studio to watch the shooting of a film directed by Satyajit Ray. Cary had to steal away early, and spent the next day in bed – he was often unwell in India. But he thought his script, which centred on irrigation projects and was entitled 'The Water of Life', was evolving satisfactorily, and he was also 'writing verse so I'm quite happy'. But Calcutta was very noisy: 'There are few real doors anywhere . . . All native bullock carts rattle and thump like falling hammers – everyone here talks very loud and they talk all night. One hears also an incessant din of bells, horns, conch shells blown to scare the demons and dogs barking in every key.'

At a brief stop in Bengal the unit was entertained by the Governor, Richard Casey, in the old Viceroy's house, built in the eighteenth century, with its 'enormous pillared rooms' and 'throne room with its silver throne'. That evening 'we dined with two Indian nationalists. Most of the Indians, of course, are fanatical nationalists and I foresee we are going to have plenty of repetition in our talks which will be numerous.'

Then they went on to New Delhi. Thorold Dickinson had been badly bitten by a dog (belonging to a member of the American Red Cross!) while in Calcutta, and would have to endure a course of anti-rabies injections. Difficulties were beginning to accumulate. Cary disliked New Delhi and was increasingly disenchanted with the project. 'We are still to be stuck in this place for five more days.' he commented on 24 January, 'and I am bored and lonely. We spend ninetenths of our time in very dull interviews either with dull officials or Indians who [are] very pleasant and friendly but, of course, tend to say the same things over and over again.' On one occasion he had to watch ten documentary films in a row. 'All the talk makes me very tired and as for sight seeing we never have time for it.'

But there were compensations. They were invited by the Viceroy, Lord Wavell, to lunch:

We were received by red coated servants who gave us drinks – then 4 A. D. C.s turned up and introduced each other. Then the other guests and household visitors came in – John Gielgud and some actresses – various soldiers. We were lined up in a row and Wavell shook hands – then he went in alone to the dining room next door and we all followed. Each of us had a servant behind his chair, in red – with Wavell's monogram on his chest, and they smoothly put our chairs under us . . . Afterwards we went into the garden. An A. D. C. fetched me to talk to Lady Wavell – and then another A. D. C. fetched me to talk to H. E. who promised us what we wanted – car transport. Afterwards John Gielgud tried to get Thorold to do a film for him . . . and we found our way out.

Meanwhile Cary had been 'trying to make something of Hindu mythology'. At a Hindu temple he 'saw the people praying before the shrines in the side chapels, heard the priests chanting from the sacred books and then great gongs were rung and a service begun.' He also visited the great Muslim Mosque, 'an enormous open courtyard surrounded by arcades . . . as we walked about in our socks, pilgrims were praying towards the big open building on the Mecca side. Hundred of other pilgrims, holy men, fanatics etc. camp out on the steps day and night, an extraordinary looking crowd from all over India and Arabia.'

He told Trudy 'I do wish terribly you were here with me – there are so many times when I want to speak to you – when you wld. enjoy looking at things with me . . . I do pray you are all right, darling and not too worried. Tho I know you must have plenty of worries and much too much work. How I wish I cld. take you away for a real holiday – in luxury – I shall try when I come back.'

Lahore, Cary decided, was 'a delightful city, and this is the best hotel we have found yet, in its old fashioned Kipling way. Kipling's father died here and we saw the old gun which figures in Kim . . .' He had to spend a morning at the Irrigation Research Institute, 'seeing model rivers washing away their banks', but there were also some opportunities for sightseeing: 'Amritsar is a real old town – with narrow streets and crowded dirty bazaars . . . The Golden Temple is a small temple covered largely with gold leaf, in the middle of a square lake . . . It is the holy temple of the Sikhs, where they keep their holy book. It is read continuously day and night in one room, in another singers chant from it day and night . . . the Sikh religion is very strict – monotheistic, egalitarian and puritan . . .'

They went on long bus journeys (driven by 'an Italian prisoner who used to be a racing motorist'), and saw a Hindu religious festival at Dipalpur (the town's narrow streets crowded with pilgrims from all over India).[4] There he jotted in his notebook 'The Shrine – the red stuff being daubed on walls – and floor – the bells struck by visitors – the children playing – and beating bells for fun – the priests seated behind taking offerings – the one lamp burning in the niche – the feeling of a business like religion – mediaeval – matter of fact – but fiercely *believing.* and traditional.'[5]

Back at New Delhi on 6 February, he found that the proofs of *The*

Moonlight had arrived, and needed 'a lot of changes at the beginning which is very bad. I shall work at it all tomorrow, I fancy I can do a great deal on the plane on the way to Bombay.' But there he found himself in a room with three other occupants, one of whom, an Indian Captain, 'snored all night and got up at 3.45 to catch a plane. I feel rather worn.' Fortunately, the hotel's manager found him a single room 'on the 5th floor looking straight on the sea and the ships'; for he had to put in four wearing days on the proofs; and even then, as he sent the proofs off, appealed to Trudy and Peter (now living at home) for help. He would tell Robert Lusty to contact them about 'any difficulty. For instance if the printer has too much or too little on any page or in any paragraph, he will apply to you and Peter and you can add a word or cut a word – or choose a shorter adjective or a longer one'; but he had tried to ensure that this would not be necessary – 'I am so tired I can hardly write . . .'

It was very hot. They drove for eight hours on rough roads to see a dam. 'Driving here is exciting because of the crowds on the roads – the bullocks and donkeys and goats etc. wandering everywhere – the bullock carts whose drivers are often asleep and the pot holes which send your head to the roof every few yards.'

He and Dickinson had decided that the film's heroine should be Indian ('Thorold could not "see" an English girl getting religion whereas I could, but I am quite happy to make her an Indian girl') and were very anxious to find a suitable actress for the role. Cary spent one whole day 'seeing stars – at lunch too – Begum Para who is the Oomph girl of the Indian film . . . Savitri Devi . . . very pretty, enormous eyes, very proper (how she and Para stabbed each other with their eyes) . . . At tea Chetins, dark, fierce, full of politics – five children tho she looks about 24 . . . In the evening a dinner of about 40 film people at the radio club . . .'

Meanwhile the Navy mutiny had begun. He hoped that the British newspapers had not been making 'too much of the Bombay trouble – I heard a good deal of firing one day – and the sailors were rushing about the harbour in motor boats cheering and shouting slogans but as far as I know there were no serious casualties. One simply avoids any street where mobs are operating.'

Cary's interest in Eastern religions had been growing steadily – 'I am reading about Indian religion,' he wrote on 16 February, 'a vast and very confused subject'. A film he was shown about the temples of Southern India excited him, and he decided to 'make a quick dash into Southern India to see some of the famous temples there'.

First he travelled some 700 miles over rough roads to see some temples near Hyderabad. 'The paintings at Ajanta are very beautiful and the gorge, surrounded by the Buddhist cells, monasteries and temples, all cut out of solid rocks, is a lovely place, but I'm not sure I didn't find the Ellera temple of Kailasa more interesting. It was so rich with the Hindu feeling of life which is something I had not discovered elsewhere in such strong expression. Buddhism is a religion of philosophers but Hinduism lies very close to the primary feelings of life.'[6] His notes at Ellora responded particularly to the temple's motif of lingam and lotus flower: 'The *freedom. sense* of a mysterious power approached from a new side – i.e. with awe and excitement and rejoicing as well as fear – *sex not vulgarized or degraded by ascetic notions.* But *feared . . .* '[7]

On 25 February he flew to Madras, only to 'find a general strike going on – even the hotel servants are out'. Cars were being stoned. But 'I managed to write some more verse in the plane and a little to-day so I don't feel that all my time is being wasted . . .' With Madras as his centre, Cary travelled to various temples by train – sometimes adventurously, sleeplessly. After seeing the Rameswaram Temple ('a wonderful place – enormous – crowded with images and holy men'), he discovered that he would have to wait four hours for the next train, 'so I lay in a 2nd class carriage and wrote verses'. At Trichinopoly, he visited ' a huge rock with temples and a bell tower on top and a view for miles'; after tipping the priest, he was given scented flowers while 'they rang the big 2 ton bells for me'. At Mahabalipuram he found 'A group of rock-cut temples with very fine early sculpture and one temple on the shore – right at the edge of the sea' – it would make a good locale for the film's religious scenes.

Back in Bombay with Dickinson at the beginning of March, he went to work revising the script. On 5 March they found an actress 'who might be able to take our star part . . . and we are both very gay. I met Mulk Anand here, the Indian writer, who turned out to be a fan of mine – I like him very much . . . The party last night was very successful – 45 guests including most of the great stars.' Then they flew to New Delhi. They would go on to Agra, Jaipur and Benares; and Cary had also decided that, before returning to England, he should visit the Kashmir to scout for scenery.[8]

In his notebook he wrote

India has been an anxious and unhappy country for her people – with continual wars, invasions, *famines* and plagues. Life is short, *uncertain* and dangerous. This naturally leads to the feeling that life is an evil, a dream – and should be escaped.

Among the superstitious, notion of force of evil leads to *worship* and *propitiation* of evil . . .

Among the philosophers it leads to the *theory* of life as a dream to be escaped, by contemplation.

And activity is the enemy of contemplation.[9]

As he travelled on through northern India, Cary's mind was turning to his own writing in preparation for his return to Parkers. 'My poem is going rather well,' he told Trudy on 31 March. 'I am quite excited about it, and I have an idea [for] my next novel – a thing – or rather two things I wrote some time ago.' He had also started to write another filmscript, *Secret People*.

On 12 April he and the Dickinsons were in New Delhi. They visited the Viceroy and 'made our report – he was quite pleased tho he said the film wld. have to wait on the political situation'.[10] In fact, the film was never made. Once widespread violence began in early 1946, such projects became impossible and irrelevant.

Cary was home by the end of April 1946 – just in time to prepare for his eldest son's wedding in May to Isabel Leslie, a South African. Tristram was still in the Navy – he was not demobbed until November 1946. Peter had resumed study at Queen's College for a degree in English, and was being tutored by Lord David Cecil; he was also taking piano lessons, and at the end of 1946 gave a solo recital. George, in his first year at Trinity College, Cambridge, had become very interested in bibliography, and during the summer catalogued Eton College's library.

Cary's social life in Oxford was now much more active. Even there he was becoming a public figure. He and Trudy were invited to Enid Starkie's gaudy parties, and got to know several of her friends – some of whom, like Audrey Beecham, felt much more at ease with Trudy than her husband. The Carys gave dinner parties, and instituted Sunday evening 'at homes'. Trudy made a potent cocktail of rum and lime juice which, in the comparative austerity of post-war Oxford, was a great attraction. (On one of these occasions Dylan Thomas, drunk on the floor, informed Trudy 'I like fat blondes'. She 'ran over to Joyce and appealed for help.')[11]

The Drunken Sailor

Cary was now becoming obsessive about his writing, increasingly anxious to complete as many as possible of the novels and other works clamouring in his mind and notebooks for release. Returning to his attic study in May, he seems to have concentrated first on completing the simplest two of the three projects he had been working on in India.

The poem he had been writing with such pleasure and urgency was now entitled *The Drunken Sailor*. It was, he explained to Robert Lusty, 'based on the legend of . . . the Flying Dutchman. The Drunken Sailor is the Captain of an ancient ship with a crew of immortals; the poets, dreamers of history. It is hailed for search by a battleship which represents the authority of [the] state. It is fired at, half-wrecked, pursued, and finally brought to action.' But it does not sink. Instead, the battleship sinks.[12]

In spite of this, Cary told an American critic 'I detest allegory – my people are real people in a real world or they are nothing'.[13] In *Art and Reality* he further justified his rejection of allegory: 'Allegory gives a clear, a definite meaning; not to the soul, but to the conceptual judgment, and in a form of dry precept whose falsity is at once detected by the soul . . . It treats the world as a mechanism whereas it is a world of free souls.' But he also said that 'Allegory is an immense temptation to the writer, especially the great, the obsessive writer'[14] – who, pervasively concerned with moral analysis, is attracted by its didactic force.

Cary, with his penchant for the didactic, had been drawn towards allegory from the beginning of his career (in Borgu he had written many 'fables' modelled on Aesop's). In his later years, he struggled against this tendency, with varying success; the open allegory of *The Drunken Sailor*, in a genre he did not consider realistic, was perhaps part of that struggle, helping him in his attempt to purge his fiction of the allegorical.

The Drunken Sailor attempts to justify Cary's myth. Writing the poem in the very shadows of the temples he found so perilously impressive, he was attacking their message that 'life is an evil . . . a dream to be escaped, by contemplation'. Phantasmagoric though it is, *The Drunken Sailor* could hardly be more strenuously active and insistent.

Drawing from an abortive long poem of the 1930s, 'The Two-Faced Angel', it is cast largely in a helter-skelter, metrically-free, rhymed verse strongly suggestive of John Skelton's. (Did Nevill Coghill's reference to *Piers Plowman* lead Cary to the fifteenth-century poet as a model for his second long poem?) And added to *The Drunken Sailor* is an intermittent prose gloss modelled on Coleridge's *Rime of the Ancient Mariner* (which was clearly another general influence).

In no other writing of Cary's is his myth more vigorously and memorably expressed than in this poem's gloss (derived from his "Essay on the Free Imagination"):

> . . . the driving spirit of creation, possessed by everlasting vehemence, salutes even conflict and danger as the mettle of life . . .
> For only by things created does the soul know life and joy; and all created things fail and die . . .
> . . . the free soul can never rest content in the accomplished thing of art, church, or government . . .
> . . . imagination by its very nature must find in all completion a gaol, in all conclusion a grave. Its lot is to navigate among storms, for ever at watch and work, in labour that achieves, by continual accomplishment, its own ransom from bitterness, knowing that there is nothing sure, nothing dependable, but the spirit of life itself and its invincible desperation, which, among the cruelty of circumstance that is the form and effect of its real being, begets for ever in newness and innocence eternal delight.[15]

'Eternal delight': with that Blakean phrase, Cary flings his activist myth against the seductive quietism of the East.

Robert Lusty sent Cary three hostile Readers' responses to the poem: 'I found Joyce Cary's poem almost unreadable . . . verbose . . . '; 'I found it extremely difficult to read and even more difficult to get more than a shadowy glimpse of what the author is driving at'; 'I had some misgivings about Cary's last long poem (the war poem), which I found uncomfortably loose in construction. The misgivings turned to dismay during my struggle with the difficulties of *The Drunken Sailor*. I recall again that in the novel about the painter there was a symptom of some sort of mental cloudiness or incoherence, which threatened to turn the master novelist of *Herself Surprised* into an eccentric writer given overmuch to gusto and caricature . . . '[16]

Cary must have been jolted; but he was not deterred, and, however reluctantly, Michael Joseph published the poem (with Cary's own pen-and-ink illustrations) in November 1947. Cary sent a copy to Dover Wilson.

Noone says anything about this poem – he doesn't know what to say but I expected some damns for which my publishers (with secret sources of information) prepared me. Yet I had to do it to get rid of it. This is one aspect of the art which no critic has dealt with – the awful weight of a work in the belly and the absolute need, at a certain point, to get rid of it. One reason why I get busier as I get older is that I have so many of these things to bring forth. [17]

Years later Cary insisted that *The Drunken Sailor* was one of the best things he ever wrote. [18]

The filmscript *Secret People* was a similarly questionable achievement. He started this filmscript in India, finished it by August 1946 and then sent it to Thorold Dickinson, who recommended that they register its plot. But by the time the film was made four years later (with the young Audrey Hepburn as its star), Cary's script had been extensively altered. The credits on the script then read 'Original story by Joyce Cary and Thorold Dickinson/Screenplay by Thorold Dickinson and Wolfgang Wilhelm'. Cary refused to allow his name to appear in the film's credits.

CHAPTER THIRTY FIVE

JOY AND GRIEF

1946–1949

A Fearful Joy

Cary's twelfth novel to be published gave him problems throughout its composition. For many of its critics *A Fearful Joy* is 'too packed, too fast moving';[1] by far his weakest and least enjoyable novel. What went wrong? In his Preface Cary mentioned 'private reasons' which are certainly part of the answer. But the new novel, in its very origins, was problematic.

Cary was a restlessly innovative writer by temperament; he was also a deeply conservative writer by temperament. The friction of this duality was creative, but, when uncontrolled, could result (as with 'They Want to Be Happy') in a grinding stasis, with imaginative fecundity and thematic irresolution beating frantically against each other. After his great gallop, he was close to exhaustion; and emotionally enervated by his clash with India. It was important, but not easy, to rein in the horse.

The two putative novels Cary had suddenly connected in India were (in two of the several titles he gave them) 'Juno' (apparently an offshoot of 'Captive and Free', the story of two sisters that had been a source of *The Moonlight*) and 'To Sleep in Ulro' (which probably evolved soon after *The Horse's Mouth*; its title, like an alternative, 'To beget spirits', is a Blake quotation).

Cary also called the latter story 'Hamper', after its protagonist, a homosexual fashion designer 'trying to be the ordinary man'. 'Theme. Love that makes the world go round . . . Arts of civilization from sex and pride.' 'Hamper rages against the modern vulgar notion of Homos . . . he is fighting his own tendency which he scorns and doesn't believe in . . .' Hamper is a spellbinder, aggressively at odds both with himself and his society, and destined to commit suicide. The background of his story was to be the rapid change of women's fashions.[2]

Juno's story Cary remembered as 'the sketch of a young girl at her first dance, who gets no partners and is in despair, when suddenly she is taken out by the beau of the evening. He flirts with her, charms her, and finally elopes with her under the delusion that she is an heiress.' (He gave this version the title 'The Heiress'.) The girl was sometimes Nina (originally in another story connected to 'Captive and Free', 'The Turkish House'), sometimes Hannah (sister of Leila in 'Captive and Free').[3] Cary linked 'Juno' and 'To Sleep in Ulro', he said in 1956, because he 'wanted to write a novel with a background of economic change and dealing especially with the role of the imaginative man in business and in invention.'[4]

His struggles with the novel resulted in a plethora of notes and versions. By March 1947, the title 'It's a Gift' had emerged. This version was again a story of two sisters, Hannah and Leila, and he considered telling it 'from two points of view, i.e. in two books. Hannah as a responsible person of principle (the plain girl) who looks after Leila and battles with her . . . and Leila as the artist . . .'[5]

One version of 'Juno' evolved at about this time into a separate story entitled 'A State of Nature'. In September 1947 Cary told Robert Lusty that this would be 'the first of a new series of novels [with] the unifying basic theme of the problem of freedom in the modern world. It is the story of Charles Gye, retired soldier and land agent, who at the age of sixty has married a much younger girl' – and later discovers that 'his wife, through the almost inevitable pressure of circumstances, is having an affair with another man . . . '[6] This clearly repeats the basic situation of *Cock Jarvis*, and was to influence the evolution of Cary's Second Trilogy. But 'A State of Nature' itself was abandoned before 1948.

Cary then returned to 'It's a Gift', creating a new story that amalgamated elements of both sources. The two women were replaced by a single heroine – first the American heiress Betty Wendt whose spellbinder is Phil Toner ('The Facts of Life'), then Tabitha Baskett, whose spellbinder is Dick Bonser.

The theme, too, changed; and the final title emerged. 'Oct. 48. Fearful Joy. Life as an adventure – i.e. *new experience*. Life itself in essence is the experience, the thrill of new or renewed delight, which is always changing. Tabitha . . . runs away with Bonser because he is *forbidden and dangerous* . . . ' 'The fearful joy is life rising from below – in anger, in love, in laughter, and at same time taking form of enterprise, and imagination, always creative.' 'A *fearful joy – the danger of love. a terrible beauty because of its instability and danger* . . . ' 'Tragedy . . . *of the instability of what is loved –* its very *essence passing away bec. essence is in creative love.*'[7]

Soon after the publication of *A Fearful Joy* one of his fans wrote severely, echoing some of the novel's professional critics (although at least one has proclaimed it Cary's finest novel): 'I can't believe that you are pleased with this book . . . it strikes me as something merely concocted. Of course the characters are living – that's your way – but that doesn't mean that they are alive . . . one at least of your old believers says No to what you are writing now.'[8]

'this frightful and unexpected blow'

But Cary had an intense need, while working on the later stages of *A Fearful Joy*, to focus on 'life rising from below – in anger, in love, in laughter . . . '

His wife was dying. And in the novel, as Tabitha runs away with Bonser (whose name combines suggestions of gift-giving and clowning) 'because he is *forbidden and dangerous*', against the background of tragic '*instability of what is loved*', Cary could both relive the precious relationship with his wife and cope with her approaching loss. The agonising intensity of the novel's conclusion, as Tabitha, dying, must laugh at the sheer vitality of the 'small square girl' who confronts her, is both protest against, and acceptance of, life's fearful joy.[9] Cary's last literary gift to Trudy, A *Fearful Joy* was published only two months before she died.

The end of 1946 had brought much family happiness, but from the start 1947 was a bad year for Cary. A sign of incipient depression is the diary entry he scrawled on 5 January. Tristram, whose company he had enjoyed over Christmas, was moving to London to begin studying musical composition. Just before this, a tree that his attic window overlooked had had to be severely pruned.

> Tristram left at 7.15 in rain for town. A cold grey morning. The feeling of a departure. He took the gargoyles I bought in Paris in 1907. I was attached to them as a feeling of that time and I was sorry when they went. But perhaps it is a good thing to be separated from such attachments – they are feelings which draw one backwards. All the same, my life cld. get too meagre and thin for want of them.
>
> The afternoon is now at 2.30 very ugly – because of the cut tree. It is nonsense to say that beauty is a simple feeling – there are different feelings for objective beauty of form. My tree was a beautiful thing with the most beautiful movement in its long branches – and I never went into my room without looking at it. The Struwelpeter thing that remains with its shock of twigs may have a beauty of its own – like the willows on the Cher[well River] or garden trees – but I detest it . . . [10]

If some of the entries in his notebooks are Gulley Jimson's this one is Tom Wilcher's.

However, the birth of his first grandchild, Lucius, had brought joy. Michael was now 'Secretary to the Air Council which is a new and more interesting job (also more important than the old)'. And Harper, a decade after Cary's unsuccessful first American publication of a novel, had contracted to publish *The Moonlight*, with an option on his other novels if sales were good. 'The American publishers up to now usually say I am too English for their public,' Cary commented; 'this has not been an objection in Sweden, France, Germany, Italy etc.' – where his novels were being published in translation. In England, his books were mostly 'unprocurable' (owing to wartime restrictions on publication and the bombing of Michael Joseph's warehouse); 'Reprints are now beginning but at long intervals and in small editions on account of shortages of papers, binders, and labour.'[11] Michael Joseph also proposed to reissue his novels in a special uniform edition – a pleasing compliment. And soon there was also good news from Harper: *The Moonlight* had sold well enough for them to decide to publish *Herself Surprised* in 1948, and probably the rest of the First Trilogy thereafter.

In August Cary wrote that he was 'fearfully busy as we go away to Ireland in September and I must before then establish my book. A book is a mood and does not travel well. Also I am very behind with my patient and anxious publisher.' That new novel may have been 'The Come Back', 'the story of an old actor named Fuljam who has gone down in the world but who is rediscovered by a BBC producer looking for "originals"'.[12] Cary soon abandoned it. He had, he told Stevenson, put aside another book (presumably the troublesome A *Fearful Joy*) 'till next year. I am a wasteful writer and Trudy despairs of my tons of unfinished and unpublished MSS. I shall not finish 1/10 of my work in my lifetime.'

Christmas came, and again 'we had all the family here – seven and the grandson – to eat Aunt Netta's Irish turkey. It contains all the things we need most, fats above all . . . a feast for the greedy eye before it becomes spiritual food upon the table'.[13] But Cary himself nearly missed Christmas dinner: he was ordered to bed for several weeks at the beginning of December with 'inflammation of the joints'. (Audrey Beecham reported to Rachel Cecil that he 'looked like an Elizabethan portrait sitting up in bed'.)[14] His health was beginning to weaken under the strain of overwork. 'I am fearfully busy,' he told Stevenson again, on 4 January 1948, 'in my new book – "in" is the word for the thing extends for miles round and darkens over my head. God knows where I am if he's interested which is possibly not and I must fight my way out before I die of it.'[15]

Later in 1948 he wrote four diary entries in a notebook:

April 25. At supper to-day T. said suddenly, 'Joyce, I've got a lump in my breast', and jumped up to make me feel it. She was flushed and excited, but I don't think frightened. I called Charlie Murray at once, who advised immediate action and then I called Heneage on the phone and arranged to see him the next afternoon. T. was all this time in her usual splendid health and had been looking forward immensely to the parties and concerts of the town.

April 27. To-day when I came back from London and went to T. I still felt confused with this frightful and unexpected blow. As T. said 'It's like a dream but now we know we're not going to wake up.'

What is strange is that I got no pleasure, in walking through the Parks and looking at the new leaves on the trees, and the buttercups which are just opening in crowds among the bright green new grass. I used to think that looking at nature wld. always give me consolation in misery but it did not do so to-day. The only thing that gave me comfort was simply a feeling for other people in misfortune and their need of love. I was made to feel, I suppose, for the first time, the *absolute need* of love to make life possible, and the continuous everlasting presence of love in the world. And so the fearful bitterness of this danger to T. and all our memories together was mixed with the sense of something that can survive any loss, the power to love.

April 28. Took T. to town. Georgina Galbraith on the train – a kind strong woman. Her expression when she said 'Old men must not be moved – they want peace.' . . . T. at hospital. An hours wait in the little waiting room – then T. coming back with her coat off and she must wait again. She says

'But it's all no good' meaning 'it won't put back the dream.' And again 'If I had not noticed the lump on Sunday we would still be happy', and her look made me nearly cry. She has loved happiness so much and we have been so happy. When I said good-bye and got in the train, she smiled at me suddenly with her look of gaiety as if amused at something in me and forgiving it and enjoying it at the same time. I don't know what was in her mind . . .

She said 'It's like an animal eating in my heart all the time.' She doesn't feel any pain, but I think this makes the idea of an animal, a kind of silent and greedy presence tearing at her all the time, still more horrible.[16]

After he got home that evening he wrote to her: 'I can't tell you how desolate Parkers seemed when I came in from the station and felt your absence. I gave your message to Peter and he had made a good supper for me, but we were both sad, missing you every moment. You have made this place so rich and happy a home for us all that we need you, all ways. Dearest, I know how fearfully hard it is for you not to worry and not to hate the treatments, but I pray you for our sakes to try to relax . . . '[17]

April 29. I telephoned to Neville Court [Heneage's home in London] to know how T. was. She answered herself, and described her day, meeting Elsie, Tristram. but what struck me again was the gaiety and youth of her voice . . . Trudy's voice is electric with vitality – not noisy or forced – it is soft and quick and without the least strain conversational – and yet it carries life with it. But it wld. do the same however ill and unhappy she were – it is her manner of speaking on a telephone.[18]

Heneage had arranged that one of the foremost London surgeons, Sir Stanford Cade, should treat Trudy. On 11 May, she wrote from Blackheath, where she was now staying with Michael and Isabel: 'I saw Sir Stanford today . . . I am to go into the treatment til the 21st . . . and then will be free till the 31st when I can go into hospital – with the op. on the 1st (our wedding day!). This brings everything rather near . . . The first few days I will love to have you near darling, though I mustn't distract you from your work . . . you will love me the same after, won't you?'[19]

The same day he told her that his cutting of A *Fearful Joy* was going well (Chapter 5 was down from 61 pages to 40). 'Darling, I'm thinking of you all the time – how happy we shall be when this nightmare is over – happier than before because we shall know how valuable happiness is to us both.'[20]

Cary stayed with Michael and Isabel to be at Trudy's side. The operation was pronounced a success. Trudy was back in Oxford convalescing by July, and in mid August Cary took her off for two weeks to Switzerland, which she had loved since skiing holidays in her childhood. They went to the same hotels and places they had visited together in the early 1920s.

Then Cary struggled on with A *Fearful Joy*. But, as he had confessed to Lionel Stevenson in late May, 'My new book is still under revision and will be held up by Trudy's illness as she is my secretary typist.'[21] Heroically, Trudy insisted on resuming that role when they returned from Switzerland. For both of them, A *Fearful Joy* had become a painful and desperate labour of love.

'she loved life'

Then another blow. Peter, after his wounding and strain during the war, had suffered from 'endless headaches' and worry; now he had the additional burden of his mother's illness. With his parents' encouragement, he went on holiday to Ireland in the late summer, exploring Inishowen with great enjoyment and then staying at The Bungalow.

Suddenly, in mid September, Cary was informed that Peter was seriously ill. He rushed over to Castledawson and wrote on 17 September to explain that '. . . to-day he seems a little better. He must have two nurses, day and night . . . I know how you feel, dear, it is wretched for you to have to stay at a distance when Peter is ill . . . but we must both have patience this week.'[22] Trudy wrote the same day 'I am longing to hear news of Peter and how things really are – it is worrying being so far away . . . I feel very alone and sad without you darling, but one of us had to be with dear Peter – only I am so sorry you have had this other and unexpected postponement of your work again – you have been very patient over it all – but I know how despairing you must feel sometimes.'[23]

She wanted to join him, but Cary, worried about her own health, suggested she wait until Peter was recovering. Meanwhile, when not with Peter, he did some writing – not of A Fearful Joy because 'I can't do connected work while I may be sent for any minute. I am working on some preliminary sketches for stories which will be useful later on.' He assured Trudy that Peter was improving.

By the end of September, Peter was much better. 'Nothing can exceed the sympathy and patience of Cary and Nurse Agnes, and Aunt Netta . . . I look forward to your coming. I told Peter you were coming and he was delighted.'[24] The crisis was over. Cary went doggedly back to his novel.

The year ended. Cary, writing to Lionel Stevenson on 2 January 1949, uncharacteristically did not mention the festivities or give any family news.

Herself Surprised had been published in the USA towards the end of 1948; it did well enough for Harper to decide that To Be a Pilgrim should follow it early in 1949. In January Cary received 'An immense batch of reviews on the Moonlight . . . We both notice that American reviewers are for the most part much more intelligent than British ones. They are in quite a different class – and take more trouble. This is odd because circulations are much lower. My books sell 4 times the number (20,000 or so) on this side . . .'[25] His first American article was published later that year – 'On the Function of the Novelist' in the New York Times Book Review. [26] Cary's popularity in America was increasing.

Otherwise, 1949 was a year of intensifying strain and sadness. Cary's friends helped him to find relief and relaxation in occasional social excursions. At the Davins' house in February, he encountered a painter, Gerald Wilde, who already had a reputation as 'the Gulley Jimson of Soho', and so began a relationship that was to interest and trouble him for several years. There were happy family occasions. At Easter, when all four sons were at home, there was a musical evening; Trudy played her cello, accompanied by her sons and her friends the Boyds. Then the whole family attended Tristram's wedding.

But Trudy's decline continued. Death had already struck the Ogilvie family the previous summer: Freddy and Mary's eldest son James was killed in a climbing accident on the Matterhorn. In May 1949, Freddy, who had been Principal of Jesus College for five years, fell seriously ill. The brother and sister who had been so close in childhood and youth now faced death together. After two operations, Freddy Ogilvie died on 10 June.

Trudy's pain had returned. Two nurses were now looking after her. In July she was admitted to Westminster Hospital for further treatment. 'I am so terribly sorry for all these last weeks darling – and the upheaval to all your work,' she wrote to Cary from her ward. 'I am so sorry if I was depressed yesterday . . . but I think this endless tummy pain is getting me down . . . possibly the radium may not be good for it – but I *don't* want to go on living a crock – I make such a rotten and useless wife for you . . . I am *so* worried about this setback to your work again darling – don't worry about me – and I do hope perhaps you will get a "feeling" again to write . . . '[27]

Cary tried to put her mind at rest:

Darling love,
I hated to leave you yesterday – it was a blessing that George cld. be with you for a short time.
I am very sorry that I ever suggested any worry about work or money. Curtis Brown writes that Harpers want to do Mister Johnson next – this gives me at least 18 months or 2 yrs run in USA (Horses Mouth + Mister Johnson + Fearful Joy) and quite possibly we will be quite well off next year. Also I got started in the train on an idea which seems very promising . . .
. . . All my love, my dearest, in this very hard time – I wish I cld. be with you especially at night when I feel that you need someone to take care of you, in your pain,
Your loving grateful husband
Joyce[28]

When she came home, Cary took her to Southwold for a short holiday. Trudy, who had been at school there, wanted to look out at the sea before she died.[29] She was now very frail. 'I am terribly sorry you have been feeling ill Zum,' Peter wrote (Zum was the pet-name that both he and George used). 'I do hope the change will really help you to get better. Congratulations on being book of the month in America [*The Horse's Mouth*], Daddy, that is wonderful news'.

Towards the end of July there was another family wedding – the last public occasion Trudy would manage. George, while an undergraduate, had tutored the children of the late Sir Eric Phipps (who had been Ambassador to Germany and France) – and fallen in love with one of them, Mig (Margaret). Trudy's presence at their wedding was an act of sheer courage, for she was failing fast. Mig's mother, Frances Phipps, wrote to Cary on 27 October: 'Ever since I left Oxford I have thought of you and Trudy, of your deep anxiety and her suffering face and of the agony of it all for you both . . . To see her so ill and be able to do so little, and yet love her so much, is just an *unbearable* agony for you just now, dear Joyce. I know it is.'[30]

A final hospital treatment was tried in November – a 'new Nitrogen Mustard prescription'.[31] But it did not arrest Trudy's cancer. She returned home for the last time. The family gathered round her. Michael had been making a clavichord for her, the best he could achieve, as a loving surprise. It was 'smuggled in', then Peter and Tristram played it for her.

Tristram, still studying at Trinity College, London, had been making a name as a composer; his 'Partita' was to be premiered at a concert in London on 12 December, and they all hoped that Trudy could be there.

Trudy's niece Antonia came to cook for the household, while the housekeeper was on holiday. One morning she saw a poignant scene: 'Joyce was lying fully clothed in a brown suit on the bed beside her, Gertie was lying under the bedclothes holding Joyce's hand. They looked like effigies on a tomb – with the sunlight streaming across the bed.'[32]

Cary's friends were awed by his stoicism. Enid Starkie:

> . . . I remember, one evening, a few days before his wife died, just as he was leaving me, I clasped his hand in mine. I wanted just to make him relax, I could not bear his stiff upper lip. He was somewhat surprised, but he understood, I think, what I wanted to suggest, though I had no words to express it. Yet all he said was: 'Bad show! Yes! a bad show!'[33]

At the beginning of December, Cary heard that he had been recommended to become a Companion of the British Empire. Michael urged him to accept: 'I am always a little, and perhaps unnecessarily, irritated, at people who refuse, perhaps because I know how long and patient are the enquiries, counter enquiries and siftings that must be gone through before an offer is made. And would it not give Mummy pleasure? Or would she feel that a K[nighthood] should have been the first step? The final decision must be yours.'[34]

He declined the CBE on 5 December. 'I take it that the honour proposed is for literary work, and not for my political books', he wrote to the Prime Minister's Secretary; 'and in that case I'm afraid I should be embarrassed by a distinction which seems to grade writers according to merit.'[35] Was it also a matter of pride? Both Trudy's brothers had been knighted; but should it matter to him, or to her, whether his success was formally endorsed? Did he also feel that the success was not his alone, but a joint achievement?

His 61st birthday was celebrated; five days later there were three curtain calls after the performance of Tristram's 'Partita' on 12 December. A cousin of Trudy's, Juliet Ogilvie, wrote to Cary the next day: 'The concert was a great success . . . We went to Tristram's flat together. It was splendid to see all your four sons but it seemed incomplete without you and Gertie also.'[36]

Trudy was already dead. She had died on the morning of 13 December, in Cary's arms.

He wrote to Enid Starkie, who was in Dublin:

> The poor child fought to the last breath – she loved life so much that she could not bear to leave it. We don't even feel sure that she knew of

Tristram's success . . . We told her and she shewed that she knew that we were trying to tell her something important but she was already too weak to speak clearly.

I never knew anyone who lived so richly and innocently – the serene and beautiful woman we buried was not the Trudy we knew – so gay – so sad – so anxious – so frank in all her passions and delights. She loved you, my dear, for your warm heart and the candour of spirit so like her own. [37]

A friend who had not heard of her death came to see Trudy. 'She left yesterday,' Cary told her. [38]

The funeral, Audrey Beecham remembered, was very formal. Cary was in full morning dress. As she had requested, Trudy was buried in her wedding dress. The coffin was carried by her four sons, Michael weeping uncontrollably. After the ceremony, Cary 'walked collectedly to the graveside, and looked sideways, with his birdlike glance, into the grave'. [39]

Mary Ogilvie wrote 'I know strength will be given to you, as it was given to me, and at the time one somehow manages to live through the days. But it is later that the real loneliness and desolation come over you. Gertie was the dearest and most affectionate sister to me. I loved her beauty, her brilliance and her warm-heartedness. She was the best company in the world. I loved being with her. She showed all of us what a home could be . . .'[40]

Another Christmas. Trudy had completed all the arangements. 'She had prepared all the Christmas cards and ordered tickets for the family to visit the pantomime – though not one for herself . . .'[41] The cards were sent off, and family and friends went to the pantomime on Boxing Day, Enid Starkie among them:

There were programmes – one for each person – and chocolates and ices in the interval, and [Cary] laughed uproariously at all the jokes – even more than they deserved – crossing and uncrossing his legs, as was his habit in moments of excitement or nervous tension. When the performance was over we went back to the house, and there were cold turkey, plum-pudding with all the trimmings, and champagne . . . Later, when he saw me home, he said: 'It has been a good Christmas!'[42]

CHAPTER THIRTY SIX

NEW WORLDS

1949–1953

'I must reorganise my life'

In 1945 Cary had written a letter of condolence to John Dover Wilson, whose only son had recently died: 'sympathy appears to be a small thing to offer in face of such a calamity which changes the whole landscape of a man's life. And if it gives a wider horizon, a deeper sky, they are also more dark and strange. And I know how I should suffer in losing a son and always suffer, except in the memory of the boy as he was in himself, and the knowledge of his own peace.'[1]

Now Cary's own life was similarly changed and he set about adjusting with his usual briskness. His life was now, more than ever, dichotomous: long lonely slogging in his study, brief excursions or social occasions. But the writing, as always, demanded precedence; and he was increasingly obsessed by his sense of unfinished work. Without Trudy to type his novels, he was reliant on paid secretaries, who could work only at set times. 'I have, for the moment, a typist,' he wrote on 12 January 1950, 'so the work goes on fast – and I work the harder because it is an escape from loneliness.'[2] But because the secretaries could not read his now almost illegible handwriting (only Trudy, he used to joke, knew what he had written), he had to dictate his text. He taught himself to type. This took time and effort, when he wanted to get on with his writing. He was undismayed. His typing, even after several years, was so idiosyncratic that it looked like a new art form; but it was a challenge met; and he was soon proudly telling his American literary agent about 'a good day's work (2000 words *composed* on typewriter). I like learning new tricks . . . '[3]

Cary's daily routine began very early. 'He was a light sleeper and usually woke about four in the morning,' Dan Davin noted. 'He would then lie in bed thinking about new novels to write or about the book on which he was at the moment concentrating. He would scribble notes of any good points that struck him . . . ' Then he might doze before getting up at about 7.30 to read the morning's mail.[4] The importance of the doze in his creative process is suggested by a comment in a letter: 'I went asleep till 7 and had some very good dreams. I prefer my horse sleep to my baby sleep because it is a boon I don't rely on and it always has good dreams.'[5]

An interviewer in 1952 described the rest of his day: 'Cary has fixed hours. He is in his study at nine, dictates till one and walks after lunch to keep fit. He then works again till late in the afternoon or even until dinner, but rarely later.'

His study on the top floor was 'the old children's nursery . . . It is the room of a tidy, but unfussy person, who will not waste time tidying up, but who knows where to find everything at once.'[6] He worked at a desk, made shortly before Trudy's death, which he had 'specially designed' for his method of writing, with eight shelves above the writing surface (later, by 1952, four more were added). On each shelf was a 'packet' which accumulated manuscript for a section of the novel he was working on. 'I've already got something in 3,' he told a visitor around 1950, 'something in 5, which is another important scene, and 7 and 8 are far on. I'm working now on the first sections and when they are done – I'll work on the whole book.'[7]

He still did his exercises every morning, and his health remained good – apart from one ailment at the end of 1951 similar to the 'inflammation of the joints' that had afflicted him four years earlier. On 7 December 1951, his sixty-third birthday, he was suddenly stricken by a 'hip pain' which prevented him walking, and the next day his leg was 'still throbbing'. He was rushed to the Wingfield-Morris Orthopaedic Hospital at Headington with suspected poliomyelitis, but there told he had bursitis, and kept for a week.

Cary's friends made sure that he was never isolated for long. Enid Starkie's flat at 41 St Giles', round the corner, and the Davins' house, 103 Southmoor Road, a short cycle ride away, were frequent venues. At a 'famous dinner' she cooked for them, he met Starkie's sparring partner, Maurice Bowra, President of Lincoln College, and Janet Vaughan, President of Somerville.[8] Cary did not like Bowra, to judge by a notebook sketch – 'The man like M. B. who collects honours and enjoys distinction of that kind'[9] – but Vaughan became a good friend, and he was often invited to grace the high table at Somerville dinners. At his own college, Trinity, he posed a minor problem by regularly attending Gryphon Club meetings. Undergraduates would fall silent in his voluble presence; so, after a while, Tommy Higham quietly persuaded him to limit his appearances.[10]

Something of a national celebrity now, he was also invited to a range of formal functions and became acquainted with many of Oxford's Lions – Isaiah Berlin, Hugh Trevor-Roper, A. J. P. Taylor, Alan Bullock, A. L. Rowse.

He was always happiest, however, with those who were on the fringe of fame, or who, ignoring their fame, behaved with a lively informality. The Davins had a wide circle of literary, artistic and academic friends. A New Zealander of Irish extraction, with the social advantage of exemption from the British class system, Dan Davin was himself a novelist, and his job at the Oxford University Press brought him into touch with many writers; his wife Winifred was a warmly gracious hostess. Although the Davins enjoyed meeting friends at a nearby pub, the 'Victoria Arms', Cary rarely joined them there. (His uneasiness in pubs, noted by Dan Davin, no doubt expressed his fear of losing self-control, and a vestigial patrician prejudice.)[11]

At the Davins' house he met several stimulating people who became his friends. Dan Davin's fellow New Zealander, Wendy Campbell Purdie, introduced Cary to jitterbugging at her Thursday evening parties, and, as provider of accommodation for the feckless Gerald Wilde, was responsible for Cary's involvement with 'the Gulley Jimson of Soho'. Like many in Oxford, Cary did all he could to help Wilde, buying his pictures, giving him money (though this, it was soon learnt, could encourage binges), even writing an article praising Wilde's work. If such activities were a distraction, they were also important in helping him fend off depression.

The Davins also had three young daughters – Anna, Delia and Bridgid – all under ten years old. He quickly became their honorary godfather, looking forward to their Wednesday afternoon visits for tea and his twice-weekly walks with the whole family. Every September he would take the Davin girls to St Giles' Fair. In 1951, to his delight, he was mistaken for a balloon vendor: 'Waiting outside a flea circus for the children of his party, he was holding a bunch of balloons which was too large to take into the flea circus. He was approached by a timid little man who asked for two balloons for himself and his companion, a big, boisterous woman. In order not to disappoint them, Cary sold them two of his own balloons.'[12] Every Boxing Day the Davin family would join him and his own family for the ritual pantomime, and afterwards go to Parkers for convivial food and drink. And so the family traditions were adapted, and perpetuated.

He also continued the Sunday evening 'open house', and an informal Cary circle came into being. Its regular members were Lord David Cecil and Enid Starkie; the Davins; Audrey Beecham, a poet; Peter Ady, an economist; Jean Bannister, a scientist; Helen Gardner and W. W. Robson, English dons; Ernest and Kathleen Stahl, he a lecturer in German (later Professor), she a historian; Iris Murdoch, a Philosophy don soon to begin her own career as a novelist (she found the group attractively kind and caring[13]). Occasional visitors included Walter Allen and Robert Lusty, the poets Dylan Thomas, Louis MacNeice and W. R. Rodgers, and Gordon Ostlere (who lived next-door for a period and, as Richard Gordon, later wrote the humorous 'Doctor' novels).

Cary's behaviour at those Sunday evening gatherings was not always predictable, and sometimes indicated stress. He might talk at insistent length, or listen in silence – or even absent himself; on one occasion, Win Davin remembered, he was found looking through the cartoons in his old *Punches*.[14] But he greatly valued this weekly opportunity to meet friends and acquaintances, and usually participated eagerly in the lively conversation.

In addition to the members of the 'Sunday crowd', old and new friends came to see him – the Highams, Herberts and Boyds; neighbours like Donald Hurst, a judge; and Oxford figures like the Norringtons, J.I.M. Stewart (English don and critic and, as 'Michael Innes', author of whodunits), the Ridlers (Vivien Ridler, the University Printer, his wife Anne, a poet), Alic

Halford Smith (Warden of New College), F. P. Wilson and Herbert Davis (Professors of English).

Lord David Cecil occasionally drove him out into the Cotswolds on the day-long expeditions that they both loved. Unlike Trudy, Cary had always been a poor driver, and the weak sight in his right eye made him a menace on the road – so the car remained in the garage and he relied on his bicycle for short journeys. Apart from cycling, and his daily walks, he also continued to skate in winter and, in summer, to go sailing at Bosham with Heneage Ogilvie.

In 1951 and 1952 Cecil took him to see several Shakespeare productions at Stratford-upon-Avon. In August 1951 they saw the Histories performed as a series. 'I had never seen them in a row and when David asked me to join him in the adventure I thought it was something like mathematics which one ought to go through . . .'; but he had immensely 'enjoyed the experience'– 'To see the same actor working out the destiny of his person . . . was highly significant – I had not expected the powerful effect of continuity.'[15] In August 1952 he reported to Stevenson that he had had 'a wonderful week at Stratford' seeing *Coriolanus*, *The Tempest*, *Macbeth*, *As You Like It*, and *Volpone* – 'the first and last I scarcely knew and they gave me a big surprise.'[16] In fact he was so deeply moved by Anthony Quayle's performance as Coriolanus that the character and play influenced his Second Trilogy ('it harrowed me up endways and sideways and throughways', he told Dover Wilson).[17]

Cary's family was growing steadily. In 1949 and 1951, two more sons, Chippy (Tristram) and Anthony, were born to Michael and Isabel. Christopher, George and Mig's son, was born in 1950. Tristram and Dorse had their first son, John – Cary's fourth grandchild – in 1952; and in the same year Peter married Beth Simon. Cary took great pleasure in visits from all the members of his family. 'I don't know where I'd be without my children and daughters in law and grandsons – I should feel like a man who jumps out of a plane and suddenly perceives that he has forgotten his parachute.'[18]

With two women – who had in common vigour, courage, intellectual sharpness, and closeness to Trudy – Cary developed especially close relations in the early 1950s: Enid Starkie and Mary Ogilvie. While Starkie was away from Oxford during 1951, he wrote her long affectionate letters. ' . . . look after yourself my dear, don't drink too much and go to bed early. This will annoy but I am fond of you my dear and so I have the right to bully you.' 'I miss you very much for tho I see little of you I always like to feel that you are there. There is a great gap in St Giles while you are away. Very much love . . .' There was in Starkie, he recognised, a bohemianism that harmonised with a persistent part of his own personality. And he confessed that he valued her judgement and encouragement highly, for 'I am not in fact a very confident writer partly because I am always venturing into new country and do not myself know quite what I have done. I write venturing but really I think I am pushed or driven by forces that I myself don't understand.'[19]

Mary Ogilvie, with her solid Scottish good sense and rectitude, appealed to the other, conservative extreme of Cary's personality. And, as sister-in-law, with her long Ogilvie connection and appreciation of Trudy, she also gave him the stability of deep personal understanding,. While he valued lively social occasions with Enid Starkie, with Mary Ogilvie he was able to enjoy relaxing holidays, both on their own and with other members of the family.

Cary did not write (or, probably, speak) of either woman to the other. Nor, apparently, did his relationship with them go beyond companionship – though he proposed marriage to Mary Ogilvie in 1951[20] and each was rumoured to be his mistress (Mary Ogilvie was still amused by this decades later[21]). With his deep capacity for friendship, he gave affection and appreciation to both of them, and from both of them received affection and appreciation.

'the perfect author'

At the beginning of 1950 – with sad irony, only a month after Trudy's death – Cary's American reputation suddenly surged upwards. *The Horse's Mouth* was published by Harper in January, and it was also a Book of the Month. Just over three months after publication, its Harper sales alone had passed 25,000. *Newsweek* sent a reporter to interview him, announcing that 'There has never been anything quite like the current enthusiasm for Cary's novels. The superlatives that are heaped upon his books . . . have the unmistakable ring of sincerity; they come from all kinds and classes of critics, right and left, high-brow and low-brow.'[22]

Harper had not originally wanted to publish *The Horse's Mouth* at all. They had rejected it in 1946; then, puzzled by. its British success, asked to reconsider. Critical reception rather than the sales of *The Moonlight*, *Herself Surprised*, and *To Be a Pilgrim*, from 1947 to 1949, had established a small American reputation for Cary. His correspondence with Harper had also established two important new friendships for him.

Cary's relations with Michael Joseph, and especially with his editor Robert Lusty, were always pleasant but rather formal. He appreciated the compliment paid him when the Carfax Edition, with its flattering Oxford reference, was inaugurated in 1951 (though he was privately disparaging about its 'sissy dove grey cover' and 'the flowery banana on the title page'[23]); and he spent much time and energy writing Prefaces for it.

Relations with his American publishers were different. He responded with immediate warmth to their businesslike informality. Elizabeth Lawrence, his editor-to-be, had written at the end of 1946 'You have a very warm following among English visitors I have met recently and I am hoping Harper's can build you a comparable following on this side of the Atlantic.'[24] Although unwilling to inflate his mandatory autobiographical statements, Cary was appreciative of all efforts to promote his novels in America, and Lawrence was soon telling Robert Lusty 'I think Joyce Cary *must* be the perfect author, at least we are finding him so. While there may be a disadvantage in having an author play shy about publicity, it is certainly preferable to over-eagerness. At this considerable distance, Mr Cary is giving us every possible cooperation.'[25] More than once he specifically thanked her 'for all the trouble you take on my behalf'; he was 'delighted that you are doing my books, and I hope you do well out of them'.[26] 'What I like about Harpers,' he commented later, 'is that they have a feeling, and tell me about it. I am far too busy, in my work, for which there is *never* enough time, to talk about the other end, the publication end.'[27]

Jack Fischer of Harper visited him towards the end of 1949, while Trudy was dying, to discuss publicity methods. From London he wrote to tell Elizabeth Lawrence that Cary

> is a wonderful man, bubbling with life, volubility, and ideas for new novels. He says he has parts of seventeen books already written, which he hopes to finish; and fragments of a dozen more he has abandoned . . . He lives almost as a recluse, and turns out two or three thousand words a day, all in long hand . . .
>
> For the first time in my life, I felt that maybe I had met a genuine 18-carat genius.[28]

Cary's correspondence with Elizabeth Lawrence became friendly very quickly, though he would not budge on matters he considered important. 'Dear Mr Cary, I want to thank you for Sara Monday,' Lawrence wrote. 'She's superb and every woman meeting her must feel – as I did – a rueful sense of self-discovery.' But might she suggest that some title other than the 'slightly Victorian' *Herself Surprised* would sell better in America?[29] She received a firm, swift reply: 'The point is that my titles are essential parts of the book. I don't forget for a moment that they appear at the top of each page. The essence of Sara is the revelation of Herself to herself – she is surprised at herself but also she is surprised, for us, in her nakedness . . .' On punctuation he was, as always, easy: ' . . . I have no tricks. I dislike anything that catches the readers eye to make him say 'Thats new', or worse 'thats smart'. I want him to be lost in the tale. So please put in any stops that are needed. Personally I don't like apostrophes etc – little spots like black measles all over the page – but rather than be spider in a trifle I always use them.' He *was* bothered by the American text's 'pretentious' chapter headings ('my chapters are not important like divisions – they are more like numbered paragraphs. Some therefore are very short, and a large division and strong point at the head of a short chapter has something [of] the air of a six foot Commissionaire outside a flea's circus'). Because he was always ready to comment on his novels, his correspondence with Lawrence is often very illuminating about his literary opinions and intentions.

Cary was moved by the thoughtfulness and generosity of his American publishers. January 1948: 'Dear Elizabeth Lawrence, Your parcel arrived this morning and caused a sensation in the family, especially as we had seven in the house for Christmas . . . Your butter stood out like an Ararat to the ark of our wandering appetites.'[30] Harper personnel sent fruit for Trudy, arranged a subscription to *The New Yorker* (which they both enjoyed) as her last Christmas present to Cary in 1949, and later bought and sent him his favourite American underpants!

Even before Trudy's death, Cary was looking forward to visiting the United States, and in February 1950 Elizabeth Lawrence urged 'On no account should you resist the temptation to come over to the States this year. Quite apart from the pleasure you will give us, your presence here will benefit the next novel.'[31]

He flew twice to America, for two and then three months (21 January to 31 March 1951 and early September to 8 December 1953), spending time in and near New York, making exhausting but stimulating lecture tours around the country, revelling in American generosity and liveliness. He was also able to see his Aunt Mab and cousin Lionel Stevenson, now Professor of English at Berkeley: 'a very pleasant experience for me – it recalled those old days at Clare when I was so happy'.[32]

He made several new friends. He had been invited to stay at the Fischers' home at White Plains, near New York, and that became his headquarters on both occasions. He felt immediately at home with the Fischer family, Jack and his English wife Betty, their two small daughters Nicky and Sarah, and Betty's sister Irene Wilson (he usually called her Rene). Sarah, about nine, became an instant pal. In the article 'A Child's Religion' written a couple of years later, he recalled her fascination with an old well in the garden ('I suppose that's where they put the bad horses'),[33] and he shared with her in the mysterious death and resuscitation of her pet goldfish. He got on well with the adults, too; and formed a particularly close friendship with Rene, newly in America, and corresponded with her until the end of his life. They would travel in to New York together by train daily; 'Listening to his conversation was like watching a bird of bright plumage dart from tree to tree through a sunlit forest'.[34]

Travelling on his own was exhilarating – even in the depths of a hard winter in 1951. On one occasion his plane was grounded by a storm at Burlington, Vermont (after 'the ugliest ride of my life'), then he was 'driven 85 miles in a blizzard to Plattsburg – gave my lecture, and went back next night in a sleeper, to find the railwaymen in New York on strike.'[35]

The lectures he enjoyed. Addressing women's literary societies could be heavy going; but he loved a lively university audience, and his informal style of lecturing made him especially effective with small groups – on his second trip he requested the organiser, Colston Leigh, to ensure that most of his lectures were of that kind.

In February 1951 he spoke to Louis Macleish's seminar in creative writing at Harvard. Walt Rostow, with whom he stayed, was a friend of Michael's and, when Harmsworth Visiting Professor at Oxford in 1946–7, had become a frequent visitor at Parkers. He recalled how Cary, at that seminar, had taken command of the 'shy. egocentric, talented group by observing how he went about writing a novel'; this 'stirred the young to talk and opened into a remarkable evening'.[36]

'tact of the heart'

Cary's friendships with Jack Fischer and Elizabeth Lawrence deepened during his trips to America. Thirty years later, Lawrence wrote that it was 'a pleasure to remember and talk about him . . . His natural ease and attentiveness invited self-assurance in others. He listened, and with interest. And there was the mind – open, far-ranging, curious, receptive, tolerant, laced with humour and a well-earned wisdom.' Although he was 'very lovable . . . romance was not a factor in our friendship', she added. When he said goodbye to her at the end of his first American visit, he gave her 'a rather shy, tentative kiss'.[37]

With another American woman he formed a much closer friendship, in which romance *was* a factor. Mrs Sewell Haggard was his American literary agent, at Curtis Brown in New York. A widow in her late forties, some fifteen years younger than Cary, she had been close to Sinclair Lewis (who had recently died), as his literary agent. She was beautiful, graceful and, like Trudy's, her voice was strong and warm. When Cary stepped into her office in January 1951, they felt an immediate rapport, and were soon friends.

It was with Edith Haggard that he was dancing in the anecdote *Time* included in its review of *Prisoner of Grace*: 'in a Manhattan restaurant whence all but two customers had departed, one of the two, a middle-aged man, left his lady companion to go to the phone. Suddenly he stopped in his tracks and cocked an ear: the Muzak had begun a waltz. He danced smilingly back to his table and bowed low to the middle-aged lady who sat there. In and out among the tables 63-year-old Joyce Cary spun his startled partner.'[38]

Edith Haggard was an excellent agent. Most of the nearly fifty articles and two dozen short stories he wrote during the next five years were placed by her, for lucrative fees, in such magazines as the *New Yorker*, *Vogue*, *Esquire*, *Holiday*. 'You are the best agent in the world as well as the nicest,' he wrote;[39] she wrote 'You are not only a great writer, but a perfect client . . . my admiration for you approaches a passion'.[40]

Although he was living at White Plains with the Fischers, he would come to her apartment near Central Park during the day, for conversation and relaxation. After March 1951, their friendship continued in long letters. Before he left America, they had decided to keep their personal and professional correspondence separate, and during the following six years wrote each other well over 150 personal letters. He knew he could speak to her, with utter confidence, out of his deepest feelings; for she had a self-abnegating loyalty and generosity like Trudy's. He wrote:

one must not think of life in terms of happiness but of achievement. My only consolation in those terrible years when my wife was fighting for her life (and she adored life – no one could be so happy) was in the thought that she had achieved so much. And in fact she never thought of herself as having achieved anything . . . she never had time to be sorry for herself. She suffered fearfully but she never despaired or ceased to be the mistress of her house and the mother of her sons. She went down fighting and I pray I may make so good and grand a death.

Of course you are lonely. I am lonely – I have a big hole inside me that will never be filled up as long as I live not even by the children's and grandchildren's claims. I rather suspect that everyone of my age, even those who have not lost their wives after 35 years, have a hole . . . But my hole is bigger and deeper and so is yours . . . The only thing to do is to forget it and there I am lucky because I have my work.

We have had a good deal of the same experience in life, and enough difference to give us plenty to discuss, and it is a common experience and common sympathies which are the true basis of friendship . . . We can tell each other anything and do tell each other everything. And I don't know why that is such a relief and joy, but it certainly is one of the greatest. It is a breaking down of walls, a breaking out of cages, it does for such solitary souls as us what confession does for the catholics.

What a delight to get to your peaceful room out of the streets. You spoilt me but how I loved to be spoilt by so clever and true a friend – you are the dearest of women – you have the tact of the heart.[41]

CHAPTER THIRTY SEVEN

A BUSY LIFE

1950–1952

The Second Trilogy

Cary was critical of his First Trilogy's structure. He agreed with those who thought it too loose. The various 'worlds' of the three novels 'were not sufficiently interlocked to give the richness and depth of actuality that I had hoped for. That's why, in planning the second trilogy, I limited it to a single subject, politics, and tied the three chief characters closely together in the same complex development.'[1] (Again his plan was to be modified in the writing.)

Cary's Second Trilogy – *Prisoner of Grace, Except the Lord* and *Not Honour More* – repeats the basic structure of its predecessor (innovator and conservative involved with a woman), but the two men of its triangle are set in constant competition, both for the woman and within a political situation. In fact, Cary returned to the central relationships and political context of *Cock Jarvis* – which became a major influence on the Trilogy, and especially on *Not Honour More*. In his First Trilogy, tension between creativity and injustice was resolved in favour of creativity; in his Second, injustice prevails. (So mirroring the difference between his early experiences of conflict in political and aesthetic domains.)

There are other similarities and differences. Both trilogies begin with the woman's account, but the order of the subsequent volumes is reversed. By ending his Second Trilogy with the conservative's statement, as well as by stressing conflict throughout, Cary promoted its sombre mood and implications. Moreover, Latter is, compared with Wilcher, a malignant and destructive conservative. Indeed all three of the later protagonists are less attractive, more ambiguous, more culpable, than their predecessors; their novels more insistently (and delusively) self-justificatory: 'I am writing this book because I understand that "revelations" are soon to appear . . . '; 'If I draw back now the curtain from my family life, sacred to memory, I do so only to honour the dead, and in the conviction that my story throws light upon the crisis that so fearfully shakes our whole civilization'; 'This is my statement, so help me God, as I hope to be hung'.[2]

In both trilogies, incarceration is a central fact. But in the First Trilogy, Sara and Jimson have been released from prison, she loves her kitchen, Wilcher's mansion is, like him, being urged into the future, Gulley's wall crumbles into sunlight. In the Second Trilogy, confinement is final, and utterly destructive: Nina is a prisoner, and executed as one; Nimmo is hunted from room to room, and murdered in a toilet; Latter waits to die in his cell. In fact, the Second Trilogy is, throughout, largely negative and tragic, where his First was largely positive and comic. Cary, stoically enduring loss, loneliness and the approach of his own death, faced the darkness squarely.

Prisoner of Grace

Prisoner of Grace was first called 'The Turkish House' – a title taken from Cary's private name for a house which, together with its occupants, had fascinated him during family holidays in Wales, in the early 1930s.[3] The originating situation of the novel (though in a story about two sisters, as in 'Juno') was connected with that house. (In *Prisoner of Grace* it is replaced by Palm Cottage, which, in a map Cary drew while writing the novel, is near Kingsbridge, that other favourite holiday area of the Carys.)

The novel's change of title reflects Cary's intuition of grace as a driving force in human experience – 'an influence as common as the weather and persistent as the heart muscle'.[4] This seems to have been, in part, a response to the power of Eastern religion as he had observed it in India. (He defines an important difference between Nina and Nimmo by introducing an 'eastern' sexual position into their lovemaking: 'At "indian move" he is shocked tho Nina says "holy in India".' In a note Cary reminded himself 'The grace relation must not be lost sight of in all its aspects. The book is about the weight of moral authority and resentment of it.'[5]

As a spellbinder, Chester Nimmo radiates grace, and it captivates not only Nina (in spite of her old and deep attraction to Jim Latter) but her son Tom, 'who is also unable to escape from Nimmo's powerful influence, and whose life is ruined by his inability to get free and make a place of his own in the world'. In Nimmo Cary again represented the creator, the innovator – but his artistry is in rhetoric, manipulation and self-deception, and his power is shown to be more often malign than beneficent in its effects. Nimmo's dominating role in Nina's novel, from her opening words onward, later faced Cary with such a serious problem that he temporarily decided to abandon the trilogy.

Prisoner of Grace

is a study of the Radical spell-binder in a real political atmosphere . . . where it is often difficult to know what is right and what is wrong . . . The story is told by Nina, and the odd plot is required both to show the personal moral situation through the eyes of a good-natured intelligent woman who can perceive its subtleties, and also to develop in Nimmo's political career, and his gradual education in the actual political world, the full theme of the political dilemma . . . [6]

That Nimmo was largely based on Lloyd George, the controversial Liberal

politician and Prime Minister, is indicated not only by Cary's notes ('Inspiration of Lloyd George') but by the draft of a letter to Lady Megan Lloyd
George in March 1953:

> My sister-in-law, Lady Ogilvie, tells me that you have read my book the
> Prisoner of Grace and liked it.
>
> This gives me much more pleasure than perhaps you think, because I had
> the greatest admiration for your father, and I was extremely anxious that no
> one should suppose the book was aimed at him. I seem to have been
> successful in this, but I was still anxious about the reactions of his family.
>
> As you see, in order to show what I thought, the really important elements
> in English political history during the last sixty years, I had to have for hero a
> radical politician who had made his way from the bottom and who was
> profoundly evangelical in his training . . .[7]

Several observations about Nina's personality in Cary's notes suggest that a
partial source was Trudy; and the novel may have had an early complimentary
intention. If so, the portrait was quickly blurred and darkened. One cause of
this was the influence of two literary sources. Cary had been deeply moved by
The Diary of Dostoevsky's Wife (a translation of the diary kept by Anna
Snitkina, Dostoevsky's second wife); he annotated it extensively, fascinated by
its revelation of the complex relationship between Anna and the volatile
creator who held her in emotional servitude.[8]

But probably a more important influence on Cary at this time was Robert
Graves's fine historical novel Wife to Mr Milton: The Story of Marie Powell
(1942). Marie Powell was an Oxfordshire girl of Royalist stock who married
John Milton in 1642 at the age of sixteen, to save her parents from financial
ruin. She then left him, but in 1645 returned, bore him three children, and
died in 1651. Graves depicted her as a lively young girl in love with a
handsome young Royalist, Mun, but forced into a loveless marriage with the
middle-aged Puritan politician-poet. In the novel she narrates her own tragic
story. Not only do the central characters and their relations coincide with
Cary's, but it seems likely that the title Not Honour More, for the third novel
of the trilogy, was suggested by the seventeenth-century setting of Graves's
novel and Marie's love for a Royalist soldier.[9]

Cary worked steadily and confidently at Prisoner of Grace but did not in fact
finish it until early 1952, largely because of other writing and his first
American visit.

He requested that all the novel's earnings be transferred to his four sons,
although this meant his bank balance was frequently fragile: 'It always seems
unfair to me,' he explained to Elizabeth Lawrence, 'that I inherited £300 a
year when that was worth 6 or 700 to-day and they get nothing'.[10] Their
financial needs were certainly greater than his. But surely this was also a way
of goading himself to even greater effort.

Walter Allen, in his Reader's report for Michael Joseph, was enthusiastic
about Prisoner of Grace as 'essence of Cary; only he could have written it; it's a
further exploration of his own special world. And in some respects I think it's

the most powerful novel he's written. There are extremely funny comic passages in it but it's not Cary the comic novelist. It's a study, an exposition, . . . of the imaginative faculty in man and how it shapes life, this time political life. And the imagination, for Cary, is always in a sense religious.'

Allen wondered if the book suffered 'from the fact that the characters are essentially similar to those we've met before in [Cary's] novels'; for Nimmo was 'essentially of the same family as Gulley Jimson . . . he feels himself in touch with the divine', Nina 'obviously of the same family as Sara in *Herself Surprised* – say, an upper-middle-class sister', and Latter 'one of those angry, inarticulate, direct men of action Cary specialises in, a man . . . governed by a sense of honour that is never questioned'. But he thought Nimmo a 'tremendous creation' and the novel 'wonderfully solid': 'it's as though we're given the story of a Lloyd George born in the West Country, with the tradition of West Country, instead of Welsh, radicalism behind him'. Allen considered that Cary's 'recreation of the very feel of political passions between 1900 and 1914' was 'brilliant' – 'the period, politically, is completely captured in all its intensity'.

In conclusion:

> As a study of a politician in action it is quite superb; one feels at the end that here, almost for the first time, is the truth about the politician, the man for whom politics is a way of life in the same dedicated sense as for the artist art may be a way of life, or religion for a priest . . . I found it in many respects a painful book; one can't help wanting Nina to get free of him, but she's caught up in the toils of a dynamic force, a force of nature almost. It seems to me that in this relationship of Nimmo and Nina Cary is at his most powerful . . . I think *Prisoner of Grace* is a great feat of imagination.[11]

The novel was published by Michael Joseph in September 1952, and by Harper in October, to critical acclaim. The novelist Brian Moore wrote: 'Mr Cary has given us three people who are wholly believable, wholly human, wholly at fault in their conduct and who jump to life in every page with an almost unbearable intensity.'[12]

'Success Story'

During the early 1950s, Cary was increasingly involved in activities that took him away from writing novels. He was a public figure now, his name an attraction. Already he had been invited to participate in professional organisations. During 1948 and 1949 he had been a member of the P.E.N. Executive Committee. In 1954 he was elected to membership of the Council of the Society of Authors (fellow members already known to him included Walter Allen, Helen Gardner, L. P. Hartley, Rosamond Lehmann and Rex Warner) and as a result he took a prominent public position on two topical issues. In April 1954 he was one of nineteen leading British writers who 'announced they would sign no new contracts . . . if the Publishers' Association went ahead with any plan to force all new authors to give them a cut of film, theatre, TV and strip cartoon rights';[13] and he argued forcefully against the popular advocacy of increased censorship in the mid 1950s ('You do not give self-respect and self-reliance by censorship; you can only foster ignorance or develop hypocrisy, the blind fear that goes with ignorance, the violence that comes from prejudice').[14]

He had agreed to write Prefaces for all his novels as they entered the Carfax edition, and this kept him intermittently busy. Three came out in 1950, another three in 1951, and six in 1952. He was ambivalent about them. On one hand, he longed to describe his intentions, explain his myth ('all novelists are preachers'); on the other, he was convinced that a novel was an imaginative construct and must embody its own meaning. That irresolution weakens his Prefaces, although many of them are useful in describing background and pointing to themes.

Towards the end of 1951 the issue of explanation was given force by Mark Schorer's *New York Times* review of *Mister Johnson* (which had just been published in the United States). Cary was stung by Schorer's statement that he had 'no central thematic core'.[15] 'This,' he complained to Fischer, 'is a bit hard on a man who did not publish a line and wasted ten good years until he was satisfied that he had a complete "thematic core".' And he continued

> It raises the whole question of my meaning in an acute form – I gave way about the introductions [Carfax Prefaces] with doubts but now I wonder if I should not have made them more explicit. I was afraid of killing the books – of turning them into theses – which is just what I want to avoid. It seemed to me a special danger in my case just because I had such a careful and extensive scheme. But now I wonder if I should not write a kind of general preface to the lot – I once thought of calling the whole set the Comedy of Freedom (e.g. Balzac's Comedie humaine) but the scheme seemed to me pretentious and the [phrase] is ambiguous.[16]

Inundated during the early 1950s with requests for articles, Cary always tried to oblige, and was not fussy about payment. He composed popular articles about writing and literature – like 'The Way a Novel Gets Written', 'A Novel is a Novel is a Novel'. 'The Period Novel'; some well-paid 'travel' pieces for *Holiday* – like 'Switzerland' and his fine evocation of the Cotswolds, 'The Heart of England'; a few topical or miscellaneous discussions – 'The Revolution of the Women', 'Britain is Strong in Herself', 'The Sources of Tension in America'; and two or three analytical essays – 'Policy for Aid', 'Political and Personal Morality', 'Britain's Liberal Influence'. Many of these shorter writings remain readable and relevant; all are unpretentiously lively and straightforward; and some are in addition important for the light they shed on his novels – 'Political and Personal Morality' in relation to the Second Trilogy, for example.

Undoubtedly his autobiographical essays are Cary's finest. Forced into reconsidering his earlier novels for the Carfax Prefaces, responding to the contemplative pull of late middle age, Cary relived and reinterpreted his past. 'Barney Magonegal' and 'Cromwell House' encapsulate vivid childhood memories; 'A Slight Case of Demolition' recreates Prichard's crucial challenge; three articles ('The Most Exciting Sport in the World', 'Africa

Yesterday: One Ruler's Burden', 'Christmas in Africa') superbly preserve Nigerian memories.

Several of Cary's shorter writings (including some of the best) were initially radio broadcasts. From 1947 he received frequent invitations and proposals from the BBC, but he did not broadcast frequently until 1952. That year, for the novelist P. H. Newby, he followed Beveridge and Bronowski in Addressing Posterity. 'If you are right in believing that the forces of integration are greater than the forces of disintegration,' Newby advised, after receiving Cary's script, 'so much will, presumably, be manifest to the 21st century. What they will want to know is why so many people in the mid twentieth century can have thought so differently.'[17] Cary told them.[18] Newby reported that a great deal of interest had been aroused by Cary's participation in the series.

He was interviewed on radio several times, and in 1950 he and Lord David Cecil enacted one of their rapid-fire literary conversations for the nation. He agreed to be the first 'contemporary novelist of repute' interviewed for a 'Woman's Hour' series.[19] And Denis Gray Stoll told him that, in the opinion of several colleagues at the BBC, 'you are a born spontaneous broadcaster'.[20] He was becoming a 'radio personality'.

He was also doing more and more lecturing. For many years he had spoken to college clubs and literary groups. In 1951 he happened to mention to Fischer that he would soon be giving a lecture at Swindon; to the immediate request for his text, he replied 'I'm sorry that I can't send you the lecture on truth in the novel . . . because it dont exist. I spoke from notes based on a sketch.'[21] When he was invited to give a series of University lectures in Oxford at the beginning of 1952, however, he prepared them carefully: 'the 3 public lectures have given me great pleasure – I feel like the village boy who has made good,' he told Fischer.[22] Delivered under the title 'The Novel as Truth', these became the nucleus for *Art and Reality*. Thereafter, largely through Helen Gardner, he was invited to contribute lectures to several summer school courses in Oxford.

Short stories were also taking more and more of Cary's time and energy. He must have smiled wrily, remembering his first success and subsequent failure in the genre, when editors as well as his literary agents begged him for any morsel of words. During the previous two decades he had written several stories – autobiographical, like 'Umaru', or about children, like 'Success Story' and 'A Special Occasion'. These he sent to Edith Haggard when, in 1950, she asked him for short stories.

'I don't believe in long short stories – they ought to be as short as possible. I rather object to short stories being paid for their length: it ought to be [for] their shortness.'[23] One of the shortest of the stories he wrote in the early fifties, 'A Glory of the Moon', was 'as short as it can be and as concentrated – like a Japanese poem. I wish I had time to do more of the same kind of thing but they take an immensity of time and trouble in proportion to their size and weight – at least as these things are measured in the market.'[24] When another story, 'Carmagnole', was criticised as 'slight', he wrote indignantly 'It deals with the revolutionary impulse in children, in the grass roots. It is about as slight as murder.'[25]

The very short 'epiphanies' that Cary enjoyed writing at this time are magnificently suited to the evocation of childhood. 'Success Story' (about 1,500 words) counterpoints a small boy and an old man in a park, a situation similar to the end of *A Fearful Joy*. Precisely, movingly, the mutual frailty and vitality of youth and age are described, the child finally 'drunk with laughter, while the old man in painful silence reasserts his life: 'At last he stood upright. He raised his chin, a trembling hand went up to set the hat straight. For a moment he stood. Then all at once he lifted his stick about two inches and struck its iron ferule hard upon the gravel. He had done it again.'[26] Even shorter is 'A Special Occasion' (less than 1,000 words), which, with superb insight, brings together two small children at a party; they fight, ferociously; then as suddenly lose themselves in creative imagination; and the story ends with one child's 'enormous sigh of relief, of very special happiness'.[27] These two stories are superb. Cary is one of the great short-story writers.

In 1952 Cary involved himself in an artistic episode that renewed the old joy of championing Gilbert Spencer against the Oxford establishment. The sculptor Jacob Epstein had recently been commissioned by New College to do a portrait bust of their Warden, Alic Halford Smith, 'a great talker' who reminded Epstein of 'the great Humanist scholars of the Renaissance'.[28]

He was also a friend of Cary's. And Cary had long admired Epstein's personality and achievement. (The 'Risen Christ' of 1917–19 he thought 'the most powerful and unforgettable work of religious art that I have ever seen';[29] some of his own sketches are Epstein-like, and the sculptor had been a likely influence on *The Horse's Mouth*.) 'Bohemian in dress and behaviour',[30] with 'the stocky build and pugnacious jaw of the fighter', Epstein had been intensely controversial since the 'Strand statues row' of 1908, when his figures for the British Medical Association building in the Strand, London, became notorious. For Cary, Epstein epitomised the 'original artist' ('he does something to you and you can't overlook or forget it'), arrogant because he must be to overcome conservative opposition.[31]

In 1948 Epstein's 'Lazarus' was exhibited and, as usual, provoked a furore. Four years later, it had still not been sold. Perhaps it was Cary who put the idea into Smith's mind: during his third sitting for Epstein, Smith said suddenly 'How wonderful [the 'Lazarus'] would look in the cloisters in New College.' Cary spoke strongly in favour of the controversial project. Eventually the statue was bought and placed at the west end of New College Chapel. Epstein thought it 'miraculous' that 'the statue should harmonise so completely with the ancient stone walls. The lofty soaring arches seemed to continue the upward thrust of my figure.'[32]

CHAPTER THIRTY EIGHT

SEIZING HAPPINESS

1952–1954

'I am very busy'

In May 1952, Cary paused to consider priorities, soon after completing *Prisoner of Grace* and before embarking on his next novel. 'I am very busy organising my work for the rest of my life,' he told Edith Haggard. 'I find I have about 10 books in various stages and lots of loose work – I am going to decide now what it is worth finishing and what must come first. I might drop dead and what then if I'd wasted a good character . . .'[1]

It was during this stock-taking that he decided not to continue the Second Trilogy. Whatever his other reasons, one was surely recognition of the overwhelmingly difficult task he had set himself. Not only had Nimmo's political and domestic activities dominated Nina's narrative (so that it would be all too easy to bore the reader through repetition), but to have Nimmo writing about those events would make it difficult to avoid identifying him with Lloyd George.

Then he opened a letter from a fan. B. Evan Owen, a critic and writer living near Oxford, had written to suggest that Cary write another trilogy. 'Your suggestion of a trilogy startled me . . . but it has great attractions,' Cary replied. 'Unluckily I am surrounded by attractions and don't know what next to finish.' At the end of 1953 he wrote again to Owen, after the publication of *Except the Lord*: 'Yes, the new book is the second of a trilogy . . . and you were certainly one of the people who encouraged me to return to my original plan of a trilogy when I was doubtful about continuing with it.'[2]

Except the Lord, like *Mister Johnson*, was written with extraordinary fluency and rapidity – though, like all the novels of this Trilogy, it required considerable research (Cary employed an assistant, Cecilia Dick, who looked up historical and other facts in the Bodleian for him). Once he had solved the conundrum of the second novel's content, his imagination flashed.

There were interruptions. One came early in 1953. 'Be happy,' Cary had often told Edith Haggard. He had picked up the expression from his youngest son, George, who died on 9 January at the age of twenty-five.

There had been at least one other recent family illness. Jack had been stricken and Cary had spent time with him at Burnside in July 1952: 'his only joy was sport shooting fishing going round the hedges with a gun. Now he is in bed with a heart attack . . . He is surprisingly patient. Every one ought to die suddenly – bang. I pray God I do – I should be a bad invalid.'[3] Jack was to outlive his elder brother by a decade.

The previous Christmas all four sons and their families had gathered at Parkers for Christmas, but at the end of 1952 there were several absences: one of Cary's grandsons, John, had pneumonia; also 'George is ill and I am anxious about him. I must go and see him to-day.'[4]

George Cary was already established as a brilliant Classical scholar. Very tall, with a 'striking face' and reserved manner, he was admired by contemporaries at Cambridge for his 'most individual and distinguished mind and . . . delightfully lovable personality'.[5] He had been awarded a major postgraduate scholarship and then a Fellowship by his College, Trinity, after achieving a First in his Tripos. Then, after immersing himself in ancient Persian literature, he had turned to a subject suggested by his brother Michael (a fine Classicist before he became an administrator), the medieval tradition of Alexander the Great. His marriage to Mig was very happy; their son was two years old.

George's health had always been fragile. Apparently nobody had suspected a congenital heart ailment – though, as an undergraduate, he had often suffered from headaches, pain in one arm, and bouts of severe lassitude;[6] and a military medical examination in 1948 had detected an abnormality. He fell seriously ill towards the end of 1952. Heneage Ogilvie consulted experts in the field of heart surgery, but at that time heart surgery was insufficiently advanced for an operation to be thought justifiable.

After his death, George's mother-in-law Frances Phipps wrote to Cary: 'if he had lived he would have been an invalid, and in fact, I know that this last year had kept him face to face with that fear, even before his last illness. And that would have been an unbearable life for him and for those who loved him.'[7]

For Cary, George's death, two years after Trudy's, repeated the double blow of his mother's and stepmother's deaths. He was stoical. But a letter to Jack Fischer gives a glimpse of his grief: 'Not many boys of 25 have had obituaries in *The Times* . . . He had really a brilliant mind, one of the best of his time. And so strong and energetic a character. I miss him terribly with his warm heart and his enthusiasm – we loved to be about together on common hobbies.'[8]

When George's *The Medieval Alexander* – still a standard text in the field – was published a few years later, Cary often spoke of it, with affectionate pride.

Back to work. There were lesser interruptions, like his own ten-day stay in hospital for a hernia operation, and a stay with Mig to help her go through George's possessions; but in May 1953, he reported that his novel was 'going great guns'[9] and, by August, a few weeks before he left for America, 'The Book is finished and gone to Elizabeth yesterday in its last proof . . . The next is in my head and will be very amusing to do.'[10]

A few weeks before, he had travelled to Edinburgh for a second happy occasion there – to receive an honorary Doctor of Laws degree from the University. (The private irony behind this compliment – Ll.D. to the recipient of a Fourth-class BA in Jurisprudence – must have salted his pleasure.)

In July 1952, Cary had spent 'a marvellous two days sailing at Cowes' with Heneage Ogilvie 'in a new boat he has designed . . . He himself fell overboard'.[11] Like his holidays with Mary Ogilvie, such family occasions were increasingly precious to him. In 1954 he had another holiday with Heneage, his last, with an exhilarating sail off Bosham, 'steering in a thunderstorm, under a black sky, in a black sea'.[12]

He often visited Burnside, too, in the early 1950s, enjoying the quiet company of Jack and Shiela; relaxing into rural life: 'This is *real* country – nothing much has happened since William the Conqueror. No tourist ever finds Wadeford . . . I slept about 6 hours last night right off and even now I am too sleepy to think.'[13] Those short visits surely influenced the subject and mood of *Except the Lord*; its depiction of country life; its distanced nostalgia (even in the phrasing, several passages echo autobiographical statements; for instance, Nimmo says, as Cary said, 'I have few memories of my mother, but they are vivid.'[14])

In June 1954, Cary was visited by Jack Middleton Murry and his wife Mary. A few years before, Murry's son Colin, then an undergraduate at Oxford, had 'received a note from Joyce Cary inviting me to have dinner with him. He had, it emerged, been corresponding with my father'. (Murry had initiated the correspondence by asking for the words of a song Cary had once taught him at Oxford, 'One Meat Ball').[15] Colin Middleton Murry had found Cary 'remarkably like some ancient Roman general just returned from a successful desert campaign' –

> a small, intensely alive man, with a prominent hooked nose, receding hair and darting, bird-bright eyes . . . He seemed to know everybody who was anybody, and he talked nineteen to the dozen. This was just as well because, to start with, I was rendered mute by shyness. However, by the time I had finished my third glass of Beaujolais I was sufficiently sloshed to be able to tell him that I doubted whether he would ever write another book as good as A *House of Children*. This had the effect of bringing him up short. He stared at me long and hard, lifted the bottle to see how much was left in, and then said: 'There speaks a Middleton Murry. Go ahead and tell me why you think so.'

After that, conversation flowed, Cary was 'a good listener but an even better talker, bubbling with anecdotes, many of them – alas – unprintable'. And he sent Colin Murry away with a comment that lodged 'like a seed of thistledown in one of the crevices of my memory: "Oh, fame's pleasant enough, but the rapture lies in the writing. You'll see."'[16]

Dan Davin, who, with his wife, the Cecils and Mary Ogilvie was at the dinner-party Cary gave for his old friend in June 1954, recalled that the evening 'went off agreeably and the Murrys themselves were charming; but it was clear enough to Joyce and Murry and the rest of us that too much time and separate experience had divided them for too long and that the old warm friendship of their youth could no more be revived than youth itself'. [17]

Murry's diary: 'There was Joyce, for all the world just as I had left him in 1912, and there was I, not at all (I felt) as he had left me. He had had a long and happy married life; I a succession of disasters. He had achieved, deservedly, a huge success, and was enjoying it vastly, sadness is: we now just don't understand each other.'[18]. To Dan Davin, Murry had seemed 'worn and scarred with life'.[19] To both Murrys, Cary had seemed very fit, 'abounding in physical energy'.[20]

Except the Lord

Except the Lord, published almost simultaneously in London and New York, was as much a surprise to Cary's publishers as to his readers. He sent them a brief description:

> In this second book we see where [Nimmo's] ideals took form. We are given his childhood as a poor boy, son of a horseman on a farm . . . Left-wing ideas are truly called radical. They have very deep roots in Protestant religion. The book, therefore, is not about politics, it is about a child's reaction to poverty and social injustice, and the effect upon that reaction of a religious education. That is, it is a study of character, and so of that region of feeling and idea in which politics have their beginning and achieve their ends.[21]

Walter Allen's report began 'It is disconcerting to this extent, that it gives us Nimmo as he was in the years before he married Nina, so that the two novels do not overlap; we don't, as perhaps we had anticipated, get a second version of the incidents of *Prisoner of Grace*; so that the two books appear to have little in common.'[22] This novel 'shows Cary at his gravest and most austere,' Allen felt. 'There is none of the famous exuberance, no farce, indeed no comedy; it is – or promises to be – his most direct and explicit rendering of the Nonconformist spirit. I say "promises" because I assume it will be followed by a further piece of Nimmo's autobiography.' (He would again be surprised.)

Allen argued that 'within the limits' Cary had set himself, *Except the Lord* was 'completely successful and a very fine novel with several memorable characters of a dignity moving because of the austerity with which they are presented'. Georgina he thought 'one of Cary's most striking representations of children, this fierce child with her sense of responsibility whose love for her father and brothers and sister is expressed through a sort of baffled indignant criticism of them'.

'The book must be a memoir a passionate tale of his experience his mother his sister killed by poverty the social order of his day and his fearful resentment continued by his religion – the *fountain* of his mind and opinions.' Cary's notes also show his concern to find the appropriate style for

Nimmo's narrative. Like Wilcher's it is to be 'biblical . . . the repetition as in psalms the rhetoric and quotations.' Moreover, he culled characteristic expressions from his copies of John Wesley's *Journal* and Lloyd George's *War Memoirs*.

'What I want is the connection between the poverty and the religion as the motive of the *scenes*.' Ruskin (the father's authority figure), Bunyan and the psalms were to be prominent; and the Italian romantic revolutionary Mazzini is referred to often in the notes as Nimmo's political inspiration. The novel's title, taken from Psalm 127 ('Except the Lord build the house: their labour is but lost that build it'), is a firm signpost to the theme's nexus of Protestantism and left-wing politics.

'Chesters feelings of *deprivation throughout the book* . . . Chester gets to feel that religion *is* opinion of people'; but also 'Chester is aware of his tendency to exaggerate i.e. to lie . . . '[23] As with one of Browning's dramatic monologues, it is necessary for the reader to follow the text's clues closely as Nimmo's personality expresses itself. Like all Cary's protagonists, he is certainly no collation of all the virtues; but neither, as he wangles in his and democracy's service, is he a villain.

Allen: 'It's a very packed novel, but everything is subordinated to the theme of the religious nature of man as manifested in the direct intercourse of man with God that is fundamental to nonconformity. In various ways Cary has dealt with this theme on many occasions; it is in fact *his* theme. But until now he had dealt with it indirectly . .•. '[24] The very purity, the poignant directness of evocation in this 'classical' novel, make its successor the more shocking.

'how happy we were'

Immediately after Christmas 1954 Cary 'set out to make a serious beginning' on *Not Honour More* but by 10 February, he was facing difficulties, not all of them literary. Pipes had burst; 'I have been flooded out and had to tear up floors . . . Now I have to put everything back again just when I am most anxious to get on with the book which is giving me trouble'. Meanwhile Gerald Wilde 'is raging through Oxford full of drink and complexes and distracts me . . . I know he will descend on me some time and I shall have to take him to the station and fire him out of Oxford. Gullys in real life are a pain and a curse.'

In spring, though, a welcome distraction. Edith Haggard arrived in London on a month's business trip. She had visited him briefly in Oxford during 1952, and they had seen a lot of each other during his recent three months in America. Now he went to London to join her in the old Stafford Hotel.

At the end of that week she visited him in Oxford. He had invited the Cecils, Mary Ogilvie (who had recently been appointed Principal of St Anne's College, Oxford) and Isaiah Berlin to dinner. 'What a good evening it was – even the shrimps had a special taste and the champagne tap gave a wonderful performance,' he wrote just before Haggard returned to America.

What good talk we had afterwards – I wish I had recorded it, it was full of stories that ought to be told. I am very glad indeed that I had the idea of taking you back to town . . . It was bad enough leaving you alone last night, to face the riot to-day and all the turmoil of packing. What a blessing we had our last delightful, gay, talking evening to remember – something that no one and nothing can take from us – a piece of permanent happiness, secure against even time and the income tax. My love, my dear, take care of your precious but fragile self . . .

And a few days later: 'I am missing you a great deal . . . It is driving me to work and I have done really an astonishing amount in the three days since you left . . . I have a . . . hole in my life which you have left – to be filled with loneliness – or work. I shall do a *lot* of work in the next year.'

She was upset by his reference to 'our last . . . evening together'. He responded:

My dear, you say I have hurt you by saying that evrything must come to an end . . . it is the way I console myself for loss or disappointment. I enjoy things so much at the time . . . It is a phrase like that of the soldier who cheers himself up in the trenches by saying One only dies once. That feeling lies very deep in my way of life. I don't expect too much from it – more than it can give. I know that all real happiness is dangerous because it can so easily be lost – and leave you weakened in face of a damned tough world. I have never run away from happiness – I think that is wrong and mean and stupid but when I am happy I never forget I cant forget that it is a lucky chance that gives it to me. I think I am the happier for that feeling – so deep in me that I think it goes very far back into my childhood. I seize anything I can get of happiness and appreciate it all the more because it is rare and lucky. I delighted in your stay here and everything about it . . . You have great powers of enjoying simple things which makes you a delightful companion. My dear, how happy we were and what fun we had . . .

By July, Cary had completed the first draft of *Not Honour More* – 'the book is all there – and it is a most exciting book to do'. But it could not be serialised in a popular journal, as Haggard had suggested: 'It is too violent and too cruel – I am going to kill Nina and I rather think I shall cut the poor darlings throat. I *feel* that she must have a brutal end. I was going to shoot her but then Jim has tried to shoot Nimmo already – and more shooting wld. be repetition . . . Besides I *feel* there must be cruelty. I must break through the damned crust.'[25]

He wrote that in Stuttgart. 1954 was a year of extensive lecture tours through Europe: he visited Italy in March, Germany in June and July, France in October, Scandinavia in November and December. In all, he spent more than four weeks in those travels.

For several years, Cary's novels had been widely published in Europe. Swedish and Czech translations in the 1940s had been followed by French and Norwegian (from 1950), Spanish (1951), Italian and Dutch (1953), German and Finnish (1954). Cary had helped some of the translators, notably the French translator of *The Horse's Mouth* when she had trouble with Gulley Jimson's racy idiom.[26] Some of the translations, like the Swedish *Prisoner of Grace* in 1953, had sold very well, and Continental critical opinion of Cary's novels was generally positive by 1954. He was encouraged by Curtis Brown to make lecture tours, and the British Council now recognised in him a good literary ambassador.

The Italian tour was exhausting yet enjoyable. His tour of Germany was also demanding and in October he joined Enid Starkie in Paris, where he was to deliver a British Institute lecture (she was there for the Rimbaud Centenary). Starkie noticed that 'there was something wrong' with him: 'I remarked how badly he was walking and suggested he should ask a doctor about it . . . '[27] He passed it off. But towards the end of November he scribbled in a letter to Edith Haggard from Oxford that he was beginning to feel that the proposed American lecture tour in 1955 might be an 'awful gap in a man of my ages life when he hasnt anyhow enough life to finish what he set out to do in his time. And do you know I've really been tired once or twice lately in quite a new way. I was quite startled by the feeling that my feet were too heavy for my legs. I don't remember that ever I had had it before.'

Just over a week later, however, he was writing gaily from Stockholm: 'This affair is the most strenuous yet – I thought the first day – a lecture, a lunch, a seminar, a cocktail party, another lecture, a radio interview, and a dinner party starting at 7 and ending at 12 – wld. kill me.'[28]

And he chortled over his Swedish publisher's revenge on the Stockholm critics. After they had all fallen over themselves to praise Cary, the publisher 'read to them over the dessert what they had said about my first Swedish translated book 11 years ago. This was embarassing for us all – the expressions of some of the critics when they saw their turn coming and tried to remember how rude they had been – the cautious glances at me to see how I was taking it all, were pure film, by Orson Welles.'[29]

Not Honour More

He had sent the typescript of *Not Honour More* to Michael Joseph before his Scandinavian tour, and on his return found a copy of Walter Allen's report.

> I think this is splendid. It rounds off the trilogy beautifully, and is as thoroughly unexpected as *Except the Lord* was. Moreover, by bringing in the third member of the triangle as spokesman it brings in too, in full force and voice as it were, a type of man the author had not presented nearly as fully anywhere in his work before. If Chester Nimmo is the God-intoxicated man, Jim Latter, who tells the story of this novel, may be regarded as his opposite: the man who has no use for inspiration or intuition but proceeds according to his sense of duty and justice, the archetype one might suppose of the soldier. He seems to me as brilliantly rendered, in the very tones of his speaking and syntax, as any personage Cary has presented in the first person. He is utterly convincing . . .

The novel, Allen went on, was not only 'an account of the final stage in the intricate relations between Nimmo, Nina and Latter' (so concluding the series of events begun in *Prisoner of Grace*); it was also 'a remarkably vivid reconstruction of the General Strike as seen from two points of view, Latter's and

Nimmo's, which is implicit . . . The invention is brilliant: just as now when one thinks of the political history of the years before 1914, it is scarcely possible not to imagine Nimmo taking a part in it, so I feel that for me my notion of the General Strike is henceforward going to be coloured by Cary's imaginative rendering of it.'[30] To recreate the General Strike of 1926 Cary drew on his own memories and reading, and notes by Cecilia Dick, his research assistant; he also consulted his neighbour, Judge Donald Hurst, on legal issues.

A particular influence on Jim Latter's personality and thought was D. H. Lawrence, as several notes indicate: 'cf Lawrence and his hatred of the intellectual *the clever* who can make black white in order to wangle the people and himself'; 'D. H. Lawrence is in battle with the concept i.e. Russell, Keynes, and appeals to the blood.' Latter is also like Horace Plunkett: 'monomaniac gives all his money to the movement'. And Cary may have had in mind *Othello* (the subject of Helen Gardner's 1955 British Academy lecture[31]) as well as *Coriolanus*. And of course he reincarnated aspects of the early Cock Jarvis.

Cary expected his readers to recognise how ironic is the novel's title. Juxtaposing love and honour in a military context, it quotes the last words of the Cavalier poet Richard Lovelace's 'To Lucasta, Going to the Wars' ('I could not love thee (Dear) so much,/Lov'd I not honour more'). Cary noted that *'Jim's honour* . . . only artificial. Highest honour to sacrifice oneself. Afraid of public opinion – of what people will say. this "honour" is artificial, trivial, it is *really cowardice.'* 'Jealousy a key.' *'Jim's hatred of Nimmo devouring – absorbed.'*

In his political behaviour Latter is an idiot – culpably innocent. 'Jim must have rules'. And that, in a world where change is ineluctable, where frequent adjustment is necessary, results in confusion, anger, hatred, violence.

As in all Cary's first-person narratives, the style of *Not Honour More* helps to judge the protagonist: 'his style shews unbalance'. While revising the novel in July 1954: 'Style. Begin officialese but throw in . . . slang In quick passages slide into exclamatory . . .'[32]

Radical uncertainty about the novel's meaning – critical response was confused and sometimes hostile – resulted from failure to read the text with sufficient care. Cary wrote in a letter that 'The curse of the world is the fanatic, the partisan; who will not even try to understand the other man's case. The rage and hatred of the fanatic is based on fear, the fear that after all he mayn't be right.'[33] Elsewhere he called Latter's a 'Fascist mind',[34] and in the Preface he wrote for the German translation (the publisher was fearful, presumably because he suspected the novel of endorsing extremist values), he commented that Latter 'states the fundamental conservative view'; both he and Nimmo have a case that deserves to be considered, for the clash between them is that 'between fundamental temperaments and these temperaments are permanent in the world'. The only hope for peace is compromise, tolerance.[35] But that, of course, is to side with Nimmo's point of view (though not necessarily the man himself); for of the two, only Nimmo believes in democracy, and, as Cary argued in *Power in Men*, only democracy fosters compromise and tolerance.

Walter Allen foresaw that *Not Honour More* and the Second Trilogy as a whole, would be widely misunderstood. For him *Not Honour More* offered

> triumphant proof that its author is still growing, developing, experimenting, is still, within the context of his view of life, unpredictable. *Except the Lord* had an absurdly silly press. It was evidence, I thought, that reviewers as a body were a long way behind Cary, still stuck somewhere about *The Horse's Mouth*. I suspect they will never quite catch up . . . And if that is not being alive and creative I don't know what is.[36]

CHAPTER THIRTY NINE

CRASHES

1954–1956

'I have got off lightly'
With Michael, Peter, Tristram, and their families due to arrive the following day, Cary wrote on 23 December 1954 that he was 'in a whirl of presents', and would also 'have to clear my room of some of the mess as I shall be sleeping here during the week. I rather enjoy sleeping among my work tho I am always in danger of falling out of bed.'[1] In mid January he was due to fly to Greece and Cyprus for a three-week lecture tour, under the auspices of the British Council. Mary Ogilvie, noticing how tired he looked, persuaded him to go on a short holiday to Brighton over the New Year.

Back in Oxford, he settled down to a final revision of *Not Honour More*. Edith Haggard had noticed several discrepancies in the text he had sent her. For instance, early in the novel Latter had referred to the time as eight o'clock; 'he says he's been blacked out for over four hours, yet on page 4 . . . he had returned at six o'clock'. That was easily remedied. More seriously, she found herself confused about the ages of major characters: 'How old is Nina at the moment? She has a young child and it would be stretching it a bit for her to be nearly sixty, wouldn't it? I had a feeling she was in her early fifties, but Nimmo is seventy and Nina was seventeen at their marriage and he thirty, it doesn't work out right.' The confusion was caused, Cary confessed, by 'a bad mistake at the beginning of *Prisoner of Grace*. Nina was born in 1876, Nimmo in 1857. There are nineteen years between them. This doesn't agree with their remarks at the beginning of *Prisoner of Grace* which were meant to be changed but got missed.'[2]

As critics have noticed, several such discrepancies remain in the Second Trilogy, especially in *Not Honour More*. These seem to indicate strain and haste in composition. But Cary's anxiety to amend the text where possible shows his concern about textual detail. Although he argued in *Art and Reality* that accuracy in minor details is much less important than effective expression of a novel's theme,[3] he habitually drew plans of his imagined houses, and set out chronologies for characters, to try to avoid errors. Only one of Edith

Haggard's points did he reject firmly. She wondered if the passage 'came running into the room who hit me on the jaw and knocked me black' should read 'came running into the room, hit me on the jaw and knocked me black'. Cary's reply indicates how carefully considered were all aspects of style in his first-person novels: 'Your suggestion is better grammar, but the thing as written is Jim's grammar. As you see throughout, I have to suggest a man without much literary ability and yet not vulgarly illiterate. This was rather difficult to manage and I found that clumsy grammar was one of the best methods.'[4] He may also have felt that if some errors remained in the text, they would serve to discredit Latter still further.

He was glad that Haggard had 'enjoyed the thing' but was keen to hear what Elizabeth Lawrence thought of it. Clearly he was apprehensive about the novel's reception. He was probably disquieted, as much as relieved, by her opinion that 'it will rank with your strongest work. And for the public it has the kind of pace and rumbustiousness that are associated with you. Jim Latter engages one's sympathies deeply.'[5]

On Sunday 16 January, Cary was aboard a British Airways Viscount at Heathrow Airport. It was a foggy morning.

> The pilot turned onto the wrong runway, an old takeoff strip no longer in use. Roaring into the mist at eighty miles an hour the plane suddenly swerved violently and plowed into a steel barrier.
>
> The Undercarriage collapsed. The two port engines flew off and all four of the propellors sailed through the air. The fuel tanks burst open and Kerosene washed around the wrecked plane, which also lost its tail.[6]

The Viscount had been thrown completely round by the force of impact, yet only two of its thirty passengers were injured. Cary was not one of them – or so it seemed. He was interviewed by a journalist immediately after the accident – as he had been in Montenegro forty years earlier, after his first escape from explosive death; and he was just as nonchalant.

Cary flew on to Greece by the first possible flight, later that day. When expressions of relief and concern reached him in Athens a few days later, he responded calmly and humorously, even flippantly. Enid Starkie was told 'How nice it was not to be burnt.'[7] After admitting to Betty Fischer that, just for a moment, he had thought he was 'finished', he added jauntily, 'I think I was about due for a crash after 100,000 miles, so I have got off lightly and start my second 100,000 with a reasonable security'.[8]

Cary set out determinedly to enjoy himself in Greece. He was enthusiastic about Delphi; 'most strange and unexpected with its little temples and ex-voto shrines . . .' 'I've also been at the Acropolis and I'm going to Mycenae to-morrow if the weather is not too wet.' He was delighted when his sightseeing was unexpectedly extended by the cancellation of a lecture in Corfu, where 'there was some threat of political opposition'. He was, he insisted, very relaxed. 'I am being very idle and do no work at all – get up late and doze half the afternoon. I think I needed a holiday and hope I am getting the good of it. But the chief immediate effect is to make me still lazier.'[9]

The novelist Francis King, a friend of Liddell's and a member of the British Council, was often responsible for escorting Cary and so saw a lot of him in Athens. Cary, he remembered, 'repeatedly said that he was none the worse after the near-fatal plane accident' and his demeanour was usually 'extremely pleasant' – but there were occasional outbursts of 'petulance'. It seemed to King that, although Cary 'put up a cheerful front, he was not really enjoying the tour and wanted to get back to his desk . . . All in all, I got the impression of a man work-obsessed'.

Nor did Cary's conversation and lecturing impress King:

> . . .I was disappointed, as were other people who met him, that, although he would talk about the practicalities of writing in general and of his own highly idiosyncratic methods of writing in particular, he was reluctant to venture beyond these parameters. His lectures . . . broke no new ground and were not notable for the sort of brilliance of composition or delivery that so often conceals that kind of lack of originality.

Uncharacteristically, Cary failed to observe social niceties: he did not tip his Athenian driver, and did not write later to thank King for his help.

The evidence suggests that Cary was suffering, however courageously he concealed it, from delayed shock as he soldiered on through his holiday and the duties that paid for it. His distress was most startlingly registered by an act of physical courage emblematic not only of the 'rider' in him but of protagonists stretching back from his most recent, Latter, to Cock Jarvis – and behind them all the figure of Arthur Cary, famous in Inishowen for his dangerous rock-jump. Francis King:

> At a party given by (I think) the then Librarian of the British Council . . . [Cary] asked me to show him the lavatory. He was absent so long that I wondered what had happened to him. Suddenly he appeared through a door to the terrace. He explained that he had got locked into the lavatory, and had not wanted to bother people by shouting, and had therefore climbed out of the lavatory window and made his way along the ledge to the terrace. Even at about half his then age, I should never have attempted anything so hazardous. [10]

And this at a time when he was very weak; so weak that, as he later admitted in notes for a doctor, he had found himself unable to open a door with his left hand soon after arriving in Athens. 'A few days later while climbing ruins,' those notes continued, 'sudden fall due to collapse of left leg. Also nearly fell in descending from lecture platform. Legs very stiff. Noticed now general weakness in legs.' [11]

That perilous journey along the ledge to the terrace was perhaps an attempt to push himself to the limit, to restore morale by 'seizing safety from the nettle danger'. And he did bring an honourable conclusion to the job in hand, giving eight lectures for the British Council in Athens, Salonica, Nicosia, Limassol, Famagusta. It was his last lecture tour.

The physical and emotional strain of the plane crash and those three weeks in Greece and Cyprus did not deprive Cary of his capacity for subtly ironic humour ('the most Irish thing about him,' said Enid Starkie[12]). On one occasion Francis King was talking to him about the difficulty of writing novels while working full-time for the British Council. Cary said, 'with what appeared to be complete sincerity and not as a joke: "You should try to find a well-to-do woman to marry. That's what I did. Then you can concentrate on what is important."'[13]

'the whole thing turns on him'

In May 1954 Cary had received a letter from Spencer Curtis Brown: 'A man called Norman Rosten in America has asked us to forward you this letter because he is taken with the idea of writing a play based on *Mister Johnson.*' Curtis Brown was not impressed by the project – he had 'never seen how this book could make a play' and doubted 'if Mr Rosten is the man to try, since his record to date is depressing'.[14] This was not the way to influence Cary. He read the enclosed letter sympathetically, pleased by Rosten's enthusiasm (Johnson 'is a delight and a wonder . . . I love him and wish dearly to put him in a play'[15]) and by the fact that he was a poet, with five books of poetry already published.

A contract was drawn up, including (at Curtis Brown's insistence) a clause stipulating that Rosten submit his final version to Cary 'before it is offered for production'. To Rosten Cary explained that the clause had been added in case the play 'contains anything that I couldn't pass. As you understand, there are all kinds of angles upon government service, and the West African situation generally, which are important to me but which would probably not be known to you.' He would be happy to answer questions and to give what help he could.[16]

According to Dan Davin, those who knew Cary well were amused by the arrangement: 'Joyce was only able to criticise another man's work – novel or play or film – in terms of what he himself would have done'.[17] He received a copy of Rosten's script early in January 1955, and, before leaving for Greece, sent a preliminary response to Rosten: 'The play is very interesting from a dramatic point of view, but it will require a certain number of alterations in details about Service life. Also I find the dialogue between Bulteel and Rudbeck a bit comic in the wrong way.'[18]

He told Edith Haggard, on his return from Greece, that he was rewriting that dialogue. In fact, he was rewriting a good deal: it took him well over a month of hard work. As was his habit in revision, he cut the play extensively – 'If they want it longer they can enlarge the native scenes which cld. bear extension'.[19]

Rosten, perplexed by the delay in signing a contract, telegraphed to say 'Producer and Director have integrity intelligence enthusiasm . . . While awaiting your notes and doing revisions may we not clear up contracts . . . Anxious not to jeopardise production plans by protracted delay'.[20]

Cary dug in his heels:

> His dialogue between the Englishmen is extraordinarily unEnglish and also uncharacteristic, and naturally he has little idea of the way a political officer works in Africa, Another problem is that he puts the story in the present

time. It refers actually to a situation thirty or forty years ago when I was in the Service. This has also required changes.

But Rosten's framework remains and the play would not have been done without his initiative. I don't suggest, therefore, that my name should appear as joint author. I must only insist that my revision is accepted before we sign contracts.

Between ourselves I think the play as I have handled it is a very much better job, it moves at about twice the pace.[21]

The final remark is revealing, and endorses Dan Davin's reservations. Cary had been unable to forget his own aspirations as playwright, or to refrain from imposing his own aesthetic principles on another man's interpretation of the novel. Already he had allowed himself to be drawn far beyond his original intentions, at a high cost in time and energy. He sent off the annotated and heavily revised script on 15 March and simultaneously a letter to Rosten justifying the changes.

Rosten replied objecting to the excision of 'several wonderful lines from your own book in the final scene' and expressing concern about Cary's assumption that the revised version was now 'the play'.[22]

In his letter, Cary had skirted a much more fundamental difference of opinion: although he disagreed, very strongly, with the playwright's general conception and treatment, he had merely questioned Rosten's use of offstage 'Voices' as 'an ancient and rather corny device, for suggesting some cosmic significance; but that's just what you don't want. You've got a simple and powerful tragedy. Why trim it down into some kind of metaphysical fable? And I needn't remind you that there's nothing critics hate more (and they're quite right) than the phony sublime.'[23]

But when in June he received a list of questions from Rosten, his fundamental objection suddenly blazed out. He attacked a statement in Rosten's introductory description of the play that 'We have here an allegory – a picaresque comi-tragedy – that calls for bravado and style. In the air, there will be clouds, echo of drums, voices, and laughter; on the ground, simply the thin scrub area, a constant glaze of sun – all part of the destiny of a land trambling between reason and fantasy, the present and a faint primordial wonder.'[24]

> I see in your script you write of [the] play as allegory.
> I think this would absolutely ruin it. The book is not an allegory – not on your life. Allegory seems to me absolute poison in literature or drama, because it destroys personality. Characters just become stock figures as in Everyman. And you cease to sympathise with them as people. It is crude – you can't express anything but the crudest meanings in allegory. It is pretentious. It says 2 x 2 = 4 with more fuss than Einstein stated relativity. It is a champion bore.
> I do very much hope you agree with me here. I'm sure the producer will agree. I speak from a pretty long experience of all kinds of writing.[25]

He was now ambivalent about the play. He felt his advice was being disregarded. Apart from other issues, he wanted Johnson to be utterly central – 'the whole thing turns on him. Everything else is background and subordinate'

– and he wanted the action to be 'quick and simple to convey the *native* characterisation of Johnson, Bamu, Ajali, Benjamin, etc'.

However, he did not wish to prevent the play's production. When he replied to a letter from Edith Haggard – who had been dragged into the affair – he showed how uneasy he was. 'I WANT THE PLAY DONE and fully appreciate what I owe to Rosten for all his trouble[26]'.

When Rosten finally agreed to accept all the revisions to the text, and not to identify the time of action as 'the present', Cary gave way and signed the contract. It was almost too late. And Cary made it clear that he still expected to see the final script some months before the play opened.[27]

Saved at the last moment, the production of Rosten's *Mister Johnson* went ahead, and Cary was informed that rehearsals would begin in mid December. He wrote to Alan Collins of Curtis Brown, New York, to express his pleasure; but also to enlist support: 'I have every confidence in Rosten, we understand each other and you can be sure that I am not going to be fussy about the script, but frankly the original . . . so far as it dealt with British characters, was impossible . . . Rosten promised a finished script this month, but it has not arrived yet . . . I just want to make sure that I do see it while there is still time to discuss points.'[28]

At the beginning of December Cary received a copy of the final script, with a request from Rosten that he return it as quickly as possible. He told Collins that the characterisation of Celia was still unsatisfactory, and that the 'voices' still upset him. But, very busy with other work, he decided not to criticise the play any further. It was to open in New Haven, Connecticut, at the end of March 1956; go on to Philadelphia; then move to Broadway.

Collins went to a performance in Philadelphia. He was impressed by the 'terrific performance given by Earl Hyman' as Johnson. This young Black actor, just beginning his career, was playing the role with such intensity that the director was trying to 'calm [him] down'.

The New York reviewers were respectful – with the one, unfortunately crucial, exception of Brooke Atkinson in the *New York Times*. Ruefully Collins told Cary 'there is something in what he says, "that it does not come into sharp focus and make a single impression". This is in part due, I think, to the heavy emphasis placed on the Rudbeck-Celia-Bamu theme which tends to draw interest away from Johnson.'

Cary must long since have rued his profligate expenditure of time and energy on the play. But his loyalty was engaged – especially as several American friends, including Edith Haggard, had supported the production financially and publicly he stuck by it. In mid April he learned from Collins that the play was 'limping along at a weekly financial loss'[29] and he readily agreed to allow his royalties to be halved so that the New York run could continue. Various explanations had been given to Cary for the play's 'precarious state' – 'opening in Holy Week, and all the fuss about segregation which has made New York rather tired of any negro problem. But I suppose the real reason was that it did not get hold of people.'[30]

At the end of April 1956, *Mister Johnson* folded after running for a month on Broadway. Rosten found consolation in the audiences' response: 'It is a triumph of Mister Johnson that we overwhelm the audience; they love it – and we get ovations every night; but the *larger* public has simply not responded at the box office. Is it their fear of tragedy? Does Johnson hold up some mirror of guilt?'[31]

Cary's last letters to Rosten after the New York closing, were sympathetic, if somewhat tactless: 'I can't say how sorry I am for you and for Hyman in this disaster which is so little deserved . . . Every original work of art runs against this problem, that critics cannot understand or appreciate real originality . . . You remember Chekov's troubles in his beginning. He was considered one of the worst playwrights ever to attempt the stage.'[32]

For Rosten and Hyman the play was valuable experience in their respective careers. But for Cary the episode was a fiasco; a waste of time and energy fast running out.

'Gulley gets away with everything'

As Cary struggled with Norman Rosten's dramatisation of *Mister Johnson*, he was also becoming entangled with the complications of a project to film *The Horse's Mouth*. Just as his earlier attempts at writing plays had fuelled his involvement with the play, so his film work of the 1940s now became a strong influence. Moreover his son Tristram was becoming prominent as a composer of film music. Cary was very proud of Tristram's 'triumph with his music for the new Guinness film',[33] *The Ladykillers*, in 1955. He enjoyed hearing all that Tristram could tell him about personalities and events in the British film world.

Proposals for films based on his novels had reached him intermittently from the early 1950s. In March 1952, for instance, Hettie Hilton of Curtis Brown, London, had told him 'Word has gone round that you have delivered *Prisoner of Grace* and you have no idea how the American film companies are yapping at my heels for a sight of it.'[34] Four years later, in March 1956, Jerry Wald of Columbia Pictures wrote to Cary expressing interest in *Charley is My Darling* (true, he had not read the book – could Cary tell him how he could get a copy?); he was also interested in filming *The Horse's Mouth*.[35]

In fact negotiations over filming *The Horse's Mouth* had been going on for over five years, involving several producers and directors, British and American. In April 1954 a Wardour Street producer had written to ask permission to try to persuade Charlie Chaplin to portray Gulley Jimson; there were problems, he confessed, in that Chaplin usually wrote and directed his own films, 'a director of genius' like John Huston was essential, and so was £500,000.[36] Nothing more was heard of that project.

In the same year, the actor Alec Guinness, his reputation soaring after a series of admired film performances, began a filmscript based on *The Horse's Mouth* and discussed the project with his friend Ronald Neame, producer of *Oliver Twist* and recently director of *The Card* (based on Arnold Bennett's novel), both starring Guinness. They decided to approach Cary for an option. Neame lunched with Cary in Oxford on 9 September 1954; a contract was drafted.

The first problem came when Neame had difficulty persuading Rank to finance the film. After hearing nothing for eight months, Cary wrote to Alan Collins of Curtis Brown, New York, noting that Neame's option would expire at the end of November. Would a Hollywood contract be possible then? 'The story, of course, will have to be changed, but I am quite ready to do that.'

Before Collins gave his opinion, Cary wrote again:

> What I want to do now is to tell you my own suggestions for making a film story. I want to be sure that I have priority in them as they seem to me very likely to occur to someone else.
>
> The three chief characters in the book are Gulley Jimson, Nosey Barbon, devoted disciple, and Coker, the barmaid who nurses the old man.
>
> The problem for a film is a good woman's part, and also the end. My suggestion for the end simply is that Coker and Barbon could console each other . . .
>
> As I say, I am giving you these suggestions merely in order to secure them for my own story. Neame's (between ourselves) is quite different. He wants to give the thing a happy ending. Gulley gets away with everything. This could be done, but mine is much better. I didn't suggest it to Neame because he so loved his own. Coker could be a magnificent part for a character actress. We can throw in a child too, if required . . . [37]

Hettie Hilton informed him on 15 November that Neame was 'full of contrition that you have not heard from him for so long. He and Guinness have worked out a full screen play, on which it was and still is their intention to ask you to work'. Neame had 'severed his connection with Rank', was committed to making a film for Fox immediately, but was 'absolutely confident that he can fix up *The Horse's Mouth* starring Guinness, who will also be free, next Spring'. [38]

Cary wrote to explain this situation to Collins, adding that his son Michael 'says we shld. not give Neame an option unless he can produce a contract and I agree with this. I doubt very much if he will get a *good* contract in England . . . What do you advise? Ranks were offering £4,000 . . . which seemed small for a book that is known all over the world.' [39] Next day he received an apologetic and optimistic letter from Neame; Metro-Goldwyn-Mayer, for whom Alec Guinness had just been filming *The Bridge on the River Kwai*, had agreed to finance the project. [40] Cary told Neame he could go ahead, but Collins wrote recommending an approach to Hollywood directors and followed this up by saying he had now advised Hettie Hilton that '£4,000 is, in my opinion, a low price for your most saleable book for films'. 'Your desire is to secure money for the boys [Cary had allocated all proceeds of the film to his sons] and . . . I can't see that this property will ever be worth less than it is now and may well be worth more.' [41] Collins had already received two enquiries from Hollywood, and in the following months there were at least two British approaches too.

Neame and Guinness were equal to the challenge. On 19 March Collins informed Cary that the *New York Times* movie section had run an item 'quoting Ronald Neame as saying that he intends to make *The Horse's Mouth* for Metro in London later this year starring Alec Guinness. He further says that he and Guinness have already done the script.'[40] Almost simultaneously Hettie Hilton told Cary that Neame was now offering £7,500 for a renewed option and that 'Guinness will only make this film in conjunction with Neame, and using the script which he and Neame concocted together'. She reminded Cary of Guinness's 'enormous reputation in America'.[42]

Cary was annoyed. 'These reports are cropping up all the time,' he told Collins. 'Neame had an option for one year . . . and the option expired. My children refused to renew the option and the rights are therefore wide open. There are offers buzzing about on all sides, but at the moment, none has been accepted.' He wrote again on 4 April: 'Tom Morahan, a producer over here, is also after *The Horse's Mouth*; that's to say, he has joined the queue . . . Of course if Neame wants to do the thing and can pay Hettie's price we will deal with him, though I didn't much like his suggestion for a script.'[43]

But it was checkmate, as first Hettie Hilton and then Collins made clear: 'If you decide finally that you do not want to do business with Ronnie it may mean not selling the book for a long time';[44] MGM 'don't want the book without Guinness'.[45] Cary sent a final appeal to Collins: 'I hear from Hettie that the American offer . . . has fallen through. She seems doubtful if they will even pay the option. I wish I knew what had been going on, and if Neame queered the pitch with suggestions that he had rights or had some claim when he had neither. He is now in the market again, but of course he won't offer much. What do you think I should do?'[46] Collins replied that *The Horse's Mouth* was 'a hard property to make a film of for the reason that you need a producer, a director and a star who all feel personally compelled by it. That always presents difficulties and tends to keep the price down since you can almost never develop a competitive situation. I would think £10,000 would be a good price for it and probably you ought to accept £7,500.'[47]

Cary signed the contract at the end of September 1956. Shooting began late in 1957 (on the set Guinness learned that he had won an Oscar for his performance in *The Bridge on the River Kwai*). When it came out on 1958, *The Horse's Mouth* was selected for the Venice Film Festival and for the 1959 Royal Film Performance; the script was nominated for an Oscar.

The film's reviews were mixed, however – ranging from extravagant admiration to contemptuous hostility. Some critics praised Guinness's bravura performance. Some did not: 'an external performance, never truly felt', 'turning Gulley Jimson's pantheistic exuberance into mere eccentricity', 'completely at odds with the original Gulley Jimson'.[48] Several critics complained about the filmscript and its tacked-on 'extremely pointless finale'; one assailed Guinness's 'merciless butchery of a fine book to make a spluttering British farce'.[49] Many critics found the film disappointing – 'too much caricature, too much slapstick, too much general *bonhomie*'; 'the film is guilty of every fault which the novel successfully dodged'.[50]

For Cary the episode was another show-business fiasco; a second draining away of precious time and energy. While he was writing *Not Honour More*, Win Davin had observed that Cary's behaviour became notably Latter-like.[51] His conduct in regard to the film was similarly unreasonable. Complaints about the manoeuvring of Neame and Guinness are unconvincing when he had himself politicked; annoyance about a fake happy ending rings hollow against his readiness to compromise with Hollywood's crassest commercialism. But he was now a sick man.

CHAPTER FORTY

ILLNESS

1955–1956

'don't write me off yet'

Just after his return from Greece and Cyprus in early February 1955, Cary had dislocated a finger in a bad fall while staying with Michael and Isabel in Blackheath, after the birth of their fourth child, Kate. They urged him to seek medical advice immediately.

Once back in Oxford, however, Cary found himself very busy. There was a domestic crisis when his housekeeper gave notice; Mary Ogilvie quickly found a replacement, 'rather young and I fear she is partly moved by some notion of the glamour and she will find me very silent absorbed and remote in my own house, I read at meals and meditate all the time on work and don't like interruptions even to ask what I wld. like for dinner'.[1]

He threw himself into the task of revising Norman Rosten's *Mister Johnson* script. 'This has taken all my time and energy for a month,' he told Edith Haggard on 15 March. Then he spent a week writing two short stories, 'A Hero of our Time' and 'Out of Hand', and on 22 March started work on an article about Westminster Abbey for *Holiday*. From 26 March to 4 April he went on holiday with Mary Ogilvie in the Scilly Isles. On his return he corrected typescripts of the two short stories and 'Westminster Abbey', and started an article he had promised Henry Kissinger, then Editor of the Harvard journal *Confluence*. Meanwhile problems continued with Rosten's play. On 19 April he travelled to Swansea to lecture on 'The Novel as Truth', and a week later told Edith Haggard he was writing another short story while revising 'Policy for Aid'.

And only then, after this sweep of frenetic activity, did he pause to pay attention to his physical state. Perhaps he feared that his writing would be curtailed before long: during the three months since his return from Greece, his left hand and foot had continued to weaken and, as he mentioned nonchalantly a little later, he had had several more bad falls. After examining him, Cary's doctor immediately set up an appointment for him with Dr W. Ritchie Russell, Consulting Neurologist to the United Oxford Hospitals.

In preparation for this examination, at the Radcliffe Infirmary on 26 April, Cary wrote a dispassionate summary of his general physical condition: 'Left foot flops when walking and is apt to trip. Left hand weak and apparently wasting. In any attempt to run, both legs are apt to seize up. Slight shakiness in hands, especially left hand. Sudden falls, due probably to a slight trip and inability to make any quick compensating movement, or to cramp. With care, and a stick, these falls have lately been avoided.'[2]

Russell's report to Cary's doctor was not optimistic. He noted extensive atrophy of muscles in the left leg and left arm, and fasciculation (bunching of the fibres) in many muscles on both sides of the body. Diagnosis would be easier in a few months; but it seemed likely that Cary was developing motor neurone disease (one of the names for what is also called, more technically, amyotrophic lateral sclerosis, and, more popularly, progressive muscular atrophy).

Cary requested a second opinion, and was sent to an eminent Harley Street neurologist. This time there was no room for doubt about the seriousness of his condition and he had to cancel the American lecture tour planned for September. But he contined to make light of his illness. On 27 April, the day after Russell's examination, he travelled to London to attend a lecture by Helen Gardner to the British Academy, dined that night with the Dover Wilsons, and on 29 April attended the opening of the Royal Academy's Summer Exhibition with his daughter-in-law Beth. He also continued to keep all his engagements, lecturing to the Oxford English Society and the Exeter College Literary Society early in May, and spending two days in Wadeford with Jack and Shiela.

With characteristic reticence and stoicism, he had said little or nothing about his illness to friends; only Edith Haggard had had cause for mild concern, asking him about 'the finger still being stiff, and your sprained foot which you had not mentioned before'.[3] Colston Leigh's announcement that Cary's lecture tour had been cancelled was a bombshell for Curtis Brown and Harper in New York. But Cary told Jack and Betty Fischer on 21 May, that he still hoped to visit them: 'I've not by any means given up hope even now, I cld. easily come over and give a few lectures in or near New York, just to pay my fare . . . So don't write me off yet.'[4]

Cary travelled to Bristol on 24 May, the day before he was due to record a radio talk for the BBC. There he discussed with Dr Malcolm Campbell a new experimental treatment using calcium versonate that was being offered him. Campbell 'was quite frank. He said that his method is empirical and I gathered he has cured only one person.' Because no beds were available at the Churchill Hospital, Oxford, Cary would become a patient at Stoke Mandeville Hospital in Aylesbury (about twenty miles west of Oxford) from 31 May to 19 June.

'They gave me 5 transfusions last week of some chemical in saline,' he wrote on 7 June, 'and they're going to give me 5 more this week and then some physio-therapy . . . I get rather impatient as you may imagine lying quite still for 5 or 6 hours while the needle is in my arm but I read a lot and think more.'[5] He also made notes of what was going on round him; as always, they began to turn into stories even as he jotted them down.

The child taken to see father in physio-therapy room, fascinated by strangeness. The strangeness which is not depressing because it is purposeful and *calm*.

The triumph of walking a step the concentration of the walker (man tired of life learning to walk again) . . .

He is worried about his wife and daughter, but especially his grand-daughter. He is trying to *arrange something* – and he *uses me* to take messages. I am ill too but he doesn't realise it.

And he meditated on his new situation of intensified loneliness:

A serious illness is another world. You can't even describe it. If you tried, people would no more understand you than if you talked about the moon, in Chinese . . .

But since they know you are ill, since you are suffering and in danger of death, perhaps a horrible death, you can't just pretend that nothing is the matter. That would be as bad as trying to explain the real situation. Your real feelings. They would be embarrassed. They wld. think you were playing some kind of game with them.

Back home, he recorded moments of immense pleasure at being still alive: 'A warm summer night with a heavy scent in the air–tobacco plant mixed with something too indefinable – too rich and sweet like old malt. The sky was a strange blue, dark but not clear, and the stars came out by ones and twos very bright, and then faded suddenly.'[6]

The treatment at Stoke Mandeville had no discernible effect. On 26 June, Russell was still unsure whether it had been of any benefit at all. His examination that day found Cary's arms unchanged but his legs weaker, and a continuous 'fluttering' in his chest. Cary, Russell noted, had not been at all upset by the treatment, insisting that he was very well 'in himself'.

But during the next few months there was rapid deterioration. Cary's family and friends became alarmed. He wrote to Russell on 7 August to say he had completed the second course of versonate tablets, and to ask advice about possible vaccine treatment. While Russell was sceptical about the use of vaccines to try to cure obscure diseases, he did not think such treatment would do Cary any harm; but would prefer him to finish the course of versonate tablets first – advice which Cary accepted.

He had not yet accepted his death sentence. He had not even told his family the experts' diagnosis of his illness. If indeed he had amyotrophic lateral sclerosis, then his muscles would waste away steadily, from the extremities inwards, and he would be lucky to last another two years. Could nothing be done? Would a different treatment be more effective? Was it possible that his symptoms had a completely different, and remediable, cause?

'It struck me,' he wrote to Russell in mid August, 'that aluminium is a soft metal and is cleaned with steel wool – how much aluminium do people swallow with their soup.' This line of reasoning led him to conclude, a few months later, that he might be suffering from lead poisoning. 'I have discovered about forty feet of lead pipe in my own house which has been shut off at some time at the top so that, for an unknown number of years, it has been full of dead water . . . If the water was contaminated, it would explain why each treatment seemed to do me good, and then after returning home I began to go back again.'[7] He approached the Counties Public Health Laboratories, who agreed to analyse a sample of the water. The report was unequivocal: 'All metals (Iron, Lead, Zinc, Copper, Manganese) are *absent* from the water.'[8]

'visits of old friends'

Cary now had seven grandchildren. Kate's birth in February had delighted him ('the first female Cary in fifty years'). In the same month Robert, second child of Tristram and Dorse, was born. In July, Cary managed to travel to London for Robert's christening, and in August Michael and Isabel and their children spent two weeks with him at Parkers. He enjoyed sitting in the garden with Kate rocking in her cradle beside him.

Lucius, his eldest grandson, was now a boarder at the Dragon School, and Cary looked forward to his regular visits. 'Lucius is doing *very* well at school both in work and games,' he told Edith Haggard, 'and is the nicest small boy – I love having him.'[9]

If Cary's zest was unimpaired, by the end of 1955 his physical deterioration had gone far. He could no longer write or sleep upstairs, after several falls on the stairs, and the downstairs back sitting-room had to be converted into a study. In September, just before his next examination by Russell, he was forced to ask the Department of Neurology at the Radcliffe Infirmary 'If I come by taxi to the door would it be possible for me to have a wheel-chair in the hospital? I can manage fifty yards or so on my own feet but no more, and last time I was completely exhausted by the time I reached the consulting room.'[10]

After he had examined Cary at the end of September, Russell, recognising that the versonate treatment was helping little if at all, informed Cary's physician, Dr Kirkham, that he had now decided to try the vaccine treatment earlier suggested by Cary.

So Cary went back into Stoke Mandeville for a week at the beginning of October, and was given a course of the toxoid *crotalus terrificus* by intravenous drip. At first the signs were hopeful. He returned optimistic to Oxford, just before Edith Haggard's arrival.

She stayed for a week at Parkers. Worried by his news, she had told him at the beginning of August that she would like to use her annual leave to visit him, suggesting that, to save embarassment, he tell Alan Collins that the visit was his suggestion. Cary refused to do that: 'I hate any kind, even the most innocent kind, of deception with my friends. Its one thing to keep personal secrets even among friends but another to start any kind of mystification.' But he told her he would very much like her to come. 'I shall work in the mornings and perhaps all day if the fit takes me,' he warned her, 'because it is a fit I can't put off and because if I don't put things down they get lost': he had 'a new novel in hand, as well as the Clark lectures for next year'. But 'what I like above all is to know I have a friend in the house and in fact since I have been so house bound in the last two or three months I have enjoyed nothing so much as the visits of old friends.'

After she had left on 20 October, he wrote

> I *did* miss you last night – no one to pour my bath, light my fire – and tuck me up. You don't know what a pleasure it was to end the day like that and to have that last peaceful talk with you afterwards by the fire light. I suppose it is true as one gets older one does become more like a child – like poor old Tolstoy one simply longs for a mother again. I am by nature, as you know, rather a lone ass of the desert . . . even as a small boy I used to spend . . . hours alone exploring or simply dreaming. I suppose after my mother's death I got used to having a certain independence whether I liked it or not and learnt to do without company. But also I was a gang leader and loved family enterprise and parties and crowds and noise. And I always had very close friendships. I was in love at nine with a cousin and I was generally in love from that date. I needed affection to give and receive it almost as much as I needed the hours alone for thinking and dreaming – perhaps all the more because of those hours.
>
> And thats why it was so delightful to have you in the house and *know* you were there all the time so that when I came out of my working time I would find you. I can't thank you enough my dear for coming over at such an expense of time and money just to give me those days of love and happiness. You are an extraordinary woman only to think of such an enterprise much less to carry it out.[11]

Among the thoughtful, generous gifts she had brought him was a silver whistle which he could hang round his neck and blow to summon help.

'a good year'

On 8 November Cary informed Russell that, much to his surprise, his weight had increased by about three pounds. 'I am puzzled myself by this improvement as there is still a good deal of flutter and my strength has declined, but there is no doubt about it.'[12] However, when Russell next saw Cary, a month after the vaccine treatment, he had to inform Kirkham that their patient seemed to be getting slowly worse. 'There is no reason to suppose that our most recent treatment did any good.' His only positive observation was that, although Cary had 'lost more muscle', his right hand 'remains excellent'.[13]

Cary, convinced that the versonate treatment had helped him, requested another course by intravenous drip. This time he was admitted, on 16 November, to the Chesterfield Nursing Home in Clifton, near his old school, so that Dr Campbell could supervise the treatment personally. Again Cary judged that the treatment had improved his condition; but Campbell told Kirkham this was 'wishful thinking'.[14]

Christmas came, with its ritual of cheerful festivities, the family around him. It was, Cary told Edith Haggard, 'one of the most successful in family history – even the pantomime was unusually good'.[15] He told Jack Fischer that 'all the sons came and four of the grandsons' – and he went on to describe his sons' latest achievements. Michael had just been appointed a member of the British Delegation to NATO, and would be spending two years in Paris from spring 1956. And 'George's posthumous work, to be published by the Cambridge University Press, will come out in a few months. Altogether we have had a good year.'[16]

In January he suffered from a bad bout of flu. Then, because of his debilitated condition, he suffered the additional discomfort of a broken rib, when his portable typewriter slid back on to him while he was typing in bed. By the time the rib had healed, it was clear to everyone that he would not be able to leave the house on his own again. A wheel-chair became necessary. He would not walk again. His family were desperate with helpless concern. On 18 April 1956, Tristram wrote to Ritchie Russell:

> we are all so worried about my father, Joyce Cary, that I thought I would ask your advice.
>
> The main trouble is that he will do nothing himself to alleviate his difficulties. He feels, I think, that he has been given up as hopeless, but characteristically this doesn't depress him at all, at least not outwardly or enough to damage his work. But it is impossible to get him to seek help except when he has an actual accident . . .
>
> Trying to establish a possible timetable of the course of the disease, we found that his symptoms correspond with those of Amiotrophic Lateral Sclerosis, and this seems to have a fearfully short course before it kills its victim. This amateur diagnosis is probably wrong, but we are seeking any means to try to help him and forestall possible events. His decline since Christmas has been dramatically rapid, and I was shocked when I saw at Easter how weak he is.
>
> Do you think it would be a good idea to arrange for regular visits by a doctor who could at least relieve ordinary aches and pains as they turn up, and in my opinion be a great psychological comfort simply by making his visit regular. The suggestion would of course have to come from the doctor, because my father would say it is unnecessary . . .
>
> If you have occasion to see him, please don't tell him that I wrote, because he would not want me to go behind his back. Our great friends, the Davins of 103 Southmoor Rd, whom I believe you know, are my father's constant helpers, and will do anything to cooperate in any scheme to help him. Miss Millen, his secretary, is also a nurse, which is a great help, but I still think he should have the feeling that a medical man is thinking of ways to help him along.

And he ended, in love and anguish, 'My mother died so tragically of cancer that it seems almost impossibly unfair for my father also to be struck down by a malignant destroyer.'[17]

Russell agreed that regular medical visits were desirable. It was a matter between patient and doctor, but 'there is no reason why you should not press your father or his doctor to make some firm arrangement . . . I am afraid your diagnosis is perfectly correct and your father fully understands the position and is facing it with remarkable courage . . . I am sorry we can do so little for him.'[18]

CHAPTER FORTY ONE

SUFFERING & MIRACLES

1955–1956

The Captive and the Free
In the early stages of his final illness, Cary had suffered two disappointments in his professional life, both in genres that were not central to his creative achievement – drama and film. In both cases he had struggled, and failed, to exert a strong influence over projects not his own. The strain and uncertainty caused by his illness, the frustration of having to give up cherished plans, the unsettled existence imposed by the several periods of treatment in hospital: these undoubtedly contributed to his difficulty in reasserting priorities.

But now, in the final stages of his illness, he seized the reins and rode for victory, with all his horsemanship, and against all odds. The two failures were triumphantly redeemed by two successes, in the two genres he knew best. For the last time, he worked on a treatise and a novel together – Art and Reality and The Captive and the Free.

Both titles are emphatically dualistic, yet each work attempts a final resolution: The Captive and the Free of the two themes that had dominated Cary's thought and writing – injustice and creativity; Art and Reality of the two fundamental aspects of his life – experience and its interpretation in art.

Cary did not begin writing The Captive and the Free until the late summer of 1955, nearly a year after completing Not Honour More. In May he told Edith Haggard 'I haven't started a new novel yet but the ideas are bubbling'. Two months later he still could not 'make up my mind which to go with', and it was mid August before he announced 'I have a new novel in hand, as well as the Clark lectures for next year . . .'[1]

During those final months of indecision, while he was undergoing his first treatment in Stoke Mandeville Hospital, he had been working at a putative novel closely related to his personal situation called 'The Firing Line'. '. . . the *experience* of being old . . . the world of illness and sudden death . . . the sudden change of view by the man devoted to his things who becomes ill and must give them up.'

The protagonist of this story then became an old woman, Kate, 'trying to hold on to her life and to make them believe she isn't really ill . . . She is *fighting the illness* . . .' 'Dying makes her feel essentials . . . ' 'The Firing Line' now drew to its centre the issue of miracle cures; 'Kate *expects* miracles. ie expects the thing to stop',[2] and began to evolve into *The Captive and the Free* – which, Cary said on his deathbed, 'is about religion and deals partly with faith-healing, for faith-healing raises some fundamental problems of religion . . .'[3]

Edith Haggard had been making enquiries in New York about developments in treating diseases like Cary's. 4 November 1955: 'To write that I am sorry not to have news of some miracle cure is to indulge in a kind of understatement that is preposterous.'[4] But Cary did not believe in 'what are called physical miracles. That is to say, any interference in the natural order of things, so far as it is revealed by scientific research.' His reasons were grounded firmly on his long-established myth: 'God could not abolish the power of doing evil because if he did he would also have to abolish the power of doing good. The world would be a machine . . . if physical miracles were possible, there is no reason why any child should die in agony. To believe in their possibility makes God responsible for that evil.'[5]

Nevertheless he was often tempted to pray for a miracle; especially when, as news of his illness spread, he received letters suggesting 'crank' cures or advocating faith-healing ('I have put your name on the distant healing list of the Glasgow Psychic Healing Centre'[6]). Some of these letters he added to the research notes he was now accumulating about the phenomenon of faith-healing and about religious denominations like Christian Science. He explored the Anglican Church's views, and read relevant books (like C. S. Lewis's *Surprised by Joy*).

The connection between faith-healing and the media increasingly interested him as he read and thought; and it became thematically important as the novel developed. Billy Graham, then very prominent, was only the latest in a long line of publicity-exploiting evangelists; Cary included references to him, as well as to Buchmanism, the 'inner light' movement that had fascinated him in the 1930s. Also mentioned in the novel are Hitler and Mussolini, spellbinders who had used the media to promote hatred through religious fervour. And Bertrand Russell, who 'wants publicity all the time. describe him . . . mischievous and silly . . . cold hatred and arrogant'.[7] Russell, first sketched as Professor Hoopey in *Arabella* twenty-five years earlier, returns in *The Captive and the Free* as a minor character, the physicist Sir Robert Tinney.

The central character of the novel was, at first, Kate Rideout. In the final version she is an important secondary character, whose return home from hospital poignantly fictionalises Cary's just before he began the novel: 'All those familiar things with their associations', her beloved furniture, 'had suddenly become hostile . . . They did not give anything to her weakness, they made demands on it. They demanded attention . . . The room was like a grave-yard, full of family tombs. And it had been waiting for her, to bury her in . . . a loneliness, a darkness, far more remote from the living world than the hospital.' And Kate turns to her daughter Joanna, 'Don't leave me.'[8]

In writing this novel, Cary purged himself of self-pity and resentment. An early version of the character later central as Preedy was the faith-healer John Pargeter. The novel opened

> Pargeter was the son of an Irish Squire, burnt out and ruined in the twenties. The family had been resident landlords, popular with their tenants. The house was burnt by the village boys, none over sixteen, in league with the cook who acted as spy. They were sent for the purpose from Dublin and enjoyed the job. What a triumph for four lads from the slums, to burn even a small mansion, to soak fine things in petrol and see them blaze; to watch the gentry, educated people, standing helpless in their night clothes while their house was destroyed.
>
> Old Pargeter tried to start again. He came to England and bought a small farm. But his heart was broken, as much by the senseless injustice of his fate, as the loss of the place. He began to drink . . .[9]

But Cary quickly discarded this version, with its expression of personal bitterness and its lapse into the negative obsession with injustice that had characterised Jim Latter and the early Cock Jarvis. He countered with a resurgent emphasis on creativity: 'The man who stands aside – the mystic etc . . . is a traitor to some cause of good. There is always some affirmation, some good, to be done.'[10]

Cary was 'deeply engaged' with *The Captive and the Free* from August 1955: 'the new novel has laid hold of me and carried me off to a new world of feeling and among a lot of new people.'[11] He often spoke of the novel to Dan Davin as 'his most cherished and difficult project, something that was to be the capstone of his work. The title itself gnomically summed up his view of the condition of man . . . ' He wanted the novel to express 'his maturest views about religion, the summa of his whole belief as an artist and a man'.[12]

The title was indeed deeply significant. Like 'The Horse's Mouth', it had evolved in the 1930s and carried with it an explicit concern with religion and, as Cary's notes from late 1955 indicate, an accretion of the fundamental beliefs first articulated polemically in *Power in Men*. In religious terms, freedom (Cary wrote now), exists only 'in love, in creation, in the knowledge of what is'. Nobody can escape a degree of mental captivity (if only by 'some kind of duty'), but 'he may still be free in his general grasp of the whole situation and his attitude to that situation':

> He can accept that world as he knows it to be. He can understand that any good he gets out of it is a gift. That love and beauty which make life worth living are inseparable from the evil of its contingency. He must *know* God, he must live *in* God.
>
> The real captivity, that is, is in superstition, hatred, fear, egoism, jealousy, in all the blind passions good and bad which bind men even when they realise they are being bound and driven; and in *ignorance*, in a bad map, a bad idea.[13]

It was probably while he still intended Kate Rideout to be his protagonist that Cary was planning the work as a trilogy – his third, to complete a tripartite analysis of the human condition focussed progressively on art, politics and religion. But he soon realised that his illness would not permit him to complete such a big project. Traces of the trilogy intention remain (for instance, in the lack of a central character, the division of interest between Preedy and Syson, whose conflict, of innovator and conservative, repeats a dominant element of Cary's trilogy form). These, together with the incursion of sub-themes (like the role of the newspaper) and a large number of undeveloped characters, weaken unity and coherence. The wonder is that a man so ill managed to drive the novel so close to his intention. 'I shall die if I don't finish this book,' he joked to Win Davin.[14]

Cary was profoundly impressed and disturbed by Dostoevsky's *The Brothers Karamazov*, and one chapter in that novel became especially influential on *The Captive and the Free*. It is 'that great scene . . . where Ivan argues against his brother Alyosha's faith, the chapter called "Pro and Contra"'. This episode, Cary wrote, 'is a monument to the integrity of the artist who loved truth a great deal better than he knew. And it also shows us how deep and strong were the effects of Dostoevsky's religious education as a child.'[15]

In *The Captive and the Free* Cary institutes a similar debate, between Syson and Preedy. They represent, too, to some extent, what Cary, in some of his late articles, called 'the split mind of the west' – a recurrent 'battle between science and religion.'[16]

Even more influential on Cary's novel were the references in the 'Pro and Contra' chapter to the deaths of children. Of *The Captive and the Free* Cary wrote '*Centre is faith*. Dostos child. The child dying in pain . . . Problem of evil. Why does God allow it. Can God do miracles. If he can, why does he allow suffering . . . '[17] 'Dostos child' is the child Ilusha – one of several examples of the deaths of children – which, for Dostoevsky, as for Cary, epitomised cosmic injustice, and raised ultimate questions abut the existence and nature of God.

In *The Captive and the Free* the death of a child provokes a climactic epiphany for Syson, the Anglican priest, whose spiritual odyssey and final views are close to Cary's own. Angered because he can no longer believe in 'a God of love and truth who hated cruelty and injustice', hating the charismatic faith-healer Preedy who has forced him to recognise in his conventional Christianity 'a muddle of wish-fulfilment and time-serving', Syson sinks towards nihilism, yearning to be 'a puppet pulled about on strings'. Then, suddenly, he receives a letter from a woman whose child has died: 'you were right, and God could not save my poor child. But still you were wrong too for he can do miracles. He has done one for me, for he has given me forgiveness and peace.' And Syson apprehends the only sort of miracle Cary could accept: 'the miracle of God's love in the world'.

It is a truth that Preedy, the spellbinder, apprehends too, in his own way. In a moving sermon near the end of the novel, he raises his face to the sky as the sun breaks through clouds, and points to the wintered trees around him:

'See the trees are standing as if dead. To themselves they are dead. But the sun will not allow them to die. He sends his light to their roots, and there, unknown to the bare branches, the sap is rising, the life they deny is rising through their cells.

'So the life rises in the souls of men, whether they would or not. And so the light of grace drives the sap through dead words and brings them to life, to a new harvest of beauty and at last the seed. So men by grace realise their living power and their death.'[18]

Art and Reality

At the end of 1954 Cary had accepted an invitation to deliver the 1956–7 Clark Lectures, at Trinity College, Cambridge. Among his predecessors were John Middleton Murry and John Dover Wilson.

Very busy, and knowing that he would base his lectures on the series he had given in Oxford in 1952 ('The Novel as Truth'), he did not start preparing his text until August 1955. By then his illness was severely reducing his time and energy, and after *The Captive and the Free* took fire he found it difficult to give attention to other writing. By the middle of March 1956 he was getting worried: 'those Cambridge lectures hang over me – Cambridge says if I can't give them myself they'll have them read. So they must be done.'[19]

He struggled on. It was his duty to fulfil the undertaking. Moreover, the six lectures had importance for him beyond their prestige and the scholarly applause they implied: 'he hoped to bring together – did eventually bring together – and expound in theoretical form the views about art and life which he had so stubbornly pondered for so many years and which his novels presented in fictional form . . . these lectures became for him another summa, parallel with and eventually competing for time with "The Captive and the Free".'[20]

In late October 1956, barely able to write at all, he was still revising the last three lectures. Meanwhile his nephew Robert Ogilvie (youngest son of Freddy and Mary, and an undergraduate at Clare College) had been reading the first three on his behalf. The series ran from 19 October to 23 November, and was well attended.

Published in 1958 as *Art and Reality*, Cary's revised Clark Lectures were widely and sympathetically reviewed though Elizabeth Jennings, like other reviewers, assessed them as 'a very personal picture of the world . . . altogether too subjective' in the handling of 'technical terms such as "the real", "the concept", "intuition", and so on.'[21] These comments recognised recurrent characteristics of Cary's treatises. *Art and Reality* is undeniably discursive, repetitive, sometimes confusing; but it is also lively, stimulating, and peppered with enjoyable personal illustration. As J. B. Priestley pointed out, it is 'more like eager intelligent talk than a carefully planned essay, and it is no worse for that'.[22]

In *The Nature of Experience* (1959), Sir Russell Brain wrote 'Cary combined the training of an artist with experience as a novelist . . . Not being himself a philosopher, he did not achieve a coherent philosophical view of art nor did he analyse what he meant by intuition or symbol. Nevertheless his book is full of pregnant insights . . . '[23]

Much in Cary's discussion had been voiced earlier in articles and Carfax Prefaces. What is significantly new is his stress on intuition and memory. This was surely a recognition, as he faced death, of the deepest source of his own writing.

At the beginning of his career, he had sought desperately for intellectual coherence, convinced that it was essential as a foundation for his literary achievement; and perhaps it was. But now, as he looked back, he saw the even more fundamental importance of 'the dream world in which we spend so much of our lives, not only when we are asleep. I suspect that the inspirations of the artist and scientist both arise from the logic of the subconscious, carried on by a method far more rapid and effective than that of conceptual logic, by short cuts of pure association.'

One of his examples came from a writer and a novel that had long impressed him: Tolstoy's intuition, through noticing the embroidery on his dressing-gown, of 'a woman's life, a woman's mind, and woman's world' – the essential theme of *Anna Karenina*.

Another example was drawn from his own experience when, in 1953, Elizabeth Lawrence had taken him 'round Manhattan Island in a steamer' and a woman aboard attracted his sympathetic and speculative notice. Weeks later he awoke 'at 3 o'clock in the morning with so acute a sense of a story that I turned on a light and wrote two or three key pages of talk and description'.[24] This evolved into the short story 'A Good Investment', which culminates in the protagonist's agonised recognition that 'the very things for which he loves [his wife], her unselfishness, her strength of affection, are breaking her health, and may take her from him'.

Revising that story, Cary had noticed a repeated physical detail that suddenly connected the fictional wife with 'that girl on the Manhattan boat . . . and I realised where the story had come from . . . the essentials were straight from the subconscious where they had formed themselves round an intuition . . . ' And that intuition, Cary continued, 'was itself conditioned by an attitude to life'.[25] He would surely not have been surprised by a suggestion that behind the girl on the boat stood Trudy; and behind Trudy, the mother who had died more than half a century before.

'I've got to carry on and do it myself'

In April 1956 the American scholar and critic Andrew Wright began a six-month stay in Oxford in order to prepare a book about Cary's novels. Characteristically Cary's response had been generous and welcoming: 'I should be delighted and most flattered that you should write a book about me, and if you want any material or references I should be eager to give them . . .

As for biographical facts, ask anything you like.'[26] He was even better than his word, replying 'fully, thoughtfully and frankly' to questions in Wright's letters during the year before his arrival in Oxford.

He gave Wright his vacated upstairs study as an office, and told him he was free to read and use any material he found there or in the attic. Wright went to Parkers almost daily, and was deeply impressed by the 'unstinting generosity' of this 'extremely busy man', his friendliness, his 'entire candour' – 'most people conceal or withhold some at least of the facts. Cary did not . . . We became friends, and I shall always think of knowing Joyce Cary as one of the luckiest and best things that has happened to me.'

Cary, he perceived, was 'fully aware of the imminence of his own death,' but remained 'vigorous in spirit', 'a generous and lively man who gave and responded to affection'.[27] Other visitors at that time were not always aware that their host was ill, so effectively did Cary exercise his self-control.

Edith Haggard arrived at the end of May for another short stay. Distrusting aeroplanes, she always travelled across the Atlantic by boat. Although this cut down the time she could spend in England, it enabled her to bring several trunks of clothes – on this occasion, they acompanied her in a taxi up from Southampton.

'How lovely it has been these nine days while you have been here – a time to remember as a high spot,' Cary wrote afterwards. 'And what I appreciated so much was you brought your best frocks and put them on for me. My only regret was I couldn't parade you round town, and ask people to see what a woman had come to see me. A really high-toned woman who did high-toned things as naturally as she breathed.'

But she had been deeply upset to see him so weak and ill, and from New York wrote emotionally. He responded 'I saw your letters getting more distressed but thought it better . . . to say nothing . . . If anyone offers me sympathy my instinct is to recoil and say . . . "I'm feeling fine." And this isn't all pride, its a precaution. I've got to carry on and do it myself. No one on earth can help me in the real fundamental situation.'

He told her about events that cheered him up. W. H. Auden, championed by Enid Starkie, Lord David Cecil and Nevill Coghill, had recently been elected Oxford's Professor of Poetry. He visited Cary 'and talked for 2 1/2 hours without stopping . . . David C. was here too – it was a good evening. At intervals A. said how he loved being here after the House [Christ Church, his college] . . . He burst out "You want to say 'Fuck the Pope'" . . . I took to him very much and hope he'll come again.' Visits were beginning to fire him seriously, however. 'I simply haven't time to waste on odd people with whom I have nothing whatever in common. I've too much work to do and too few nerve cells left.'[28]

At the beginning of August 1956, Cary wrote again to Ritchie Russell: 'There has been a great deal of deterioration in the last months, and I should be very glad of your advice about possible mechanical aids; for instance, for my hands. My right is now following the left which is almost useless at present, but I feel that you may know of some attachment which may keep it in use for a little longer . . . '[29]

Russell asked his colleague Dr Whitty of Stoke Mandeville to see what could be done, and the latter visited Cary on 11 August. He reported to Dr Kirkham that Cary was thinking of getting a hospital-type bed which would allow the attachment of springs to help his turning and his arm movements. In the event, however, Cary kept his old four-poster bed and all its memories of a happy marriage; finally accepting its replacement with a bed from Stoke Mandeville only two months before his death.

Long before then, however, he had begun a series of adjustments. The enemy's advance might be inexorable, but Cary marshalled his forces so brilliantly, planned each retreat so skilfully, that he was able to hold his ground to the last possible moment.

When he abandoned the study upstairs, Trudy's old ground-floor sitting-room, overlooking the back garden, had been turned into his study. He must have found comfort in the room's associations, as well as convenience in its situation next door to his bedroom and close to the bathroom. Julian Fane saw him there not long before he was confined to his wheelchair: 'His illness was in an early stage, not noticeable, and curable, it was hoped. He was up and about, and took me into a small study-room at the back of the raised ground-floor of his house, where he sat on a stool in front of the window . . .'[30] The Irish novelist and critic John Jordan, a close friend of Enid Starkie's, also visited Cary at this time: 'He sat on a sofa, with an Eastern immobility, a small ivory image who listened carefully but seldom spoke. Not until long after his death . . . did I learn, with a pang, that my ivory image had been dying of a progressive muscular paralysis.'[31]

He had handrails fitted to his bath, then 'metal grips fitted into the walls of the passages at various strategic points, and with their aid and that of a stick could for a time get about without other help'.[32] In fact he had two walking-sticks, one black and the other brown, and soon had to use both to get about.

From June he was increasingly confined to a wheelchair. He wore Edith Haggard's whistle round his neck all the time, to summon help quickly – especially as his breathing became weaker. He was having to harbour his strength carefully. 'As you know,' he told Edith Haggard on 22 August, 'the illness has now cut down my hours of work, so that, while I *can* work, I have to be at it nearly all the time simply to keep level.'

He invented gadgets, after consulting his doctors, to compensate for his disabilities. A sling with an elastic band, suspended from the ceiling, supported his right wrist sufficiently, as the muscles of his right hand weakened through mid 1956, to help him continue writing. When he found that the tray he wrote on tended to slide away, he had 'a special table made into which [the tray] can be fitted when I am sitting up in my wheelchair. It is really a very neat design and I am lucky enough to have a carpenter who enjoys carrying out my designs. In fact, he told Miss Millen that he always likes working out my ideas because they always do work.'

When he could no longer sit in a wheelchair for long periods, he devised a writing-board that enabled him to write in bed. Made for him by his old friend and neighbour Donald Hurst, this ingenious machine allowed a roll of blank paper to be pushed forward from one spool to another by light pressure from the writing hand. (Among the Cary papers are several of these rolls of thin paper, covered with his huge, staggering scrawl – remnants of the daily struggle to keep writing.) When he could no longer push the paper forward, the carpenter J. R. Harris, who had made the table and other furniture for Cary, modified the writing-board: 'It has just been electrified and runs on a dynamo. You touch a button and the paper jumps as far as you like. The children haven't seen it yet – they will like it too much.'[33]

Another very useful device was the nursing-hoist designed and manufactured for him by the engineer John Payne. Later patented and marketed as the 'Oxford Hoist', it benefited the sick and handicapped around the world – a result of his illness that pleased Cary immensely. It originated during a conversation in an Oxford pub during the early summer of 1956. Cary's friends Audrey Beecham and Peter Ady had joined Payne, who owned a small garage, for lunch. Deeply concerned about Cary's increasing paralysis, Beecham was describing the problem of lifting him from bed to bath and back. Payne sat meditating, head in hands, then said, 'I think I might be able to help him.'[34]

By mid August Dr Whitty was able to tell Edith Millen, Cary's secretary, that he had 'spoken to Payne's about the nursing hoist and they tell me that the model is made and needs only a coat of paint and the slings'.[35] A small crane on three wheels, suspending two slings, the nursing-hoist was used to lift and lower Cary, one sling under his knees and the other under his back, and carry him smoothly from one room to another. Cary, as an inventor himself, appreciated the machine's ingenuity; and Ritchie Russell was able to observe it in action before giving it his imprimatur.

The hoist was delivered at the end of August. By November Payne could write to Cary enclosing a pamphlet describing the advantages of the 'Oxford Hoist' ('This machine is primarily designed for the safe and easy handling of disabled persons in the hospital or at home'); he noted in a covering letter that 'improvements have been made in the light of experience gained in which connection the observations made by your goodself have been much appreciated'.[36]

But the hoist had to be used with great care if the patient was not to be jarred. Win Davin recalled an occasion when, despite preliminary practising with her children (who loved going rides in it), she narrowly missed banging Cary against a door jamb. Frail as he was, he looked up at her with a twinkle and murmured 'A man has to be very strong to be ill.'[37]

She spent several nights in Parkers looking after Cary when he was in a bad way. Mostly, though, he was looked after by Edith Millen and his housekeeper Mrs Lightburne. They had come into his service at about the same time during the summer of 1955, and gave him devoted service to the end.

That September he made his last excursions out of doors. He went on a 'last Cotswold trip' in Tristram's old London taxi (they 'spent the afternoon driving round the countryside').[38]

And on a last visit to his beloved St Giles' Fair with the Davins. They hired a wheelchair from the Red Cross, and pushed him through the noisy throng around the booths lining each side of the wide road. Knowing he was unlikely to experience it again, he squeezed every ounce of joy from the occasion, and even insisted on accompanying the two younger Davin girls, Delia and Brigid, when they went for a ride on the Big Wheel. Dan Davin: 'Although he was barely able to totter from the wheelchair to his seat, once the wheel began to turn, he was full of gaiety, laughing, eyes shining, waving to my wife and turning to each of the girls in turn, to enjoy their enjoyment.'[39]

CHAPTER FORTY TWO

LAST THINGS

1956–1957

'Seize the day'

In August 1956 Cary began to sketch illustrations for Andrew Wright's edition of *The Horse's Mouth*, to be published by George Rainbird. This project had come about largely because Ruari McLean (an old friend of Michael's who had married Trudy's niece Antonia Carlisle) was Rainbird's partner. McLean informed Wright on 8 August that Cary had agreed to do eight illustrations for the book, on the lines of his illustrations for the edition of 'The Old Strife at Plant's' (printed the year before, by Cary's friend Professor Herbert Davis, on the hand-press of the New Bodleian Library). Recalling that the illustrations had been the 'original *raison d'être*' of their project, McLean mourned 'I do not think we will ever get these, he is losing the strength in his hands so quickly'.[1]

That was to underestimate the strength of Cary's mind. He accomplished all eight illustrations, and in addition four versions of a moving self-portrait, one of which was used as frontispiece. The book's Note on the illustrations describes the circumstances of their composition:

> It was agreed that he would make the drawings on zinc lithographic plates, a medium which he had not previously used, and which has the advantage that no photographic process is interpolated between artist and public. The plates were provided and the self-portrait . . . was the first result. But he was losing the use of his wrists and hands so rapidly that he was unable to draw any more on zinc, and resorted to pencil on paper. On 1 September 1956, he wrote: 'I have now decided to do the illustrations . . . in the correct size as I found the larger ones too tiring. But I am drawing much more easily by holding my pencil in a different way between the fingers, and you can be sure of getting the set of eight quite soon. I am deliberately using a sketchy technique to go with the book.' The drawings were delivered a week later, six months before he died.[2]

However sketchy the technique – as always, Cary was able to adjust triumphantly to contingency – there can be no doubt about their liveliness, their freshness. In one, Rubens-plump Sara is seen emerging, delectably self-conscious, from her bath, while fierce emaciated Gulley Jimson immortalises her. In the last of the series, Jimson, spreadeagled on air, plummets from 'The Creation' to the accompaniment of the onlookers' mirth. He will not live much longer.

Cary dedicated this beautiful edition of his most successful novel 'to my wife, in memory'. It was published soon after he died. He was shown the proofs on his deathbed, and smiled.

The self-portrait – 'a superb likeness of a suffering, wise, and courageous man: the head of a man about to confront his last, indeed his only, enemy' – puzzled one of the Davin girls. 'It's very like you, Joycie, but why do you look so grim?' 'Because I was looking in a mirror, my dear.'[3]

His physical decline seemed ever swifter. But still he fought for life – not raging against the dying of the light, but eager to wring more precious time and energy for work and enjoyment. On 9 October 1956 he wrote his last letter to Ritchie Russell: 'Do you know anything about the Zeillis Institute at Gallspach, Austria, which treats neurological conditions . . . . ? I have now had a letter from an American woman about a son of hers who, she says, has received considerable benefit. It is a sensible letter and, according to the symptoms described, the son's disease is like mine.'[4]

Russell had no knowledge of the Institute, 'and of course I should point out that if your correspondent's son is under 40 it is extremely improbable that the condition from which he is suffering is the same as your own. We have recently been trying other new drugs on your condition but I have not as yet found one which is effective. I shall let you know at once if our researches turn out to be slightly encouraging.'[12]

On 13 October, Dan Davin noted in his diary 'He can scarcely use a pen at all now. Dictates, but the voice is beginning to go. A desperate, slow tragedy. The development of this will overcast our whole winter and I fear he cannot live much beyond that.'

In November Cary went into Stoke Mandeville yet again, this time to be treated with one of the new experimental drugs Russell had mentioned. While there he answered a letter from Brigid Davin; like all his letters to children it was radiant with sympathy; and it was quite bare of self-pity: 'My darling Brigid. How well you write. When my mail came in, on my breakfast tray, I looked at all the writings and said: Who's *this* from Oxford – which professor – and I was terrifically astonished to see that it was from you. I'm writing my best now but I can't write so well as you and usually my writing is quite atrocious – poor Miss Millen has a fearful struggle to make out my M.S.S.'[6]

At the beginning of November Cary was informed that the Hebdomadal Council of Oxford University had 'resolved to propose to Convocation that the degree of Doctor of Letters *honoris causa* be conferred upon you'. When he replied that he would not be able to receive the degree, the Council 'decided . . . to have the degree voted by Convocation and this was done on 4 December'.[7]

Those who saw Cary in his last weeks were immutably touched by the experience. Julian Fane:

The last time I met him he was terribly ill. He was . . . lying in a four-poster bed, unable to move much, with a contraption of slings and pulleys to help him to lift his arms. He was thin and pale, but his complexion had kept a hint of weathered freshness that was more like a moral than a physical trait. It was difficult for him to talk: due to the deterioration of his throat muscles he coughed continually. His expression reminded me of Rembrandt's in the final self-portraits. The eyebrows were raised in the same way, as if to question once again, gently and tiredly, the harsh decisions of fate, and the mouth was drawn up at the corner into the same long-suffering, patient line.[8]

Enid Starkie: 'his fortitude and stoicism in face of death were sublime, and made him like some legendary hero of antiquity. I never heard him complain or repine, and there was no self-pity in his realization of his doom.'[9]

His death was indeed becoming a legend, and what he was thinking and feeling was of increasing interest around the world. Fleet Street, which, ironically, Cary was still anatomising in *The Captive and the Free*, led the way into his bedroom; other news media were not far behind. Captive, he maintained freedom through the simple dignity of his response.

Early in September 1956, Edith Haggard had written:

Last week I saw on the London office sales record three articles to be written by you on commission for The Daily Mail. I . . . asked what they were and if, by any chance, you were writing about your illness . . .

When the newspapers here first carried word of your illness, two weeks or more ago, Cal Whipple of Life telephoned me to ask if I thought you might write about it and, if so, Life would be enormously interested. After much discussion, we decided we could not ask you and now we find we, in a sense, out-scooped ourselves.

She reminded him that his first-reading agreement with the *New Yorker* 'precludes your writing for anyone else except in the circumstances set forth in that agreement'.[10] Clearly she was under pressure from editors anxious to exploit the glamour of a famous writer's deathbed.

Cary responded firmly but with his usual grace and affection:

The articles in the Daily Mail were articles with some reminiscence mixed in . . . When you get the carbons you will see what I mean. I thought the New Yorker priority only applied to stories and set pieces of family history, like Cromwell House . . . Otherwise I don't think it would be possible for me to go on with it. I must be able to write for the English or foreign press when they ask me . . . I haven't written any article about my illness. There have only been interviews . . .

The Daily Mail certainly wanted first publication . . . They sent a woman to sit in the house till the first article was done, so they were certainly in a hurry.

And he ended 'I am looking forward to the 'phone call tomorrow. I hope you will get through. Tristram will be here with me. He has just got another big film. My love, my dear.'[11]

Even before this the *Daily Express* had come out with a scoop, on 27

August, headlined 'If you could face your problems today as this man faces his . . . AN ASTONISHING INTERVIEW BY MERRICK WINN'. While Cary 'lay there, propped up on five pillows in a four-poster bed,' he had 'laughed a lot' as they conversed.

Death has not touched his features yet, except to shade the eyes a little, to pinch the cheeks. This it has done with dignity, even beauty.

And if death has touched his spirit it has done so magnificently. He is almost unafraid . . .

Given the chance would he barter the books he had written for a few more years of life? '"No," he said. "I wouldn't barter one. Not for 10 more years of life. It isn't that I think my books so good, but they're me and they're something I have done with my life . . . I look upon life as a gift from God. I did nothing to earn it. Now the time is coming to give it back I have no right to complain."' Finally: what was the most important thing life had taught him? '"I would leave this message: Seize the day, for there isn't much time."'[12]

'We live . . . in the creation'

During 1956, in the interstices of his work on Art and Reality and The Captive and the Free, he had written some ten short stories and half a dozen articles (including the fine retrospective meditation 'Cromwell House', for which the New Yorker paid him $2,000). On 10 October he sent Edith Haggard two of those short stories, 'The Breakout' and 'First Love', telling her 'After this I am going straight back to the novel, so I shan't have any more stories for some time; possibly till after Christmas, unless, that is, there is an urgent need.'[13] (He meant financial exigency, for he was earning his way towards death, anxious to pay all bills and leave no debt.)

Christmas came, and New Year, his last. All through 1956 his family and close friends had gathered more and more frequently around him. He looked forward to his Wednesday afternoon visit from his grandson Lucius and the Davin girls, and, as long as he could, he kept his labyrinthine serials going. 'We are old friends,' he told a reporter from Life in December 1956. 'They elected me God-papa. I told them a story over the years. One episode made Delia an Indian goddess with six tigers and a huge shield. But the one they liked best was about the man who was a bigamist 11 times.'[14]

So rapid was his physical decline now that all those close to him feared that he 'could not live till Christmas . . . But we underestimated his stubborn spirit and the force over him that was exercised by a family occasion to which he could look forward.' When the family gathered again round the Christmas tree (which he had carefully ordered well in advance of Christmas), he could not join them; when they sang the familiar carols, he could only listen from the next room; and there could be no thought of an expedition to the pantomime.

But he showed them how much he was enjoying it all – 'his presence in the adjoining room, though we were all filled with sorrow and foreboding, still radiated courage and cheerfulness and made the ritual celebrations a success against the odds, something not macabre'. Only once did Dan Davin see Cary's self-control fail. 'On Christmas Eve, his grandson Lucius, at Joyce's request, sang "O Little Town of Bethlehem". The doorway of the bedroom was open so that Lucius, standing in the doorway, could hear the piano. When it was over, Joyce burst into tears.'

The festivities over, he threw himself back into work, continuing with *The Captive and the Free* until, in mid January, it clashed with his revision of the Clark lectures for publication as *Art and Reality* – a task which, Dan Davin says, he regarded as a duty. Only then did he lay the novel aside, accepting that he could not complete it; but it was 'in the bag'; he entrusted it to Win Davin's revision and completion. When *Art and Reality* was sent off at the end of February to Cambridge University Press (and, as he had promised, to Harper's World Perspectives series for American publication), he did not turn back to *The Captive and the Free*; but continued a series of short stories that he had begun early in the New Year – 'things he knew he could finish because they were short'.

Astonishingly, these five short stories show no decline in his creativity; indeed, they are among his finest works, and secure his claim to be considered a modern master of the genre. 'It was typical of him,' Dan Davin commented, 'that these last stories should be full of an ironical gaiety'.[15] It was also typical that they should draw together themes that had preoccupied him throughout his career, and that in their very titles the word 'new' should recur.

'New Women' is a cheerfully ironic anatomy of Feminism. 'The Tunnel' and 'Period Piece', are moving celebrations of sexual love and marriage. Irony plays over all three stories, qualifying apparent simplicities, challenging the reader to sensitive response.[16]

And then there are two stories dealing directly with the themes that reverberate through all Cary's writing: injustice and creativity. And a final balance is struck. 'New Boots' is an almost unbearably dispassionate evocation of the injustice endemic in daily life. It is one of Cary's greatest triumphs. Surrounded by emblems of purity and beauty, the little schoolgirl Milly, in her new boots, is impelled by what she is – human – into violence; before our appalled gaze, she becomes a fascist, marching 'with her new discovered goose-step' around a small boy, her brother, who has built a 'lop-sided tower' of wooden blocks. She kicks it down 'with a magnificent kick'. Then 'Milly planted the boot deliberately and firmly in her brother's face. His roar became a shriek. Milly lifted the boot again and saw blood running from the child's nose. She blushed deeply and thrust out her lips in a tremor of excitement and triumph; she stooped forward hastily to look once more at the boots. She frowned with admiration and curiosity, as if she had never before fully experienced them.'[17]

Set against this, Cary's last and most powerful vignette of childhood, is a story that recreates a basic situation of *A Fearful Joy* and the Trilogies. Irony is signalled by its title, 'The Sheep'; but the irony is multiple. Tomlin is a variant of Tom Wilcher – 'he was always the one to be ordered about'; his nemesis and 'friend' Blew (significantly named) is a liar, a cheat, vindictive, selfish, evil – and a source of vitality. The plot, narrated throughout in the present tense, subjects Tomlin to inconvenience and injustice involving Blew's daughter Florrie. But, unexpectedly, first Blew and then Florrie evaporate from the hard-tried Tomlin's life. And the conservative impulse triumphs, if only temporarily, as Tomlin is left peaceful in his 'shining house', toasting muffins and unfolding his *Times* and feeling a 'gratitude beyond expression. At last he admits it to himself. "No doubt about it, I'm a sheep, a born sheep. And what luck that is, what marvellous luck."'[18] Irony crackles around Tomlin's haven; but is it not a haven all the same? Here, in one of his last works, Cary appears to vindicate the joy and creativity of the conservative impulse in his own personality; linking, full circle, with his childhood letter to Queen Victoria.

Those final stories, astringent or affectionate, superbly vigorous and controlled, have the jubilee taste of champagne. He also dictated a couple of final celebratory articles. Early in the New Year, Edith Haggard, not knowing how fast he was now sinking, had asked if he would write a short piece for *Holiday* (up to 500 words, for $500). 'The Meaning of England', a luminous glance back at his life, was in her hands within weeks. The editors of *Holiday* were 'delighted and tremendously grateful to you for writing it so beautifully, movingly, and quickly'.[19]

A more extended retrospective essay was the aptly titled 'Joyce Cary's Last Look at his Worlds', written for *Vogue*. In it, he gathered up, calmly, coolly, the folds of his varied life, Ireland, Nigeria, England, and laid out its pattern.[20]

'Soon I'll be free'

His end was near now, and of course he knew it. In the middle of January it became necessary for him to be attended by a full-time nurse; Miss N. E. Williams of the British Nursing Asociation lived in the house from then until his death. His voice was weakening. Edith Haggard, who telephoned Cary every Sunday, wrote on 18 February 'Your voice sounded very good yesterday – only at the end, I feared you were tired and hastily closed the conversation, but I heard the "Bless you" clearly.'[21]

When news of his condition reached Sarah Fischer, then twelve years old, in February 1957, she wrote with a suggestion. 'In writing,' she recalled, 'I had been torn between feeling too presumptuous telling him my idea, and thinking maybe it really could be helpful. I'm happy . . . that he didn't take my suggestion (whistling in Morse code) amiss.'[22] Far from being offended, Cary was touched. He managed to dictate a reply on 12 February, and even add a shaky signature.

My dear Sara,
       Thank you so much for your letter and its very good suggestion. The only thing is that now the laryngitis has cleared up it has been discovered that my trouble is weakness of the diaphragm, which produces breathlessness and difficulty in speech, so I am afraid whistling would be just as difficult as speaking; but Morse code might certainly help communication.

I am so glad that you are enjoying life as you grow up. In my experience, life is much more fun when you do grow up.

My love to you, my dear,
Ever yours affectionately,
Joyce Cary [21]

The second paragraph reads like a farewell. And – expecially from a man whose childhood had been ecstatically happy so often, and who was enduring a long death – like a gallant affirmation.

Two days later he could barely sign the last letter he sent to Helen Gardner. Although she was widely considered deserving of election as Merton Professor of English Literature at Oxford, the post had gone to Nevill Coghill. Cary dictated a note to say 'I couldn't tell you while people were here, but I think it was a great shame for the University that you were not made Professor. I do hope you are not taking it too much to heart; after all, your reputation is secure.'[24] Nearly thirty years later, Dame Helen, one of the most admired scholars and critics of her time, was grateful and deeply moved by that generous gesture of a dying friend.[25]

Now within weeks of death, bereft of almost all power of movement, his voice a whisper, he was still receiving visits – farewell visits now – from old friends. Some friends could not travel to Oxford. Jack Middleton Murry had written a poignant letter at the end of August 1956 reminding Cary of their meeting in 1954 when 'real communication' had not been possible. He had thought over their meeting for some while and 'came to the conclusion that you were a real creative artist, and I was not. You lived in the world of your imaginative creations, whereas I – but what I do doesn't matter . . . I felt you were, in the best sense, self-contained . . . But I do want to say how much I cherish the memory of our old friendship . . . '[26] Murry was himself ill when he wrote; he was to die within months of Cary.

Other friends who did not live in Oxford – like Spencer Curtis Brown, his literary agent for twenty-five years – asked if they could pay farewell visits. Robert Lusty, who had seen so many of Cary's books into print, found him

immaculate, with almost the look of a dandy. He lay on his couch in the neatest of jumpers, and carefully pressed linen trousers rather deeper in colour; his socks were gay and his shoes neat and highly polished. A monocle dangled from a chain; his face, a little pale, achieved nobility and his eyes had lost nothing of their brilliance. He seemed more relaxed than I had ever seen him. He gave the impression of having done with the worries of the world.[27]

Cary's oldest friend, Heneage Ogilvie, had a similar impression: 'I have recently watched my dearest friend dying. He was one of the greatest British writers and philosophers and the malady that was slowly creeping upon him had left his mind unclouded. "Dying is something you must do alone," he said to me on my last visit.'[28]

Lord David Cecil was there almost daily. 'I miss him more than I can say,' Cecil wrote to Edith Haggard soon after Cary's death. 'It was not kindness that made me drop in; I did it for my own pleasure.'[29] He was, Dan Davin felt, 'able to disguise better than any of us the grief he felt for Joyce and find a steady stream of interesting and amusing talk that left it unnecessary for Joyce himself to strain his resources by trying to whisper a bridge across silences.'

And Cary was 'adamant that his friends should gather every Sunday night as of old and have drinks and talk. To him "laughter in the next room" was not something to make him feel cut off and repine but an affirmation that life went on and would go on after him.'[30]

Whenever they could, his family would be with him. The profound joy he received from their presence is illustrated in a dialogue he scrawled into a notebook, probably late in 1956. His grandson Chippy (Tristram, Michael's third son, then about seven years old) was with him.

I don't think you'll last much longer.
I *am* rather old.
I should say about 30 years.
Then I'd be nearly 100.
Well, ten years. Perhaps not more than five years.
That's more likely.
You're so awfully weak aren't you. You couldn't be a soldier any more, like you were before.
No, but that was a long time ago.
You're too lame and weak.[31]

Cary, more profoundly the soldier than ever before as he faced death, was delighted by the conversation. He frequently joked on his deathbed. 'A few days before his death he said to one visitor, "I'm a captive now, soon I'll be free." And he smiled, as if he had said something very funny.'[32]

Until the last week, he could still, with extreme effort, work. Win Davin would write down his whispered words, Edith Millen would type them. But then his throat muscles gave way, and he went into a final silence, able to respond only with glances and weak smiles. His mind, all agree, was clear to the end.

Two days before he died, Edith Millen wrote to Edith Haggard:

. . . When I read your letter to him this morning, he listened, and when I had finished he nodded to me, closed his eyes, and then smiled, a tiny smile. He was most certainly thinking of you, and his expression was one of utter serenity. He is quite clear mentally when he is awake, and though he can hardly speak, it is quite obvious that he understands perfectly what is said to him.

One other small detail is that he is still in complete control of his bodily functions. I tell you this because so many people in his weak state are not, and you know how distressed he would be that were so.

The LIFE article which you sent arrived yesterday and I held it up for Mr Cary to see. The portrait is indeed a good one; a companion for that wonderful self-portrait. He still looks the same; his face is perhaps a little thinner, but just as beautiful as ever.

Tristram is staying here now and is such a tower of strength to us all.

Unfortunately he has to go back to London, but Isabel, Michael's wife, is coming to stay for a few days. I don't know if you have met her; she is a dear, kind and sensible and devoted to Mr Cary. I know he will be glad that she is here. Michael himself is unable to get away from his work at the moment, though he did have a short visit last week to see his father.

. . . You know I consider myself very greatly privileged to have had these months of working with Mr Cary. He is the most wonderful person that I am ever likely to know, and in my humble way, I love him dearly too. [33]

Nora Lightburne wrote to Edith Haggard on 29 March 1957:

I feel you would like a few lines to-day from me.

Mr Cary died very peacefully in his sleep at 10 am to-day. Miss Millen was with him. It is the way we all hoped the end would come. For him we are so very glad, but he has left a great gap and will be terribly missed by all his dear ones and his friends. I feel it is a privilege to have known such a brave man – such a gentleman through and through.

His son Peter was here at the time – Tristram had gone back to London the day before, but is now back again. Michael is expected on Monday. His wife came yesterday.

The funeral is on Tuesday at 2.15 pm. A service in St Giles' Church first and burial at the cemetery in North Oxford.

I filled Mr Cary's room with lovely flowers from you and will keep them replenished until Tuesday. I feel sure you would like me to order a wreath as from you? I have heaps of money left – £13.15.4. [34]

And Tristram wrote to Edith Haggard on 10 April:

Your generosity and completely unselfish devotion to my father helped him more than anyone can say over the last months. We were all grateful that there was not a long period of complete and unproductive frustration at the end. This could have happened, and was what you and all of us feared. But the will to live began to wane when he could no longer work, and the very end was quite calm and peaceful. [35]

T. S. Matthews was at the funeral service, conducted by Canon F. R. Diggle, brother of the man with whom Cary had alternated in administering Borgu forty years earlier: 'Funerals are seldom cheerful affairs, but his was. The church . . . was crowded with his friends and family – you could see the Cary nose, the Cary cheekbones, the Cary head, all around you. A family affair, the service was straightforward Church of England, with no frills, and the hymns were good old thumpers that everyone knew and sang with a will.' [36]

NOTES

The following abbreviations have been used throughout:
JC: Joyce Cary
GC: Gertrude Cary
C (followed by box number): Cary Papers (The Osborn Collection of Joyce Cary MSS), Bodleian Library, Oxford
CAF: *The Case for African Freedom and Other Writings on Africa*
CC: *Castle Corner*
HC: *A House of Children*
SE: *Selected Essays*
SS: *Spring Song and Other Stories*
  All writings unattributed below are by JC.

Introduction

1 Title of interview by Graham Fisher, *Coronet*, XLI (January 1957), 41–44; also in *SE*, 251–5.
2 Subtitle of 'A Valedictory of a Great Writer', *Life*, 25 March 1957, 105–6, 108.
3 'If you could face your problems today as this man faces his . . . ', interview by Merrick Winn, *Daily Express*, 27 August 1956, 4.
4 Lord David Cecil, 'Mr JC: Tenderness of Heart' (obituary notice), *The Times*, 4 April 1957, 14.
5 Cecil to author, 1981.
6 Enid Starkie, 'JC, a Portrait', *Essays by Divers Hands*, n.s. XXXII, ed. Joanna Richardson (London: Oxford University Press, 1963), 133, 126.
7 Julian Fane, *Memoir in the Middle of a Journey* (London: Hamish Hamilton, 1977), 27.
8 Pamela Hansford Johnson, letter to Enid Starkie, 4 January 1961.
9 Jean Bannister to author, 1983.
10 Peter Ady to author, 1982.
11 Kathleen Stahl, letter to Enid Starkie, 16 November 1957.
12 Audrey Beecham to author, 1982.

13 Starkie, 126.
14 Fane, 24.
15 Quoted in Editors' Preface, *Mister Johnson*, Time Reading Program Special Edition (New York: Time Incorporated, 1962), v.
16 Dan Davin, *Closing Times* (London: Oxford University Press), 108–9.
17 Elizabeth Lawrence, Introduction, *The Horse's Mouth*, Time Reading Program Special Edition (New York: Time Incorporated, 1965), xvii–xviii.
18 Sylvia Lynd, letter to JC, 4 July 1938, C Adds.
19 J. B. Priestley, 'J. B. Priestley says You Hear JC Talking', *Reynolds News*, 11 May 1958.
20 Davin, 93.
21 Beecham to author, 1982.
22 M. M. Mahood to author, 1982.
23 W. W. Robson, letter to author, 17 June 1986.
24 Helen Gardner, Foreword, *SE*, vii.
25 Gardner in 'JC and his Vision of Life', presented by David Lytton, BBC Radio 3, 27 June 1977.
26 T. S. Matthews. *Angels Unwares* (New York: Ticknor and Fields, 1985), 239.
27 Davin, 70, 108.
28 Lawrence, xix–xx.
29 Walter Allen, *As I Walked Down New Grub Street* (London: Heinemann, 1981), 185.
30 Robson, letter to author.
31 Tristram Cary to author, 1983.
32 Gardner, 'The Novels of JC', *Essays and Studies*, n.s. XXVIII, ed. Robert Ellrodt (London: John Murray, 1975), 81.
33 Robert Lusty, *Bound to Be Read* (London: Jonathan Cape, 1975), 81.
34 Harvey Breit, 'A Talk with JC', *New York Times Book Review*, 18 February 1951, 14.
35 Davin, 'Lecture on JC' (unpublished).
36 Penelope Lively, *According to Mark* (Harmondsworth: Penguin, 1985), 210.
37 Davin, *Closing Times*, 106–7.
38 Tristram Cary to author, 1983; and see his 'Background to *The Horse's Mouth*', 24 *Hours* (Australia), May 1980, 12.
39 Dorse Cary, Elizabeth Cary, Isabel Cary, Margaret Robertson, to author, 1982, 1983.
40 Isabel Cary to author, 1982.
41 Lawrence, xxii–xxiii.
42 Starkie, 130.
43 Edith Haggard to author, 1987.
44 Starkie, 131, 133, 130, 134, 129, 143.
45 Peter Cary to author, 1982.
46 Starkie, 128, 130.
47 Gardner, 'The Novels of JC', 90.
48 Starkie, 126, 127.
49 Pamela Hansford Johnson, 'JC', *Sunday Times*, 31 March 1957.
50 Starkie, 128.
51 Peter Cary to author, 1982.
52 Gardner to author, 1983.
53 David Lytton, in 'JC and his Vision of Life'.
54 Starkie, 131.
55 Gardner, 'The Novels of JC', 77.
56 Donald Barr, 'A Careful and Profound Thinker', *Adam International Review* (JC issue), XVIII: 212–13 (November–December 1950), 31.

57 Gardner, 'The Novels of JC', 77.
58 Andrew Wright, *JC: A Preface to his Novels* (London: Chatto and Windus, 1958).
59 Robert Bloom, *The Indeterminate World* (Philadelphia: University of Pennsylvania Press, 1962), ix, viii.
60 Hazard Adams, *JC's Trilogies* (Tallahassee: University Presses of Florida, 1983), xi, 264.
61 Dennis Hall, *JC: A Reappraisal* (London: Macmillan, 1983), 1, 153.
62 John Updike, 'Writers I Have Met', *New York Times Book Review*, 11 August 1968, 2.
63 Doris Lessing. 'Personal Choice', *The Good Book Guide*, 16 (Autumn–Winter 1982), 26.
64 Paul Theroux, 'An English Visitor', *New Statesman*, 25 June 1976, 852; also in his *Sunrise with Seamonsters* (London: Hamish Hamilton, 1985), 139.
65 James Simmons, 'JC in Ireland', in *On the Novel*, ed. B. S. Benedikz (London: Dent, 1971), 140.
66 Jonah Raskin, *The Mythology of Imperialism* (New York: Dell, 1971), 311–3.
67 Davidson Nicol, 'JC's African Novels', *West African Review*, December 1957, 1199.
68 D. C. R. A. Goonetilleke, *Developing Countries in British Fiction* (London: Macmillan, 1977), 243.
69 Michael Echeruo, *JC and the Novel of Africa* (London: Longmans, 1973) and *JC and the Dimensions of Order* (London: Macmillan, 1979): S. H. Kanu, *A World of Everlasting Conflict* (Ibadan: Ibadan University Press, 1974).
70 Chinua Achebe, quoted in Alex Hamilton, 'African Explorer', *Guardian*, 23 February 1972, 8.
71 JC, 'Morality and the Novelist', *SE*, 156.
72 JC, letter to GC, 7 December 1916.
73 Beecham to author, 1982.
74 JC, letter to GC, 24 October 1919.
75 Stanley Parker, 'JC or What is Freedom?' (interview), *Oxford Mail*, 15 December 1942, 3.
76 'JC's Last Look at His Worlds', *SE*, 247.

Chapter 1 – Beginnings, 1066–1887

Genealogical and historical information relating to the Cary family has been collated from various sources, including a family-tree owned by the family, cemeteries in Inishowen, reference works like *Burke's Landed Gentry*, *Burke's Guide to Country Homes*, the *Dictionary of National Biography*, Edward MacLysaght's *Irish Families*, research notes on the Cary family compiled by W. F. Carey of Londonderry, and, especially, Lionel Stevenson's *The Cary Family of Inishowen* (Durham, North Carolina: Privately published, 1963).

Historical information about Ireland has been gleaned mainly from J. C. Beckett's *The Making of Modern Ireland* (New York: Knopf, 1977), Oliver MacDonagh's *Ireland* (Englewood Cliffs, New Jersey: Prentice-Hall, 1968), and books noted below.

1 HC, 161.
2 See Sir Newman Chambers, letter to JC, 1 February 1907, C321.
3 JC, letters to GC, 25 September and 24 October 1919.
4 Lionel Stevenson, *The Cary Family of Inishowen*, 14.
5 See Violet Powell, *The Constant Novelist: A Study of Margaret Kennedy* (London: Heinemann, 1983), 17.
6 See A. J. Langguth, *Saki* (London: Hamish Hamilton, 1981), 209.
7 See Will Ready, 'JC: A Biographical Sketch', *Critic*, XVIII (June–July 1960), 10.

8 JC, letters to GC, 23 and 28 November 1919.
9 Prefatory Essay, *Charley is My Darling*, 6. For six weeks during the summer of 1897, the Montgomeries were at New Park, the family house at Moville; see Alan Chalfont, *Montgomery of Alamein* (London: Weidenfeld and Nicolson, 1976), 39.
10 John Aubrey, *Aubrey's Brief Lives*, ed. Oliver Lawson Dick (London: Secker and Warburg, 1958), 56.
11 J. R. Green. *History of the English People* (New York: Harper, 1890), III: 308.
12 S. R. Gardiner, entry in *Dictionary of National Biography*, III: 1159.
13 J. A. R. Marriott, *The Life and Times of Lucius Cary, Viscount Falkland* (London: Methuen, 1907), 1.
14 Clarendon, Earl of, *Selections*, ed. G. Huehns (Oxford: Oxford University Press, 1978), 58.
15 'The Front-Line Feeling', *Listener* (17 January 1952), 92.
16 Mary Ogilvie to author, 1982.
17 *Penguin Dictionary of Surnames*.
18 'The Meaning of England', *SE*, 71.
19 From the opening line of 'Innishowen' by C. G. Duffy.
20 Stevenson, 5.
21 David Thomson, *Woodbrook* (London: Barrie and Jenkins, 1974), 33
22 Brendan Behan, *The Hostage*, Act I.
23 Terence de Vere White, *The Anglo-Irish* (London: Victor Gollancz, 1972), 36.
24 Thomson, 65, 34, 154, 33.
25 JC, of Henry Miller, in letter to Graham Ackroyd, 11 November 1946; C Adds 4.
26 Stevenson, 5.
27 JC, letter to GC, 27 February 1919.
28 Letter to GC, 19 December 1918.
29 'Speaking for Myself', *SE*, 19.
30 Elizabeth Bowen, *Bowen's Court*, in *Bowen's Court & Seven Winters* (London: Virago, 1984), 360.
31 CC, 25, 24, 14.
32 JC, letter to GC, 21 October 1919.
33 'Speaking for Myself', *SE*, 19.
34 'Speaking for Myself', 19.
35 CC, 18.
36 Thomson, 71, 20.
37 JC, autobiographical draft, C293/S22I.
38 Peter Cary, Margaret Robertson, Winifred Davin, in conversation with the author, 1982.
39 James Morris, *Pax Britannica* (London: Faber, 1968), 464, 236.
40 Bowen, *Seven Winters*, in *Bowen's Court & Seven Winters*, 32.
41 Cyril Connolly, *Enemies of Promise* (London: André Deutsch, 1973), 155.
42 Victoria Glendinning, *Elizabeth Bowen* (London: Weidenfeld and Nicolson, 1977), 14.
43 White, 19.
44 J. C. Beckett, *The Anglo-Irish Tradition* (London: Faber, 1976), 144.
45 CC draft, C 35.
46 'The Meaning of England', *SE*, 71–2.
47 JC, letter to GC, 5 November 1919.
48 Caroline Curry, letter to JC, C 328.
49 JC, letter to GC, 5 November 1919.
50 Edward MacLysaght, *Irish Families* (New York: Crown, 1957), 73, 189.
51 See Charlotte Joyce, letter to Arthur Joyce, n.d., C Adds.
52 Charlotte Joyce, diaries, C 332.

53 Charlotte Joyce, letters to Jane and Olive Cary, 3 September 1883, C. Adds.
54 Stevenson, 7.
55 Charlotte Joyce, letters to Arthur Cary, 4 September 1883 to 18 July 1886.
56 'Carrig Cnoc', *SE*, 30.
57 Charlotte Joyce, letters to Arthur Cary, 14 October 1886 to 31 July 1887.
58 James Joyce, letter to Arthur Cary, January 1887, C Adds.
59 Charlotte Joyce, letter to Arthur Cary, 14 July 1887.
60 Londonderry *Standard*, 17 August 1887.
61 Charlotte Joyce, letter to Arthur Cary, 18 May 1887.

Chapter 2 – Loss, 1888–1899

1 JC, letter to GC, 27 May 1919.
2 Hessie Cary's sketchbook is owned by the family.
3 'Freedom of Mind', incomplete essay, C 331.
4 'What Christ has Taught Me', C 249; published in translation in V*art Kristus Idärt mig* (Stockholm: Bokforlagt Natur och Kultur, 1957).
5 Letter to GC, 6 December 1916.
6 'What Christ has Taught Me'.
7 'A Child's Religion',*SE*, 23.
8 'What Christ has Taught Me'.
9 C 265 / N63.
10 'Freedom of Mind'.
11 The other account is in Prefatory Essay, *Charley is My Darling*, 5–7.
12 'Freedom of Mind'.
13 JC, letter to GC, 3 February 1919; Charlotte Joyce's letters to Arthur Cary, C Adds 16.
14 'Freedom of Mind'.
15 Untitled draft, C 214.
16 Charlotte Joyce, letter to Arthur Cary, 28 September 1885.
17 Virginia Woolf, 'A Sketch of the Past', in *Moments of Belief*, ed. Jeanne Schulkind (London: Hogarth, 1985), 80.
18 Stevenson, 7.
19 JC, letter to GC, 28 October 1919.
20 Caroline Curry, letter to JC, n.d., C 328.
21 JC, letter to GC, 22 January 1919.
22 Prefatory Essay, *HC*, 6; also mentioned in letter to GC, 4 January 1919.
24 Stanley Parker, 'Joyce Cary or What is Freedom?'
25 JC, Letter to GC, 8 January 1919.
26 Letters to GC, 28 August 1917, 22 November 1918, 12 February 1919.
27 Jane Cary, letter to JC, 22 March 1899.
28 JC, untitled, incomplete essay, C 331.

Chapter 3 – Inishowen, 1892–1900

1 'Speaking for Myself', *SE*, 19.
2 JC, letter to GC, 25 September 1919.
3 Copy of letter, C Adds 4.
4 Family-tree in letter to GC, 8 September 1917.
5 *HC*, 206.
6 *HC* draft, C 53.
7 Prefatory Essay, *HC*, 5–6.
8 CC draft, C 28.

9 JC painted several copies as gifts for John Dover Wilson, family and friends.
10 *HC*, 18.
11 JC, letter to GC, 5 September 1919.
12 *CC*, 27.
13 'Speaking for Myself', 19.
14 *CC*, 18, 29.
15 *HC*, 12.
16 JC, letter to GC, 28 July 1917.
17 Autobiographical draft, C 293 / S22I.
18 Autobiographical draft, C 301.
19 *HC* draft, C 270 / S11J.
20 Autobiographical draft, C 301.
21 JC, letter to GC, 5 November 1919.
22 *HC*, 205–6, 214–5.
23 *HC*, 82–3.
24 JC, letter to GC, 5 November 1919.
25 *HC*, 205–6, 214–5.
26 'Speaking for Myself', 19.
27 Autobiographical draft, C 293 / S22I.
28 *HC*, 99.
29 *CC*, 18–19.
30 *HC*, 160.
31 *HC*, 97–8, 100, 108–9, 104.
32 *HC* draft, C 55.
33 'Sergeant Umaru', C 265 / N76.
34 In a sketch-book owned by the family.
35 'Uncle Jim Joyce', C 270 / S11J.
36 *HC*, 47.
37 JC, letter to GC, 24 March 1917.
38 Draft of Prefatory Essay, *HC*, C 244.
39 JC, letter to GC, 8 September 1917.
40 See Barbara Fisher, *JC: The Writer and his Theme* (Gerrards Cross: Colin Smythe, 1980), 21.
41 "Out of Hand", *SS*, 86–91.
42 'Speaking for Myself', *SE*, 20.
43 *HC*, 114.
44 'Horror Comics', *SE*, 26–7.
45 'Freedom of Mind', C 331.
46 *HC* drafts, C 53.
47 JC, letter to GC, 13 September 1919.
48 'Mills' notes, C 253 / N8.
49 GC, letter to JC, 17 December 1916.
50 *HC*, 184, 238–9, 193, 204–6, 186.
51 C293 / S22I Autobiographical draft.
52 Quoted in Wright, *JC*, 24.
53 'Speaking for Myself', *SE*, 20.
54 *HC*, 66.
55 N80, in Barbara Fisher's transcription.

Chapter 4 – School, 1900–1904

Apart from the sources noted below (especially Christie's *History*), information about Clifton College was gathered during a visit in 1982. All Cary's references to

Cromwell House are from 'Barney Magonagel' or 'Cromwell House', *SE*, 32–65.

1 JC, letter to Arthur Cary, 2 September 1900, C Adds 4.
2 Letter to GC, 22 April 1919.
3 Arthur Cary, letter to JC, 5 March 1901, C321.
4 See Foster, *JC*, 28.
5 Information from various Hurstleigh School programme, C 333.
6 *HC*, 158–9.
7 *Tottenham*, C 180.
8 *HC*, 34.
9 'The Meaning of England', *SE*, 72.
10 Autobiographical draft beginning 'My own religious history', C 331.
11 *HC*, 223–4.
12 Dorothy Cary, letter to JC, 23 September [1900], C 321.
13 Quoted in Virginia Woolf, *Roger Fry* (Toronto: Macmillan, 1940), 36.
14 Quoted in Derek Winterbottom, *Henry Newbolt and the Spirit of Clifton* (Bristol: Redcliffe, 1986), 23.
15 Winterbottom, 49.
16 Valerie Pakenham, *The Noonday Sun* (London: Methuen, 1955), 57.
17 Mark Girouard, *The Return to Camelot* (New Haven: Yale University Press, 1981), 172.
18 GC, letter to JC, 11 December 1916.
19 Report in *The Cliftonian*, XVII (July 1904); JC's copy, C 337.
20 Refrain of 'Vitai Lampada'.
21 *The Cliftonian*, XVII.
22 Winterbottom, 27.
23 O. F. Christie *A History of Clifton College* (Bristol: J.W. Arrowsmith, 1935), 38.
24 Quoted in Andrew Wright, *JC*, 20.
25 'Darley', C169.
26 *Art and Reality*, 46–8.
27 C 250 / N1.
28 C261 / N45.
29 *Art and Reality*, 47–8.
30 C261/N45.

Chapter 5 – Shock & Recovery, 1904–1906

1 Arthur Cary, letter to JC, 11 May 1904, C321.
2 Charles Tait, letter to JC, 12 May 1904, C 321.
3 Arthur Cary, letters to JC, 3, 10, and 13 June 1904.
4 *The Cliftonian*, XVII (July 1904), 228.
5 'Cromwell House, *SE*, 57.
6 JC, letter to GC, 19 February 1919.
7 'On His Own Method', C 237 (published in translation as 'Notes sur l'art et la liberté, *Preuves*, August 1954).
8 Prefatory Essay, *The Horse's Mouth*, 10.
9 Basil Taylor, Introduction, *The Impressionists and Their World* (London: Phoenix House, 1953), 7.
10 Quoted in 'Cheerful Protestant', *Time*, 20 October 1952, 48.
11 *Art and Reality*, 74–6; other accounts in Prefatory Essay, *The Horse's Mouth* and 'The Way a Novel Gets Written', *SE*, 125.
12 JC, letter to Arthur Cary, 11 March 1906, C Adds 4.

13 Heneage Ogilvie, *No Miracles Among Friends* (London: Max Parrish, 1959) 14.
14 Quoted in 'Cheerful Protestant', 48.
15 JC, personal letter to Edith Haggard, 29 July 1951.
16 *HC*, 160–70.
17 JC, letter to GC, 14 April 1917.
18 'My own religious history'; see also 'A Slight Case of Demolition', *SE*, 69.
19 JC, letter to Arthur Cary, 11 March 1906.
20 *The Cliftonian*, XVIII (July 1905), 41 (published anonymously); a copy of the poem is in C Adds 4.
21 *The Cliftonian*, XIX (June 1906), 194–5 (published anonymously).

Chapter 6 – Artist, 1906–1909

1 Memie Agar, letter to JC, 12 June 1906, C 321.
2 Caroline Curry, letter to JC, 2 February [1907], C321.
3 Memie Cary, letter to JC, 4 December 1909.
4 Arthur Cary, letter to JC, 15 February 1912, C 322.
5 JC, letter to GC, 24 March 1917.
6 Autobiographical draft, 'Sketch for an idea of life', C 271 / N82.
7 Sketch-books owned by the family.
8 Charles Mackie, letter to JC, 27 May 1907, C321.
9 'Sketch for an idea of life'.
10 Stuart Cloete, *A Victorian Son* (London: Collins, 1972), 116, 58, 155.
11 'On His Own Method', C 237.
12 JC, letter to John Dover Wilson, 18 September 1942, National Library of Scotland.
13 Draft of acceptance speech for Honorary D.Ll., Edinburgh University, 1943, C 301.
14 Arthur Cary, letter to JC, 16 March 1907.
15 C 261 / N45.
16 Mary Yule, letter to GC, 24 January 1919, C Adds.
17 JC, letters to Arthur Cary, 29 October 1908 and n.d., C Adds 4.
18 Archibald Sturrock, letter to JC, 8 November 1909, C 321.
19 Acceptance speech draft.
20 *Art and Reality*, 48–9.
21 'Sketch for an idea of life'.
22 Autobiographical draft entitled 'Sketch', C 272 / P52.
23 JC, letter to Arthur Cary, n.d. [October 1907].
24 Fr Brocard Sewell, ed., *Two Friends: John Gray and André Raffalovich* (Aylesford, Kent: St Albert's Press, 1963), 32, 34.
25 'My own religious history'.
26 JC, letter to Arthur Cary, 29 October 1908.
27 Quoted in Wright, 21.
28 Quoted in 'Cheerful Protestant', *Time* (20 October 1952), 49.
29 In a sketch-book owned by the family.
30 JC, letter to Arthur Cary, 20 June 1907.
31 Quoted in Wright, 42.
32 JC, letter to Lionel Stevenson, 23 January 1927, Duke University Library.
33 Quoted in Wright, 42.
34 Wright, 42.
35 JC, letter to Arthur Cary, 29 October 1908.
36 S. T. Irwin, letter to JC, 9 October 1908, C 321.
37 JC, letter to Arthur Cary, n.d. [January 1909].

38 Arthur Cary, letter to JC, 27 February 1909.
39 JC, letters to Arthur Cary, n.d. [spring 1909].
40 Letter to Jack Cary, 25 September 1909, C 329.

Chapter 7 – Oxford, 1909–1910

Historical information about the University has been gleaned from the Histories by Charles Mallett and V. H. H. Green, and *Oxford and Its Colleges* by J. Wells, as well as from books listed below.

1 'The Oxford Scholar', *Holiday*, XIII (June 1953), 139.
2 Quoted in Jan Morris, ed., *The Oxford Book of Oxford* (Oxford: Oxford University Press, 1978), 322.
3 Quoted in Morris, 182.
4 CC draft, C 28.
5 'The Oxford Scholar', 134.
6 'Tod' draft, C 178.
7 'The Oxford Scholar', 134–5.
8 'Carrig Cnoc', *SE*, 30.
9 JC, letter to Arthur Cary, 17 November 1909.
10 'The Oxford Scholar', 135.
11 'Sketch', C 272 / P52.
12 JC, letter to Arthur Cary, 17 November 1909.
13 'Sketch for an idea of life', C 271 / N82.
14 JC, 'A Slight Case of Demolition', *SE*, 68.
15 'Tod', C 178.
16 JC, letter to GC, 30 January 1919.
17 C 261 / N45.
18 Harold Nicolson, 'Marginal Comment', *Spectator*, 10 August 1945.
19 Quoted by Nicolson.
20 'Sketch', C 272 / P52.
21 'Sketch for an idea of life'.
22 Maurice Bowra, *Memories*, (London: Weidenfeld and Nicolson, 1966), 112.
23 Sir Isaiah Berlin, 'Austin and the Early Beginnings of Oxford Philosophy', in *Essays on J. L. Austin* (Oxford: Clarendon Press, 1973), 2.
24 'Sketch for an idea of life.'
25 'A Slight Case of Demolition',*SE*, 67–70.
26 Christopher Hollis, *Oxford in the Twenties*, 13.
27 'The Oxford Scholar', 137.
28 TS of speech for Addison Society, 30 May 1952, C 233.
29 C 333.
30 See Ronald Knox, *Let Dons Delight* (London: Sheed and Ward, 1939).
31 Milton Club Minute Book, C338.
32 Anthony Alpers, *The Life of Katherine Mansfield*, (New York: Viking, 1980), 131.
33 F. A. Lea, *The Life of John Middleton Murry* (London: Methuen, 1959), 15.
34 Murry in *Coming to London*, ed. John Lehmann (London: Phoenix House, 1957), 98.
35 'Tod' drafts, C 178.
36 *Coming to London*, 98.

Chapter 8 – Bohemian, 1910–1911

Cary's account of his two weeks in Paris is entirely drawn from his 'Paris Diary', C 253 / N9.

1 Bill, Pension de Famille Bazin, Montparnasse, C321.
2 Murry, *Between Two Worlds* (London: Cape, 1935), 144–5, 150.
3 Margaret Morris, Introduction, *Café Drawings in Edwardian Paris from the Sketch Books of J. D. Fergusson* (Glasgow: Blackie, 1974), 5.
4 Murry, 150–4.
5 J. D. Fergusson, *Modern Scottish Painting* (Glasgow: W. Maclenan, 1943), 18, 19, 76, 25, 123.
6 Murry, 141.
7 Murry, 160.
8 Murry, 155–7.
9 Richard Rees, entry in *Dictionary of National Biography 1951–1960*, ed. E. T. Williams and Helen Palmer (Oxford: Oxford University Press), 1971, 761.
10 Virginia Woolf, *Collected Essays*, I, 321.
11 C. A. Hankin, Introduction, *The Letters of John Middleton Murry to Katherine Mansfield* (London: Constable, 1983), 4.
12 Untitled review by 'A. J. C.', *Rhythm* I: 4 (Spring 1912), 36.
13 Quoted in F. A. Lea, *The Life of John Middleton Murry*, 25.
14 Murry, 173.
15 Murry, postcard to JC, 3 April 1911, C 321.
16 Murry, 182–3.
17 *Coming to London*, 101.
18 Dan Davin, *Closing Times*, 94.
19 Arthur Cary, letter to JC, 1 December 1911, C 321.
20 *Coming to London*, 100.
21 Quoted in 'Cheerful Protestant', *Time*, 20 October 1952, 50.
22 C 251 / P15.
23 Quoted in Wright, *JC*, 23.
24 JC, letter to GC, 22 February 1917.
25 Murry, *Still Life* (London: Constable, 1916), 320, 223, 224.
26 C 274 / P60.
27 *Still Life*, 368.

Chapter 9 – The Ogilvies, 1911–1912

1 Information from W. M. Ogilvie, *Reminiscences* (privately published, 1929).
2 JC, letter to GC, 5 March 1919.
3 W. M. Ogilvie, 6–7.
4 JC, letter to GC, 28 October 1919.
5 Quoted in 'Cheerful Protestant', *Time*, 51.
6 JC, letter to GC, 16 April 1917.
7 Letters to GC, 29 June, 12 May, 24 September 1919, 7 June and 24 November 1917, 28 October 1919.
8 GC, letter to JC, 30 September 1917.
9 Quoted in GC, letter to JC, 29 September 1917.
10 C 263 / N56.
11 JC, letter to GC, 21 November 1917
12 Letter to GC, 1 March 1919.
13 Letter to GC, 14 August 1917.
14 GC, letters to JC, 26 April and 7 October 1917, 1 June and 3 August 1919.
15 Mary Anna Ogilvie, letters to Gertrude Ogilvie, C Adds.
16 GC, letters to JC, 14 September and 1 July 1917, 18 August 1918, 18 October 1916.
17 GC, letter to JC, 7 July 1917.

18 JC, letters to GC, 10 August 1918, 18 August and 7 November 1916.
19 'The Oxford Scholar', 134, 136.
20 GC, letter to JC, 15 January 1919.
21 'The Oxford Scholar', 142–3.
22 JC, letter to GC, 14 September 1917.
23 GC, letter to JC, 24 May 1917.
24 JC, letters to GC, 12 October 1916, 16 October 1917, 6 March 1919.
25 'Sketch', C 272 / P52.
26 'My own religious history', C 331.
27 'Sketch'.
28 'An Interview with JC', *SE*, 10. (But to Elizabeth Lawrence, 21 June 1949, he recalled learning about 'creative evolution' from Bergson.)
29 Draft of letter to Mr Vaughan of the Blake Society, n.d., C 233.
30 'My own religious history'.
31 Telegram, n.d. [July 1912], C 321.
32 JC, letters to GC, 15 April and 5 March 1917, 1 June 1919.
33 GC, letter to JC, 1 July 1917.
34 JC, letter to GC, 1 June 1919.
35 GC, letter to JC, 1 July 1917.
36 JC, letter to GC, 7 December 1916.
37 [F. R. Barry], letter to JC, 1 December 1912, C 321.
38 C 329.
39 C 297.

Chapter 10 – Montenegro, 1912–1913

MB: *Memoir of the Bobotes*

1 Arthur Cary, letter to JC, 28 October 1912, C 322.
2 Untitled article about Montenegro, C 332.
3 *MB*, 27.
4 Article about Montenegro.
5 *MB*, 30.
6 Alphonse Courlander, 'The Man who was Blown Up', *Daily Express*, 8 November 1911.
7 Netta Clark, letter to JC, 19 November 1912, C 322.
8 Dorothy Cary, letter to JC, 17 November 1912, C 322.
9 *MB*, 41, 44.
10 Article about Montenegro.
11 *MB*, 49.
12 JC, letter to Arthur Cary, 16 October 1912, C Adds 4.
13 Letter to GC, 21 December 1919.
14 *MB*, 57.
15 Preface, *MB*, 14.
16 *MB*, 70, 60.
17 See *MB*, 76.
18 *MB*, 78, 80.
19 JC, letter to GC, 14 October 1918.
20 GC, letter to JC, 19 May 1919.
21 Dan Davin, *Closing Times*, 100.
22 A. Martin-Leake, letter to JC, n.d., C 328.
23 *MB*, 85, 82, 97, 98.
24 JC, letter to Arthur Cary, 11 April [1913], C Adds 4.

25 *MB*, 119–20, 123.
26 Article about Montenegro.
27 *MB*, 123.
28 *MB*, 129–30.
29 *MB*, 146, 147.
30 Quoted in Wright, *JC*, 24.
31 JC, letter to Arthur Cary, 1 July 1913.
32 Walter Allen, Foreword, *MB*, 9, 10.
33 Allen, 9.
34 Allen, 10.
35 *MB*, 86, 154, 134, 17, 164.
36 Allen, 11.
37 *MB*, 32, 108.

Chapter 11 – Rejections, 1913

In addition to books noted below, information about the Irish Co-operative Movement has been gleaned from Edward E. Maclysaght, *Sir Horace Plunkett* (Dublin: Maunsel, 1916), and research in the Library of the Plunkett Foundation for Co-operative Studies, Oxford.

1 JC, letter to GC, 29 January 1917.
2 GC, letter to JC, 19 August 1917.
3 JC, letter to Arthur Cary, 1 July [1913] C Adds 4.
4 Horace Plunkett, quoted in Margaret Digby, *Horace Plunkett* (Oxford: Basil Blackwell, 1949), 17, and in Patrick Bolger, *The Irish Co-operative Movement*, (Dublin: Institute of Public Administration, 1977), 61.
5 Digby, 294.
6 Menu, St Patrick's Club Dinner, Randolph Hotel, Oxford, 11 June 1910, C 333.
7 Autobiographical draft, C 293 / S 22 I.
8 Gertrude Ogilvie, diary, 14 July 1913, C Adds.
9 GC, letter to JC, 19 January 1917.
10 Gertrude Ogilvie, diary, 14 July 1913.
11 GC, letters to JC, 19 May 1919 and 19 January 1917.
12 Plunkett, letter to JC, 20 July 1913, C 322.
13 GC, letter to JC, 29 January 1917.
14 Digby, 156.
15 Plunkett, diary, 25 and 26 July 1913, Library of the Plunkett Foundation, Oxford.
16 Autobiographical draft, C293 / S 22I.
17 JC, letter to GC, 30 May 1919.
18 See R. A. Anderson, *With Horace Plunkett in Ireland* (London: Macmillan, 1935), 11.
19 Plunkett, letter to Adams, 29 September 1913, Plunkett Foundation.
20 Gerald Heard, quoted in Digby, 303, 302.
21 Digby, 302, 300.
22 Bolger, 56.
23 C 261 / N45.
24 JC, letters to GC, 11 January and 2 September 1917.
25 GC, letter to JC, 1 June 1919.
26 Gertrude Ogilvie, diary.
27 GC, letter to JC, 7 March 1919.
28 GC, letters to JC, 18 October 1916, 11 May 1917, 20 November 1916.
29 JC, letter to GC, 23 June 1917.
30 GC, letters to JC, 3 August 1917, 12 January 1919, 18 November 1917.

31 Autobiographical statement for Harper, 1949; see Mary Harvey, M.A. thesis (Appendix A), C 344.
32 Lionel Stevenson, *The Cary Family of Inishowen*, 10.

Chapter 12 – Bauchi, 1914

Historical and administrative information about Nigeria has been gleaned from several books apart from those listed below: A. H. M. Kirk-Greene, ed., *The Principles of Native Administration in Nigeria* (London, 1965); W. R. Crocker, *Nigeria: A Critique of Colonial Administration* (London, 1936); I. F. Nicolson, *The Administration of Nigeria 1900–1960* (Oxford, 1969); Michael Crowder, *The Story of Nigeria* (London, 1966); S. J. Hogben and A. H. M. Kirk-Greene, *The Emirates of Northern Nigeria* (London, 1966); *Gazetteer of Bauchi Province*, comp. F. B. Gall (London, 1920); A. C. G. Hastings, *Nigerian Days* (London, 1925); Margery Perham, *Lugard* (London, 1956, 1960).

1 JC, *The Case for African Freedom*, in CAF, 56.
2 See C 250/ N12, N13.
3 Unpublished Preface for American edition of *The African Witch* (1936).
4 *The Case for African Freedom*, 56.
5 *The Case for African Freedom*, 180.
6 F. D. Lugard, *The Dual Mandate* (Edinburgh: Blackwood, 1922), 215.
7 *The Case for African Freedom*, 181.
8 Preface for *The African Witch*.
9 *The Case for African Freedom*, 57.
10 Alan Burns, *History of Nigeria* (London: Allen and Unwin 1969), 206.
11 *The Case for African Freedom*, 54–5.
12 Cary's copy, C 337.
13 'Railway Camp', C 189.
14 'Too Good to Be True', C 181.
15 H. S. W. Edwardes, diary, 21 May 1914; Edwardes Papers, Rhodes House Library, Oxford.
16 'Too Good to Be True'.
17 C 261 / N45.
18 *The Case for African Freedom*, 182–3.
19 'Policy for Aid', SE, 97–8.
20 C 276 / N86.
21 [H. S. W. Edwardes], *On the Improvement of Native Paths in Northern Nigeria* (privately published, 1913); copy in Rhodes House Library.
22 Edwardes, letter to JC, 22 September 1915, C 322.
23 Edwardes, diary, 7 and 9 April 1916.
24 F. B. Gall, letter to Governor General of Nigeria, N Kaduna SNP 8 / 29 / 1916.
25 'Memoranda by H. S. W. Edwardes on the Gandi Canal' and associated material, N Kaduna SNP 9 / 1888 / 1918.
26 Robert Huessler, *The British in Northern Nigeria* (London: Oxford University Press, 1968), 90, 128–9.

Chapter 13 – Gombe, 1914–1915

1 Edwardes, diary, June–July 1914.
2 HC, 135.
3 JC, letter to Arthur Cary, 3 August 1914, C Adds 4; also C 265 / N63, and 'Darley', C 169.
4 Letter to Arthur Cary, 3 August 1914.

5 Edwardes, diary, 5 August 1914.
6 'Marching as to War', C 187.
7 J. F. J. Fitzpatrick, 'Mr Johnson', *Blackwood's Magazine*, CCI (February 1917), 250–1.
8 Fitzpatrick, letter to JC, n.d., C 322.
9 Edwardes, letter to JC, 2 September 1914, C 322.
10 Fitzpatrick, letter to JC, 27 August 1914.
11 JC, letter to Arthur Cary, 1 October 1914.
12 Fitzpatrick, letters to JC, n.d., C 322.
13 Edwardes, diary, 9 June 1915.
14 N Kaduna SNP 8 / 56 / 1920.
15 JC, letter to GC, 28 February 1917.
16 N Kaduna SNP 17 / 9/ C218, and *Colonial Office List* 1926.
17 Fitzpatrick, 'Nigeria's Curse – the Native Administration', *National Review*, December 1924, 618.
18 Fitzpatrick, letters to JC, 18 December and 21 October 1914.
19 JC, letter to GC, 19 October 1916.
20 Letter to Arthur Cary, 1 October 1914.
21 Fitzpatrick, letter to JC, 18 December 1914.
22 JC, letters to Arthur Cary, 1 and 19 October 1914.
23 Draft entitled 'Politics and Freedom', C 267 / N65.
24 JC, letter to Arthur Cary, 22 November 1914.
25 F. H. Ruxton, Resident of Bornu, extract from report enclosed by F. B. Gall in letter to Resident of Yola, 21 April 1915, C 322.
26 C 257 / N39.
27 *HC*, 135.
28 C 265 / N63.
29 'Adamu', C 181.
30 Edwardes, letter to JC, 2 September 1914.
31 E. L. Mort, letter to M. M. Mahood, 5 September 1962.
32 JC, letter to GC, 15 February 1917.
33 See his memo 'Pagan Training', and associated material, N Kaduna SNP 10 / 370P / 1921.
34 T. F. Carlyle, letter to JC, 8 November 1914, C 322.
35 E. W. Pemberton, letter to M. M. Mahood, 10 September 1962.
36 'Politics and Freedom', C 267 / N65.
37 JC, letter to GC, 20 December 1916.
38 Draft of letter to Gollancz, 19 June 1936, C 268 / S10D.
39 *Mister Johnson*, 46.

Chapter 14 – Bush Fighting, 1915–1916

Information about the Cameroons conflict has been taken mainly from Brigadier General E. Howard Gorges, *The Great War in West Africa* (London: Hutchinson, n.d.) and Brigadier General F. J. Moberly, *Military Operations: Togoland and the Cameroons 1914–1916* (London: HM Stationery Office, 1931).

1 Quoted in John Buchan, *Nelson's History of the War*, III: 149.
2 'Bush River'. *SS*, 11.
3 'Guda', C 184.
4 JC, letter to GC, 4 July 1917.
5 C 265 / N63.
6 'Buying a Horse', *SS*, 50, 51, 53–4.

7 Carlyle, letter to JC, 1 August 1915, C 322.
8 Sir J. A. Hammerton, ed., *A Popular History of the Great War*, II: 461.
9 JC, letters to Curtis Brown (New York), 15 July and 30 December 1952, Columbia University Libraries.
10 'Bush River', *SS*, 9.
11 J. Chartres, letter to M. M. Mahood, 7 September 1962.
12 'Bush River', *SS*, 15, 10–11, 16.
13 'Sergeant Umaru' (draft of 'Umaru'), C 265 / N76.
14 'Umaru', *SS*, 19, 21, 23–4.
15 'Instructions by Brigadier General F. H. G. Cunliffe for the attack on Mora Mountain', 1 September 1915; copy in C 322.
16 'Britain's Colonial Record' Bulletins from Britain, 104 (26 August 1942), 8.
17 *A Popular History of the Great War*, II: 466.
18 JC, letter to GC, 3 March 1917.
19 'Cheerful Protestant', *Time*, 20 October 1952, 50.
20 Arthur Cary, letter to JC, 17 September 1915, C 322.
21 Frederick Ogilvie, letter to JC, 30 October 1915, C 322.
22 Heneage Ogilvie, letter to JC, 19 November 1915.
23 Autobiographical draft, C 293.
24 Autobiographical draft, C 279 / S16A
25 *A Popular History of the Great War*, II: 461.
26 C 265 / N63.
27 JC, letter to Curtis Brown (New York), 30 December 1952.
28 Letters to GC, 5 November and 3 March 1917.
29 Letter to GC, 24 September 1917.
30 JC, letters to GC, 15 September and 25 April 1917.
31 GC, letters to JC, 8 October 1916, 2 September 1917.
32 JC, letters to GC, 5 July 1919, 20 November 1918, 2 September 1917.
33 GC, letter to JC, 9 September 1917.
34 JC, letter to GC, 20 September 1917.
35 GC, letter to JC, 11 May 1917.
36 Letter to JC, 9 November 1917.
37 JC, letter to GC, 21 October 1917.
38 GC, letter to JC, 26 April 1919.
39 JC, letter to GC, 5 October 1917.
40 GC, letter to JC, 1 July 1917.
41 Heneage Ogilvie, letter to JC, 8 May 1916, C 323.
42 JC, letters to GC, 1 June 1919, 11 January 1917.
43 GC, letter to JC, 30 May 1919.
44 C323
45 JC, letter to GC, 6 August 1916.

Chapter 15 – Officer in Charge, 1916–1917

1 Valerie Pakenham, *The Noonday Sun* (London: Methuen, 1985), 57.
2 GC, letters to JC, 23 and 16 December 1916, 29 August and 7 July 1917.
3 JC, letters to GC, 10, 21, 25, 27, 29 and 30 August, 3, 4, 8, 13, 18 and 19 September 1916.
4 Letters to GC, 22, 24, 29 and 30 September 1916.
5 Letters to GC, 4 and 6 October 1916.
6 GC, letters to JC, 21 August and 1 September 1916.
7 JC, letters to GC, 13, 15 and 16 October 1916.
8 Letters to GC, 19, 20, 27, 20 and 22 October, 11 November 1916.

9 'The Most Exciting Sport in the World'. *SE*, 77, 79, 76.
10 JC, letters to GC, 2 and 7 November, 19 December, 27 November 1916, 15 February 1917, 12 December 1916, 16 February 1917.

Chapter 16 – *Transition, 1916–1917*

Information about Borgu and its history has been gleaned from Michael Crowder's *Revolt in Bussa* (London, 1973), the books noted below, and research in Northern Nigeria during 1981.

1 JC, letters to GC, 25 October, 18 and 19 November, 7 December 1916.
2 Letters to GC, 7 and 30 December, 20 December, 11 November, 5 December 1916, 4 January 1917, 27 October 1916, 27 and 1 January 1917.
3 Letters to GC, 3 and 5 January, 17, 18, 13, 28 February, 8 March 1917.
4 Letters to GC, 24, 27 and 28 March, 10 and 16 April 1917.
5 Personal letter to Edith Haggard, 21 October 1955.
6 Letters to GC, 4 March, 5 May 1917
7 Letter to Curtis Brown (New York), 15 May 1951.
8 'Borgu, Handing-Over Notes. November 1919', N Kaduna, DOB / HIS / 82.
9 Kaiama Assessment Report, 1919, N Kaduna DOB / ASR / 10.
10 Kaiaima Assessment Report.
11 Lugard, in *Northern Nigeria: Colonial Report 1905–1906*, 84.
12 Crowder, *Colonial West Africa* (London: Frank Cass, 1970), 151.
13 Major W. Hamilton–Browne, quoted in Crowder, 161.
14 Edwardes, diary, 1 June 1911.
15 JC, letters to GC, 29 April and 1 May 1917.
16 GC, letter to JC, 10 June 1917.
17 JC, letter to GC, 7 May 1917.
18 Letter to GC, 5 May 1917.
19 C 251 / P10.
20 H. W. Cowper, letter to Co Moody, 27 February 1962, C Adds 4.
21 JC, letters to GC, 12, 13, 14, 16 and 15 May 1917.
22 Frederick Ogilvie, letter to JC, 1 July 1917, C 323.
23 Arthur Cary, letter to JC, 26 April 1917.
24 Mary Anna Ogilvie, letter to JC, 8 May 1917.
25 JC, letters to GC, 15, 16, and 17 May 1917.
26 Heneage Ogilvie, letter to JC, 14 November 1917.

Chapter 17 – *A. D. O. Borgu, 1917*

1 H. W. Cowper, letter to Colonel Moody, 27 February 1962.
2 JC, letters to GC, 26 and 27 June 1917.
3 Kaiama District Assessment Report, 1919, N Kaduna DNB / ASR /10.
4 JC, letters to GC, 1 and 7 July 1917.
5 Letter to GC, 9 June 1917.
6 Autobiographical draft, C 331.
7 'Africa Yesterday: One Ruler's Burden', *SE*, 83, 84–5.
8 JC, letters to GC, 3, 7, 6, 5, 15 July, 5 June 1917.
9 Letters to GC, 14 July, 6 August, 17, 19, 20 and 25 July 1917.
10 W. Hamilton-Browne, letter to JC, 2 August 1917, C 323.
11 JC, letters to GC, 27 July, 3, 4, 5 and 8 August 1917.
12 Poem owned by the family.

Chapter 18 – Problems 1917–1918

1 GC, letter to JC, 21 June 1917.
2 JC, letters to GC, 10, 17, 18, 19, 22 and 23 August 1917.
3 Letters to GC, 28 and 29 August, 4 and 10 September 1917.
4 Letters to GC, 26 and 30 September 1917.
5 Letters to GC, 22 September, 2, 4 and 6 October 1917.
6 Letters to GC, 30 October, 6, 1, 15, 23, 24, and 25 November 1917.
7 W. Hamilton-Browne, letter to Secretary, Northern Nigeria, n.d. (with JC, 'Kaiama Assessment Report, 1919'), N Kaduna DOB / ASR /10.
8 JC, letter to GC, 21 November 1918.
9 Personal letter to Edith Haggard, 13 February 1954.
10 Letter to GC, 5 February 1919.
11 GC, letters to JC, 27 January 1919, 19 November, 14 September and 13 August 1918.
12 JC, letter to GC, 27 July 1919.
13 Mary Anna Ogilvie, letter to GC, 9 April 1918, C Adds.
14 JC, letter to GC, 16 August 1917.
15 GC, letter to JC, 7 May 1919.
16 JC, letter to GC, 1 April 1919.
17 GC, letters to JC, 2 and 7 May 1919.
18 JC, letters to GC, 1 April, 13, 12, 13 June 1919.

Chapter 19 – Trials & Reports, 1918–1919

1 JC, letter to GC, 7 August 1918.
2 GC, letters to JC, 4 and 24 October, 18 August 1918.
3 JC, letters to GC, 6 and 7 September 1918.
4 GC, letter to JC, 10 August 1918.
5 JC, letter to GC, 8 October 1918.
6 'Africa Laughs', C 273 / S12B.
7 Report on 'Provincial Court Case 26 / 1918 . . . Rex v Jarimi,. December 2nd, 1918', *Borgu Court Minute Book*, N Kaduna Borgdist 4.
8 'Africa Laughs'.
9 JC, letters to GC, 1 August and 5 July 1919.
10 Report on 'Case No 788 / 56 / 1919', 5 July 1919, N Kaduna SNP 13/1, O/PC / 228 / 1919.
11 Preface for American edition of *African Witch* (1936), C 271 / N85.
12 Report on 'Rex v Makoshi, Lafia, Ajemkem, Magaji', 20 August 1919, *Borgu Court Minute Book*.
13 *The Case for African Freedom*, CAF, 20.
14 JC, letter to GC, 4 November 1919.
15 Letters to GC, 30 August and 4 November 1919.
16 E. C. Duff, Confidential Report No 22/18 to Governor, 26 April, and reply 31 May, N Kaduna SNP 8 / 54 / 1918.
17 JC, letter to GC, 29 January 1919.
18 Emir of Borgu, in conversation with author, 1981.
19 JC, letter to GC, 28 January 1919.
20 Letters to GC, 16, 30 and 31 October 1918.
21 Letters to GC, 3 November, 23 October 1918, 5 May 1919.
22 Prefatory Essay. *Aissa Saved*, 5.
23 JC, letter to GC, 3 January 1919.
24 Kaiama and Yashikera Assessment Reports, 1919, and ancillary documents, N Kaduna Borgdist / DOB / ASR / 9 and 10.

25 Crowder, *Revolt in Bussa* (London: Faber, 1973), 172.
26 Kaiama Assessment Report.
27 T. Hostyns-Abrahall, Okuta Assessment Report, 1922, N Ibadan, 111/51245.
28 JC, letter to GC, 27 October 1918.
29 Observed during visit to Kaiama, 1981.
30 JC, letters to GC, 4, 13 and 18 December 1918.
31 'Christmas in Africa', *SE*, 91–2, 94, 95.

Chapter 20 Bridges & Roads, 1919

 1 *The Case for African Freedom*, CAF, 115, 25, 115–6.
 2 Yashikera Assessment Report, N Kaduna Borgdist / DOB / ASR / 9.
 3 'Policy for Aid', *SE*, 99–100.
 4 JC, letters to GC, 17, 12 and 15 February 1919.
 5 'Primitive Freedom', C 271 / N85.
 6 JC, letters to GC, 18 and 24 February 1919.
 7 Yashikera Assessment Report.
 8 *The Case for African Freedom*, CAF, 35, 133.
 9 JC, letter to GC, 3 October 1919.
10 Letter to GC, 8 March 1919
11 GC, letters to JC, 30 October, 6 November, 29 December 1918, 5 February, 2 January, 18 February 1919.
12 Jack Cary, letter to JC, 1941, C Adds.
13 Arthur Cary, letter to JC, 22 December 1918, C 324.
14 GC, letter to JC, 18 February 1919.
15 JC, letters to GC, 27 February and 13 March 1919.
16 C261 / N45.
17 JC, letters to GC, 17 and 22 March, 6, 12 and 14 April 1919.
18 Letters to GC, 21 and 24 April 1919.
19 Letter to GC, 28 May 1919.
20 'Africa Yesterday: One Ruler's Burden', *SE*, 83.
21 JC, letter to GC, 25 May 1919.
22 GC, letter to JC, 14 April 1919.
23 JC, letter to GC, 30 May 1919.
24 Letters to GC, 4 April, 28 January, 20 April, 13, 14, 19 and 24 May, 4 June 1919.

Chapter 21 – Departures, 1919

 1 JC, letters to GC, 11, 22 and 27 June, 8 and 22 July 1919.
 2 GC, letters to JC, 17 June, 8 July, 16 October 1919.
 3 William Maxwell Ogilvie, letter to JC, 31 August 1919, C 324.
 4 JC, letter to GC, 17 October 1919.
 5 Mary Anna Ogilvie, letter to JC, 20 November 1919.
 6 GC, letters to JC, 4 June and 26 July, 1919. The book was C. L. Temple's *Native Races and Their Rulers*.
 7 JC, letters to GC, 12 and 13 August 1919.
 8 *The Case for African Freedom*, CAF, 36; and see Prefatory Essay, *Mister Johnson*, 5–7.
 9 George Graves, letter to Colonel Moody, 7 May 1962, C Adds 4.
10 JC, letters to GC, 18 and 14 August 1919.
11 *The Case for African Freedom*, 36.
12 JC, letter to GC, 22 August 1919.

13 Handing-Over Notes, 18 December 1919, N Kaduna Borgdist / DOB / HISD / 82.
14 Hoskyns-Abrahall, diary, 8 April 1921, Rhodes House Library.
15 JC, letter to GC, 23 September 1919.
16 Emir of Borgu to author, 1981.
17 JC, letters to GC, 9, 6 and 19 October 1919.
18 Graves, letter to Colonel Moody.
19 'An Interview with JC', *SE*, 10.
20 *Daventry*, C 169.
21 JC, letters to GC, 19 and 27 October 12, 21, 23 and 28 November 1919.

Chapter 22 – *Delight, 1919*

1 JC, letters to GC, 29 April and 13 January 1919, 5 October and 7 May 1917, 16 October, 1 April and 6 August 1919.
2 Letters to GC, 6, 13, 14 and 29 November, 2 December 1919.
3 Emir of Borgu, in conversation with author, 1981.
4 A Campbell-Irons, Handing Over Notes, 13 October 1920, N Kaduna Borgdist DOB / HIS / 82
5 JC, Handing Over Notes.
6 N. P. M. Jones, Handing Over Notes, September 1931, N Kaduna Borgdist DOB / HIS / 78.
7 Hoskyns-Abrahall, diary, 7 May 1921 and subsequent entries, Rhodes House Library.
8 JC, Handing-Over Notes.
9 Suleiman dan Galadima, in conversation with author, 1981.
10 Isak Dinesen, *Shadows on the Grass* (New York: Random House, 1961), 91.
11 'Government Baby', *SS*, 225.
12 M. M. Mahood, 'JC in Africa, 1913–1920', *New Statesman*, 1 October 1960, 478.
13 Leonard Woolf, *Beginning Again* (London: Hogarth Press, 1964), 99.
14 Woolf, *The Village in the Jungle* (London: Hogarth Press, 1961).
15 Woolf, *Growing* (London: Hogarth Press, 1961), 120, 246–7, 180.
16 'Sketch for an idea of life', C 271/N82.
17 H. W. Cowper, letter to Moody, 27 February 1962.
18 'The Meaning of England', *SE*, 73.

Chapter 23 – *A New Start, 1920–1921*

1 John Burrow and Alex Hamilton, 'An Interview with Joyce Cary', *SE*, 3.
2 Mary Anna Ogilvie, letter to GC, 5 May [1920], C 313.
3 The Under–Secretary of State, Colonial Office, to JC, 24 July 1920, C Adds.
4 JC, letter to GC, 3 May 1917.
5 GC, letter to JC, 10 June 1917.
6 JC, letter to GC, 14 November 1919.
7 Thomas Joyce, 'The Springs of Youth', *Saturday Evening Post*, 6 March 1920, 32.
8 Thomas Joyce, 'Salute to Propriety', *Saturday Evening Post*, 9 October 1920, 40.
9 Thomas Joyce, 'The Reformation', *Saturday Evening Post*, 22 May 1920, 124.
10 'The Springs of Youth', 189.
11 Wright, *JC*, 26.
12 Thomas Joyce, 'A Piece of Honesty', *Saturday Evening Post*, 26 June 1920, 66.

13 Thomas Joyce, 'A Consistent Woman', *Saturday Evening Post*, 21 August 1920, 82.
14 'Salute to Propriety', 46.
15 'The Reformation', 21.
16 'A Consistent Woman', 82.
17 'Salute to Propriety', 46.
18 JC, letter to GC, n.d. [Summer 1921], C 312.
19 'William' notes, C 254 / N17.
20 'Georgy' drafts, C 254 / N19.
21 E. M. Forster, *A Passage to India*, Chapters 2 and 3.
22 'Prue', C 254 / N18.
23 JC, letters to GC, 4 and 7 June, 20 July, [25 July], and n.d. [Summer 1921], C 311 and C 312.
24 GC, letters to JC, 27 and 30 July 1921.
25 Mary Ogilvie, in conversation with author, 1982.
26 C 261 / N45.
27 JC, letters to GC, [16], 22 and 23 November 1921.
28 GC, letter to JC, 24 November [1921].

Chapter 24 – Settling Down, 1922–1926

1 JC, letter to GC, [28 July 1921].
2 Introduction to 1944 edition of *The Case for African Freedom*, CAF, 14.
3 'Unfinished Novels', SE, 110.
4 W. B. Yeats, 'If I were Four-and-Twenty' (1919).
5 'Whick MacArthur' drafts, C 252 / S3D.
6 C 251 / P5.
7 JC, letters to GC, [24 July] and 28 July, 1 August and [2 August] 1922.
8 Thomas Joyce, 'Not Wholly Matrimony', *Strand Magazine*, LXVI (December 1923), 660–1.
9 JC, letter to GC, 17 [April 1925].
10 Elsie Carlisle, letter to GC n.d., C 313.
11 William Maxwell Ogilvie, 'Reminiscences'.
12 JC, letter to GC, 7 July 1924.
13 JC, letter to GC, 3 August 1925.
14 GC, letter to JC, 4 September [1925], C 320.
15 JC, letters to GC, 24, 26 and 25 August 1925.
16 Instructions 'For a girl', C 313.
17 C 258 / S5J.
18 C 254 / N30.
19 C 251 / P2.
20 A. J. P. Taylor, *A Personal History* (London: Hamish Hamilton, 1983), 79.
21 A. L. Rowse, *A Cornishman at Oxford* (London: Cape, 1963), 295.
22 Philip Gibbs, *The Pageant of the Years* (London: Heinemann, 1946), 354.
23 JC, letters to GC, 11 May and [15 May] 1926.
24 *The Horse's Mouth*, 11.
25 Heneage Ogilvie, *Fifty* (London: Max Parrish, 1962), 155.
26 JC, letter to GC, 11 September 1926.

Chapter 25 – Injustice & God, 1922–1928

1 Prefatory Essay, *An American Visitor*, 9, 10.
2 'An Interview with JC', SE, 12.
3 'My own religious history', C 331.

4 'Cheerful Protestant', *Time*, 52.
5 'Unfinished Novels', *SE*, 110–11.
6 C 251 / P3.
7 Walter Allen, Foreword to JC, *Cock Jarvis*, xiv.
8 'The Way a Novel Gets Written', *SE*, 119.
9 'The Novelist at Work' (conversation with Lord David Cecil) XVIII: 212–3 (November–December 1950), *Adam*, 15.
10 'The Way a Novel Gets Written', 127–8.
11 'The Approach, the Formal Construction, the Style', C 233.
12 'The Way a Novel Gets Written', 127–8.
13 'Theme and Impression', C 249.
14 'The Approach, the Formal Construction, the Style'.
15 'Interview with JC', 12.
16 'My First Novel', *Listener*, 16 April 1953, 637.
17 'The Way a Novel Gets Written', 117.
18 'Theme and Impression'.
19 JC, letter to GC, 22 May 1933.
20 C 363 / N25.
21 See C 251 / P11.
22 Draft of letter to Ernest Benn about *Aissa Saved*, 1932.
23 Mahood, *JC's Africa*, 99; and see Hastings, *Nigerian Days*, 3, 33.
24 *Cock Jarvis*, 37.
25 See *Britain and West Africa*, CAF, 170.
26 *Cock Jarvis*, 179, 181.
27 C 363 / N26.
28 'Sketch for an idea of life', C 271 / N82.
29 See E. F. Carritt, *The Theory of Beauty*, C B308.
30 'Sketch for an idea of life'.
31 John MacMurray, 'Objectivity in Religion', in *Adventure*, ed. Burnett H. Streeter (London: Macmillan, 1927), 183; C B66.
32 'A Great Author Faces up to Death' *SE*, 253.
33 'The Split Mind of the West' (unpublished essay), C 247.
34 MacMurray, 193.
35 'Unfinished Novels', *SE*. 113.
36 'On his Own Method', C 237.
37 'Sketch for an idea of life'.

Chapter 26 – Published Novelist, 1928–1932

1 JC, letters to GC, 4 and 6 August 1929, C 311.
2 C 257 / N37.
3 JC, letter to GC, 3 May 1933.
4 Draft for Prefatory Essay, *An American Visitor*, C 244.
5 C 254 / N30.
6 Drafts of letter to Ernest Benn Ltd, C 258 / S5E.
7 C258 / S5E.
8 C251 / P4.
9 C 254 / N23.
10 C251 / P7.
11 Owned by the family.
12 Draft for Prefatory Essay, *Aissa Saved*, C 244.
13 C 254 / N30.
14 *Aissa Saved*, 211.

15 Prefatory Essay, *Aissa Saved*, 8.
16 C 258 / S5E.
17 *An American Visitor*, 38–9.
18 *John O'London's*, 26 August 1933; *Times Literary Supplement*, 17 August 1933.
19 Graham Greene, letter to JC, 19 January 1954, C Adds.
20 Draft of letter to Ernest Benn, C 258 / S5S.
21 JC, letter to Edwardes, 2 January 1034, C Adds 4.
22 'Essay on the Free Imagination', C 210.
23 Draft of letter to Benn, C 258 / S5S.
24 Prefatory Essay, *An American Visitor*, 7.
25 C 258 / S5K.
26 G. K. Hibbert, *The Inner Light* (London: Ernest Benn, 1928).
27 'Essay on the Free Imagination'.
28 *An American Visitor*, 234–9.
29 Quoted in Garth Lean, *Frank Buchman* (London: Constable, 1985), 1.
30 C 251 / P15.
31 JC, letter to GC, 3 May 1933.
32 See Bertrand Russell, *What I Believe* (London: Kegan Paul, 1925); C B334.
33 *Arabella*, C 155.

Chapter 27 – Failure & Success, 1932–1935

1 JC, letter to Edwardes, 2 January 1934, C Adds 4.
2 Prefatory Essay, *The African Witch*, 11.
3 'The Jew Story' notes, C 297.
4 'Tod' notes, C 259 / N44.
5 'Tod' notes, C 260 / S6A.
6 'Tod' drafts C 178.
7 'Tod' notes, C 297.
8 'Moore' notes, C 170.
9 'Tod' notes, C 259 / N44.
10 Draft letter to John Wilkes of Eton College, verso of *An American Visitor* draft, C 6.
11 JC, letters to GC, 9 May and n.d. [May–June 1933].
12 Letters to GC, 18 July and 14 December 1933.
13 Prefatory Essay, *The African Witch*, 11.
14 *Cock Jarvis* notes, C 254 / N27.
15 *Cock Jarvis* notes, C 254 / N25.
16 C 251 / P21.
17 C 251 / P5.
18 C 251 / P7.
19 'An Interview with JC', *SE*, 7.
20 Owned by the family.
21 Prefatory Essay, *The African Witch*, 9.
22 'Aladé', C 251 / P8.
23 Victor Gollancz, copy of letter to JC, 3 January 1936, Victor Gollancz Ltd.
24 Reader's report, Victor Gollancz Ltd.
25 JC, letter to Gollancz, 4 November 1935.
26 Prefatory Essay, *The African Witch*, 11, 12.

Chapter 28 – Creativity & Happiness, 1935–1938

1 *Cock Jarvis*, 239–40.
2 Gilbert Spencer, *Memoirs of a Painter* (London: Chatto and Windus, 1974), 111.
3 Dan Davin, *Closing Times*, 110.

4 CC draft, C 31.
5 Gollancz, copy of letter to JC, 3 January 1936.
6 JC, letter to Gollancz, 21 September 1936.
7 'Account of C. C. sent to Gollancz Sep. 1936', C 268 / S10D.
8 Arthur Cary, letter to JC, C 263 / N51; see CC, 348–9.
9 C 263 / N55.
10 Autobiographical draft, C 301.
11 GC, letters to JC, 3 June [1933] and 13 September 1936.
12 C 263 / N55; entries dated 8, 9 and 13 September 1936, and n.d.
13 JC, letter to GC, 3 April 1936, C 312.
14 'Marta', C 175.
15 JC, letter to Gollancz, 2 April 1937.
16 Tristram Cary to author, 1982.
17 N80 (as transcribed by Fisher).
18 C 265 / N 61.
19 JC, letter to Lionel Stevenson, 15 February 1938.
20 'Account of C. C. sent to Gollancz'.
21 JC, letter to GC, 16 April 1937.
22 Letter to Gollancz, 2 June 1937.
23 Letters to GC, 10, 13 and 16 August 1937.
24 Letter to Gollancz, 2 September 1937.
25 Reader's report, Victor Gollancz Ltd.
26 *Observer, News Chronicle, The Times, Star*, 17 January 1938.
27 See, 'The Tough World of Surtees', *SE*, 179–85.

Chapter 29 – Freedom 1938–1940

1 Dorothy MacGregor, letter to GC, 29 March [1937], Cary Adds.
2 Desmond MacCarthy, Preface to Robert Lynd, *Essays in Life and Literature* (London: Dent, 1951), xi.
3 J. B. Priestley *Margin Released* (London: Heinemann, 1962), 148.
4 Sylvia Lynd, *English Children* (London: Collins, 1942); see JC's copy, C Adds B32.
5 Antonia McLean, letter to author, 3 February 1988.
6 JC, letter to GC, 23 August [1936], C 312.
7 C263 / N58; entries dated 11 August and n.d. [summer 1936 and 1937].
8 JC, letters to Lionel Stevenson, 1 and 28 November [1937].
9 C 263 / N55; entry dated 28 November [1937].
10 *The Case for African Freedom*, CAF, 14.
11 J. W. Gough, *The Social Contract* (Oxford: Clarendon Press, 1936), 255.
12 'Political and Personal Morality', *SE*, 229.
13 *Britain's Liberal Influence*, *SE*, 210, 216.
14 Kathleen Nott, *A Soul in the Quad* (London: Routledge and Kegan Paul, 1969), 177, 180, 181.
15 *Power in Men*, 195, 198.
16 Draft of letter to Mr Harcourt-Johnstone of the Liberal Party, 29 May 1939, C 271 / N85.
17 JC, letter to Edwardes, 5 August 1939, C Adds 4.
18 Letter to Stevenson, 12 February 1939.
19 Prefatory Essay, *CC*, 8.
20 Prefatory Essay, *Mister Johnson*, 10.
21 *Mister Johnson* notes, C 265 / N73.
22 J. F. J. Fitzpatrick, 'Mr Johnson', *Blackwood's Magazine*, CCI (February 1917), 258.

23 Prefatory Essay, *Mister Johnson*, 5, 7.
24 A. J. N. Tremearne, *The Ban of the Bori* (London: Heath, Cranston and Ouseley, [1914]), 329.
25 JC, letter to Gollancz, 18 April 1939.
26 Reader's report, Victor Gollancz Ltd.
27 Gollancz, copy of letter to JC, 25 July 1939.
28 Hugh Walpole, letter to JC, 23 April 1939.
29 J. B. Priestley, letters to JC, 16 January and 16 February 1939, C Adds and C 326.
30 *Happy Valley*, C 217.
31 Priestley, letter to JC, 13 July 1939, C 326.
32 Frederick Ogilvie, letter to Carys, 17 February 1939.
33 *The King is Dead, Long Live the King*, C219.
34 It was produced as a BBC radio play in 1967, with music by Tristram Cary.

Chapter 30 – War & Childhood, 1939–1941

1 JC, letter to Edwardes, 28 January 1941, C Adds 4.
2 Letter to Stevenson, 28 April 1939.
3 Letter to GC, 28 April 1942, C 312.
4 Letter to Edwardes, 28 January 1941.
5 Spencer Curtis Brown, letter to JC, 15 August 1939, C 326.
6 As recalled by Robert Lusty, in 'JC and his Vision of Life', presented by David Lytton, BBC Radio 3, 27 June 1977.
7 JC, letter to Mab Stevenson, 27 November 1938.
8 N80 (as transcribed by Fisher).
9 Prefatory Essay, *Charley is My Darling*, 5, 10.
10 Quoted in 'JC or What is Freedom?', *Oxford Mail*, 15 December 1942.
11 *Charley is My Darling*, 157, 172, 72.
12 C 270 / S11C.
13 *Charley is My Darling*, 343.
14 Mary Higgins and Julian Orde, letters to JC, 13 November 1942 and 2 August 1941, C Adds.
15 *News Chronicle, The Times, Observer, Time and Tide*, April 1940; *quotations, C* 57.
16 *HC* notes, C 270 / S11J.
17 Prefatory Essay, *HC*, 5, 8.
18 'Carrig Cnoc', *SE*, 30.
19 Prefatory Essay draft, *HC*, C244.
20 *HC*, 223.

Chapter 31 Cantering, 1940–1944

1 'Note on Trilogy for U. S. A.' (draft of Preface, *First Trilogy*), C 292 / N148.
2 Preface, *First Trilogy* (New York: Harper, 1958), ix.
3 'Note on trilogy for U. S. A.'; autobiographical draft, C 279 / S16A.
4 Preface, *First Trilogy*, x.
5 *Art and Reality*, 74.
6 Draft of Preface, *First Trilogy*, C 245.
7 JC, letter to Graham Ackroyd, 11 November 1946, C Adds 4.
8 JC's copy (C B141) was given to him by GC on 1 June 1939 and is heavily annotated.
9 Herbert Read, *The End of a War* (London: Faber, 1933).
10 See Alan Kennedy, *The Protean Self* (London: Macmillan, 1974), 104–7.
11 Immanuel Kant, *Critique of Pure Reason*, tr. J. Meiklejohn (1893); C B321.

12 'An Interview with Joyce Cary', *SE*, 7.
13 C 272 / P46, P43, P47.
14 'Song of Lally', C 275 / S13F; 'A Woman's Confession', C 275 / S13F.
15 Preface, *First Trilogy*, x–xi.
16 Description of *The Horse's Mouth* for Harper 1949.
17 J. R. Harris, in conversation with author, 1982.
18 'Morality and the Novelist', *SE*, 162.
19 'The Revolution of the Women', *Vogue*, 15 March 1951, 100.
20 Spencer Curtis Brown, letter to JC, 31 December 1941.
21 Quoted in Bernard Crick, *George Orwell* (London: Secker and Warburg, 1946), 272.
22 George Orwell, Introduction to *The Case for African Freedom*, CAF, 3.
23 Arthur Creech Jones, letter to JC, 27 July 1941.
24 Edwardes, letter to JC, 29 July 1941.
25 Davidson Nicol, 'JC's African Novels', *West African Review*, December 1957, 1199.
26 Description of *The Horse's Mouth* for Harper.
27 *To Be a Pilgrim* notes, C 71; and see *To Be a Pilgrim*, 342.
28 Preface, *First Trilogy*, xi.
29 L. P. Hartley, letter to JC, 10 January 1943.
30 *To Be a Pilgrim* notes, C 71.
31 *To Be a Pilgrim*, 241.
32 Michael Joseph, letter to JC, 'Mid October 1942'.
33 Frederick Ogilvie, letter to GC, 23 January 1942.
34 Heneage Ogilvie, letter to GC, 29 November 1942.
35 Tristram Cary, 'Background to *The Horse's Mouth*', *24 Hours*, May 1980, 12.
36 L. P. Hartley, letter to JC, 16 March 1941.
37 A. L. Rowse, *A Cornishman at Oxford*, 145.
38 Maurice Bowra, *Memories*, 117.
39 Lord David Cecil, in conversation with author, 1982.
40 Enid Starkie, letter to JC, 3 December 1942.
41 Joanna Richardson, *Enid Starkie*, 2–3.
42 Starkie, letter to GC, 20 January 1943; quoted in following.
43 GC, letter to JC, 21 January 1943.

Chapter 32 Galloping 1942–1944

1 JC, letters to John Dover Wilson, 31 January and 1 February 1942.
2 Letter to C.B. Young, 24 August 1942.
3 C 272 / P57.
4 JC, letter to Andrew Wright, 9 March 1957.
5 *The Horse's Mouth* notes, C 82.
6 JC, letter to Dover Wilson, 26 September 1942.
7 'Tolstoy's Theory of Art', *SE*, 130, 135.
8 'Morality and the Novelist', *SE*, 154.
9 'Tolstoy's Theory of Art', 137.
10 John Dover Wilson, *Milestones on the Dover Road* (London: Faber, 1969), 130.
11 Dover Wilson, letter to Helen Gardner, 20 June 1957.
12 Dover Wilson, *The Fortunes of Falstaff* (Cambridge: Cambridge University Press, 1953), 1, 9.
13 JC, letter to Dover Wilson, 5 December 1942.
14 Autobiographical draft, C 279 / S16A.
15 G. W. L. Day, 'Men of Two Worlds', C 339.

16 Thorold Dickinson, contribution to *Men of Two Worlds* progranmme, First Presentation, 22 July 1946, C 339.
17 JC, letters to GC, 17, 20 and 19 January 1943.
18 Dickinson, letter to Merja Makinen, 11 May 1982.
19 JC, letter to GC, 5 February 1943.
20 Dickinson, in *Men of Two Worlds* programme.
21 JC, letters to GC, 2, 12 and 15 March 1943.
22 Day, '*Men of Two Worlds*'.
23 JC, letters to GC, 17, 20 and 25 March 1943.
24 Letter to Curtis Brown, 22 April 1943, C Adds 16.
25 Day, '*Men of Two Worlds*'.
26 Dickinson, letter to Merja Makinen, 14 May 1982.
27 'Introduction for Braille version', *The Horse's Mouth*, C 79.
28 *The Horse's Mouth* notes, C 82, C 272 / P59.
29 'Introduction for Braille version'.
30 Bowra, *Memories*, 193.
31 Information about Stanley Spencer from several sources including George Behrend's, *Stanley Spencer at Burghclere*, Duncan Robinson's *Stanley Spencer: Visions of a Berkshire Village* and Maurice Collis's *Stanley Spencer*.
32 Isabel Cary, in conversation with author, 1988.
33 Dan Davin, *Closing Times*, 101.
34 'An Interview with JC', *SE*, 13.
35 C 255 / N36.
36 'An Interview with JC', 14.
37 See C B14.
38 Comments on *The Horse's Mouth* for Madeleine Lebetue–Laforte, French translator, 6 June 1952, C Adds.
39 *The Horse's Mouth* note, C 82.
40 *The Horse's Mouth*, 41, 42, 227.
41 JC, letter to Andrew Wright, 31 January 1956, C Adds 4.
42 *The Horse's Mouth*, 87.
43 *The Horse's Mouth* notes, C 82.
44 Description of *The Horse's Mouth* for Harper.
45 *The Horse's Mouth* draft, C 80.
46 *The Horse's Mouth*, 60.
47 Edwin Muir, *Listener*, 5 October 1944.
48 G. W. Stonier, *New Statesman*, 18 December 1948.
49 JC, letter to Augustus John, 2 January 1951, Tate Gallery.
50 J. B. Priestley, *Reynolds News*, 11 May 1958.
51 *Two Men of Letters*, ed, Rupert Hart-Davis (London: Michael Joseph, 1979), 86.
52 Preface, *First Trilogy*, xiii.
53 Julian Fane, *Memoir in the Middle of a Journey*, 23.
54 JC, letter to Andrew Wright, 16 August 1955, C Adds 4.
55 Letter to Graham Ackroyd, 30 November 1946, C Adds 4.

Chapter 33 – *Soldiers & Women, 1943–1946*

1 Description of *The Process of Real Freedom*, C 299.
2 Arthur Clark, letter to JC, 8 January 1944, C Adds.
3 *The Battle Axe*, C 216.
4 Tax statement, 9 April 1945–5 April 1946, C 329.
5 JC, letters to Stevenson, 2 December 1943 and 7 April 1944.
6 Peter Cary, letters to JC and GC, n.d. [1944–45].

7 Nevill Coghill, letter to JC, 22 July 1945, C Adds.
8 Vita Sackville-West, letter to JC, 4 November 1944.
9 JC, letters to Stevenson, 15 September and 2 December 1945.
10 Pamela Hansford Johnson, 'JC', *Sunday Times*, 31 March 1957.
11 JC, letter to Ivy Compton-Burnett, 3 August 1956, C Adds 4.
12 Ivy Compton-Burnett, letter to Elizabeth Taylor, quoted in Robert Liddell, *Elizabeth and Ivy* (London: Peter Owen, 1986), 48–9.
13 JC, letters to Stevenson, 15 September and 30 May 1945.
14 C 276 / N114, and other notebooks.
15 Prefatory Essay, *The Moonlight*, 9–10; and 'The Way a Novel Gets Written', *SE*, 118.
16 Prefatory Essay, *The Moonlight*, 10.
17 'The Novelist at Work', *Adam*, 15.
18 'The Way a Novel Gets Written', *SE*. 118–9.
19 'Captive and Free' notes C 281 / N92 and C 277 / S14C.
20 *The Moonlight* draft, C 94.
21 C 176 / N114.
22 GC, letter to JC, 25 January 1946.
23 Rachel Cecil, letter to JC, 31 May [1946], C Adds.
24 *Britain and West Africa*, CAF, 189, 191–2, 194.
25 'Policy for Aid', *SE*, 104.

Chapter 34 – Faith & Myth, 1946

1 GC, letter to JC, 3 January 1946.
2 JC, letter to GC, 3 January 1946.
3 'British Film Team Surveys India: 12-Week Study Tour', *Times of India*, 12 February 1946.
4 JC, letters to GC, 7, 11, 12, 14, 24, 18, 23, 20 and 28 January, 1, 2, and 4 February 1946.
5 C 280 / N124.
6 JC, letters to GC, 6, 9, 11, 14, 16, 21 and 22 February 1946.
7 C 280 / N124.
8 JC, letters to GC, 25, 26 and 28 February, 2, 5 and 11 March 1946.
9 C 280 / N124.
10 JC, letters to GC, 31 March, 12 April 1946.
11 Tristram Cary to author, 1988.
12 Description of *The Drunken Sailor*, C 279 / S16B.
13 JC, draft of letter to Mark Schorer, 13 October 1951, C 302.
14 *Art and Reality*, 162–3.
15 *The Drunken Sailor*, 32, 37, 59, 60–3.
16 Readers' reports, Michael Joseph Ltd, C 301.
17 JC, letter to Dover Wilson, 7 January 1948.
18 Jack Fischer, letter to Elizabeth Lawrence, 18 September 1949, C Adds 1.
19 *Secret People*, C 223.

Chapter 35 – Joy & Grief, 1946–1949

1 Prefatory Essay, *A Fearful Joy*, 6–7.
2 'They Sleep in Ulro' and 'Hamper' notes, C 282 / N153, C 286 / S19A–E.
3 Prefatory Essay, *A Fearful Joy*, 5 (and see 'Unfinished Novels', *SE*, 111–3); 'Juno' and 'Captive and Free' notes are in C 281 / N 92, N104, N130, N131, C 282 / S17A–K, C 283 / N137, N138, and drafts in C156–61.

4 'Unfinished Novels', *SE*, 112.
5 C281 / N130, N131, and C 174.
6 Description of 'A State of Nature', in Robert Lusty, letter to JC, 3 September 1947, C 326.
7 A *Fearful Joy* notes, C 283 / N134, C 282 / N130.
8 Mary McHugh, letter to JC, 30 October 1949, C Adds.
9 A *Fearful Joy*, 388.
10 C 257 / N37.
11 JC, letters to Stevenson, 25 March and 11 April 1947.
12 Wright, *JC*, 50; and see C 286 / S19I.
13 JC, letters to Stevenson, 8 August and 26 December 1947.
14 Quoted in Rachel Cecil, letter to JC, 8 December 1947 C Adds.
15 JC, letter to Stevenson, 4 January 1948.
16 C 257 / N37.
17 JC, letter to GC, 28 April 1948, C Adds.
18 C 257 / N37.
19 GC, letter to JC, n.d. [April 1948].
20 JC, letter to GC, 11 May 1948
21 Letter to Stevenson, 28 May 1948.
22 Letter to GC, 17 September 1948.
23 GC, letter to JC, 17 September 1948, C Adds.
24 JC, letters to GC, n.d. [September 1948], 21 and 25 September 1948.
25 Letter to Stevenson, 2 January 1949.
26 In *SE*, 150–3.
27 GC, letter to JC, n.d. [July 1949], C Adds.
28 JC, letter to GC, n.d. [July 1949], C Adds.
29 Antonia McLean, letter to author, 31 January 1988.
30 Frances Phipps, letter to JC, 27 October 1949, C Adds.
31 Heneage Ogilvie, letter to JC, 11 October 1949, C Adds.
32 Antonia McLean, letter to author, 1988.
33 Enid Starkie, 'JC, A Portrait', 131.
34 Michael Cary, letter to JC, n.d. [December 1949], C Adds 16.
35 JC, letter to Prime Minister's Private Secretary, 5 May 1949; quoted in Foster, *JC*,
36 Juliet Ogilvie, letter to JC, 13 December 1949, C Adds 4.
37 JC, letter to Starkie, 18 December 1949.
38 Quoted in Davin, *Closing Times*, 104.
39 Audrey Beecham, in conversation with author, 1982.
40 Mary Ogilvie, letter to JC, 15 December [1949], C Adds 16.
41 Davin, 104.
42 Starkie, 132.

Chapter 36 – New Worlds, 1949–1950

1 JC, letter to John Dover Wilson, 14 May 1945.
2 Personal letter to Jack Fischer, 12 January 1950.
3 Business letter to Edith Haggard, 29 April 1951.
4 Davin, *Closing Times*, 97.
5 JC, letter to Elizabeth Lawrence, 26 October 1951.
6 Ruth Miller, 'Novelist-Impersonator' (based on 1952 interview), C Adds.
7 C 288 / S20A.
8 Joanna Richardson, *Enid Starkie*, 225.
9 C 283 / N140.
10 Michael Maclagan to author. 1988.

11 Davin, lecture on JC.
12 Ruth Miller.
13 Iris Murdoch, letter to author, 23 June 1986.
14 Winifred Davin to author, 1981.
15 JC, letter to Starkie, 4 September 1951.
16 Letter to Stevenson, 27 August 1952.
17 Letter to Dover Wilson, 29 August 1952.
18 Letter to Irene Wilson, 3 July 1951.
19 Letters to Starkie, 29 July 1951, 26 November 1953.
20 David Ogilvie, letters to author, 1 and 23 May 1988.
21 Mary Ogilvie to author, 1982.
22 'Well-Neglected Genius', *Newsweek*, 30 January 1950, 74.
23 JC, personal letter to Edith Haggard, 21 August 1951.
24 Elizabeth Lawrence, letter to JC, 4 November 1946.
25 Lawrence, letter to Robert Lusty, 14 June 1949, C Adds 1.
26 JC, letters to Lawrence, 27 June and 22 August 1949.
27 Letter to Jack Fischer, 12 November 1949.
28 Jack Fischer, letter to Lawrence, 18 September 1949.
29 Lawrence, letter to JC, 21 November 1947.
30 JC, letters to Lawrence, 17 December 1947, 21 January and 20 April 1948, n.d. [September 1948] and 8 January 1948.
31 Lawrence, letter to JC, 8 February 1950.
32 JC, letter to Mab and Lionel Stevenson, 11 March 1951.
33 'A Child's Religion', *SE*, 22.
34 Irene Wilson Laune, letter to Edwin Christian, 9 November 1982.
35 JC, letter to Starkie, 18 February 1951; and see 'The Sources of Tension in America', *SE*, 220–1.
36 Walt Rostow, letter to Christian, 8 October 1952.
37 Elizabeth Lawrence Kalashnikoff, letters to Christian, 15 October and 11 November 1982.
38 'Cheerful Protestant', *Time*, 20 October 1952, 48.
39 JC, personal letter to Edith Haggard, 16 September 1955.
40 Haggard, letter to JC, 12 May 1952.
41 JC, personal letters to Haggard, 11 August 1951, 18 and 29 October, 10 December 1953.

Chapter 37 – A Busy Life, 1950–1952

1 Preface, *First Trilogy*, xiv.
2 Openings of *Prisoner of Grace*, Except the Lord and *Not Honour More*, the three novels that compose the Trilogy.
3 See 261 / N45. C 284 / P106, C 287 / N145.
4 Prefatory Essay, *Prisoner of Grace*, 7.
5 *PG* note, C 288 / S20C.
6 JC, letter to Elizabeth Fischer, 15 November 1952.
7 Draft of letter to Lady Megan Lloyd George, 9 March 1953, C Adds 6.
8 JC's copy of *Diary of Dostoevsky's Wife* (C B213), given to him by GC in 1928, is extensively annotated.
9 See Robert Graves, *Wife to Mr Milton* (London: Cassell, 1943).
10 JC, letter to Lawrence, 27 May 1951.
11 Walter Allen, Reader's report, Michael Joseph Ltd; in C Adds.
12 Brian Moore, review in *Montreal Gazette*, 15 November 1952.
13 See *Bookseller*, 24 April 1954, 1220.

14 'Horror Comics', *SE*, 28.
15 Mark Schorer, 'Native Boy in Patent Leather Shoes', (review of *Mister Johnson*), *New York Times Book Review*, 7 October 1951.
16 JC, letter to Fischer, 13 October 1951. (He did write to Schorer, explaining his 'scheme' at length; see draft of letter, 13 October 1951, C 302.)
17 P. H. Newby, letter to JC, 3 January 1952, C Adds 5.
18 See 'The Front Line Feeling', *Listener*, 17 January 1952, 92–3.
19 Lorna Pegram, letters to JC, 22 December 1955 and 4 January 1956.
20 Denis Gray Stoll, letter to JC, 9 June 1955, C Adds 5.
21 JC, personal letter to Fischer, 21 September 1951.
22 Letter to Fischer, 19 October 1951, C Adds 2.
23 Letter to Haggard, 2 June 1952.
24 Personal letter to Fischer, 13 March 1954.
25 Letter to Haggard, 19 June 1954.
26 'Success Story', *SS*, 31–2.
27 'A Special Occasion', *SS*, 27.
28 Jacob Epstein, *Epstein: An Autobiography* (London: Hulton Press, 1935), 232.
29 'On Jacob Epstein', unpublished essay, C 237.
30 Evelyn Silber, *The Sculpture of Epstein* (Lewisburg: Bucknell University Press, 1986), 9, 14.
31 'On Jacob Epstein'.
32 Epstein, 232.

Chapter 38 – Seizing Happiness, 1952–1954

1 JC, letter to Edith Haggard, 9 May 1952.
2 Letters to B. Evan Owen, 15 July 1952 and 12 December 1953.
3 Letter to Haggard, 16 July 1952.
4 Letter to Mab and Lionel Stevenson, 26 December 1952.
5 Obituary by D. S. R., *Cambridge University Review*, March 1953.
6 George Cary, letters to JC and GC, n.d.
7 Frances Phipps, letter to JC, n.d., C 134 (with *Not Honour More* notes).
8 JC, letter to Jack Fischer, 18 March 1953.
9 Letter to Haggard, 5 May 1953.
10 Letter to Elizabeth Fischer, 30 August 1953.
11 Letter to Haggard, n.d. [July 1952].
12 Letter to Fischer, 25 August 1954.
13 Letter to Haggard, 17 July 1952.
14 *Except the Lord*, 10.
15 John Middleton Murry, letter to JC, 6 October 1950, C 326.
16 Colin Middleton Murry, *Shadows on the Grass* (London: Gollancz, 1977), 154–5.
17 Davin, *Closing Times*, 111–2.
18 Quoted in F. A. Lea, *The Life of John Middleton Murry* (London: Methuen, 1959), 337–8.
19 Davin, 111.
20 Mary Middleton Murry, *To Keep the Faith* (London: Constable, 1959), 172.
21 Description of *Except the Lord*, C Adds 6.
22 Walter Allen, Reader's report for Michael Joseph, C Adds 6.
23 *Except the Lord* notes, C 289 / N154.
24 Allen, Reader's report.
25 JC, personal letters to Haggard, 10 February, 4, 6 and 26 May, 7 July 1954.
26 See correspondence with Yvonne Davet, Madeleine Lebetue-Laforte, 1952–4, C Adds.

27 Quoted in Richardson, *Enid Starkie*. 209.
28 JC, personal letters to Haggard, 22 November and 3 December, 1954.
29 Letter to Davin, 5 December 1954.
30 Allen, Reader's report.
31 See Helen Gardner, *The Noble Moor* (Proceedings of the British Academy, 1955).
32 *Not Honour More* notes, C 289 / N154 and N158.
33 JC, letter to Dorothy Erskine Muir, 28 April 1955, C Adds 4.
34 'The Writer's World', C 243.
35 Preface for German edition of *Not Honour More*, C 242.
36 Allen, Reader's report.

Chapter 39 – Crashes, 1954–1956

1 JC, personal letter to Edith Haggard, 23 December 1954.
2 Haggard, letter to JC, 30 December 1954.
3 *Art and Reality*, 122.
4 JC, letter to Haggard, 6 January 1955.
5 Elizabeth Lawrence, letter to JC, 7 January 1955.
6 'Taking Off in London Fog', *New York Herald Tribune*, 17 January 1955.
7 JC, letter to Enid Starkie, 24 January 1955.
8 Letter to Elizabeth Fischer, 23 January 1955.
9 Letter to Starkie, 24 January 1955.
10 Francis King, letter to author, 9 June 1986.
11 JC, notes for doctor, [April 1955], C Adds.
12 Starkie, 'JC, A Portrait', 143.
13 King, letter to author.
14 Spencer Curtis Brown, letter to JC, 30 March 1954.
15 Norman Rosten, letter to JC, 18 March 1954.
16 JC, letter to Rosten, 11 June 1954.
17 Davin, *Closing Times*, 115.
18 JC, letter to Rosten, 15 January 1955.
19 Letter to Edith Haggard, 9 February 1955.
20 Rosten, telegram to JC, 9 March 1955.
21 JC, letter to Mrs James Byrne, Curtis Brown (NY), 10 March 1955.
22 Rosten, letter to JC, 12 April 1955.
23 JC, letter to Rosten, 15 March 1955.
24 *Mister Johnson* (play), C 43.
25 JC, letter to Rosten, 28 June 1955.
26 Letter to Haggard, 5 April 1955.
27 Letter to Mrs Byrne, 15 April 1955.
28 Letter to Alan Collins, 29 September 1955.
29 Collins, letters to JC, 16 March, 2 and 24 April 1956.
30 JC, letter to Collins, 23 April 1956.
31 Rosten, letter to JC, 5 May [1956].
32 JC, letter to Rosten, 9 May 1956. The play was produced in London during 1960, with little success.
33 Personal letter to Fischer, 30 December 1955.
34 Hettie Hilton, letter to JC, 11 March 1952, C Adds 14.
35 Jerry Wald, letter to JC, 14 March 1956.
36 H. Vernon Beste, letters to JC, 22 March and 15 April 1954.
37 JC, letters to Collins, 23 August and 8 October 1955. Information about Alec Guinness from books by Alan Hunter and John R. Taylor.
38 Hettie Hilton, letter to JC, 15 November 1955.

39 JC, letter to Collins, 22 November 1955.
40 Ronald Neame, letter to JC, 22 November 1955.
41 Collins, letters to JC, 19 December 1955 and 19 March 1956.
42 Hilton, letter to JC, 26 March 1956.
43 JC, letters to Collins, 24 March and 4 April 1956.
44 Hilton, letter to JC, 10 May 1956.
45 Collins, letter to JC, 16 May 1956.
46 JC, letter to Collins, 10 May 1956.
47 Collins, letter to JC, 16 May 1956.
48 *Amateur Cine World*, April 1959; *Times Educational Supplement*, 6 March 1959; *Financial Times*, 9 February 1959.
49 *Times Educational Supplement*, 6 March 1959; *Sunday Express*, 8 February 1959.
50 *Blackfriars*, April 1959; *Amateur Cine World*, April 1956.
51 Winifred Davin to author, 1981; and see Dan Davin, *Closing Times*, 112.

Chapter 40 – *Illness, 1955–1956*

1 JC, personal letter to Edith Haggard, 20 February 1955.
2 Notes for doctor, [April 1955], C Adds.
3 Haggard, letter to JC, 5 May 1955.
4 JC, letter to Fischers, 21 May 1955.
5 Personal letters to Haggard, 28 May amd 7 June 1955.
6 C 296 / P170.
7 JC, letters to Ritchie Russell, 7 and 15 August 1955, 24 January 1956.
8 Report, Counties Public Health Laboratories, 27 April 1956.
9 JC, personal letters to Haggard, 29 August 1955 and 13 February 1956.
10 Letter to Department of Neurology, Radcliffe Infirmary, 23 September 1955.
11 Personal letters to Haggard, 8 and 17 August, 21 October.
12 Letter to Ritchie Russell, 8 November 1955.
13 Ritchie Russell, letter to Kirkham, 1 November 1955.
14 Dr Campbell, letter to Kirkham, 3 December 1955.
15 JC, personal letter to Haggard, 28 December 1955.
16 Letter to Jack Fischer, 30 December 1955.
17 Tristram Cary, letter to Ritchie Russell, 18 April 1956.
18 Ritchie Russell, letter to Tristram Cary, 23 April 1956.

Chapter 41 – *Suffering & Miracles, 1955–1956*

1 JC, personal letters to Edith Haggard, 12 May, 14 July and 17 August 1955.
2 C 296 / P172, P171, P170.
3 'A Great Author Faces up to Death', *SE*, 252.
4 Haggard, personal letter to JC, 4 November 1955.
5 'A Great Author Faces up to Death', 252.
6 One of two letters to JC, both advocating faith-healing, with *The Captive and the Free* notes, C 294 / N164.
7 C296 / P175.
8 *The Captive and the Free*, 144.
9 *The Captive and the Free* draft, C 142.
10 C 294 / N161.
11 JC, letter to Dan Davin, 8 August 1955.
12 Davin, *Closing Times*, 114.
13 C 294 / N162.
14 Davin, 114.

15 *Art and Reality*, 41–2.
16 'The Split Mind of the West', unpublished essay, C 247.
17 C 162.
18 *The Captive and the Free*, 282–4, 298.
19 JC, personal letter to Haggard, 18 March 1956.
20 Davin, 115.
21 Elizabeth Jennings, *Observer*, 20 April 1958.
22 J. B. Priestley, *Reynolds News*, 11 May 1958.
23 Sir Russell Brain, *The Nature of Experience* (London: Oxford University Press, 1959), 72.
24 *Art and Reality*, 126, 107, 127–8.
25 *Art and Reality*, 131; and see 'A Good Investment', SS, 62–78.
26 JC, letter to Andrew Wright, 15 March 1955, Cary Adds 4.
27 Wright, Foreword, *Joyce Cary*, 7–8.
28 JC, personal letters to Haggard, 3 May, 9 July, 3 June, 23 September and 8 July 1956.
29 Letter to Ritchie Russell, 7 August 1956.
30 Julian Fane, *Memoir in the Middle of a Journey*, 28.
31 John Jordan, 'Seeking the mystic experience', *Irish Independent*, 24 July 1976.
32 Davin, 114.
33 JC, personal letters to Haggard, 22 August and 21 October 1956, 29 January 1957.
34 Audrey Beecham, in conversation with author, 1982.
35 Dr Whitty, letter to Edith Millen, 11 August 1956.
36 'Nursing Hoists', pamphlet by W. Ritchie Russell, and accompanying letter by John Payne to JC, 16 November 1956, C Adds.
37 Winifred Davin, in conversation with author, 1981.
38 Tristram Cary to author, 1988.
39 Dan Davin, *Closing Times*, 116.

Chapter 42 – Last Things, 1956–1957

1 Ruari McLean, letter to Andrew Wright, 8 August 1956, C Adds 4.
2 'A Note on Illustrations', Rainbird Edition of *The Horse's Mouth*, ed. Andrew Wright, [vi].
3 Dan Davin, *Closing Times*, 116.
4 JC, letter to Ritchie Russell, 9 October 1956.
5 Ritchie Russell, letter to JC, 12 October 1956.
6 Quoted in Davin, 118 and 117.
7 Douglas Veale, Oxford University Registry, letters to JC, 5 and 13 December 1956.
8 Julian Fane, *Memoir in the Middle of a Journey*, 29.
9 Starkie, 'JC, A Portrait', 131.
10 Edith Haggard, letter to JC, 4 September 1956.
11 JC, letter to Haggard, 8 September 1956.
12 Merrick Winn, 'If You Could Face Your Problems Today as This Man Faces His . . .', *Daily Express*, 27 August 1956.
13 JC, letter to Haggard, 10 October 1956.
14 'A Valedictory of a Great Writer', *Life*, 25 March 1957, 106.
15 Davin, 119–20.
16 In SS, 189–95, 181–5, 196–203.
17 'New Boots', SS, 148, 149, 150.
18 'The Sheep', SS, 205, 213, 220.
19 Haggard, letter to JC, 8 March 1957.

20 'JC's Last Look at His Worlds', *SE*, 239–47.
21 Haggard, letter to JC, 18 February 1957.
22 Sarah Fischer Gleason, letter to Ed Christian, 24 October 1982.
23 JC, letter to Sarah Fischer, 12 February 1957.
24 Letter to Helen Gardner, 14 February 1957.
25 Helen Gardner, in conversation with author, 1983.
26 John Middleton Murry, letter to JC, 29 August 1983.
27 Robert Lusty, *Bound to Be Read*, 81–2.
28 Heneage Ogilvie, *No Miracles Among Friends*, 173.
29 Lord David Cecil, letter to Haggard, 18 April 1957.
30 Davin, 119.
31 C296 / N178.
32 Emery Barcs, 'Zest for Life in a Wheelchair', *Sydney Daily Telegraph*, 2 April 1957.
33 Edith Millen, letter to Haggard, 27 March 1957.
34 Nora Lightburne, letter to Haggard, 29 March 1957.
35 Tristram Cary, letter to Haggard, 10 April 1957.
36 T. S. Matthews, *Angels Unawares*, 241.

SELECT BIBLIOGRAPHY

Only writings mentioned in this biography are listed below. JC: Joyce Cary.

Published Works by Joyce Cary

Novels (*hardback British and American, in order of first publication*).
Quotations in this biography are from the Carfax edition where possible.

Aissa Saved. London: Ernest Benn, 1932. London: Michael Joseph, 1949; Carfax edition, 1952. New York: Harper, 1962.

An American Visitor. London: Ernest Benn, 1933. London: Michael Joseph, 1949; Carfax edition, 1952. New York: Harper, 1961.

The African Witch. London: Victor Gollancz, 1936. New York: William Morrow, 1936. London: Michael Joseph, 1950; Carfax edition, 1951. New York: Harper, 1962.

Castle Corner. London: Victor Gollancz, 1938. London: Michael Joseph, 1950; Carfax edition, 1952. New York: Harper, 1963.

Mister Johnson. London: Victor Gollancz, 1939. London: Michael Joseph, 1947; Carfax edition, 1952. New York: Harper, 1951.

Charley is My Darling. London: Michael Joseph, 1940; Carfax edition, 1951. New York: Harper, 1960.

A House of Children. London: Michael Joseph, 1941; Carfax edition, 1951. New York: Harper, 1956.

Herself Surprised. London: Michael Joseph, 1941; Carfax edition, 1951. New York: Harper, 1948.

To Be a Pilgrim. London: Michael Joseph, 1942; Carfax edition, 1951. New York: Harper, 1949.

The Horse's Mouth. London: Michael Joseph, 1944; Carfax edition, 1951. New York: Harper, 1950. London: George Rainbird, 1957 (ed. Andrew Wright).

First Trilogy. New York: Harper, 1958. (The above three novels in one volume.)

The Moonlight. London: Michael Joseph, 1946; Carfax edition, 1952. New York: Harper, 1947.

A Fearful Joy. London: Michael Joseph, 1949; Carfax edition, 1952. New York: Harper, 1950.

Prisoner of Grace. London: Michael Joseph, 1952; Carfax edition, 1954. New York: Harper, 1952.

Except the Lord. London: Michael Joseph, 1953. New York: Harper, 1953.

Not Honour More. London: Michael Joseph, 1955; Carfax edition, 1966. New York: Harper, 1955.

The Captive and the Free. London: Michael Joseph, 1959; Carfax edition, 1963. New York: Harper, 1959.

Cock Jarvis: An Unfinished Novel, ed. A. G. Bishop. London: Michael Joseph, 1974. New York: St Martin's, 1974.

Short Fiction

Spring Song and Other Stories. London: Michael Joseph, 1960; Carfax edition, 1974. Not included in *Spring Song* are early short stories published as by 'Thomas Joyce' or 'T. Joyce':

'Thus Crime is Punished'. *Idler*, XXXVII (May 1910), 895–8.

'The Springs of Youth'. *Saturday Evening Post*, 6 March 1920, 30, 32, 189, 190.

'The Reformation'. *Saturday Evening Post*, 22 May 1920, 20, 21, 124. Also published as 'The Sins of the Mothers'. *Grand Magazine*, XXXVII (July 1920), 439–46.

'A Piece of Honesty'. *Saturday Evening Post*, 26 June 1920, 66, 69, 70.

'A Consistent Woman'. *Saturday Evening Post*, 21 August 1920, 30, 32, 81, 82.

'Salute to Propriety'. *Saturday Evening Post*, 9 October 1920, 40, 42, 45, 46. *Hutchinson's Magazine*, IV (January 1921), 54–65.

'The Uncle'. *Hutchinson's Magazine*, IV (June 1921), 601–15.

'Not Wholly Matrimony'. *Strand Magazine*, LXVI (December 1923). 655–65.

'The Old Strife at Plant's' (rejected chapter of *The Horse's Mouth*). *Harper's Magazine*, CCI (August 1950), 80–96. *World Review*, February 1951, 45–62. Also published privately in 100 copies, with illustrations by Cary, at the New Bodleian, Oxford, 1956.

Poetry

Published anonymously:

'To My Pen'. *The Cliftonian*, XVIII (July 1905), 41.

'A Lawn, and in the midst a Silken Pool'. *The Cliftonian*, XIX (June 1906), 194–5.

As Arthur Cary:

Verse. Edinburgh: Robert Grant, 1908.

Marching Soldier. London: Michael Joseph, 1945.

The Drunken Sailor. London: Michael Joseph, 1947.

Treatises

Power in Men. London: Nicholson and Watson (for the Liberal Book Club), 1939.

The Case for African Freedom. London: Secker and Warburg (Searchlight Series), 1941; revised and enlarged, 1944. In *The Case for African Freedom and Other Writings on Africa by Joyce Cary* (Austin: University of Texas Press, 1962), 1–136.

Process of Real Freedom. London: Michael Joseph, 1943.

Britain and West Africa. London: Longmans, Green, 1946; revised, 1947. In *The Case for African Freedom and Other Writings on Africa*, 137–200.

Art and Reality: Ways of the Creative Process (revised Clark Lectures, 1956). Cambridge: Cambridge University Press, 1958.

Memoir of the Bobotes. Austin: University of Texas Press, 1960. London: Michael Joseph, 1964.

Essays

Prefatory Essays to all novels up to *Prisoner of Grace* are in the Carfax edition.

Selected Essays, ed. A. G. Bishop. London: Michael Joseph, 1976. New York: St Martin's, 1976.
Not included in *Selected Essays* are:
'Britain's Colonial Record'. *Bulletins from Britain*, No 104 (26 August 1942), 7–10.
'The Revolution of the Women'. *Vogue* (US), CXVII (15 March 1951), 99–100, 149.
'The Front-Line Feeling'. *Listener*, 17 January 1952, 92–3.
'My First Novel'. *Listener*, 16 April 1953, 637–8.
'The Oxford Scholar'. *Holiday*, XIII (June 1953), 96, 98, 100, 132, 134, 136, 137, 139–43.
'Switzerland'. *Holiday*, XVI (August 1954), 28–32.
'Britain is Strong in Herself'. *New York Times Magazine*, 22 April 1956, 12, 32, 33.
'Gerald Wilde', *Nimbus*, III: 2 (1955), 47–54.

Interviews and conversations
Two are included in *Selected Essays*: John Burrow and Alex Hamilton, 'An Interview with JC' (1953), 3–16; and Graham Fisher, 'A Great Author Faces Up to Death' (1957), 251–5.
Stanley Parker. 'JC or What is Freedom?' *Oxford Mail*, 15 December 1942, 3.
'The Novelist at Work: A Conversation between JC and Lord David Cecil' (transcribed from a telediphone recording of the BBC, made 7 July 1950). *Adam International Review*, XVIII: 212–13 (November–December 1950), 15–25.
Harvey Breit. 'A Talk with JC'. *New York Times Book Review*, 18 February 1951, 14; *The Writer Observed* (New York: World, 1956), 167–9.
'Cheerful Protestant'. *Time*, 20 October 1952, 118–30. (Partly a review of *Prisoner of Grace*, this article incorporates quotations from JC as well as some of his friends.)
Merrick Winn. 'If you could face your problems today as this man faces his . . . '. *Daily Express*, 27 August 1956, 4.
Anne Tennant. 'Because I am about to Die.' *Daily Mail*, 28 August 1956, 4.
Nathan Cohen. 'A Conversation with JC' (conducted September 1956, broadcast CBC January 1957). *Tamarack Review*, 3 (Spring 1957), 5–15.
'A Valedictory of a Great Writer' (largely composed of JC's written replies to questions sent in December 1956). *Life*, 25 March 1957, 105, 106, 108.

Unpublished Works of Joyce Cary and others

Most unpublished writings by, or related to, JC are in the vast Osborn Collection (abbreviated below as C) in the Bodleian Library, Oxford. (MSS. Cary 1–347; Cary Adds 1–12 and 26 uncatalogued boxes).

Typescript and manuscript drafts of the novels, short stories, poetry, plays and filmscripts, treatises, essays, lectures – published and unpublished – occupy 245 large numbered boxes, chronologically arranged for the published novels.

There are 50 boxes of notes. JC's notebooks have been classified by size (large notebooks and files, N; pocket-notebooks, P); pages of notes found elsewhere among the Papers have been added (S). It has been further attempted to classify the notes as 'practice' or 'background', and to arrange them chronologically.

Correspondence: JC's letters to his wife, 1913–49, are in C 305–12; letters by others to her, C 313; her letters to him, C 314–20; letters to JC from family and friends, C 321–8; miscellaneous letters, C 329. Further correspondence is in C Adds: 1–3, between JC and his American publishers, Harper; 4, letters by JC to Arthur Cary, H. S. W. Edwardes, Andrew Wright and others; 5–8, mainly relating to broadcasts and British publication: 9–12 and uncatalogued boxes, a wide range of correspondence added recently.

There are also nearly 20 boxes of autobiographical and miscellaneous material –

sketches and photographs, printed items (especially programmes), newspaper cuttings, theses and articles about JC's writing.

Autobiographical drafts
'Sketch', C 272 / P52; 'Sketch for an idea of life', C 271 / N82; typescript for Harper, C 344; untitled drafts, C 279 / S16A, C 293 / S22I, C 301, C 331.

Essays
'Africa Laughs', C273 / S12B: 'The Approach, the Formal Construction, the Style', C233; 'Essay on the Free Imagination', C 210; 'Freedom of Mind', C331; 'Introduction for Braille Version [of *The Horse's Mouth*], C 79; article about Montenegro, C 332; 'My own religious history', C 331; 'On his Own Method', C237; 'On Jacob Epstein', C237; 'The Pattern of a Free Man', C 258/S5E; 'Politics and Freedom', C 267/N65; Preface for American edition of *The African Witch*, C 271/N85; Preface for German edition of *Not Honour More*, C 242; 'Primitive Freedom', C 271/N85; 'The Split Mind of the West', C247; 'Theme and Impression', C249; 'What Christ has Taught Me', C 249; 'The Writer's World', C 243.

Novels
'Aladé', C 151; *Arabella*, C 152–5; 'Captive and Free', C 156–61; 'The Come Back', C 168; 'Darley', C 169; *Daventry*, C 169; 'Georgy', C 172; 'The Homely Nurse', C 173; 'It's a Gift', C 174; 'The Jew Story', C 297; 'Juno', C174; 'Marta', C 175; 'Mills', C 176; 'They Want to Be Happy'. C 22–38; 'Tod' ('T.B.'), C 170–1, 178–9; *Tottenham*, C 180–2; 'To Sleep in Ulro', C 177; 'Whick MacArthur', C252 / S3D, C 303.

Short Stories
'Adamu', C 181; 'Guda', C 184; 'Marching as to War', C 187; 'The Pantry Door', C 297; 'Railway Camp', C 189; 'Sergeant Umaru', C 265/N76; 'Too Good to Be True', C 181; 'T.R.', 'Uncle Jim Joyce', C 270 / S11J.

Plays and filmscripts
The Battle Axe, C 216; *Happy Valley*, C 217–19; *The King is Dead, Long Live the King*, C 219; *Secret People*, C222–3

Other
Addison Society talk, C 233; letter to Blake Society, C 233; Borgu notebook, C 250 / N16; 'Account of C[astle] C[orner] for Gollancz', C 268/S10D; Edinburgh acceptance speech, C 301; Paris diary, C 253 / N9; poetry, C 214; 'Notes on [First] Trilogy for USA', C292/N148; descriptions (for publishers) of *The Drunken Sailor* (C 279/S16B), *Except the Lord* (C Adds 6), *The Horse's Mouth* (C 245), *Process of Real Freedom* (C 299).

Biographical and critical article about JC
Ruth Miller. 'Novelist-Impersonator.' C Adds 9.

In addition to the Cary Papers, I have gratefully made use of the following:
  in the Library of the Plunkett Foundation for Co-operative Studies (Oxford), the Horace Plunkett papers;
  in the National Archives of Nigeria (Kaduna and Ibadan), JC's official reports, court records, handing-over notes, and other documents relating to his administrative service and to colleagues in Northern Nigeria;

in Rhodes House Library (Oxford), the H. S. W. Edwardes and Sir Chandos Hoskyns-Abrahall papers;

in Duke University Library (Durham, North Carolina), the Lionel Stevenson papers;

in the National Library of Scotland (Edinburgh), the John Dover Wilson papers;

in the Bodleian Library, the Enid Starkie papers;

in the Tate Gallery Archives (London), the Augustus John and Stanley Spencer papers;

in the Columbia University Rare Books and Manuscripts Library (New York), the Curtis Brown (New York) papers;

in the possession of their recipients, JC's letters to the Davin and Fischer families, Dame Helen Gardner, Mrs Sewell Haggard, Elizabeth Lawrence Kalashnikoff, Irene Wilson Laune, Antonia and Ruari McLean, Lady Ogilvie, B. Evan Owen, Norman Rosten, Norman Shrapnel;

in the possession of Dan Davin and Winifred Davin, his 'Lecture on JC', and documents by, or relevant to, JC;

in the Cary family's possession, sketch-books and paintings, the family-tree, letters and other documents.

Biographical and Critical Works referring to Joyce Cary

This list generally excludes reviews, details of which will be found in the Notes.

Adams, Hazard. *JC's Trilogies: Pursuit of the Particular Real*. Tallahassee: University Presses of Florida, 1983.

Allen, Walter. *As I Walked Down New Grub Street: Memories of a Writing Life*. London: Heinemann, 1981.

Foreword to JC, *Cock Jarvis: An Unfinished Novel*, ed. A. G. Bishop (London: Michael Joseph, 1974), vii–xiv.

Foreword to JC, *Memoir of the Bobotes* (London: Michael Joseph, 1964), 7–12.

Alpers, Anthony. *The Life of Katherine Mansfield*. New York: Viking, 1980.

Barcs, Emery. 'Zest for Life in a Wheelchair.' *Sydney Daily Telegraph*, 2 April 1957.

Barr, Donald. 'A Careful and Profound Thinker'. *Adam International Review*, XVIII: 212–13 (November–December 1950), 30–31.

Bloom, Robert. *The Indeterminate World: A Study of the Novels of JC*. Philadelphia: University of Pennysylvania Press, 1962.

Brain, Sir Russell. *The Nature of Experience*. London: Oxford University Press, 1959.

Cary, Tristram. 'Background to *The Horse's Mouth*', *24 Hours* (Australia), May 1980, 12–13.

Cecil, Lord David. 'Mr JC. Tenderness of Heart' (obituary). *The Times*, 14 April 1957, 14.

Christian, Edwin. *JC's Creative Imagination*. New York: Peter Lang, 1988.

Cook, Cornelia. *JC: Liberal Principles*. London: Vision Press, 1981.

Courlander, Alphonse. 'The Man who was Blown Up'. *Daily Express*, 8 November 1912.

Davin, Dan. *Closing Times*. London: Oxford University Press, 1975.

Day, G.W. 'Men of Two Worlds'. (Cutting in C 339.)

Dictionary of National Biography 1951–1960, ed. E. T. Williams and Helen Palmer. Oxford: Oxford University Press, 1971.

Echeruo, Michael. *JC and the Novel of Africa*. London: Longman, 1973.

JC and the Dimensions of Order. London: Macmillan. 1979.

Editors' Preface. JC, *Mister Johnson* (New York: *Time* Reading Program Special Edition), v–ix.

Fane, Julian. *Memoir in the Middle of the Journey*. London: Hamish Hamilton, 1971.

Fisher, Barbara. *The House as a Symbol: JC and 'The Turkish House'*. Amsterdam: Rodopi, 1986.
    JC: The Writer and his Theme. Gerrards Cross, Colin Smythe, 1980.

Foster, Malcolm. *JC: A Biography*. Boston: Houghton Mifflin, 1968.

Gardner, Helen. Foreword. *JC, Selected Essays*, ed. A. G. Bishop (London: Michael Joseph, 1976), vii–xii.
    'The Novels of JC'. *Essays and Studies: 1975*, n.s. XXVIII, ed. Robert Ellrodt (London: John Murray, 1975), 76–93.

Goonetilleke, D.C.R.A. *Developing Countries in British Fiction*. London: Macmillan, 1977.

Hall, Dennis. *JC: A Reappraisal*. London: Macmillan, 1983.

Hart-Davis, Rupert, ed. *Two Men of Letters: Correspondence between R. C. Hutchinson and Martyn Skinner, 1957–1974*. London: Michael Joseph, 1979.

Johnson, Pamela Hansford. 'JC'. *Sunday Times*, 31 March 1957.

Kanu, S. H. *A World of Everlasting Conflict*. Ibadan: Ibadan University Press, 1974.

Kennedy, Alan. *The Protean Self: Dramatic Action in Contemporary Fiction*. London: Macmillan, 1974.

Lawrence, Elizabeth. Introduction. JC, *The Horse's Mouth* (New York: Time Reading Program Special Edition), xvii–xxiii.

Lea, F. A. *The Life of John Middleton Murry*. London: Methuen, 1959.

Lessing, Doris. 'Personal Choice.' *The Good Book Guide*, 16 (Autumn–Winter 1982), 26.

Lusty, Robert. *Bound to Be Read*. London: Jonathan Cape, 1975.

Lytton, David (presenter). *JC and his Vision of Life*. BBC Radio 3, 27 June 1977. (Contributions by Lytton, Lord David Cecil, Dan Davin, Denis Duerden, Dame Helen Gardner, Sir Robert Lusty, Prof Molly Mahood).

Mahood, M. M. 'JC in Africa, 1913-1920'. *New Statesman*, 10 October 1960, 477–8.
    JC's Africa. London: Methuen, 1964.

Matthews, T. S. *Angels Unawares*. New York: Ticknor and Fields, 1985.

Murry, Colin Middleton. *Shadows on the Grass*. London: Gollancz, 1977.

Murry, John Middleton. *Between Two Worlds: The Autobiography of John Middleton Murry*. London: Cape, 1935.
    ['Coming to London.'] *Coming to London*, ed. John Lehmann (London: Phoenix House, 1957), 94–107.

Murry, Mary Middleton. *To Keep Faith*. London: Constable, 1959.

Nicol, Davidson. 'JC's African Novels', *West African Review*, December 1957, 1197, 1199, 1201, 1203, 1205.

Nott, Kathleen. *A Soul in the Quad*. London: Routledge and Kegan Paul, 1969.

Ogilvie, (William) Heneage. *Fifty: An Approach to the Problems of Middle Age*. London: Max Parrish, 1962.
    No Miracles Among Friends. London: Max Parrish, 1959.

Ogilvie, William Maxwell. *Reminiscences*. London: privately published, 1929.

Orwell, George, Foreword. JC, *The Case for African Freedom* (London: Secker and Warburg, 1941 – Searchlight Books), 5–6.

Priestley, J. B. 'J. B. Priestley says You Hear JC Talking.' *Reynolds News*, 11 May 1958.

Raskin, Jonah. *The Mythology of Imperialism: Rudyard Kipling, Joseph Conrad, E. M. Forster, D. H. Lawrence and JC*. New York: Dell, 1971.

Ready, William. 'JC: A Biographical Sketch'. *Critic: A Catholic Review of the Books and Arts*, XVIII (June–July 1960), 9–10, 59–60.

Richardson, Joanna. *Enid Starkie*. London: John Murray, 1973.

Rosten, Norman. *Mister Johnson* (based on JC's novel). New York: Dramatists Play Service, 1969.

Simmons, James. 'JC in Ireland.' B. S. Benedikze, ed., *On the Novel* (London: Dent, 1971), 140–60.

Spencer, Gilbert. *Memoirs of a Painter*. London: Chatto and Windus, 1974.

Starkie, Enid. 'JC, A Portrait' (Tredegar Memorial Lecture). *Essays by Divers Hands*, n.s. XXXII, ed. Joanna Richardson (London: Oxford University Press, 1963), 125–44.

Stevenson, Lionel. *The Cary Family of Inishowen*. Durham, North Carolina: privately published, 1963.

'Taking Off in London Fog.' *New York Herald Tribune*, 17 January 1955.

Theroux, Paul. 'An English Visitor.' *New Statesman*, 25 June 1976, 851–2.

Updike, John. 'Writers I Have Met.' *New York Times Book Review*, 11 August 1968, 2.

Wilson, John Dover. *Milestones on the Dover Road*. London: Faber, 1969.

'Well-Neglected Genius.' *Newsweek*, 30 January 1950, 74–5.

Wright, Andrew. *JC: A Preface to his Novels*. London: Chatto and Windus, 1958.

Works that probably influenced Cary's thought and writing

The following are among books owned and annotated by JC (many of these are in the Cary Papers), or read by him. Where possible, they are noted in the edition he read.

Ashford, Daisy. *The Young Visiters*. London: Chatto and Windus, 1918.

Aubrey, John. *Brief Lives*, ed. Andrew Clark. 1898.

Austen, Jane. *Pride and Prejudice*. 1813.

Bennett, Arnold. *Clayhanger, Hilda Lessways, These Twain*. London: Methuen, 1910, 1911, 1916.
    The Old Wives' Tale. 1908.

Blake, William. *The Works* (3 vols.), ed. Edwin Ellis and W. B. Yeats. London: Bernard Quaritch, 1893.
    Poems and Prophecies, ed. Max Plowman. London: Dent (Everyman's Library), 1942.

Bosanquet, Bernard. *Philosophical Theory of the State*. London: Macmillan, 1899.

Brown, Ivor. *The Meaning of Democracy*. London: Cobden-Sanderson, 1920.

Cannan, Gilbert. *Mendel: A Story of Youth*. London: Fisher Unwin, 1916.

Carritt, E. F. *The Theory of Beauty*. London: Methuen, 1923 (2nd ed.).

Cary, George. *The Medieval Alexander*, ed. D. J. A. Ross. Cambridge: Cambridge University Press, 1956.

Cellini, Benvenuto. *The Life of Benvenuto Cellini*, trans. John Addington Symonds. London: Macmillan, 1908.

Clarendon, Earl of. *The History of the Rebellion and Civil Wars in England*. 1702–4.

Conrad, Joseph. *Arrow of Gold*. London: Fisher Unwin, 1919.
    Heart of Darkness. 1899.
    Victory. London: Methuen, 1915.

De Morgan, William. *When Ghost Meets Ghost*. London: Heinemann, [1914].

Dostoevskaya, Anna. *The Diary of Dostoevsky's Wife*, trans. Madge Pemberton. London: Gollancz, 1928.

Dostoevsky, Fyodor. *The Brothers Karamaazov*, trans. Constance Garnett. London: Heinemann, 1930.

[Edwardes, H. S. W.] *On the Improvement of Native Paths in Northern Nigeria*. Northern Nigeria: privately published, 1913.

Fergusson, J. D. *Modern Scottish Painting*. Glasgow: W. Maclenan, 1943.

Fitzpatrick, J. F. J. 'Mr. Johnson'. *Blackwood's Magazine*, CC (September 1914), 247–58.

'Nigeria's Curse – The Native Administration'. *National Review*, December 1924, 617–24.

Frazer, Sir James. *The Golden Bough* (abridged). London: Macmillan, 1922.

Freud, Sigmund. *Totem and Taboo*, trans. A. A. Brill. London: Routledge, 1919.

Gardner, Helen. *The Noble Moor*. Proceedings of the British Academy, 1955. (Read 27 April 1955.)

Gazetteer of the Kontagora Province, comp. E. L. Duff, rev. W. Hamilton-Browne [with contributions by JC]. London: HMO, 1920.

Gordon, General. *The Journals of Major-Gen. C. G. Gordon, C.B., at Kartoum*. London: Kegan Paul, 1885.

Gorst, Mrs Harold. *The Thief on the Cross*. London: Eveleigh Nash, 1908.

Gough, J. W. *The Social Contract: A Critical Study of its Development*. Oxford: Clarendon Press, 1936.

Graves, Robert. *Wife to Mr Milton: The Story of Mary Powell*. London: Cassell, 1942.

Green, J. R. *History of the English People*, 1874.

Haecker, Theodor. *Soren Kierkegaard*, trans. Alexander Dru. London: Oxford University Press, 1937.

Hardy, Thomas. *Jude the Obscure*. London: Osgood, McIlvaine, 1896.
    The Woodlanders. London: Macmillan, 1887.

Hastings, A. C. G. *Nigerian Days*. London: Bodley Head, 1925.

Hibbert, G. K. *The Inner Light*. London: Ernest Benn, 1928.

Hitschmann, Eduard. *Freud's Theories of the Neuroses*, trans. C. Payne. London: Kegan Paul, 1921.

James, William. *The Varieties of Religious Experience: A Study in Human Nature*. London: Longmans, Green, 1928.

Jefferies, Richard. *Wild Life in a Southern County*. London: Nelson [1908].

Joad, C. E. M. *Common-Sense Theology*. London: Fisher Unwin [1922].

Joyce, James. *Finnegans Wake*. London: Faber, 1939.
    A Portrait of the Artist as a Young Man. London: Egoist, 1917.
    Ulysses. London: Bodley Head, 1937.

Jung, C. G. *Psychology of the Unconscious*, trans. B. Hinkle. London: Kegan Paul, 1921.

Kant, Immanuel. *Critique of Pure Reason*, trans. J. Meiklejohn. London: George Bell, 1893.

Kierkegaard, Soren, See. Haecker, Theodor.

Lawrence, D. H. *Fantasia of the Unconscious*. London: Martin Secker, 1923.
    The Rainbow. London: Methuen, 1915.

Lewis, C.S. *Surprised by Joy*. London: Geoffrey Bles, 1955.

Lindsay, A. D. *The Nature of Religious Truth: Sermons Preached in Balliol College Chapel*. London: Hodder and Stoughton, 1927.

Lloyd George, David. *War Memoirs of David Lloyd George*. London: Odhams Press, 1938.

Lugard, F. D. *The Dual Mandate in British Tropical Africa*. Edinburgh: Blackwood, 1922.
    Political Memoranda. Northern Nigeria. [To 1919.]

Lynd, Sylvia. *English Children*. London: Collins, 1942.

McDougall, William. *Psychology: The Study of Behaviour*. Oxford: Oxford University Press (Home University Library), [1912].

MacMurray, John. 'Beyond Knowledge' and 'Objectivity in Religion'. Burnett H. Streeter, ed., *Adventure: The Faith of Science and the Science of Faith* (London: Macmillan, 1927).

Marett, R. R. *Threshold of Religion*. London: Methuen, 1909.

Marriott, J. A. R. *The Life and Times of Lucius Cary, Viscount Falkland*. London: Methuen, 1907.

Mill, J. S. *On Liberty*. 1859.

Moore, George. *Confessions of a Young Man*. London: Heinemann, 1917.

Murry, John Middleton. *The Life of Jesus*. London: Cape, 1926.
    Still Life. London: Constable, 1916.
    William Blake. London: Cape, 1933.

Otto, Rudolf. *The Idea of the Holy*, trans. John Harvey. London: Humphrey Mitford, 1926.

Paul, Maurice and Cedar. *Creative Revolution: A Study of Communist Ergatocracy*. London: Allen and Unwin, 1920.

Plato. *Republic*, trans. B. Jowett. 1871.

Proust, Marcel. *Remembrance of Things Past* (7 vols.), trans. London: Chatto and Windus, 1929–41.

Read, Herbert. *The End of a War*. London: Faber, 1933.

Rhythm: Art, Music, Literature, I: 1–4. London, 1911–12.

Russell, Bertrand. *What I Believe*. London: Kegan Paul, 1925.

Spinoza, Benedict de. *The Chief Works* (2 vols.), trans. R. Elwes. 1883.

Stone, Irving. *Lust for Life: The Novel of Vincent Van Gogh*. London: John Lane, 1934.

Temple, C. L. *Native Races and Their Rulers*. Cape Town, Cape Argus Press, 1918.

Thackeray, William. *The History of Pendennis*. 1849.

Tolstaya, Gratinya. *The Diary of Tolstoy's Wife 1860–1891*, trans. Alexander Werth. London: Gollancz, 1928.

Tolstoy, Leo. *Anna Karenina*, trans. Constance Garnett. London: Heinemann, 1901.
    The Kreutzer Sonata and Other Stories, trans. J. D. Duff and Aylmer Maude. London: Oxford University Press (World's Classics), 1926.
    Master and Man and Other Tales. London: Dent (Everyman), [1910].
    What is Art? and Essays on Art, trans. A Maude. London: Oxford University Press. 1904.

Tremearne, A. J. N. *The Ban of the Bori: Demons and Demon-dancing in West and North Africa*. London: Heath, Cranston and Ouseley, [1914].

Walpole, Hugh. *The Secret City*. London: Macmillan, 1919.

Wells, H. G. *Mr Britling Sees It Through*. London: Cassell, 1916.

Wesley, John. *John Wesley's Journal* (abridged by Percy Livingstone). London: Isbister, 1903.

Whitehead, A. N. *Religion in the Making*. Cambridge: Cambridge University Press, 1927.

Whittaker, Thomas. *Schopenhauer*. 1908.

Wilson, John Dover. *The Fortunes of Falstaff*. Cambridge: Cambridge University Press, 1944. (Clark Lectures, May 1943.)

Zola, Emile. *Paris*, trans. E. Vizetelly. 1898.

Works of Background Relevance

Anderson, R. A. *With Horace Plunkett in Ireland*. London: Macmillan, 1935.

Aubrey, John. *Aubrey's Brief Lives*, ed. Oliver Lawson Dick. London: Secker and Warburg, 1958.

Beckett, J. C. *The Anglo-Irish Tradition*. London: Faber, 1976.
    The Making of Modern Ireland: 1603–1923. New York: Knopf, 1977.

Behrend, George. *Stanley Spencer at Burghclere*. London: Macdonald, 1965.

Berlin, Isaiah. 'Austin and the Early Beginnings of Oxford Philosophy'. *Essays on J. L. Austin* (Oxford: Clarendon Press, 1973.)

Bolger, Patrick. *The Irish Co-operative Movement: Its History and Development.* Dublin: Institute of Public Administration, 1977.

Bowen, Elizabeth. *Bowen's Court and Seven Winters.* London: Virago, 1984.

Bowra, Maurice. *Memories 1898–1939.* London: Weidenfeld and Nicolson, 1966.

Buchan, John. *Nelson's History of the War* (III). London: Nelson, n.d.

Burns, Alan. *History of Nigeria.* London: Collins, 1963.

Chalfont, Alan. *Montgomery of Alamein.* London: Weidenfeld and Nicolson, 1976.

Christie, O. F. *A History of Clifton College 1860–1934.* Bristol: J. W. Arrowsmith, 1935.

Clarendon, Earl of. *Clarendon: Selections from 'The History of the Rebellion' and 'The Life by Himself'*, ed. G. Huehns. Oxford: Oxford University Press, 1978.

Cloete, Stuart. *A Victorian Son: An Autobiography 1897–1922.* London: Collins, 1972.

Collis, Maurice. *Stanley Spencer: A Biography.* London: Harvill Press, 1962.

Connolly, Cyril. *Enemies of Promise.* London: Deutsch, 1973.

Crick, Bernard. *George Orwell: A Life.* London: Secker and Warburg, 1980.

Crocker, W. R. *Nigeria: A Critique of Colonial Administration.* London: Allen and Unwin, 1936.

Crowder, Michael. *Colonial West Africa: Collected Essays.* London: Frank Cass, 1978.

    Revolt in Bussa: A Study of British 'Native Administration' in Nigerian Borgu, 1902–1935. London: Faber, 1973.

    The Story of Nigeria (rev. ed.). London: Faber, 1966.

Digby, Margaret. *Horace Plunkett: An Anglo-American Irishman.* Oxford: Basil Blackwell, 1949.

Dinesen, Isak (Karen Blixen). *Shadows on the Grass.* New York: Random House, 1961.

Epstein, Jacob. *Epstein: An Autobiography.* London: Hulton Press, 1935.

Gibbs, Philip. *The Pageant of the Years.* London: Heinemann, 1946.

Girouard, Mark. *The Return to Camelot: Chivalry and the English Gentleman.* New Haven and London: Yale University Press, 1981.

Glendinning, Victoria. *Elizabeth Bowen: Portrait of a Writer.* London: Weidenfeld and Nicolson, 1977.

Gorges, Brigadier General E. Howard. *The Great War in West Africa.* London: Hutchinson, n.d.

Green, J. R. *A Short History of the English People* (III). New York: Harper, 1890.

Green, V. H. H. *A History of Oxford University.* London: Batsford, 1974.

Hammerton, Sir John, ed. *A Popular History of the Great War* (II). London: Fleetway House, n.d.

Hankin, C. A., ed. *The Letters of John Middleton Murry to Katherine Mansfield.* London: Constable, 1983.

Hogben, S. J. and A. H. M. Kirk-Greene. *The Emirates of Northern Nigeria: A Preliminary Study of their History and Traditions.* London: Oxford University Press, 1966.

Hollis, Christopher. *Oxford in the Twenties: Recollections of Five Friends.* London: Heinemann, 1976.

Huessler, Robert. *The British in Northern Nigeria.* London: Oxford University Press, 1968.

Hunter, Alan. *Alec Guinness on Screen.* Edinburgh: Polygon, 1982.

Kirk-Greene, A. H. M., ed. *The Principles of Native Administration in Nigeria: Selected Documents 1900–1947.* London: Oxford University Press, 1965.

Knox, Ronald. *Let Dons Delight: Being Variations on a Theme in an Oxford Common-Room.* London: Sheed and Ward, 1939.

Langguth, A. J. *Saki: A Life of Hector Hugh Munro*. London: Hamish Hamilton, 1981.

Lean, Garth. *Frank Buchman*. London: Constable, 1985.

Liddell, Robert. *Elizabeth and Ivy*. London: Peter Owen, 1986.

Lively, Penelope. *According to Mark*. Harmondsworth: Penguin, 1985.

MacDonagh, Oliver. *Ireland*. Englewood Cliffs, New Jersey: Prentice-Hall, 1968.

MacLysaght, Edward E. *Irish Families: Their Names, Arms and Origins*. New York: Crown, 1957.

   Sir Horace Plunkett and his Place in the Irish Nation. Dublin and London: Maunsel, 1916.

Mallet, Charles E. *A History of the University of Oxford* (3 vols.) London: Methuen, 1927.

Moberly, Brigadier General F. J. *Military Operations: Togoland and the Cameroons, 1914–1916*. London: HM Stationery Office, 1931.

Morris, James (Jan). *Pax Britannica: The Climax of an Empire*. London: Faber, 1968.

Morris, Jan, ed. *The Oxford Book of Oxford*. Oxford: Oxford University Press, 1978.

Morris, Margaret. Introduction to *Cafe Drawings in Edwardian Paris: From the Sketch Books of J. D. Fergusson*. Glasgow: Blackie, 1974.

Nicholson, I. F. *The Administration of Nigeria 1900–1960*. Oxford: Clarendon Press, 1969.

Nicolson, Harold. 'Marginal Comment'. *Spectator*, 10 August 1945.

Northern Nigeria: Colonial Report 1905–1906. London: HMO, 1906.

Pakenham, Valerie. *The Noonday Sun: Edwardians in the Tropics*. London: Methuen, 1985.

Perham, Margery. *Lugard* (2 vols.). London: Collins, 1956, 1960.

Powell, Violet. *The Constant Novelist: A Study of Margaret Kennedy*. London: Heinemann, 1983.

Priestley, J. B. *Margin Released: A Writer's Reminiscences and Reflections*. London: Heinemann, 1962.

Rowse, A. L. *A Cornishman at Oxford*. London: Cape, 1965.

Sewell, Fr Brocard, ed. *Two Friends: John Gray and André Raffalovich*. Aylesford, Kent: St Albert's Press, 1963.

Silber, Evelyn. *The Sculpture of Epstein*. Lewisburg: Bucknell University Press, 1986.

Stanley Spencer, R. A. (Catalogue of Exhibition, 20 September–14 December 1980). London: Royal Academy of Arts, 1980.

Taylor, A. J. P. *A Personal History*. London: Hamish Hamilton, 1983.

Taylor, Basil. Introduction to *The Impressionists and Their World*. London: Phoenix House, 1953.

Taylor, John R. *Alec Guinness: A Celebration*. London: Pavilion Books, 1984.

Thomson, David. *Woodbrook*. London: Barrie and Jenkins, 1974.

Wells, J. *Oxford and Its Colleges*. London: Methuen, 1923.

White, Terence de Vere. *The Anglo-Irish*. London: Gollancz, 1972.

Winterbottom, Derek. *Henry Newbolt and the Spirit of Clifton*. Bristol: Redcliffe, 1986.

Woolf, Leonard. *Beginning Again: An Autobiography of the Years 1911–1918*. London: Hogarth Press, 1964.

   Growing: An Autobiography of the Years 1904–1911. London: Hogarth Press, 1961.

   The Village in the Jungle. London: Edward Arnold, 1913.

Woolf, Virginia. *Moments of Being*, ed. Jeanne Schulkind. London: Hogarth, 1985.

   Roger Fry: A Biography. Toronto: Macmillan, 1940.

INDEX